✓ checklists

spotlights

FIRST CANADIAN EDITION

Contemporary Business Communication

Scot Ober
Ball State University

Brad Quiring
Mount Royal

Houghton Mifflin Company
Boston   New York

To my wife and five sons, with deep affection: Diana, Jeff, Andy, Ken, Tony, and Casey

Executive Publisher: George Hoffman
Project Manager: Timothy Cullen
Development Editor: Glen Herbert
Senior Project Editor: Margaret Park Bridges
New Title Project Manager: James Lonergan
Senior Marketing Manager: David Tonen

Cover image: Jigsaw Puzzle Pieces, courtesy of Malcolm Piers, Getty Images.

The model letters provided on authentic company stationery have been included by permission to provide realistic examples of company documents for educational purposes. They do not represent actual business documents created by these companies.

Credits appear on page 597, which is considered an extension of the copyright page.

Printed in the U.S.A.

Library of Congress Control Number: 2006937982

ISBN-10: 0-618-73806-1
ISBN-13: 978-0-618-73806-9

Instructor's Edition and Student Study supplements are available online. Please contact us for details at Canada@hmco.com

1 2 3 4 5 6 7 8 9-CRK-11 10 09 08 07

brief contents

contents

Part Two ■ Developing Your Business Writing Skills

Part Three   Basic Correspondence

11 Writing the Report   378

Part Five   Oral and Employment Communication

12 Business Presentations   433

13 Employment Communication   480

Reference Manual

preface

Students don't have to be convinced of the need for competent communication skills. By the time they enter the business communication class, they already know enough about the business environment to appreciate the critical role communication plays in the contemporary organization. They're also aware of the role that communication will play in helping them secure an internship or get a job and be successful at work.

Scot Ober

To sustain this inherent interest, students need a textbook that is current, fast-paced, and interesting—just like business itself. Thus, a major objective of the Canadian edition of *Contemporary Business Communication* is to present comprehensive coverage of real-world concepts in an interesting and lively manner.

This edition of *Contemporary Business Communication* will provide students with the skills they need to communicate effectively in the complex and ever-changing contemporary work environment. It is based on the input of numerous Canadian business communication instructors, addressing the discipline and the work world that students will enter.

Objective-Based Organization   To a greater extent than is true for most other business courses, the content and organization of the basic business communication course differs markedly, depending on the institution at which it is taught, the department that teaches the course, the level of the student, and the like. For example, some institutions place major emphasis on business report writing, while others give the topic scant coverage. The same is true, of course, for other topics such as oral communication, basic English skills, and employment communications. Even more important, there are topics within chapters that, because of time constraints or coverage in other courses, some instructors choose not to cover. Thus, every chapter communication objective (CO) may not be relevant for every business communication class.

Contemporary Business Communication lets instructors easily customize their course to meet their particular needs. Each communication objective that is presented at the beginning of each chapter has been defined to cover an important element of that chapter's content. Each chapter is then organized around these objectives, and the particular objective being covered is identified in the margins. All content relating to one objective is presented before moving on to the next objective. Further, the chapter summary is organized around each objective, as are the end-of-chapter exercises.

This means that instructors can easily assign an entire chapter or only components of the chapter, based on the communication objectives, and then easily identify the related end-of-chapter exercises and test-bank items.

Business Communication—In Context

Business communication problems in the real world do not occur in a vacuum. Events have happened before the problem and will happen after the problem, affecting its resolution. Thus, in addition to typical end-of-chapter exercises, three learning tools in this text provide more complete, long-term situations that provide a "slice-of-life" reality students will actually face on the job.

An Insider's Perspective   Each chapter begins with a profile of a manager discussing some facet of business communications. All opening profiles continue at the end of each chapter with a 3Ps (Problem, Process, and Product) activity.

Continuing Text Examples and End-of-Chapter Exercises   Continuing examples are often used throughout the chapter (and sometimes carried forward to the next chapter) in both the text and end-of-chapter exercises. Such situations are realistic because they provide a sense of following a problem through to completion. They are interesting because they provide a continuing thread to the chapters. They also reinforce the concept of audience analysis because students must first assume the role of sender and later the role of receiver for the same communication task.

Northern Lights: An Ongoing Case Study   Every chapter ends with a case study involving Northern Lights, a small entrepreneurial start-up company whose primary product is Ultra Light, a new paper-thin light source that promises to revolutionize the illumination industry. A company profile is contained in the Appendix to Chapter 1, and each chapter presents a typical communication problem faced by one of the employees. As students systematically solve these 13 case studies, they face communication problems similar to those typically found in the workplace. The continuing nature of the case studies provides these positive learning experiences.

- Students are able to use richer contextual clues to solve communication problems than is possible in the shorter end-of-chapter exercises.

- Students become intimately familiar with the managers and the company and must select what is relevant from a mass of data, thereby learning to handle information overload. For added realism, each case includes an action photograph illustrating that particular communication situation.

- Because the same situations frequently carry over into subsequent chapters, students must face the consequences of their earlier decisions.

- Many cases require students to solve the same communication problem from two different perspectives—thereby enhancing the concept of audience analysis.

- The cases provide realistic opportunities for practicing work-team communication and critical-thinking skills.

Focus on Contemporary Issues

Throughout the text, boxed features called Spotlights illustrate how business communication is affected by three contemporary issues: the increasing international and intercultural nature of today's business world, technology in the workplace, and the growing importance of the ethical dimensions of communicating.

Also in this edition are "Communication Snapshots"—colourful graphics that present up-to-date factoids about issues directly relating to contemporary business communication.

Today, if there is one business buzzword, it has to be "technology"—and with good reason. Every aspect of contemporary business communication—from determining what information to communicate to processing the information and sharing it—depends on technology. In *Contemporary Business Communication* students learn to:

- compose, format, and manage e-mail,
- evaluate the quality of the information accessed from the Internet,
- format electronic and HTML résumés and search online for jobs,
- give electronic presentations, including preparing effective audience handouts, and
- cite electronic sources such as Web pages, online journals and directories, email, and other Internet sources in business, APA, and MLA formats.

Throughout, the text places major emphasis on newer technologies (such as teleconferencing, video conferencing, and video and electronic presentations). In addition, numerous end-of-chapter exercises provide experience in obtaining, evaluating, and using Internet data sources.

The 3Ps (Problem, Process, and Product) Model

The 3Ps (Problem, Process, and Product) models and activities, with their step-by-step analyses of typical communication tasks, have been one of the most popular features of previous editions. These models comprise the *problem* (the situation that requires a communication task), the *process* (step-by-step guidance for accomplishing that task), and the *product* (a fully formatted finished document).

The 3Ps activities require students to focus their efforts on developing a strategy for any message (including email messages) before beginning to compose it, and they serve as a step-by-step model for students when they compose their own messages.

The 3Ps activities within each chapter all contain the solutions to the process questions. The 3Ps exercises at the end of the chapter pose process questions and then require the students themselves to provide the solutions, thereby more actively engaging the student in the problem-solving process.

Annotated Models and Checklists

Full-page models of each major writing task appear in this edition, shown in complete ready-to-send format, so that students become familiar with the appropriate format for every major type of writing assignment. Each model provides marginal step-by-step composing notes as well as grammar and mechanics notes that point out specific illustrations of the grammar and mechanics rules presented in the Reference Manual.

The Checklists recap the essential points for composing each major type of communication and serve as a blueprint when students compose their own documents.

Basic Skills First

Language Arts Basics (LABs) No one can communicate effectively if he or she cannot communicate correctly. It is an unfortunate fact of life that many contemporary students today have not had the advantage of the nuts-and-bolts grammar and mechanics instruction that their instructors took for granted in their own education. Students must learn these basic skills at some point, and the collegiate business communication course is probably their last opportunity.

The six LAB exercises in the appendix of *Contemporary Business Communication* systematically teach and test the most frequently occurring and most frequently misused rules of English grammar and mechanics:

1. Parts of Speech
2. Punctuation—Commas
3. Punctuation—Other Marks
4. Grammar
5. Mechanics
6. Word Usage

Each chapter in the text ends with a LAB test that systematically reinforces the language arts rules presented in the appendix. Instructors can use the LAB exercises and LAB tests as needed to ensure that their students have an opportunity to demonstrate their strategic business communication skills without allowing grammar and mechanics deficiencies to interfere with their communication goals.

Revising—The Real Communication Skill   Students learn at least as much from revising as from drafting their documents. Recognizing the importance of drafting first and revising later, *Contemporary Business Communication* offers a unique approach to the writing process, dedicating one full chapter to planning, organizing, and drafting messages (Chapter 3) and two full chapters to revising messages for style and tone (Chapters 4 and 5). By isolating the revision process and focusing on three levels of revision—the word, the sentence, and the paragraph—this textbook aims to help students develop a comprehensive set of writing and rhetorical skills that can be applied to any document. In addition, annotated first-draft/second-draft models in the correspondence chapters show how a document evolves through rewriting and refining.

Supplemental Materials

For the Instructor

Instructor's Resource Manual   Available on the Instructors' Web Site, the Instructor's Resource Manual provides chapter overviews, supplemental lecture and discussion notes, and suggested answers to chapter exercises. Includes scoring rubrics for evaluation of letters and reports; suggestions for assigning a writing portfolio; student handout masters (containing essential checklists, additional exercises, and selected answer keys), which can be duplicated for distribution to students; and a SCANS correlation chart. Also includes teaching tips for writing exercises and case problems, sample reports, additional 3P samples with solutions, an answer key to grammar and mechanics exercises, supplementary lectures, an answer key to LAB tests, and answers to the exercises in the Reference Manual. Also included are Handout masters to detach for easy duplication.

Print test Bank   Includes over 1700 test items, including multiple-choice, short answer, true-false, revision exercises, and writing cases.

HM ClassPrep with HM Testing CD-ROM   Provides PowerPoint for classroom presentations and Word files from the Instructor's Resource Manual, which can be easily edited. HMTesting, an electronic version of the Print Test Bank, allows instructors to generate and change tests easily on the computer. The program will print an answer key for each version of the text.

Instructor Web Site • www.hmco.ca/ober The Online Teaching Centre provides a monthly newsletter with additional teaching tips and hot-off-the-press current event items that illustrate business communication concepts (sign-up on the site); detailed lecture and supplemental discussion notes; additional application exercises and cases; downloadable **PowerPoint** slides; alternative versions of the complete report included in the Instructor's Manual, so that those who prefer the APA, MLA, or business styles can have access to all three; and a forum for exchanging ideas with the author, publisher, and other instructors around the country.

Eduspace powered by Blackboard™, is Houghton Mifflin's online learning environment. By pairing the widely recognized tools of Blackboard with quality, text-specific content from Houghton Mifflin, Eduspace makes it easy for instructors to create all or part of a course online. Includes the BusCom Writer Tutorials: a set of interactive computer modules that guide students through the development of 15 basic business documents. Each module is based on the textbook's 3Ps (Problem, Process, Product) model, such that students are presented with a unique business situation, are guided through the process of analyzing the situation, developing communication goals, preparing the document, and then prompted to proofread and revise the finished product to meet proper writing guidelines.

Blackboard/WebCT CD-ROM This online course allows flexible, efficient, and creative ways to present learning materials and opportunities. In addition to course management benefits, instructors may make use of an electronic gradebook, receive papers from students enrolled in the course via the Internet, and track student use of communication and collaboration functions.

Classroom Response System (CRS) Content Using state-of-the-art wireless technology and text-specific Ober content, a Classroom Response System (CRS) provides a convenient and inexpensive way to gauge student comprehension, deliver quizzes or exams, and provide "on-the-spot" assessment. Ideal for any classroom, a CRS is a customizable handheld response system that will complement any teaching style. Various answering modes, question types, and display options mean that a CRS is as functional as you want it to be. As a testing platform, as an assessment tool, or simply as a way to increase interactivity in the classroom, a CRS provides the technology you need to transform lecture into a dynamic learning environment.

Houghton Mifflin Instructional Videos Video case studies of well-known companies reinforce text concepts by directly relating them to the footage being shown. In addition, discussion questions and suggested writing assignments are provided for each video.

PowerPoint® Consists of more than 300 slides, including summaries of key concepts, good/bad paired examples, and supplementary information such as answers to selected exercises. For added interest, the examples used in the slides are all different from those used in the text.

Transparencies Over 100 full-colour acetates provide summaries of key concepts, good/bad paired examples, writing examples, text figures, and answers to selected exercises.

For the Student

Student Web Site • www.hmco.ca/ober   The student site offers electronic flash-cards, ACEonline practice quizzes, online writing labs, internet exercises, enrichment exercises, discussion and review questions, sample reports, 3Ps chapter mini-cases, and a complete business glossary.

Acknowledgments

Thanks to everyone within the Houghton Mifflin international division who worked to make this new edition a reality. I would also like to thank Glen Herbert, the developmental editor, for both talking me into the project and supporting me throughout. To Debbie Underhill, with whom I've worked for many years, and the rest of the Canadian sales team who have worked so hard on this project, I extend my sincerest gratitude. Thanks also to the various members of the production team, especially the copy editor, Catherine Leek, for her patience with my numerous questions. And of course to many of my colleagues, particularly Bill and Don, I owe much thanks and appreciation for their eagerness to lend a hand whenever needed. And finally, I wish to thank the two most important people in the world—my wife, Sara, and daughter, Kael.

Thanks to the following reviewers for their thoughtful contributions:

Carl Bridges, *Arthur Andersen Consulting;* Annette Briscoe, *Indiana University Southeast;* Mitchel T. Burchfield, *Southwest Texas Junior College;* Janice Burke, *South Suburban College;* Leila Chambers, *Cuesta College;* G. Jay Christensen, *California State University, Northridge ;* Connie Clark, *Lane Community College;* Miriam Coleman, *Western Michigan University;* Anne Hutta Colvin, *Montgomery County Community College;* Doris L. Cost, *Metropolitan State College of Denver;* L. Ben Crane, *Temple University;* Ava Cross, *Ryerson Polytechnic University;* Nancy J. Daugherty, *Indiana University-Purdue University, Indianapolis;* Rosemarie Dittmer, *Northeastern University;* Gary Donnelly, *Casper College;* Graham N. Drake, *State University of New York, Geneseo;* Kay Durden, *The University of Tennessee at Martin;* Phillip A. Holcomb, *Angelo State University;* Larry R. Honl, *University of Wisconsin, Eau Claire;* Kristi Kelly, *Florida Gulf Coast University;* Michelle Kirtley Johnston, *Loyola University;* Alice Kinder, *Virginia Polytechnic Institute and State University;* Emogene King, *Tyler Junior College;* Richard N. Kleeberg, *Solano Community College;* Patricia Laidler, *Massasoit Community College;* Lowell Lamberton, *Central Oregon Community College;* E. Jay Larson, *Lewis and Clark State College;* Michael Liberman, *East Stroudsburg University;* Julie MacDonald, *Northwestern State University;* Marsha C. Markman, *California Lutheran University;* Diana McKowen, *Indiana University, Bloomington;* Maureen McLaughlin, *Highline Community College;* Sylvia A. Miller, *Cameron University;* Billie Miller-Cooper, *Cosumnes River College;* Wayne Moore, *Indiana University of Pennsylvania;* Gerald W. Morton, *Auburn University of Montgomery ;* Jaunett Neighbors, *Central Virginia Community College;* Judy Nixon, *University of Tennessee at Chattanooga;* Rosemary Olds, *Des Moines Area Community College;* Richard O. Pompian, *Boise State University;* Karen

Sterkel Powell, *Colorado State University;* Seamus Reilly, *University of Illinois;* Jeanette Ritzenthaler, *New Hampshire College;* Betty Robbins, *University of Oklahoma;* Joan C. Roderick, *Southwest Texas State University;* Mary Jane Ryals, *Florida State University;* Lacye Prewitt Schmidt, *State Technical Institute of Memphis;* Sue Seymour, *Cameron University;* Sherry Sherrill, *Forsyth Technical Community College;* John R. Sinton, *Finger Lakes Community College;* Curtis J. Smith, *Finger Lakes Community College;* Craig E. Stanley, *California State University, Sacramento;* Ted O. Stoddard, *Brigham Young University;* Vincent C. Trofi, *Providence College;* Deborah A. Valentine, *Emory University;* Randall L. Waller, *Baylor University;* Maria W. Warren, *University of West Florida;* Michael R. Wunsch, *Northern Arizona University;* Annette Wyandotte, *Indiana University, Southeast;* Betty Rogers Youngkin, *University of Dayton*

I also wish to thank the following reviewers who contributed to the Canadian Edition:

Richard Almonte, *George Brown College;* Sandy Dorley, *Conestoga College;* Amanda Hardman, *Douglas College;* Kathleen Greenfield, *McGill University;* Daniel Guo, *Conestoga College;* Kathryn Pallister, *Red Deer College;* Al Parkin, *St. Lawrence College;* David Patient, *Simon Fraser University;* Pat Post, *University of New Brunswick;* Diane Klempner Russell, *McGill University;* Alberta Smith, *Algonquin College;* Robert Soroka, *Dawson College;* Ruth Tracy, *St. Lawrence College.*

Scot Ober
askober@ober.net

Contemporary Business Communication

1

Understanding Business Communication

communication OBJECTIVES

After you have finished this chapter, you should be able to

1. Understand the role of communication within organizations.

2. Describe the characteristics of the grapevine.

3. Describe the components of communication.

4. Identify the common forms of written and oral communication.

5. Identify the major verbal barriers to communication.

6. Explain the legal and ethical dimensions of communicating.

Look to the Communication Objectives (COs) as a guide to help you master the material. You will see references to the COs throughout the chapter.

Steering communication upward, downward, horizontally, and across business and borders—at full throttle—is part of a race that never ends for Debra Sanchez Fair. As vice president of corporate communications for Nissan North America, she and her 43-person staff drive all communications for the automaker's operations in Canada, the United States, and Mexico. Communication is considered so critical to building internal and external relationships that Fair reports to senior management, the global head of communications, and directly to Nissan's CEO in Tokyo; she is also part of a six-person team handling the corporation's overall communication strategy. Fair always maintains a global perspective because Nissan is headquartered in Japan, has an alliance with France's Renault, and conducts business on every continent. English is the firm's official language.

an insider's
perspective

DEBRA SANCHEZ FAIR
Vice President,
Corporate Communications,
Nissan North America, Inc.

Fair uses a variety of media to share information within the organization, ranging from email, video conferencing, and satellite television to more traditional newsletters, meetings, and memos. Before selecting any medium, however, she carefully plans what she wants to achieve. "First, you have to think about your objective, the audiences you are targeting, and your communication strategies," she says. "Then you think about the tactics. Every situation or initiative may require a different approach."

Several times each year, Fair serves as moderator for internal "town hall meetings," during which senior executives provide updates on key issues and answer questions from employees. "Often, we field questions in advance from the employee base," Fair notes. "We also take emailed questions during the meeting." If time runs out, questions are answered in the company's internal *Dateline* newsletter and posted on their intranet.

One of Fair's biggest challenges was to handle communication related to the Nissan Revival Plan, an aggressive three-year strategy calling for massive organizational changes to restore the company's profitability and growth. Not only did Nissan need internal support to achieve its goals, but it also needed to explain the plan to industry media, financial analysts, shareholders, and other outsiders. "The only way to galvanize the employee base and get the message to external audiences was to get the communication function involved at the start," Fair explains. "The key was developing clear, consistent messages to be communicated internally and externally."

To find out whether audiences understand the Nissan Revival Plan messages, Fair conducts twice-yearly global employee surveys and annual surveys of business leaders and media representatives. "We ask, 'Did your employees understand the key messages?'" she says. "How do they feel about it? Are they on board? Is there a more effective tool we should be using for communication?" Monitoring this feedback helps Fair and her team analyze audience response and keep Nissan's communication on track in the race that never ends.

"The key was developing clear, consistent messages to be communicated internally and externally."

■ Communicating Within Organizations

CO1. **Understand the role of communication within organizations.**

The margin note above shows which communication objective is being addressed in this text.

Communication is necessary if an organization is to achieve its goals.

Walk through the halls of a contemporary organization—no matter whether it's a small start-up entrepreneurial firm, a Fortune 500 global giant, a government office, or a non-profit organization—and what do you see? You will see managers and other employees reading reports, drafting email messages, attending meetings, conducting interviews, talking on the telephone, conferring with subordinates, holding business lunches, reading mail, dictating correspondence, and making presentations. In short, you see people *communicating*.

An organization is a group of people working together to achieve a common goal, and communication is a vital part of that process. Indeed, communication must have occurred before a common goal could even be established. And a group of people working together must interact; that is, they must *communicate* their needs, thoughts, plans, expertise, and so on. Communication is the means by which information is shared, activities are coordinated, and decision making is enhanced.

Understanding how communication works in business and how to communicate competently within an organization will help you participate more effectively in every aspect of business. Indeed, the importance of acquiring communication skills for success in the workplace cannot be understated. A 2005 BackDRAFT survey of 2700 workers in Canada and the US revealed the following[1]:

- Financial/insurance employees spend over 36 percent of their workdays writing (up 6 percent over the past five years)

- Writing in the wholesale industry accounts for 24 percent of the overall workday (up 25 percent)

- Writing in the government accounts for 37 percent of the workday (up 18 percent)

- Business service professionals spend over 31 percent of their workday writing (up 16 percent)

- Transportation/utilities writing now accounts for more than 21 percent of the workday (up 12 percent)

These designers from Bruce Mau Design Studios in Toronto are engaging in both non-verbal communication (such as body movement, voice qualities, and use of space) and verbal communication (speaking, listening, reading, and writing).

Real people in real organizations are highlighted in these photos, most of which are taken from magazines and newspapers.

Yet, in spite of this growing demand for good communication skills, a Conference Board of Canada survey revealed that eight out of ten organizations surveyed said new recruits lack important communication skills in writing, speaking, and listening.[2]

Clearly, good communication skills are crucial to your success in the organization. Competent writing and speaking skills will help you get hired, perform well, and earn promotions. If you decide to go into business for yourself, writing and speaking skills will help you obtain venture capital, promote your product, and manage your employees. These same skills will also help you achieve your personal and social goals.

It is no wonder then that, according to Mark H. McCormack, chairman of International Management Group and best-selling author of *What They Don't Teach You at Harvard Business School,* "People's written communications are probably more revealing than any other single item in the workplace."[3]

■ Directions of Communication

For an organization to be successful, communication must flow freely through formal and informal channels.

The Formal Communication Network

Within the organization, information may be transmitted from superiors to subordinates (downward communication), from subordinates to superiors (upward communication), among people at the same level on the organizational chart (horizontal communication), and among people in different departments within the organization (cross-channel communication). These four types of communication make up the organization's **formal communication network.** We'll use part of Northern Lights' organizational chart, shown in Figure 1.1, to illustrate the directions of communication. (See page 34 in the Appendix to Chapter 1 for a more complete chart.)

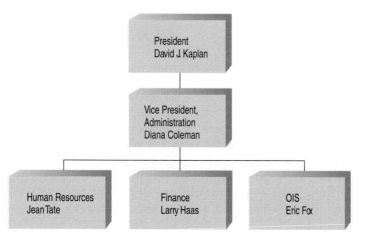

figure1.1

Part of the Formal Communication Network at Northern Lights

spotlight 1

Overcoming Information Anxiety

Executives, like nearly everyone else in this information-laden society, are being bombarded by more data than they can absorb. According to Richard Wurman, author of *Information Anxiety*, to function in business, we are being forced to assimilate a body of knowledge that is expanding by the minute.

For example, consider these statistics:

- The total amount of unique information generated worldwide each single year is about 1.5 exabytes (one exabyte is 1 followed by 18 zeroes). Stored on floppy disks, this amount of information would stack over 3.2 million kilometres high.
- Office workers spend 60 percent of their days processing documents.
- It is estimated that one weekday edition of each day's *New York Times* contains more information than the average person in seventeenth-century England was likely to come across in an entire lifetime.

Wurman believes it's a myth that the more choices you have, the more freedom you enjoy. More choices simply produce more anxiety. So as you decrease the number of choices, you decrease the fear of having made the wrong one.

The Black Hole

Trying to process all this information can induce "information anxiety"—apprehension about the ever-widening gap between what we understand and what we think we should understand. In other words, it is the black hole between data and knowledge. Here are some symptoms of information anxiety as Wurman describes them:

- Nodding your head knowingly when someone mentions a book, artist, or news story that you have actually never heard of.
- Feeling guilty about that ever-higher stack of periodicals waiting to be read.
- Feeling depressed because you don't know what all the buttons on your DVD player do.

Wurman believes that "the System" is at fault—too many people are putting out too much data.

Nobody Knows It All

The first step in overcoming information anxiety is to accept that there is much you won't ever understand. Let your ignorance be an inspiration to learn, not something to conceal. Wurman recommends standing in front of a mirror and practicing, "Could you repeat that?" or "I'm not sure I understand," instead of pretending to understand what you do not.

Other suggestions include the following:

- Separate what you are really interested in from what you merely think you should be interested in.
- Minimize the time you spend reading or watching news that isn't relevant to your life.
- Reduce your pile of office reading.

If all else fails, heed Wurman's conclusion: "Most information is useless. Give yourself permission to dismiss it."[4]

Boxed features called Spotlights illustrate how business communication is affected by three contemporary issues: across cultures, technology, and ethics.

Downward Communication   In most organizations the largest number of vertical communications move downward—from someone of higher authority to someone of lower authority. For example, Dave Kaplan, president of Northern Lights (Figure 1.1), sends an email message to Diana Coleman about a computer report; she, in turn, confers with Eric Fox. Through written and oral channels, information regarding job performance, policies and procedures, day-to-day operations, and other organizational information is communicated. (We'll become quite familiar with Dave and his company in the coming chapters.)

Higher-level management communicates with lower-level employees through such means as email, voice mail, blogs (weblogs), memorandums, conferences, telephone conversations, company newsletters, and policy manuals. One of the problems with written downward communication is that management may assume that what is sent downward is received and understood. Unfortunately, that is not always the case. If you're the boss, you should also recognize that your downward messages will receive more attention, faster responses, and more approval than messages coming from peers or superiors. The fact that those in subordinate positions seek your goodwill does not necessarily mean that your ideas are of higher quality or that they are communicated more effectively.

Upward Communication   Upward communication is the flow of information from lower-level employees to upper-level employees. In Figure 1.1, for example, Jean Tate sends a monthly status report to the president regarding human resource actions for the month, and Diana responds to Dave's memo regarding the computer report. Upward communication can take the form of email, voice mail, blogs, memorandums, conferences, reports, suggestion systems, or union publications, among others.

The free flow of communication upward helps prevent management isolation.

Upward communication is important because it provides higher management with the information needed for decision making. It also cultivates employee loyalty by giving employees an opportunity to be heard, to air their grievances, and to offer suggestions. Finally, upward communication provides the feedback necessary to let supervisors know whether subordinates received and understood messages that were sent downward.

Horizontal Communication   Horizontal communication is the flow of information among peers within the same work unit. For example, the administration division holds a weekly staff meeting at which the three managers (Jean, Larry, and Eric) exchange information about the status of their operations.

Horizontal communication is important to help coordinate work assignments, share information on plans and activities, negotiate differences, and develop interpersonal support, thereby creating a more cohesive work unit. The more that individuals or departments within an organization must interact with each other to accomplish their objectives, the more frequent and intense will be the horizontal communication.

The most common form of horizontal communication is the committee meeting, where most coordination, sharing of information, and problem solving take place. Intense competition for scarce resources, lack of trust among co-workers, or concerns about job security or promotions can sometimes create barriers to the free flow of horizontal information.

Cross-Channel Communication   Cross-channel communication is the exchange of information among employees in different work units who are neither subordinate nor superior to one another. For example, each year a payroll clerk in Jean Tate's department sends out a request to all company employees for updated information about the number of exemptions they claim on their tax forms.

Staff specialists use cross-channel communications frequently because their responsibilities typically involve many departments within the organization. Because they lack line authority to direct those with whom they communicate, they must often rely on their persuasive skills, as, for instance, when the human resources department encourages employees to complete a job-satisfaction questionnaire.

The informal communication network is important in helping an organization achieve its objectives. Obongo, a California tech start-up company, sponsors a monthly potluck lunch for its multicultural management team.

The Informal Communication Network

The **informal communication network** (or the *grapevine*, as it is called) is the transmission of information through nonofficial channels within the organization. Carpooling to work, waiting to use the photocopier, jogging at noon, eating in the cafeteria, or chatting at a local community association meeting—wherever workers come together, they are likely to hear and pass on information about possible happenings in the organization. Employees often say that the grapevine is their most frequent source of information on company plans and performance. In one survey of 451 executives, 91 percent reported that employees typically use the grapevine for information on company "bad news" such as layoffs and takeovers. Office politics was cited as a grapevine topic by 73 percent, whereas only 41 percent said their employees turned to the grapevine for "good news." Another survey found that 39 percent of the managers thought that business matters were the most common subject discussed at the office water cooler—and 17 percent admitted they didn't have a clue.[5]

CO2. Describe the characteristics of the grapevine.

The informal communication network (grapevine) transmits information through non-official channels within the organization.

These are the common characteristics of the grapevine:[6]

- Most of the information passed along the grapevine (about 80 percent) is business related, and most of it (75 to 95 percent) is accurate.

- The grapevine is pervasive. It exists at all levels in the organization—from the corporate boardroom to the assembly line.

- Information moves rapidly along the grapevine.

- The grapevine is most active when change is taking place and when one's need to know or level of fear is highest—during layoffs, plant closings, acquisitions, mergers, and the like.

- The grapevine is a normal, often vital, part of every organization.

As with any medium, the grapevine has both advantages and disadvantages. Experts advise that managers, rather than trying to eliminate the grapevine (a futile effort), should accept its existence and pay attention to it. Doing so will give them a sense of organizational morale, an understanding of employees' anxieties, and insight into how well formal communication networks are working. Moreover, ignoring the grapevine can lead to the spreading of misinformation, lower morale, and lower productivity.[7]

Managers who are aware of the grapevine can act promptly to counteract false rumours. More importantly, they can use the formal communication network (including meetings, memos, newsletters, and bulletin boards) to ensure that all news—positive and negative—gets out to employees as quickly and as completely as possible. The free flow of information within the organization not only stops rumours, but is also simply good business.

■ The Process of Communication

Because communication is such a vital part of the organizational structure, it's important to understand its components. **Communication** is the process of sending and receiving messages—sometimes through spoken or written words and sometimes through such non-verbal means as facial expressions, gestures, and voice qualities. Thus, if someone communicates the following message to you and you receive it, communication will have taken place. However, only if you understand Chinese will the communication have been successful.*

危机

*Illustrated above is the Chinese word for *crisis,* which is composed of the words *danger* and *opportunity,* perhaps an inspirational reminder to always remain hopeful.

As illustrated in Figure 1.2, the communication model consists of five components: the stimulus, filter, message, medium, and destination. Ideally, the process ends with feedback to the sender, although feedback is not necessary for communication to have taken place.

To illustrate the model, let us have another look at Northern Lights. Dave Kaplan was a chemical engineer at Industrial Chemical, Inc. In 2000, in the process of working on another project, Dave developed Ultra Light, a flat, electroluminescent sheet of material that serves as a light source. Dave could see the enormous business opportunity offered by a paper-thin light fixture such as Ultra Light, which was bendable and could be produced in a variety of shapes and sizes.

The market for lighting is vast, and Dave, even though an engineer at the time and not a business person, felt the sting of inventing a device that had great potential but that belonged to somebody else (Industrial Chemical, Inc.). He was disappointed in IC's eventual decision not to manufacture and market this product. As we learn what happened to Dave Kaplan after IC's decision, we'll examine the components of communication, one at a time.

CO3. Describe the components of communication.

Communication is the sending and receiving of verbal and non-verbal messages.

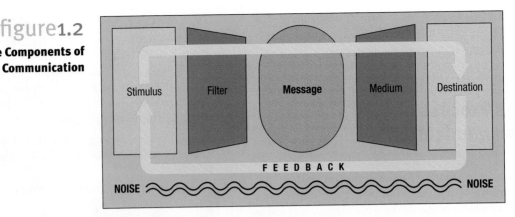

figure1.2

The Components of Communication

Incident	Communication Component
Dave receives a memorandum from the head of R&D.	Dave receives a *stimulus*.
He interprets the memo to mean that IC has no interest in his invention.	He *filters* the stimulus.
He decides to relay this information to his brother.	He forms a *message*.
He telephones Marc.	He selects a *medium*.
His brother receives the call.	The message reaches its *destination*.
Marc listens and gives Dave his reaction.	Marc provides *feedback*.

The Stimulus

Step 1: A stimulus creates a need to communicate.

In order for communication to take place, there first must be a **stimulus,** an event that creates within an individual the need to communicate. This stimulus can be internal or external. An internal stimulus is simply an idea that forms within your mind. External stimuli come to you through your sensory organs—your eyes, ears, nose, mouth, and skin. A stimulus for communicating in business might be an email message you just read, a bit of gossip you heard over lunch, or even the hot air generated by an overworked heating system (or colleague!).

You respond to the stimulus by formulating a message: a **verbal message** (written or spoken words), a **non-verbal message** (non-written and non-spoken signals), or some combination of the two. For Dave Kaplan, the stimulus for communication was a memorandum he received from the head of the research and development (R&D) department informing him that IC was not interested in developing Ultra Light but would, instead, sell the patent to some company that was interested.

The Filter

If everyone had the same perception of events, your job of communicating would be easier; you could assume that your perception of reality was accurate and that others would understand your motives and intent. Instead, each person has a unique perception of reality, based on his or her individual experiences, culture, emotions at the moment, personality, knowledge, socio-economic status, and a host of other variables. These variables act as a **filter** in shaping everyone's unique impressions of reality.

> *Step 2: Our knowledge, experience, and viewpoints act as a filter to help us interpret (decode) the stimulus.*

Once your brain receives a message, it begins to interpret the stimulus to derive meaning from it so that you will know how to respond or whether any response is even necessary.

> *The brain attempts to make sense of the stimulus.*

The memo Dave received from R&D simply reinforced what he had come to expect at his company, which showed little interest in exploiting unexpected discoveries such as Ultra Light. Dave's long involvement in the research that had led to this product caused him to assume a protective, almost paternalistic, interest in its future. Besides, after so many years in the lab, Dave was ready for a new challenge. These factors, then, acted as a filter through which Dave interpreted the memo and formulated his response—a phone call to his brother in Toronto.

At the time of Dave's call, Marc Kaplan was sitting alone in his office at a Toronto advertising agency sampling different brands of pizza (see the photo below, right). As a marketing manager in charge of a new pizza account, he was preoccupied with finding a competitive edge for his client's product, and his perception of Dave's message was filtered by his current situation.

To hear his scientist brother, the McGill graduate who all his life had preferred to pursue solitary scholarly research, suddenly erupting over the phone with the idea of starting a business, contradicted Marc's lifelong preconceptions about Dave and acted as a strong filter resisting Dave's urgent message. Furthermore, Marc's emotional and physical frame of reference—hunkered down as he was over several pizzas—did not put him in a receptive mood for a grand scheme that would take tens of thousands of dollars and many years of hard work. But Marc's background—his economic status, his education, and his current job—added another point of view, in this case a highly favourable filter for taking in Dave's message.

If Dave is convincing in communicating his message, he might be able to persuade Marc to join him in buying the Ultra Light patent from IC and starting a business of their own.

The Message

Dave's message to Marc was, "Let's form our own company." The extent to which any communication effort achieves its desired goal depends on how well you construct the **message** (the information to be communicated). Success at communicating depends not only on the purpose and content of the message but also on how skillful you are at communicating, how well you know your **audience** (the person or persons with whom you're communicating), and how much you hold in common with your audience. As a scientist, Dave Kaplan did not have an extensive business vocabulary. Nor did

An example of communication at work.

Let's form a company, Marc.

This is my brother? I don't believe this.

Step 3: We formulate (encode) a verbal or non-verbal response to the stimulus.

he have much practice at oral business presentations and the careful pacing and selective reinforcement required in such circumstances. In effect, Dave was attempting to make an oral business proposal, unfortunately without much technique or skill.

"You're crazy, Dave. You don't know what you're talking about." This initial response from Marc made it clear to Dave that his message wasn't getting through. But what Dave lacked in skill, he made up for in knowing his audience (his kid brother) backward and forward.

"You're chicken, Marc," had always gotten Marc's attention and interest in the past, and it worked again. Dave kept challenging Marc, something he knew Marc couldn't resist, and kept reminding him of their common ground: all the happy adventures they had shared as kids and adults.

The Medium

Step 4: We select the form of the message (medium).

Once the sender has encoded a message, the next step in the process is to transmit that message to the receiver. At this point, the sender must choose the **medium,** that is, the means of transmitting the message. Oral messages might be transmitted through a staff meeting, personal conference, telephone conversation, voice mail, or even such informal means as the company grapevine. Written messages might be transmitted through a memorandum, a report, a brochure, a bulletin board notice, email, a company newsletter, or an addition to the policies and procedures manual. And non-verbal messages might be transmitted through facial expressions, gestures, or body movement. (See Spotlight 2, "The Medium is the Message," on page 14.)

Because Dave is in the process of talking with Marc over the phone, his medium is a telephone conversation. You should be aware that the most commonly used forms of communication are not necessarily the most effective ones. The International Association of Business Communicators (IABC) recently surveyed nearly 1000 organizations about their communication practices. As shown in Figure 1.3, although email was found to be the most frequently used medium of communication, it was not considered the most effective medium.[8]

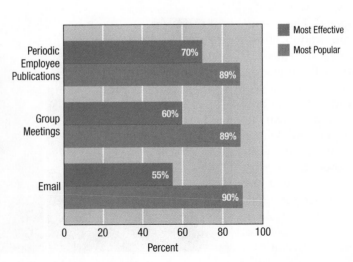

figure1.3

Effectiveness Versus Popularity of Communication Media

The Destination

The message is transmitted and then enters the sensory environment of the receiver, at which point control passes from the sender to the receiver. Once the message reaches its destination, there is no guarantee that communication will actually occur. We are constantly bombarded with stimuli, and our sensory organs pick up only part of them. Even assuming your receiver does perceive your message, you have no assurance that it will be interpreted (filtered) as you intended. Your transmitted message then becomes the source, or stimulus, for the next communication episode, and the process begins anew.

Step 5: The message reaches its destination and, if successful, is perceived accurately by the receiver.

After Dave's enthusiastic, one-hour phone call, Marc promised to consider the venture seriously. Marc's response provided **feedback** (reaction to a message) to Dave on how accurately his own message had been received. In time, it led to many more versions of the communication process, both written and oral, before the two brothers founded Northern Lights, a small "start-up" company whose primary product is Ultra Light. The company employs 178 people at its corporate headquarters in Calgary, and at a completely automated manufacturing plant in Winnipeg.

The Dynamic Nature of Communication

From our look at the components of communication and the model presented in Figure 1.2 on page 10, you might erroneously conclude that communication is a linear, static process—flowing in an orderly fashion from one stage to the next—and that you can easily separate the communicators into senders and receivers. That is not at all the case.

Communication is not a linear, static process.

Two or more people often send and receive messages simultaneously. At the same time you are receiving one message, you may be sending another. For example, the look on your face as you are receiving a message may be sending a new message to the sender that you either understand, agree with, or are baffled by the message being sent. And the feedback thus given may prompt the sender to modify his or her intended message.

Therefore, artificially "freezing" the action in order to examine each step of the communication process separately causes us to lose some of the dynamic richness of that process in terms of both its verbal and non-verbal components.

Northern Lights: A Continuing Case Study

As we join Northern Lights (NL), Dave and Marc's company has annual sales in the $30 million range, with a net profit last year of $1.4 million. It is considered a progressive company by the investment community, with skillful management and healthy earnings potential. The local community considers NL to be a good corporate citizen; it is non-polluting, and its officers are active in community affairs.

A Northern Lights continuing case problem is at the end of each chapter.

You will be seeing more of the Kaplan brothers and Northern Lights in the chapters ahead, as communication within the organization serves as an ongoing case study for each of the major areas of business communication—from this basic model of communication all the way through to the final chapter. You'll have the opportunity to get to know the people in the company and watch from the inside as they handle every type of business communication in concrete terms. Right now, you can learn more of the background of Northern Lights by reading the Appendix to Chapter 1 (beginning on page 33), which contains an overview of the company's history, products, financial data, and all-too-human personnel.

The Medium Is the Message

Marshall McLuhan (1911–1980) is considered by many to be the world's most influential scholar in the area of communications and technology. Born in Edmonton, and spending much of his career at the University of Toronto as Director of the Centre for Culture and Technology, McLuhan is perhaps best known for coining "The medium is the message." McLuhan argued that the content of the message you send is actually subordinate to the medium you choose. Each medium has unique characteristics that affect the reader in different ways, and thus your choice of medium is at least as important as the message itself. And exactly how does the medium affect the message you send?

Situation A: Telephone

Assume that your travel plans for two weeks from now just changed and you find that you'll have to stay overnight in Winnipeg instead of continuing on to Vancouver. You decide to use the evening to wine and dine a good customer in nearby Ste. Anne. Which medium should you use to invite her and her spouse to dinner?

The simplest and fastest thing to do, of course, is to pick up the phone and call your customer. But because you're both busy people (isn't everyone, these days?), you should be prepared to leave a voice mail message, if necessary:

Voice Mail

Hi, Marge. Stan Petrie here from Eastern Container Corporation. It's 2:30 p.m. on Monday, October 1. I just found out that I'm going to be in town Wednesday night, October 17, and hope you and Casper can be my guests for dinner at Cordon Bleu Restaurant. If you can come, let's plan to meet in the lobby at 7:00 p.m. Please give me a call back at 416-555-8221 to let me know if you can join me. I look forward to seeing you. Bye.

Notice how your choice of telephone communication affected the content of your message. First, because some answering machines and voice-message systems don't record the time, you included the time and date of your call. Also, recognizing that some systems have limited capacity, you cut out the small talk and left a concise, to-the-point

message (after all, you don't want to get disconnected midsentence). You were also considerate enough to provide your phone number, which also encourages a prompt callback.

Because you were leaving a voice message, you were able to use certain non-verbal clues—such as enthusiasm and warmth in your tone of voice—to help convey a friendly message and encourage this important customer to accept your invitation. As you can see, oral messages generally assume a more informal tone than do written messages.

Situation B: Email

Uh, oh. You just realized that (1) Marge and Casper might not know where Cordon Bleu Restaurant is, and (2) they have young children and will need to leave some emergency location information with their sitter. Phone messages work best for one-way calls or for requests that require a short, simple response. They do not work well for detailed messages because the listener must listen and try to take notes at the same time.

Instead of phoning, you decide to send Marge an email:

Email

Hi, Marge:
I will be in town on Wednesday, October 17, and invite you and Casper to be my guests for dinner at Cordon Bleu Restaurant (15 La Verendrye Ave; Phone: 204-555-8766).

If you can join me, let's plan to meet in the lobby at 7:00 p.m. We should be finished with dinner by 9:30 p.m.

It will be good to visit with you and Casper again.
Stan Petrie
Eastern Container Corporation
416-555-8221
spetrie@ecc.com

One advantage of email (of any written communication, in fact) is that you can revise your message before sending it—to make it more effective. Also, the recipient can save or print the message if desired, thereby providing documentation. Another advantage is that responding is simple; the recipient can simply click the Reply button and either accept or decline your invitation. Note also that because your phone number is included in your "signature," you don't need to include it in the body of the email itself.

Situation C: Letter

Now assume a different scenario. For some reason, Marge has not placed an order with Eastern Container Corporation in more than a month, and you want to gently broach this subject with her to find out why. Given the fact that she may be embarrassed at not swinging any business your way lately, Marge might be reluctant to accept your invitation and might need some "incentive" to join you.

Wanting to make a favourable impression on this good customer and realizing that email is not always free from prying eyes, you decide to invite her to dinner in a letter. (After all, the dinner is still two weeks away, so you have time to go the "snail mail" route.)

Business Letter

Dear Marge:

Your company's feedback earlier this spring helped us redesign our series of corrugated shipping cartons, and I'd like to thank you in person.

Would you and Casper be my guests for dinner at Cordon Bleu Restaurant on Wednesday, October 17? The restaurant is located at 15 La Verendrye Ave; its phone

---

number is 204-555-8766. If you can join me, let's plan to meet in the lobby at 7:00 p.m. We should be finished with dinner by 9:30 p.m.

It will be good to see you again—and also to let you in on a few "surprises" we discovered along the way to redesigning these cartons.
Sincerely,

Notice how the medium affects the message in this version. First, in the transmitted document, the message will be formatted in regular business letter format and on letterhead stationery, which will give it a more formal appearance. Second, note the differences in the organization of the message—for example, the persuasive opening and the "teaser" at the end. Finally, because space is not at a premium, you can include more information in a business letter than is advisable in voice mail and email messages (remembering, however, that conciseness is a virtue in any form of communication).

The overall tone of the business letter also differs from that of the voice mail message. To illustrate the differences, read the voice mail message aloud; then read the business letter aloud. You will immediately note the difference in the naturalness of each message for its intended medium. The medium is the message—at least, in part.

Sometimes in your communications, you have a choice as to which medium to use (of course, sometimes you do not). Competent communicators ensure that both the medium and the message itself help them achieve their communication objective.

■ Verbal Communication

It is the ability to communicate by using words that separates human beings from the rest of the animal kingdom. Our verbal ability also enables us to learn from the past—to benefit from the experience of others.

CO4. Identify the common forms of written and oral communication.

Oral Communication

Oral communication is one of the most common functions in business. Consider, for example, how limiting it would be if a manager could not attend meetings, ask questions of colleagues, make presentations, appraise performance, handle customer complaints, or give instructions.

Oral communication is different from written communication in that it allows more ways to get a message across to others. You can clear up any questions immediately;

Verbal messages are composed of words—either written or spoken.

use non-verbal clues; provide additional information; and use pauses, emphasis, and voice tone to stress certain points.

According to research, these are the most annoying voice qualities, listed in decreasing order of annoyance:[9]

Whining, complaining, or nagging tone	44%
High-pitched, squeaky voice	16%
Mumbling	11%
Talking very fast	5%
Weak, wimpy voice	4%
Flat, monotonous tone	4%

For oral communication to be effective, a second communication skill— listening—is also required. No matter how well-crafted the content and delivery of an oral presentation, it cannot achieve its goal if the intended audience does not have effective listening skills. Some research has found that nearly 60 percent of all communication problems in business are caused by poor listening.[10]

Written Communication

Writing is more difficult than speaking because you have to get your message correct the first time; you do not have the advantage of immediate feedback or nonverbal clues such as facial expressions to help you achieve your objective. Examples of typical written communication in industry include the following:

- *Email (electronic mail):* **Email** (see Figure 1.3 on page 12) is a message transmitted electronically over a computer network. Often, in the contemporary office, email has replaced traditional memorandums and, in many cases, letters.

- *Web site:* A **Web site** comprises one or more pages of related information that is posted on the World Wide Web and is accessed via the Internet; the main page of a Web site is called its "home page."

- *Weblog:* A Weblog (often shortened to **blog**) is a Web site where regular entries are made, much like an online diary. In business, blogs may be used by the organization to disseminate information to and solicit feedback from employees or the public.

- *Memorandums:* A **memorandum** is a written message sent to someone working in the same organization.

- *Letters:* A **letter** is a written message sent to someone outside the organization.

- *Reports:* A **report** is an orderly and objective presentation of information that assists in decision making and problem solving. Examples of common business reports include policies and procedures, status reports, financial reports, personnel evaluations, and computer printouts.

- *Miscellaneous:* Other examples of written communication include contracts, sales literature, newsletters, and bulletin board notices.

Writing is crucial to the modern organization because it serves as the major source of documentation. A speech may make a striking impression, but a memorandum leaves a permanent record for others to refer to in the future in case memory fails or a dispute arises.

For written messages to achieve their goals, they must, of course, be read. The skill of efficient reading is becoming more important in today's technological society. The abundance of widespread computing and word processing capabilities, along with the proliferation of convenient and economical photocopying and faxing, has created more paperwork rather than less. It is estimated that the typical manager reads about a million words every week.[11] Thus, information overload is one of the unfortunate by-products of our times (see Spotlight 1, "Overcoming Information Anxiety," on page 6). These and other implications of technology on business communication are discussed throughout this text.

Most oral communication is temporary; written communication is permanent.

Barriers to Verbal Communication

Considering the complex nature of the communication process, your messages may not always be received exactly as you intended. As a matter of fact, sometimes your messages will not be received at all; at other times, they will be received incompletely or inaccurately. Some of the obstacles to effective and efficient communication are verbal; others are non-verbal. As illustrated in Figure 1.4, these barriers can create an impenetrable "brick wall" that makes effective communication impossible.

CO5. Identify the major verbal barriers to communication.

Verbal barriers are related to what you write or say. They include inadequate knowledge or vocabulary, differences in interpretation, language differences, inappropriate use of expressions, over-abstraction and ambiguity, and polarization.

Inadequate Knowledge or Vocabulary   Before you can even begin to think about how you will communicate an idea, you must, first of all, *have* the idea; that is, you must have sufficient knowledge about the topic to know what you want to say. Regardless of your level of technical expertise, this may not be as simple as it sounds. Assume, for example, that you are Larry Haas, manager of the finance department at Northern Lights. Dave Kaplan, president of the company, has asked you to evaluate an investment opportunity. You've completed all the necessary research and are now ready to write your report. Or are you?

Have you analyzed your audience? Do you know how much the president knows about the investment so that you'll know how much background information to include? Do you know how familiar Dave is with investment terminology? Can you safely use abbreviations like *NPV* and *RRR,* or will you have to spell out and perhaps define *net present value and required rate of return?* Do you know whether the president would prefer to have your conclusions at the beginning of the report, followed by your analysis, or at the end? What tone should the report take? The answers to such questions will be important if you are to achieve your objective in writing the report.

You must know enough about both your topic and your audience to express yourself precisely and appropriately.

Differences in Interpretation   Sometimes senders and receivers attribute different meanings to the same word or attribute the same meaning to different words. When this happens, miscommunication can occur.

Every word has both a denotative and a connotative meaning. **Denotation** refers to the literal, dictionary meaning of a word. **Connotation** refers to the subjective, emotional meaning that you attach to a word. For example, the denotative meaning of the word *plastic* is "a synthetic material that can be easily molded into different forms." For some people, the word also has a negative connotative meaning— "cheap or artificial substitute." For other people, the word means a credit card, as in "He used plastic to pay the bill."

A word's denotation defines its meaning; its connotation indicates our associations with the word.

figure1.4

Verbal Barriers to Communication

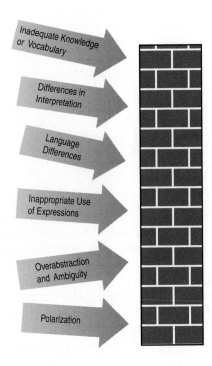

Inadequate Knowledge or Vocabulary

Differences in Interpretation

Language Differences

Inappropriate Use of Expressions

Overabstraction and Ambiguity

Polarization

Most of the interpretation problems occur because of the personal reactions engendered by the connotative meaning of a word. Do you have a positive, neutral, or negative reaction to the terms *broad, bad, aggressive, hard-hitting, workaholic, corporate raider, headhunter, golden parachute,* or *wasted?* Are your reactions likely to be the same as everyone else's? The problem with some terms is not only that people assign different meanings to the term but also that the term itself might cause such an emotional reaction that the receiver is "turned off" to any further communication with the sender.

Language Differences   In an ideal world, all managers would know the language of each culture with which they deal. International business people often say that you can buy in your native language anywhere in the world, but you can sell only in the language of the local community. Most of the correspondence between Canadian and foreign firms is in English or French; in other cases, the services of a qualified interpreter (for oral communication) or translator (for written communication) may be available. But even with such services, problems can occur. Consider, for example, the following blunders:[12]

- In Brazil, where Portuguese is spoken, an airline advertised that its Boeing 747s had "rendezvous lounges," without realizing that rendezvous in Portuguese implies prostitution.

- In China, Kentucky Fried Chicken's slogan "Finger-lickin' good" was translated "So good you suck your fingers."

- In Puerto Rico, General Motors had difficulties advertising Chevrolet's Nova model because the name sounds like the Spanish phrase "No va," which means "It doesn't go."

To ensure that the intended meaning is not lost during translation, important documents should first be translated into the second language and then retranslated into English. Be aware, however, that communication difficulties can arise even among native English speakers. For example, a British advertisement for Electrolux vacuum cleaners displayed the headline "Nothing Sucks Like An Electrolux." Copywriters in Canada would never use this wording!

Inappropriate Use of Expressions   Expressions are groups of words whose intended meanings are different from their literal interpretations. Examples include slang, jargon, and euphemisms.

- **Slang** is an expression, often short-lived, that is identified with a specific group of people. Business, of course, has its own slang, such as *24/7, bandwidth, hardball, strategic fit,* and *window of opportunity.* Teenagers, construction workers, immigrants, knowledge professionals, and just about every other subgroup you can imagine all have their own sets of slang. Using appropriate slang in everyday speech presents no problem; it conveys precise information and may indicate group membership. Problems arise, however, when the sender uses slang that the receiver doesn't understand. Using slang when communicating with someone whose native language is not English can cause misunderstandings. Slang that sends a negative non-verbal message about the sender can also be a source of problems.

- **Jargon** is the technical terminology used within specialized groups; it has sometimes been called "the pros' prose." Technology, for example, has spawned a whole new vocabulary. Do you know the meaning of these common computer terms?

The use of slang, jargon, and euphemisms is sometimes appropriate and sometimes inappropriate.

applet	FAQ	JPEG	plug'n'play
blog	flame	killer app	ROFL
BRB	hacker	locked up	spam
BTW	HTML	patch	worm
CU	IMO	PDA	WYSIWYG
e-commerce			

As with slang, the problem is not in using jargon—jargon provides a very precise and efficient way of communicating with those familiar with it. The problem comes either in using jargon with someone who doesn't understand it or in using jargon in an effort to impress others.

- **Euphemisms** are inoffensive expressions used in place of words that may offend or suggest something unpleasant. Sensitive writers and speakers use euphemisms occasionally, especially to describe bodily functions. How many ways, for example, can you think of to say that someone has died?

Slang, jargon, and euphemisms all have important roles to play in business communication—so long as they're used with appropriate people and in appropriate contexts. They can, however, prove to

CANADIAN-ISMS   *word*wise

Washroom	Canadians head for the washroom when they need to use the toilet. Bathrooms are places with bathtubs in them.
Allophone	Someone whose first language is neither English nor French.
Caisse pop	A kind of co-op bank, found mostly in Quebec. Formally known as a caisse populaire.
Toonie	Canadian two-dollar coin, "Give me a couple toonies and a loonie for this five-dollar bill."
Keener	Someone who tries to impress people of authority for their own personal gain. "He's such a keener."

be barriers to effective communication when used to impress, when used too often, or when used in inappropriate settings.

Overabstraction and Ambiguity

An **abstract word** identifies an idea or a feeling instead of a concrete object. For example, *communication* is an abstract word, whereas *memorandum* is a **concrete word,** a word that identifies something that can be seen or touched. Abstract words are necessary in order to communicate about things you cannot see or touch. However, communication problems result when you use too many abstract words or when you use too high

a level of abstraction. The higher the level of abstraction, the more difficult it is for the receiver to visualize exactly what the sender has in mind. For example, which sentence communicates more information: "I acquired an asset at the store" or "I bought a laser printer at Staples"?

Similar communication problems result from the overuse of ambiguous terms such as a *few, some, several,* and *far away,* which have too broad a meaning for use in much business communication.

The word transportation is abstract; the word automobile is concrete.

Polarization

At times, some people act as though every situation is divided into two opposite and distinct poles, with no allowance for a middle ground. "You are with me or against me," is a common example of a viewpoint that artificially divides the world into two opposing categories. Of course, there are some true dichotomies. You are either human or non-human, and your company either will or will not make a profit this year. But most aspects of life involve more than two alternatives.

Thinking in terms of all or nothing limits our choices.

For example, you might assume that a speaker either is telling the truth or is lying. In fact, what the speaker actually says may be true, but by selectively omitting some important information, he or she may be giving an inaccurate impression. Is the speaker telling the truth or not? Most likely, the answer lies somewhere in between. Likewise, you are not necessarily either tall or short, rich or poor, smart or dumb. Competent communicators avoid inappropriate either/or logic and instead make the effort to search for middle-ground words when such language best describes a situation.

It is generally more effective to depend on logic instead of emotions when communicating.

■ Ethics and Communication

co6. Explain the legal and ethical dimensions of communicating.

Each of us has a personal code of **ethics,** or rules of conduct, that might go beyond legal rules to tell us how to act when the law is silent. When composing a business proposal, drafting a sales letter, writing a human resources policy, or recruiting a

Other Ethical Considerations

Sometimes being legally right is not sufficient justification for our actions (see Spotlight 3, "How Would You Respond?," on page 22). Many corporations have developed their own codes of ethics to govern employee behaviour. For the business communicator, the matter of ethics governs not only one's behaviour but also one's communication of that behaviour. In other words, how we use language involves ethical choices.

A message can be true and still be unethical.

When you have doubts about the ethical propriety of your writing, ask yourself these questions:

1. Is this message true?
2. Does it exaggerate?
3. Does it withhold or obscure information that should be communicated?
4. Does it promise something that cannot be delivered?
5. Does it betray a confidence?
6. Does it play unduly on the fears of the reader?
7. Does it reflect the wishes of the organization?

Competent communicators use their knowledge of communication to achieve their goals while acting in an ethical manner.

■ Introducing the 3Ps (Problem, Process, Product) Model

Every chapter in this text concludes with a 3Ps model designed to illustrate important communication concepts covered in the chapter (see the following section).

The 3Ps model guides you step-by-step through a typical writing assignment by posing and answering relevant questions about each aspect of the message.

These short case studies of typical communication assignments include the *problem*, the *process*, and the *product* (the 3Ps). The *problem* defines the situation and discusses the need for a particular communication task. The *process* is a series of questions that provides step-by-step guidance for accomplishing the specific communication task. Finally, the *product* is the result—the finished document.

The 3Ps model provides a practical demonstration of a particular type of communication, shown close up so that you can see the *process* of writing, not just the results. This process helps you focus on one aspect of writing at a time. Use the 3Ps steps regularly in your own writing so that your written communications will be easier to produce and more effective in their results.

Pay particular attention to the questions in the Process section and ask yourself similar questions as you compose your own messages. Finally, read through the finished document and note any changes made from the draft sentences composed in the Process section.

WRITING AN ETHICAL STATEMENT

Problem

Assume the role of Jason, a quality control engineer for an automobile manufacturer. You are responsible for testing a new airbag design. Your company is eager to install the new airbags in next year's models because two competitors have similar airbags on the market. However, your tests of the new design have not been completely successful. All of the airbags tested inflated on impact, but 10 airbags out of every 100 tested inflated only 60 percent. These partially inflated airbags would still protect passengers from most of a collision impact, but the passengers might receive more injuries than they would with fully inflated bags.

Before reporting the test results, you tell your supervisor that you would like to run more tests to make sure that the airbags are reliable and safe. But your supervisor explains that the company executives are eager to get the airbags on the market and want the results in a few days. You now feel pressured to certify that the airbags are safe (and indeed, they all inflated—at least partially).

Process

1. What is the problem you are facing?

   I must decide exactly how I will phrase the certification sentence in my report.

2. What would be the ideal solution to this problem?

   I would be given additional time to conduct enough tests to assure myself that the airbags are reliable and safe.

3. Why can't the ideal solution be recommended?

   The company is pressuring me to certify the airbags now because two competitors have already introduced similar airbags.

4. Brainstorm possible certification statements that you might make.
   - All the airbags inflated.
   - None of the airbags failed to inflate.
   - Ninety percent of the airbags inflated fully; the rest inflated only 60 percent.

5. How will you determine which is the best statement? In other words, what criteria will you use to evaluate the statements?
   - Would the statement be in the best interests of the company?
   - Would the statement be in the best interests of the public?
   - Would the statement be in my own best interests?

6. Now evaluate each alternative in terms of these criteria.

All the airbags inflated.

This statement is true and is a positive statement that will probably satisfy management. However, it overstates the success of the tests and is somewhat misleading in what it omits—that 10 percent of the airbags inflated only partially. I may be harming potential users by giving them a false sense of security; in addition, I may be leaving the company open to lawsuits resulting from failure of airbags to inflate fully.

None of the airbags failed to inflate.

Again, this statement is true but omits important information the consumer needs. In addition, it is a negative statement, which will not please management.

Ninety percent of the airbags inflated fully; the rest inflated only 60 percent.

This statement provides the most accurate assessment of the test results. It emphasizes the positive and does state that some problems exist. The most serious risk with this alternative is that it could delay the release of the new design on the market. If this happens, my job might be at risk. In addition, it doesn't interpret the meaning of the partially inflated airbags.

7. Using what you've discovered about each alternative, construct the certification statement you will include in your report to management.

Product

Results of my testing of the new airbag design indicate that 90 percent of the airbags inflate fully on impact; the remaining 10 percent inflate 60 percent, which is sufficient to protect passengers from most of a collision impact.

■ Summary

co1. Understand the role of communication within organizations.

The organization's formal communication network consists of downward communication from superiors to subordinates, upward communication from subordinates to superiors, horizontal communication among people at the same level, and cross-channel communication among people in different departments within the organization.

co2. Describe the characteristics of the grapevine.

The informal communication network (also called the grapevine) consists of information transmitted through non-official channels. Rather than try to eliminate it, managers should accept its existence and pay attention to it.

co3. Describe the components of communication.

The communication process begins with a stimulus. On the basis of your unique knowledge, experience, and viewpoints, you filter, or interpret, the stimulus and formulate the message you wish to communicate. The next step is to select a medium of transmission for the message. Finally, the message reaches its destination. If it is successful, the receiver perceives it as a source for communication and provides appropriate feedback to you.

co4. Identify the common forms of written and oral communication.

Verbal communication includes oral (speaking and listening) and written (writing and reading) communication. Common forms of written communication in business include email messages, blogs, Web sites, memorandums, letters, and reports.

co5. Identify the major verbal barriers to communication.

Sometimes barriers are present that interfere with effective communication. Examples of verbal barriers are inadequate knowledge or vocabulary, differences in interpretation, language differences, inappropriate use of expressions, overabstraction and ambiguity, and polarization.

co6. Explain the legal and ethical dimensions of communicating.

Regardless of the size and type of organization, every business writer faces ethical questions when communicating orally and in writing. Legal questions arise with regard to defamation, invasion of privacy, and fraud or misrepresentation. In choosing what information to convey, and which words and sentences to use, we make ethical choices—moral decisions about what is right, even when no question of law is involved.

■ Key Terms

You should now be able to define the following terms in your own words and give an original example of each:

abstract word (20)	ethics (20)
audience (11)	euphemism (19)
blog (16)	feedback (13)
communication (9)	filter (11)
concrete word (20)	formal communication network (5)
connotation (17)	fraud (21)
defamation (21)	informal communication network (8)
denotation (17)	invasion of privacy (21)
email (16)	jargon (19)

letter (16)

libel (21)

medium (12)

memorandum (16)

message (11)

misrepresentation (22)

non-verbal message (10)

report (16)

slander (21)

slang (19)

stimulus (10)

verbal message (10)

Web site (16)

■ Exercises

1 **Nissan North America, Inc. Revisited**   By regularly asking for feedback from employees, media representatives, business leaders, and others, Debra Sanchez Fair is able to gauge whether her audiences have received and understood the messages sent by Nissan North America. If changes are necessary, she and her staff decide whether to switch to another medium, repeat key points for reinforcement, or entirely change the message content. Fair knows that good communication starts with a clear sense of purpose and a thorough knowledge of the audience.

The first Exercise in each chapter relates back to An Insider's Perspective. Exercises also contain continuing examples used throughout the chapters.

Problem

You are in charge of dealer relations for Nissan North America. At the end of the workday, you receive a call from an angry dealer in Ottowa who yells about being repeatedly disconnected during calls to Nissan's Tokyo headquarters. Over and over, this dealer screams about the rude treatment he says he has received when trying to talk with people in Nissan's Japanese headquarters. You doubt any employees would be rude on purpose, yet it is your job to ensure smooth relations with dealers.

CO1. **Understand the role of communication within organizations.**

Process

a. What is the problem you are facing in this situation?
b. What verbal barriers to communication seem to be operating here?
c. What options do you see for resolving this problem?
d. What criteria can you use to determine the option that will best solve this problem?
e. Using these criteria, evaluate your options and identify the best one.

Product

What opening statement can you make to the dealer as a way of implementing the option you have selected as the best solution to this problem?

2 **Grapevine**   Read a journal article about the company grapevine. Then write a one-page summary of the article. Proofread for content and language errors and revise as needed. Staple a photocopy of the article to your summary and submit both to your instructor.

CO2. **Describe the characteristics of the grapevine.**

3 **The Digital Grapevine**   The international airline Swissair has an excellent safety record, but its management knows that accidents can occur at any time.

As a result, Swissair has developed a plan to guide the company's communication response to emergencies. The purpose is to ensure that employees, media representatives, and other audiences have fast and convenient access to accurate information. As part of this plan, the airline is always ready to post a special Web page with crisis contacts and other details. The company had to put its plan into effect not long ago when a Swissair jet crashed near Nova Scotia. Immediately after the crash, management posted a Web page with facts about the accident and created a prominent link to the page from the airline's home page at www.swissair.com so the public—and Swissair employees—could get up-to-the-minute news.

Now Swissair has hired you to evaluate its management of the digital grapevine and to suggest additional ways of improving internal communication during emergencies. With what types of emergencies should Swissair be concerned? What kind of information would employees need during these crises? How do you recommend that Swissair use the Internet to provide its employees with accurate, updated information during such emergencies? Prepare a brief memorandum to management, summarizing your recommendations.

4 Slanguage   Using Google or some other search engine, enter the search terms *Canadian slang*. You will find dozens of Web sites on Canadian slang, many of which focus on the differences between Canadian and American slang.

Identify ten common slang expressions that are uniquely Canadian. Writing for an American audience, write a one-page report, in your own words, that explains the meaning of each of these expressions.

5 Communication Process   Use an incident from a recent television program to illustrate each of the five components of the communication process. Identify any communication barriers that you observed.

CO3. Describe the components of communication.

6 Communication Components   Working with a partner, identify the five components of communication in the following situation:

> Alice Liston has had a dream of going to university. She has maintained a 95 percent average in high school and was both class president and valedictorian. Because her family is not in a position to pay her tuition, Alice applied for a Canada Millennium Scholarship. Two weeks later Alice receives a letter from the scholarship committee. She nervously reads the letter and then runs to her bedroom to email her best friend, letting her know that she had received the scholarship. Her friend reads the email message two hours later.

After identifying the five components in this scenario, working in pairs, prepare your own communication scenario and identify the five components of communication for it.

CO4. Identify the common forms of written and oral communication.

7 Internet Exercise   This chapter discussed how email messages are replacing traditional memorandums and letters in the contemporary office. But are email messages sent or received by managers and employees really private? Using Internet search tools such as Google.ca, search such word combinations as *email (or e-mail) + privacy* to investigate the issue of email privacy at work. Why are companies concerned about employee use of email? What are they doing to monitor email messages? How are employees reacting to this situation? Share your findings in a brief classroom presentation; be sure to include your views about whether companies should be allowed to monitor email messages by employees.

8 **Communication Directions**   Think of an organization to which you belong or a business with which you are familiar. Provide a specific illustration of each of the four directions in the formal communication network. Then develop an organizational chart similar to the one in Figure 1.1 on page 5.

9 **Communicating at Northern Lights**   Using the organizational chart from the Appendix to Chapter 1 (page 34), determine the direction (downward, upward, horizontal, or cross-channel) and the formality (formal or informal) being used in each of the following situations:
a. David J. Kaplan sends an email message to Paul Yu regarding a recent drop in sales.
b. Mary Lyons talks to Larry Haas by telephone about financing for some new manufacturing equipment.
c. O.J. Drew visits with C.B. Odom over lunch about possible changes on the production line.
d. Ann Stetsky meets with Marc Kaplan to review their upcoming presentation to the company's employees.
e. Wendy Janish emails O.J. Drew asking questions about the latest Ultra Light product to help her prepare the new advertising campaign.
f. Luis Diaz talks with Thomas Mercado while playing golf about adding a new storage facility.
g. Marc Kaplan gets a voice mail message from Thomas Mercado asking him for information about a presentation to David J. Kaplan.
h. Diana Coleman receives a report from Jean Tate outlining the new hiring policy.
i. Eric Fox calls Mary Lyons at home to ask her about the layoff rumours.

10 **Diversity**   "I'll never understand our people in Pakistan," Eileen said. "I wrote our local agent over there, who's supposedly a financial wizard, this note: 'If your firm wants to play ball with us, we'll need the straight scoop. What's your bottom-line price on the STX model with all the bells and whistles? Also, if you pull out all the stops, can we get delivery by Xmas?' And you know what he did? He wrote me back a long letter, inquiring about my health and my family, but never answering my questions! If they don't get on the ball, I'm going to recommend that we stop doing business with them." From a communication standpoint, what is happening here? What advice can you give Eileen? Rewrite her message to the Pakistani agent to make it more effective.

CO5. Identify the major verbal barriers to communication.

11 **Code of Ethics**   Working with several classmates, develop a code of ethics for this class. Share your code of ethics with the other groups in the class. Based on the items presented to the class, as a class, select a code of ethics that all class members can abide by for the semester.

CO6. Explain the legal and ethical dimensions of communicating.

12 **You Are Invited**   Recently, two million people opened their mailboxes to find what they thought was a wedding invitation. It was the same size as a wedding invitation, was printed on pale-gray card stock, had the words *RSVP* in silver on the envelope, and was sent using a regular postage stamp. Only after opening the envelope did readers discover that the message was an "invitation" to subscribe to a high-speed Internet service.

You've probably received mail like this, because companies have found these come-ons effective. Do you think it is ethical for companies to use gimmicks like this to induce customers to read their sales letters? If so, which gimmicks are acceptable and which are not? Would a sales message contained in an envelope that was made to look like an official government communication be ethical?

Write a one-page, double-spaced report giving your view of this practice. Use logic, rather than emotionalism, to discuss why you think as you do.

13 **Legal**   Sam was thinking of hiring Olivia Mason for an open sales territory. Knowing she had previously worked at Kentron, he called his friend there, Barry Kelley, to ask about her performance. "She's very smart, but I wouldn't hire her again, Sam," Barry said. "She's a little lazy. Sometimes she wouldn't begin making her calls until late morning or even after lunch. And she was also sloppy with her paperwork. I assume she's honest, but I never could get her to file receipts for all her expenses. Of course, she was going through a messy divorce then, so maybe that affected her job performance." Sam thanked his friend and notified Olivia that she was not being hired for the job.

If Olivia learned of Kelley's comments, would she have the basis for a legal suit? If so, what type and on what grounds? How could Kelley have reworded his comments to convey the information in a businesslike, ethical manner?

14 **Ethics**   You are the office manager of the Natural-Disaster Recovery Team for People Helping People. After testing several new word processing programs, you wrote a memo to your supervisor requesting the purchase of 15 copies of Microsoft Word Vista so that each member of your office staff would have a copy. You have just received your memo back from your supervisor with this handwritten note attached to it:

> I'm tired of purchasing software and then not having it do what it says it will do. Let's order one copy of the program first and make copies for all your staff. If in two months everyone is still happy with the program, I'll buy 14 more copies to make us legitimate. After all, we have to be careful with the funds donated to our organization.

How do you respond?

continuing
case 1

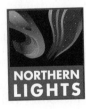

NORTHERN LIGHTS

Each chapter ends with a case study on Northern Lights. By solving these cases, students will encounter communication problems typical to the workplace.

Northern Lights Sees the Light

Marc Kaplan asked Dave to approve the following draft sales letter, which Marc wanted to mail out next month to the 4200 members of the Office Furniture Dealers' Association (OFDA) as the kickoff campaign for Northern Lights' Ultra Light Strips. After reading the letter twice, Dave had still not approved it. Something about the tone of the letter bothered him.

Dear Manager:

Would you like us to come visit you in jail?

Now, it's true that you probably won't be put in jail for requiring your computer operators to sit in front of a monitor eight hours a day, but you just might get slapped with a lawsuit from a disgruntled employee who complains of back problems or failing eyesight. One pregnant employee even won damages by blaming her miscarriage on emotional stress caused by too many hours sitting at her computer! And two studies published this past year that warn of dangers from long periods of working at a computer don't help the situation any.

Before going to your lawyer, come to NL—to Northern Lights—for the answer to your problems. We have recently patented a new strip lighting system for modular furniture that will throw precisely the right amount of soft light around the monitor. With Ultra Light Strips, your operators won't have to put up with glare from their monitors, they won't have to position themselves in a certain way just to read the monitor, and they won't have shadows falling on their copy holders. As a result, they will be happier as well as more productive.

And if wiring is in place, just about anyone can install Ultra Light Strips. Just order the lengths you need—from 0.3 to 6.0 metres long. They are completely flexible, so that you can easily bend them around your modular furniture. And because they attach with Velcro strips, you can move them around and reuse them as your needs change.

We're really the only game in town when it comes to flexible task lighting. For example, the Mod Light by GME produces 200 foot-candles—far too much light to provide the needed contrast between the screen and surrounding light; your operators will soon begin to make careless errors from visual fatigue. And the Light Mite from Tedesco has long had a reputation for poor reliability. In addition, both GME and Tedesco produce their light fixtures abroad, while Ultra Light Strips are 100 percent Canadian-made! With Ultra Light Strips lighting the way, your operators' increased productivity will easily cover the cost of these strips within the first six months of use. Crush the competition. And avoid those costly legal battles. Call us toll-free at 1-800-555-2883 for a free on-site demonstration. We can also show you the many other uses of Ultra Light that will save your company money.

Sincerely,
Marc Kaplan
Vice-President, Marketing

Dave Kaplan edits a sales memo his brother, Marc, drafted for potential customers.

Critical Thinking

1. What is your reaction to this letter? Is the letter effective? Is it ethical? Explain.

2. If this letter represented your only knowledge of Northern Lights, what would be your opinion of the company? In other words, what kind of corporate image does the letter portray?

3. Without actually rewriting the letter, what revisions can you suggest for giving Marc's letter a more ethical tone?

LABtest 1

Retype the following email message from Dave, inserting any needed commas according to the comma rules introduced in LAB (Language Arts Basics) 2 on page 534.

Fort Garry in Winnipeg Manitoba has been chosen to host the largest most comprehensive lighting exhibit and conference ever held in Canada. This conference which is known as the International Lighting Expo will be held on June 14–16 2006 and is expected to draw more than a thousand

5   participants. "This will be the first such conference ever held in Canada " noted the program chair Dave Kaplan "and we also intend for it to be the best."

Exhibitors are invited to enter their best new lighting products for judging in the "Best of Show" competition and all lighting companies are invited

10   to compete for the "Energy Miser" awards. Entries for each award will be evaluated by an international panel of lighting experts and will be awarded at the closing session of the three-day conference.

The purpose of this message Ms. Allison is to inquire whether your company would be interested in supplying a speaker for one of the sessions.

15   Although your company would be responsible for all expenses we will supply a coordinator overhead projector and screen for each session. We can in addition, provide other reasonable accommodations if arrangements are made in advance. If you would be interested in participating please call me at 555-1038 to discuss the details of your sponsorship of this important

20   industry event.

Northern Lights, Inc.

The Company

Northern Lights, Inc. (NL) is a small "start-up" company whose primary product is Ultra Light, a new, paper-thin light source that promises to revolutionize the illumination industry. The company employs 178 people at its corporate headquarters in Calgary, Alberta, and in a completely automated manufacturing plant in Winnipeg, Manitoba. It is incorporated under the *Canadian Business Corporations Act,* with all stock privately held by the founders and their families.

Northern Lights has annual sales in the $30 million range, with a net profit last year of $1.4 million. It is considered a progressive company by the investment community, with good management and good earnings potential. The local community considers NL to be a good corporate citizen; it is a non-polluting firm, and its officers are active in the local chamber of commerce and in community affairs.

Northern Lights headquarters in Calgary, Alberta.

The Product

Ultra Light is a flat, electroluminescent sheet of material that serves as a light source. It is capable of replacing most fluorescent, neon, and incandescent light fixtures. Physically, Ultra Light is a paper-thin sheet of chemically-treated material laminated between thin layers of clear plastic. In effect, it is a credit-card-thin light fixture that is bendable and that can be produced in a variety of shapes and sizes. Operated by either battery or wall current, it generates a bright white or coloured light.

Ultra Light is cost-competitive with other, more conventional lighting, and its life expectancy is measured in years. All of this, combined with the appeal of its very thin profile, battery operation ("use it anywhere"), the evenly distributed light it produces, and the way it can conform to a variety of physical shapes, makes Ultra Light a new product with a lot of potential.

Company History

NL was founded in 2001 by two brothers, David and Marc Kaplan. Dave was a chemical engineer at Industrial Chemical, Inc., when he developed the basic concept of Ultra Light while working on another project. Because IC was not interested in pursuing the manufacturing and marketing of this product, Dave bought all rights to Ultra Light from IC and patented it in 2000. Then he and his younger brother Marc, formerly a marketing manager for an advertising agency in Toronto, started Northern Lights in an empty warehouse in Calgary.

The company received start-up funds through personal investments of $50 000 by Dave Kaplan and $35 000 by Marc and a $68 500 five-year loan from the Business Development Bank of Canada. Because of Marc's advertising background, the company's five-year business plan focused on marketing Ultra Light initially for advertising purposes—to illuminate signs, point-of-purchase displays, and the like. Later, as the company became better established in the marketplace, plans were to expand into industrial, office, and consumer applications.

After a somewhat uneven start, NL had become profitable by the end of its fourth year of operations and had outgrown its original building. The company recently built a 1300-square-metre facility in an attractive office park in Calgary, to house its administrative, marketing, and R&D functions. The company also moved its manufacturing operations to Winnipeg, in a leased facility. The manufacturing facility is completely automated, with state-of-the-art robotics, just-in-time inventory control, and a progressive union-management agreement. The latest three-year labour contract expires next year.

Personnel

A partial organization chart for Northern Lights is shown in Figure 1. Each corporate position and the person currently occupying that position are described below.

Board of Directors   The board comprises David J. Kaplan, chair; Marc Kaplan, vice-chair; Judith Klehr Kaplan (David Kaplan's wife), secretary/treasurer; Thomas V. Robertson, general counsel; and Eileen Jennings (vice-president of Calgary Credit Union). As required by the articles of incorporation, the board meets quarterly at company headquarters.

Dave Kaplan, age 46, is a professional engineer-turned-manager. He graduated with honours from McGill University with a degree in chemical engineering. Upon graduation from McGill, he began working as a chemical engineer in the polymer division at Industrial Chemical,

President
Dave Kaplan

where he worked until 2001 when he started NL. During his time at IC, he attended graduate school part-time at the University of Calgary, where he received his MBA degree in 1989. Although he was offered numerous management positions at IC, he elected to continue working as a chemical engineer. His work resulted in numerous profitable patents for IC, and he was considered a highly respected member of the scientific staff.

Dave has published numerous articles in scholarly journals, has presented papers in his area of specialty at several international conferences, and has served as president of the Alberta Society of Chemical Engineers.

Although he manages his new company effectively, Dave will tell you that some of his happiest times were working in the lab at IC—pursuing some esoteric research project alone and at his own pace. He will also tell you

figure1   **Northern Lights Organizational Chart**

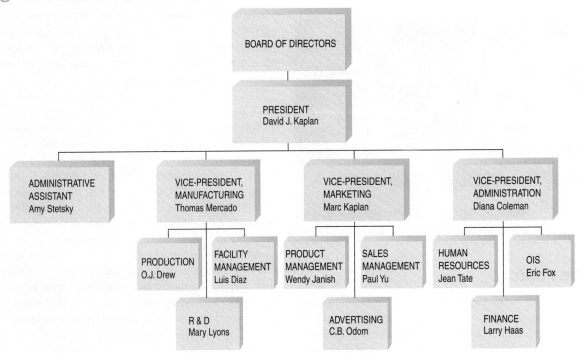

that the aspects of managing Northern Lights that he dislikes the most are attending the incessant meetings and having to manage and be responsible for the work of others. At NL, Dave is considered a perfectionist and a workaholic. Although not an especially warm person, he is highly respected by his staff.

Amy Stetsky, or "Stetsky" as she is called by nearly everyone who knows her, was one of the first people hired by Dave Kaplan. She is 32 years old, has an associate's degree in office systems, and recently earned the Certified Administrative Professional (CAP) designation as a result of passing an intensive exam administered by the International Association of Administrative Professionals (IAAP). She is highly respected and well-liked by everyone in the organization.

Administrative Assistant
Amy Stetsky

Thomas Mercado knows the production business from top to bottom. He is 47 years old and has been with the company from the beginning, having been hired away from a similar job at Steelcase Corporation. Tom has earned the respect of both Dave and his subordinates, including the engineers in the R&D unit.

Tom gives his staff wide latitude in running their units. He supports them, even when they make mistakes. He does insist, however, on being kept informed at every step of the way. He is a very direct type of person—you always know where you stand with him. If any of his subordinates have some bad news to convey, they know he wants to know immediately and directly—with no beating around the bush.

Vice-President, Manufacturing
Thomas Mercado

Although he gets along well with both Dave and his subordinates, he and Marc Kaplan have had several run-ins during the past five years. Privately, he would tell you that he believes Marc is a "lightweight" who is not particularly effective in marketing the firm's products. Tom is especially upset that Marc has shot down several new product ideas proposed by Tom's R&D staff.

People who know both Dave and Marc Kaplan cannot believe they are brothers. Marc, age 42, is the complete opposite of Dave. He is warm and outgoing, with a wide circle of friends both in and out of business. His extensive network of personal and professional contacts has resulted in numerous large and lucrative orders for the firm.

Vice-President, Marketing
Marc Kaplan

Marc depends heavily on his three managers, especially for in-house operations. He spends a great deal of time away from the office—entertaining customers and prospective customers, attending conventions where NL exhibits its products, and making the rounds of golf tournaments and after-hours cocktail parties.

Marc is aware of Tom's feelings about him but brushes them aside as normal jealousy. He believes that if he could get Tom to go on a golf outing with him a few times, things could be patched up. As it is, although their relationship is somewhat strained, it is not affecting either's ability to do his job.

Age 38, Diana Coleman has a master of science degree in management information systems from Trent University. She was promoted to her present position only last year, having served as manager of the Office and Information Systems (OIS) unit at Northern Lights for four years prior to that.

Vice-President, Administration
Diana Coleman

Diana is an ardent feminist. She is also very involved in politics and worked extensively in the unsuccessful campaign of Eric Leavitt, the NDP candidate for the riding of Calgary Southeast.

Diana manages the division that houses both the human resources function and the office function; the office function employs a large number of clerical and secretarial workers (all of whom are female). When Dave Kaplan offered her the promotion to vice-president, Diana informed him that one of her goals would be to institute policies that would upgrade the role of women within the company. Although she gets along well with Tom Mercado, she resents Marc Kaplan's sometimes condescending attitude toward her and what she considers his chauvinistic attitude toward many of the females on his staff.

Financial Data

By year's end, assets for Northern Lights totalled $23.2 million, with net income of $1.4 million. Earnings per share for the current year were $1.08; and a dividend of $0.64 per share was paid on the 1.3 million outstanding shares (all of which are held by the two Kaplan families).

2

Work-Team Communication

communication

OBJECTIVES

After you have finished this chapter, you should be able to

1. Communicate effectively in small groups.

2. Communicate effectively within a diverse environment.

3. Communicate effectively by telephone.

4. Communicate effectively via electronic media.

5. Plan, conduct, and participate in a business meeting.

an insider's perspective

JOHN RYAN
CEO, Farm Credit Canada

As the CEO of a company recognized for the third consecutive year by *The Globe and Mail* Report on Business and Hewitt Associates as among the top 50 employers in Canada, John Ryan understands the importance of good communication between members of his team. Indeed, Ryan himself has been lauded internationally for his outstanding communication skills: he was the recipient of the International Association of Business Communicators EXCEL award for excellence in business communication in 2004—only the fifth Canadian CEO to win the award in IABC's 42-year history.

Ryan has been the CEO of Farm Credit Canada since 1997, a crown corporation that employs approximately 1100 employees across the country, providing financial support and business services for farmers and agribusiness across Canada. With their head office in Regina, FCC has enjoyed 13 consecutive years of portfolio growth, with a current lending portfolio of over $12 billion.

So what makes Ryan such a great communicator? And more importantly, what makes his team so happy to work at FCC? According to Ryan, "Our success depends on the calibre and frequency of communication with staff and stakeholders." Paramount for Ryan is accountability among all members of his team. "The most important principle is holding people accountable for respectful, team-oriented, high performance behaviour day in and day out," he stresses. And to underscore the importance of accountability and open communication, Ryan recently instituted FCC's "Cultural Practices"—an explicit code of conduct to further encourage employees to build trusting relationships.

And Ryan practices what he preaches, insisting that cultural practices "only work when employees see they are being modeled at the senior level."

To further encourage open communication, Ryan doesn't insist that employees follow a strict protocol when giving or soliciting input: "We believe employees should have their choice of channel, so we mix it up with our Intranet, our internal publication (AgriCulture), a senior management dine around program, and an online forum where employees can ask tough questions and get honest answers."

Even corporate strategy is pushed down to all levels of the team through open and honest communication: "Strategy is one thing, but if we can't explain what the strategy is, or people can't understand it at all levels, we're not going to be able to execute . . . an understanding of communication is part of creating outstanding strategy development. You have to get people to take ownership of the strategy and that's where communication comes in. . . . You need buy-in across the company."

Part of developing effective communication within a team is the ability to recognize, respect, and encourage diversity among members. Ryan recently instituted *French Fridays* across their English speaking offices (and *English Fridays* in Quebec). For French Fridays, a French word or expression of the day is emailed to all staff, who are then "encouraged to speak French on that day in the spirit of collaboration." Such commitment to promoting linguistic duality won Ryan yet another award—the Leon Leadership Award, an award that recognizes Ryan's leadership in providing bilingual service to the public, creating a workplace conducive to the use of both French and English, and supporting official language minority communities.

In Ryan's words, the strength of his team can be attributed to a simple set of beliefs that he and his team put into practice every day: "We believe that employees are at the heart of high-performing companies; we believe that great customer experiences emerge from organizations that fully engage their employees; we believe in the power of people to make the impossible happen; and we believe in the power of communication as a tool to help forge strong relationships, mobilized for a larger and more compelling purpose."

"The most important principle is holding people accountable for respectful, team-oriented, high performance behaviour day in and day out."

■ Communicating in Work Teams

A **team** is a group of individuals who depend on one another to accomplish a common objective. Teams are often superior to individuals because they can accomplish more work, are more creative, have more information available to them, and offer more interpersonal communication dynamics. There is a synergy at work in which the group's total output exceeds the sum of each individual's contribution.

A recent study compared the performance of virtual teams (whose members had not met but communicated only by speakerphone) and traditional in-person teams. The researchers found that virtual teams were more productive at brainstorming, whereas face-to-face teams were more productive in tasks where they had to negotiate and reach a decision.[1]

On the other hand, teams can waste time, accomplish little work, and create an environment in which interpersonal conflict can rage. As anyone who has ever worked in a group can attest, there is also the danger of *social loafing,* the psychological term for avoiding individual responsibility in a group setting.

Two to seven members seems to be the most appropriate size range for most effective work teams. Small-team research indicates that five is an ideal size for many teams.[2] Smaller teams often do not have enough diversity of skills and interests to function effectively as a team, whereas larger teams may lack healthy team interaction because just a few people may dominate the discussions.

CO1. Communicate effectively in small groups.

If the group is too large, members may begin to form cliques, or subgroups.

The Variables of Group Communication

Three factors—conflict, conformity, and consensus—greatly affect the efficiency with which a team operates and the amount of enjoyment members derive from it.

Conflict   Managers who demonstrate skill in resolving workplace conflicts are seen as effective leaders—which, in turn, enhances their advancement potential.[3] Conflict is a greatly misunderstood facet of group communication. Many group leaders work hard to avoid conflict because they think it detracts from a group's goals. Their attitude is that a group experiencing conflict is not running smoothly and is destined to fail.

In fact, conflict is what group meetings are all about. One purpose of collaborating on a project is to ensure that various viewpoints are heard so that agreement as to the most appropriate course of action can emerge. Groups can use conflict productively to generate and test ideas before they are implemented. Rather than indicating that a meeting is disorderly, the presence of conflict indicates that members are actively discussing the issues. If a group does not exhibit conflict by debating ideas or questioning others, there is very little reason for it to exist. The members may as well be working individually.

Conflict, then, is the essence of group interaction. Competent communicators use conflict as a means to determine what is and what is not an acceptable idea or solution. Note, however, that the conflict we are talking about involves debate about *issues,* not about *personalities.* Interpersonal conflict can, indeed, have serious negative consequences for work teams.

Debate issues, *not* personalities.

Conformity   Conformity is agreement with regard to ideas, rules, or principles. Members may be encouraged to disagree about the definition of a problem or possible solutions, but certain fundamental issues—such as how the group should operate—should be agreed to by everyone.

Although group conformity and group cohesiveness are necessary for successful small-group communication, too much cohesiveness can result in what has been termed **groupthink,** the barrier to communication that results from an overemphasis on unity, which stifles opposing ideas and the free flow of information (see Figure 2.1).[4]

The pressure to conform can become so great that negative information and contrary opinions are never even brought out into the open and discussed. Thus, the group loses the advantage of hearing and considering various perspectives. In effective work-team communication, conflicts, different opinions, and questions are considered an inevitable and essential part of the collaborative process.

Consensus   Consensus means reaching a decision that best reflects the thinking of all team members. It is finding a solution that is acceptable enough that all members can support it (perhaps, though, with reservations) and that no member actively opposes it. Consensus is not necessarily a unanimous vote, or even a majority vote. In a majority vote, only the majority are happy with the end result; people in the minority may have to accept something they don't like at all.

Not every decision, of course, needs to have the support of every member; to push for consensus on every matter would require a tremendous investment of time and energy. The group should decide ahead of time when to push for consensus—for example, when reaching decisions that have a major effect on the direction of the project or the conduct of the team.

Consensus does not mean a unanimous vote—or even necessarily a majority vote.

Initial Group Goals

The group's first task is to get to know one another.

It is difficult to work effectively as a team if the team members do not know one another well and are not aware of each member's strengths and weaknesses, styles of working, experiences, attitudes, and the like. Thus, the first task of most new teams is to get to know one another. For small teams to function effectively, not only the task dimension, but also the social dimension, must be considered. Some amount of "small talk" about family, friends, current happenings, and the like before and after the meetings is natural and helps to establish a supportive and open environment. You want to be able to compliment each other without embarrassment and to disagree without fear.

figure2.1

Effect of Excessive Conformity on a Group's Productivity

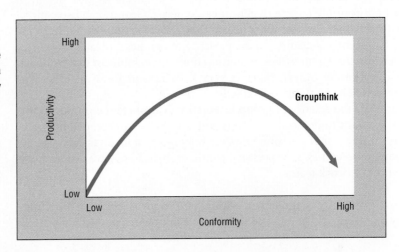

Too often, decisions just "happen" in a team; members may go along with what they think everyone else wants. Teams should therefore discuss how they will make decisions and should develop operating rules. They should talk about what would be legitimate reasons for missing a meeting, establish a procedure for informing others of an absence beforehand and of keeping the absent member informed of what was accomplished at the meeting, and decide what being "on time" means. In short, they should develop "norms" for the team.

Giving Constructive Feedback

The single most important skill to have in working through any problem is the ability to give constructive feedback. There are proven methods for giving and receiving criticism that work equally well for giving and receiving praise.[5]

Acknowledge the Need for Feedback   Feedback is vital; it is the only way to find out what needs to be improved and should be an overall part of the team's culture. Thus, your team must agree that giving and receiving feedback is an acceptable part of how you will improve the way you work together. This way, no one will be surprised when he or she receives feedback.

Give Both Positive and Negative Feedback   Many people take good work for granted and give feedback only when there are problems. Unfortunately, this habit is counterproductive. People are far more likely to pay attention to your complaints if they have also received your compliments.

Learn How to Give Feedback   Use these guidelines for compliments as well as complaints:

1. *Be descriptive.* Relate objectively what you saw or what you heard. Give specific examples: the more recent, the better.
2. *Avoid using labels.* Words like *undependable, unprofessional, irresponsible,* and *lazy* are labels that we attach to behaviours. Instead, describe the behaviours and drop the labels.
3. *Don't exaggerate.* Be exact. To say, "You're always late for meetings" is probably untrue and therefore unfair.
4. *Speak for yourself.* Don't refer to absent, anonymous people ("A lot of people here don't like it when you . . .").
5. *Use "I" statements.* This is perhaps the most important guideline. For example, instead of saying, "You are frequently late for meetings," say, "I feel annoyed when you are late for meetings." "I" statements create an adult/peer relationship (see Figure 2.2).

Conflict Resolution

Most conflicts in groups can be anticipated or prevented if a group spends time developing itself into a team, getting to know one another, establishing ground rules, discussing norms for group behaviour, and the like. However, no matter how much planning is done or how conscientiously team members work, conflicts occasionally show up.

One of the worst tactics to take is to accept problems blindly. Problems rarely disappear on their own. However, you should neither overreact nor under react to

Giving and receiving feedback should be a part of every team's culture.

"I" statements tell specifically how someone's behaviour affects you.

Lucent put its managers through a paper-plane management exercise to foster team-building, increase intra-office communications, and improve client relations.

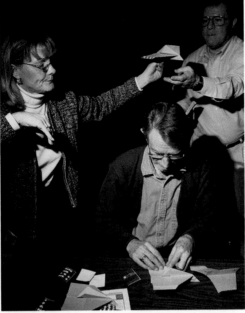

React to problems appropriately, consider them "group" problems, and have realistic expectations about the group process.

group problems. Some behaviours are only fleeting disruptions and can be ignored. Others are chronic and disruptive and must be resolved.

Think of each problem as a group problem. Groups should avoid the temptation to defuse conflicts by making a scapegoat of one member—for example, "We'd be finished with this report now if Sam had done his part; you never can depend on him." Rarely is one person solely responsible for the success or failure of a group effort. Examine each problem in light of what the group does to encourage or allow the behaviour and what the group can do differently to encourage more constructive

figure 2.2

Using "I" Statements When Giving Feedback

Sequence	Explanation
1. "When you . . ."	Start with a "When you . . ." statement that describes the behaviour without judgment, exaggeration, labelling, attribution, or motives. Just state the facts as specifically as possible.
2. "I feel . . ."	Tell how the behaviour affects you. If you need more than a word or two to describe the feeling, it's probably just some variation of joy, sorrow, anger, or fear.
3. "Because I . . ."	Now say why you are affected that way. Describe the connection between the facts you observed and the feelings they provoke in you.
4. (Pause for discussion)	Let the other person respond.
5. "I would like . . ."	Describe the change you want the other person to consider . . .
6. "Because . . ."	. . . and why you think the change will help alleviate the problem.
7. "What do you think?"	Listen to the other person's response. Be prepared to discuss options and compromise on a solution.

How the feedback will work:

When you [do this], I feel [this way], because [of such and such]. What I would like you to consider is [doing X], because I think it will accomplish [Y]. What do you think?

Example:

"When you are late for meetings, I get angry because I think it is wasting the time of all the other team members and we are never able to get through our agenda items. I would like you to consider finding some way of planning your schedule that lets you get to these meetings on time. That way we can be more productive at the meetings, and we can all keep to our tight schedules."

Source: From Peter R. Scholtes, *The Team Handbook,* 2d ed., Madison, WI: Joiner Associates, 1996, pp. 6–27. Copyright © 1996 Joiner Associates Inc. Reprinted with permission.

behaviour. Because every member's role is a function of both his or her own personality and the group's personality, the group should consider how to help every person contribute more to the collaborative efforts.

Finally, be realistic. Don't assume responsibility for the happiness of others. You are responsible for behaving ethically and for treating other group members with respect, but the purpose of the group is not to develop lifelong friendships or to solve other people's time-management or personal problems.

Competent communicators welcome all contributions from group members, regardless of whether the members agree or disagree with their own views. They evaluate each contribution objectively and respond in a non-threatening manner, with comments that are factual, constructive, and goal-oriented. If the atmosphere becomes tense, they make a light comment, laugh, compliment, recall previous incidents, or take other helpful actions to restore harmony and move the group forward. If interpersonal conflict appears to be developing into a more or less permanent part of the group interactions, the group should put the topic of conflict on its agenda and then devote sufficient meeting time to discussing and working through the conflict.

> **TECH ADDICTION** *word*wise
>
> According to WordSpy.com, the term crackberry was first used by Geoff Colvin, CEO of Waterloo's Research in Motion in September, 2000. The site also lists associated terms such as "thumb candy," "thumb culture," "heroinware," and "BlackBerry thumb" that reflect the appeal and popularity of PDAs in the work world.

Team Writing

The increasing complexity of the workplace makes it difficult for any one person to have either the time or the expertise to be able to identify and solve many of the problems that arise and prepare written responses. This situation especially applies to long or complex documents. The differing talents, skills, and perspectives of several individuals are often needed in a joint effort to analyze a given situation and generate proposals or recommendations. Thus, team writing is becoming quite prevalent in organizations.

Writing as part of a team is a common task in contemporary organizations.

In addition to the general team-building guidelines discussed in the previous section, writing teams should follow these strategies.

Form a Group   Frequently team writing will occur within a group whose composition has been predetermined by a supervisor or project manager. Occasionally, however, group members will have the luxury of choosing their own writing team. When choosing members to work with, be sure to select members based on two main criteria: appropriate skill set for the task and appropriate personality mix to ensure success and to minimize personality conflicts. Too often groups are selected based on the popularity of their members rather than the ability of members to work well together and to complete the task effectively.

Keep in mind that large writing tasks can often be broken into several sub-tasks: researching the problem, planning and organizing the content, drafting and revising the content, style, and mechanics, formatting the document, and finally proofreading for errors. Most writers are better at some of these tasks than others. Whenever possible try to select a writing team with skills in all of the above tasks.

Assign Tasks and Develop a Schedule   Start by determining the goals of the project and identifying the reader. Determine the components of the project, the research needed, and the date when each aspect needs to be completed. Then divide

Develop a work schedule—and stick to it.

table2.1

Common Pitfalls in Group Writing Projects		
Problem	**Result**	**Prevention**
Poor group composition	Conflict	Choose members based on compatibility of personalities and on complementary skill sets.
Poor task allotment	Skills unsuited to task	Be open and honest about strengths and weaknesses and assign tasks according to member strengths.
Poor timeline estimation	Latter stages of project are rushed.	Keep firm deadlines and reassign tasks if deadlines are not met.
	Poor finished product.	Overestimate the time required for final stages of project.

the tasks equitably, based on each member's needs, interests, expertise, and commitment to the project.

Estimating the time and effort each task or component of the project takes practice and can be difficult. A common problem is underestimating the time it takes to revise, format and proofread a document (see Table 2.1). Too often, groups allow too much time for the researching and writing tasks and too little for the formatting and editing tasks. In many cases, especially for novice writers, these tasks can take longer than the actual writing and researching tasks. A rushed final product, with sloppy formatting or glaring errors in spelling, grammar, or punctuation, will quickly negate all the work put into the researching and writing tasks.

Ideally, tasks should be divided equitably and based on each member's needs, interest and commitment to the project. Of greater significance, however, is that tasks be assigned to members with skill in that area.

Meet Regularly   Schedule regular meetings throughout the project to pool ideas, keep track of new developments, assess progress, avoid overlap and omissions, and, if necessary, renegotiate the workload and redefine tasks. As soon as you have finished gathering data, meet as a group to develop an outline for the finished project. This outline should show the sequence of major and subordinate topics in the document. Beware of a "data-dump," in which every bit of information gathered is dumped into the final document. Not *all* of the information that you collect may need to be included in the report.

Draft the Document   The goal at this stage is not to prepare a finished product but to draft all of the content. You have two options:

- *Assign parts to different members.* Having each member write a different part of the document provides an equitable distribution of the work and may produce a draft more quickly. You must ensure, however, that each member is writing in his or her area of expertise and that all have agreed on such style issues as the degree of formality, direct versus indirect organization, and use of preview and summary techniques.

- *Assign one person to draft the entire document.* Assigning one member (presumably the most talented writer) to draft the entire document helps guarantee a more consistent writing style and lessens the risk of serious omissions or duplication. You must, however, provide sufficient guidance to the writer and allow ample time for one person to complete the entire writing task.

✔checklist1

Commenting on Peer Writing

✔ Read first for meaning; that is, comment on the large issues first—issues such as the paper's focus, organization, appropriateness for the intended audience, and overall clarity.

✔ Assume the role of reader—not instructor. Your job is to help the writer, not to grade the assignment.

✔ Point out sections that you liked, as well as those you disliked, explaining specifically why you thought they were effective or ineffective (not "I liked this part" but "You did a good job of explaining this difficult concept").

✔ Prefer "I" language (not "You need to make this clearer" but "I was confused here").

✔ Comment helpfully—but sparingly. There is no need to point out the same misspelling a dozen times.

✔ Emphasize the *writer* when giving positive feedback: for example, "I'm glad you were able to get the most current figures from the company's home page." And emphasize the *text* (rather than the writer) when giving negative feedback: for example, "This argument would be more persuasive for me if it contained the most current figures."

✔ Avoid taking over the text. Accept the fact that it is someone else's writing—not your own. Make constructive suggestions, but avoid making decisions or demands.

One common pitfall in team writing is the failure to achieve a single "voice" in the project. Regardless of who prepares each individual part of the report, the final report must look and sound as though it were prepared by one writer. Think of the report as a single document, rather than as a collection of parts. Organize and present the data so that the report comes across as coherent and unified.

Ensure that the final group document "speaks with one voice"—that is, that it is coherent and unified.

Provide Helpful Feedback on Team Writing Commenting on the writing of peers can be helpful both to you and to the colleague whose writing you're reviewing. As you respond to the writing of others, you practice techniques that will help you react more effectively to your own writing. As a writer, you benefit from the viewpoints of multiple audiences and from learning what does or doesn't work in your writing. In a team environment, peer comments create more active involvement and can help foster a sense of community within the team.

When reviewing a colleague's writing, follow the guidelines presented in Checklist 1, "Commenting on Peer Writing," above.

Revise the Draft Be sure to allow enough time for editing the draft. This task is best accomplished by providing each member with a copy of the entire draft beforehand (to allow time for reading and making notes) and then meeting as a group to review each section for errors in content, gaps or repetition, and effective writing style.

Decide who will be responsible for making the changes to each section, how the document will be formatted, and who will be responsible for proofreading the final document. Typically, one person (preferably not the typist) will be assigned to review the final draft for consistency and correctness in content, style, and format.

The Ethical Dimension of Work-Team Communication

Accepting membership on a team implies acceptance of certain standards of ethical behaviour. One of the most basic of these standards is to put the good of the team ahead of personal gain. Team members should set aside private agendas in their

Concentrate on group goals rather than individual goals.

team actions and avoid advocating positions that might benefit them personally but that would not be best for the team.

Team members also have an ethical responsibility to respect the integrity and emotional needs of one another. Everyone's ideas should be treated with respect, and no action should be taken that results in a loss of self-esteem for a member.

Finally, each member has an ethical responsibility to promote the team's welfare—by contributing his or her best efforts to the team's mission and by refraining from destructive gossip, domination of meetings, and other counterproductive actions.

■ Communicating in a Diverse Environment

CO2. Communicate effectively within a diverse environment.

Canada is among the most multicultural nations in the world. According to a Statistics Canada study, roughly one in every five people could be a member of a visible minority by the year 2017, the year Canada celebrates its 150th anniversary. (Canada's *Employment Equity Act* defines visible minorities as "persons other than the Aboriginal peoples, who are non-Caucasian in race and non-white in colour.") **Diversity** in the workplace, of course, includes more than just an increasingly multicultural workforce. A diverse workplace is one that embraces any traditionally under-represented group and one that recognizes the business advantage of doing so. The *Employment Equity Act* seeks to "correct the conditions of disadvantage in employment" of four specific groups: women, Aboriginal peoples, persons with disabilities, and members of visible minorities. These four groups are a wealth of human capital, comprising six of every ten able Canadians. Kamil Dib, a senior economist with Human Resources and Skills Development Canada (HRDC), argues that removing barriers to their entry into the workforce is making Canada more competitive in a global economy that relies increasingly on knowledge over natural resources.[6]

spotlight4
ACROSS CULTURES

Workplace Diversity

Workplace diversity rests on three pillars:

Direction Only the CEO or company head has the clout to lead an equity/diversity plan and process. "The message has to come from the top," says Norma Tombari, manager of workforce flexibility at the Royal Bank of Canada. "It is invaluable and gives a lot of credibility." Brenda Jean Lycett, president of Toronto-based human resources consulting company 4Change agrees: "This cannot just be something that is seen as an HR issue—it has to come from the top down, and there have to be quarterly reports to the CEO."

Strategy Improved policies and practices are fine, but not nearly enough. You must incorporate equity plans into overall strategy. As Prem Benimadhu, vice-president of

organizational performance at the Conference Board of Canada explains, "Systemic barriers prevent organizations from fully benefiting from the heterogeneity of the Canadian labour force." Only a well-planned strategy can change that.

Perseverance "If you do not sustain your efforts, the cynics and naysayers will say it is just the flavour of the day," says Laraine Kaminsky, executive vice-president of Graybridge Malkam, a language training and consulting firm in Ottawa. Keep refining diversity and equity measures; regularly assess where you are. And don't be discouraged. "You are helping to build a culture," says Rose Patten, senior executive vice-president of human resources and strategic management at BMP Financial Group. "These things take time." [7]

Of course, working within a diverse environment poses some challenges. Learning to recognize, accept, and even promote differences, both within the Canadian workforce and within the worldwide marketplace, will have increasingly profound effects on our lives and will pose a growing challenge for managers (see, for example Spotlight 5, "Internationally Yours," below).

spotlight5
ACROSS CULTURES

Internationally Yours

Most of the correspondence between Canadian firms and foreign firms takes place in English. Even when the language is the same, however, different meanings can result.

Losing Something in the Translation

Consider, for example, the miscommunication that occurred when these phrases were translated from English into the local language:

North American English:	"The Electrolux is the strongest vacuum available."
British English:	"Nothing sucks like an Electrolux."
English:	"Come alive with Pepsi."
Thai:	"Bring your ancestors back from the dead with Pepsi."
English:	"I'm just tickled to death to be here."
Russian:	"Scratch me until I die."

Très Chic: Communicating Continentally

When communicating with international business colleagues, customers, venture capitalists, and other important audiences, you will often find not only language differences but also other differences in usage and style.

Phone Numbers Continental (European) style calls for the use of periods rather than hyphens or parentheses to separate parts of a phone number: for example, 317.555.1086 rather than 317-555-1086 or (317) 555-1086. Dot-style telephone numbers seem to be gaining popularity in Canada, where they are sometimes viewed as classier and more elegant.

Spelling and Word Choice In Canada, some spellings are preferred though they differ from accepted spellings in the United States. Examples include *behaviour, centre, cheque, labour, legalise, organization,* and *theatre.* While Canadian spelling is becoming more and more standard-

ized, there has historically been disagreement in whether Canadians should adopt the British or the American spelling for certain words. In 1998, Canadian Press finally recognized the -*our* spellings of words such as colour and honour—until then it had insisted in its style manual that such words be spelled without the *u.* As explanation, CP noted that the spelling issue was not settled in Canada until 1890, when John A. Macdonald personally ruled in favour of -*our* so that "the same system should obtain in all portions of the British Empire."

There still remain regional differences that make a sweeping consensus on Canadian spelling somewhat elusive. When communicating with Americans, the task of using familiar spelling is much easier—simply set your spelling checker's dictionary language to English (US).

Punctuation In the style most common in Canada, commas and periods are placed inside closing quotation marks, whereas the British place them outside. Also, British usage calls for single quotation marks where Canadian usage calls for double quotation marks. Thus, Canadians would type "I see." The British would type 'I see'. Also, British and Continental style omits periods after *Dr., Mr., Ms.,* and other courtesy titles, as well as after *Jr.* and *Sr.*

Decimals Canadians, Americans, and the British use a period to indicate a decimal point (1.57 percent), whereas some countries (including France) use a comma instead (1,57 percent).

Dates In Canada, writers have typically used a month/day/year format (such as May 15, 2006, or 05/15/06). However, the influential International Organization for Standardization, a 130-nation federation dedicated to global uniformity, has issued ISO 8601, which requires putting the year first, month second, and day last (2006-06-15). Because so many companies seek ISO approval to simplify international trade, this year-month-day style will likely become more prevalent everywhere.

Cultural Differences

Cultures differ widely in the traits they value. For example, as shown in Table 2.2, international cultures differ widely in their emphasis on individualism, long-term orientation, time orientation, power distance, uncertainty avoidance, formality, materialism, and context-sensitivity.

Each person interprets events through his or her mental filter, and that filter is based on the receiver's unique knowledge, experiences, and viewpoints. For example, the language of time is as different among cultures as the language of words.

> *Cultures differ not only in their verbal language but also in their non-verbal language. Very few non-verbal messages have universal meanings.*

table2.2

Cultural Values

Value	High	Low
Individualism: Cultures in which people see themselves first as individuals and believe that their own interests take priority.	*Canada* United States Great Britain Australia Netherlands	Japan Taiwan Mexico Greece Hong Kong
Long-Term Orientation: Cultures that maintain a long-term perspective.	*Canada* United States	Pacific Rim countries
Time Orientation: Cultures that perceive time as a scarce resource and that tend to be impatient.	*Canada* United States	Pacific Rim and Middle Eastern countries
Power Distance: Cultures in which management decisions are made by the boss simply because he or she is the boss.	France Spain Japan Mexico Brazil	*Canada* Israel Germany Ireland
Uncertainty Avoidance: Cultures in which people want predictable and certain futures.	Israel Japan Italy Argentina	*Canada* United States Australia Singapore
Formality: Cultures that attach considerable importance to tradition, ceremony, social rules, and rank.	Latin American countries	*Canada* United States Scandinavian countries
Materialism: Cultures that emphasize assertiveness and the acquisition of money and material objects.	Japan Austria Italy	Scandinavian countries
Context Sensitivity: Cultures that emphasize the surrounding circumstances (or context), make extensive use of body language, and take the time to build relationships and establish trust.	Asian, Arab, Hispanic and African countries	Northern European countries

Source: From *Human Relations* by A. J. DuBrin. © 1997. Adapted by permission of Prentice-Hall, Inc. Upper Saddle River, NJ.

Canadians, Americans, Germans, and Japanese are very time-conscious and very precise about appointments; Latin American and Middle Eastern cultures tend to be more casual about time. For example, if your Mexican host tells you that he or she will meet with you at three, it's most likely *más o menos* (Spanish for "more or less").

Business people in both Asian and Latin American countries tend to favour long negotiations and slow deliberations. They exchange pleasantries at some length before getting down to business. Likewise, many non-Western cultures use the silent intervals for contemplation, whereas business people from Canada tend to have little tolerance for silence in business negotiations. As a result, Canadians may rush in and offer compromises and counterproposals that would have been unnecessary if they had shown more patience.

Body language, especially gestures and eye contact, also varies among cultures. For example, our sign for "okay"—forming a circle with our forefinger and thumb—means "zero" in France, "money" in Japan, and a vulgarity in Brazil (see Figure 2.3). Canadians generally consider eye contact important, although of course there are cultural differences here, too. Some aboriginal cultures, for example, consider sustained eye contact a sign of disrespect. In Asian and many Latin American countries, looking a partner full in the eye is considered an irritating sign of ill breeding.

Touching behaviour is very culture-specific. Many Asians do not like to be touched, except for a brief handshake in greeting. However, handshakes in much of Europe tend to last much longer than in Canada, and Europeans tend to shake hands every time they see each other, perhaps several times a day. Germans typically use a firm grip and one shake; Asians typically grasp the other's hand delicately and shake only briefly. In much of Europe, men often kiss each other upon greeting; unless a Canadian business person is aware of this custom, he or she might react inappropriately.

Our feelings about space are partly an outgrowth of our culture and partly a result of geography and economics. For example, Canadians are used to wide-open spaces

When in doubt about how to act, follow the lead of your host.

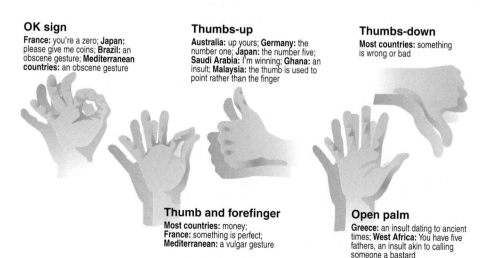

OK sign
France: you're a zero; **Japan:** please give me coins; **Brazil:** an obscene gesture; **Mediterranean countries:** an obscene gesture

Thumbs-up
Australia: up yours; **Germany:** the number one; **Japan:** the number five; **Saudi Arabia:** I'm winning; **Ghana:** an insult; **Malaysia:** the thumb is used to point rather than the finger

Thumbs-down
Most countries: something is wrong or bad

Thumb and forefinger
Most countries: money; **France:** something is perfect; **Mediterranean:** a vulgar gesture

Open palm
Greece: an insult dating to ancient times; **West Africa:** You have five fathers, an insult akin to calling someone a bastard

figure 2.3
Same Sign, Different Meanings

Adapted from Ben Brown, "Atlanta Out to Mind Its Manners," *USA Today*, March 14, 1996, p. 7c. Copyright © 1996 *USA Today*. Reprinted with permission.

and tend to move about expansively, using hand and arm motions for emphasis. But in Japan, which has much smaller living and working spaces, such abrupt and extensive body movements are not typical. Likewise, Canadians tend to sit face to face so that they can maintain eye contact, whereas the Chinese and Japanese (to whom eye contact is not as important) tend to sit side by side during negotiations.

Also, the sense of personal space differs among cultures. In Canada, most business exchanges occur at about 1.5 metres, within the so-called social zone discussed earlier. However, both in the Middle East and in Latin American countries, this distance is too far. Business people there tend to stand close enough to feel your breath as you speak. Most Canadians tend to back away unconsciously from such close contact.

Finally, social behaviour is very culture-dependent. For example, in the Japanese culture, the matter of who bows first upon meeting, how deeply the person bows, and how long the bow is held is very dependent upon one's status.

Competent communicators become familiar with such role-related behaviour and also learn the customs regarding giving (and accepting) gifts, exchanging business cards, the degree of formality expected, and the accepted means of entertaining and being entertained.

Group-Oriented Behaviour

As shown earlier in Table 2.2 on page 48, the business environment in a capitalistic society such as Canada places great value on the contributions of the individual toward the success of the organization. Individual effort is often stressed more than group effort, and a competitive atmosphere prevails. In other cultures, however, originality and independence of judgment are not valued as highly as teamwork. The Japanese say, "A nail standing out will be hammered down." Thus, the Japanese go to great lengths to reach decisions through consensus, wherein every participating member, not just a majority, is able to agree.

Expect negotiations to take longer when unanimous agreement, rather than majority rule, is the norm.

Closely related to the concept of group-oriented behaviour is the notion of "saving face." The desire to save face simply means that neither party in a given interaction should suffer embarrassment. Human relationships are highly valued in Japanese cultures and are embodied in the concept of *wa*, or the Japanese pursuit of harmony. This concept makes it difficult for the Japanese to say "no" to a request because it would be impolite. They are very reluctant to offend others—even if they unintentionally mislead them instead. Thus, a "yes" to a Japanese colleague might mean "Yes, I understand you" rather than "Yes, I agree." In intercultural communications, one has to read between the lines, because what is left unsaid or unwritten may be just as important as what is said or written.

Strategies for Communicating Across Cultures

Perhaps, up to this point, you have been inferring that our encounters with those of other cultures will take place primarily when travelling abroad. Nothing could be further from the truth. Intercultural communication occurs even within a country. Many people from northern Canada have recognizable cultural differences, including their languages and many of their traditions, than those born and raised in southern parts of Canada. This is also true of many people from Quebec in comparison to people from other parts of Canada. Indeed, Canada contains a broad array of cultures within its borders, and such diversity is both promoted and protected by law. See

Communication Snapshot 1 for a breakdown of visible minorities in Canada. The multiculturalism policy of Canada seeks to "recognize and promote the understanding that multiculturalism is a fundamental characteristic of the Canadian heritage and identity" (*Canadian Multiculturalism Act*, s. 3).

Having such a multicultural workforce poses tremendous advantages in a global economy. According to *Canadian Business* magazine, "Diverse companies are more likely to succeed in today's national and international marketplace."[8] And according to the Royal Bank of Canada, "Valuing someone who has a different point of view or a different experience can enhance problem solving and spark innovation."[9] In short, diversity makes good business sense.

So how does a good communicator adapt within such a diverse environment? When communicating with people from different cultures, whether abroad or at home, consider the following strategies.

Maintain Formality   Compared to the traditional Canadian cultures, most other cultures value and respect a much more formal approach to business dealings. Call others by their titles and family names unless specifically asked to do otherwise. By both verbal and non-verbal clues, convey an attitude of propriety and decorum. Most other cultures do not equate formality with coldness.

Show Respect   Withhold judgment, accepting the premise that attitudes held by an entire culture are probably based on sound reasoning. Listen carefully to what is being communicated, trying to understand the other person's feelings. Learn about your host country—its geography, form of government, largest cities, culture, current events, and the like.

Communicate Clearly   To ensure that your oral and written messages are understood, follow these guidelines:

■ Avoid slang, jargon, and other figures of speech. Expressions such as "They'll eat that up" or "out in left field" are likely to confuse even a fluent English speaker.

■ Be specific and illustrate your points with concrete examples.

■ Provide and solicit feedback; summarize frequently; provide a written summary of the points covered in a meeting; ask your counterpart to paraphrase what has been said; encourage questions.

■ Use a variety of media: handouts (distributed before the meeting to allow time for reading), audiovisual aids, models, and the like.

communication snapshot 1

Who are Canada's visible minorities?

Chinese	990 385	26.1%
South Asian	896 225	23.6
Black	593 335	15.6
Filipino	216 980	7.7
Latin American	216 980	5.7
Arab	194 680	5.1
Southeast Asia	191 820	5.0
West Asian	109 285	2.9
Korean	98 325	2.6
Japanese	55 880	1.5
Others	98 920	2.6
Multiple minorities	750	1.6

The Visible Minority Population in Canada's Biggest Cities

Vancouver	36.9%
Edmonton	14.6
Calgary	17.5
Winnipeg	12.4
Toronto	36.8
Ottawa-Hull	14.1
Montreal	13.6
Halifax	7.0

Source: *Canadian Business*, 3/29/2004, Vol. 77, Issue 7, p. 53.

Showing respect is probably the easiest strategy to exhibit—and one of the most important.

- Avoid attempts at humour; humour is likely to be lost on your counterpart.

- Speak plainly and slowly (but not so slowly as to appear condescending), choosing your words carefully.

Value Diversity　Those who view diversity among employees as a source of richness and strength for the organization can help bring a wide range of benefits to their organization. Whether you happen to belong to the majority culture or to one of the minority cultures where you work, you will share your work and leisure hours with people different from yourself—people who have values, mannerisms, and speech habits different from your own. This statement is true today, and it will be even truer in the future. The same strategies apply whether the cultural differences exist at home or abroad.

Cultural diversity provides a rich environment for solving problems and for expanding horizons.

A person who is knowledgeable about, and comfortable with, different cultures is a more effective manager because he or she can avoid misunderstandings and tap into the greater variety of viewpoints that a diverse culture provides. In addition, such understanding provides personal satisfaction.

Strategies for Adapting to Others

In addition to adapting to cultural differences, good communicators also recognize the myriad other differences that can influence how we communicate. Much has been written, for example, about the numerous differences between the communication styles of men and women. Our goal here is not to discuss specific differences in detail, but to offer some insight that may further help you adapt to others in the workplace.

Men and women often communicate differently.

Gender Issues in Communication　Gender roles consist of the learned behaviour associated with being male or female. Certain differences typically exist in male/female communication patterns:[10]

1. Women communicate largely to build rapport; men communicate primarily to preserve independence and status by displaying knowledge and skill.
2. Men prefer to work out their problems by themselves, whereas women prefer to talk out solutions with another person.
3. Women are more likely to compliment the work of a co-worker; men are more likely to be critical.
4. Men tend to interrupt to dominate a conversation or to change the subject; women tend to interrupt to agree with or to support what another person is saying.
5. Men tend to be more directive in their conversation, whereas women emphasize politeness.
6. Men are more interested than women in calling attention to their own accomplishments.
7. Men tend to dominate discussions during meetings.
8. Men tend to internalize successes ("That's one of my strengths") and to externalize failures ("We should have been given more time"). Women tend to externalize successes ("I was lucky") and to internalize failures ("I'm just not good at that").
9. In the workplace, men speak differently to other men than they do to women, and women speak differently to other women than they do to men.
10. Even when gender is not readily apparent in online communication, men and women have recognizably different styles in posting to the Internet.

Recognize that these differences often (but not always) do exist (see Figure 2.4). Thus, women should not take it personally if a male co-worker fails to praise their work; he may simply be engaging in gender-typical behaviour. If a male manager feels that a female colleague is more interested in relating to others in the group and seeking consensus than in solving the problem, she may simply be engaging in gender-typical behaviour.

Competent communicators seek to understand and adapt to these differences. According to Alice Sargeant, author of *The Androgynous Manager,*

Relate versus **Debate**
Rapport versus **Report**
Cooperation versus **Competition**

figure2.4

Goals of Gender Communication

Do you know women and men who defy these gender stereotypes?

Men and women should learn from one another without abandoning successful traits they already possess. Men can learn to be more collaborative and intuitive, yet remain result-oriented. Women need not give up being nurturing in order to learn to be comfortable with power and conflict.[11]

Communicating with People with Disabilities Since the *Employment Equity Act* was passed in 1996, more physically disabled individuals than ever before have been able to enter the workplace. According to Statistics Canada, nearly a million disabled Canadians were part of the workforce as of 2001.

While Canadian equity and human rights legislation protects disabled individuals from discrimination, competent communicators go beyond the legal requirements. Depending on each individual situation, some reasonable changes in the way you communicate will be appreciated. For example, when being introduced to someone who uses a wheelchair, bend over slightly to be closer to eye level. If the person is able to extend his or her hand for a handshake, offer your hand. For lengthy conversations, sit down so that you are both eye to eye. People who use wheelchairs may see their wheelchairs as extensions of their personal space, so avoid touching or leaning on their wheelchair.

Most hearing-impaired people use a combination of hearing and lip reading. Face the person to whom you're speaking, and speak a bit slower (but not louder) than usual. When talking with a person who is blind, deal in words rather than in gestures or glances. As you approach him or her, make your presence known; if in a group, address the person by name so that he or she will know to whom you are talking. Identify yourself and use your normal voice and speed.

Everyone needs help at one time or another. If someone with a disability looks as if he or she needs assistance, ask whether help is wanted and follow the person's wishes. But resist the temptation to take too much care of an individual with a disability. Don't be annoying or patronizing.

Always, everywhere, avoid using language like "Are you deaf?," "He's a little slow," or "What are you, blind?" Such language is disrespectful to those with physical or cognitive disabilities; in fact, such language is disrespectful to everyone.

When making presentations, consider the needs of those with disabilities—in terms of seating, handouts and other visual aids, and the like. As always when

Making reasonable accommodations for workers with disabilities is a normal part of the contemporary workplace.

communicating, the best advice is to know your audience. Also, see the "unseen." Recognize that some disabilities are invisible. Be alert and sensitive to colleagues who may have allergies or other sensitivities, unseen physical disabilities, addictions, or other life-threatening (or even fatal) conditions.

Accept accommodations as a normal part of the workplace. We all need accommodations of some sort, not necessarily a wheelchair but perhaps a standard office chair that needs adjustment for users of different height. Embrace the idea that accommodating co-workers, customers, and guests with disabilities is a normal function of the workplace. In short, show that you are a team player who values social inclusion.

Most important, relax. Insofar as possible, forget about the disability, and treat the person as you would anyone else. That person was hired because of the contribution he or she could make to the organization—not because of the disability.

■ Communicating by Telephone

co3. Communicate effectively by telephone.

Communicating effectively by telephone is a critical managerial skill, one that becomes increasingly important as the need for instantaneous information increases. Your telephone demeanour may be taken by the caller as the attitude of the entire organization. Every time the phone rings, your organization's future is on the line.

Your Telephone Voice

Sit or stand tall and greet the caller with a smile.

Because the person to whom you're speaking has no visual clues to augment the auditory clues, a voice that is raspy, hoarse, shrill, loud, or weak can make you sound angry, excited, depressed, or bored—even when you aren't. Therefore, try to control your voice and project a friendly, competent, enthusiastic image to the other party.

To make your voice as clear as possible, sit or stand tall and avoid chewing gum or eating while talking. If your head is tilted sideways to cradle the phone between your head and shoulder, your throat is strained and your words may sound unclear.

Greet the telephone caller with a smile—just as you would greet someone in person. Your voice sounds more pleasant when you're smiling. An experiment was once conducted in which telephone salespeople were instructed to smile when they talked to their customers on one day and to scowl on the next. The salespeople sold almost twice as much on the days they were smiling.[12]

When the phone rings, pause, shift gears mentally, smile, and then answer the phone. Some firms even attach a sticker to the phone to remind employees to smile. "Smile," the sticker says, "it might be the boss calling."

Your Telephone Technique

Although every office worker will answer phones, the people who answer the firm's main number are vital to the firm's public image. These people must be trained and highly qualified—not the newest or least informed workers, as is often the case. These people's contacts with customers can have more impact on the organization's public image than the best advertising and promotional campaign.

Always answer the phone by the second or third ring. Regardless of how busy you are, you do not want to give the impression that your company doesn't care about its callers. Answer clearly and slowly, giving the company's name. Remember that even if you give the same greeting 50 times a day, your callers probably hear it only once. Make sure they can understand it.

Be a good listener. Just as you would never continue writing or reading while someone speaks to you in person, do not engage in such distracting activities during phone calls. Pay attention especially to getting names correct and use the person's name during the conversation to personalize the message.

Give the caller your undivided attention.

As with most other communication forms, emphasize positive language. Instead of saying, "I don't know," say, "Let me check and call you right back." Instead of "you'll have to...," say, "We'll be happy to handle that if you'll just. . . ."

One study estimated that 70 percent of all business calls are placed on hold at some time during the conversation.[13] If you must put a caller on hold, always ask, "May I put you on hold?" and then give the caller an opportunity to respond. Long-distance callers may prefer to call back rather than to be put on hold. When you get back on the line, do not appear rushed or exasperated. Give the patient caller your complete attention.

Voice Mail

Whether you love it or hate it, voice mail (for example, "Press 1 to leave a message or press 2 to speak to an operator") is here to stay. Although some callers find voice mail impersonal and irritating, most are grateful for the opportunity to leave a message when they're unable to reach their party.

Plan what message you will leave before you make the call.

Before you even make a call, recognize that you might have to leave a message, so plan your message beforehand. Be polite and get to the point quickly. Clearly define the purpose of the call and the desired action and always give your phone number—even if the caller has it on file. The calls that get returned the fastest are those that are easiest to make.

If you have voice mail on your own phone, follow these guidelines:

- Never use voice mail as a substitute for answering your phone when you are available. Your customers, suppliers, and fellow workers deserve more consideration than that.

- Record your outgoing message in your own voice and keep it short. Here is an example: "Hello, this is John Smith. Please leave me a message and I'll get back to you as quickly as I can. Thank you." Change your message when you will be away from the office for an extended period of time.

- Check your messages at least daily and return calls promptly. Callers assume that you've received their messages and may interpret a lack of response as rudeness.

Telephone Tag

The telephone would be a much more efficient instrument if we could be assured of reaching our party each time we call. Instead, we're often forced to play an unproductive game of telephone tag, in which Party A calls Party B, is unable to reach her, and leaves a message. Party B then returns A's call, is unable to reach him, and leaves a message. And the process continues until the connection is finally made or until one party gives up in frustration.

Only 17 percent of business callers reach their intended party on the first try, 26 percent by the second try, and 47 percent by the third try. Thus, it takes the majority of business callers at least three tries to reach their intended party.[14]

To avoid telephone tag, plan the timing of your calls. Try to schedule them at times when you're most likely to reach the person. Also, announce when you're returning a call. If you're returning someone's call and get a secretary on the line, begin by saying you're returning the boss's call. This will clue the secretary that the boss wants to speak to you.

If necessary, find out what time would be best to call back or whether someone else in the organization can help. Finally, know when to call it quits. If you haven't reached your intended party after numerous attempts, it is unlikely that further attempts will be successful. When all else fails, stop calling and write a letter or use email.

Cellphones and Paging Devices

Turn your cellphone off during social occasions.

Nothing is more disconcerting than to have your business presentation interrupted by the ringing of someone's cellphone or the beeping of someone's pager. In public locations where conversation is expected (such as in airline terminals), using a cellphone or answering a page is appropriate. However, at formal meetings, restaurants, movies, and social occasions, you should either turn off your device or switch to the "silent-alert" mode (typically either a light or a vibrating device).

When calling someone on a cellphone, get down to business quickly; both you and the recipient are paying by-the-minute charges for using the phone. And when driving, remember that safety comes first. Do not make (or answer) a call while manoeuvring in difficult traffic.

■ Communicating Electronically

co4. Communicate effectively via electronic media.

Technology helps us not only access information but also share it with others. A variety of technological innovations—some quite recent and others that have been around for several decades—enable work teams and people with similar interests and objectives to communicate quickly and efficiently.

Email and Instant Messaging

In email (electronic mail), messages are composed, transmitted, and usually read on computer screens. Today, email has replaced the telephone as the preferred medium to communicate in business. There are nearly a billion email addresses assigned in the world. Consumers comprise 60 percent of the email accounts, equivalent to one address for every 13 people on the planet.[15]

Email has, in fact, become so popular that it can be time-consuming to read and answer. Another problem relates to the fact that email is typically written "on the fly"—composed and sent while keyboarding. Writers therefore sometimes tend to ignore effective writing principles. According to Charles McGoon, email may be:

> desensitizing us to egregious grammatical gaffes. . . . Would you write a printed memo to your boss with typos in it? To what earthly purpose? How can someone on the other end of an email message know that you're really an intelligent person?[16]

Competent communicators follow the guidelines shown in Checklist 2, "Effective Email Practices," on page 58, to ensure that their email messages achieve their objectives. (Also see Spotlight 6 on Technology on pages 59–61.)

Instant messaging (IM) works much like email, but because information is exchanged in real time, IM facilitates a digital "conversation" much more readily than email. One author describes the advantages of IM over email this way:

> Where IM rises above email is in its speed—converse as fast as you can type—and in something called 'presence awareness'. Unlike email, where you fire the message off into Cyberspace and pray the recipient is near a computer and not in Tofino having forgotten to activate their vacation responder, IM allows users to have buddy lists with indicators showing which of your co-workers are available to chat. No more having to phone people to see if you can email them. If their PC is off, so is the green light beside their name on your buddy list.[17]

Of course, with these advantages come some pitfalls. To keep an IM conversation moving (often while typing with your thumbs on a BlackBerry), users frequently employ a much more compressed style of writing (short or even incomplete sentences and plenty of shorthand and acronyms), which can lead to miscommunication. Moreover, the addictive nature of IM means many users, believing themselves to be productively multi-tasking, are constantly distracted from giving their full attention to a person or task. One critic decries the trend toward trying to make ourselves constantly accessible: "While we are hypnotized by the constant beeping and buzzing of virtual machines that keep us tuned in, we may actually be tuning out, not only on critical pieces of information which we may need to do a good job, but even on real-life smiles and conversations and the rain and the sunshine around us."[18]

IM security is another problem. Because consumer instant messaging programs such as Yahoo and MSN do not normally allow screening by a company server, IM exposes business to threats of viruses, worms, and the like. Moreover, many IM systems delete messages as soon as the computer is turned off, making records retention impossible.[19]

Avoiding these pitfalls is actually quite simple. For individuals, know when to turn your instant messaging off—during important meetings, when performing tasks that require careful attention, and when communicating with others face to face. For businesses, monitor how IM is being used in your workplace, set up policies to govern its use, and acquire business-class software that includes security and archiving abilities.[20]

Groupware

Groupware is a form of software that automates information sharing between two or more remote users and enables them to communicate electronically and coordinate their efforts easily.

One form of groupware—a *group-authoring system*—enhances the process of collaborative writing by enabling different people to comment with ease on one another's writing. This type of program keeps an "edit trail" of changes made, who made them, and when. Because group members can comment on both the original draft and other members' comments and can raise and answer questions, such programs can reduce the need for time-consuming face-to-face meetings. Today, in fact, most word processing software can function quite effectively as groupware for editing team-writing projects (see Spotlight 6, "Using Microsoft Word to Edit a Team Document," on pages 59–61).

✓checklist 2

Effective Email Practices

Format

✓ **Use short lines and short paragraphs (especially the first and last paragraphs).** They are much easier to read. Avoid formatting a long message as one solid paragraph.

✓ **Don't shout.** Use all-capital letters only for emphasis or to substitute for italicized text (such as book titles). Do NOT type your entire message in all capitals. It is a text-based form of *shouting* at your reader and is considered rude (not to mention being more difficult to read).

✓ **Proofread your message before sending.** Don't let the speed and convenience of email lull you into being careless. Although an occasional typo will probably be overlooked by the reader, excessive errors or sloppy language creates an unprofessional image of the sender.

Content

✓ **Choose your recipients carefully.** Don't send a message to an entire mailing list (for example, the whole department) if it applies to only one or two people. This practice has been dubbed the "reply-all" syndrome and is the bane of many workplaces.

✓ **Use a descriptive subject line.** Most email programs allow the reader to preview new messages by date received, sender, and subject, so the wording of the subject line may determine not only *when* but *if* a message is read. Use a brief, but descriptive, subject line.

✓ **Greet your recipient.** Downplay the seeming impersonality of computerized mail by starting your message with a friendly salutation, such as "Hi, Amos" or "Dear Mr. Fisher."

✓ **Insert previous messages appropriately.** Most email programs allow you to insert the original message into your reply. Use this feature judiciously. Occasionally, it may be helpful for the reader to see his or her entire message replayed. More often, however, you can save the reader time by establishing the context of the original message in your reply—for example, "Here is my opinion of the AlphaBat system that you asked for in your May 28 email."

✓ **Use a direct style of writing.** Put your major idea in the first sentence or two. If the message is so sensitive or emotionally laden that a more indirect organization would be appropriate, you should reconsider whether email is the most effective medium for the message.

✓ **Think twice; write once.** Because it is so easy to respond immediately to a message, you might be tempted to let your emotions take over. Such behaviour is called "flaming" and should be avoided. Always assume the message you send will never be destroyed.

✓ **Provide an appropriate closing.** Some email programs identify only the email address (for example, "70511.753@aol.com") in the message header. Don't take a chance that your reader won't recognize you. Include your name, email address, and any other appropriate identifying information at the end of your message. Most email programs can automatically insert a "signature" containing this information at the end of every message.

No matter which software you use, follow these guidelines:

- Assign someone the role of manager of the document to keep the discussion on track and to edit comments as needed.
- Determine beforehand how often each participant should check for changes.
- Minimize clutter by encouraging the use of email or other communication channels for one-on-one communication. Provide everyone with email addresses and phone numbers of all participants.
- If you're an inexperienced user, copy the newest file before making your comments—to simplify reverting to the original if you later change your mind.

spotlight6
ON TECHNOLOGY

Using Microsoft Word to Edit a Team Document

Once upon a time, to edit a group report you would first print out several copies of the report and distribute them to your team members. The team, in turn, would handwrite their comments on their copies and send them back to you. Finally, you'd manually collate the copies, make whatever changes were necessary, and print out a final copy of the report.

Today, anyone with access to a computer and email can easily coordinate team efforts and collaborate electronically. In fact, you can accomplish group editing simply by using a word processing program such as Microsoft Word.

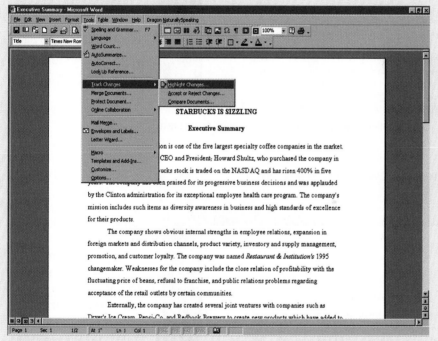

Assume, for example, that your team is conducting a company analysis of the popular Starbucks coffee shops. As the designated writer for the team, you create the draft of your document. Then, to keep track of changes that others make to the document, from the Word menu bar you select Tools, Track Changes, Highlight Changes (see screen A). You then send your two other team members—Lanying Zhao and Sandy Overton—the document as an email attachment and ask for their comments.

Screen A: With Microsoft Word, you can easily keep track of any changes made to your document.

(continued)

Teleconferencing and Video Conferencing

A **teleconference** (that is, a telephone conference call) is a meeting of three or more people, at least some of whom are in different locations, who communicate via telephone. The primary advantage of teleconferences is that they save time and money because participants do not have to leave their offices. As in all telephone communications, however, this medium limits the amount of non-verbal cues available to the participants.

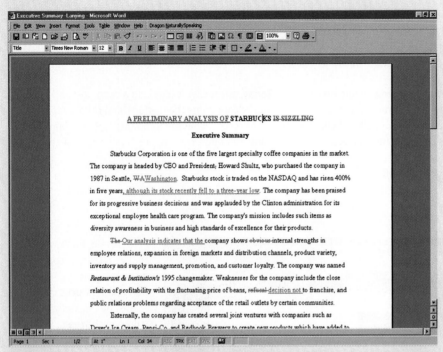

Screen B: Microsoft Word automatically underlines inserted text and strikes through deleted text.

Lanying prefers to do line-by-line editing, so she first makes a copy of the report (saving the original in case she later changes her mind) in Microsoft Word and then makes her changes on the document itself. Because the document has been saved with Track Changes enabled, Lanying's proposed changes show up in color on the screen. In screen B, for example, she proposes changing the report title from "Starbucks Is Sizzling" to "A Preliminary Analysis of Starbucks."

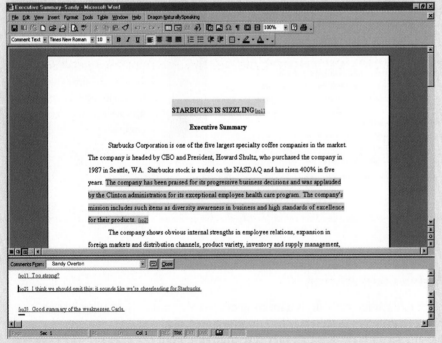

Screen C: In Microsoft Word, it's a simple task for a team member to add comments and questions to the original document.

Sandy receives the same draft of the report; he prefers to comment on the text rather than make line-by-line changes. He highlights the text he wants to comment on and then selects Comment from the Insert menu. A comment window opens at the bottom of the screen where he can type in his comments. In screen C, for example, Sandy has highlighted the last two sentences in the first paragraph and makes this comment: "I think we should omit this; it sounds like we're cheerleading for Starbucks."

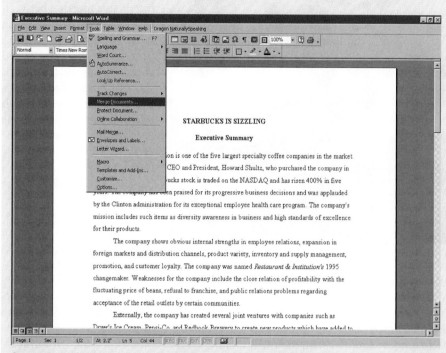

Screen D: As the designated writer for the team, you can easily produce a final document by merging the comments and suggested changes from all team members.

When Lanying and Sandy are finished, they email their annotated documents back to you. As the designated writer, you must decide which of their changes to accept or reject. You begin by opening your original document and then merging both sets of annotations into your document. To do so, you select Tools, Merge Documents from the menu (see screen D).

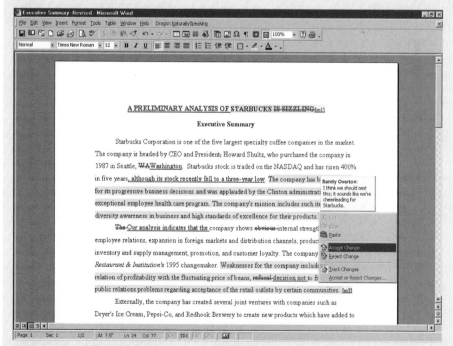

Screen E: Each team member's comments and proposed changes are shown in a different color for you to accept or reject.

The merged document (screen E) shows your original material along with comments and changes suggested by Lanying and Sandy. Because Lanying made her changes on the document itself, it's easy to follow her changes. To see Sandy's comments, you pause the mouse over the highlighted text so that his comments appear on screen. For every suggested change, you can accept or reject the revisions by right-clicking while pausing the mouse over the comment.

Despite the failure of many large dot-com start-ups, a surprising number of small web start-ups, called mini-dots, are surviving by sticking to niches they know well and using Net resources, from email to customer-sharing arrangements. According to Aron Benon, founder of Florist.com, "Today, the Internet is what the telephone was when it was invented—a way to further our reach."

A **video conference** is an interactive meeting between two or more people using video link-ups at two or more sites. The audio and video signals that transmit the live voices and images may be transmitted through telephone lines, direct cable connections, microwave, or satellite. Video conferencing has grown tremendously in recent years, spurred by the increasing cost of travel, more affordable transmission rates, and the advent of more effective hardware. As with other distant technologies, however, participants may miss some non-verbal cues and may prefer the personal chemistry that develops more easily in face-to-face meetings. Also, some users are uncomfortable in front of a camera and worry about how they look, act, and sound. These self-conscious feelings are likely to diminish, however, as managers become more familiar with the medium and develop more experience in conducting business this way.

Personal one-on-one video conferencing is becoming popular as people take advantage of the advent of inexpensive personal webcameras attached to personal computers. This technology allows two people to conduct an on-the-spot video conference using nothing more than their personal computers and Internet hookup.

Using a small webcam, you can hold your own video conference directly from your computer.

Follow these guidelines when conducting a teleconference or video conference:

- Plan ahead. Prepare a detailed agenda and follow it.

- Involve all participants frequently during the call. Try to avoid having most conference participants in a single room and only one or two elsewhere.

- Speak normally. There's no need to shout—or to drum your fingers on the table, play with your pen, or make other distracting sounds.

- Be prepared. Provide participants with copies of the agendas, handouts, other visual aids, and the like ahead of time. Follow up with meeting minutes.

- In a teleconference, encourage folks to position themselves near the phone when talking, but avoid noisily sliding the phone around the table. Always address individuals by name to assure their attention, and ask participants to identify themselves before speaking.

- In a video conference, when you want to speak, introduce yourself; then wait until the camera is focused on you before beginning to speak. (High-end video cameras are able to automatically focus on the person speaking.)

- Prepare any graphics with video in mind. Wait until the camera focuses on your visual aid before discussing it, and make sure that your visual aids are simple, with readable fonts.

■ Avoid sudden movements. Current technology cannot handle as many frames per second in video conferences as television can. Maintain a quiet posture, avoid moving around unnecessarily, and limit unnecessary gestures. Rely more on your voice than your hands.

REQUIRED READING   *wordwise*

Actual book titles published within the past ten years, according to *Bookseller* magazine.

- *The Flat-Footed Flies of Europe*
- *Fancy Coffins to Make Yourself*
- *Tea Bag Folding*
- *The Art and Craft of Pounding Flowers*
- *Lightweight Sandwich Construction*

Mailing Lists and Newsgroups

A **mailing list** is a discussion group in which messages are sent directly to members via email. On the Internet, these mailing lists are called *listservs*. To become a member, you must first subscribe to the list (typically by sending an email message to the listserver). From then on, any messages posted to the list are automatically sent to your email address. Listservs are usually created to enable members to exchange information and views about a particular topic. Your instructor, for example, may create a mailing list for your class. Any message posted to that mailing list either by the instructor or by one of the students will then be sent to (and presumably read by) all members of the class. Such a list would be discontinued at the end of the school term. Some more-or-less permanent mailing lists provide searchable archive files that contain all of the old messages.

A **newsgroup** is a discussion group in which messages (called *articles*) are posted at the newsgroup site. Anyone can connect to the site via an Internet *Usenet* connection as frequently as desired to read any newly-posted articles. Newsgroups differ from mailing lists in that newsgroup members have to "visit" the newsgroup site to see any new messages, whereas new messages are automatically sent as email to mailing-list members. The news administrator determines how long old articles remain archived (and, therefore, available for searching).

Figure 2.5 shows a typical email message posted from a listserv (top) and a newsgroup article (bottom).

Web 2.0

Web 2.0 is defined by Wikipedia as "a second generation of services available on the World Wide Web that lets people collaborate and share information online. In contrast to the first generation, Web 2.0 gives users an experience closer to desktop applications than the traditional static Web pages." Comprising a number of technologies (such as weblogs and wikis) designed to promote open communication, Web 2.0 promises to shake up traditional business models as it challenges the old "command and control mindset of corporations" and flattens "organizational boundaries—between managers and employees and between the company and its partners and customers."[21]

A **weblog** (frequently shortened to blog) was defined in Chapter 1 as a Web site where regular entries are made. More specifically, a blog is a Web site that may be created by an individual, interest group, or organization, often to provide a forum for discussion and dissemination of information. A blog can also comprise videos, photos, or links to other blogs and Web sites. As with any communication technology, blogs can be powerful tools or dangerous foes for business.

While blogs can and do serve some of the same functions as email, they are much more versatile. According to Microsoft blogging guru Robert Scoble (author of

figure2.5

Listserv Email Posting (top) and Newsgroup Posting (bottom)

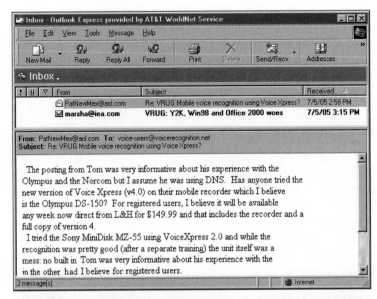

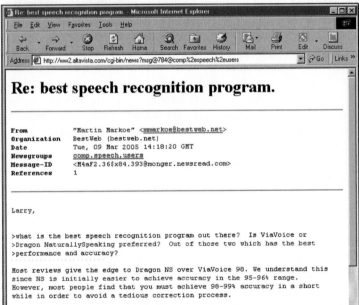

Naked Conversations), blogs are better than email when the subject being discussed does not require a response (e.g., a progress report) or when the subject requires multiple audiences to view the material and perhaps offer feedback.[22] Email is a one-to-one conversation; a blog is a community forum.

A great fear of many businesses is that their own employees may keep personal blogs (often anonymously) that can do great harm to the business. There have been many cases of employees being terminated for taking liberties with a company's information or reputation. In one instance, a US airline attendant posted an innocuous photo of herself in her uniform on her personal blog, accompanied by the caption "Queen of the Sky." She was terminated for doing so.[23] Other more sinister cases have revealed employees leaking confidential business information through their blog.

Of course, the greatest danger of blogs is also their greatest asset—the speed at which information can travel to a wide audience. Indeed, many companies are taking advantage of blogs as a powerful way to do business. CEOs of major corporations, such as GM and Sun Microsystems, keep their own blogs, even to the point of occasionally conversing with customers directly.

In a business context, blogs can be broadly divided into two categories: internal and external. Internal blogs exists only on the company's Intranet, and are thus not available for public consumption. They can be effective tools at sharing information and opinions—upwardly, downwardly, and horizontally. External blogs, which exist on the Internet and can be viewed by anyone with a computer and an Internet connection, can be a great way for organizations to promote products and solicit feedback from the public.

When used internally, the key to an effective blog, according to Canadian HR reporter, is to ensure it's a two-way medium that's kept up to date: "Blogging can play a key role in enhancing communication, but it is important to remember that blogs won't work if they are just a different pipeline for the same old memos. To be successful, CEOs and senior leaders who blog must have a good track record in communicating confidently and openly with employees. . . . Likewise, a blog must be current and timely."[24]

 Fredrik Racka, as expert on corporate blogging, offers these reasons on his Web site, www.corporateblogging.com, why companies might consider setting up their own blogs:

■ To establish relationships with customers beyond just the objective to sell them something

■ To create a channel for the media to check regularly on what the organization has to say

■ To provide internal collaboration, using blogs as a workspace where members can keep each other up to date

■ To establish your company as a "thought leader" in the industry, thereby gaining public attention both for sales and recruitment purposes

■ To informally test products or ideas while soliciting feedback from the public

A **podcast** is an audio program made available for downloading as an MP3. (The name owes its origin to Apple's iPod.) Many radio stations now make their programs available as downloadable podcasts as an alternative to traditional real-time formats. Growing out of the success of blogs, podcasts are now used by a growing number of businesses to serve many of the same functions as blogs, most notably in the area of internal communications—as an alternative medium to the traditional newsletter—and in marketing.

Where blogs are somewhat akin to on-line journals, podcasts are more like radio programs made available over the Internet. Nanette Matys, of Toronto law firm Osier Hoskin and Harcourt, uses podcasts (linked to their Web site) as a "way of showcasing the firm's expertise." She maintains that "there's a nuance and a directness of the spoken word that doesn't always get captured in print."[25]

A **wiki** is a web page that is set up to be edited by groups of people (i.e., typically, anyone who's a register user on the site). The best known wiki is probably Wikipedia, an enormous online encyclopedia, constantly under revision by thousands of contributors. Perhaps the main difference between a blog and a wiki is that a blog is typically sponsored and controlled by an individual, who posts his or her entries and invites feedback, whereas a wiki is controlled by all participants—who not only add their own material, but also edit the postings of other members. Because of the flexibility and simplicity of wikis, they are ideal tools for collaborative writing.

Businesses can use wikis in endless ways. One investment bank recently began posting meeting agendas, schedules, and other project-related documents on its wiki Web site, which allows each member of the project to append the material with changes or comments. After exploring the use of wikis as an alternative to the endless number of emails typically sent back and forth during a project, the bank discovered a 75 percent drop in emails, a considerable improvement in communication efficiency.[26]

A Word of Caution

As we have seen, our need for up-to-date and accurate information is insatiable, and technology helps satisfy this need. Some argue that one downside of technology is a fragmenting of society as our number of shared experiences diminishes in the resulting glut of information. Says David Shenk, author of *Data Smog, Surviving the Information Glut:*[27]

> Technically, we possess an unprecedented amount of information; however, what is commonly known has dwindled to a smaller and smaller percentage every year. This should be a sobering realization for a democratic nation, a society that must share information in order to remain a union.

Also, according to historian Daniel Boorstin, "Every advance in the history of communications has brought us in closer touch with people far away from us, but at the expense of insulating us from those nearest to us."[28] Of course, users and advocates of Web 2.0 would argue that this particular technological advancement has just the opposite effect, actually bringing more and more people together and expanding our collaborative knowledge.

Whatever your views on the usefulness of the various technological advancements discussed here, know that competent communicators use technology to full advantage to accomplish their communication goals but are mindful of the need for shared personal interactions as well. In short, they practice both high-tech *and* high-touch communication.

■ Communicating Through Business Meetings

CO5. Plan, conduct, and participate in a business meeting.

Effective managers know how to run and participate in business meetings.

Much of the listening you'll do in the workplace will be in the context of business meetings. Meetings serve a wide variety of purposes in the organization. They keep members informed of events related to carrying out their duties; they provide a forum for soliciting input, solving problems, and making decisions; and they promote unity and cohesiveness among the members through social interaction.

Considering these important purposes, it is not surprising the average executive spends 25 percent to 70 percent of his or her day in meetings (an average of three hours per day, according to research by MCI WorldCom Conferencing). No wonder, then, many managers complain that "meetingitis" has become a national plague in Canadian business. (Someone once described a meeting as an occasion for a group of people to keep minutes and waste hours.) The typical business meeting is a staff meeting held in a company conference room for just under two hours, with no written agenda distributed in advance.[29]

The ability to conduct and participate in meetings is a crucial managerial skill. One survey of more than 2000 business leaders showed that executives who run a meeting well are perceived to be better managers by both their superiors and their peers.[30]

To use meetings as an effective managerial tool, you need to know not only how to run them but also when to call them and how to follow up afterward. Like so many decisions you will have to make about communication, your choices will be guided by what you hope to accomplish.

Planning the Meeting

When you add up the hourly salaries and fringe benefits of those planning and attending a meeting, the cost can be considerable. Managers must make sure they're getting their money's worth from a meeting, and that requires careful planning: identifying the purpose and determining whether a meeting is really necessary, preparing an agenda, deciding who should attend, and planning the logistics.

Identifying Your Purpose   The first step is always to determine your purpose. The more specific you can be, the better results you will get. A purpose such as "to discuss how to make our marketing representatives more effective" is vague and therefore not as helpful as "to decide whether to purchase cellular phones for our marketing representatives." The more focused your purpose, the easier it will be to select a means of accomplishing that purpose.

Determining Whether a Meeting Is Necessary   Sometimes meetings are not the most efficient means of communication. For example, a short memo or email message is more efficient than a face-to-face meeting to communicate routine information. Similarly, it doesn't make sense to use the weekly staff meeting of ten people to hold a long discussion involving only one or two of the members. A phone call or smaller meeting would accomplish that task more quickly and at less cost.

Determine whether a meeting is the best way to accomplish your goal.

However, alternative means of conveying or securing information often present their own problems. Some people don't read written messages carefully, or they interpret them differently. Time is lost in transmitting and responding to written messages. And information may be garbled as it moves from person to person and from level to level.

Preparing an Agenda   Once you've established your specific purpose, you need to consider in more detail what topics the meeting will cover and in what order. This list of topics, or **agenda,** will accomplish two things: (1) it will help you prepare for the meeting by showing what background information you'll need, and (2) it will help you run the meeting by keeping you focused on your plan.

An agenda helps focus the attention of both the leader and the participants.

Knowing what topics will be discussed will also help those attending the meeting to plan for the meeting effectively—reviewing needed documents, bringing pertinent records, deciding what questions need to be raised, and the like. The survey of 2000 business leaders mentioned earlier revealed that three-fourths of the managers consider agendas to be essential for efficient meetings; yet nearly half the meetings they attend are *not* accompanied by written agendas.[31]

Formal, recurring business meetings might follow an agenda like this one; of course, not every meeting will contain all these elements:

1. Call to order
2. Roll call (if necessary)

3. Reading and approval of minutes of previous meeting (if necessary)
4. Reports of officers and standing committees
5. Reports of special committees
6. Old business
7. New business
8. Announcements
9. Program
10. Adjournment

Each item to be covered under these headings should be identified, including the speaker (if other than the chair); for example:

7. New business
    a. Review of December 3 press conference
    b. Recommendation for annual charitable contribution
    c. Status of remodelling—Jan Fischer

Everyone at the meetings should have a specific reason for being there.

Deciding Who Should Attend   A great number of ad hoc meetings take place each business day for the purpose of solving a specific problem. If you must decide who will attend a particular meeting, your first concern is how the participants relate to your purpose. Who will make the decision? Who will implement the decision? Who can provide needed background information? On the one hand, you want to include all who can contribute to solving the problem; on the other hand, you want to keep the meeting to a manageable number of people.

Consider also how the potential group members differ in status within the organization, in knowledge about the issue, in communication skills, and in personal relationships. The greater the differences, the more difficult it will be to involve everyone in a genuine discussion aimed at solving the problem.

Don't underestimate the impact of potential group members' hidden agendas. If any member's personal goals for the meeting differ from the group goals, conflicts can arise, and the quality of the resulting decisions can be impaired. Meeting separately with some of the important participants ahead of time might help to identify sources of potential dissension and provide clues for dealing with them.

Membership in recurring meetings (such as a committee meeting) is relatively fixed. Even for these meetings, the planner must decide whether outsiders should be invited to observe, participate, or simply be available as resource people.

Plan carefully the physical arrangement of the meeting room.

Determining Logistics   It would be unwise to schedule a meeting that requires extensive discussion and creative problem solving at the end of the workday, when members may be exhausted emotionally and physically. Likewise, it would be counterproductive to schedule a three-hour meeting in a room equipped with uncushioned folding chairs, poor lighting, and extreme temperatures.

Instead, facilitate group problem solving by making intelligent choices about the timing and location of the meeting, room arrangements, types of audiovisual equipment, and the like. Doing so will increase the likelihood of achieving the goals of the meeting.

With regard to seating arrangements, the most important tip is to make the decision *consciously;* that is, if you have a choice, use the arrangement that best fits your purpose (see Figure 2.6):

■ The rectangular arrangement is most commonly used for formal meetings, with the chairperson sitting at the head of the table, farthest from the door.

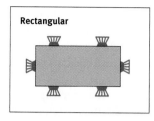

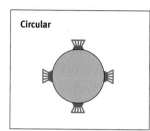

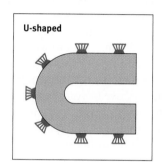

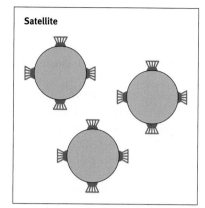

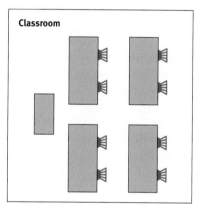

figure2.6
Meeting Room Setups

- The circular arrangement is more informal and encourages an equal sharing of information and leadership functions.

- For larger meetings, a U-shaped setup is desirable because it allows each attendee to see all other meeting participants.

- A satellite arrangement is often useful for training sessions or when participants are to be divided into groups. This arrangement allows the chair to move freely around the room, addressing each group separately.

- A classroom arrangement is appropriate when most of the information is one way—from the leader to the audience; but even in this setup, the leader should encourage interaction among group members.

Conducting the Meeting

Planning for a meeting goes a long way toward ensuring its success, but the manager's job is by no means over when the meeting begins. A manager must be a leader during the meeting, keeping the group focused on the point and encouraging participation.

Punctuality   Unless a high-level member or one whose input is vital to the business at hand is tardy, make it a habit to begin every meeting on time. Doing so will send a powerful non-verbal message to chronic late arrivals that business will be conducted and decisions made whether or not they're present.

An efficient leader begins and ends each meeting on time.

If you wait for latecomers, you send the message to those who *were* punctual that they wasted their time by being prompt. As a result, they will probably arrive late for subsequent meetings. And the habitual late arrivals will then begin arriving even later! Avoid this vicious cycle by beginning (and ending) at the appointed times.

Following the Agenda   One key to a focused meeting is to follow the agenda. At formal meetings you will be expected to discuss all items on the published agenda and no items not on the agenda. The less formal the meeting, the more flexibility you have in allowing new topics to be introduced. It's always possible that new information that has a bearing on your problem may arise. To prevent discussion simply because you didn't include the item on your agenda would make it more difficult for you to achieve your purpose. But as leader of the meeting, you must make certain that new topics are directly relevant.

Leading the Meeting   Begin the meeting with a statement of your purpose and an overview of the agenda. As the meeting progresses, keep track of time. Don't let the discussion get bogged down in details.

Preventing people from talking too much or digressing from the topic requires tact. Comments like "I see your point, and that relates to what we were just discussing" can keep you on track without offending the speaker. You'll also need to encourage the participation of the quieter members of the group with comments like "Juan, how does this look from the perspective of your department?"

Determine which problem-solving strategy is appropriate.

At the end of the meeting, summarize for everyone what the meeting has accomplished. What was decided? What are the next steps? Review any assignments and make sure that everyone understands his or her responsibilities.

During the meeting, someone—either an assistant, the leader, or someone the leader designates—should record what happens. That person must report objectively and not impose his or her own biases.

Following Up the Meeting

Routine meetings may require only a short memorandum or email as a follow-up to what was decided. Formal meetings or meetings where controversial ideas were discussed may require a more formal summary.

Formal meetings require formal minutes of what took place.

Minutes are an official record of the proceedings; they summarize what was discussed and what decisions were made. Generally, they should emphasize what was *done* at the meeting, not what was *said* by the members. Minutes may, however, present an intelligent summary of the points of view expressed on a particular issue, without names attached, followed by the decision made. Avoid presenting minutes that are either so short they lack the "flavour" of what transpired or so long they tend to be ignored.

The first paragraph of minutes should identify the type of meeting (regular or special); the meeting date, time, and place; the presiding officer; the names of those present (or absent) if customary; and the fact that the minutes of the previous meeting were read and approved.

The minutes should be accurate, objective, and complete.

The body of the minutes should contain a separate paragraph for each topic. According to parliamentary procedure, the name of the maker of a motion, but not the seconder, should be entered in the minutes. The precise wording of motions, exactly as voted on, should also appear in minutes. It is often helpful to use the same subheadings as in the agenda. A sample portion of the minutes of a business meeting follows:

Review of December 3 Press Conference

A videotape of the December 3 press conference conducted by Donita Doyle was viewed and discussed. Roger Eggland's motion that "Donita Doyle be commended for the professional and ethical manner in which she presented the company's view at the December 3 press conference" was adopted unanimously without debate.

Recommendation for Annual Charitable Contribution

Tinrah Porisupatani moved "that Maritime Chemical donate $15 000 to a worthwhile charity operating in Essex County." Linda Peters moved to amend the motion by inserting the words "an amount not exceeding" after the word "donate." On a motion by Todd Chandler, the motion to make a donation, with the pending amendment, was referred for further study to the Social Responsibility Committee with instructions to recommend a specific amount and charity and report at the next meeting.

The last paragraph of the minutes should state the time of adjournment and, if appropriate, the time set for the next meeting. The minutes should be signed by the person preparing them. If someone other than the chair prepares the minutes, the minutes should be read and approved by the chair before being distributed.

Guidelines for conducting business meetings are summarized in Checklist 3, "Business Meetings" (see below), and an agenda for a meeting is shown in Model 1, "Agenda for a Meeting" (see page 72).

✔**checklist 3**

Business Meetings

Planning the Meeting

✔ Identify the purpose of the meeting.

✔ Prepare an agenda for distribution to the participants.

✔ Decide who should attend the meeting.

✔ Determine the logistics of the meeting—timing, location, room and seating arrangements, and types of audiovisual equipment needed.

✔ Assign someone (even if it is you) the task of taking notes during the meeting. These notes should be objective, accurate, and complete.

Conducting the Meeting

✔ Encourage punctuality by beginning and ending the meeting on time.

✔ Begin each meeting by stating the purpose of the meeting and reviewing the agenda.

✔ Establish ground rules that permit the orderly transaction of business.

✔ Control the discussion to ensure that it is relevant, that a few members do not monopolize the discussion, and that all members have an opportunity to be heard.

✔ At the end of the meeting, summarize what was decided, what the next steps are, and what each member's responsibilities are.

Following Up the Meeting

✔ If the meeting was routine and informal, follow it up with a memorandum or e-mail summarizing the major points of the meeting. For more formal meetings, prepare and distribute minutes.

model 1

AGENDA FOR A MEETING

Indentifies purpose and length of meeting.

Uses a numbered list to aid readability.

Provides only enough detail to give an indication of what will be discussed.

1

COMPUTER USE COMMITTEE

Regular Meeting Agenda

May 18, 20—

10:00–11:30 a.m.

1. Call to order

2. Approval of agenda

3. Approval of minutes of previous meeting

2   4. Report of the budget subcommittee   Zoe Petropoulu (15 minutes)

Appendix A–attached

5. Old business   Rafik Kurji (10 minutes)

3

6. New business

    a. Standardization of Web Page Development Software   Jenny West (25 minutes)

    b. Standardization of Voice Recognition Software   Shannon Lindsey (25 minutes)

7. Announcements   Peter Wu (15 minutes)

8. Adjournment

Grammar and Mechanics Notes

1 Unless a different format is traditional, use regular report format for meeting agendas.

2 Identify the speakers and the anticipated length of discussion for each agenda.

3 Use parallel language for enumerated or bulleted items.

The **3Ps**
Problem, Process, Product

A PLAN FOR A BUSINESS MEETING

Problem

You are Dieter Ullsperger, director of employee relations for the city of Halifax. The city manager has asked your department to develop a policy statement regarding the solicitation of funds from employees during work hours for employee weddings, retirements, anniversaries, and the like.

Despite the good intentions of such efforts, the city manager questions whether they put undue pressure on some employees and take unreasonable time from official duties. You have already gathered secondary data regarding this matter and have spoken with your counterparts in Montreal, Ottawa, and Edmonton. You are now ready to begin planning a first draft of the policy statement.

Process

1. What is the purpose of your task?

   To prepare a policy statement on soliciting funds from employees during office hours.

2. Is a meeting needed?

   Because this policy will affect every employee in city government, it should be developed on the basis of input from representatives of the work force. Therefore, a planning meeting is desirable.

3. What will be the agenda?

   My first reaction is that the meeting agenda is to write the new policy. I recognize, however, that it is not reasonable for a policy statement to be written during a meeting. Thus, the real agenda is to develop the broad outlines for the policy. The policy will be planned collaboratively; drafted individually; reviewed collaboratively; and finally, revised individually.

4. Who should attend the meeting?

   Because I want to ensure broad consensus on this policy, I'll ask the union representatives to attend. (I'll represent management.) I'll also ask the city's lawyer to attend to ensure that our policy is legal. Finally, I'll ask Lyn Paterson in Transportation to attend; she is a veteran city employee who is well respected among her peers and has served as the unofficial social chairperson for numerous fundraising events over the past several years. I'll telephone each of those people to ask for his or her voluntary participation in this project.

5. What about logistics?

Because I want the meeting to be informal, we'll hold it in the small conference room downstairs, which has an oval table. The only audiovisual equipment I'll need is a chalkboard to display any ideas we might have. I'll ask my assistant to take minutes. Since I was not given a specific deadline, I'll delay the meeting for three weeks because two retirement parties are already scheduled in the meantime.

Product

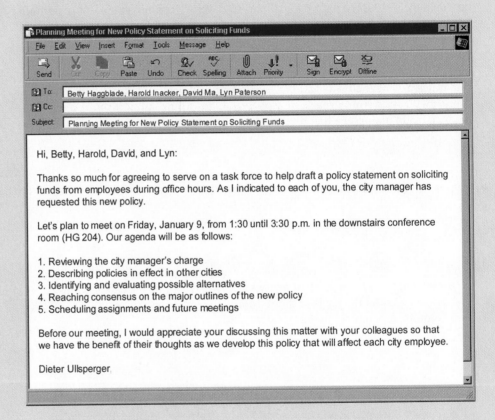

■ Summary

Teams can accomplish more and better-quality work in less time than individuals can *if* the teams function properly. Otherwise, teams can waste time and cause interpersonal conflicts. Conflict about ideas is a helpful part of the group process, whereas interpersonal conflicts are detrimental. An appropriate emphasis on consensus and conformity is productive, but too much emphasis can lead to groupthink, wherein legitimate differences of opinion are not even discussed.

CO1. Communicate effectively in small groups.

At the beginning, group members should get to know one another and set operating rules. They should also acknowledge the need for positive and negative feedback and know how to give productive feedback, including providing helpful feedback on team writing. When problems arise, group members should react to them appropriately, consider them as group problems, and be realistic about what to expect from the group.

For group writing projects, team members should develop a work schedule and meet regularly to ensure proper coordination. Either one person can be assigned to write the draft, or the parts can be divided among group members. Everyone, however, should be involved in revising the draft.

Competent communicators maintain formality, show respect, remain flexible, and write and speak clearly when communicating with people of different cultures. Even if you live and work in a small community in Canada, you will be communicating with, and should learn to be comfortable with, people with different ethnic backgrounds, different genders, and different types of disabilities.

CO2. Communicate effectively within a diverse environment.

When communicating by telephone, give the person to whom you're speaking your undivided attention, speak clearly, listen carefully, and treat the other party with courtesy. Take positive steps to avoid the inconvenience of not being able to reach your party (telephone tag) and use voice mail appropriately. Use cell phones and paging devices only in public places, and practise courtesy when using a speakerphone for conference calls.

CO3. Communicate effectively by telephone.

Today, email is the preferred medium of communicating in business. Competent communicators ensure that they use appropriate formats (especially a descriptive subject line) and content for their email messages. They also make appropriate use of other emerging technologies, including groupware, teleconferencing, video conferencing, blogs, and wikis.

CO4. Communicate effectively via electronic media.

Planning a business meeting requires determining your purpose and deciding whether a meeting is the most efficient way of accomplishing that purpose. You must then determine your agenda, decide who should attend, and plan such logistics as timing, location, and room arrangements.

CO5. Plan, conduct, and participate in a business meeting.

When conducting a meeting, begin with a statement of your purpose and agenda. Then follow the agenda, keeping things moving along. Control those who talk too much, and encourage those who talk too little. Use whatever strategies seem appropriate for solving problems and managing conflicts. At the end of the meeting, send a follow-up memo if needed or distribute minutes of the meeting.

■ Key Terms

You should now be able to define the following terms in your own words and give an original example of each.

agenda (67)   podcast (65)

diversity (46)   team (39)

groupthink (40)   teleconference (59)

groupware (57)   video conference (62)

mailing list (63)   weblog (63)

minutes (75)   wiki (65)

newsgroup (63)

■ Exercises

1 **The 3Ps (Problem, Process, and Product) Model: Communication Applications at Farm Credit Canada.**   As you saw in the chapter-opening profile, John Ryan believes strongly in engaging employee input and collaboration, even to the point of encouraging employees to participate in online forums to discuss the direction of the organization.

Problem

Imagine that you are a special assistant to Ryan. He has called a senior management meeting for October 19 to discuss next year's corporate strategy and to assess the changing economic conditions within the farming and agribusiness industries. You have been asked to prepare a brief email message asking all employees to participate in a meeting to discuss suggestions for specific topics for the meeting agenda.

Process

a. What is the purpose of this meeting, and is a meeting even necessary?
b. Why would Ryan ask employees for suggestions about the agenda in advance of the actual meeting?
c. What information should you include in this message?

Product

Write a subject line for your email message and list two points you should make in the body of the message.

CO1. Communicate effectively in small groups.

2 **Work Rules in Practice**   Interview a business executive and have him or her explain how work teams are used in his or her organization. Try to find out if teams are used, how often teams are used, how the teams are usually formed, how successful the team process is, what problems come up in team settings, and anything else you think would be meaningful regarding the use of teams in business. Prepare a short report of your findings.

3 **Work-Team Communications**   Think of the last team or group setting in which you were involved. Briefly describe for the class (in two or three minutes) the purpose of the group, how the group was formed, how well (or not so well) the group functioned, and if ground rules were established before working on the project. Describe how the variables of group communication—conflict, conformity, and consensus—were or were not incorporated. Was groupthink an issue? Did the group struggle with any problems related to gender, culture, or ethnicity? What were the group's decisions, and did the decisions work effectively?

4 Providing Feedback Everyone had agreed to have his or her part of the five-year marketing plan drafted by the time your team met today. What would be an appropriate response to each of the following incidents at today's meeting? Where appropriate, use the steps shown in Figure 2.2, "Using 'I' Statements When Giving Feedback," on page 42, to compose your response.

a. Fred did not have his part ready (although this is the first time he has been late).
b. Thales did not have his part ready (the third time this year he has missed a deadline).
c. Anita not only had her part completed but also had sketched out an attractive design for formatting the final document.
d. Sunggong was 45 minutes late for the meeting because his car had skidded into a ditch as a result of last night's snowstorm.
e. Elvira left a message that she would have to miss the meeting because she was working on another report, one due tomorrow.

5 Diversity Assume that you are a supervisor in a firm where one-third of the work force is of Asian descent, about half from Taiwan and the other half from mainland China. All are either Canadian citizens or landed immigrants. Because both groups speak Mandarin as their native language, can you assume that both groups have similar cultures? Do some research (including Internet research) on both groups in terms of their typical educational backgrounds, political beliefs, job experiences, and the like. Organize your findings into a two-page report.

CO2. Communicate effectively within a diverse environment.

6 Diversity As a manager, how would you respond to each of the following situations? What kind of helpful advice can you give to each party?

a. Alton gets angry when several of the people he works with talk among themselves in their native language. He suspects they are talking and laughing about him. As a result, he tends to avoid them and to complain about them to others.
b. Jason, a slightly built office worker, feels intimidated when talking to his supervisor, a much larger man who is of a different racial background. As a result, he often is unable to negotiate effectively.
c. Raisa is embarrassed when she must talk to Roger, a subordinate who suffered major facial disfigurement when a grenade exploded in Afghanistan. She doesn't know how to look at him. As a result, she tends to avoid meeting with him face to face.
d. Sheila, the only female manager on staff, gets incensed whenever her colleague Alex apologizes to her after using profanity during a meeting. First, she tells him, he shouldn't be using profanity at all. Second, if he does, he should not apologize just to her for using it.
e. When Jim arrived as the only male real estate agent in a small office, it was made clear to him that he would have to get his own coffee and clean up after himself—just like everyone else. Yet whenever the FedEx truck delivers a heavy carton, the women always ask him to lift the package.

7 International   Joe arrived 15 minutes late for his appointment with Itaru Nakamura, sales manager for a small manufacturer to which Joe's firm hoped to sell parts. "Sorry to be late," he apologized, "but you know how the local drivers are. At any rate, since I'm late, let's get right down to brass tacks." Joe began to pace back and forth in the small office. "The way I see it, if you and I can come to some agreement this afternoon, we'll be able to get the rest to agree. After all, who knows more about this than you and me?" Joe sat down opposite his colleague and looked him straight in the eye. "So what do you say? Can we agree on the basics and let our assistants hammer out the details?" His colleague was silent for a few moments, and then said, "Yes." Discuss Joe's intercultural skills. Specifically, what did he do wrong? What did Nakamura's response probably mean?

8 International Communication   Working with a teammate, select a foreign country. Using two or more Internet sites, outline various cultural differences of the selected country that might impact international business dealings. Look for differences regarding customs, use of space, hand gestures, time orientation, social behaviour, the manner in which business is conducted, and other business-related issues. Prepare an outline of your findings, and submit it and the Internet sources to your instructor.

CO3. Communicate effectively by telephone.

9 Communicating by Telephone   Role-play the situation described below. Record the conversations for later evaluation. While two students are role-playing, the others in the class should be making notes of what went well and what might have been improved. To help simulate a telephone environment, have the two student actors sit back to back so that they cannot see each other or the other class members.

Situation

You are Chris Renshaw, administrative assistant for Ronald Krugel, the marketing manager at Kraft Canada. Terry Plachta, an important customer whom you've never met, calls your boss with a complaint that an item ordered two weeks ago does not work as advertised. Your boss won't be back in the office until tomorrow afternoon.

10 Evaluating Telephone Communications   Telephone two organizations in your area. Your purpose is to speak to the director of human resources to learn how much time he or she spends in meetings each week and to get an evaluation of the effectiveness of these meetings. Call at least three times if you're not successful the first time. Leave a message if necessary. Keep a log of each person with whom you speak at each organization and evaluate the effectiveness of that person's telephone communication skills. Finally, write a summary of what you learned about meetings in that organization. Submit both your log and your summary to your instructor.

11 Leaving Effective Telephone Messages   Assume that on your third try (see Exercise 10) you were still unsuccessful in reaching the director of human resources by telephone. Instead you got a recording asking you to leave a message of no more than 30 seconds. Compose the message you would leave.

CO4. Communicate effectively via electronic media.

12 Technology in Business   Working with a classmate, interview two to four business people. Ask them about the role technology plays in their business operations. Summarize your findings and email the results to your instructor. Find answers to the following questions:

a. What kind of technologies do they routinely use on the job?
b. How has technology impacted their job?
c. What do they enjoy most about using technology?
d. What do they dislike about technology?
e. How often do they use technology?
f. What technology do they use the most?
g. What advantages or disadvantages do they see regarding their use of technology?
h. Has technology made them more effective in the workplace, or has it just made it faster to get things done?

13 The Invisible Web   Much information stored on the Web cannot be identified through normal search engines. The reason is that such information is stored in databases that cannot be accessed directly or is stored in a format (such as Adobe's PDF files) that cannot be indexed by Web crawlers. Using your favourite search engine, do a search for "invisible Web" (don't forget the quotation marks), and study some of the sources you identify. Based on your research, what strategies can you use to access this "invisible" information? Try out some of them and analyze their effectiveness. Create an example of a research problem where you would not be successful using traditional search engines, and then explain step-by-step how you were able to access this information using some of the strategies you've uncovered. Write up your findings in a one- or two-page, double-spaced report.

14 Communication Technology   Select which communication technology, if any, would be best for delivering messages in the following situations, and explain why.

a. A departmental meeting will be held on Friday at 2 p.m. in the conference room.
b. A worker needs to be notified that he or she is going to be laid off.
c. Plant managers located throughout North America need to be trained on a new operation.
d. A salesperson needs to ask a potential customer in the same city about meeting for lunch to discuss a new product.
e. A salesperson needs to get a contract signed by his or her supervisor and returned quickly.
f. The CEO needs to let all employees know of some major changes in the company's dress code.
g. The vice-president is traveling to Mongolia in February and needs to know what the weather will be like.
h. The marketing manager wants to let all of his or her customers throughout Canada know about an upcoming sale.

15 Effective Email Practices   Evaluate the following email message in terms of the guidelines provided in Checklist 2 (see page 58). Specifically, what would you change to make it more effective? Should this message have been sent as an email message in the first place? Discuss.

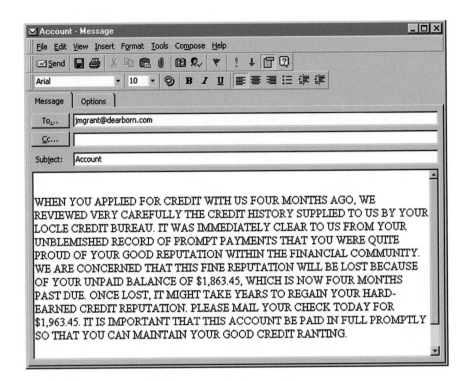

WHEN YOU APPLIED FOR CREDIT WITH US FOUR MONTHS AGO, WE REVIEWED VERY CAREFULLY THE CREDIT HISTORY SUPPLIED TO US BY YOUR LOCLE CREDIT BUREAU. IT WAS IMMEDIATELY CLEAR TO US FROM YOUR UNBLEMISHED RECORD OF PROMPT PAYMENTS THAT YOU WERE QUITE PROUD OF YOUR GOOD REPUTATION WITHIN THE FINANCIAL COMMUNITY. WE ARE CONCERNED THAT THIS FINE REPUTATION WILL BE LOST BECAUSE OF YOUR UNPAID BALANCE OF $1,863.45, WHICH IS NOW FOUR MONTHS PAST DUE. ONCE LOST, IT MIGHT TAKE YEARS TO REGAIN YOUR HARD-EARNED CREDIT REPUTATION. PLEASE MAIL YOUR CHECK TODAY FOR $1,963.45. IT IS IMPORTANT THAT THIS ACCOUNT BE PAID IN FULL PROMPTLY SO THAT YOU CAN MAINTAIN YOUR GOOD CREDIT RANTING.

16 Revising an Email Message Revise the email message shown above, following the email guidelines in Checklist 2 on page 58. List at the bottom of your message the specific practices of effective emails that you were able to follow in your communication.

17 The Downside of Technology As noted in the section entitled "A Word of Caution," historian Daniel Boorstin believes that "every advance in the history of communications has brought us in closer touch with people far away from us, but at the expense of insulating us from those nearest to us." Take a position—either for or against—and give some evidence for your position in a classroom discussion.

18 Teleconferencing Your instructor will divide you into teams with three members. Hold a short team meeting with this brief agenda: introduce yourselves (if necessary), exchange phone numbers and email addresses, elect a team leader, and decide on a convenient time to have a conference call. The purpose of the conference call is to (a) discuss any disadvantages you can identify of using the Web and (b) agree on the three most serious disadvantages of Web use. You will then assign each team member to write a one-half-page discussion of one of the three factors. Do *not* discuss the project at all during your brief team meeting. All discussions will be held during the teleconference and, later, using email. The team leader will place the conference call, tape-record the call, and lead the discussion.

19 Revising a Team Document Electronically Send your one-half-page discussion (see Exercise 18) as an email attachment to your other two team members. When you receive their drafts, open the attachments in a word processing program, turn on Track Changes, make whatever changes you feel would improve the documents, and then email them back to the appropriate writers. Copy yourself on every email you send and print out the copy when you receive it. When you receive your team members' revisions to your document, merge their revised copies with your original copy and make whatever changes you feel are needed. Continue this process, with the team leader in charge, until you have one unified team document discussing the three disadvantages of our reliance on the Internet. Submit to your instructor: (a) the tape recording of your conference call, along with the short report you prepared as a result of the call; and (b) the final team report, including copies of all email messages as an appendix to the report.

20 **Communication in Meetings**   Attend a departmental meeting, an academic council meeting, a city council meeting, a school of business meeting, a student association meeting, a business meeting, or some other meeting. Identify such variables as the following:

CO5. Plan, conduct, and participate in a business meeting.

- Purpose of the meeting

- Role of an agenda

- Members present and their punctuality

- Layout of the room

- Person presiding

- Use of parliamentary procedure

- Outcomes of the meeting

Take minutes of the meeting, answer all of the questions listed in this exercise, and submit both to your instructor.

continuing
case 2

Don't Let the Smoke Get in Your Eyes

Outside on a smoke break, Marc Kaplan ground his cigarette into the ashtray in the lovely courtyard that Northern Lights maintained for its employees. "Won't those save-the-earth people ever be satisfied?" he thought. Even before it became law, NL had enforced a policy of no smoking anywhere within the building—including private offices. Now Diana had just sent a memo to Dave Kaplan asking that the no-smoking policy be extended to outside areas owned by the company as well. This policy would mean that smokers would have to journey across a busy intersection to the small municipal park across the street to light up.

Diana cited health dangers, reduced air quality, rights of non-smokers, and damage to company property. Marc knew he could cite some arguments also: the rights of smokers, the unfairness of imposing new restrictions that were not in place when employees were hired, the reduced productivity due to increased time spent on outside smoking breaks, and the fact that other health-related productivity hazards (such as gross obesity) were not banned. He felt he could enlist the support of

O.J. Drew and Wendy Janish—the other two smokers in the management offices. Tom Mercado, an ex-smoker, was an unknown.

At any rate, Dave Kaplan had decided to hold a special meeting of the executive committee, made up of him and the three vice-presidents, the following week to discuss and resolve the issue. Parliamentary procedure is followed at these meetings.

Oral and Written Communication Projects

1. Assume the role of Dave Kaplan. Compose a memo to the executive committee announcing the meeting and outlining the agenda.

2. Have four members play the roles of Dave and the three vice-presidents; Dave conducts the meeting. The other class members should listen actively, take notes, and be prepared to discuss the events afterward. Each observer should also serve as the secretary and submit a set of minutes for the meeting.

At the executive committee meeting, Marc presents his reasons for not extending the no-smoking policy.

Critical Thinking

3. After role-playing, discuss the situation. How did each actor feel? Was anyone arguing a position with which he or she didn't really agree? Was correct parliamentary procedure followed? Was the meeting successful? Did anyone win? Lose?

LABtest 2

Dave Kaplan prepared a draft of the monthly column that he writes for *Home Remodelling*. Retype the following passage, inserting any needed punctuation according to the punctuation rules introduced in LAB 3 on page 541.

Rita Nguyen of Montreal, Quebec, wants to know this I've heard that replacing my old-fashioned bulbs with compact fluorescents will save $50 per bulb and reduce global warming. Will this type of bulb create that drab, corpselike appearance in everybodys home?

5   The answer is that modern fluorescent bulbs produce excellent colour quality rather than the drab bluish hue of older ones. I use them exclusively in my own home no one has checked my pulse lately to see if I am still breathing. To quote Jim Dulley in Cut Those Bills," published in the Daily Telegraph, You can lose the blues and still cut costs.

10   There are decorative globe, bullet, candelabra, and bent tube designs and recessed, task, and spot lighting will focus the light where you need it. Fluorescent lightings main advantage is its economy. Fifty five dollars is the typical annual savings on homeowners utility bills.

For more information, contact the Industry Conservation Council at

15   905-555-8016 and ask for George Mandrake, energy analyst Betty Bow, economist or Bob Onwood, staff analyst.

3

The Process of Writing

After you have finished this chapter, you should be able to

1. **Specify the purpose of your message and analyze your audience.**

2. **Compose a first draft of your message.**

3. **Revise for content, style, and correctness.**

4. **Arrange your document in a standard format.**

5. **Proofread your document for content, typographical, and format errors.**

A s president of Daydream Communications, a company specializing in technical and marketing communications, Bill Bunn writes and edits technical documents for a varied set of clientele, including the Petroleum Joint Venture Association, Alberta Mortgage Broker's Association, and Metro Graphics Advertising and Design.

"Everything is tied to the process," Bunn emphasizes, which he defines as a set of stages used to create a written document. Generally, his writing process includes the following stages: research and analysis, first draft, review, second draft, review, and final draft. "This process is one that everyone involved in a project contributes to, and it is one that I write into all the contracts I sign. It's that important."

Most importantly, the process gives structure to a writing project." Clients, he points out, often don't know where to begin and what to do. The process serves as a reliable guide as to what needs to be done. "Plus," he says, "it sets out a clear set of milestones that can be assigned to people with deadlines." Once the process is underway, those involved can get a good handle on where the project is at because the process provides that sense of how much has been done, and how much is left to do. "As a professional writer, payment is tied to milestones, which are tied to process. So for me, money is synonymous with process."

A clearly defined process is also critical to achieving quality. "Good communication is rarely ever an accident. Though process can't guarantee good communication, it goes a long, long way. Since I work for an advertising agency one day and an oil company the

an insider's
perspective

BILL BUNN
President,
Daydream Communications

next, there often isn't much else I can rely on. But regardless of where I go and what I'm writing, the process should be the same."

Bunn believes when things go wrong with the writing process, it's a sign that the project is going off the rails. "I have to work with clients sometimes to help them understand why it's so important," he says. "One recent client would not respect the process. I had been working with several executives on a brochure, and we were completing the second draft. Another executive came to one of our meetings and said, 'we have to start over. I had a different idea.'" Obviously, the group did not have a clear idea of what they wanted in the first place, and the process revealed some fundamental differences that these executives had with what the brochure should do. "Of course," Bunn points out, "the whole group wanted me to start over again, which resulted in higher costs and delayed project deadlines."

Generally speaking, Bunn says, if a company has good processes in place, the company has a commitment to quality. "Big companies, good ones, all use strict processes. Those are good companies to work for. If a company refuses to use a process, or violates it, it's difficult to achieve quality, and, typically, these are not clients a writer wants to work for."

"In this business, the writing process is sacred. It serves me in such important ways that I can't be a professional writer without it. The stronger and better the process becomes, the better I become as a writer."

"In this business, the writing process is sacred."

The writing process consists of planning, drafting, revising, formatting, and proofreading.

Stages of the Writing Process

There is no single "best" writing process. In fact, all good writers develop their own process that suits their own ways of tackling a problem. But one way or another, competent communicators typically perform the following five steps when faced with a business situation that calls for a written response (see Figure 3.1):

1. *Planning:* Determining what the purpose of the message is, who the reader will be, what information you need to give the reader to achieve your purpose, and in what order to present the information.
2. *Drafting:* Composing a first draft of the message.
3. *Revising:* Editing for content, style, and correctness.
4. *Formatting:* Arranging the document in an appropriate layout.
5. *Proofreading:* Reviewing the document to check for content, typographical, and format errors.

The amount of time you devote to each step depends on the complexity, length, and importance of the document. Not all steps may be needed for all writing tasks. For example, you may go through all the steps if you are writing a business plan to get funding for a small business but not if you are answering an email message inviting you to a meeting. Nevertheless, these steps are a good starting point for completing a writing assignment—either in class or on the job.

figure3.1
The Five Steps in the Writing Process

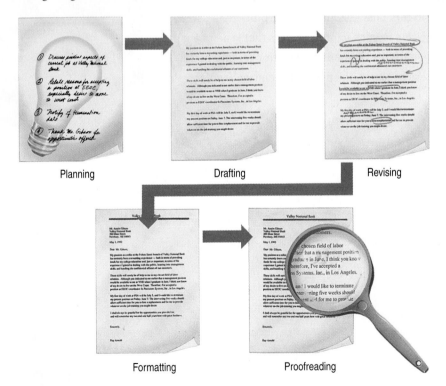

Planning   Drafting   Revising

Formatting   Proofreading

Planning

co1. Specify the purpose of your message and analyze your audience.

Planning, the first step in writing, involves making conscious decisions about the purpose, audience, content, and organization of the message.

Purpose

The first decision relates to the purpose of the message. If you don't know why you're writing the message (that is, if you don't know what you hope to accomplish), then later you'll have no way of knowing whether you've achieved your goal. In the end, what matters is not how well-crafted your message was or how attractive it looked on the page; what matters is whether you achieved your communication objective. If you did, your communication was successful; if you did not, it was not.

In writing for his weekly show, *The Mercer Report*, Rick Mercer mines the political landscape for targets of satire, a process made easier by accessible politicians. "It's Canada. You just call them up. Not only do they call you back, but half the time they answer the phone themselves."[1]

Most writers find it easier to start with a general purpose and then refine the general purpose into a specific one. The specific purpose should indicate the response desired from the reader.

Assume, for example, that you are a marketing manager at Sunshine Coast Resorts, a chain of small hotels in British Columbia. You have noted that many of the larger hotel chains have instituted "frequent-stay" plans, which reward repeat customers with free lodging, travel, or merchandise. You want to write a message recommending a similar plan for your small hotel. Your general purpose might be this:

The purpose should be specific enough to serve as a yardstick for judging the success of the message.

> **General Purpose:** To describe the benefits of a frequent-stay plan at Sunshine Coast Resorts.

Such a goal is a good starting point, but it is not specific enough. To begin with, it doesn't identify the intended audience. Are you writing a memo to the vice-president of marketing recommending this plan, or are you writing a letter to frequent business travelers recommending that they enrol in this plan? Assume, for the moment, that you're writing to the marketing vice-president. What is she supposed to *do* as a result of reading your memo? Do you want her to simply understand what you've written? agree with you? commit resources for further research? agree to implement the plan immediately? How will you know if your message achieves its objective? Perhaps you decide that your specific purpose is this:

> **Specific Purpose:** To persuade Cynthia to approve the development and implementation of a frequent-stay plan for a 12-month test period in two of Sunshine Coast hotels.

Now you have a purpose that's specific enough to guide you as you write the memo and to permit you to judge, in time, whether your message achieved its goal.

In another situation, your general purpose might be to resolve a problem regarding a shipment of damaged merchandise, and your specific purpose might be to persuade the manufacturer to replace the damaged shipment at no cost to you within ten days. Or your general purpose might be to refuse a customer's claim, and your specific purpose might be to convince the customer that your refusal is reasonable and to maintain the customer's goodwill.

Having a clear-cut statement of purpose lets you focus on the content and organization, eliminating any distracting information and incorporating all relevant information.

A clearly stated purpose helps you avoid including irrelevant and distracting information.

Audience Analysis

To maximize the effectiveness of your message, you should perform an **audience analysis;** that is, you should identify the interests, needs, and personality of your receiver. Each person perceives a message differently because of his or her unique mental filter. Thus, we need to determine the level of detail, the language to be used, and the overall tone by answering the pertinent questions about audience discussed in the following sections (see Figure 3.2).

Who Is the Primary Audience?
For most correspondence, the audience is one person, which simplifies the writing task immensely. It is much easier to personalize a message addressed to one individual than a message addressed to many individuals. Sometimes, however, you will have more than one audience. In this case, you need to identify your **primary audience** (the person whose cooperation is crucial if your message is to achieve its objectives) and then your **secondary audience** (others who will also read and be affected by your message). If you can satisfy no one else, try to satisfy the needs of the primary decision maker. If possible, also satisfy the needs of any secondary audience.

If, for example, you're presenting a proposal that must be approved by the general manager but that will also require the cooperation of your colleagues in other departments, the general manager is the primary audience and your colleagues are the secondary audience. Gear your message—its content, organization, and tone—mainly to the needs of the general manager. Most often (but not always), the primary audience will be the highest-level person to whom you're addressing your communication.

Your relationship with the reader determines the tone and content of your message.

What Is Your Relationship with the Audience?
Does your audience know you? If not, you will first have to establish your credibility by assuming a reasonable tone and giving enough evidence to support your claims. Are you writing to someone inside or outside the organization? If outside, your message will often be a little

figure3.2

Questions for Audience Analysis

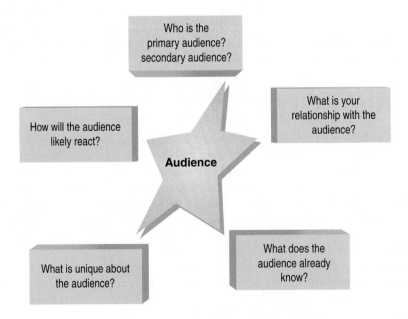

more formal and will contain more background information and less jargon than if you are writing to someone inside the organization.

What is your status in the organization in relation to your audience? Communications to your superiors are obviously vital to your success in the organization. Such communications are typically a little more formal, less authoritarian in tone, and more information-filled than communications to peers or subordinates. In addition, such messages are typically "front-loaded"—that is, they use a direct organizational style and present the major idea in the first paragraph. Study your superior's own messages to get a sense of his or her preferred style and diction, and adapt your own message accordingly.

Most communications to your superiors will probably be organized in a direct style.

When you communicate with subordinates, be polite but not patronizing. Try to instill a sense of collaboration and of corporate ownership of your proposal. When praising or criticizing, be specific; and criticize the action—not the person. As always, praise in public but criticize in private.

How Will the Audience React?   If the reader's initial reaction to both you and your topic is likely to be *positive,* your job is relatively easy. You can use a direct approach—beginning with the most important information (for example, your conclusions or recommendations) and then supplying the needed details. If the reader's initial reaction is likely to be *neutral,* you may want to use the first few lines of the message to get the reader's attention and convince him or her that what you have to say is important and that your reasoning is sound. Make sure your message is short and easy to read and that any requested action is easy to take.

Suppose, however, that you expect your reader's reaction—either to your topic or to you personally—to be *negative.* Here you have a real sales job to do. If the reader shows a personal dislike of you, your best strategy is to call on external evidence and expert opinion to bolster your position. Show that others, people whom the reader is likely to know and respect, share your opinions. Use courteous, conservative language, and suggest ways the reader can cooperate without appearing to "give in"—perhaps by reminding the reader that new circumstances and new information call for new strategies.

If the expected reader reaction is negative, present lots of evidence and expert testimony.

If you anticipate that your reader will oppose your proposal, your best strategy is to supply extra evidence. Instead of one example, give two or three. Instead of quoting one external source, quote several. Begin with the areas of agreement, stress reader benefits, and try to anticipate and answer any objections the reader might have. Through logic, evidence, and tone, build your case for the reasonableness of your position.

What Does the Audience Already Know?   Understanding the audience's present grasp of the topic is crucial to making decisions about content and writing style. You must decide how much background information is necessary, whether the use of jargon is acceptable, and what readability level is appropriate. If you are writing to multiple audiences, gear the amount of detail to the level of understanding of the key decision maker (the primary audience). In general, it is better to provide too much rather than too little information.

Determine how much information the reader needs.

What Is Unique About the Audience?   The success or failure of a message often depends on little things—the extra touches that say to the reader, "You're important, and I've taken the time to learn some things about you."

What can you learn about the personal interests or demographic characteristics of your audience that you can build into your message? Is the reader a "take-charge"

Make the reader feel important by personalizing the content.

kind of person who would prefer to have important information up front—regardless of whether the news is good or bad? What level of formality is expected? Would the reader be flattered or be put off by the use of his or her first name in the salutation? Have good things or bad things happened recently at work or at home that may affect the reader's receptivity to your message?

Competent communicators analyze their audience and then use this information to structure the content, organization, and tone of their messages.

Example of Audience Analysis   To illustrate the crucial role that audience analysis plays in communication, let's consider three different scenarios for the memo to the marketing vice-president requesting a pilot test of a frequent-stay incentive program.

First, assume that Cynthia Haney, vice-president of marketing and your immediate superior, will be the only reader of your memo; that is, she has the authority to approve or reject your proposal. Ms. Haney is an old hand in the hotel business, having had 20 years of managerial experience, and she respects your judgment. She has made it clear that she likes directness in writing and wants the important information up front—so that she can get the major ideas first and then skim the rest of the communication as necessary. The first paragraph of your memo to her might then use a direct approach, as follows:

Some readers like a direct approach, regardless of the purpose of the message.

> The purpose of this memo is to recommend implementing a frequent-stay plan for a 12-month test period at two of our hotels. This recommendation is based on a review of the policies of our competitors and on an analysis of the costs and benefits of instituting such a program. The pertinent data is presented below.

In the next scenario, assume that Haney assumed her position at Sunshine Coast Resorts just six months ago and that she is still "learning the ropes" of the hospitality industry. Up to this point, your relationship with her has been cordial, although she is probably not very familiar with your work. That being the case, the first paragraph of your memo might use an indirect approach, in which you discuss your procedures and present the evidence before making a recommendation.

> The attached *National Post* article discusses four small hotel resorts that have started frequent-stay plans. The purpose of this memo is to describe such plans and analyze their costs and benefits. Then I will recommend what action Sunshine Coast might take in this regard.

In a third scenario, suppose that instead of having confidence in your skills, Haney has given some indication that she *doesn't* yet completely trust your judgment. You might then be wise to add a second paragraph to establish your credibility.

Establish credibility by showing the basis for your recommendations.

> To gather the needed data, I studied published reports prepared by the Hotel and Restaurant Association. Then, I interviewed the person in charge of frequent-stay programs at three hotels. Finally, Dr. Kenneth Lowe, professor of hospitality services at B.C.I.T., reviewed and commented on my first draft. Thus, this proposal is based on a large body of data collected over two months.

As can be seen, the type of information you include in your message, the amount, and the organization reflect what you know (or can learn) about your audience.

The Role of Persuasion in Communicating

Any business communication—no matter how routine—involves more than just information dumping. You must select and organize the information with a specific audience and purpose in mind. In a real sense, persuasion is a major purpose of any communication. Whether your goal is to sell, to motivate, to convey bad news, or simply to inform, your ability to persuade ultimately determines the degree of success or failure that you will achieve. Your motivations may vary from greed to altruism, and your methods may vary from overt to subtle, but in the end you seek to direct others' behaviour toward a desired course of action or point of view.

Persuasion, of course, is not *coercion*—far from it. In some cases, people may be forced to do something, but they can't be forced to believe something. They must be persuaded in ways that are agreeable to them. The word *persuade,* in fact, stems from a Latin root that means *agreeable.*

Social worker Mona Munro must use the persuasive methods of ethos (credibility) and pathos (emotion) to win the confidence of those she counsels.

In his work *Rhetoric,* Aristotle identified three methods by which people can be persuaded:

- *Ethos,* an appeal based on credibility

- *Pathos,* an appeal based on emotion

- *Logos,* an appeal based on logic

These methods remain as relevant today as they were when Aristotle wrote about them more than two thousand years ago.

Every document you write seeks to persuade—through credibility, emotion, or logic.

Ethos

Ethos is an ethical appeal based on who you are and how your audience perceives you. Advertisers use this type of appeal frequently—for example, in celebrity endorsements. Your audience must believe that you know what you are talking about. Sometimes your credibility comes from your audience's prior knowledge and experience in dealing with you; at other times, you must first establish your credibility with your audience before they will buy your message. To grasp the importance of credibility, assume that you just heard that a giant meteor would crash onto Earth in 24 hours. How would your reaction differ if this announcement came from the Psychic Hot Line versus Stephen Hawking?

Competent communicators know their audience—and ensure that their audience knows them.

Pathos

Pathos appeals to an audience's emotions. You might, for example, use examples or what-if situations to make an audience happy, sad, or scared. You are probably familiar, for example, with the American Express commercials highlighting the problems faced by customers who lost their credit cards while vacationing abroad. The message: "To avoid this type of stress and fraud, always carry American Express."

Competent communicators are careful in their use of emotional appeals, however, recognizing that such appeals can be overused and that audiences may assume that you're appealing to emotions because you're short on objective, logical reasons.

Logos

For most business communication situations, logic is the most effective form of persuasion—facts, inferences, and opinion. Aristotle defined the three aspects of logic this way:

Which is more persuasive—a fact, an inference, or an opinion?

- *fact:* that which is indisputably true
- *inference:* that which is probably true
- *opinion:* that which is possibly true

The more factual data you can bring to bear on your position, the more likely you are to persuade. Nevertheless, inferences that can be drawn based on available data and opinion (especially expert opinion) are also persuasive.

Competent communicators tend to rely on logical appeals and ensure that the facts, inferences, and expert opinion they use have relevance—both to their position and to their audience.

Content

Once you have determined the purpose of your message and identified the needs and interests of your audience, the next step is to decide what information to include. For simple messages, such as routine email, this step presents few problems. However, many communication tasks require numerous decisions about what to include. How much background information is needed? What statistical data best supports the conclusions? Is expert opinion needed? Would examples, anecdotes, or graphics aid comprehension? Will research be necessary, or do you have what you need at hand?

> *Do not start writing until you have planned what you want to say.*

The trick is to include enough information so that you don't lose or confuse the reader, yet avoid including irrelevant material that wastes the reader's time and obscures the important data. Different writers use different methods for identifying what information is needed. Some simply jot down notes on the points they plan to cover. For all but the simplest communications, the one thing you should *not* do is to start drafting immediately, deciding as you write what information to include. Instead, start with at least a rudimentary outline of your message—whether it's in your head, in a well-developed typed outline, or in the form of notes on a piece of scratch paper.

One useful strategy is **brainstorming**—jotting down ideas, facts, possible leads, and anything else you think might be helpful in constructing your message. Aim for quantity, not quality. Don't evaluate your output until you've run out of ideas. Then begin to refine, delete, combine, and otherwise revise your ideas to form the basis for your message.

Another possible strategy is **mind mapping** (also called *clustering*), a process that avoids the step-by-step limitations of lists. Instead, you write the purpose of your message in the middle of a page and circle it. Then, as you think of possible points to add, write them down and link them by a line either to the main purpose or to another point. As you think of other details, add them where you think they might fit. This visual outline offers flexibility and encourages free thinking. Figure 3.3 on page 94 shows an example of mind mapping for our frequent-stay memo.

Organization

The final step in the planning process is to establish the **organization** of the message—that is, to determine in what order to discuss each topic. After you have brainstormed or mapped out your ideas around a main idea, you need to organize them into an outline that you can use to draft your message into its most effective form.

Classification (grouping related ideas) is the first step in organizing your message. Once you've grouped related ideas, you then need to differentiate between the major and minor points so that you can line up minor ideas and evidence to support the major ideas.

The most effective sequence for the major ideas often depends on the reaction you expect from your audience. If you expect a positive response, you may want to use a direct approach, in which the conclusion or major idea is presented first, followed by the reasons. If you expect a negative response, you may decide to use an indirect approach, in which the reasons are presented first and the conclusion after.

Because of the importance of the sequence in which topics are discussed, the recommended organization of each specific type of communication is discussed in detail in the chapters that follow. (See also coverage of paragraph unity, coherence, and length in Chapter 4—all of which are important elements of organization.)

DRESSED FOR SUCCESS   *word*wise

A lawyer wears a suit to work. Here's what other people wear:

Electrician:	Shorts
Boxer:	Socks
Golfer:	T-shirt
Psychiatrist:	Slip
Painter:	Coat
Firefighter:	Hose

To maintain good human relations, base your organization on the expected reader reaction.

■ Drafting

Having now finished planning, you are finally ready to begin **drafting**—that is, composing a preliminary version of a message. The success of this second stage of the process depends on the attention you gave to the first stage. The warning given earlier bears repeating: Don't begin writing too soon. Some people believe they have weak writing skills; when faced with a writing task, their first impulse is therefore to jump in and get it over with as quickly as possible. Avoid the rush. Follow each of the five steps of the writing process to ease the journey and improve the product. As shown in Communication Snapshot 2 on page 95, the quality of the writing is enhanced when writers not only plan what they want to write but also jot down notes to guide them.

Probably the most important thing to remember about drafting is to just let go—let your ideas flow as quickly as possible onto paper or computer screen, without worrying about style, correctness, or format. Separate the drafting stage from the revising stage. Although some people revise as they create, most find it easier to first get their ideas down on paper in rough-draft form, then revise. It's much easier to polish a page full of writing than a page full of *nothing*. As one writing authority has noted:

> Writing is art. Rewriting is craft. Mix the two at your peril. If you let your inner editor (who, according to popular theory, lives in the left side of your brain) into the process too early, it's liable to overpower your artist, blocking your creative flow.[2]

So avoid moving from author to editor too quickly. Your first draft is just that—a *draft*. Don't expect perfection, and don't strive for it. Concentrate, instead, on recording in narrative form all the points you identified in the planning stage. When you have finished and then begin to revise, you will likely discover that a surprising amount of your first draft is usable and will be included in your final draft.

If a report is due in five weeks, some managers (and students) spend four weeks worrying about the task and one week (or even one long weekend) actually writing the report. Similarly, when given 45 minutes to write a letter or memo, some people

CO2. **Compose a first draft of your message.**

Do not combine drafting and revising. They involve two separate skills and two separate mindsets.

Employ the power of positive thinking: You can write an effective message!

figure3.3
A Sample Mind Map

spend 35 minutes anxiously staring at a blank page or blank screen and ten minutes actually writing. These people are experiencing **writer's block**—the inability to focus on the writing process and to draft a message. The causes of writer's block are typically one or more of the following:

- *Procrastination:* Putting off what we dislike doing.

- *Impatience:* Growing tired of the naturally slow pace of the writing process.

- *Perfectionism:* Believing that our draft must be perfect the first time.

These factors naturally interfere with creativity and concentration. In addition, they undermine the writer's self-image and make him or her even more reluctant to tackle the next writing task. The treatment for writer's block lies in the strategies discussed in the following paragraphs.

1. **Choose the right environment.** The ability to concentrate on the task at hand is one of the most important components of effective writing. The best

environment may *not* be the same desk where you normally do your other work. Even if you can turn off the phones and shut the door to visitors, silent distractions can bother you—a notation on your calendar reminding you of an important upcoming event, notes about a current project, even a photograph of a loved one. Many people write best in a library-type environment, with a low noise level, relative anonymity, and the space to spread out notes and other resources on a large table. Others find a computer room conducive to thinking and writing, with its low level of constant background noise and the presence of other people similarly engaged.

2. **Schedule a reasonable block of time.** If the writing task is short, you can block out enough time to plan, draft, and revise the entire message at one sitting. If the task is long or complex, however, schedule blocks of no more than two hours or so. After all, writing is hard work. When your time is up or your work completed, give yourself a reward—take a break or get a snack.

3. **State your purpose in writing.** Having identified your specific purpose during the planning phase, write it at the top of your blank page or tack it on the bulletin board in front of you. Keep it visible so that it will be uppermost in your consciousness as you compose.

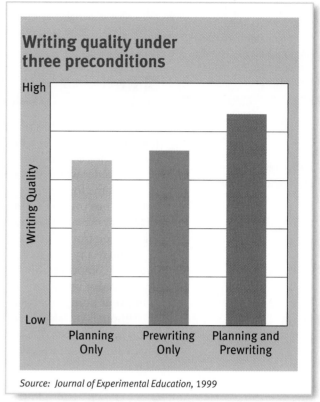

communication snapshot 2

Writing quality under three preconditions

Source: *Journal of Experimental Education, 1999*

4. **Engage in free writing.** Review your purpose and your audience. Then, as a means of releasing your pent-up ideas and getting past the block, begin **free writing;** that is, write continuously for five to ten minutes, literally without stopping. Although free writing is typically considered a pre-drafting technique, it can also be quite useful for helping writers "unblock" their ideas.

    While free writing, don't look back and don't stop writing. If you cannot think of anything to say, simply keep repeating the last word or keep writing some sentence such as, "I'll think of something soon." Resist the temptation to evaluate what you've written. At the end of five or ten minutes, take a breather, stretch and relax, read what you've written, and then start again, if necessary.

5. **Avoid the perfectionism syndrome.** Remember that the product you're producing now is a *draft*—not a final document. Don't worry about style, coherence, spelling or punctuation errors, and the like. The artist in you must create something before the editor can refine it.

6. **Think out loud.** Some people are more skilled at *speaking* their thoughts than at writing them. Picture yourself telling a colleague what you're writing about, and explain aloud the ideas you're trying to get across. Hearing your ideas will help sharpen and focus them.

7. **Write the easiest parts first.** The opening paragraph of a letter or memo is often the most difficult one to compose. If that is the case, skip it and begin in the middle. In a report, the procedures section may be easier to write than the recommendations. Getting *something* down on paper will give you a sense of accomplishment, and your writing may generate ideas for other sections.

Try each of these strategies for avoiding writer's block at least once, then build into your writing routine those strategies that work best for you. Just as different athletes and artists use different strategies for accomplishing their goals, so do different writers. There is no one best way, so choose what is effective for you.

You need not write the parts of a message in the order in which they will finally appear. Begin with the easiest parts.

■ Revising

Revising is the process of modifying a document to increase its effectiveness. Having the raw material—your first draft—in front of you, you can now refine it into the most effective document possible, considering its importance and the time constraints under which you are working. If possible, put your draft away for a period of time—the longer the better. Leaving time between creation and revision helps you distance yourself from your writing. If you revise immediately, the memory of what you "meant to say" rather than what you actually wrote may be so strong that it keeps you from spotting weaknesses in logic or diction.

CO3. Revise for content, style, and correctness.

If you're a typical writer, you will have made numerous minor revisions even as you were composing; however, as noted earlier, you should save the major revisions until later. For important writing projects, you will probably want to solicit comments about your draft from colleagues as part of the revision process.

Although we have discussed revising as the third step of the writing process, in fact it involves several steps. Most writers revise first for content, then for style, and finally for correctness. All types of revision are most efficiently done from a typed copy of the draft rather than from a handwritten copy.

Revising for Content

After an appropriate time interval, first reread your purpose statement and then the entire draft to get an overview of your message. Your most important concern is whether your document has addressed the needs of your audience. The mantra of the journalist is worth reciting: Have you answered for your reader the questions who, what, where, when, why and how? In addition to ensuring your document addresses these questions, also ask yourself such questions as the following:

Ensure that all needed information—and only needed information— is included.

- Is the content appropriate for the purpose I've identified?

- Will the purpose of the message be clear to the reader?

- Have I been sensitive to the needs of the reader?

- Is all the information necessary?

- Is any needed information missing?

- Is the order of presentation of the points effective?

Although it is natural to have a certain pride of authorship in your draft document, don't be afraid to make whatever changes you think will strengthen your document—even if it means striking out whole sections and starting again from scratch. The aim is to produce a revised document in which you can have even more pride.

Revising for Style

Revising for style is one of the most important—and most difficult—business writing skills you will learn. Because there are so many facets of style—clarity, conciseness, vigour, and overall tone, to name a few—you will be guided through this part of the revision process in detail in Chapters 4 and 5. As you revise each sentence of your draft you will be applying the 16 criteria contained in Checklist 5 in Chapter 5 on page 172 as the basis for your evaluation. Reading aloud gives you a feel for the rhythm and flow of your writing. Long sentences that made sense as you wrote them may leave you out of breath when you read them aloud.

If time permits and the importance of the document merits it, try reading your message aloud to friends or colleagues, or have them read your revised draft. Ask them what is clear or unclear. Can they identify the purpose of your message? What kind of image do they get of the writer just from reading the message? Adhering to the principles you will learn in Chapters 4 and 5 and securing feedback from colleagues will help you identify areas of your message that need revision.

"I'm unbelievably nit-picky about every word. I could never turn something in until I've dealt with every semicolon five times."
—Dave Barry

Revising for Correctness

The final phase of revising is **editing,** the process of ensuring that writing conforms to standard English. Editing involves checking for correctness—that is, identifying problems with grammar, spelling, punctuation, and word usage. You may want to use your word processor's grammar checker as a starting point for editing (see Spotlight 8, "Use You're Grammar Check Her—Four What Its Worth," on pages 100–101). Editing should follow revision because there is no need to correct minor errors in passages that may later be revised or deleted. Writers who fail to check for grammar, mechanical, and usage errors risk losing credibility with their reader. Such errors may distract the reader, delay comprehension, cause misunderstandings, and reflect negatively on the writer's abilities.

While you'll want to do much of your revising on computer, always print a hard copy when editing for correctness. In particular, typographical errors and errors in spelling, punctuation, and word usage can often be missed on the computer screen. Section A of the Reference Manual at the back of this text offers detailed guidelines on punctuation, grammar, mechanics, and word usage.

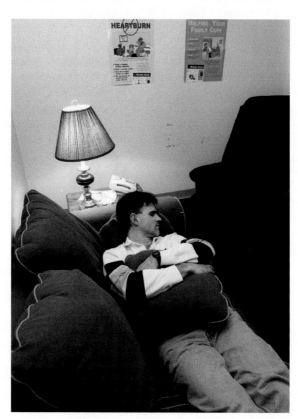

Sometimes the best thing to do before editing is to take a break, or even a nap. In fact, many Canadian businesses are waking up to the benefits of napping on the job. Here Nova Chemicals employee, Rich Verwegen, relaxes in the Operations Alertness Recovery Room at the company in Corunna, Ontario.

spotlight
ACROSS CULTURES

Canadian English

Katherine Barber, known to many as Canada's Word Lady, is passionate about English—specifically, Canadian English. As the Editor-in-Chief of the *Canadian Oxford Dictionary*, Barber has dedicated her career to uncovering the distinctive nature of Canadian English since 1991, when she was hired to begin the daunting project of developing a uniquely Canadian dictionary. "A Canadian English dictionary is proof that there is a distinct Canadian identity, because obviously most Canadians, the thing they want more than anything else in life is for people to understand that we're not Americans. It's very gratifying to produce this dictionary and say that, yes, Canadian English does exist."[3]

Katherine Barber in Toronto showing off the *Canadian Oxford High School Dictionary*.

Since the first edition rolled off the press in 1998, Barber has become something of a minor celebrity. "Quite often, I'll be introduced to somebody and they'll ask 'Aren't you the word lady?'" She adds, "Sometimes I think it's my mission in life to convince people that there is more to Canadian English than 'eh'! There are actually thousands of distinctly Canadian words."[4]

One of her favourites is "double-double." "It was a word we knew about when we were working on the first edition of the dictionary; we didn't put it in that one because at that point someone had said, 'This is a Tim Horton's thing,' and if that was true, it didn't constitute general Canadian English. But we kept on with it. We have a group of Canadians across the country that we email when we're trying to determine regionalisms and pronunciations and so on, and we asked them, 'Do you say double-double, do you understand what it means, and do you only use it in Tim Horton's?' They overwhelmingly said, 'Oh yes, I know what it means, I would use it myself, and not just at Tim Horton's.' We also found some evidence in other sources, books, papers like *The Globe and Mail*, of people using it as a generic term."[5]

Here's a list of some of Ms. Barber's other favourites:[6]

Bangbelly: A dense cake made of cooked rice, flour, molasses, raisins, salt pork, and spices.

Blueberry buckle: A cake topped with blueberries and a crumbly topping, most common in the Maritimes.

Bumbleberry: A mixture of berries.

Idiot string: A string attached to each of two mittens or gloves and strung through the sleeves of a child's coat.

Jambuster: A jelly-filled doughnut.

■ Formatting

CO4. Arrange your document in a standard format.

Letters are external documents sent to people outside the organization; *memos* are internal documents sent to people inside the same organization as the writer. Today, most traditional memos have been replaced by email; and, in fact, many letters are now sent as email attachments rather than through the mail. Email and reports may be either internal or external. No one format for any type of business document is universally accepted as standard; a fair amount of variation is common in industry. Detailed guidelines for the most common formatting standards are presented in the Reference Manual at the back of this text.

To some extent, technology is changing formatting standards. For example, although formatting is traditionally the next-to-last step in the writing process, you may, in fact, make some formatting decisions at the planning or drafting stages. For example, your word processing program has probably been set with default side margins of 2.54 to 3.18 centimetres, which are appropriate for most documents.

In addition, email messages all look like memorandums—whether they are sent to someone inside or outside the organization. They typically contain *To:*, *From:*, *Date:*, and *Subject:* lines, just as memos do, and they do not contain an inside address as is typical in letters. The important point is to use the format that is appropriate for each specific message.

Regardless of who actually types your documents, *you* are the one who signs and submits them, so *you* must accept responsibility for not only the content but also the mechanics, format, and appearance of your documents. In addition, executives now keyboard many of their own documents—without the help of an assistant.

Another advantage of standard formatting is simply that it is more efficient. Formatting documents the same way each time means that you do not need to make individual layout decisions for every document. Thus, a standard format not only saves time but also gives a consistent appearance to the organization's documents.

Finally, readers *expect* to find certain information in certain positions in a document. If the information is not there, the reader is unnecessarily distracted. For all these reasons, you should become familiar with the standard conventions for formatting documents.

■ Proofreading

Proofreading is the final quality-control check for your document. Remember that a reader may not know whether an incorrect word resulted from a simple typo or from the writer's ignorance of correct usage. And even one such error can have adverse effects (see Figure 3.4). Being *almost perfect* is not good enough; for example, if your telephone directory were only 99 percent perfect, each page would contain about four wrong numbers! And imagine the embarrassment of the tax preparer who submitted supporting statements for a client's tax return that contained this direction: "Please reference *Lie 12* on Schedule C." (Would a computer's spell-checker have caught this error?) Or how about the newspaper ad that Continental Airlines ran in the *Boston Herald,* in which the company advertised one-way fares from

CO5. Proofread your document for content, typographical, and format errors.

Typographical errors may send a negative non-verbal message about the writer.

figure3.4
The Need for Competent Proofreading Skills

If 99.9% accuracy is acceptable to you, then

Every hour:
- 18 300 pieces of mail will be mishandled.
- 22 000 checks will be credited to the wrong bank accounts.
- 72 000 phone calls will be misplaced by telecommunication services.

Every day:
- 12 newborn babies will be given to the wrong parents.
- 107 incorrect medical procedures will be performed.

Every year:
- 2.5 million books will be shipped with the wrong cover.
- 20 000 incorrect drug prescriptions will be written.

Not to mention that:
- 315 entries in *Webster's Third New International Dictionary of the English Language* will be misspelled.

spotlight8
ON TECHNOLOGY

Use You're Grammar Check Her—Four What Its Worth

Most of us can use all the help we can get when it comes to writing, and that's where grammar checkers come in. These tools, which are now standard features of most word processing programs, identify spelling and typographical problems as well as possible examples of awkward writing, clichés and jargon, passive voice, mismatched punctuation marks, and the like. They then propose alternatives that you can accept, reject, or mark for subsequent fixing.

Grammar checkers compare words and phrases in a document with built-in lists of words and phrases. Some even go beyond the compare-and-mark function by using artificial intelligence to identify incorrectly used homonyms such as *there, their,* and *they're.*

In addition to flagging possible spelling, grammar, and style problems, many programs identify such common punctuation problems as placing a comma after (instead of before) a quotation mark or leaving two spaces between words. Finally, many programs provide a word count and readability grade level.

How well do such programs work? Some of the suggestions identified are close to nitpicking. Typically, a large percentage of the words and phrases that are flagged as possible errors are, in fact, used appropriately; conversely, other more serious errors or stylistic problems are not identified. Moreover, not only are spelling checkers occasionally inaccurate, Canadian spelling checkers adapted from American software don't always catch the preferred Canadian spelling.

Let's apply MicrosoftWord's grammar and spelling checker to the first draft of the student-written passage in The 3Ps (Problem, Process, and Product) model exercise on page 103. Here is the draft:

1. The Mount Royal Chapter of A.C.E. (Advancing Canadian Entrepreneurship) shares your
2. interest in increasing the number of scholarships available to business majors.
3. We recently voted to establish an annual $1,000 scholarship for a first- or second-year student
4. majoring in Entrepreneurship. To fund this scholarship, we propose selling
5. doughnuts and coffee in the main lobby from 7:30–10:30 A.M. daily. All of the
6. profits will be earmarked for the Scholarship fund. A secondary benifit of this
7. project is that it will provide practical work experience for our members. We
8. will purchase out own supplies and equipment, and keep careful records. When
9. they are not in use, the supplies and equipment will be stored in the office of
10. Professor Grant Edwards, our Sponsor. DPMA follows similar procedures with
11. it's fund raising project of selling computer disks in the main lobby.
12. We need your approval of this scholarship project in time for us to begin in
13. January. This project also provides a convenient service for faculty, staff, and
14. students.

Boston to Los Angeles for $48? The actual one-way fare was *$148.* That typographical error cost Continental $4 million, because it sold 20 000 round trip tickets at a loss of $200 each.[7]

Don't depend on having an assistant catch and correct every mistake; become a "super blooper snooper" yourself. It's your reputation that is at stake. Take responsibility for ensuring the accuracy of your communications, just as you take responsibility for your other managerial tasks. Proofread for content, typographical, and format errors. While much of the revision process can be accomplished efficiently on a computer, always print a hard copy to proofread. You can often overlook spelling, punctuation, and even grammatical errors when proofreading a document on a computer screen. Why are such errors more easily spotted on a hard copy?

Spelling Alerts

The spell-checker correctly identified the one misspelling in the passage ("benifit" in line 6) and suggested the correct spelling "benefit." Not surprisingly, the checker also identified the abbreviation "DPMA" in line 10 (actually, the abbreviation is correct) and incorrectly suggested "DAMP" instead.

Grammar Alerts

The grammar checker correctly identified the misused "it's" in line 11 and suggested the correct form "its." However, it incorrectly identified the sentence in lines 8 to 10 ("When they are not in use, the supplies and equipment will be stored in the office of Professor Grant Edwards, our Sponsor") as a sentence fragment when, in fact, it is a complete sentence.

In addition, the grammar checker flagged the sentence "All of the profits will be earmarked for the Scholarship fund" in lines 5 and 6 as being in the passive voice and suggested that it be changed to the active voice. On closer inspection, however, the sentence is more effectively stated in the passive voice because the receiver of the action "the profits" is more important than the doer "A.C.E." You want your grammar checker to provide this kind of alert so that you can make a case-by-case decision as to whether your original wording is more effective or should be changed.

Errors Not Identified

More important, however, are the errors that the checker did *not* identify:

- Line 3: "$1,000" should be formatted as "$1000."
- Line 4: "Entrepreneurship" should not be capitalized.
- Line 5: "from 7:30–10:30 A.M." should be reformatted as "from 7:30 to 10:30 a.m."
- Line 6: "Scholarship fund" should be "scholarship fund."
- Line 8: "out" should be "our"; in addition, the comma should be omitted after the word "equipment."
- Line 10: "Sponsor" should be lower case.
- Line 11: "fund raising" should be one word: "fundraising."

Finally, the grammar checker did not identify that the opening paragraph is 164 words long, much longer than the 60 to 80 words recommended for a typical paragraph in business writing.

Results of Relying on the Computer Grammar and Spell-Checker

In summary, applying the grammar and spell-checker in Microsoft Word gave these results:

- Identified 20 percent (2 of 10) of the actual errors, missing 80 percent of the errors.
- Identified 3 "errors" that were, in fact, correct.
- Missed 1 stylistic error (excessively long first paragraph).

Would you (or your instructor—or your boss) consider these results acceptable?

Not only is a printed page of text typically larger than what's shown on a computer screen, the resolution of printed text is much higher, making it easier to spot errors.

- *Content Errors:* First, read through your document quickly, checking for content errors. Was any material omitted unintentionally? Unfortunately, writers who use word processing to move, delete, and insert material sometimes omit passages unintentionally or duplicate the same passage in two different places in the document. In short, check to be sure that your document *makes sense.*

- *Typographical Errors:* Next, read through your document slowly, checking for typographical errors. Watch especially for errors that form a new word—for example, "I took the figures *form* last month's reports." Such errors are difficult to spot, and your spell checker won't recognize them as errors. Also be on the lookout for repeated or omitted words. Double-check all proper names and all figures, using the original source if possible. Professional proofreaders find that

✔checklist 4

The Writing Process

Planning

✔ Determine the purpose of the message.

- Make it as specific as possible.
- Identify the type of response desired from the reader.

✔ Analyze the audience.

- Identify the audience and your relationship with this person.
- Determine how the audience will probably react.
- Determine how much the audience already knows about the topic.
- Determine what is unique about the audience.

✔ Determine what information to include in the message, given its purpose and your analysis of the audience.

✔ Organize the information.

- Prefer a direct approach for routine and good-news messages and for most messages to superiors: present the major idea first, followed by supporting details.
- Prefer an indirect approach for persuasive and bad-news messages written to someone other than your superior; present the reasons first, followed by the major idea.

Drafting

✔ Choose a productive work environment and schedule a reasonable block of time to devote to the drafting phase.

✔ Let your ideas flow as quickly as possible, without worrying about style, correctness, or format.

✔ Do not expect a perfect first draft; avoid the urge to revise at this stage.

✔ If possible, leave a time gap between writing and revising the draft.

Revising

✔ Revise for content: determine whether all information is necessary, whether any needed information has been omitted, and whether the content has been presented in an appropriate sequence.

✔ Revise for style: follow the guidelines discussed in Chapters 4 and 5.

✔ Revise for correctness: use correct grammar, mechanics, punctuation, and word choice (see the Reference Manual).

Formatting

✔ Format the document according to commonly used standards (see the Reference Manual).

Proofreading

✔ Proofread for content errors, typographical errors, and format errors.

writers often overlook errors in the titles and headings of reports, in the opening and closing parts of letters and memos, and in the last paragraph of all types of documents.

- *Format Errors:* Visually inspect the document for appropriate format. Are all the parts included and in the correct position? What will be the receiver's first impression before reading the document? Does the document look attractive on the page? Do not consider the proofreading stage complete until you are able to read through the entire document without making any changes. There is always the possibility that in correcting one error you inadvertently introduced another.

The **3Ps**
Problem, Process, Product

A SIMPLE MEMO

Today is December 3, 20—, and you are Alice R. Stengren, president of the Mount Royal chapter of ACE (Advancing Canadian Entrepreneurship). ACE is the newest of the six student organizations in the school of business and has 38 members. It was formed two years ago when the department of management instituted a major in entrepreneurship.

The association recently voted to institute an annual $1000 ACE scholarship. The scholarship will be awarded on the basis of merit to a first- or second-year business student majoring in entrepreneurship at Mount Royal. Funds for the scholarship will be raised by selling coffee and doughnuts each day from 7:30 to 10:30 a.m. in the main lobby of the building. Write a memo to Dean Richard Wilhite, asking permission to start this fundraising project in January.

1. What is the purpose of your memo?

   To convince the dean to let ACE sell coffee and doughnuts in the main lobby from 7:30 to 10:30 a.m. daily, beginning in January.

2. Describe your primary audience.

   Dean Richard Wilhite:

   - Former president of Wilhite Energy Systems (started the company—an entrepreneur himself)
   - 46 years old; has been business dean at Mount Royal for six years (very familiar with the school and college)
   - Nationally known labour expert
   - Holds tenure in the School of Business at Mount Royal (which offers an entrepreneurship major)
   - Has spoken about the need to increase scholarships
   - Devotes a great deal of time to lobbying the legislature and raising funds (recognizes the need for fundraising)
   - Doesn't know me personally but is familiar with ACE.

3. Is there a secondary audience for your memo? If so, describe.
   - No secondary audience.

4. Considering your purpose, what information should you include in the memo? (Either brainstorm and jot down the topics you might cover or construct a mind map.)

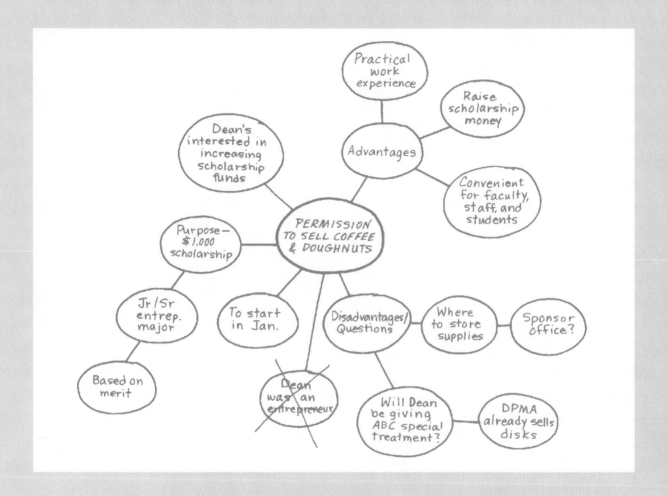

5. Jot down the major topics in the order in which you'll discuss them.

   a. Dean's interest in increasing scholarships

   b. Introduce scholarship and our fundraising proposal

   c. Practical work experience that members will get

   d. Possible drawbacks (where to store supplies; special treatment for ACE.)

   e. Other needed details

   f. Close—convenient for faculty, staff, students

6. Using the rough outline developed in Step 5, write your first draft. Concentrate on getting the needed information down. Do not worry about grammar, spelling, punctuation, transitions, unity, and the like at this stage.

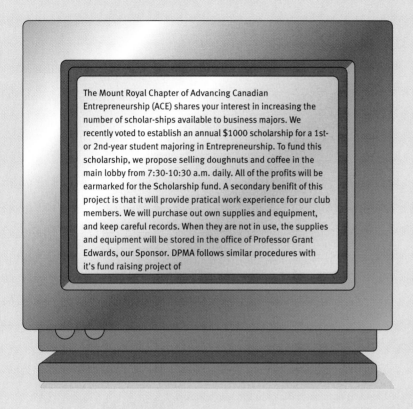

The Mount Royal Chapter of Advancing Canadian Entrepreneurship (ACE) shares your interest in increasing the number of scholar-ships available to business majors. We recently voted to establish an annual $1000 scholarship for a 1st- or 2nd-year student majoring in Entrepreneurship. To fund this scholarship, we propose selling doughnuts and coffee in the main lobby from 7:30-10:30 a.m. daily. All of the profits will be earmarked for the Scholarship fund. A secondary benifit of this project is that it will provide pratical work experience for our club members. We will purchase out own supplies and equipment, and keep careful records. When they are not in use, the supplies and equipment will be stored in the office of Professor Grant Edwards, our Sponsor. DPMA follows similar procedures with it's fund raising project of

7. Print your draft and revise it for content, style, and correctness. (See the revised draft on page 106.)

8. How will you transmit this message; that is, what format will you use?

   I could, of course, send the dean an email message. Given the importance of this request, however, I'll format it as a memo on our college's letterhead. That way the request will look more professional, and the dean will have a printed copy for review.

9. Format your revised draft, using a standard memo style. Then proofread.

Product

The Mount Royal Chapter of Advancing Canadian Entrepreneurship

(ACE) shares your interest in increasing the number of scholarships available

to business majors. *Toward that end,* We recently voted to establish an annual $1,000

scholarship for a (1st-) or (2nd-year) student majoring in Entrepreneurship. To

fund this scholarship, we propose selling doughnuts and coffee in the

main lobby from 7:30 *to* 10:30 A.M. daily. All ~~of the~~ profits will be

earmarked for the scholarship fund. A secondary benefit of this

project is that it will provide practical work experience for our club

members. We will purchase ~~out~~ *our* own supplies and equipment and keep

careful records. When ~~they are~~ not in use, the supplies and equipment

will be stored in the office of Professor Grant Edwards, our sponsor.

(DPMA) follows similar procedures with it's fund-raising project of

selling computer disks in the main lobby.

We look forward to receiving ~~We need~~ your approval of this ~~scholarship~~ *fundraising* project in time for us

to begin in January. ~~This project also provides~~ a convenient service

for faculty, staff, and students.

In addition to raising new scholarship money and providing work experience for our members, we will also be providing

Revised Draft

Mount Royal University
4622 Maurice Road
Calgary, AB T2N 1P7
Telephone: 403-440-6841
Fax: 403-440-6842

MEMO TO: Dean Richard Wilhite

FROM: Alice R. Stengren, President   *ARS*
Mount Royal Chapter of Advancing Canadian Entrepreneurship

DATE: December 3, 20—

SUBJECT: Establishment of ACE Scholarship

Mount Royal Chapter of Advancing Canadian Entrepreneurship (ACE) shares your interest in increasing the number of scholarships available to business majors. Toward that end, we recently voted to establish an annual $1000 scholarship for a first- or second-year student majoring in entrepreneurship. To fund this scholarship, we propose selling doughnuts and coffee in the main lobby from 7:30 to 10:30 a.m. daily. All profits will be earmarked for the scholarship fund.

A secondary benefit of this project is that it will provide practical work experience for our club members. We will purchase our own supplies and equipment and keep careful records. When not in use, the supplies and equipment will be stored in the office of Professor Grant Edwards, our sponsor. The Data Processing Management Association follows similar procedures with its fundraising project of selling computer disks in the main lobby.

We look forward to receiving your approval of this fundraising project in time for us to begin in January. In addition to raising new scholarship money and providing work experience for our members, we will also be providing a convenient service for faculty, staff, and students.

Mount Royal University 4622 Maurice Road   Calgary, AB T2N 1P7   Telephone: 403-440-6841   Fax: 403-440-6842

Finally, after planning, drafting, revising, formatting, and proofreading your document, transmit it—confident and satisfied that you've taken all reasonable steps to ensure that it achieves its objectives. The steps in the writing process are summarized in Checklist 4.

■ Summary

CO1. **Specify the purpose of your message and analyze your audience.**

Before writing, identify the purpose of your intended message. Carefully analyze your audience (or audiences) and determine what information to include. Determine whether a direct or indirect organizational plan will help you achieve your goals better.

CO2. **Compose a first draft of your message.**

Select an appropriate environment for drafting, and schedule enough time. Concentrate on getting the information down, without worrying about style, correctness, or format. Leave a time gap between writing and revising the draft.

CO3. **Revise for content, style, and correctness.**

Revise first for content—to determine whether all the needed information (and no unneeded information) has been included. Then revise for style, ensuring that the manner in which you present your ideas is effective. Finally, revise for correctness, being sure to avoid any errors in grammar, mechanics, punctuation, and word choice.

CO4. **Arrange your document in a standard format.**

Use a generally accepted format for your letters, memos, email, and reports to provide efficiency for the writer, readability for the receiver, and a consistent appearance for the organization's documents.

CO5. **Proofread your document for content, typographical, and format errors.**

Read through your document to ensure that the document makes sense. Be on the lookout for typos. Finally, visually inspect the document for appropriate format.

■ Key Terms

You should now be able to define the following terms in your own words and give an original example of each.

audience analysis (88)

brainstorming (92)

drafting (93)

editing (97)

free writing (95)

mind mapping (92)

organization (92)

primary audience (88)

revising (96)

secondary audience (88)

writer's block (94)

■ Exercises

① **The 3Ps (Problem, Process, and Product) Model: Communication Applications at Daydream Communications.** Bill Bunn follows a strict writing process when he manages projects and communications for his clients. He adheres to the process rigorously to ensure that projects remain on budget and on time. Even when writing routine correspondence such as email, he follows a process of planning, drafting, proofreading, and revising before hitting "send" to ensure his message is clear and his tone appropriate.

Problem

Assume you are Bill Bunn and must coordinate a group of subject matter experts in putting together a promotional brochure for a new piece of computer software to be marketed to the oil and gas industry around the globe. You have asked each of those involved in the project—including engineers, geologists, programmers, and graphical designers—to describe the software's advantages over competing products and submit their descriptions to you. Your job is to interpret each of the descriptions and then simplify them enough so they appeal to a broad audience. Unfortunately, each of the contributors has sent a very detailed and often highly technical description of the software—descriptions that will need significant revising before they appear on the brochure.

You are now sending an email requesting that each contributor review the first draft of the brochure and offer feedback. Of course, you're hoping that all will agree with your description of the product, but you're well aware that each of the content experts has a different perspective on the product and a different opinion on how it should be described. At the same time, you want to be sure that your synthesis of all the contributions hasn't inadvertently changed their meaning. Prepare an email message to accompany the draft of the brochure.

Process

a. What is the specific purpose of your email message?
b. Describe your audience.
c. Is pathos or logos most appropriate for this message?
d. What topics should you include in this message?
e. What phrase will you write on the subject line of your email message?

Product

Using your knowledge of the writing process, prepare a one-page email message, creating any reasonable data needed to complete this assignment.

2 Communication Purpose   Compose a specific goal for each of the following:

CO1. **Specify the purpose of your message and analyze your audience.**

a. A memo to a professor asking him to change a grade.
b. A letter to MasterCard about an incorrect charge.
c. A letter to the president of a local bank thanking her for speaking at your student organization meeting.
d. A memo of reprimand to a subordinate for leaving the warehouse unlocked overnight.

3 Communication Purpose and Reader Response   For each of the following communication tasks, indicate the specific purpose and the desired response:

a. A letter to a premier about a proposed provinical surcharge on college tuition.
b. A memo to your payroll department head about an incorrect paycheque.
c. A letter to the college newspaper discussing the quality of the cafeteria food in recent months.
d. A memo to your assistant asking about the status of an overdue report.

4 Audience Analysis   Assume you must write an email message to your current business communication professor, asking him or her to let you take your final examination one week early so that you can attend your cousin's wedding.

a. Perform an audience analysis of your professor. List everything you know about this professor that might help you compose a more effective message.

b. Write two good opening sentences for this message, the first one assuming that you are an A student who has missed class only once this term and the second assuming you are a C student who has missed class six times this term.

5 Audience Analysis Revisited   Now assume the role of the professor (see Exercise 4) who must reply to the request of the student with the C grade who has missed class six times. You'll tell the student that you are not willing to schedule an early exam.

a. Perform an audience analysis of yourself (as the student).What do you know about yourself that would help the professor write an effective message?
b. Should the professor use a direct or an indirect organization? Why?
c. Write the first sentence of the professor's message.

6 Audience Reaction   Read the following situations and decide what the audience reaction would be and whether a direct or indirect organizational plan would be better. Explain your answers.

a. As the manager of a small retail clothing store, you are preparing a memo to let the employees know they are getting a 50¢-per-hour raise.
b. As the assistant manager of a hotel, you are writing to a customer letting her know that the jewellery she left in her room when she departed has not been found.
c. As a newly-hired advertising director, you are emailing the president of the company requesting a 10 percent increase in your advertising budget.
d. You are writing a letter to customers announcing a new product that will be available in the store starting next month.

7 Ethos, Pathos, and Logos   You and a partner are working for an advertising firm. You have recently landed the account for a national tire company. You know about three appeals for persuasion: ethos, pathos, and logos. You decide to write three television commercials for the tire company—each using one of these appeals. Explain how you might use each appeal in a television commercial for tires. Turn the assignment in to your instructor for evaluation.

8 Group Brainstorming   Working in groups of three or four, come up with as many uses for a brick as you can. Make a list of all the suggestions and then share your list with the other groups in the class. How does your list compare to the other groups? How many new ideas did the other groups come up with that your group hadn't thought of? How big was the combined list?

CO2. Compose a first draft of your message.

9 Free Writing   As office manager for station CKUA, a non-profit, publicly-owned radio station in Calgary, Alberta, you want to buy a scanner to use with the three computers in your office. The scanner would let you input graphics (charts and pictures) into your computer documents and enter data without having to re-keyboard it. A scanner operates like a photocopier: you feed a copy of a picture or a page of text into the machine, and the picture or text then appears on your computer screen, where it can be used by your word processing or other software programs.

   You must write a memo, the goal of which is to convince the general manager to let you buy a scanner and related software for $425. Think about ways you could use this equipment. Then free write for 10 to 15 minutes without stopping and without worrying about the quality of what you're writing. (You may first want to reread the discussion of free writing on page 95 of this chapter.) Now examine what you have written. If you were actually going to write the memo, how much of your output could you use after revision?

10 **Mind Mapping (Clustering)**   Assume you must write a two-page, double-spaced summary of the important points of this chapter. *Without reviewing the chapter*, prepare a mind map of the points you might want to cover.

11 **Organizing**   Prepare a rough outline for the summary, using the mind map as your guide. List the major and minor points you will cover and the order in which you will cover them. (You do not have to follow your mind map precisely; it's only for guidance.)

12 **Brainstorming, Organizing, and Drafting**   Assume you are going to write a letter to your provincial minister of education about a proposed 6 percent increase in university tuition fees next year.

a. Determine a specific purpose of your letter.
b. Brainstorm at least six facts, ideas, and questions you might want to raise in your letter.
c. Determine an effective sequence of the points you decide to include in the letter.
d. Type the specific purpose at the top of a blank page.
e. Write the easiest part of the letter first. With which part did you start? Why?
f. Continue to draft the remaining sections of the letter.
g. Did you use every fact, question, or idea on your list? Explain your choices.

13 **Revising for Content**   Bring in a one-page composition you have written in the past—an essay exam response, business letter, or the like. Make sure your name is not on the paper. Exchange papers among several colleagues (so that you are not revising the paper of the person who is revising yours). Read the paper once and, using the guidelines presented in this chapter, revise only for content. Specifically, make sure the content is appropriate to the writer's purpose and the audience's needs. Additionally, ensure all key questions (who, what, where, why, when and how) have been answered.

CO3. Revise for content, style, and correctness.

Return the paper to the writer. Then, using the revisions of your paper as a guide only (after all, *you* are the author), prepare a final version of the page. Submit both the marked-up version and the final version of your paper to your instructor.

14 **Work-team Communication**   You will work in groups of four for this assignment. Assume that a large shopping centre is next to your campus and many day students park there for free while attending classes. The shopping centre management is considering closing this lot to student use, citing the need for additional space for customer parking. The four members of your group represent four student organizations (a writers' club, an athletic club, a business student organization, and a campus service organization), which have decided to write a joint letter to the manager of the shopping centre, trying to convince him to maintain the status quo.

CO4. Arrange your document in a standard format.

Following the five-step process outlined in this chapter, compose a one-page letter to the manager. Brainstorm to generate ideas for the content of the letter;

have each member of the group call out possible points to include while one person writes down all the ideas. Don't evaluate any of the ideas until you have worked for 10 to 15 minutes. Then discuss each point listed and decide which ones to include and in what order.

Format your letter in block style. Address it to Mr. Martin Uthe, Executive Manager, Fairview Shopping Centre, P.O. Box 1083, Edmonston, NB, E3V 4L4. Type an envelope, sign and fold the letter, and insert it into the envelope before submitting it to your instructor.

co5. Proofread your document for content, typographical, and format errors.

15 Proofreading   Assume that you are Michael Land and you wrote and typed the following letter. Proofread the letter, using the line numbers to indicate the position of each error. Proofread for content, typographical errors, and format. For each error, indicate by a *yes* or *no* whether the error would have been identified by a computer's spelling checker. (*Hint:* Can you find 30 content, typographical, or format errors?)

1   April 31 2005
2   Mr. Thomas Johnson, Manger
3   JoAnn @ Friends, Inc.
4   222 3rd Ave North
5   Saskatoon, SK S7K 0J5

6   Dear Mr. Thomas:

7   As a writing consultant, I have often aksed aud-
8   iences to locate all teh errors in this letter.
9   I am allways surprised if the find all the errors.
10   The result being that we all need more practical
11   advise in how to proof read.

12   To aviod these types of error, you must ensure that
13   that you review your documents carefully. I have
14   preparred the enclosed exercises for each of you
15   to in your efforts at JoAnne & Freinds, Inc.

16   Would you be willing to try this out on you own
17   workers and let me know the results.

18   Sincerly Yours

19   Mr. Michael Land,
20   Writing Consultant

16 Organizing Messages—Eyeing Discount Contact Lens Sales   Your boss, Roger Vincent Hardy, has his eye on a better way to retail contact lenses. Hardy is CEO of Coastal Contacts, which sells contact lenses online and by phone. His firm's annual revenues exceed $30 million, and a large portion of their advertising budget is dedicated to targeted email campaigns.

Hardy has asked you, his executive assistant, to write an email to college and university students, encouraging them to buy their contacts online from Coastal. Should you use a direct or indirect approach to organize this information? Why? Visit the website Coastalcontacts.com for any background information you may need. Then, draft the email, based on your organization strategy.

Two Heads Are Better Than One

Last year the Office Information Systems (OIS) Department installed a voice mail system. One of the features of this system is that users can now call over the telephone and dictate their correspondence and reports. All executives and R&D engineers below the rank of vice-president use the system. Three full-time transcriptionists in the OIS department then transcribe the dictation using word processing software. Turnaround time is typically less than five hours.

Yesterday, Angela Harper, one of the three transcriptionists, told department head Eric Fox that she really wants to be able to spend more time with her three-year-old. She asked about the possibility of job-sharing. She has a friend, Li Ying Yu, who has had extensive experience as a transcriptionist and who would also like to work half-time. Angela could work from 8 a.m. until noon daily, and Li Ying could work from 1 until 5 p.m. daily. Eric has had difficulty finding workers; he does not want to lose Angela.

On the plus side, if he accepts Angela's plan, he will have two highly-qualified employees. If one employee is sick, the other might be willing to cover for her. Two employees working only half a day would probably be more productive than one employee working the entire day, and any deficiencies in one employee might be compensated for by the other (for example, if one employee is better at handling technical vocabulary, such dictation could be saved for her). On the negative side is the fact that there might be some coordination problems (especially in the beginning), and fringe benefits will be increased somewhat (he estimates about 15 percent).

Eric decides to write a memo to Diana Coleman recommending job-sharing for this one position. Because job-sharing would be a new company policy, he knows that his memo will ultimately be forwarded to Dave Kaplan for his reaction.

Angela Harper, a transcriptionist at Northern Lights, asked about the possibility of job-sharing as a means of spending more time at home with her three-year-old daughter. Contemporary organizations must address such worker-friendly issues as job-sharing, telecommuting, and on-site child care.

Critical Thinking

1. Assume the role of Eric Fox. What is the specific goal of your memo?

2. Who are the primary and secondary audiences for this memo? What do you know about the primary audience that will help you write a more effective memo?

Writing Projects

3. List the points you should cover in the memo—in order.

4. Write a draft of the memo. (You may make up any needed information, as long as it is reasonable.)

5. Revise the draft.

6. Format the memo, proofread, and submit.

LABtest 3

DIRECTIONS. Correct any comma in the following letter to the editor from Dave (according to the comma rules introduced in LAB 2 on page 534).

Your lead editorial on May 19 2005 lamented light pollution which limits our views of the night sky. As a person who loves the profound beauty of the night sky I thank you for spreading the word about the loss of this precious environmental resource.

5   A retired lighting engineer however from Halifax Nova Scotia disputed many of the points you made. He stated that streetlights were not the problem and that the average streetlight is designed to put 95 percent of its light on the street. While the best ones do they are a small minority. Many spill a quarter or more of their light

10   horizontally and upward.

The ultimate goals of lighting are security and visibility. More light does not necessarily aid these goals and it can actually defeat them if the lighting is of poor quality.

James Thurber stated "There are two kinds of light: the glow

15   that illumines and the glare that obscures." We can preserve the beauty of the night sky enhance our security and reduce our energy costs. Fellow lighting engineers I challenge you to apply the creative dedicated energies of our profession to solving this problem.

4

Revising for Style: Individual Elements

OBJECTIVES

After you have finished this chapter, you should be able to

1. Write clearly.

2. Prefer short, simple words.

3. Write with vigour.

4. Write concisely.

5. Use a variety of sentence types.

6. Use active and passive voice appropriately.

7. Use parallel structure.

8. Keep paragraphs unified and coherent.

9. Control paragraph length.

No matter who manages to stay in the ring—or who lands outside—Gary Davis uses positive language to describe the situation. He is vice-president of corporate communications for World Wrestling Entertainment (WWE), which arranges more than 300 professional wrestling events every year in Canada, the United States, Europe, Asia, and Australia. Wrestling fans follow the action through the WWE's popular *SmackDown!* and *Raw* television programs and its magazines, videos, and DVDs. Davis's role is to communicate with a diverse international audience of media representatives, investors, advertisers, business partners, government officials, and community groups.

Most of the written messages Davis sends are business letters, full-length news releases, and news alerts—brief email messages about a particular issue or development. On occasion, he prepares special oral or video presentations for specific external audiences. Whether drafting a routine announcement or explaining the company's response to an unexpected problem, the WWE executive emphasizes that "the key is to write as if the glass is half full. If you do that, your message will come out positive." To make his meaning clear, Davis is especially careful to avoid overusing negative words and to eliminate double negatives. "Someone might write something like 'He did not think it would not work,'" he says, "when the real meaning is, 'He thought it would work.'"

Another way Davis helps audiences grasp his meaning is by writing simply and concisely. "Although it is very easy to overwrite, to say too much, to be too flowery, this

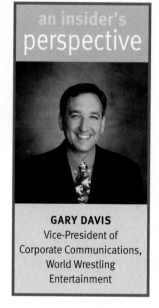

an insider's
perspective

GARY DAVIS
Vice-President of
Corporate Communications,
World Wrestling
Entertainment

115

obscures what you're trying to say," he notes. "From a business communication standpoint, less is more." Once he has developed a sentence or paragraph that concisely and accurately makes a certain point, he reuses this language, customized as appropriate, when writing about that topic in future messages.

Demonstrating the power of concrete, positive language in the service of an important ideal, Davis recently wrote a letter showcasing the SmackDown Your Vote!

initiative, supported by the WWE and a dozen partner groups. The letter, released to the media, quoted WWE stars talking about registering young voters and encouraging them to become poll workers. "We wanted to create a document that would put our wrestlers in front of the public in a different light," says Davis. "This letter is as much about the importance of the message as it is about the fact that our talent and our company are associated with putting this together." The result: hundreds of thousands of young voters are becoming involved in the election process—and the WWE is enhancing its credibility with key audiences.

"From a business communication standpoint, less is more."

■ What is Business Style?

Few would argue that there is *one* accepted style for all business writing. Good business writers understand that choices about style are really choices about what's appropriate for a given context. Firing an urgent text message off to a colleague in the middle of a board meeting would call for a particular style—colloquial, minimal detail, with perhaps only cursory attention to grammatical conventions. Writing a formal proposal for a multi-million dollar project would call for a different style—more formal language, carefully organized and detailed paragraphs, with meticulous attention to grammatical conventions, spelling, and punctuation.

What virtually all business writing has in common is that it demands a response from its reader: soliciting an opinion, setting up a meeting, exchanging information, selling a product, requesting a job interview—in all of these situations, the reader is expected to *do* something in response to the message.

For your business writing to be successful, your first concern is that it be understood and acted upon. To be understood, your message must be clear; to be easily acted upon, it must be efficient. Secondly, in virtually all business contexts, you want to present yourself as reliable, professional, and trustworthy. In making a proposal to a superior, in marketing a product to a client, or in seeking new employment, no matter how clearly your message is written, if your audience doesn't trust you, your message will fail. In short, you want your message—and by extension, yourself—to be credible.

So business writing differs from other forms of writing not so much in its style, but in its goals. The mistake many inexperienced writers (and even some experienced ones) commonly make is to assume that one style fits all situations. The excuse "that's just how I write" is a poor one. Such writers fail to adapt their style to what's appropriate for a given context. At best, their message fails to accomplish its goal; at worst, their message results in a total loss of their own credibility with their audience.

The following guidelines are intended to help make your writing more effective in achieving its goals. They are not intended as universal rules for all business-related writing. (The shorthand frequently used in text messaging, for example, would overlook many of the guidelines we discuss.) However, since most business writing demands the writer be clear, efficient, and credible, the decisions you make about your writing style are important.

What Do We Mean by Style?

If you study the six LAB (Language Arts Basics) exercises in the Reference Manual at the end of this book, you will know how to express yourself *correctly* in most business writing situations; that is, you will know how to avoid major errors in grammar, spelling, punctuation, and word usage. But a technically correct message may still not achieve its objective. For example, consider the following paragraph:

NOT: During the preceding year just past, Oxford Industries operated at a financial deficit. It closed three plants. It laid off many employees. The company's president was recently named Nova Scotia Small Business Executive of the Year. Oxford is now endeavouring to ascertain the causes of its financial exigency. The company president said that . . .

Your writing can be error-free and still lack style, but it cannot have style unless it is error-free.

This paragraph has no grammatical, mechanical, or usage errors. But it is not clear, vigorous, or coherent. For example:

- Consider the phrase "preceding year just past." *Preceding* means "just past," so why use both terms?

- In the second sentence, was closing the three plants the cause or the result of the financial deficit?

- What is the point of the sentence about the president?

- If you were speaking instead of writing, would you really say "endeavouring to ascertain," or would you use simpler language, like "trying to find out"?

- Finally, there are no transitions, or bridges, between the sentences; as a result, they don't flow smoothly.

Style refers to the effectiveness of the words, sentences, paragraphs, and overall tone of your message.

Although the paragraph is technically correct, it lacks an effective **style.** By style, we mean the way in which an idea is expressed (not its *substance*). Style consists of the particular words the writer uses and the manner in which those words are combined into sentences, paragraphs, and complete messages.

Now compare the first-draft paragraph above with this revised version:

BUT: Last year Oxford Industries lost money and, as a result, closed three plants and laid off 200 employees. Now the company is trying to determine the causes of its problems. In an explanation to stockholders, Oxford's president, who was recently named Nova Scotia Small Business Executive of the Year, said that . . .

Mechanics refers to how an idea is expressed in writing.

The revised version is more direct and readable. It clarifies relationships among the sentences. It uses concise, familiar language. It presents ideas in logical order. In short, it has an effective *style.* Chapters 4 and 5 discuss the principles of effective writing style for business, illustrated in Figure 4.1. Apply these principles of style as you write and revise the letters, memos, emails, and reports that are assigned in later chapters.

As you learned in Chapter 3, while writing the first draft of a message, you should be more concerned with content than with style. Your major objective should

figure4.1

Steps to an Effective Writing Style

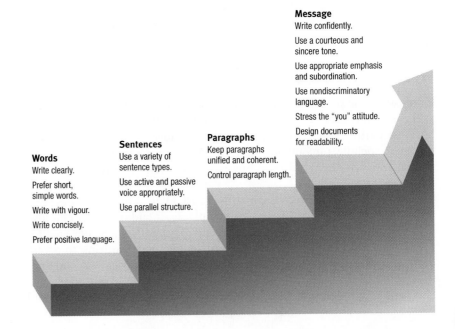

Message
Write confidently.
Use a courteous and sincere tone.
Use appropriate emphasis and subordination.
Use nondiscriminatory language.
Stress the "you" attitude.
Design documents for readability.

Paragraphs
Keep paragraphs unified and coherent.
Control paragraph length.

Sentences
Use a variety of sentence types.
Use active and passive voice appropriately.
Use parallel structure.

Words
Write clearly.
Prefer short, simple words.
Write with vigour.
Write concisely.
Prefer positive language.

be to get your ideas down in some form, without worrying about style and mechanics. (**Mechanics** are elements in communication that show up only in written form, including spelling, punctuation, abbreviations, capitalization, number expression, and word division.)

Having planned and composed your draft and having revised it for content, you are now ready to revise for style. As you become more comfortable with the principles of this chapter you will begin to incorporate many of them at the drafting stage, making your writing process more efficient. Even experienced writers, however, find it easier to draft a message first and worry about style afterwards.

■ Choosing the Right Words

Individual words are our basic units of writing, the bricks with which we build meaningful messages. All writers have access to the same words. The care with which we select and combine words can make the difference between a message that achieves its objective and one that does not. Discussed below are four principles of word choice to help you write more effectively.

Clarity

The basic guideline for writing, the one that must be present for the other principles to have meaning, is to write clearly—to write messages the reader can under-

CO1. Write clearly.

Dr. Jacqueline Shan understands the importance of making complex information accessible. As the Chief Scientific Officer, President, and CEO of CV Technologies—the makers of Cold FX—Dr. Shan has learned to communicate the science behind her product to both the scientific community and the general public. Cold FX is used by many professional sports teams, including the Montreal Canadiens, the Edmonton Oilers, and the Calgary Flames.

stand, depend on, and act on. You can achieve clarity by making your message accurate, by using familiar words, and by avoiding dangling expressions and unnecessary jargon.

Accuracy is the most important attribute in business writing. It involves more than freedom from errors.

Be Accurate   A writer's credibility is perhaps his or her most important asset, and credibility depends greatly on the accuracy of the message. If by carelessness, lack of preparation, or a desire to manipulate, a writer misleads the reader, the damage is immediate and long-lasting. A reader who has been fooled once may not trust the writer again.

Accuracy can take many forms. The most basic is the truthful presentation of facts and figures. But accuracy involves much more. For example, consider the following sentence from a memo to a firm's financial backers:

> The executive committee of Mitchell Financial Services met on Thursday, May 28, to determine how to resolve the distribution fiasco.

Suppose, on checking, the reader learns that May 28 fell on a Wednesday this year—not on a Thursday. Immediately, the reader may suspect everything else in the message. The reader's thinking might be, "If the writer made this error that I *did* catch, how many errors that I *didn't* catch are lurking there?"

Now consider more subtle shades of truth. The sentence implies that the committee met, perhaps in an emergency session, for the *sole* purpose of resolving the distribution fiasco. But suppose this matter was only one of five agenda items being discussed at a regularly scheduled meeting. Is the statement still accurate? Suppose the actual agenda listed the topic as "Discussion of Recent Distribution Problems." Is *fiasco* the same as *problems?*

Ethical communicators make sure the overall tone of their message is accurate.

The accuracy of a message, then, depends on what is said, how it is said, and what is left unsaid. Competent writers assess the ethical dimensions of their writing and use integrity, fairness, and good judgment to make sure their communication is ethical. Closely related to accuracy is completeness. A message that lacks important information may create inaccurate impressions. A message is complete when it contains all the information the reader needs—no more and no less—to react appropriately.

As a start, answer the five Ws: Tell the reader *who, what, when, where,* and *why.* Leaving out any of this information may result either in decisions based on incomplete information or in extra follow-up correspondence to gather the needed information.

Use language that you and your reader understand.

Use Familiar Words   Your message must be understood before someone can act on it. So you must use words that are both familiar to you (so that you will not misuse the word) and familiar to your readers.

Marilyn vos Savant (identified by the *Guinness Book of World Records* as the smartest person alive) once asked her readers what the following paragraph meant:

> When promulgating your esoteric cogitations or articulating your superficial sentimentalities and amicable philosophical and psychological observations, beware of platitudinous ponderosity. Let your verbal evaporations have lucidity, intelligibility, and veracious vivacity without rodomontade or thespian bombast. Sedulously avoid all polysyllabic profundity, pompous propensity, and sophomoric vacuity.[1]

Her translation: Don't use big words!

The push towards using familiar words in business and government has been underway for over two decades in Canada. Brian Dickson and Antonio Lamer, former Canadian Supreme Court judges, are credited with spearheading the movement toward making Supreme Court judgments readable to the general population.

Indeed, newly appointed judges are now encouraged to take courses that include instruction on writing clearly understandable decisions. Other organizations, including both the British Columbia and the Ontario Securities Commissions, have also joined the movement towards using plain language in their decisions.

Consider this October 1945 decision of the Supreme Court of Canada:

The judgment ordering the probate of a holograph will does not constitute re judicata. . . . In an action where a holograph will duly probated is contested, the burden of proof still continues to impose upon the beneficiaries the obligation to establish the genuineness of the writing or of the signature of the testator. The probate has not the effect of shifting such burden to the party repudiating the will, the latter not having the incumbent duty of proving that the writing or the signature was forged.

Now consider how much clearer and more familiar the language is in this June 2005 Supreme Court decision:

In any constitutional climate, the administration of justice thrives on exposure to light— and withers under a cloud of secrecy. That lesson of history is enshrined in the Canadian Charter of Rights and Freedoms. Section 2(b) of the Charter guarantees, in more comprehensive terms, freedom of communication and freedom of expression. These fundamental and closely related freedoms both depend for their vitality on public access to information of public interest. What goes on in the courts ought therefore to be, and manifestly is, of central concern to Canadians.

Don't assume that only long words cause confusion. Consider the following sentences:

NOT: Rejecting *ruth*, the candidate would *limn* about how he *fain* would be the *birr* to *moil* for the *ruck* if the nation's *weal* were ensured.

BUT: Rejecting pity, the candidate would describe how he gladly would be the driving force to work hard for the great masses if the nation's prosperity were ensured.

The seven short italicized words in the first version would probably be understandable only to a crossword puzzle addict (or a speller at the National Spelling Bee, from whose Web site the words came). Most readers, however, would understand the second version.

Long words are sometimes useful in business communication, of course, and should be used when appropriate. The larger your vocabulary and the more you know about your reader, the better equipped you will be to choose and use correctly those words that are familiar to your reader.

Avoid Dangling Expressions

A **dangling expression** is any part of a sentence that doesn't logically fit in with the rest of the sentence. Its relationship with the other parts of the sentence is unclear; it *dangles*. The two most common types of dangling expressions are misplaced modifiers and unclear antecedents.

To correct dangling expressions, (1) make the subject of the sentence the doer of the action expressed in the introductory clause; (2) move the expression closer to the word that it modifies; (3) make sure that the specific word to which a pronoun refers (its *antecedent*) is clear; or (4) otherwise revise the sentence.

NOT: After reading the proposal, a few problems occurred to me. *(As written, the sentence implies that "a few problems" read the proposal.)*

BUT: After reading the proposal, I noted a few problems.

NOT: Dr. Ellis gave a presentation on the use of drugs in our auditorium. *(Are drugs being used in the auditorium?)*

BUT: Dr. Ellis gave a presentation in our auditorium on the use of drugs.

NOT: Robin explained the proposal to Joy, but she was not happy with it. *(Who was not happy—Robin or Joy?)*

BUT: Robin explained the proposal to Joy, but Joy was not happy with it.

> *Jargon is sometimes appropriate and sometimes inappropriate.*

Avoid Unnecessary Jargon   Jargon is technical vocabulary used within a special group. Every field has its own specialized words, and jargon offers a precise and efficient way of communicating with people in the same field. But problems arise when jargon is used to communicate with someone who does not understand it. For example, to a banker the term CD means a "certificate of deposit," but to a music lover or computer user it means a "compact disc." Even familiar words can be confusing when given a specialized meaning.

Does the field of business communication have jargon? It does—just look at the Key Terms list at the end of each chapter. The word *jargon* itself might be considered communication jargon. In this text, such terms are first defined and then used to make communication precise and efficient. Competent writers use specialized vocabulary to communicate with specialists who understand it. And they avoid using it when their readers are not specialists.

Short, Simple Words

> co2. **Prefer short, simple words.**

Short and simple words are more likely to be understood, less likely to be misused, and less likely to distract the reader. Literary authors often write to *impress;* they select words to achieve a specific reader reaction, such as amusement, excitement, or anger. Business writers, on the other hand, write to *express;* they want to achieve *comprehension.* They want their readers to focus on their information, not on how they convey their information. Using short, simple words helps achieve this goal.

NOT: To recapitulate, our utilization of adulterated water precipitated the interminable delays.

BUT: In short, our use of impure water caused the endless delays.

DILBERT

It is true, of course, that often no short, simple word is available to convey the precise shade of meaning you want. For example, there is no one-syllable replacement for *ethnocentrism* (the belief that one's own cultural group is superior), a concept introduced in Chapter 2. Our guideline is not to use *only* short and simple words but to *prefer* short and simple words. (As Mark Twain, who was paid by the word for his writing, noted, "I never write *metropolis* for seven cents because I can get the same price for *city*. I never write *policeman* because I can get the same money for *cop*.")

One analysis of more than 2500 actual industry documents found that more than half of all word occurrences in these documents contained four or fewer characters and just one syllable. As shown in Communication Snapshot 3, the average word used in business writing contains five characters.[2]

Here are some examples of needlessly long words, gleaned from various business documents, with their preferred shorter substitutes shown in parentheses:

ascertain (learn)	indispensable (vital)	substantial (large)
endeavor (try)	initiate (start)	termination (end)
enumerate (list)	modification (change)	utilization (use)
fluctuate (vary)	recapitulate (review)	

You need not strike these long words totally from your written or spoken vocabulary; any one of these words, used in a clear sentence, would be acceptable. The problem is that a writer may tend to fill his or her writing with very long words when simpler ones could be used. Use long words in moderation.

spotlight9
ACROSS CULTURES

Same Rules the World Over

The strategies for writing effective business messages discussed in this chapter are common across many cultures. The passage below, from a business communication text for Chinese business executives, recommends substituting concise phrases for long, empty ones.[3]

"简洁"是有客观标准的。虽然西方国家的作者之间在怎样用词才算"简洁"方面还是有争论的,不过他们的一些看法还是有一定参考价值的。现把他们所做的某些词句的"不简洁"与"简洁"的比较列在下面供参考:

不 简 洁　　　　　　　　　　　简 洁

Wordy	Concise	Wordy	Concise
enclosed herewith	enclosed	under separate cover	separately
enclosed you will find	enclosed is	a long period of time	a long time
please be advised that	(four wasted words)	continuous and uninterrupted	continuous (*or:* uninterrupted)
please don't hesitate to call upon us	please write us	during the year of 1971	during 1971
please feel free to write	please write	endorse on the back of this check	endorse this check
prior to	before	for a price of $300	for $300
this is to advise you	(five wasted words)		

You've probably heard the advice "Write as you speak." Although not universally true, such advice is pretty close to the mark. Of course, if your conversation is peppered with redundancies, jargon, and clichés, you would not want to put such weaknesses on paper. But typical conversation uses mostly short, simple words—the kind you *do* want to put on paper. Don't assume that the bigger the words, the bigger the intellect. In fact, you need a large vocabulary and a well-developed word sense to select the best word. And more often than not, that word is short and simple. Write to express—not to impress.

Vigour in Writing

co3. Write with vigour.

Vigorous language is specific and concrete. Limp language is filled with clichés, slang, and buzzwords. Vigorous writing holds your reader's interest. But if your reader isn't even interested enough to read your message, your writing can't possibly achieve its objective. A second reason for writing with vigour has to do with language itself. Vigorous writing lends vigour to the ideas presented. A good idea looks even better dressed in vigorous language, and a weak idea looks even weaker dressed in limp language.

Use Specific, Concrete Language   In Chapter 1, we discussed the communication barriers caused by overabstraction and ambiguity. When possible, choose *specific* words—words that have a definite, unambiguous meaning. Likewise, choose concrete words—words that bring a definite picture to your reader's mind.

NOT: The vehicle broke down several times recently.

BUT: The delivery van broke down three times last week.

communication snapshot 3

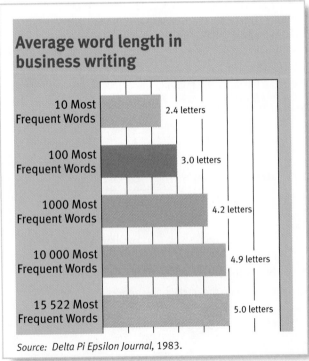

Average word length in business writing

10 Most Frequent Words	2.4 letters
100 Most Frequent Words	3.0 letters
1000 Most Frequent Words	4.2 letters
10 000 Most Frequent Words	4.9 letters
15 522 Most Frequent Words	5.0 letters

Source: Delta Pi Epsilon Journal, 1983.

In the first version, what does the reader imagine when he or she reads the word *vehicle*—a golf cart? automobile? boat? space shuttle? Likewise, how many times is *several*—two? three? 15? What is *recently*? The revised version tells precisely what happened.

Sometimes we do not need such specific information. For example, in "The president answered *several* questions from the audience and then adjourned the meeting," the specific number of questions is probably not important. But in most business situations, you should watch out for words like *several, recently, a number of, substantial, a few,* and *a lot of.* You may need to be more exact.

Likewise, use the most concrete word that is appropriate; give the reader a specific mental picture of what you mean. That is, learn to talk in pictures:

NOT: The vice-president was bored by the presentation.

BUT: The vice-president kept yawning and looking at her watch.

Bored is an abstract concept. "Yawning and looking at her watch" paints a vivid picture.

Be sure that your terms convey as much meaning as the reader needs to react appropriately. Watch out for terms like *emotional meeting* (anger or gratitude?), *bright colour* (red or yellow?), *new equipment* (postage metre or cash register?), and *change in price* (increase or decrease?).

Employment experts urge employers to be specific and concrete when listing required skills and qualifications. Job seekers should do likewise when submitting their résumés.

Businesses realize the value of using specific, concrete language that paints a picture. You should, too.

Concrete words present a vivid picture.

Avoid Clichés, Slang, and Buzzwords

A **cliché** is an expression that has become monotonous through overuse. It lacks freshness and originality and may also send the unintended message that the writer couldn't be bothered to choose language geared specifically to the reader.

NOT: Enclosed please find an application form that you should return at your earliest convenience.

BUT: Please return the enclosed application form before May 15.

Here are some examples of other expressions that have become overused (even in other countries; see Spotlight 9, "Same Rules the World Over," on page 123) and that therefore sound trite and boring. Avoid them in your writing.

Picture a person finding "thank you for your recent letter" in all 15 letters he or she reads that day. How sincere and original does it sound?

According to our records	It goes without saying that
Company policy requires	Needless to say
Do not hesitate to	Our records indicate that
For your information	Please be advised that
If I can be of further help	Take this opportunity to
If you have any other questions	Under separate cover

As noted earlier, slang is an expression, often short-lived, that is identified with a specific group of people. If you understand each word in an expression but still don't understand what it means in context, chances are you're having trouble with a slang expression. For example, read the following sentence:

It turns my stomach the way you can break your neck and beat your brains out around here, and they still stab you in the back.

To anyone unfamiliar with North American slang (a non-native speaker, perhaps), this sentence might seem to be about the body because it refers to the stomach, neck, brains, and back. The real meaning, of course, is something like this:

I am really upset that this company ignores hard work and loyalty when making personnel decisions.

Avoid slang in most business writing, for several reasons. First, it is informal, and much business writing, although not formal, is still *businesslike* and calls for standard word usage. Second, slang is short-lived. A slang phrase used today may not be in use—and thus may not be familiar—in three years, when your letter is retrieved from the files for reference. Third, slang is identified with a specific group of people, and others in the general population may not understand the intended meaning. For these reasons, avoid expressions like these in most business writing:

ace in the hole	divide and conquer
back to the drawing board	drop in the bucket
bark up the wrong tree	fair shake
beggars can't be choosers	filled to the brim
can of worms	fly the coop
cart before the horse	pay through the nose
chip off the old block	

Clichés and buzzwords go in and out of style too quickly to serve as effective components of written business communication.

A **buzzword** is an important-sounding expression used mainly to impress other people. Because buzzwords are so often used by government officials and high-ranking business people—people whose comments are "newsworthy"—these expressions get much media attention. They become instant clichés and then go out of fashion just as quickly. At either end of their short life span, they cause communication problems. If an expression is currently being used by everyone, it sounds monotonous, lacking originality. If it is no longer being used by anyone, readers may not understand the intended meaning. Here are examples of recent "in" expressions:

big picture	manage expectations	think outside the box
bottom line	multitasking	touch base
cutting edge	state of the art	value-added
going forward	team player	win win

Be especially careful of turning nouns and other types of words into verbs by adding *-ize*. Such words as *agendize, prioritize, strategize, unionize,* and *operationalize* quickly become tiresome.

Conciseness

CO4. **Write concisely.**

Business people are busy people. The information revolution has created more paperwork, giving business people access to more data. Having more data to analyze (but presumably not being able to read any faster or having more time in which to do so), managers want information presented in the fewest possible words. To achieve conciseness, make every word count. Avoid redundancy, wordy expressions, hidden verbs and nouns, and other "space-eaters."

Avoid Redundancy   A **redundancy** is the unnecessary repetition of an idea that has already been expressed or intimated. Eliminating the repetition contributes to conciseness.

NOT: Signing both copies of the lease is a necessary requirement.

BUT: Signing both copies of the lease is necessary.

NOT: Combine the ingredients together.

BUT: Combine the ingredients.

A *requirement* is, by definition, *necessary,* so only one of the words is needed. And to *combine* means to bring *together,* so using both words is redundant. Don't confuse redundancy and repetition. Repetition—using the same word more than once—is occasionally effective for emphasis (as we will discuss in the next chapter). Redundancy, however, serves no purpose and should always be avoided.

Redundancy and repetition are not the same.

Some redundancies are humorous, as in the classic Samuel Goldwyn comment, "Anybody who goes to a psychiatrist ought to have his head examined," or the sign in a jewellery store window, "Ears pierced while you wait." Most redundancies, however, are simply *verbiage*—excess words that consume time and space. Avoid them. (See Figure 4.2.)

Make every word count.

Do not use the unnecessary word *together* after such words as *assemble, combine, cooperate, gather, join, merge,* or *mix.* Do not use the unnecessary word *new* before such words as *beginner, discovery, fad, innovation,* or *progress.* And do not use the unnecessary word *up* after such words as *connect, divide, eat, lift, mix,* and *rest.* Also avoid the following common redundancies (use the words in parentheses instead):

advance planning (planning)	but nevertheless (but *or* nevertheless)
any and all (any *or* all)	
basic fundamentals (basics *or* fundamentals)	each and every (each *or* every)
repeat again (repeat)	free gift (gift)
over again (over)	sum total (sum *or* total)
past history (history)	true facts (facts)
plan ahead (plan)	when and if (when *or* if)

Another type of redundancy to avoid is needlessly adding a noun to an abbreviation that already stands for that noun. For example, you should not write *ATM machine* because ATM stands for "automated teller machine." Similarly, avoid *PIN number, HIV virus, OPEC countries,* and *RSVP requested.*

Avoid Wordy Expressions   Although wordy expressions are not necessarily writing errors (as redundancies are), they do slow the pace of the communication and should be avoided. For example, try substituting one word for a phrase whenever possible.

Use the fewest number of words that will achieve your objective.

NOT: In view of the fact that the model failed twice during the time that we tested it, we are at this point in time searching for other options.

BUT: Because the model failed twice when we tested it, we are now searching for other options.

The original sentence contains 28 words; the revised sentence, 16. You've "saved" 12 words. In his delightful book, *Revising Business Prose,* Richard Lanham speaks

~~new~~ beginner	assemble ~~together~~	connect ~~up~~
~~new~~ discovery	combine ~~together~~	divide ~~up~~
~~new~~ fad	cooperate ~~together~~	eat ~~up~~
~~new~~ innovation	gather ~~together~~	lift ~~up~~
~~new~~ progress	mix ~~together~~	rest ~~up~~

figure4.2

Avoid Unnecessary Words

of the "lard factor": the percentage of words saved by "getting rid of the lard" in a sentence. In this case,

$$28 - 16 = 12; 124 \div 28 = 43 \text{ percent}$$

Thus, 43 percent of the original sentence was "lard," which fattened the sentence without providing any "nutrition." Lanham suggests, "Think of a lard factor (LF) of ⅓ to ½ as normal and don't stop revising until you've removed it."[4]

Here are examples of other wordy phrases and their preferred one-word substitutes in parentheses:

are of the opinion that (believe)	for the amount of (for)
as to whether (whether)	in order to (to)
despite the fact that (although)	in the event that (if)
due to the fact that (because)	pertaining to (about)
for the purpose of (for *or* to)	with regard to (about)

> *Changing verbs to nouns produces weak, uninteresting sentences.*

Avoid Hidden Verbs and Subjects   A hidden verb is a verb that has been changed into a noun form, thereby weakening the action. Verbs are *action* words and should convey the main action in the sentence. They provide interest and forward movement. Consider this example:

NOT: Carl made an announcement that he will give consideration to our request.

BUT: Carl announced that he will consider our request.

What is the real action? It is not that Carl *made* something or that he will *give* something. The real action is hiding in the nouns: Carl *announced* and will *consider*. These two verb forms, then, should be the main verbs in the sentence. Notice that the revised sentence is much more direct—and four words shorter (LF = 33 percent). Here are some other actions that should be conveyed by verbs instead of being hidden in nouns:

arrived at the conclusion (concluded)	has a requirement for (requires)
came to an agreement (agreed)	held a meeting (met)
gave a demonstration of (demonstrated)	made a payment (paid)
performed an analysis of (analyzed)	gave an explanation (explained)

> *A pronoun in an expletive does not stand for any noun.*

Like verbs, subjects play a prominent role in a sentence and should stand out, rather than being obscured by an expletive beginning. An **expletive** is an expression such as *there is* or *it is* that begins a clause or sentence and for which the pronoun has no antecedent. Because the topic of a sentence beginning with an expletive is not immediately clear, you should use such sentences sparingly in business writing. Avoiding expletives also contributes to conciseness.

NOT: There was no indication that it is necessary to include John in the meeting.

BUT: No one indicated that John should be included in the meeting.

Imply or Condense   Sometimes you do not need to explicitly state certain information; you can imply it instead. In other situations, you can use adjectives and adverbs instead of clauses to convey the needed information in a more concise format.

NOT: We have received your recent letter and are happy to provide the data you requested.

BUT: We are happy to provide the data you recently requested.

NOT: This brochure, which is available free of charge, will answer your questions.

BUT: This free brochure will answer your questions.

Because words are the building blocks for your message, choose them with care. Using short, simple words and writing with clarity, vigour, and conciseness will help you construct effective sentences and paragraphs. If you are one of the many students learning business communication for whom English is a second language, see Spotlight 10, "So You're an ESL Speaker," on page 132.

■ Writing Effective Sentences

A sentence has a subject and predicate and expresses at least one complete thought. Beyond these attributes, however, sentences vary widely in style, length, and effect. They are also very flexible; writers can move sentence parts around, add and delete information, and substitute words to express different ideas and emphasize different points. To build effective sentences, you should be able to identify phrases and clauses. Once you understand these, you can learn to use a variety of sentence types and to use active and passive voice appropriately.

CO5. Use a variety of sentence types.

Understanding Clauses and Phrases

Sentences are made up of words, phrases, and clauses. There are two types of clauses and several types of phrases. While it's not essential that you understand all the different types of phrases, it is essential that you can identify both types of clauses. Not only does understanding clauses help you add variety to your sentences, this understanding also helps you make correct decisions about punctuation.

Phrases A **phrase** is a group of related words that does not have *both* a subject and a predicate. A **subject** is the word or group of words that does something, has something done to it, or is identified or described. A **predicate** is the word or group of words that tells what the subject does, what is done to it, or how it is identified or described.

Noun Phrase

Between Thanksgiving and Christmas is our busiest season.

Verb Phrase

Nguen *will be attending* the national conference.

Prepositional Phrase

Lab tests *of many kinds* were then ordered.

Adverbial Phrase

We will finish the tests *before lunch.*

Clauses   A **clause** is a group of related words that contains both a subject and a predicate. (A phrase may contain either a subject or predicate—but not both.) An **independent** (or *main*) **clause** expresses a complete thought and can stand alone as a complete sentence. Every sentence has at least one independent clause. A **dependent** (or *subordinate*) **clause** does not express a complete thought and cannot stand alone as a complete sentence. A dependent clause must be accompanied by an independent clause to express a complete thought.

Adverbial Phrase

After the break, we'll continue.

Dependent Clause

After we take a break, we'll continue.

Gerund Phrase

Reading the computer program was difficult.

Dependent Clause

When I was reading the computer program, I discovered an error.

Verb Phrase

By 2007, Jonathan Stein *will have been working for 30 years.*

Independent Clause

By 2007, *Jonathan Stein will have been working for 30 years.*

Types of Sentences

There are four basic sentence types—simple, compound, complex, and compound-complex—all of which are appropriate for business writing.

Simple Sentence   A **simple sentence** contains one independent clause. Because it presents a single idea and is usually short, a simple sentence is often used for emphasis. Although a simple sentence contains only one independent clause, it may have a compound subject or compound verb (or both). All of the following sentences are simple:

> I quit.

> Individual Retirement Accounts are a safe option.

> Both Individual Retirement Accounts and Simplified Employee Pension Plans are safe and convenient options as retirement investments for the entrepreneur.

Compound Sentence   A **compound sentence** contains two or more independent clauses. Because each clause presents a complete idea, each idea receives *equal* emphasis. (If the two ideas are not closely related, they should be presented in two separate sentences.) Here are three compound sentences:

> Stacey listened, but I nodded.

> Morris Technologies made a major acquisition last year, and it turned out to be a disaster.

> Westmoreland Mines moved its headquarters to Sudbury in 1984; however, it stayed there only five years and then moved back to St. John.

Use a simple sentence for emphasis and variety.

Use a compound sentence to show coordinate (equal) relationships.

Complex Sentence   A **complex sentence** contains one independent clause and at least one dependent clause. For example, in the first sentence below, "The scanner will save valuable input time" is an independent clause because it makes sense by itself. "Although it cost $235" is a dependent clause because, though it contains both a subject and a predicate, it does not make sense by itself.

> Although it cost $235, the scanner will save valuable input time.
>
> George Bosley, who is the new CEO at Avro, made the decision.
>
> I will be moving to Calgary when I assume my new position.

The dependent clause provides additional, but *subordinate,* information related to the independent clause.

Use a complex sentence to express subordinate relationships.

Compound-Complex Sentence   A **compound-complex sentence** contains *two or more* independent clauses and *one or more* dependent clauses.

> Although I wanted to write the report myself, I soon realized I needed legal advice, so I consulted our lawyer. *(two independent clauses and one dependent clause)*
>
> If I can, I'll do it; if I cannot, I'll ask Sheila to do it. *(two independent clauses and two dependent clauses)*

Sentence Variety   Using a variety of sentence patterns and sentence lengths helps keep your writing interesting. Note how simplistic and choppy too many short sentences can be and how boring and difficult too many long sentences can be.

Too Choppy:

Fairmont Resorts will not purchase the Montclair Hotel. The hotel is 160 years old. The asking price was $210 million. It was not considered too high. Fairmont Resorts had wanted some commitments from the Montreal municipal government. The government was unwilling to provide such commitments. Some observers believe the refusal was not the real reason for the decision. They blame the weak Quebec economy for the cancellation. Fairmont Resorts purchased the Stake House in Niagara Falls in 2000. It lost money on that purchase. It does not want to repeat its mistake in Montreal.
(Average sentence length = 9 words)

Too Difficult:

Fairmont Resorts will not purchase the Montclair Hotel, which is 160 years old, for an asking price of $210 million, which was not considered too high, because the company had wanted some commitments from the Montreal municipal government, and the government was unwilling to provide such commitments. Some observers believe the refusal was not the real reason for the decision but rather that the weak Quebec economy was responsible for the cancellation; and since Fairmont Resorts purchased the Stake House in Niagara Falls in 2000 and lost money on that purchase, it does not want to repeat its mistake in Montreal.
(Average sentence length = 50 words)

The sentences in these paragraphs should be revised to show relationships between ideas more clearly, to keep readers interested, and to improve readability. Use simple sentences for emphasis and variety, compound sentences for coordinate (equal) relationships, and complex sentences for subordinate relationships.

So You're an ESL Speaker

If English is your second language, you have already noticed that there are a number of idiomatic expressions and structures that can cause communication problems. Here are some tips to help you with some of the more common ESL errors. You also will need to get a good English dictionary, a handbook for ESL speakers, and be prepared to ask a lot of questions in order to learn all the exceptions to the rules of grammar and usage.

Articles with Count and Non-Count Nouns

The indefinite articles *a* and *an* are usually used with singular count nouns—nouns that can be counted—where the specific identity of the noun is unknown to the reader. The article *an* is used in those cases where the noun starts with a vowel or where the *h* is unvoiced.

> Ex.   a banana   an apple
>   a mechanical pencil an honour
>   a meeting   an exact replica

The definite article *the* is used with most nouns whose specific identity is known to the reader. Usually, the identity is clear to the reader because the word has been mentioned before, the noun is in some way restricted or modified, or the context itself makes the identity known.

> Ex.   A report needs a title page.
>   *The* title page will not be numbered.
>   *The* computer on my desk is slow.
>   Remember to turn off *the* lights when you leave.

As a general rule, *a, an,* or *the* are not used with plurals or with non-count nouns—nouns that cannot be counted. Some non-count nouns commonly used in a business context are as follows: mail, transportation, work, research, money, advice, confidence, employment, knowledge, wealth, intelligence, truth, coffee, tea, and information. There are some exceptions to the rules for articles, so if in doubt, ask a native speaker.

Prepositions for Time and Place

Prepositions, at least in the English language, are often very idiomatic, but the following examples outline how four of the most common prepositions are used to show time and place.

Time

At a specific time (at 8:00 a.m.)
On a specific day or date (on Tuesday)
In a part of the day, a year, or month (in the morning, in 2008, in July)
By a specific time or date (by 8:00, by July 6)

Place

At a location or the edge or corner of something (at the gym, at my desk)
On a surface or electronic medium (on the table, on television)
In an enclosed space or print medium (in the office, in the newspaper)

Verbs

There are a number of rules governing which verb form is used when—too many, in fact, to deal with here. However, there are a few simple rules that can help you avoid some common mistakes with verb forms.

Some verbs need helping verbs in order to be complete. These helping verbs are either some form of *to be, to have,* or *to do,* which show tense; or *could, can, may, might, must, shall, should, will, would,* which don't reveal a tense and are called modals. These "helping" verbs always appear before the main verb.

When using any of the modals as a helping verb, the main verb will be in its base form (the one found in the dictionary).

> ■ Ex.   During oral presentations, you should speak clearly and loudly.

When using *do, does,* or *did* as helping verbs, the main verb will be in its base form.

> ■ Ex.   The manager does not need the report until tomorrow.

When *has, had,* or *have* as the helping verb, the main verb will be in its past participle form.

> ■ Ex.   The CEO has agreed to answer any questions after the speech.

When using any form of *to be,* the main verb will be in its present participle form.

▪ Ex. The manager was using a flipchart for his presentation.

When writing a sentence in passive voice, and using *to be,* the verb will be in past participle form.

▪ Ex. The meeting was re-scheduled for next Tuesday.

There are exceptions to all of these rules, so if in doubt, ask a native speaker. Studying the written language is also helpful. When you're writing an assignment, take time to study the samples in the text. What words are used in the samples of proper usage? How long are the sentences, and how are they combined to form paragraphs? How do the samples of proper usage differ from the samples of poor usage? These contrasts can help you avoid common mistakes as you become more proficient in English. Always proofread your written work carefully and, as a final check, ask a native English speaker to read it and point out any errors so that you can correct them before submitting your assignment.

When you're speaking with a classmate who uses an English word that you don't know, politely ask about the word's meaning. This exercise is a good way to enlarge your vocabulary while learning about contemporary usage. Whenever possible, look for opportunities to interact with students who are native English speakers by participating in class discussions and personal conversations, joining a school club or another student activity, or organizing a study group. You'll learn English more quickly if you hear it spoken by native speakers and practice formulating a response in formal and informal settings.

Some schools offer additional support to their ESL students, so ask whether your school has any ESL programs or can provide a tutor for one-on-one assistance with assignments.

Don't be discouraged if you read, write, or speak English slowly at first. As your comprehension improves, you'll be able to increase your speed and communicate with less effort. Meanwhile, be sure to recognize and celebrate even your smallest gains—because small steps forward, over time, can add up to giant leaps in learning.[5]

More Variety:

Fairmont Resorts will not purchase the 160-year-old Montclair Hotel, even though the $210 million asking price was not considered too high. The company had wanted some commitments from the Montreal municipal government, which the government was unwilling to provide. However, some observers blame the cancellation on the weak Quebec economy. Fairmont Resorts lost money on its 2000 purchase of the Stake House in Niagara Falls, and it does not want to repeat its mistake in Montreal.
(Average sentence length 19 words)

The first two sentences in the revision are complex, the third sentence is simple, and the last sentence is compound. The lengths of the four sentences range from 11 to 26 words. To write effective sentences, use different sentence patterns and lengths. Most sentences in good business writing range from 16 to 22 words.

Use a variety of sentence patterns and lengths.

Active and Passive Voice

Voice is the aspect of a verb that shows whether the subject of the sentence acts or is acted on. In the **active voice,** the subject *performs* the action expressed by the verb. In the **passive voice,** the subject *receives* the action expressed by the verb.

CO6. Use active and passive voice appropriately.

ACTIVE: A and B Sound offers a full refund on all orders.

PASSIVE: A full refund on all orders is offered by A and B Sound.

ACTIVE: Deloitte and Touche audited the books in 2005.

PASSIVE: The books were audited in 2005 by Deloitte and Touche.

Passive sentences add some form of the verb *to be* to the main verb, so passive sentences are always somewhat longer than active sentences. In the first set of sentences just given, for example, compare *offers* in the active sentence with *is offered by* in the passive sentence.

In active sentences, the subject performs the action; in passive sentences, the subject receives the action.

In active sentences, the subject is the doer of the action; in passive sentences, the subject is the receiver of the action. And because the subject gets more emphasis than other nouns in a sentence, active sentences emphasize the doer, and passive sentences emphasize the receiver, of the action. In the second set of sentences, either version could be considered correct, depending on whether the writer wanted to emphasize *Deloitte* or *the books*.

Use active sentences most of the time in business writing, just as you naturally use active sentences in most of your conversations. Note that verb *voice* (active or passive) has nothing to do with verb *tense,* which shows the time of the action. As the following sentences show, the action in both active and passive sentences can occur in the past, present, or future.

> **NOT:**   A very logical argument was presented by Hal. *(passive voice, past tense)*

> **BUT:**   Hal presented a very logical argument. *(active voice, past tense)*

> **NOT:**   An 18 percent increase will be reported by the eastern region. *(passive voice, future tense)*

> **BUT:**   The eastern region will report an 18 percent increase. *(active voice, future tense)*

Passive sentences are generally more effective than active sentences for conveying negative information.

Passive sentences are most appropriate when you want to emphasize the *receiver* of the action, when the person doing the action is either unknown or unimportant, or when you want to be tactful in conveying negative information. All the following sentences are appropriately stated in the passive voice:

> Protective legislation was blamed for the drop in imports. *(emphasizes the receiver of the action)*

> Transportation to the construction site will be provided. *(the doer of the action is not important)*

> Several complaints have been received regarding the new policy. *(tactfully conveys negative news)*

Parallel Structure

CO7. **Use parallel structures.**

The term **parallelism** means using similar grammatical structure for similar ideas—that is, matching adjectives with adjectives, nouns with nouns, infinitives with infinitives, and so on. Much widely quoted writing uses parallelism—for example, Julius Caesar's "I came, I saw, I conquered" or Pierre Trudeau's "Our hopes are high. Our faith in the people is great. Our courage is strong. And our dreams for this beautiful country will never die." Parallel structure smoothly links ideas, adding both clarity and rhythm to sentences.

Parallelism refers to consistency.

> **NOT:**   The new dispatcher is competent and a fast worker.

> **BUT:**   The new dispatcher is competent and fast.

NOT: The new grade of paper is lightweight, nonporous, and it is inexpensive.

BUT: The new grade of paper is lightweight, nonporous, and inexpensive.

NOT: The training program will cover
1. Vacation and sick leaves
2. How to resolve grievances
3. Managing your workstation

BUT: The training program will cover
1. Vacation and sick leaves
2. Grievance resolution
3. Workstation management

NOT: One management consultant recommended either selling the children's furniture division or its conversion into a children's toy division.

BUT: One management consultant recommended either selling the children's furniture division or converting it into a children's toy division.

NOT: Gladys is not only proficient in word processing but also in desktop publishing.

BUT: Gladys is proficient not only in word processing but also in desktop publishing.

In the last two sets of sentences above, note that correlative conjunctions (such as *both/and, either/or,* and *not only/but also*) must be followed by words in parallel form. Be especially careful to use parallel structure in report headings that have equal weight and in numbered and bulleted lists.

■ Developing Logical Paragraphs

A paragraph is a group of related sentences that focus on one main idea. The main idea is often identified in the first sentence of the paragraph, which is then known as a *topic sentence*. The body of the paragraph supports this main idea by giving more information, analysis, or examples. A paragraph is typically part of a longer message, although one paragraph can contain the entire message, especially in such informal communications as memorandums and email.

Paragraphs organize the topic into manageable units of information for the reader. Readers need a cue to tell them when they have finished a topic so they can pause and refocus their attention on the next topic. To serve this purpose, paragraphs must be unified and coherent and be of an appropriate length.

Use a new paragraph to signal a change in direction.

Keeping Paragraphs Unified and Coherent

Although closely related, unity and coherence are not the same. A paragraph has *unity* when all its parts work together to develop a single idea consistently and logically. A paragraph has *coherence* when each sentence links smoothly to the sentences before and after it.

CO8. Keep paragraphs unified and coherent.

Unity   The rationale behind striving for paragraph unity is the same as the rationale behind choosing your words carefully and constructing your sentences effectively: unified paragraphs make your writing easier to follow. A unified paragraph gives information that is directly related to the topic, presents this information in a logical order, and omits irrelevant details. The following excerpt is a middle paragraph in a memorandum arguing against the proposal that Collins, a baby-food manufacturer, should expand into producing food for adults:

NOT: [1] We cannot focus our attention on both ends of the age spectrum. [2] In a recent survey, two-thirds of the under-35 age group named Collins as the first company that came to mind for the category "baby-food products." [3] For more than 50 years we have spent millions of dollars annually to identify our company as the baby-food company, and market research shows that we have been successful. [4] Last year, we introduced Peas 'N Pears, our most successful baby-food introduction ever. [5] To now seek to position ourselves as a producer of food for adults would simply be incongruous. [6] Our well-defined image in the marketplace would make producing food for adults risky.

Before reading further, rearrange these sentences to make the sequence of ideas more logical. As written, the paragraph lacks unity. You may decide that the overall topic of the paragraph is Collins's well-defined image as a baby-food producer. So Sentence 6 would be the best topic sentence. You might also decide that Sentence 4 brings in extra information that weakens paragraph unity and should be left out. The most unified paragraph, then, would be Sentences 6, 3, 2, 5, and 1, as shown here:

BUT: Our well-defined image in the marketplace would make producing food for adults risky. For more than 50 years we have spent millions of dollars annually to identify our company as the baby-food company, and market research shows that we have been successful. In a recent survey, two-thirds of the under-35 age group named Collins as the first company that came to mind for the category "baby-food products." To now seek to position ourselves as a producer of food for adults would simply be incongruous. We cannot focus our attention on both ends of the age spectrum.

The topic sentence usually goes at the beginning of the paragraph.

A topic sentence is especially helpful in a long paragraph. It usually appears at the beginning of a paragraph. This position helps the writer focus on the topic, so the paragraph will have unity. And it lets the reader know immediately what the topic is.

Coherence   A coherent paragraph weaves sentences together so that the discussion is integrated. The reader never needs to pause to puzzle out the relationships or reread to get the intended meaning. The major ways to achieve coherence are to use transitional words and pronouns and to repeat key words and ideas.

Coherence is achieved by using transitional words, pronouns, repetition, and parallelism.

Transitional words help the reader see relationships between sentences. Such words may be as simple as *first* and other indicators of sequence.

Ten years ago, Collins tried to overcome market resistance to its new line of baby clothes. <u>First</u>, it mounted a multi-million-dollar ad campaign featuring the Mason quintuplets. <u>Next</u>, it sponsored a Collins Baby look-alike contest. <u>Then</u> it sponsored two network specials featuring Barbara Coloroso. <u>Finally</u>, it brought in the Bay Street firm of Hendrickson and Co. to broaden its image.

The words *first, next, then,* and *finally* clearly signal step-by-step movement. Now note the following logical transitions, aided by connecting words:

I recognize, <u>however</u>, that Collins cannot thrive on baby food alone. <u>To begin with</u>, since we already control 73 percent of the market, further gains will be difficult. <u>What's more</u>, the current baby boom is slowing. <u>Therefore</u>, we must expand our product line.

Transitional words act as road signs, indicating where the message is headed and letting the reader know what to expect. Here are some commonly used transitional expressions grouped by the relationships they express:

Relationship	Transitional Expressions
addition	also, besides, furthermore, in addition, moreover, too
cause and effect	as a result, because, consequently, hence, so, therefore, thus
comparison	in the same way, likewise, similarly
contrast	although, but, however, in contrast, nevertheless, on the other hand, still, yet
illustration	for example, for instance, in other words, to illustrate
sequence	first, second, third, then, next, finally
summary/conclusion	at last, finally, in conclusion, therefore, to summarize
time	meanwhile, next, since, soon, then

A second way to achieve coherence is to use pronouns. Because pronouns stand for words already named, using pronouns binds sentences and ideas together. The pronouns are underlined here:

If Collins branches out with additional food products, one possibility would be a fruit snack for youngsters. Funny Fruits were tested in Montreal last summer, and <u>they</u> were a big hit. Roger Johnson, national marketing manager, says <u>he</u> hopes to build new food categories into a $200 million business. <u>He</u> is also exploring the possibility of acquiring other established name brands. <u>These</u> acquired brands would let Collins expand faster than if it had to develop a new product of <u>its</u> own.

A third way to achieve coherence is to repeat key words. In a misguided attempt to appear interesting, writers sometimes use different terms for the same idea. For example, in discussing a proposed merger, a writer may at different points use *merger, combination, union, association,* and *syndicate.* Or a writer may use the words *administrator, manager, supervisor,* and *executive* all to refer to the same person. Such "elegant variation" only confuses the reader, who has no way of knowing whether the writer is referring to the same concept or to slightly different variations of that concept. Avoid needless repetition, but use purposeful repetition to link ideas and thus promote paragraph coherence. Here is a good example:

Purposeful repetition aids coherence; avoid needless repetition.

Collins has taken several <u>steps</u> recently to enhance profits and project a stronger leadership position. One of these <u>steps</u> is streamlining operations. Collins's line of children's clothes was <u>unprofitable</u>, so it discontinued the line. Its four produce farms were likewise <u>unprofitable</u>, so it hired an outside professional <u>team</u> to manage them. This <u>team</u> eventually recommended selling the farms.

Ensure paragraph unity by developing only one topic per paragraph and by presenting the information in logical order. Ensure paragraph coherence by using transitional words and pronouns and by repeating key words.

Paragraph Length

CO9. Control paragraph length.

How long should a paragraph of business writing be? As with other considerations, the needs of the reader, rather than the convenience of the writer, should determine the answer. Paragraphs should help the reader by signalling a new idea as well as by providing a physical break. Long blocks of unbroken text look boring and needlessly complex. And they may unintentionally obscure an important idea buried in the middle (see Figure 4.3). On the other hand, a series of extremely short paragraphs can weaken coherence by obscuring underlying relationships.

figure4.3

The Effect of Paragraph Length on Readability

<table>
<tr>
<td>

Books&More
623 Northfield Road
Waterloo, ON, N2L 6G4
519.555.3000

MEMO TO: Max Dillion, Sales Manager
FROM: Richard J. Hayes
DATE: February 25, 20--
SUBJECT: New-Venture Proposal

The purpose of this memorandum is to propose the purchase or lease of a van to be used as a mobile bookstore. We could then use this van to generate sales in the outlying towns and villages throughout the province. We have been aware for quite some time that many small towns around the province do not have adequate bookstore facilities, but the economics of the situation are such that we would not be able to open a comprehensive branch and operate it profitably. However, we could afford to stock a van with books and operate it for a few days at a time in various small towns throughout the province. As you are probably aware, the laws of this province would permit us to acquire a provincewide business license fairly easily and inexpensively. With the proper advance advertising, we should be able to generate much interest in this endeavour. It seems to me that this idea has much merit because of the flexibility it offers us. For example, we could tailor the length of our stay with the size of the town and the amount of business generated. In addition, we could tailor our inventory to the needs and interests of the particular locales. We might spend a day or two at a retirement community, where we would stock books on hobbies, fiction, gardening, and investments. The next week we might visit a town that is celebrating an anniversary, and we would stock books relating to provincial events and history. In addition, when various organizations are holding conventions in the province, we might make arrangements to park the van at a convenient spot at the convention centre and feature books of interest to the particular group attending. The driver of the van would act as the salesperson, and we would, of course, have copies of our complete catalogue so that mail orders could be taken as well. Please let me have your reactions to this proposal. If you wish, I can explore the matter further and generate cost and sales estimates.

jmc

</td>
<td>

Books&More
623 Northfield Road
Waterloo, ON, N2L 6G4
519.555.3000

MEMO TO: Max Dillion, Sales Manager
FROM: Richard J. Hayes
DATE: February 25, 20--
SUBJECT: New-Venture Proposal

The purpose of this memorandum is to propose the purchase or lease of a van to be used as a mobile bookstore. We could then use this van to generate sales in the outlying towns and villages throughout the province.

We have been aware for quite some time that many small towns around the province do not have adequate bookstore facilities, but the economics of the situation are such that we would not be able to open a comprehensive branch and operate it profitably. However, we could afford to stock a van with books and operate it for a few days at a time in various small towns throughout the province. As you are probably aware, the laws of this province would permit us to acquire a province-wide business license fairly easily and inexpensively.

With the proper advance advertising, we should be able to generate much interest in this endeavour. It seems to me that this idea has much merit because of the flexibility it offers us. For example, we could tailor the length of our stay with the size of the town and the amount of business generated. In addition, we could tailor our inventory to the needs and interests of the particular locales.

We might spend a day or two at a retirement community, where we would stock books on hobbies, fiction, gardening, and investments. The next week we might visit a town that is celebrating an anniversary, and we would stock books relating to provincial events and history. In addition, when various organizations are holding conventions in the province, we might make arrangements to park the van at a convenient spot at the convention centre and feature books of interest to the particular group attending.

The driver of the van would act as the salesperson, and we would, of course, have copies of our complete catalogue so that mail orders could be taken as well. Please let me have your reactions to this proposal. If you wish, I can explore the matter further and generate cost and sales estimates.

jmc

</td>
</tr>
</table>

These two memorandums contain identical information. Which is more inviting to read?

Essentially, there are no fixed rules for paragraph length, and occasionally one- or ten-sentence paragraphs might be effective. However, most paragraphs of good business writers fall into the 60- to 80-word range—long enough for a topic sentence and three or four supporting sentences. Notable exceptions to this rule of thumb are email and instant messages, where paragraphs are frequently only one to three sentences long.

Excessively long paragraphs look boring and difficult.

A paragraph is both a logical unit and a visual unit. It is logical in that it discusses only one topic. It is visual in that the end of the paragraph signals readers to pause and digest the information (or, perhaps, just to rest). Although a single paragraph should never discuss more than one major topic, complex topics may need to be divided into several paragraphs. Your purpose and the needs of your reader should ultimately determine paragraph length.

Words, sentences, and paragraphs are all building blocks of communication. You have seen how using a variety of sentence types, using active and passive voice appropriately, and using parallel structures can help you revise your sentences to make them more effective. You have also seen how sentences can be combined to form unified and coherent paragraphs. In the next chapter, you will examine how to further revise these elements to improve the tone of your message.

WRITING A CONCISE MESSAGE

Problem

You are Lyn Poe, administrative assistant for the Office and Information Systems Department at Dalhousie University. You have drafted the following announcement that you intend to post to the university computer network bulletin board (the line numbers are shown for editing purposes only). You now wish to make the announcement as concise as possible—not only to make it more effective but also to have it take up less space (bandwidth) on the computer network.

Administrative Professionals Workshop Scheduled for April 21

1 Wednesday, April 22, is Administrative Professionals Day, which is a
2 part of the larger observance that is known as Administrative Professionals
3 Week®, which spans April 19–25. Businesses have observed Administrative
4 Professionals Week® or its predecessor annually since 1952 to recognize sec-
5 retaries and other administrative professionals, upon whose skills, loyalty,
6 and efficiency the functions of business and government offices depend.
7   In keeping with this occasion, the Office and Information Systems
8 Department of Dalhousie University makes an announcement of its 11th
9 Annual Administrative Professionals Workshop on Tuesday, April 21,
10 between 8:30 a.m. and 3 p.m. at the Salty's Restaurant in
11 downtown Halifax.
12   Dr. Lee Stafford will begin our workshop by speaking on "How to
13 Manage Conflict, Criticism, and Anger." Stafford motivates and educates
14 people to be the best they can be, but nevertheless he likes to have a
15 good time doing it. His humour-filled presentations are packed with
16 practical information that promotes positive change. He is a licensed
17 psychologist, holds a Ph.D. in motivation, and has more than 30 years of
18 experience in speaking, consulting, and training.
19   Conflict is a hard thing to like. However, whether it involves a 19
20 client with an overdue bill or an office quarrel with a co-worker,
21 conflict is an integral part of the working world. Stafford helps his
22 clients learn that there is value to conflict. He will make a
23 presentation of techniques to handle and give criticism without
24 offense, deal with anger, and respond to hostility from others.
25   Stafford's second presentation is "Life on the High Wire: Balancing
26 Work, Family, and Play." Society has raised the ante on what it takes
27 to be a "normal" human being. There are ever-increasing demands to be,
28 do, and own more and more. Today, for the first time in our history, we
29 talk openly about burnout. Stafford will hold a discussion of the
30 successful balancing of work, family, and play.
31   Our closing session will feature Tom Graves, a professional magician
32 for more than 20 years. Graves was first influenced by watching various

magicians and ventriloquists on the *Johnny Carson Show*. He will give a   33
demonstration of puppetry, mental telepathy, expert close-up magic,   34
comedy, juggling, and balloon-animal sculpture. It would appear that   35
Graves's talents are the most unique in the world. Drawings for free   36
gifts will be held following his performance.   37
There is a cost for this all-day workshop in the amount of $125 per   38
participant. For registration or more information, call 555-7821 or   39
visit our Web site at www.workshop.du.edu.   40

Process

1. The fourth guideline in this chapter discusses four techniques for writing more concisely. Review your draft. Do you have any redundant phrases that can be eliminated?

   Oops! I see two redundancies: In line 36 I'll change "most unique" to "unique" and in lines 36–37 I'll change "free gifts" to "gifts."

2. Does your document contain any wordy expressions?

   Yes—and I can simply delete both: "It would appear that" in line 35 and "in the amount" in line 38.

3. How about hidden verbs?

   Ouch!—four of them. Here's what I'll do:
   - Line 8: Shorten "makes an announcement of" to "announces."
   - Lines 22–23: Shorten "make a presentation of" to "present."
   - Line 29: Shorten "hold a discussion of" to "discuss."
   - Lines 33–34: Shorten "give a demonstration of" to "demonstrate."

4. Any hidden nouns?

   Actually, my draft contains two hidden nouns, but I want to change only one. In line 38, I'll change "There is a cost for this all-day workshop" to "This all-day workshop costs." In line 27, I want to keep "There are ever-increasing demands to." It sounds natural, and because the announcement contains no other expletive beginnings, I think it's okay.

5. Now reread the draft to see if you can shorten other phrases either by implying them instead of stating them outright or by condensing them.

   The very first sentence contains two—"which is" and "that is"; and I can simply omit both of them.

Product

Here is the final version of the announcement, which, incidentally, contains 32 fewer words, making it more concise—and more economical.

**ADMINISTRATIVE PROFESSIONALS WORKSHOP
SCHEDULED FOR APRIL 21**

Wednesday, April 22, is Administrative Professionals Day, part of the larger observance known as Administrative Professionals Week®, which spans April 19–25.

Businesses and secretaries have observed this week annually since 1952 to recognize the secretary and other administrative professionals, upon whose skills, loyalty, and efficiency the functions of business and government offices depend.

In keeping with this occasion, the Office and Information Systems Department of Dalhousie University announces its 11th Annual Administrative Professionals Workshop on Tuesday, April 21, between 8:30 a.m. and 3 p.m. at the Salty's Restaurant in downtown Halifax.

Dr. Lee Stafford will begin our workshop by speaking on "How to Manage Conflict, Criticism, and Anger." Stafford motivates and educates people to be the best they can be, and he likes to have a good time doing it. His humour-filled presentations are packed with practical information that promotes positive change. He is a licensed psychologist, holds a Ph.D. in motivation, and has more than 30 years of experience in speaking, consulting, and training.

Conflict is a hard thing to like. However, whether it involves a client with an overdue bill or an office quarrel with a co-worker, conflict is an integral part of the working world. Stafford helps his clients learn that there is value to conflict.

He will present techniques to handle and give criticism without offence, deal with anger, and respond to hostility from others.

Stafford's second presentation is "Life on the High Wire: Balancing Work, Family, and Play." Society has raised the ante on what it takes to be a "normal" human being. There are ever-increasing demands to be, do, and own more and more. Today, for the first time in our history, we talk openly about burnout. Stafford will discuss the successful balancing of work, family, play.

Our closing session will feature Tom Graves, a professional magician for more than 20 years. Graves was first influenced by watching various magicians and ventrilquists on the *Ed Sullivan Show.* He will demonstrate puppertry, mental telepathy, expert close-up magic, comedy, juggling, and balloon-animal sculpture. Graves's talents are unique. Drawings for gifts will be held following his performance.

The total cost for this all-day workshop is $125 per participant. For registration or to receive more information, call 555-7821 or visit our website at www.workshop.msc.edu.

■ Summary

CO1. Write clearly.

Achieve clarity by making your message accurate, by using familiar words, and by avoiding dangling expressions and unnecessary jargon.

CO2. Prefer short, simple words.

Write to express—not to impress. Short, simple words are more likely to be understood, less likely to be misused, and less likely to distract the reader. Prefer longer words only if they express your idea more clearly.

CO3. Write with vigour.

Use specific, concrete language and avoid clichés, slang, and buzzwords. Be especially careful of turning nouns and other types of words into verbs by adding *-ize* (such as *operationalize* or *strategize*).

CO4. Write concisely.

To achieve conciseness, make every word count. Avoid redundancy, wordy expressions, hidden verbs and subjects, and other "space-eaters." Sometimes it is not necessary to explicitly state certain information; instead, it can be implied. In other situations, the use of adjectives or adverbs instead of clauses can convey the needed information in a more concise format.

CO5. Use a variety of sentence types.

Because it presents a single idea and is usually short, prefer simple sentences for emphasis. Prefer compound sentences to communicate two or more ideas of equal importance. When communicating two or more ideas of unequal importance, prefer complex sentences and place the subordinate idea in the dependent clause. A compound-complex sentence contains two or more independent clauses and one or more dependent clauses.

CO6. Use active and passive voice appropriately.

Use active voice to emphasize the doer of the action and passive voice to emphasize the receiver of the action.

CO7. Use parallel structure.

Express similar ideas in similar grammatical structure. For example, match adjectives with adjectives, nouns with nouns, infinitives with infinitives, and so on. Be especially careful to use parallel structure in report headings and in numbered lists.

CO8. Keep paragraphs unified and coherent.

Your paragraphs should be unified and coherent. Develop only one topic per paragraph, and use transitional words, pronouns, and repetition to move smoothly from one idea to the next.

CO9. Control paragraph length.

Although paragraphs of various lengths are desirable, most should range from 60 to 80 words. To help the reader follow your logic, avoid very long paragraphs and avoid strings of very short paragraphs.

■ Key Terms

You should be able to define the following terms in your own words and give an original example of each.

active voice (133)	dangling expression (121)
buzzword (126)	dependent clause (130)
clause (130)	expletive (128)
cliché (125)	independent clause (130)
complex sentence (131)	mechanics (119)
compound-complex sentence (131)	passive voice (133)
compound sentence (130)	parallelism (134)

phrase (129)   simple sentence (130)

predicate (129)   subject (129)

redundancy (126)   style (118)

■ Exercises

1 **The 3Ps (Problem, Process, and Product) Model: Communication Applications at World Wrestling Entertainment**   Gary Davis makes every word count as he writes letters, news releases, and email news alerts for a diverse international audience. He also develops oral and video presentations to keep external audiences updated about certain issues. Knowing that some of his messages reach many thousands of people, Davis uses simple, positive, and concise wording to clarify his meaning.

Problem

Imagine that you are helping Davis write a news release announcing a special series of appearances supporting the SmackDown Your Vote! program. Several World Wrestling Entertainment stars will be traveling to five university campuses to encourage voter registration among students who are at least 18 years old. This news release will be sent to the five campus newspapers as well as to newspapers and radio stations in the surrounding towns. Think about how you can use words, sentences, and paragraphs to explain the program, publicize these appearances, and encourage student attendance.

Process

a. What do you want to accomplish with this news release?
b. Who are your primary and secondary audiences?
c. What should you know about these audiences before you start to write?
d. Would you use any negative language in this news release? Why or why not?
e. Would you use any passive voice in this news release? Why or why not?

Product

Write a concise headline for this news release and identify three specific points you should include in the body.

2 **Clear Writing**   Re-write the following message to make sure it uses familiar words, avoids dangling expressions, and avoids unnecessary jargon. Add details as needed to make the message complete.

CO1. Write clearly.

A family plans carefully, invests cautiously, and spends wisely; then suddenly it faces pecuniary disaster because the old man is hospitalized by an out-of-the-blue illness. As a patron of Valley Insurance Company, this supplemental hospital protection is indispensable for your family's welfare. Not only will the new-fangled Group Hospital Supplement Insurance Plan help them meet their needs, but it is also as plain as the nose on your face that it is affordable as well.

As one of our cherished customers, we guarantee your acceptance. You cannot be turned down. For only pennies a day, you can ensure your financial safekeeping.

3 Jargon   Revise this paragraph to get rid of jargon and to make the passage appropriate for a first-year college student who has never taken a communication or business course.

Regardless of the medium selected, noise may be encountered after the communication stimulus enters the receiver's filter. Such a problem occurs in both the formal and the informal communication networks. Workers experiencing ethnocentrism may have special problems with language connotations.

4 Dangling Expressions   Revise these sentences to eliminate dangling expressions.

a. As a young child, his father took him on business trips to London and Paris.
b. The various levels of government maintain excellent relations with the educational institutions, but they are still not doing as much as they had expected.
c. As a community of business academics, excellent teaching is our top priority.
d. Driving through Fredericton in the fog, the street signs were hard to read.
e. To become law, the Senate must pass the bill by the end of the session.
f. Falling from the tree limb, the boy's lip was cut open.
g. Walking down the street, the crowded van drove right by the two children.
h. Trying to close the deal, the bonus offer was presented to the customers.
i. While drilling a hole to bring in the 220 wiring, a crack was created in the wall.
j. After attending the meeting, the minutes were prepared by the secretary.

5 Checking Out Chequing Accounts   When Michael Sherman, founder of Sherman Assembly Systems in Vancouver, B.C., learned that one of his employees had been robbed after cashing a paycheque, he became concerned. Sherman Assembly makes electronic cable equipment, and some of its manufacturing employees are former welfare recipients who have little experience with financial institutions. Digging deeper, Sherman learned that many of these employees used cheque-cashing services on payday because they didn't understand how bank accounts worked. He decided to educate his employees by arranging for a local bank manager to visit the factory, explain how chequing accounts work, and help employees fill out applications for special low-minimum-balance accounts.

As Sherman's assistant, you have volunteered to write an announcement about the bank manager's visit, explaining in simple and straightforward terms how employees will benefit from using chequing accounts. Follow this chapter's principles of style as you draft this brief memo, making up any details you need to complete this assignment, such as the bank name, the manager's name, and the time and date of the visit.

CO**2.** Prefer short, simple words.

6 Simple Language   Revise this paragraph to make it more understandable.

The consultant demonstrated how our aggregate remuneration might be ameliorated by modifications in our propensities to utilize credit for compensating for services. She also endeavoured to ascertain which of our characteristics were analogous to those of other entities for which she had fabricated solutions. She recommended we commence to initiate innumerable modifications in our procedures to increase cash flow, which she considers indispensable for facilitating increased corporate health.

7 Specific and Concrete Words   Revise this paragraph to use more specific, concrete language.

To stimulate sales, Mallmart is lowering prices substantially on its line of consumer items. Sometime soon, it will close most of its stores for several days to provide store personnel time to change prices. Markdowns will range from very little on its line of laundry equipment to a great deal on certain sporting equipment. Mallmart plans to rely on advertising to let people know of these price reductions. In particular, it is considering using a popular television star to publicize the new pricing strategy.

8 **Clichés, Slang, and Buzzwords**   Make this paragraph more vigorous by eliminating clichés, slang, and buzzwords.

CO3. **Write with vigour.**

At that point in time the corporate brass were under the gun; they decided to bite the bullet and let the chips fall where they may. They hired a head honcho with some street smarts who would be able to interface with the investment community. Finance-wise, the new top dog couldn't be beat. He was hard as nails and developed a scenario that would have the company back on its feet within six months. Now it was up to the team players to operationalize his plans.

9 **Conciseness**   Revise the following paragraphs to make them more concise.

CO4. **Write concisely.**

a. In spite of the fact that Fox Inc. denied wrongdoing, it agreed to a settlement of the patent suit for a price of $6.3 million. Industry sources were surprised at the outcome because of the fact that the original patent had depreciated in value. In addition to the above, Fox also made an agreement to refrain from the manufacture of similar computers for a period of five years in length. It appears that with the exception of Emerson's new introductions, innovations in workstations will be few in number during the next few years.

b. First and foremost, David Dodge is a pragmatist. The favourable advantage of that approach is that he is able to reach a consensus of opinion on most matters. He will announce his latest interest rate change at a news conference at 3 p.m. in the afternoon.

10 **Wordy Expressions**   Revise the following sentences to eliminate wordy phrases by substituting a single word wherever possible.

a. Push the red button in the event that you see any smoke rising from the cooking surface.

b. More than 40 percent of the people polled are of the opinion that government spending should be reduced.

c. Please send me more information pertaining to your new line of pesticides.

d. Due to the fact that two of the three highway lanes were closed for repairs, I was nearly 20 minutes late for my appointment.

11 **Hidden Verbs**   Revise the following sentences to eliminate hidden verbs and convey the appropriate action.

a. After much deliberation, the group came to a decision about how to make a response to the lawsuit.

b. Although Hugh wanted to offer an explanation of his actions, his boss refused to listen.

c. Nationwide Call Systems is performing an analysis of our calling patterns to determine how we can save money on long-distance telephone calls.

12 Hidden Subjects   Re-write the following sentences to eliminate the hidden subjects.

a. There are four principles of marketing that we need to consider.
b. It is a good time to invest in the stock market.
c. The new manager said it is not his duty to complete the weekly report.
d. There are several new assignments that should be made.
e. It is our intent to complete the project by Friday at 3 p.m.
f. If you are confused about the assignment, there are some diagrams that you should review.
g. It is going to be much better having this procedure in place.
h. There is a possible solution to this problem that we haven't considered.

13 Internet Exercise   Go to the Human Resources and Skills Development (HRSDC) Web site sponsored by the Government of Canada or go to any provincial government Web site. Find an article about the use of plain language in government documents, read it, and summarize it in an email to your instructor.

CO5. Use a variety of sentence types.

14 Sentence Categories   Identify what type of sentence—simple, compound, complex, or compound-complex—each of the following sentences is. Internal punctuation has been omitted to avoid giving hints.

a. Walking down the street with my sister I saw two men dressed in dark suits running out of the bank.
b. Hillary went to see the new branch manager but the manager had gone to lunch.
c. See the coach and turn in your gear.
d. When you have finished your homework please clean your room.
e. You will have 12 hours to complete the job.
f. Allen had gone to see his brother in London so he was not able to speak at the conference.
g. We will take the test on Monday although you should be ready by Friday.
h. If you want I will call her but if I don't call she will not come.
i. I will try to get the project finished and shipped to you by tomorrow.
j. The fifth order arrives today it should be the last one.

15 Sentence Types   For each of the following lettered items, write a simple, a compound, and a complex sentence that incorporates both items of information. For the complex sentences, emphasize the first idea in each item.

a. Tim was given a promotion/Tim was assigned additional duties.
b. Eileen is our corporate counsel/Eileen will write the letter on our behalf.

16 Sentence Length   Write a long sentence (40 to 50 words) that attempts to make sense. Then revise the sentence so that it contains ten or fewer words. Finally, rewrite the sentence so that it contains 16 to 22 words. Which sentence is the most effective? Why?

17 Variety in Sentences   Write a 250-word paper on any topic in this chapter using only simple sentences (one independent clause). Then, re-write the paper using the same information but using simple, compound, and complex sentences. Explain why you decided to use each type of sentence in the second version. Submit both versions and your explanation to your instructor.

18 Active and Passive Voice   For each of the following sentences, first identify whether the sentence is active or passive. Then, if necessary, revise the sentence to use the more effective verb voice.

CO6. Use active and passive voice appropriately.

a. We will begin using the new plant in 2005, and the old plant will be converted into a warehouse.
b. A very effective sales letter was written by Paul Mendleson. The letter will be mailed next week.
c. You failed to verify the figures on the quarterly report. As a result, $5500 was lost by the company.

19 Parallelism   Determine whether the following sentences use parallel structure. Revise sentences as needed to make the structure parallel.

CO7. Use parallel structure.

a. The store is planning to install a new cash-register system that is easier to operate, easier to repair, and cheaper to maintain than the current system.
b. According to the survey, most employees prefer either holding the employee cafeteria open later or its hours to be kept the same.
c. The quarterback is expert not only in calling plays but also in throwing passes.
d. Our career-guidance book will cover
   ▪ Writing résumés
   ▪ Application letters
   ▪ Techniques for interviewing

20 Paragraph Unity and Coherence   From the following sentences, select the best topic sentence; then list the other sentences in an appropriate order.

CO8. Keep paragraphs unified and coherent.

a. Businesses will spend $150 billion a year on goods and services marketed by telephone.
b. The telephone is becoming one of the nation's chief time savers.
c. Telephones save time, save money, and establish goodwill.
d. Telephones can sell an idea, service, or product.
e. Telephones can be used to answer questions, clear up confusion, and produce immediate responses.
f. More and more business is being conducted by telephone.
g. The telephone is on its way to becoming a number one marketing tool.

21 Transitions   Insert logical transitions in the blanks to give the following paragraph coherence:

Columbia is widening its lead over Kraft in the computer-magazine war. _____ its revenues increased 27 percent last year, whereas Kraft's increased only 16 percent. _____ its audited paid circulation increased to 600 000, compared to 450 000 for Kraft. _____ Kraft was able to increase both the ad rate and the number of ad pages last year. One note of worry _____ is Kraft's decision to shut down its independent testing laboratory. Some industry leaders believe much of Kraft's success has been due to its reliable product reviews.

_____ Columbia has just announced an agreement whereby the University of British Columbia's engineering department will perform product testing for Columbia.

co9. Control paragraph length.

22 Paragraph Length   Read the following paragraph and determine how it might be divided into two or more shorter paragraphs to help the reader follow the complex topic being discussed.

Transforming a manuscript into a published book requires several steps. After the author submits the manuscript, the copy editor makes any needed grammatical or spelling changes. The author reviews these changes to be sure that they haven't altered the meaning of any sentences or sections. Then the publisher sends the manuscript out for typesetting. Next, the author proofreads the typeset galleys and gives the publisher a list of any corrections. These corrections are incorporated into the page proofs, which show how the pages will look when printed. The author and publisher review these page proofs for any errors. Only after all corrections have been made does the book get published. From start to finish, this process can take as long as a year.

continuing
case 4

Stetsky Corrects the Boss

Well, Amy Stetsky opened Dave Kaplan's Microsoft Word document on her computer and prepared to edit the hard copy she had printed. It was the first draft of a speech that Dave had written and emailed to her. He was going to deliver the speech next month at a meeting of the Vancouver chapter of the Organizational Systems Research Association. Here's what Stetsky read:

Extensive research shows that lighting has a direct affect on worker productivity and job satisfaction. Lighting that is of appropriate quantity and quality provides efficient comfortable illumination and a safe work environment. They also help to develop a feeling of visual comfort and an aesthetically attractive work area. Which increases job satisfaction.

Appropriate lighting makes the task more visible thus increasing both the speed and the accuracy of the work performed. Inadequate amounts of light causes poor workmanship inaccurate work and lowered production. For example one study conducted by the general industrial corporation showed that when illumination was temporarily reduced by no more than five percent the output of word processing operators decreased by twelve percent. In addition the accuracy of all the operators each of who were paid according to the number of correct lines they produced decreased by eight percentage.

An other study at a national bank showed that errors in processing checks decreased by forty percent when lighting was increased. The productivity of the cash register clerks at a large outlet of united food marts was reduced by twenty eight percent when they were forced to work in reduced lighting for three weeks because of store remodeling. According to the researchers they also spoke with several clerks whom complained

As she types, Stetsky routinely edits Dave's memos and speeches for style, grammar, and mechanics.

about headaches and eyestrain and customers whom complained about slow lines and errors in register receipts.

As a result of such vision research forward looking facilities managers human development personnel and labor unions are all beginning to monitor carefully the quality and quantity of illumination by which employees preform their jobs. Furthermore they are looking to technology to bring more flexibility more efficiency and to provide higher quality illumination for the seeing environment. In short they are looking at light in a new light!

Critical Thinking

1. How effective would this speech section be if it were delivered exactly as written?

Writing Project

2. With Dave's permission, Stetsky routinely edits his documents, correcting minor grammar and usage errors. As she edits, she corrects punctuation, capitalization, spelling, and word division. In short, Stetsky is a professional, and her work reflects it. Assuming the role of Stetsky, transcribe the original dictation in double-spaced format (leaving one blank line between each line of type and indenting each paragraph). Make whatever changes are needed to correct errors in grammar, mechanics, punctuation, and usage. (If necessary, refer to the LABs in the Reference Manual at the back of the text.)

LABtest

Retype the following press release from Northern Lights, correcting any mechanical errors (including misspellings) according to the rules introduced in LAB 5 on page 554.

From the most northern territories to the *Maritimes* maritimes, lighting is a major component of educational costs that often is taken for granted, except when it comes to energy bills. Lighting upgrades can result in an average return on investment of *forty* forty percent. *Two* 2 years is the average pay-
5   back period.

According to the *Minister* Min. of the Environment, lighting in institutional *facilities* facilitys can consume up to one-third of a building's total energy cost. A common upgrade is the *replacement* replacment of old lamps and magnetic ballasts with new lamps and electronic ballasts. According to
10   D. J. Hill, *CMA* C.M.A. and *vice principal* Vice Principal of MacLuhan *High School* high school in Edmonton, *Alberta* Ab. "*When* when we made the upgrade, we immediately realized a savings of $30 000 a year in energy costs, which we then put directly into the classroom." The *school system's* School System's energy-savings programs are detailed in *Table 3 on page 45*
15   table 3 on Page 45 of the May *10* 10th issue of the *Business of Education Magazine* the Business Of Education Magazine.

Charlottown *Community College* community college installed more than 11 700 electronic ballasts on *three* 3 *campuses* campusses as replacements for existing magnetic ballasts. The projected payback of the $234 000 cost is
20   calculated to be less than *2 1/2 (or 2$\frac{1}{2}$)* two and one-half years.

The cost-savings aspect of occupancy sensors was demonstrated by Aurora *College* college, which turned on its new sensors at 7 *a.m.* am and turned them off at 11 *p.m.* pm. The upgrade cost the college $23 800 in *materials* materiels and labour and resulted in an energy savings of $11 500
25   per year.

5

Revising for Style: Overall Tone and Readability

an insider's perspective

ROBIN HEPPELL
Director, Heppell Funeral Solutions

As a funeral director and owner of his own consultancy firm, Robin Heppell wears a number of hats, each one demanding that he adapt his communication style, and particularly his tone, to meet the needs of a different audience. As a funeral director, Heppell assists bereaved families; as an advance funeral planner and consultant, he sells funeral services to individuals and consulting services to funeral home owners; and as a manager, he trains and motivates sales staff.

So how does he vary his style of communication to be successful in such a diverse environment? He first starts by understanding his audience.

"All scenarios are forms of negotiation," says Heppell. "The first stage of any negotiation involves listening—finding out what the other party wants and understanding their current position. The second stage involves questioning—determining the level of the other party's knowledge and also uncovering if there are needs that have not been addressed. And the final stage is educating—suggesting various options and the associated benefits."

"Know your audience and situation, and adjust your tone accordingly," Heppel stresses. Once he clearly understands his audience's needs and the demands of the situation, Heppell adapts his communication style. "When speaking with a bereaved family, I adjust to their needs by showing support and empathy; when in a managerial role, I strive for a tone of authority," he adds. And when in a sales role, Heppell understands the need for audiences to perceive that whatever they are purchasing is of value,

153

so in this environment he strives for a tone that exudes expertise and elicits trust. "It's important to sound confident, without being overbearing, pompous, or arrogant," adds Heppell. In some sales situations, Heppell actually prefers to "tone down" his expertise, "in order to gain more information or not to be seen as a know-it-all."

In one particularly tricky negotiation, Heppell was required to employ all of these tools. "I was contacted by an elderly woman's son, who thought I'd taken advantage of his mother and wanted me to explain the value of his mother's purchase of an advanced funeral plan a year earlier," Heppell explains. "With the son, I knew better than to start into a sales pitch; I just listened and kept the conversation focused on the issue. With the mother, I carefully walked her through the arrangements made a year ago, while also reselling her on the benefits of making these arrangements in advance." By the end of the telephone call—now with a crowd of bemused staff standing around his desk—Heppell had resolved the issue. "By weaving various communication strategies—listening, clarifying, directing, and diplomacy—I managed to preserve the agreement to both the mother's and the son's satisfaction."

In written communication, Heppell prefers using an indirect style for various reasons. "When dealing with clients of the funeral home, you occasionally have to sacrifice brevity to avoid appearing too direct and rigid." This indirect approach also holds true when writing to other funeral service professionals, since this is the style they're used to in communicating with their own clients. "However, when dealing with grieving families or when closing deals with funeral home owners, converting to a more direct style at the appropriate time can bring the situation to a close and to the desired outcome for all parties."

"Know your audience and situation, and adjust your tone accordingly."

■ Creating an Appropriate Tone

Having chosen the right words to construct effective sentences and then having combined these sentences into logical paragraphs, we now examine the tone of the complete message—the complete letter, memorandum, report, or the like. **Tone** in writing refers to the writer's attitude toward both the reader and the subject of the message. The overall tone of your written message affects your reader just as your tone of voice affects your listener in everyday exchanges. You also, of course, want to ensure that the overall tone of your electronic message is appropriate (see Spotlight 11, "Electronic Communication").

The business writer should strive for an overall tone that is confident, courteous, and sincere; that stresses the positive; that uses emphasis and subordination appropriately; that contains non-discriminatory language; that stresses the "you" attitude; and that is enhanced by effective design. (Style Principles 1–9 were presented in Chapter 4.)

Writing with Confidence

Your message should convey the confident attitude that you have done a competent job of communicating and that your reader will do as you ask or will accept your decision. If you believe that your explanation is complete, that your request is reasonable, or that your decision is based on sound logic, you are likely to write with confidence. Such confidence has a persuasive effect on your audience. Avoid using language that makes you sound unsure of yourself. Be especially wary of beginning sentences with "I hope," "If you agree," and similar self-conscious terms.

CO1. Write confidently.

NOT: If you'd like to take advantage of this offer, call our toll-free number.

BUT: To take advantage of this offer, call our toll-free number.

NOT: I hope that you will agree that my qualifications match your job needs.

BUT: My qualifications match your job needs in the following respects.

In some situations, the best strategy is simply to omit information. For example, you should not provide the reader with excuses for denying your request, suggest that something might go wrong, or intimate that the reader might not be satisfied.

NOT: I know you are a busy person, but we would really enjoy hearing you speak.

BUT: The fact that you are involved in so many different enterprises makes your views on small business all the more relevant for our audience.

NOT: Let us know if you experience any other problems.

BUT: Your GrassMaster lawn mower should now give you many years of trouble-free service.

A word of caution: Do not appear *overconfident;* that is, avoid sounding presumptuous or arrogant. Be especially wary of using such strong phrases as "I know that" and "I am sure you will agree that."

Electronic Communication

With workers being flooded everyday with dozens and sometimes hundreds of electronic messages in the form of email, text or instant messages, the efficient and courteous use of electronic communication is essential. Unfortunately, when electronic communication is not used efficiently, it can cost businesses millions of dollars in lost productivity. Indeed, when one British company with 25 000 employees requested employees not to email each other, they discovered that three hours a day in employee time were saved, translating to $1.6 million a month. Like any other form of written communication, electronic communication should be used courteously and effectively. Here's a distillation of what some experts have to say about the cautious use of electronic communication.

1. Keep the message short and limit it to a single subject.

One recent study predicted that by 2005, 60 billion unwanted email messages would be sent each day. With many inboxes receiving dozens of electronic messages every day, courtesy demands you keep your message short and to the point: some experts suggest no more than 35 words. While including numerous subjects may save you time, it can actually have the reverse effect on the reader's time.

2. Edit carefully and be wary of shorthand.

Wait until your email is completed and edited for spelling and grammar before typing in the recipient's address. This prevents your from hitting send before you've had a chance to edit. Remember, electronic messages are still written documents, and they say a lot to others about your credibility. While acronyms, abbreviations and other forms of electronic shorthand may reduce keystrokes, they can also create confusion. Avoid shorthand in business situations unless you know your recipient well and can be sure he or she favours this form of writing.

3. Be careful with your subject line.

Courtesy calls for a concrete subject line. Leaving a subject line blank requires the reader to open the email to find out the subject of the message. Busy readers find this frustrating and may simply hit delete without reading the message at all.

4. Create an email thread but respect bandwidth.

For ongoing discussions of a specific topic, including a copy of the original message can create continuity and streamline the discussion. Threads also give you a record of the conversation all in one place. However, as these threads grow longer, they take up more and more bandwidth, so only create threads when necessary, not as a matter of course.

5. Include contact information.

Occasionally your reader may wish to respond by phone or fax. Be sure to make it easy to do so by providing all your contact information as part of your signature.

6. Respond after receiving.

With the exceptions of SPAM and other forms of junk mail, courtesy and common sense demand that you respond to each electronic message. Even if you can't provide your reader with the answer he or she may be looking for, you should at least acknowledge receipt of the message. Not responding to messages can give you a reputation as unreliable or simply rude.

7. Use folders.

Keep your inbox free of clutter. Move important messages to folders and delete anything not essential. Some use their inbox as a kind of to-do list—only those messages still needing attention are kept there.

8. Think twice before hitting "send".

Because electronic communication allows us to respond instantly to a message, it invites quick—and sometimes poorly considered—responses. And although electronic messages are forms of written communication, sometimes their immediacy and intimacy make them more like a phone conversation than an exchange of letters or memos. But the rich non-verbal cues that are such an important and natural part of conversations (pauses, voice tone, emphasis, and the like) are missing in electronic exchanges.

Without some device to indicate tone of voice, misunderstandings might result and might lead to an abrupt or even angry response. Such a response, called "flaming," can weaken your ability to accomplish your objective.

Particular care is needed when sending messages that express disagreement or any form of negative emotion. When writing such messages, save them first, then revisit them later and decide whether the tone is appropriate.

9. Remember that nothing is private.

"You shouldn't write anything in an email that you would not broadcast at high noon in the centre of town," says Richard Rosenberg, author of *The Social Impact of Computers*.[1] Keep in mind that even if you don't intend for others to see your message, electronic messages can be easily forwarded and circulated.

Most workplaces in Canada now have acceptable use policies that deter the misuse of email, instant messaging, the internet, and anything else related to computer usage. Typically, these policies state that anything on a user's workplace computer is owned by the company and that, although a user's email is confidential, it is not private. In one high profile case, Canadian Imperial Bank of Commerce launched a lawsuit against another company, alleging it used information confidential to CIBC. To build its case, CIBC used emails sent between employees of the two companies, primarily through BlackBerrys. "People tend to look at electronic communication as less formal" says Robert Reimer, national partner of information security services for PricewaterhouseCoopers, "so they don't really believe that the information will ever resurface."[2]

NOT: I'm sure you'll agree our offer is reasonable.

BUT: This solution should enable you to collect the data you need while still protecting the privacy of our clients.

Competent communicators are *confident* communicators. They write with conviction, yet they avoid appearing to be pushy or presumptuous.

Modest confidence is the best tactic.

Positive Language

Words that create a positive image are more likely to help you achieve your objective than are negative words. For example, you are more likely to persuade someone to do as you ask if you stress the advantages of doing so rather than the disadvantages of not doing so. Positive language also builds goodwill for you and your organization and often gives more information than negative language. Note the differences in tone and amount of information given in the following pairs of sentences:

CO2. Prefer positive language.

NOT: The briefcase is not made of cheap imitation leather.

BUT: The briefcase is made of 100 percent belt leather for years of durable service.

NOT: We cannot ship your merchandise until we receive your cheque.

BUT: As soon as we receive your cheque, we will ship your merchandise.

NOT: I do not yet have any work experience.

BUT: My two terms as secretary of the Management Club taught me the importance of accurate record keeping and gave me experience in working as part of a team.

Expressions like *cannot* and *will not* are not the only ones that convey negative messages. Other words, like *mistake, damage, failure, refuse,* and *deny,* also carry negative connotations and should be avoided when possible.

NOT: Failure to follow the directions may cause the blender to malfunction.

BUT: Following the directions will ensure many years of carefree service from your blender.

NOT: We apologize for this error.

BUT: We appreciate your calling this matter to our attention.

NOT: We close at 7 p.m. on Fridays.

BUT: We're open until 7 p.m. on Fridays to give you time to shop after work.

Sometimes you can avoid negative language by switching to the subjunctive mood, which uses words like *wish, if,* and *would* to refer to conditions that are impossible or improbable. Such language softens the impact of the negative message, making it more palatable to the reader. Here are two examples:

NOT: I cannot speak at your November meeting.

BUT: I wish it were possible for me to speak at your November meeting.

NOT: I cannot release the names of our clients.

BUT: Releasing the names of our clients would violate their right to privacy.

In short, stress what *is* true and what *can* be done rather than what is not true and what cannot be done. This is not to say that negative language has no place in business writing. Negative language is strong and emphatic, and sometimes you will want to use it. But unless the situation clearly calls for negative language, you are more likely to achieve your objective and to build goodwill for yourself and your organization by stressing the positive.

Courtesy and Sincerity

CO3. Use a courteous and sincere tone.

A tone of courtesy and sincerity builds goodwill for you and your organization and increases the likelihood that your message will achieve its objective. For example, lecturing the reader or filling a letter with **platitudes** (trite, obvious statements) implies a condescending attitude. Likewise, readers are likely to find offensive such expressions as "you failed to," "we find it difficult to believe that," "you surely don't expect," or "your complaint."

A platitude is a statement so obvious that including it in a message would insult the reader.

NOT: Companies like ours cannot survive unless our customers pay their bills on time.

BUT: By paying your bill before May 30, you will maintain your excellent credit history with our firm.

NOT: You sent your complaint to the wrong department. We don't handle shipping problems.

No one understands the importance of a courteous and sincere tone better than those who work in the service industry. Here, Alexandra Melia, teen Concierge at the Four Seasons Hotel, advises teen guests on fun, cool things to do in Toronto.

BUT: We have forwarded your letter to the shipping department. You should be hearing from them within the week.

Your reader is sophisticated enough to know when you're being sincere. To achieve a sincere tone, avoid exaggeration (especially using too many modifiers or too strong modifiers), obvious flattery, and expressions of surprise or disbelief.

Obvious flattery and exaggeration sound insincere.

NOT: Your satisfaction means more to us than making a profit, and we shall work night and day to see that we earn it.

BUT: We value your goodwill and have taken these specific steps to ensure your satisfaction.

NOT: I'm surprised you would question your raise, considering your overall performance last year.

BUT: Your raise was based on an objective evaluation of your performance last year.

Competent communicators use both verbal and non-verbal signals to convey courtesy and sincerity. However, it is difficult to fake these attitudes. The best way to achieve the desired tone is to truly assume a courteous and sincere outlook toward your reader.

Emphasis and Subordination

Not all ideas are created equal. Some are more important and more persuasive than others. Assume, for example, that you have been asked to evaluate and compare the

CO4. **Use appropriate emphasis and subordination.**

Copy Cat and the Repro 100 photocopiers and then to write a memo report recommending one for purchase. Assume that the two brands are alike in all important respects except these:

Feature	Copy Cat	Repro 100
Speed (copies per minute)	15	10
Cost	$2750	$2100
Enlargement/Reduction?	Yes	No

> Let your reader know which ideas you consider most important.

As you can see, the Copy Cat has greater speed and more features. Thus, a casual observer might think you should recommend the Copy Cat on the basis of its additional advantages. Suppose, however, that most of your photocopying involves fewer than five copies of each original, all of them full-sized. Under these conditions, you might conclude that the Repro 100's lower cost outweighs the Copy Cat's higher speed and additional features; you therefore decide to recommend purchasing the Repro 100. If you want your recommendation to be credible, you must make sure your reader views the relative importance of each feature the same way you do. To do so, use appropriate emphasis and subordination techniques.

Techniques of Emphasis   To emphasize an idea, use any of the following strategies (to subordinate an idea, simply use the opposite strategy):

> To subordinate an idea, put it in the dependent clause.

1. Put the idea in a short, simple sentence. However, if you need a complex sentence to convey the needed information, put the more important idea in the independent clause. (The ideas communicated in each independent clause of a *compound* sentence receive equal emphasis.)

   SIMPLE: The Repro 100 is the better photocopier for our purposes.

   COMPLEX: Although the Copy Cat is faster, 98 percent of our copying requires fewer than five copies per original. (*Emphasizes the fact that speed is not a crucial consideration for us.*)

2. Place the major idea first or last. The first paragraph of a message receives the most emphasis, the last paragraph receives less emphasis, and the middle paragraphs receive the least emphasis. Similarly, the middle sentences within a paragraph receive less emphasis than the first sentence in a paragraph.

   The first criterion examined was cost. The Copy Cat sells for $2750 and the Repro 100 sells for $2100, or 24 percent less than the cost of the Copy Cat.

3. Make the noun you want to emphasize the subject of the sentence. In other words, use active voice to emphasize the doer of the action and passive voice to emphasize the receiver.

   ACTIVE: The Repro 100 costs 24 percent less than the Copy Cat. (*Emphasizes the Repro 100 rather than the Copy Cat.*)

   PASSIVE: The relative costs of the two models were compared first. (*Emphasizes the relative costs rather than the two models.*)

4. Devote more space to the idea.

   The two models were judged according to three criteria: cost, speed, and enlargement/reduction capabilities. Total cost is an important consideration for our firm because of the large number of copiers we use and our large volume of copying. Last year our firm used 358 photocopiers and duplicated more than 6.5 million pages. Thus, regardless of the speed or features of a particular model, if it is too expensive to operate, it will not serve our purposes.

5. Use language that directly implies importance, such as "most important," "major," or "primary."

The most important factor for us is cost.

(In contrast, use terms such as "least important" or "a minor point" to subordinate an idea.)

6. Use repetition (within reason).

However, the Copy Cat is expensive—expensive to purchase and expensive to operate.

7. Use mechanical means (within reason)—enumeration, italics, solid capitals, second color, indenting from left and right margins, or other elements of design—to emphasize key ideas.

But the most important criterion is cost, and the Repro 100 costs 24 percent *less* than the Copy Cat.

The Ethical Dimension   In using emphasis and subordination, your goal is to ensure a common frame of reference between you and your reader; you want your reader to see how important you consider each idea to be. Your goal is *not* to mislead the reader. For example, if you believe that the Repro 100 is the *slightly* better choice, you would certainly not want to intentionally mislead your reader into concluding that it is *clearly* the better choice. Such a tactic would be not only unethical but also unwise. Use sound business judgment and a sense of fair play to help yourself achieve your communication objectives.

> *Use language that expresses your honest evaluation; do not mislead the reader.*

Making Language Non-discriminatory

Non-discriminatory language treats everyone equally, making no unwarranted assumptions about any group of people. Using non-discriminatory language is smart business because (a) it is the ethical thing to do and (b) we risk offending others if we do otherwise. Consider the types of bias in this report:

> **CO5. Use non-discriminatory language.**

> The finishing plant was the scene of a confrontation today when two ladies from the morning shift accused a foreman of sexual harassment. Amna Badri, a Sudanese inspector, and Margaret Sawyer, an assembly-line worker, accused Mr. Engerrand of making suggestive comments. Mr. Engerrand, who is 62 years old and an epileptic, denied the charges and said he thought the girls were trying to cheat the company with their demand for a cash award.

> *Be sensitive to your readers' feelings.*

Were you able to identify the following instances of bias or discriminatory language?

> *Use language that implies equality.*

■ The women were referred to as *ladies* and *girls,* although it is unlikely that the men in the company are referred to as *gentlemen* and *boys.*

■ The term *foreman* (and all other-*man* occupational titles) has a sexist connotation.

■ The two women were identified by their first and last names, without a personal title, whereas the man was identified by a personal title and last name only.

■ Badri's ethnicity, Engerrand's age, and Engerrand's disability were identified, although they were irrelevant to the situation.

Competent communicators make sure that their writing is free of sexist language and free of bias based on such factors as race, ethnicity, religion, age, sexual orientation, and disability.

Sexist Language   It makes no business sense to exclude or perhaps offend half the population by using sexist language. To avoid sexism in your writing, follow these strategies:

1. Use neutral job titles that do not imply that a job is held by only men or only women.

Instead of	*Use*
chairman	chair, chairperson
foreman	supervisor
salesman	sales representative
woman lawyer	lawyer
workman	worker, employee

2. Avoid words and phrases that unnecessarily imply gender.

Instead of	*Use*
best man for the job	best person for the job
executives and their wives	executives and their spouses
housewife	homemaker
manmade	artificial, manufactured
manpower	human resources, personnel

3. Avoid demeaning or stereotypical terms.

Instead of	*Use*
My girl will handle it.	My assistant will handle it.
Watch your language around the ladies.	Watch your language.
Housewives like our long hours.	Our customers like our long hours.
He was a real jock.	He enjoyed all types of sports.
Each nurse supplies her own uniforms.	Nurses supply their own uniforms.

By permission of John L. Hart FLP and Creators Syndicate, Inc.

4. Use parallel language.

Instead of	*Use*
Joe, a broker, and his wife, a beautiful brunette	Joe, a broker, and his wife, Mary, a lawyer (*or* homemaker)
Ms. Wyllie and William Poe	Ms. Wyllie and Mr. Poe
man and wife	husband and wife

5. Use appropriate personal titles and salutations.

   ■ If a woman has a professional title, use it (Dr. Martha Ralston, the Rev. Deborah Connell).

   ■ Follow a woman's preference in being addressed as *Miss, Mrs.,* or *Ms.*

   ■ If a woman's marital status or her preference is unknown, use *Ms.*

   ■ If you do not know the reader's gender, use a non-sexist salutation (Dear Investor:, Dear Friend:, Dear Customer:, Dear Policyholder:).

   ■ Alternatively, you may use the full name in the salutation (Dear Chris Andrews:, Dear Terry Brooks:).

6. Whether it is appropriate to use *he* or *his* as generic pronouns in referring to men or women (for example, "Each manager must evaluate *his* subordinates annually") is currently a matter of some debate. Proponents argue that its use is based on tradition and on the fact that no genderless alternative pronoun exists. Opponents argue that its use appears to exclude females. Although many business people would not be offended by such use, some would be. The conservative approach is to avoid such usage whenever possible by adopting any of these strategies:

> *Excessive use of the term he or she or his or hers sounds awkward.*

   ■ Use plural nouns and pronouns.

   All managers must evaluate their subordinates annually.

   ■ *But not:* Each manager must evaluate their subordinates annually.

   ■ Use second-person pronouns (*you, your*).

   You must evaluate your subordinates annually.

   ■ Revise the sentence.

   Each manager must evaluate subordinates annually.

   ■ Use *his* or *her* (sparingly).

   Each manager must evaluate his or her subordinates annually.

Other Discriminatory Language   We are all members of different groups, each of which may have different customs, values, and attitudes. If you think of your readers as individuals, rather than as stereotypical members of some particular group, you will avoid bias when communicating about race, ethnic background, religion, age, sexual orientation, and disabilities. Group membership should be mentioned only if it is clearly pertinent. As illustrated in Communication Snapshot 4, many groups in Canada report unfair treatment or discrimination based on ethnocultural characteristics.

> *Mention group membership only if it is clearly relevant.*

NOT:	Richard McKenna, noted black legislator, supported our position.
BUT:	Richard McKenna, noted legislator, supported our position.
NOT:	Because of rising interest rates, he welshed on the deal.
BUT:	Because of rising interest rates, he backed out of the deal.
NOT:	Anita Voyles performed the job well for her age.
BUT:	Anita Voyles performed the job well.
NOT:	Patricia Barbour's lesbianism has not affected her job performance.
BUT:	Patricia Barbour's job performance has been exemplary.
NOT:	Mary, an epileptic, had no trouble passing the medical examination.
BUT:	Mary, who has epilepsy, had no trouble passing the medical examination. *(When the impairment is relevant, separate the impairment from the person.)*

The "You" Attitude

CO6. Stress the "you" attitude.

Are you more interested in how well *you* perform in your courses or in how well your classmates perform? When you hear a television commercial, are you more in-

Interestingly, age has no bearing on ability. Hazel McCallion, shown here, remains one of Canada's best known and longest serving mayors, despite being well into her 80s.

terested in how the product will benefit *you* or in how your purchase of the product will benefit the sponsor? If you're like most people reading or hearing a message, your conscious or unconscious reaction is likely to be "What's in it for *me?*" Knowing that this is true provides you with a powerful strategy for structuring your messages to maximize their impact: stress the "you" attitude, not the "me" attitude.

The **"you" attitude** emphasizes what the *receiver* (the listener or the reader) wants to know and how he or she will be affected by the message. It requires developing *empathy*—the ability to project yourself into another person's position and to understand that person's situation, feelings, motives, and needs. To avoid sounding selfish and uninterested, focus on the reader—adopt the "you" attitude.

> *Answer the reader's unspoken question, "What's in it for me?"*

NOT:	I am shipping your order this afternoon.
BUT:	Your order should arrive by Friday.

NOT:	We will be open on Sundays from 1 to 5 p.m., beginning May 15.
BUT:	You will be able to shop on Sundays from 1 to 5 p.m., beginning May 15.

One way to assess how well you've emphasized the "you" attitude in your own writing is to compare the number of "you" and "your" pronouns to the number of "I" and "we" pronouns. In most cases, the former should outnumber the latter.

Receiver Benefits   An important component of the "you" attitude is the concept of **receiver benefits**—emphasizing how the *receiver* (the reader or the listener) will benefit from doing as you ask. Sometimes, especially when asking a favour or refusing a request, the best we can do is to show how *someone* (not necessarily the reader) will benefit. But whenever possible, we should show how someone *other than ourselves* benefits from our request or from our decision.

NOT:	We cannot afford to purchase an ad in your organization's directory.
BUT:	Advertising exclusively on television allows us to offer consumers like you the lowest prices on their cosmetics.

NOT:	Our decorative fireplace has an oak mantel and is portable.
BUT:	Whether entertaining in your living room or den, you can still enjoy the ambience of a blazing fire because our decorative fireplace is portable. Simply take it with you from room to room.

Note that the revised sentences, which stress reader benefits, are longer than the original sentences—because they contain *more information*. Yet they are

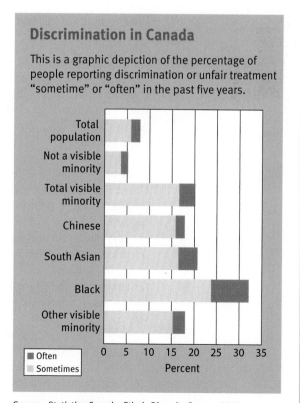

communication snapshot 4

Discrimination in Canada

This is a graphic depiction of the percentage of people reporting discrimination or unfair treatment "sometime" or "often" in the past five years.

Source: Statistics Canada, Ethnic Diversity Survey, 2002.

not verbose; that is, they do not contain unnecessary words. You can add information and still write concisely.

Exceptions   Stressing the "you" attitude focuses the attention on the reader, which is right where the attention should be—most of the time. In some situations, however, you may want to avoid focusing on the reader; these situations all involve conveying negative information. When you refuse someone's request, disagree with someone, or talk about someone's mistakes or shortcomings, avoid connecting the reader too closely with the negative information. In such situations, avoid second-person pronouns (*you* and *your*), and use passive sentences or other subordinating techniques to stress the receiver of the action rather than the doer.

NOT: You should have included more supporting evidence in your presentation.

BUT: Including more supporting evidence would have made the presentation more convincing.

NOT: You failed to return the merchandise within the ten-day period.

BUT: We are happy to give a full refund on all merchandise that is returned within ten days.

Note that neither of the revised sentences contains the word *you*. Thus, each helps to separate the reader from the negative information, making the message more tactful and palatable.

Electronic Communication and Style

The principles we've been discussing in Chapter 4 and this chapter will help you communicate your ideas clearly and effectively. They provide a solid foundation for the higher-order communication skills you will be developing in the following chapters. At first, you may find it somewhat difficult and time-consuming to constantly assess your writing according to these criteria. Their importance, however, merits the effort. Soon you will find that you are applying these principles automatically as you compose and revise messages.

Since many of you will do the bulk of your writing on computer, and much of what you write will in fact be sent to others electronically, the influence of electronic communication on style merits some discussion. Relatively new forms of communication within organizations—email, instant messaging, and text messaging being the most common—are changing, not only the way we communicate, but the very nature of communication itself. It is now common for office workers, sitting in offices mere feet from each other, to email one another rather than simply walk down the hall. Indeed, in many workplaces, the majority of employees actually prefer email over the telephone and even over face-to-face communication. And with the recent explosion in popularity of wireless email devices such as the BlackBerry, written communication, especially in the form of email and instant messaging, is quickly becoming the dominant communication channel in business. With this in mind, good writing skills may now be more important than ever.

So how does electronic communication affect writing style? Email and instant messaging (IM) often invite a more casual, even playful, approach to style. They're seen by many as a medium not restricted to the conventions of traditional writing. Take, for example, this IM conversation recorded by two researchers:[3]

Jeff: There are so much bad design
Matt: no kidding
Matt: But I still get surprised sometimes
Jeff: And so much bad grammar
Matt: Bad grammar are everywhere

Some would cite such a casual approach to writing as clear evidence that good writing is vanishing from the workplace. Others would argue that we're simply seeing a new style of writing emerge alongside the more traditional ones. The important point is, good writers know how and when to adapt their style. Because instant messaging serves the primary purpose of asking quick questions, coordinating impromptu meetings, and keeping in touch, it invites an informal style. When email is serving these functions, it too may call for an informal style.

Too often, however, writers extend this informal, even sloppy, writing style to situations that demand more care and attention. One recent study by Information Mapping Inc. revealed that 40 percent of workers surveyed said they waste between 30 minutes and three hours a day reading poorly written email.[4]

Another danger is that many writers treat electronic communication so casually that they fail to take the same precautions they do when composing traditional documents such as memos or letters. One scholar has noted that perhaps the main reason why instant written communications pose such risks is that, while they're treated by the sender as simply another form of face-to-face (i.e., casual and spontaneous) conversation, they're interpreted by the reader as written text (i.e., carefully planned and authoritative). For example, in person, a sarcastic remark made to a colleague might be accompanied by a smile, a wink, or a vocal cue to emphasize the sender's intention. With email, a similar remark, lacking the accompanying non-verbal cues, can easily be misinterpreted as offensive.

Recall that your goals for any piece of workplace communication are not only to be clear and efficient, but also to be credible. And electronic communication, like any other form of written communication, can become a permanent record, even permissible in a court of law.

In one notorious example, an angry CEO fired an email off to his subordinates, chastising them for being lazy and threatening them with dismissal. His email was quickly forwarded to stockholders, who interpreted the email as a sign of poor company morale, resulting in a 22 percent drop in the company's share price in just three days.

So while new forms of communication may invite new conventions of writing, the goal of business communication hasn't changed. Clarity, efficiency, and credibility still demand—in all but the most informal business situations—that careful attention be paid to writing and revising the message, whether in paper or electronic form. And because electronic communication can be forwarded, instantly, to numerous parties not originally intended to see your message, even greater precautions need to be taken to present your message and yourself in a professional manner.

■ Effective Page Design

The term **readability** refers to the ease of understanding a passage based on its style of writing and physical appearance. Various readability formulas, such as the Gunning Fog Index, are available that estimate the complexity of a passage on the basis of an

CO7. Design documents for readability.

*Although readability for-
mulas are helpful, other
factors are also important.*

analysis of such factors as sentence length, number of syllables per word, and word frequency. Although applying a readability formula is helpful in judging the readability of your message, you should use the results as a guide only. You could, for example, artificially change your readability score by using shorter sentences and shorter words. But sometimes a longer word is more precise and more familiar than a shorter word. Likewise, lowering the score by using all short sentences (for example, all simple sentences) might obscure the relationships among ideas because then all ideas would receive equal emphasis.

The physical appearance of your document also affects its readability. Contemporary word processing software makes it easy for writers to *design* their documents for maximum impact and effectiveness. Although the product is always more important than the packaging, there is no denying that an attractively formatted document, with legible type and plenty of white space, will help you achieve your communication objectives.

Consider the following design guidelines, which are illustrated in Spotlight 12, "Designing Documents," on page 170. Both versions of the Spotlight report contain the same information. Compare the typed version with the designed version for impact and readability.

*Use a simple, consistent
design.*

Keep It Simple   The most important guideline is to use a simple, clean, and consistent design. It would be distracting, for example, to use many different type styles and sizes in the same document. Instead, select one serif typeface (*serifs* are the small strokes at the tops and bottoms of characters, such as the "feet" at the bottom of a *T*; sans serif typefaces have no such ornamental strokes) for the body of your report and one sans serif typeface for headings and subheadings. One popular combination is Times Roman for body type and Arial (or Helvetica) for special treatments such as headings, subheadings, and captions for figures.

> This is an example of Times Roman in 10-point type. Because the serifs aid in readability, Times Roman is a good choice for the body of your report.

> **This is an example of Helvetica in 10-point type. Because it contrasts nicely with Times Roman, Helvetica is a good choice for headings.**

Similarly, it would be distracting if a reader is accustomed to seeing lists arranged in a certain format but then encounters a list formatted differently. The reader would have to pause to figure out what is different, and why. Make sure that whatever decisions you initially make about margins, spacing, headings, and the like are followed consistently throughout your report.

*The empty space on a
page also communicates.*

Use White Space to Advantage   Use generous top, bottom, and side margins to make your document inviting to read. Consider white space (the blank sections of the document) as part of your overall design. In general, the more white space, the better. Break up long paragraphs into shorter ones, and leave generous space before and after headings. Separate lengthy areas of text with subheadings. Subheadings not only break up solid blocks of type but also enhance readability by periodically providing signals for the reader.

Select a Suitable Line Length and Type Size   Line length can have a major effect on the readability of a document. Lines that are too short weaken coherence because they needlessly disrupt the normal horizontal pattern of reading. Lines that are too long cause readers to lose their place when they return to the beginning of the next line. In general, use a line no shorter than 25 characters and no longer than 75 characters for business documents. Although one column is standard for business reports, any business document can also be typed in two or three columns on a standard-sized page.

For the body of most business reports, select a type size between 10 points (elite size) and 12 points (pica size); 1 point equals 1/72 of an inch. Proportionately larger type should be used for headings and subheadings.

Determine an Appropriate Justification Format

All text lines in the body of your document should be left-justified; that is, they should all begin at the left margin. However, the end of each line may be either right-justified (sometimes called *full justification*) or ragged right. In general, a justified line presents a clean, formal look, whereas a ragged-right line gives an informal, casual appearance.

> **I'M WARNING YOU**   *word*wise
>
> **Actual product labels:**
>
> On a portable stroller: "Caution: Remove infant before folding for storage."
>
> On a package of fireplace logs: "Caution: Risk of fire."
>
> On a dessert box: "Product will be particularly hot after heating."
>
> On a hair dryer: "Do not use while sleeping."
>
> On a musical birthday candle: "Do not use soft wax as earplugs."

This is an example of a justified column, which produces even left and right margins. You should have the hyphenation feature of your word processor turned on when justifying lines.

This is an example of a column with a ragged-right margin—that is, one where the lines end unevenly. Ragged-right lines provide a more interesting, casual appearance.

Use full justification for a formal appearance and an uneven right margin for an informal appearance.

Format Paragraphs Correctly   Designed documents use only single spacing. New paragraphs are indicated either by leaving a blank line before the paragraph or by indenting the first line. Do not, however, both indent *and* leave a blank line; that would be too much. Even when paragraphs are indented, designed documents typically do not indent the first line of a paragraph that immediately follows a heading or subheading; it is obvious that what follows a heading is a new paragraph.

Writers sometimes use various techniques at the start of a document to engage the reader immediately: beginning the first word of the document with an extra-large, decorative letter; typing the first three or four words in solid capitals; or setting the first paragraph in larger type than the rest of the document. The purpose of such techniques is to make the copy attractive and inviting to read.

Emphasize Words and Ideas Appropriately   On a typewriter, underlining and solid capitals were about the only way to emphasize a word or idea. Designed documents, however, have a variety of techniques readily available—larger type size, boldface lettering, and italic type, for example. Any of these techniques is preferable to underlining and solid capitals. Solid capitals are appropriate only for very short headings. Unlike lower case letters, capital letters are all the same size and are therefore more difficult to read. Non-standard type styles, such as outline or shadow type, are inappropriate in business documents; they provide visual clutter and are distracting.

Use boldface for strong emphasis and italic for medium emphasis in the body of a document. Both boldface and italic type, along with a larger type size, may be used for headings and subheadings; just be sure your main headings stand out more than your subheadings. When headings are displayed prominently, they may be typed in

Use special emphasis techniques sparingly.

spotlight12
ON TECHNOLOGY

Designing Documents

STAFF EMPLOYEES' EVALUATION OF THE BENEFIT PROGRAM
AT ACADIA UNIVERSITY

Employee benefits are
important form of empl
non-profit organizatio
of HRDC Survey, benefi
roll costs, averaging $
1997, p. 183). Thus, o
zation's benefit prog
evaluated.

To ensure that the ben
sity's 2500 staff pers
possible, David Riggi
this report on January

Purpose and Scope

Specifically, the fol
in this study: What a
Acadia University rega
this question, the fol

1. How knowledgeable
   program?
2. What are the empl
   benefits now avai
3. What benefits, if
   added to the prog

This study attempted t
Whether the preference
in the scope of the st

Procedures

A list of the 2489 sta
fits was generated fro

Plain Version

Staff Employees' Evaluation
of the Benefit Program
at Acadia University

EMPLOYEE BENEFITS ARE a rapidly growing and an increasingly important form of employee compensation for both profit and non-profit organizations. According to a recent HRDC survey, benefits now constitute 37% of all payroll costs, averaging $9732 yearly for each employee (Berelson, 1997, p. 183). Thus, on the basis of cost alone, an organization's benefit program must be carefully monitored and evaluated.

To ensure that the benefit program for Acadia University's 2500 staff personnel is operating as effectively as possible, David Riggins, director of personnel, authorized this report on January 21, 2007.

Purpose and Scope

Specifically, the following problem statement was addressed in this study: What are the opinions of staff employees at Acadia University regarding their benefits? To answer this question, the following sub-problems were addressed:

• How knowledgeable are the employees about the benefit program?
• What are the employees' opinions of the value of the benefits now available?
• What benefits, if any, would the employees like to have added to the program?

This study attempted to determine employee preferences only. Whether the preferences are economically feasible is not within the scope of the study.

Procedures

A list of the 2489 staff employees who are eligible for benefits was generated from the January 21 payroll run. By means of a 10% systematic sample, 250 employees were selected for the survey. On February 11, each of the selected employees was sent via campus mail the cover letter and questionnaire shown in Appendixes A and B. A total of 206 employees completed questionnaires, for a response rate of 82%.

In addition to the questionnaire data, personal interviews were held with Lois White, compensation specialist at AU; Roger Ray, chair of the Staff Personnel Committee at AU; and Lewis Rigby, Nova Scotia Department of Environment and Labour. The primary data provided by the survey and personal interviews was then analyzed and compared with findings from secondary sources to determine

Designed Version

upper and lower case letters or with only the first word and proper names in upper case. Any of the following three styles would be appropriate for a heading:

Opinions of Present Benefits

Opinions of Present Benefits

Opinions of present benefits

Format Lists for Readability   Because lists or enumerations are surrounded by white space, with each item by itself on a separate line, they tend to stand out more than when the same material is presented in narrative form. You have the choice of using either numbered lists or bulleted lists. Number your lists when *sequence* is important ("Here are the five steps for requesting temporary help") or when the list is long and numbering will help when referring to a specific point. When sequence is not important and the list is short, use bullets (small squares or circles) to call attention to each item. Keep the bullets small and close to the items to which they relate. For both numbered and bulleted lists, either a first-line-indented style or a hanging style may be used. Both of the following lists are formatted appropriately:

> Use numbered lists when order is important; otherwise, use bulleted lists.

To begin using Dragon NaturallySpeaking, follow these steps:

1. Double-click the NatSpeak icon on the desktop.
2. If you wish to dictate directly into your word processing program, open that program.
3. Connect your microphone to the computer.
4. Begin dictating directly into the microphone, speaking in a normal voice and enunciating clearly. The text you dictate will appear in the active window.

Each typeface can vary in a number of important ways:

- Posture: Roman (vertical) and italic (oblique)
- Weight: Hairline, thin, light, book, regular, medium, demi-bold, bold, heavy, black, and ultra
- Width: Condensed, regular, and expanded
- Size: Text (all type sizes up to 12 points) and display (type sizes larger than 12 points)

Note how the above examples treat end punctuation differently. Typically, listed items in the form of full sentences or questions use end punctuation, whereas listed items in the form of words, phrases, or sentence fragments omit any form of end punctuation. There are certainly exceptions to this rule of thumb, and many organizations will have their own "house" style for the various elements of document design.

Use Graphics—In Moderation   When used in moderation, graphics can add interest and aid comprehension:

> Use graphics only when they help you achieve your report objectives.

   Central Airlines has been designated as the official carrier for this year's international conference in London. To receive a 15 percent discount off most coach fares, call 225-555-2525 and use this event number: XJ-1056. The reduced fares are available for one week before and one week after the conference.

This is especially the case when using charts and tables.

In addition, writers today can use files of computerized drawings, called *clipart*, that can be electronically inserted into their documents. To be effective, such clipart

✓checklist5

Revising for Style

Words

- *Write clearly.* Be accurate and complete; use familiar words; avoid dangling expressions and unnecessary jargon.

- *Prefer short, simple words.* They are less likely to be misused by the writer and more likely to be understood by the reader.

- *Write with vigour.* Use specific, concrete language; avoid clichés, slang, and buzzwords.

- *Write concisely.* Avoid redundancy, wordy expressions, and hidden subjects and verbs.

Sentences

- *Use a variety of sentence types.* Use simple sentences for emphasis and variety, compound sentences for coordinate relationships, complex sentences for subordinate relationships, and compound-complex sentences for both coordinate and subordinate relationships. Most sentences should range from 16 to 22 words.

- *Use active and passive voice appropriately.* Use active voice in general and to emphasize the doer of the action; use passive voice to emphasize the receiver.

- *Use parallel structure.* Match adjectives with adjectives, nouns with nouns, infinitives with infinitives, and so on.

Paragraphs

- *Keep paragraphs unified and coherent.* Develop a single idea consistently and logically; use transitional words, pronouns, and repetition when appropriate.

- *Control paragraph length.* Use a variety of lengths, although most paragraphs should range from 60 to 80 words.

Overall Tone and Readability

- *Write confidently.* Avoid sounding self-conscious (by overusing such phrases as "I think" and "I hope"), but also avoid sounding arrogant or presumptuous.

- *Prefer positive language.* Stress what you *can* do or what *is* true rather than what you cannot do or what is not true.

- *Use a courteous and sincere tone.* Avoid platitudes, exaggeration, obvious flattery, and expressions of surprise or disbelief.

- *Use appropriate emphasis and subordination.* Emphasize and subordinate through the use of sentence structure, position, verb voice, amount of space, language, repetition, and mechanical means.

- *Use non-discriminatory language.* Avoid bias about gender, race, ethnic background, religion, age, sexual orientation, and disabilities.

- *Stress the "you" attitude.* Emphasize what the receiver wants to know and how the receiver will be affected by the message; stress reader benefits.

- *Design your documents for readability.* Write at an appropriate level of difficulty so that your readers can understand the passage; design your documents so that they are attractive and easy to comprehend.

must be used sparingly and be well drawn, relevant, and in proper scale. Unless you are certain that a particular piece of clipart will help you tell your story more effectively, save clipart for more informal communications such as company newsletters and advertising documents. Most business reports should have a dignified, business-like appearance.

Horizontal and vertical lines (called *rules*), another graphic device, can also be used in moderation to separate different elements of the document. Horizontal rules can be narrow or wide; vertical rules (sometimes used to separate columns) should be very narrow. If horizontal rules are used at the top and bottom of a page, the top rule is generally wider than the bottom.

The 3Ps
Problem, Process, Product

WRITING AN UNBIASED MESSAGE

As chair of the employee grievance committee, you must approve the minutes of each meeting before they are distributed. Following is the draft of a paragraph from the minutes that the committee secretary has forwarded for your approval:

> Mr. Timmerman argued that the 62-year-old Kathy Bevier should be replaced because she doesn't dress appropriately for her seamstress position in the alteration department. However, the human resources director, who is female, countered that we don't pay any of the girls in the alteration department well enough for them to buy appropriate attire. Mr. Timmerman did acknowledge that the seamstress performs her job well, considering her age and the fact that she suffers from arthritis. He added that he just wished she would dress more businesslike instead of wearing the colourful clothes and makeup that reflect her immigrant background.

1. List any examples of gender bias contained in this paragraph.
   - "Mr. Timmerman" versus "Kathy Bevier"
   - "seamstress"
   - "who is female"
   - "any of the girls"

2. Are there examples of age bias?
   - "62-year-old"
   - "considering her age"

3. Are there instances of other discriminatory biases that you would want to correct?
   - Disability bias: "suffers from arthritis"
   - Nationality bias: "colourful clothes and makeup that reflect her immigrant background"

Product

Ralph Timmerman argued that Kathy Bevier should be replaced because she doesn't dress appropriately for her sewing position in the alteration department. However, the human resources director countered that we don't pay these employees well enough for them to buy appropriate attire. Timmerman acknowledged that Bevier performs her job well. He added that he just wished she would dress more businesslike.

■ Summary

Your message should convey the attitude that you have done a competent job of communicating and that your reader will do as you ask or will accept your decision. Avoid, however, sounding presumptuous or arrogant.

CO1. **Write confidently.**

Stress what is true and what can be done rather than what is not true or what cannot be done. Words that create a positive image are more likely to help you achieve your communication objective than will negative words.

CO2. **Prefer positive language.**

Use a tone of courtesy and sincerity to build goodwill and to help you achieve your objectives. Avoid lecturing the reader or using platitudes.

CO3. **Use a courteous and sincere tone.**

Not all ideas are equally important, so use techniques of emphasis and subordination to develop a common frame of reference between writer and reader. To emphasize an idea, put the idea in a short, simple sentence; place the major idea first or last; make the noun you want to emphasize the subject of the sentence; devote more space to the idea; use language that directly implies importance; or use mechanical means.

CO4. **Use appropriate emphasis and subordination.**

Use non-discriminatory language in your writing by treating everyone equally and by not making unwarranted assumptions about any group of people.

CO5. **Use non-discriminatory language.**

Keep the emphasis on the reader—stressing what the reader needs to know and how the reader will be affected by the message.

CO6. **Stress the "you" attitude.**

Use the design techniques introduced on pages 167–172 of this chapter to make your messages physically attractive, inviting to read, and easy to understand.

CO7. **Design documents for readability.**

■ Key Terms

You should now be able to define the following terms in your own words and give an original example of each.

non-discriminatory language (161)   receiver benefits (165)

platitudes (158)   tone (155)

readability (167)   "you" attitude (165)

■ Exercises

The 3Ps (Problem, Process, and Product) Model: Communication Applications at Heppell Funeral Solutions   Robin Heppell finds that many situations he faces require some form of negotiation, not just in selling his services but in ensuring both parties are satisfied with the result. This process includes *listening* to the problem or need, *questioning* to ensure the problem or need is truly understood, and finally *educating* the client so that he or she can make an informed decision. To be successful at each stage of the process, Heppell not only carefully plans his content, but he also pays particular attention to his style and tone.

Problem

Heppell has received a written letter from a funeral home owner who is asking about the benefits of having a Web site for his business. It is evident from the letter that the owner is not computer literate and is reluctantly bowing to pressure from his staff, who are trying to convince him the funeral home needs a Web site. As the strongest writer on Heppell's team, you have been asked to draft a letter to the funeral home owner and to describe the following benefits of having a Web site. Web sites are efficient: they are inexpensive to set up and to run, and they can provide a large quantity of information on funeral-related issues with just a few clicks of the mouse. Unlike newspapers, Web sites are not restricted by geography: they can provide funeral service information worldwide, including directions to various chapels and churches for upcoming services. Finally, Web sites are interactive: they can allow family members and friends to send condolences from around the world.

Process

a. Why are you writing this letter?
b. What do you need to know about your audience?
c. How can you stress the "you" attitude in your letter?

Product

Draft your letter; considering which points you will cover and in what order.

CO1. Write confidently.

2 Writing Like You Mean It Revise the paragraph to create a more confident tone.

If you believe my proposal has merit, I hope that you will allocate $50 000 for a pilot study. It's possible that this pilot study will bear out my profit estimates so that we can proceed on a permanent basis. Even though you have several other worthwhile projects to consider for funding, I know you will agree the proposal should be funded prior to January 1. Please call me before the end of the week to tell me that you've accepted my proposal.

3 Writing Confidently Revise the following sentences to convey an appropriately confident attitude.

a. Can you think of any reason not to buy a wristwatch for dressy occasions?
b. I hope you agree that my offer provides good value for the money.
c. Of course, I am confident that my offer provides good value for the money.
d. You might try to find a few minutes to visit our gallery on your next visit to galleries in this area.

CO2. Prefer positive language.

4 Positive Tone Re-write the following sentences to reflect a more positive tone.

a. You made three mistakes on your report.
b. You failed to submit the correct information.
c. If you don't get this project finished soon, your days here are numbered.
d. We will not repair your car until we get your authorization.
e. You cannot be selected without signing the enclosed form.
f. We do not sell that product in the extra large size.

CO3. Use a courteous and sincere tone.

5 Being Courteous and Sincere Revise this passage to avoid platitudes, obvious flattery, and exaggeration.

You, our loyal and dedicated employees, have always been the most qualified and the most industrious in the industry. Because of your faithful and dependable service, I was quite surprised to learn yesterday that an organizational meeting for union representation was recently held here. You must realize that a company like ours cannot survive unless we hold labour costs down. I cannot believe that you don't appreciate the many benefits of working at Allied. We will immediately have to declare bankruptcy if a union is voted in. Please don't be fooled by empty rhetoric.

6 **Evaluating Writing Style**   As a college student with a potentially bright future, you no doubt frequently receive letters from credit-card companies, department stores, insurance firms, and the like, soliciting your business. Select a letter that you or a colleague has received, and analyze it for courtesy and sincerity. Does it follow the guidelines discussed in this chapter? What is your overall reaction to the letter? Write a statement of evaluation.

7 **Evaluating Job Candidates**   Assume that you have evaluated two candidates for the position of sales assistant. This is what you have learned:

CO4. **Use appropriate emphasis and subordination.**

a. Carl Barteolli has more sales experience.
b. Elizabeth Larson has more appropriate formal training (university degree in marketing, attendance at several three-week sales seminars, and the like).
c. Elizabeth Larson's personality appears to mesh more closely with the prevailing corporate attitudes at your firm.

You must write a memo to Nahza Hammoud, the vice-president, recommending one of these candidates. First, assume that personality is the most important criterion and write a memo recommending Elizabeth Larson. Second, assume that experience is the most important criterion and write a memo recommending Carl Barteolli. Use appropriate emphasis and subordination in each message. You may make up any reasonable information needed to complete the assignment.

8 **Using Techniques of Emphasis**   Revise each sentence by applying the indicated technique of emphasis. In each case, emphasize the problems of cold weather.

a. Use one complex sentence.

Outdoor workers in Fort McMurray, Alberta, have to battle severe winter conditions. However, outdoor workers in Victoria, B.C., face mild winter conditions.

b. Choose the noun you want to emphasize as the subject of the sentence.

Telephone and utility repair personnel who work outdoors have to cope with dangerous working conditions created by sub-zero temperatures.

c. Use language that directly implies importance.

Outdoor workers generally face a range of weather conditions, but frigid temperatures can pose particularly severe problems.

d. Use repetition.

Utilities in northern Canada frequently remind outdoor workers about the cold-weather dangers of frostbite and hypothermia.

CO5. Use non-discriminatory language.

9 Using Non-discriminatory Language   Revise the following sentences to eliminate discriminatory language.

a. The mayor opened contract talks with the union representing local policemen.
b. While the salesmen are at the convention, their wives will be treated to a tour of the city's landmarks.
c. Our company gives each foreman the day off on his birthday.
d. Our public relations director, Heather Marshall, will ask her young secretary, Cheryl Lebeuf, to take notes during the president's speech.
e. Neither Rev. Batista nor his secretary, Doris Brozinic, had met the new family.

10 Sexist Language   Identify at least one non-sexist word for each of the following words: *businessman, policeman, fireman, manhole cover, waitress, stewardess, mankind, male nurse, repairman,* and *mailman.*

CO6. Stress the "you" attitude.

11 Stressing the "You" Attitude   Revise the following paragraph to make the reader the centre of attention.

We are happy to announce that we are offering for sale an empty parcel of land at the corner of Mission and High Streets. We will be selling this parcel for $89,500, with a minimum down payment of $22 500. We have had the lot rezoned M-2 for student housing. We originally purchased this lot because of its proximity to the university and had planned to erect student housing, but our investment plans have changed. We still feel that our lot would make a profitable site for up to three 12-unit buildings.

12 Reader Benefits   Revise the following sentences to emphasize reader benefits.

a. We have been in the business of repairing sewing machines for more than 40 years.
b. We need donations so we can expand the free-food program in this community.
c. Company policy requires us to impose a 2 percent late charge when customers don't pay their bills on time.
d. Although the refund department is open from 9 a.m. to 5 p.m., it is closed from 1 p.m. to 2 p.m. so our employees can take their lunch breaks.

13 Readability Level   Select a passage of at least 500 words from a textbook used in another class. Re-write the passage using the principles outlined in Chapters 4 and 5. Discuss the changes you made and the reasons you made them. Submit the copy and your revised version to your instructor for evaluation.

CO7. Design documents for readability.

14 Document Readability   Working with a partner, write a summary of Principle 7—Design Your Documents for Readability. Incorporate at least four of the design techniques presented in this section as you prepare the document. Present the document to your instructor for evaluation.

15 Document Design   Working in groups of three, reformat the press release shown in LAB Test 5 to incorporate the elements of effective document design discussed in this chapter. You may edit the document as needed as long as you do not change the basic information.

continuing
case 5

Drew Drafts a Drab Memo

Here is a first-draft memo written by O.J. Drew to Tom Mercado:

MEMO TO: Thomas Mercado, vice president, manufacturing
FROM: O. J. Drew, production manager
DATE: October 13, 20—
SUBJECT: Winnipeg Expansion

As you will remember, when we opened our Winnipeg plant, we made plans to increase capacity within three years. We're now approaching the end of our third year, and even though sales are increasing, I suggest we delay any expansion plans for another two years.

To begin with, interest rates are heading up across the board. Last week, RBC and CIBC both raised their prime rates quite a bit. This is the highest it has been in several years. Other big banks are likely to follow with similar increases. Both RBC and CIBC financed our initial efforts in Winnipeg—at a lower rate. The *Globe and Mail* predicts that interest rates will remain high for at least the next 18 months. A second reason for my suggestion is that present capacity is sufficient to support our present level of sales. If sales continue to grow substantially, we will continue to have sufficient capacity for three more years. We can increase production for minimal plant cost by simply adding a third shift. Adding a third shift will lower per-unit costs and enable us to convert numerous part-time positions to full-time positions, with a corresponding savings in fringe benefits. Finally, our union contract expires next year. Although our plant is automated, we still employ 95 unionized workers. These men's wage demands are high, and we will simply not be able to afford an expansion. I predict getting a reasonable union contract this time will be a hard nut to crack. In addition, Diana believes that if a strike is at all possible, we won't even be using the capacity we presently have—let alone expanded capacity.

For these reasons, I recommend we delay any expansion plans for another two years at least. I hope you will agree with me. Kyle Baleux does; and if you desire, we can produce a formal report of our recommendation for you to present to the board. Let me know if you have any questions.

Critical Thinking

1. In terms of what you know about Tom Mercado (see Appendix to Chapter 1 on page 35), assess the readability of this memo for its intended audience. What factors not measured by readability formulas affect the readability of this memo?

Thomas depends on specific and accurate information to successfully manage the manufacturing operations at Northern Lights.

Writing Projects

2. Analyze each paragraph, using Checklist 5 on page 172 as the basis for your analysis. What effective and ineffective techniques has Drew used?

3. List each transitional expression that was used in the second paragraph to achieve coherence. Does the paragraph have unity? Explain.

4. Revise this memorandum, making whatever changes are necessary to increase its effectiveness. You may make up any needed facts as long as they are reasonable.

LABtest 5

Retype the following press release from Dave, correcting any word-usage problems according to the rules introduced in LAB 6 on page 561.

After a hundred years, you *could've* could of assumed that there would be nothing new to say about the flashlight. With a bulb, batteries, and tube, *its* it's function hasn't changed much. However, you should not *infer* imply that the flashlight itself hasn't changed.

5   Today's flashlights are smaller and lighter than the one invented in 1898. *Regardless* Irregardless of the fact that it hasn't changed much in function, its form is now *different from* different than earlier versions.

Surely Sure, part of the flashlight's evolution *lies* lays in commercialism, but it also stems from childhood memories. You can't repeat these memories,

10   but you can create new ones to *complement* compliment them. Some of the new flashlights are already on the market; others are *imminent* eminent.

Remember the watch *whose* who's tiny built-in flashlight lets you tell the time in the dark? The next generation is a nightlight and clock, in case *you're* your really interested in the time when you visit the john.

15   In *principle* principal, a bendable flashlight is a traditional flashlight, but it also fastens to the forehead or hangs over your neck so that you don't *lose* loose your place when reading. A musical version lets *anyone* any one keep two of life's necessities at hand.

Finally, there is a flashlight designed to combat Seasonal Affective

20   Disorder, in which insufficient light *affects* effects a person's personality; it turns your entire pillow into a reading lamp.

6

Routine Messages

communication
OBJECTIVES

After you have finished this chapter, you should be able to

- Compose a routine request.
- Compose a routine reply.
- Compose a routine claim.
- Compose a routine adjustment.
- Compose a goodwill message.

Writing letters on behalf of her bunny mascot takes up a good portion of entrepreneur Ann Withey's time. Withey is co-founder of Annie's Homegrown, a $10 million business that makes packaged, all-natural macaroni and cheese products. The company is Withey's second business venture, started after she and a partner sold their first business, Smartfood Popcorn, to Frito-Lay for $15 million in 1989. These days, she lives with her family on an organic farm in Connecticut and, in between weekly visits to the company's Massachusetts office, stays in contact with employees via phone, fax, and email.

Competing against corporate giants, Withey has built her business through social responsibility and folksy communication, seeking to connect with customers on a more personal level. That's why every package carries information about social causes along with a chatty letter signed "Annie" and a drawing of Bernie, the "Rabbit of Approval." "One of the things that attracts people to our products is that Annie is real and not a made-up Madison Avenue icon," Withey explains. (Bernie is real, too; his niece, Scout, recently succeeded him as company mascot.)

While another staff member handles email messages, Withey responds to roughly 1500 letters every month. Most are requests for free information about one of the causes promoted on product packages, such as a listing of scholarships or a "Be Green" bumper sticker. Although these items are routine requests, "90 percent of the time, people add a positive line or two saying 'we love your pasta,'" she says. In response,

an insider's
perspective

ANN WITHEY
Cofounder,
Annie's Homegrown

181

Withey sends a form letter headed "Dear Friend," which opens with an expression of sincere appreciation for the reader's support and loyalty. The letter refers to the enclosed information, again thanks the reader, and closes with Bernie's picture next to Withey's signature. Making the most of every customer contact, this routine reply also includes an order form, a coupon, and information about related products and community donations.

Out of this avalanche of correspondence, about 20 letters every week require a customized response. Withey handwrites these letters, tailoring the content for each reader. "A lot of kids write about their pets and ask me about Bernie," she says. "I keep my letters light, answering their questions and explaining that Scout has taken over for Bernie. I always mention their pet's name and say how flattered I am that they took the time to let me know how much they like our products."

Withey also handwrites letters to parents who rave about the taste and convenience of her products. "Before I write, I try to envision that person sitting at the kitchen table writing to me," she says. "This helps me plan a genuine, unique letter that addresses each person's concerns." She first thanks the reader for his or her support, then picks out a specific detail from the original letter that she can discuss in her response. Finally, she closes on a friendly note by thanking the reader for "bringing a smile to my face." Withey's highly personal approach to communication reflects her overall business philosophy: "I'm a customer, too, and I treat people the way I would want to be treated."

"Before I write, I try to envision that person. . . . This helps me plan a genuine, unique letter that addresses each person's concerns."

■ Planning the Routine Message

Most of the typical manager's correspondence consists of communicating about routine matters. For example, a small business owner asks for a catalogue and credit application from a potential supplier; a manager at a large corporation sends a memo notifying employees of a change in policy; a consumer notifies a company that an ordered product arrived in damaged condition; or a government agency responds to a request for a brochure.

Although routine, such messages are of interest to the reader because the information the message contains is necessary for day-to-day operations. For example, although no company is pleased when a customer is dissatisfied with one of its products, the company *is* interested in learning about such situations so that it can correct the problem and prevent its recurrence.

When the purpose of a message is to convey routine information and our analysis of the audience indicates that the reader will probably be interested in its contents, we use a **direct organizational plan.** The main idea is stated first, followed by any needed explanation, then a friendly closing, as illustrated in Figure 6.1.

The direct style presents the major idea first, followed by needed details.

The advantage of using a direct organizational plan for routine correspondence is that it puts the major news first—where it stands out and gets the most attention. This saves the reader time because he or she can quickly see what the message is about by scanning the first sentence or two. The **indirect organizational plan,** in which the reasons are presented before the major idea, is often used for persuasive and bad news messages and is covered in subsequent chapters.

Use an indirect plan when you present negative news or anticipate reader resistance.

You may transmit your message as an intra-office memorandum (written to someone in the same organization), a letter (written to someone outside the organization), or an electronic message such as an email, text message, or instant message (written to anyone in the world with the appropriate technology). (See Communication Snapshot 5 for research showing how long it takes businesses to respond to email queries.) Regardless of the medium used to transmit the message, the principles of effective business writing discussed in Chapters 3–5 should be applied.

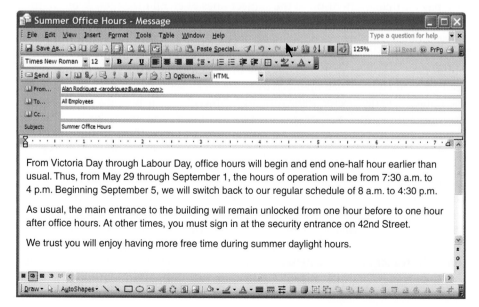

figure6.1

A Typical Routine Email Message

Unfortunately, as we discussed in Chapter 5 (see Electronic Communication and Style), many writers tend to ignore these principles when sending routine messages via electronic channels. Too often, writers using these channels view *conciseness* (incorrectly equating conciseness with efficiency) as the guiding principle of efficient electronic communication. However, sacrificing *clarity, completeness,* and *vigour* in favour of conciseness actually impedes efficiency, often requiring the reader to write back asking for clarification. This generates a greater volume of exchanges than necessary and bogs down communication. An effective routine message should accomplish its goal upon first reading; it shouldn't require the reader to ask for clarification.

Tone is another element too often forgotten in electronic communication. Numerous scholars have noted the tendency for even routine email messages to quickly and unexpectedly descend into a shouting match. Here's how one communications professional describes the pattern:

> *Employee A sends a brief request to Employee B. Because B is having a bad day, B interprets the routine request as a brusque command, and sends back a snippy response. This angers A so much that A sends a condescending reply—and copies the entire thread to B's supervisor. The supervisor reprimands B, who is now so furious with A, that B sends emails to Employees C, D, and E, saying nasty things about A. E, who is good friends with A, forwards these comments back to A . . . and on it goes.[1]*

Because routine electronic communication is often used as a substitute for face-to-face or phone conversations, and because electronic communication lacks the subtly of the spoken word (hand gestures, facial expressions, and vocal cues) the principles of tone discussed in Chapter 5 remain critically important.

Subject Lines and Routine Messages

The flood of written messages, especially email, is placing ever increasing demands on people's time. To ensure your message is given the priority it deserves, and to respect the various demands on your reader's time, always include a descriptive subject line, regardless of medium. Because of the sheer volume sent and received each day, pay particular attention to the subject lines of email messages. Avoid writing vague or misleading subject lines or leaving the subject line blank, all of which can cause problems for the reader.

Leaving the subject line blank may be fine for correspondence between friends, but in the workplace, such messages are often deleted inadvertently or they're not read until much later than intended by the sender. (Some offices even make it common practice to delete *everything* without a subject line.) Including a subject doesn't guarantee your email will be attended to, but it certainly increases the chances. Vague subject lines also present a problem. Using a subject line such as "For your consideration", or "I thought you might be interested" can be interpreted as spam by the reader—or even by overzealous spam filters. Such phrasing also shows a lack of courtesy as it expects the reader to open the message to see what it's really about. Forcing the reader to hunt for the subject of the message can delay response times and even create animosity. Misleading subject lines can actually do more harm than good. Subject lines that suggest the message is of crucial importance—using "Urgent" or "Reply immediately" for example—when in fact the message is merely routine forces the reader to give the message a priority it doesn't deserve. Writers who mislead their readers or artificially inflate their message's importance quickly lose credibility. Finally, avoid using exclamation marks in subject lines—if the message is that important, perhaps a phone call or face-to-face meeting is more appropriate.

Before learning how to write routine messages, you should know that many times a written message is not the most effective means of achieving your objective. Often a quick phone call or a walk down the hall to a colleague's office will work faster and at less expense than a written message. However, when you need a permanent record of your message (or of the reader's response to your message) or when the topic requires elaboration, a written message is more effective.

For example, if you want to confirm that the staff meeting starts at 10 a.m. tomorrow, you would probably telephone a colleague. However, if you want to confirm that a colleague has agreed to share the cost of a new advertising campaign, you would probably want to have this information on file in a written memo or email.

Of course, not all messages are routine, as we will see in the following chapters. Messages that the reader is likely to resist require persuasion and are discussed in Chapter 7, and messages that contain bad news are discussed in Chapter 8.

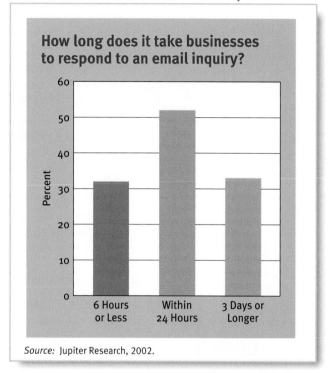

communication snapshot 5

How long does it take businesses to respond to an email inquiry?

Source: Jupiter Research, 2002.

■ Routine Requests

A request is routine if you anticipate that the reader will readily do as you ask without having to be persuaded. For example, a request for specific information about an organization's product is routine because all organizations appreciate the opportunity to promote their products. However, a request for free samples of a company's product to distribute at your store's anniversary sale might not be routine because the company might have concluded that such promotion efforts are not cost-effective; thus, you would have to *persuade* the reader to grant the request.

CO1. Compose a routine request.

Major Idea First

When making a routine request, present the major idea—your request—clearly and directly in the first sentence or two (see, however, Spotlight 13, "When in Rome . . . ," on page 187). You may use a direct question, a statement, or a polite request to present the main idea. A polite request is a statement that is phrased as a question out of courtesy but takes a period instead of a question mark, such as "May I please have your answer by May 3." Use a polite request when you expect the reader to respond by *acting* rather than by actually giving a yes-or-no answer. Always pose your request clearly and politely, and give any background information needed to set the stage. All of the following are effective routine requests:

Use a direct question, polite request, or statement to present your request.

Direct Question: Does Black & Decker offer educational discounts for public institutions making quantity purchases of tools? Pearson Junior High School will soon be replacing approximately 50 portable electric drills used by our industrial technology students.

Statement: Please let me know how I might invest in your deferred money market fund. As a Canadian currently working in Bangkok, Thailand, I cannot easily take advantage of your automatic monthly deposit plan.

Polite Request: Would you please answer several questions about the work performance of Janice Henry. She has applied for the position of industrial safety officer at Island Steel and has given your name as a reference.

Decide in advance how much detail you are seeking. If you need only a one-sentence reply, it would be unfair to word your request in such a way as to prompt the writer to provide a three-page answer. Define clearly the type of response you want and phrase your request to elicit that response.

NOT: Please explain the features of your Interact word processing program.

BUT: Does your Interact word processing program automatically number lines and paragraphs?

Do not ask more questions than are necessary. Make the questions easy to answer.

Remember that you are imposing on the goodwill of the reader. Ask as few questions as possible—and never for any information that you can reasonably get on your own. If many questions *are* necessary, number them; most readers will answer questions in the order in which you pose them and will thus be less likely to skip one unintentionally. Yes-or-no questions or short-answer questions are easy for the reader to answer; but when you need more information, use open-ended questions.

Arrange your questions in logical order (for example, order of importance, chronological order, or simple-to-complex order), word each question clearly and objectively (to avoid bias), and limit the content to one topic per question. If appropriate, assure the reader that the information provided will be treated confidentially.

Explanation and Details

Explain why you're making the request.

Most of the time you will need to give additional explanation or details about your initial request. Include any needed background information (such as the reason for asking) either immediately before or after making the request. For example, suppose you received the polite request given earlier asking about Janice Henry's job performance. Unless you were also told that the request came from a potential employer and that Janice Henry had given your name as a reference, you might be reluctant to provide such confidential information.

Or assume that you're writing to a former employer or professor asking for a letter of recommendation. You might need to give some background about yourself to jog the reader's memory. Or you might need to justify or expand on your request. Put yourself in the reader's position. What information would you need to answer the request accurately and completely?

If possible, show how others benefit from your receiving the requested information.

A reader is more likely to cooperate if you can show how he or she will benefit from agreeing to your request. In fact, it is often the communication of such benefits that makes the message routine rather than persuasive.

spotlight13
ACROSS CULTURES

When in Rome . . .

The direct organizational style is suggested for each type of message presented in this chapter. This style can be summarized in five words: *Present the major idea immediately.* North American business executives have little time and patience for needless formalities and "beating around the bush."

Such is not always the case, however, when writing to someone whose culture and experiences are quite different from your own. Business people in some countries may find letters written in the direct style too harsh and abrupt, lacking in courtesy. You should therefore adapt your writing style to the expectations of the reader.

For example, a North American manufacturer sent a form sales letter to many domestic and foreign retail stores inviting inquiries about stocking its line of fishing tackle. Note the differences in two of the responses the manufacturer received, shown below.

The moral is simple. Write as your receiver expects you to write. Take a cue from his or her writing. If the letters you receive from an international associate are written in a direct style, you may safely respond in a similar style. However, if the letters you receive are similar to the Chinese response below, you might try a more formal, less direct style when responding. Although you would not want to *adopt* the reader's style, you might need to *adapt* your own style, on the basis of your analysis of the audience.

> Would you please send me a sample of the fishing tackle you advertised in your October 3 letter, along with price and shipping information. As a long-time retailer of fishing tackle, I would be especially interested in any items you might have for fly fishing.
>
> Since the trout season starts in six weeks, I would appreciate having this information as soon as possible.

North American Request

> It was with great pleasure that we received your letter dated 3 October. We send our deepest respects and wish to inform you that Yoon Sung Fishing Tackle Company, Ltd., has been selling fishing items for 38 years.
>
> We would be pleased to consider your merchandise. May we ask you to please send us samples, prices, and shipping information. It will be a great pleasure to conduct business with your company.

Chinese Request

Will you please help us serve you better by answering several questions about your banking needs. We're building a branch bank in your neighbourhood and would like to make it as convenient for you as possible.

In general, you should identify reader benefits when they may not be obvious to the reader, but you need not belabour the point if such benefits are obvious. For example, a memo asking employees to recycle their paper and plastic trash would probably not need to discuss the value of recycling, since most readers would already be familiar with the advantages of recycling.

Friendly Closing

In your final paragraph, assume a friendly tone. Close by expressing appreciation for the assistance to be provided (but without seeming to take the recipient's cooperation

Close on a friendly note.

figure6.2

**Ineffective Example of
a Routine Request**

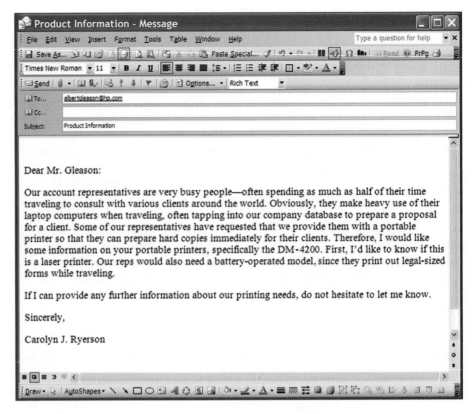

Dear Mr. Gleason:

Our account representatives are very busy people—often spending as much as half of their time traveling to consult with various clients around the world. Obviously, they make heavy use of their laptop computers when traveling, often tapping into our company database to prepare a proposal for a client. Some of our representatives have requested that we provide them with a portable printer so that they can prepare hard copies immediately for their clients. Therefore, I would like some information on your portable printers, specifically the DM-4200. First, I'd like to know if this is a laser printer. Our reps would also need a battery-operated model, since they print out legal-sized forms while traveling.

If I can provide any further information about our printing needs, do not hesitate to let me know.

Sincerely,

Carolyn J. Ryerson

for granted), by stating and justifying any deadlines, or by offering to reciprocate. Make your ending friendly, positive, and original, as illustrated by the following examples:

> Please let me know if I can return the favour.

> We appreciate you providing this information, which will help us make a fairer evaluation of Janice Henry's qualifications for this position.

> May I please have the product information by October 1, when I place my Christmas wholesale orders? That way, I will be able to include Research In Motion products in my holiday sales.

Figure 6.2 illustrates how *not* to write an effective routine request. Model 2 (page 189), a revised version of the ineffective example, illustrates the guidelines discussed previously for writing an effective routine request.

■ Routine Replies

co2. **Compose a routine reply.**

Routine replies provide the information requested in the original message or otherwise comply with the writer's request. Like the original request letters, they are organized in a direct organizational style, putting the "good news"—the fact that you're responding favourably—up front.

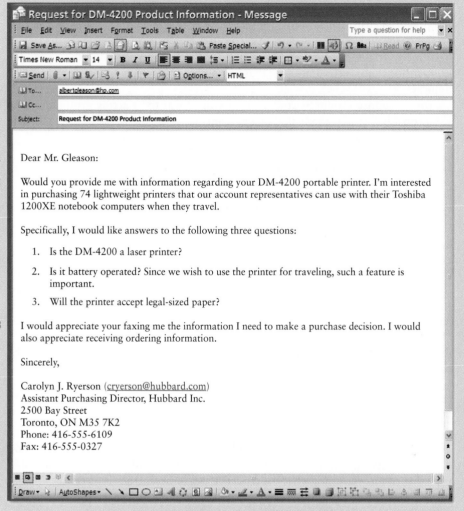

model 2

ROUTINE REQUEST

This message is from a potential customer to a manufacturer.

Presents the request in the first sentence, followed by the reason for asking.

Enumerates questions for emphasis and clarity; makes questions easy to answer.

Expresses appreciation, hints at a reader benefit.

Email screen content:

Request for DM-4200 Product Information - Message

File   Edit   View   Insert   Format   Tools   Table   Window   Help

Type a question for help

Times New Roman   14

To...   albertgleason@hp.com

Cc...

Subject: Request for DM-4200 Product Information

1   Dear Mr. Gleason:

2   Would you provide me with information regarding your DM-4200 portable printer. I'm interested in purchasing 74 lightweight printers that our account representatives can use with their Toshiba 1200XE notebook computers when they travel.

Specifically, I would like answers to the following three questions:

1. Is the DM-4200 a laser printer?

2. Is it battery operated? Since we wish to use the printer for traveling, such a feature is important.

3. Will the printer accept legal-sized paper?

3   I would appreciate your faxing me the information I need to make a purchase decision. I would also appreciate receiving ordering information.

Sincerely,

Carolyn J. Ryerson (cryerson@hubbard.com)
Assistant Purchasing Director, Hubbard Inc.
2500 Bay Street
Toronto, ON M35 7K2
Phone: 416-555-6109
Fax: 416-555-0327

Draw   AutoShapes

Grammar and Mechanics Notes

1 Format email messages for easy readability—and always proofread before sending.

2 *your DM-4200 portable printer.:* Use a period after a polite request.

3 *I would appreciate your faxing:* Use the possessive form of a pronoun *(your)* before a gerund *(faxing)*.

Respond promptly so that the information will arrive in time to be used.

Probably one of the most important guidelines to follow is to answer promptly. If a potential customer asks for product information, ensure that the information arrives before the customer must make a purchase decision. Otherwise, the time it took you to respond will have been wasted. Also, delaying a response might send the unintentional non-verbal message that you do not want to comply with the writer's request.

Your response should be courteous. If you appear to be acting grudgingly, you will probably lose any goodwill that a gracious response might have earned for you or your organization.

NOT: Although we do not generally provide the type of information you requested, we have decided to do so in this case.

BUT: We are happy to provide the information you requested.

Major Idea First

Grant the request or give the requested information early in the message. Doing so not only saves the reader's time but also puts him or her in a good state of mind immediately. Although the reader may be pleased to hear "We have received your letter of June 26," such news is not nearly so eagerly received as telling the reader "I would be pleased to speak at your Engineering Society meeting on August 8; thanks for thinking of me." Put the good news up front—where it will receive the most emphasis.

Explanation and Details

Be sure to answer all the questions asked or implied, using objective and clearly understood language. Although it is often helpful to provide additional information or suggestions, you should never fail to at least address all the questions asked—even if your answer is not what the reader hopes to hear. Questions are usually answered in the order in which they were asked, but consider rearranging them if a different order makes more sense.

The reader will probably be in a positive mood as the result of your letter, and you may consider either including some sales promotion, if appropriate, or building goodwill, by implying characteristics about your organization such as public spiritedness, quality products, social responsibility, or concern for employees. To be effective, sales promotion and goodwill appeals should be subtle; avoid exaggeration and do not devote too much space to such efforts.

CATHY   **by Cathy Guisewite**

Often the writer's questions have been asked by others many times before; in such a situation, a form letter may be the most appropriate way to respond. A **form letter** is a letter with standardized wording that is sent to different people. With word processing, it is often difficult to tell the difference between a form letter and a personal letter. If a stockholder wrote asking why your company conducted business in Sudan, a personal reply would probably be appropriate. However, if a potential stockholder wrote asking for a copy of your latest annual report, you might simply send an annual report, along with a form letter such as the following:

> We are happy to send you our latest annual report. Also enclosed is a copy of a recent profile of Dennison Industries contained in the June issue of *Profit* magazine.

> As you study our annual report, note the diversity of our product offerings—from men's clothing to massive earth movers. This diversity is one of the reasons we have shown a profit for each of the past 57 years. Our 5-, 10-, and 15-year income statements are shown on page 8 of the enclosed report.
> Dennison Industries stock is traded on the Toronto Stock Exchange, listed under "DenIn." Simply call your local broker to join the 275 000 other satisfied investors in Dennison Industries common stock.

Consider using form letters for answering frequent requests.

In the body of your message, refer to any enclosure and then add an enclosure notation at the bottom of the letter. Referring to a specific page of an enclosed brochure or to a particular paragraph of an enclosed document helps ensure that such enclosures will be read.

Refer to any enclosures in your letter to make sure they are read.

Friendly Closing

Close your letter on a positive, friendly note. Avoid such clichés as "If you have additional questions, please don't hesitate to let me know." Use original wording, personalized especially for the reader.

Model 3 on page 192 is a routine reply to the request shown in Model 2 on page 189. The original request asked three questions about the printer, and the answers are as follows:

1. No, the DM-4200 is not a laser printer.
2. No, it is not battery operated.
3. Yes, it does accept legal-sized paper.

As you can see, only one of the three questions can be answered with an unqualified "yes," and that is the question with which the respondent chose to lead off. Positive language helps soften the impact of the negative responses to the other three questions. Also, reader benefits are stressed throughout the letter. Instead of just describing the features, the writer shows how the features can benefit the reader.

Use positive language to create a positive impression.

WORDS WORTH   *word*wise

The longest word you can spell without repeating a letter: *Uncopyrightable.* It uses 15 of the 26 letters.
The longest word with just one vowel: *strengths.*
The word with the longest definition in most dictionaries: *set.*
In the *Oxford English Dictionary*, the verb *set* has over 430 meanings consisting of approximately 60 000 words.
The longest common word without an *a, e, i, o,* or *u: rhythms.*
The only two common words with six consonants in a row: *catchphrase* and *latchstring.*
Beijing has three dotted letters in a row. So does *Fiji* and *hijinks.*

model3

ROUTINE REPLY

This letter responds to the request in Model 2 on page 189.

Begins by answering the "yes" question first.

Answers all questions, using positive language and pointing out the benefits of each feature.

Uses paragraphs instead of enumeration to answer each question because each answer requires elaboration.

Gives important purchase information; closes on a forward-looking note.

Di-Mark
320 Industrial Avenue
Palo Alto, CA 94300
TEL 650.555.1200

September 12, 20—

Ms. Carolyn J. Ryerson
Assistant Purchasing Director
Hubbard Inc.
2500 Bay Street
Toronto, ON M35 7K2

Dear Ms. Ryerson:

Subject: Information You Requested About the DM-4200

Yes, our popular DM-4200 printer does accept legal-sized paper. Its 38-centimetre carriage will enable your representatives to print out complex spreadsheets while on the road. Of course, it also adjusts easily to fit standard 21.6 × 27.9 centimetre paper.

1   For quiet operation and easy portability, the Di-Mark uses ink-jet printing on plain paper. This technology provides nearly the same quality output as a laser printer at less than half the cost.

Although many travellers use their computers on a plane or in their automobiles, they typically wait until reaching their destination to print out their
2   documents. Thus, the DM uses AC power only, thereby reducing its weight by nearly half a kilogram. The extra-long 3.66-metre power cable will let you power-up your printer easily no matter where the electrical outlet is hidden.

3   To take the DM-4200 for a test drive, call your local Future Shop at 800-555-2189. They will show you how to increase your productivity while increasing your luggage weight by less than 2 kilograms.

Sincerely yours,

Albert Gleason

Albert Gleason, Sales Manager

juc
4   By Fax

Grammar and Mechanics Notes

1 *ink-jet printing:* Hyphenate a compound adjective before a noun.

2 *its:* Do not confuse *its* (the possessive pronoun) with *it's* (the contraction for "it is").

3 *a test drive,:* Place a comma after an introductory expression.

4 *By Fax:* For reference purposes, include a delivery notation if appropriate.

✓checklist6

Routine Requests and Replies

Routine Requests

- Present the major request in the first sentence or two, preceded or followed by reasons for making the request.

- Provide any needed explanation or details.

- Phrase each question so that it is clear, is easy to answer, and covers only one topic. Ask as few questions as possible, but if several questions are necessary, number them and arrange them in logical order.

- If appropriate, incorporate reader benefits and promise confidentiality.

- Close on a friendly note by expressing appreciation, justifying any necessary deadlines, offering to reciprocate, or otherwise making your ending personal and original.

Routine Replies

- Answer promptly and graciously.

- Grant the request or begin giving the requested information in the first sentence or two.

- Address all questions asked or implied; include additional information or suggestions if that would be helpful.

- Include subtle sales promotion if appropriate.

- Consider developing a form letter for frequent requests.

- Refer to any items you enclose with the letter, and insert an enclosure notation at the bottom.

- Close on a positive and friendly note, and use original wording.

Checklist 6 summarizes the points you should consider when writing and responding to routine requests. Use this checklist as a guide in structuring your message and in evaluating the effectiveness of your first draft. In addition, when composing messages that have legal implications, follow the strategies provided in Spotlight 14, "Messages with Legal Implications," on page 194.

Ed Mirvish (better known as Honest Ed) is so well respected for his customer and community focus that thousands of Torontonians attend his party each year in "Mirvish Village", the area surrounding his store, including the city's mayor and chief of police.

Messages with Legal Implications

All written messages carry certain legal implications. For example, if you knowingly write something false about a company that results in damages to that company's reputation or financial well-being, you are guilty of libel. Therefore, in all messages ensure that your information is accurate and that your message does not violate any federal or provincial laws.

Some types of messages have special legal implications. Follow these guidelines when writing letters of recommendation, letters rejecting a job applicant, and memos containing personnel evaluations.

Writing a Letter of Recommendation

1. Be fair—to yourself, to the prospective employer, to the applicant who you're recommending, and to the other applicants for the same position.
2. Begin by giving the name of the applicant, the position for which the applicant is applying, and the nature and length of your relationship with the applicant.
3. Label the information "confidential," and state that you were asked to provide this information.
4. Discuss only job-related traits and behaviours, be as objective as possible, and support your statements with specific examples.
5. If writing a recommendation for a specific position, answer all questions asked and gear your comments to the applicant's qualifications for the particular job.
6. Close by giving an overall summary of your evaluation.

Rejecting a Job Applicant

1. Keep the letter short; the candidate is anxious to learn whether your decision is "yes" or "no."
2. Provide a short, supportive buffer, thanking the candidate for applying and perhaps mentioning some specific positive comment about the candidate's résumé or interview.
3. Indicate that another candidate was chosen (not that the reader was *not* chosen), and briefly explain why.
4. Close on an off-the-topic note, perhaps thanking the reader for applying or extending best wishes.

Writing a Personnel Evaluation

1. Be fair—to yourself, to the employee, and to the organization.
2. Discuss only job-related behaviours and traits.
3. Document any praise or criticism with specific examples. Avoid exaggeration—either positive or negative.
4. Ensure that any negative information receives only the appropriate amount of emphasis.
5. Emphasize the improvement aspect of the evaluation; that is, state specifically what steps should be taken to improve performance, and discuss the specific support management will provide to assist the employee in making the desired improvements. If possible, include a reasonable timeline for improvements to be made.
6. Close with an overall summary of your evaluation or with a friendly, forward-looking comment.

■ Routine Claims

CO3. Compose a routine claim.

A **claim** (typically in the form of a letter or email) is written by the buyer to the seller, seeking some type of action to correct a problem with the seller's product or service. The purchaser may be an individual or an organization. A claim differs from a simple complaint in that it requests some type of adjustment (such as repairing or replacing the product). As a matter of fact, many written complaints would probably be more successful if they carried an implied claim that the writer wanted some adjustment to be made as a result of poor service, unfair practices, or the like. The desired adjustment might be nothing more than an explanation or apology, but the mere fact that you request some direct action will increase your chances of getting a satisfactory response.

A claim can be considered routine if you can reasonably anticipate that the reader will comply with your request. If, for example, you ordered a shipment of shoes for your store that were advertised at $23.50 each and the wholesaler charged you $32.50 instead, you would write a routine claim, asking the seller to correct the error. But suppose the wholesaler marked the price down to $19.50 two days after you placed your order. Then instead of writing a routine claim, you might want to write a persuasive claim, trying to convince the wholesaler to give you the lower price. (Persuasive claims are discussed in the next chapter.)

Contemporary corporate culture places a premium on product quality and customer service, and most companies make a genuine effort to settle claims from customers. They want to know if their customers are dissatisfied with their products so that they can correct the situation. A dissatisfied customer may not only refuse to purchase additional products from the offending company but may also tell others about the bad experience. One study of consumers showed that the typical dissatisfied customer tells 9–13 other people about the incident and that each of them, in turn, tell four or five more people. The typical satisfied customer, on the other hand, recommends the product or service to four or five other people.[2]

Write your claim promptly—as soon as you've identified a problem. Delaying unnecessarily might not only push you past the warranty date but also raise suspicions about the validity of your claim; the more recent the purchase, the more valid your claim will appear.

Although some consumer advocates suggest sending your claim to the company president, business courtesy argues for first giving the company's order department or customer relations department an opportunity to solve the problem. Such departments are designed to handle these problems most efficiently; and their employees are the most knowledgeable about specific company policies and procedures, warranty information, and the like. Only if your claim is not settled satisfactorily at this level should you then appeal to a higher level of management in the company.

Major Idea First

Although you may be frustrated or angry as a result of the situation, remember that the person to whom you're writing was not *personally* responsible for your problem. Be courteous and avoid emotional language. Assume that the company is reasonable and will do as you reasonably ask. Avoid any hint of anger, sarcasm, threat, or exaggeration. A reader who becomes angry as a result of the strong language in your claim will be less likely to do as you ask. Instead, using factual and unemotional language, begin your routine claim directly, telling exactly what the problem is.

Assume a courteous tone; avoid emotionalism.

NOT: You should be ashamed at your dishonest advertising for the DVD *Safety Is Job One.*

BUT: The DVD *Safety Is Job One* that I rented for $125 from your company last week lived up to our expectations in every way but one.

NOT: I am disgusted at the way United Express cheated me out of $12.50 last week. What a rip-off!

BUT: An overnight letter that I mailed on December 3 did not arrive the next day, as promised by United Express.

Explanation and Details

Provide needed details.

After you have identified the problem, begin your explanation. Provide as much background information as necessary—dates, model numbers, amounts, photocopies of cancelled cheques or correspondence, and the like. Use a confident tone and logic (rather than emotion) to present your case. Write in an impersonal style, avoiding the use of "you" pronouns so as not to link your reader too closely to the negative news.

NOT: I delivered this letter to you sometime in the early afternoon on December 3. Although you promised to deliver it by 3 p.m. the next day, you failed to do so.

BUT: As shown on the enclosed copy of my receipt, I delivered this letter to United Express at 3:30 p.m. on December 3. According to the sign displayed in the office, any package received by 4 p.m. is guaranteed to arrive by 3 p.m. the following business day.

If possible, mention something positive about the product.

Tell exactly what went wrong and how you were inconvenienced. If it is true and relevant, mention something positive about the company or its products to make your letter appear reasonable.

According to the enclosed arrival receipt, my letter was not delivered until 8:30 a.m. on December 5. Because the letter contained material needed for a dinner meeting on December 4, it arrived too late to be of any use. This is not the type of on-time service I've routinely received from United Express during the eight years I've been using your delivery system.

In writing, tone is much more difficult to control than in face-to-face communication, which has a broader range of communication channels. Here, Dr. David Suzuki uses body language, tone of voice, and facial expressions to win the confidence of others.

Request for Action and Confident Close

Finally, tell what type of adjustment you expect. Do you want the company to replace the product, repair it, issue a refund, simply apologize, or what? End the letter on a confident note.

I would appreciate your refunding my $12.50, thereby re-establishing my confidence in United Express.

In some situations, you may not know what type of adjustment is reasonable; then, you would leave it up to the reader to suggest an appropriate course of action. This might be the situation when you suffered no monetary loss but simply wish to avoid an unpleasant situation in the future (such as discourteous service, long lines, or ordering the wrong model because of having received incomplete or misleading information).

Please let me know how I might avoid this problem in the future.

Model 4 on the following page illustrates a routine claim letter about a defective product, asking for a specific remedy.

■ Routine Adjustments

An **adjustment** is written to inform a customer of the action taken in response to the customer's claim letter. Few people bother to write a claim unless they have a real problem, so most claims that companies receive are legitimate and are adjusted according to the individual situation. If the action taken is what the customer asked for or expected, a routine adjustment using the direct organizational plan would be written.

You should note that *anyone* in an organization may be called upon to write claim and adjustment messages—not just those working in sales or customer service. For example, an accounting manager may send (and receive) a message complaining of poor service from an employee.

CO4. Compose a routine adjustment.

An adjustment letter responds to a claim letter.

Overall Tone

A claim represents a possible loss of goodwill and confidence in your organization or its products. Because the customer is upset, the overall tone of your adjustment message is crucial. Since you have already decided to honour the claim, your best strategy is to adopt a gracious, trusting tone. Give your customer the benefit of the doubt. It does not make sense to adopt a grudging or resentful tone and risk losing whatever goodwill you might have gained from granting the adjustment.

Adopt a gracious, confident tone for your adjustment letters.

NOT: Although our engineers do not understand how this problem could have occurred if the directions had been followed, we are nevertheless willing to repair your generator free of charge.

BUT: We are happy to repair your generator free of charge. Within ten days, a factory representative will call you to schedule a convenient time to make the repair.

Avoid using negative language when describing the basis for the claim.

Your overall tone should show confidence both in the reader's honesty and in the essential worth of your own organization and its products. To the extent possible, use neutral or positive language in referring to the claim (for example, write "the situation" instead of "your complaint"). Also avoid appearing to doubt the reader. Instead of saying "you claim that," use more neutral wording, such as "you state that."

Finally, respond promptly. Your customer is already upset; the longer this anger remains, the more difficult it will be to overcome.

Good News First

Nothing that you are likely to tell the reader will be more welcomed than the fact that you are granting the claim, so put this news up front—in the very first sentence

model 4

ROUTINE CLAIM— REMEDY SPECIFIED

This claim letter is about a defective product.

Identifies the problem immediately and tells how the writer was inconvenienced.

Provides the needed details in a non-emotional, business-like manner.

Identifies and justifies the specific remedy requested.

Closes on a confident note.

 **OTIS CANDY COMPANY**   Box 302, Winnipeg, MB, R3T 2P5 919-555-4022
                                                            www.otiscandy.com

April 14, 20—

1 Customer Relations Representative
Sir Speedy, Inc.
26722 Upper James Street
Hamilton, ON L9P 2Z7

Dear Customer Relations Representative:

Subject: Poor Quality of Photocopying

The poor quality of the 13-page full-colour handout you duplicated for me on April 8 made the handouts unsuitable for use in my recent presentation. As a result, I had to use black-and-white copies duplicated in-house instead.

2 As you can see from the enclosed handout, the colours often run together and the type is fuzzy. The photocopying is not equivalent in quality to that illustrated in
3 Sir Speedy's advertisement on page 154 of the April issue of *Report on Business*.

I have already given the presentation for which these handouts were made, so re-duplicating them would not solve the problem. Because I have not yet paid your Invoice 4073 for $438.75, would you please cancel this charge.

4 I know that despite one's best efforts, mistakes will occasionally happen, and I am confident that you will correct this problem promptly.

Sincerely,

Claire D. Scriven
Claire D. Scriven
Marketing Manager

ric
Enclosure

Grammar and Mechanics Notes

1 If an addressee's name is unknown, you may use a title in both the inside address and the salutation.

2 *run together and:* Do not insert any punctuation before the *and* separating the two independent clauses because the second clause, "the type is fuzzy," is so short.

3 April issue of *Report on Business:* Italicize magazine titles.

4 *occasionally:* Note that this word has two *c*'s and one *s*.

if possible. The details and background information will come later, as illustrated by the following examples:

A new copy of the *Oxford Canadian Dictionary* is on its way to your office, and I assure you that no pages are missing from this copy. I checked it myself!

The enclosed $17.50 cheque reimburses you for your company's delayed overnight letter. Thank you for bringing this matter to my attention.

Thanks to you, we have undertaken a new training program for our housekeeping staff. Please use the enclosed coupon for two nights' free stay at the Ambassador to see for yourself the difference your letter has made.

It is often appropriate to thank the reader for giving you an opportunity to resolve the situation, but what about apologizing? An apology, which tends to emphasize the negative aspects of the situation, is generally not advised for small, routine claims that are promptly resolved to the customer's satisfaction. Instead, emphasize the positive aspects and look forward to future transactions. If, however, the customer has been severely inconvenienced or embarrassed and the company is clearly at fault, a sincere apology would be in order. In such a situation, first give the good news and then apologize in a businesslike manner; avoid repeating the apology in the closing lines.

It is appropriate to apologize for serious problems.

I have contracted with a local mason to rebuild your home's brick walkway, which our driver damaged on February 23. I am truly sorry for the inconvenience this situation has caused you and am grateful for your understanding.

Explanation

After presenting the "good news," you must educate your reader as to why the problem occurred and, if appropriate, what steps you've taken to make sure it doesn't recur. Explain the situation in sufficient detail to be believable, but don't belabour the reason for the problem. Emphasize the fact that you stand behind your products. Avoid using negative language, don't pass the buck, and don't hide behind a "mistakes-will-happen" attitude.

Let me explain what happened. On December 4, the plane that had your letter in its cargo bay could not land at Pearson International because of a snowstorm and was diverted to Detroit. Although our Detroit personnel worked overtime to reload the mail onto a delivery truck, which was then driven to Toronto, the shipment did not arrive until early on December 5.

Explain specifically, but briefly, what went wrong.

Because the reader's faith in your products has been shaken, you also have a sales job to do. You must build into your message **resale**—that is, information that reestablishes the customer's confidence in the product purchased or in the company that sells the product. To be believable, do *not* promise that the problem will never happen again; that's unrealistic. Do, however, use specific language, including facts and figures when possible.

Use resale to reassure the customer of the worth of your products.

NOT: We can assure you that this situation will not happen again.

BUT: Fortunately, such incidents are rare. For example, even considering bad weather, airline strikes, and the like, United Express has maintained an on-time delivery record of 97.6 percent during the past 12 months. No other delivery service even comes close to this record.

If the customer is at fault, explain in tactful, impersonal language how to avoid such problems in the future.

Sometimes you may decide to honour a claim even when the customer is at fault—perhaps because the writer has been a good customer for many years or represents important potential business. In such situations, your beginning paragraph should still convey the good news that you're honouring the claim, but you might temper the enthusiasm a bit. And in the explanatory paragraphs, you would tactfully communicate to the reader the facts surrounding the case—that the reader is at fault, the product was misused, the warranty has expired, or whatever the situation requires.

On the one hand, it is necessary to inform the reader of the circumstances so that he or she won't keep repeating the problem. On the other hand, if you do so in an insulting manner, you will lose the reader's goodwill. Instead, use impersonal, tactful language, taking special pains not to lecture the reader or sound condescending. For example, in the following adjustment, note that the pronoun *you* is not used at all in the fourth sentence, where the problem—the customer's misuse of the equipment—is identified.

> Because we value your friendship, we are pleased to repair your Braniff 250 copier free of charge. Our maintenance technician tells me that she took care of the problem on September 15.
>
> Your machine's register indicated that 9832 copies had been made since the copier was installed on July 18. The Braniff 250 is designed for low-level office use—fewer than 1500 copies per month. If you find that you will continue to experience high-volume usage, I suggest trading up to the Braniff 300, which will easily handle your needs. We will gladly offer you $1300 as a trade-in allowance.

Positive, Forward-Looking Closing

Do not mention the claim in the closing. Instead, look to the future.

End your message on a positive note. Do not refer to the problem again, do not apologize again, do not suggest the possibility of future problems, and do not imply that the reader might still be upset. Instead, use strategies that imply a continuing relationship with the customer, such as a comment about the satisfaction the reader will receive from the repaired product or improved service or appreciation for the reader's interest in your products.

Include sales promotion only if you are confident that your adjustment has restored the customer's confidence in your product or service; otherwise, it might backfire. If used, sales promotion should be subtle and should involve a new product or accessory rather than promoting a new or improved model of what the reader has already bought.

NOT: Again, I apologize for the delay in delivering your letter. If you experience such problems again, please don't hesitate to write.

BUT: We have enjoyed serving your delivery needs for the past eight years, Ms. Clarke, and look forward to many more years of service.

OR: If you're the type of person who has frequent crash deadlines, Ms. Clarke, you will probably be interested in our eight-hour delivery service. It is described in the enclosed brochure.

Model 5 on the page 202 illustrates an adjustment letter, and Checklist 7 on page 203 summarizes the guidelines for writing routine claim and adjustment letters.

■ Goodwill Messages

A **goodwill message** is one that is sent strictly out of a sense of kindness and friend-liness. Examples include messages conveying congratulations, appreciation, and sympathy. These messages achieve their goodwill objective precisely because they have no true business objective. To include even subtle sales promotion in such mes-sages would defeat their purpose. Recipients are quick to see through such efforts. Messages that include sales promotion or resale are *sales* messages, as might be ex-pected, and are covered elsewhere in this text.

That is not to say, however, that business advantages do not accrue from such efforts. People naturally like to deal with businesses and with people who are friendly and who take the time to comment on noteworthy occasions. The point is that such business advantages are strictly incidental to the real purpose of extending a friendly gesture.

Often the gesture could be accomplished by telephoning instead of by writing—especially for minor occasions. But a written message, either in place of or in addition to the phone call, is more thoughtful, more appreciated, and more permanent. And because it requires extra effort and the recipient will receive fewer of them, a written message—particularly in letter form—is much more meaningful than a tele-phone message.

CO5. Compose a goodwill message.

General Guidelines

To ensure that your goodwill messages achieve their desired effect, follow these five guidelines:

Five guidelines for good-will messages: be prompt, direct, sincere, specific, and brief.

1. *Be prompt.* Too often, people consider writing a goodwill message but then put it off until it is too late. The most meaningful messages are those received while the reason for them is still fresh in the reader's mind.
2. *Be direct.* State the major idea in the first sentence or two, even for sympathy notes; since the reader already knows the bad news, you don't need to shelter him or her from it.
3. *Be sincere.* Avoid language that is too flowery or too strong. Use a conversa-tional tone, as if you were speaking to the person directly, and focus on the reader—not on yourself. Take special care to spell names correctly and to make sure your facts are accurate.
4. *Be specific.* If you're thanking or complimenting someone, mention a specific incident or anecdote. Personalize your message to avoid having it sound like a form letter.
5. *Be brief.* You don't need two pages (or, likely, even one full page) to get your point across. Often a personal note card is more appropriate than full-sized business stationery. Because they are considered personal notes, goodwill messages do not require a subject line (unless, of course, they are sent via email).

Congratulatory Messages

Congratulatory notes should be sent for major business achievements—receiving a promotion, announcing a retirement, winning an award, opening a new branch, celebrating an anniversary, and the like. Such notes are also appropriate for personal milestones—engagements, weddings, births, graduations, and other noteworthy

model5

ADJUSTMENT LETTER

This adjustment letter responds to the claim letter in Model 4 on page 198.

Tells immediately that the adjustment is being made; thanks the reader.

Explains briefly, but specifically, what happened.

Looks forward to a continuing relationship with the customer; does not mention the problem again.

April 22, 20—

1   Ms. Claire D. Scriven
Marketing Manager
Otis Candy Company
Box 302
Winnipeg, MB R3T 2P5

Dear Ms. Scriven:

Subject: Cancellation of Invoice 4073

2   Sir Speedy is, of course, happy to cancel the $438.75 charge for Invoice 4073. I appreciate your taking the time to write and send us a sample handout.

3   Upon receiving your letter, I immediately sent your handout to our quality-control personnel for closer examination. They agreed that the handouts should have been redone before they left our facilities. We have now revised our procedures to ensure that before each order is shipped, it is inspected by someone other than the person preparing it.

To better serve the media needs of our corporate customers, we are installing the Xerox DocuCentre 480 copier, the most sophisticated industrial colour copier system available. Thus, when you send us your next order, you'll see that your handouts are of even higher quality than those in the *Report on Business* advertisement that impressed you.

Sincerely yours,

David Foster

David Foster
Customer Relations

Grammar and Mechanics Notes

1 Type the position title either on the same line as the person's name or, as here, on a line by itself.

2 *Invoice 4073:* Capitalize a noun that precedes a number.

3 *personnel:* Do not confuse *personnel* (employees) with *personal* (private).

✓checklist7

Routine Claims and Adjustments

Routine Claims

- Write your claim promptly—as soon as you've identified a problem.
- Strive for an overall tone of courtesy and confidence. If true and relevant, mention something positive about the company or its products somewhere in the letter.
- Begin the claim directly, identifying the problem immediately.
- Provide as much detail as necessary. Using impersonal language, tell specifically what went wrong and how you were inconvenienced.
- If appropriate, tell what type of adjustment you expect—replacement, repair, refund, or apology. End on a confident note.

Routine Adjustments

- Respond promptly; your customer is already upset.
- Begin the message directly, telling the reader immediately what adjustment is being made.

- Adopt a courteous tone. Use neutral or positive language throughout.
- If appropriate, thank the reader for writing, and apologize if the customer has been severely inconvenienced or embarrassed because of your company's actions.
- In a forthright manner, explain the reason for the problem in sufficient detail to be believable, but don't belabour the point. If appropriate, briefly tell what steps you've taken to prevent a recurrence of the problem.
- Provide information that re-establishes your customer's confidence in the product or your company. Be specific enough to be believable.
- If the customer was at fault, explain in impersonal and tactful language the facts surrounding the case.
- Close on a positive note, implying customer satisfaction and the expectation of a continuing relationship.

occasions. Congratulatory notes should be written both to employees within the company and to customers, suppliers, and others outside the firm with whom you have a relationship.

> Congratulations, Tom, on your election to the presidency of the United Way of Alberta. I was happy to see the announcement in this morning's newspaper and to learn of your plans for the upcoming campaign.
>
> Best wishes for a successful fund drive. This important community effort surely deserves everyone's full support.

Thank-You Notes

A note of thanks or appreciation is often valued more than a monetary reward. A handwritten thank-you note is especially appreciated today, when people routinely receive so many "personalized" computer-generated messages. A handwritten note assures the reader that you are offering sincere and genuine thanks, rather than simply sending out a form letter. And if you take the trouble to send a photocopy of your note to the person's supervisor, the recipient will be twice blessed.

Thank-you notes are expected in some situations; they are unexpected (and therefore much appreciated) in others.

Thank-you notes (either typed or handwritten) should be sent whenever someone does you a favour—gives you a gift, writes a letter of recommendation for you, comes to your support unexpectedly, gives a speech or appears on a panel, and so on. Don't forget that customers and suppliers like to be recognized as well. Unexpected thank-you notes are often the most appreciated—to the salesperson, instructor, administrative assistant, copy centre operator, restaurant server, receptionist, or anyone else who provided service beyond the call of duty.

Thank you so much, Alice, for serving on the panel of suppliers for our new employee orientation program. Your comments on scheduling problems and your suggestions for alleviating them were especially helpful. They provided the kind of information that only an experienced pro like you could give.

I think you could tell from the comments and many questions that your remarks were well received by our new employees. We certainly appreciate your professional contributions.

Sympathy Notes

Begin by expressing sympathy, offer some personal memory of the deceased, and close by offering comfort.

Expressions of sympathy or condolence to a person who has experienced pain, grief, or misfortune are especially difficult to write but are also especially appreciated. People who have experienced serious health problems, a severe business setback, or the death of a loved one need to know that others are thinking of them and that they are not alone.

Some of the most difficult messages to write are those expressing sympathy over someone's death. These notes should be handwritten, when possible. They should not avoid mentioning the death, but they need not dwell on it. Most sympathy notes are short. Begin with an expression of sympathy, mention some specific quality or personal reminiscence about the deceased, and then close with an expression of comfort and affection. An offer to help, if genuine, would be appropriate (see Model 6 on the next page).

model6

GOODWILL MESSAGE

This goodwill message expresses sympathy to the husband of a co-worker who died.

1 Robert McKinley
388 Vanier Square
Vancouver, BC V2B 9X6

April 3, 20—

2 Dear Ralph,

I was deeply saddened to learn of Jane's sudden death. It was certainly a great shock to her many friends and colleagues.

Jane had a well-earned reputation here for her top-notch negotiating skills and for her endearing sense of humor. She was an accomplished manager and a good friend, and I shall miss her greatly.

3 If I can help smooth the way in your dealings with our human resources office, I would be honored to help. Please call me on my private line (555-1036) if there is anything I can do.

Affectionately,
Bob

Begins with an expression of sympathy.

Mentions some specific quality or personal reminiscence.

Closes with a genuine offer of help.

G8SF-95A8

Grammar and Mechanics Notes

1 Use either company letterhead or personal stationery for sympathy notes.

2 Insert a comma (instead of a colon) after the salutation of a personal letter.

3 Handwrite the sympathy note, if possible.

A ROUTINE ADJUSTMENT LETTER

Problem

You are Kathryn Smith, a correspondent in the customer service department of Dillard's Department Store. This morning (May 25, 20—), you received the following email from Mrs. Henrietta Daniels, an angry customer:

> Dear Customer Service Manager:
>
> I am really upset at the poor-quality shades that you sell. Two months ago I purchased two pairs of your pleated fabric shades in Wedgewood Blue at $35.99 each for my two bathroom windows. A copy of my $74.32 bill is enclosed.
>
> The colour has already begun to fade from these shades. I couldn't believe it when I checked and found that they now look tie-dyed! That is not the look I wish for my home.
>
> Since these shades did not provide the type of wear that I paid for, please refund my $74.32.
>
> Sincerely,

Was this an effective claim letter? Why or why not?

You take Mrs. Daniels' itemized bill down to the sales floor and find the model of shades she purchased. You can only conclude that Mrs. Daniels' home has large bathroom windows because the only size this particular shade comes in is 162 centimetres long by 81 centimetres wide. And printed right on the tag attached to the shade is this caution: "Warning: The imported fabric in this shade makes it unsuitable for use in areas of high humidity." Clearly, these shades were not made for bathroom use. You call up Mrs. Daniels' account on your computer and find that she has been a loyal customer for many years. You decide, therefore, to refund her $74.32, even though she misused the product. Write the adjustment email.

1. What is the purpose of your email?

   To refund Mrs. Daniels' money, tactfully explain that you were not at fault, and retain her goodwill.

2. Describe your audience.
   - An important customer
   - Angry at you at the present time
   - Now believes your product is of poor quality
   - May be the type of person who doesn't read instructions carefully

3. List in the appropriate order the topics you'll discuss.

   a. Give the refund.

   b. Explain that the shades weren't intended for bathroom use.

   c. Promote your cotton and polyester bathroom curtains.

4. Write a gracious opening sentence for your letter that tells Mrs. Daniels you're refunding the $74.32. Be warm and positive in granting her request. Remember, however, that she was at fault; therefore, do not be overly enthusiastic.

   You have been a valued and faithful customer of ours for several years, Mrs. Daniels, and we are therefore refunding your $74.32.

5. Write the sentence that explains how the shades were misused. Use tactful, neutral, and impersonal language, avoiding the use of second-person pronouns (*you* and *your*).

   As the tag attached to the shades explains, the fine imported woven material used in these shades reflects sunlight without fading but will not withstand the high humidity typical of bathrooms.

6. Now write your closing paragraph, in which you promote your cotton and polyester bathroom curtains.

   For the elegant look and durable service you want in your bathroom, please consider the cotton and polyester bathroom curtains shown in the enclosed brochure. They come in Wedgewood Blue and can be custom-ordered in the exact size you desire.

Product

Allan's, Inc.
1600 Cantrell Road – P.O. Box 486 – St. John's, NF A1A 2R8
Telephone: 709-376-5200   Fax: 709-376-5917

May 25, 20—

Mrs. Henrietta Daniels
117 Pine Forest Drive
Saskatoon, SK S7K 9K2

Dear Mrs. Daniels:

Subject: Your Refund Request for $74.32

You have been a valued customer of ours for several years, and we are, therefore, refunding your $74.32. A cheque for that amount is enclosed. You can simply return the blue shades to our customer service window the next time that you stop by Allan's.

As the tag attached to the shades explains, the fine imported woven material used in these shades reflects sunlight without fading but will not withstand the high humidity typically found in bathrooms. However, when these shades are used on windows in living rooms, dining rooms, and bedrooms, they will provide many years of beautiful and carefree service.

For the elegant look and durable service you want in your bathroom, please consider the cotton and polyester bathroom curtain shown in the enclosed brochure. They come in Wedgewood Blue and can be custom-ordered in the exact size you require. Please come in and let us show them to you.

Sincerely,

Kathryn Smith

Kathryn Smith
Customer Service Department

jmr
Enclosures

■ Summary

When composing a routine request, present the major request early, along with reasons for making the request. Word your questions so that they are clear and easy to answer. Finally, close on a friendly note.

CO1. Compose a routine request.

Answer routine requests promptly and graciously. Grant the request early in the letter and answer all questions asked. Close on a positive and friendly note, and use original language.

CO2. Compose a routine reply.

Write claims promptly, begin the message directly, and tell specifically what went wrong and what resolution you're seeking. Throughout, strive for an overall tone of courtesy and confidence. End on a confident note.

CO3. Compose a routine claim.

Answer claims promptly, use neutral or positive language, and adopt a courteous tone. Begin the message directly, telling immediately what adjustment is being made. Provide information that re-establishes your customer's confidence in the product, and close on a positive note.

CO4. Compose a routine adjustment.

Write goodwill messages to express congratulations, appreciation, or sympathy. Write promptly, using a direct pattern, and be sincere, specific, and brief.

CO5. Compose a goodwill message.

■ Key Terms

You should now be able to define the following terms in your own words and give an original example of each.

adjustment (241)

goodwill message (201)

claim (194)

indirect organizational plan (183)

direct organizational plan (183)

resale (199)

form letter (191)

■ Exercises

1 **Annie's Homegrown Revisited**   Most of the 1500 letters to which Ann Withey responds every month are routine requests for free information offered by Annie's Homegrown; the remainder are letters with specific comments on the product or the company mascot, which require a more personalized response. Because her goal is to strengthen relationships with customers, Withey uses an upbeat tone, expresses appreciation for the customer's loyalty, and carefully tailors each letter to the reader's interests.

Problem

As Ann Withey's executive assistant, you are writing a letter in response to a customer's request for information about your firm's position on environmental protection. The customer, Jeff Biancolo, is a long-time fan of your products and is particularly interested in the company's recycling efforts. In addition to addressing his specific concerns, you plan to include a copy of the company's preprinted statement of support for environmental initiatives.

Process

a. What is the purpose of your letter?
b. Describe your audience.
c. List in order the topics to be discussed.
d. Write an opening paragraph, letting Mr. Biancolo know the purpose of the letter and conveying the firm's strong commitment to environmental protection.
e. Write a sentence referring to the preprinted statement you are enclosing with the letter.
f. Write a closing paragraph thanking Mr. Biancolo for his interest in, and loyalty to, the company.

Product

Using your knowledge of routine messages, write this letter to Jeff Biancolo (at 35 Catton Blvd., Montreal, QC, H1Z 3K8).

2 The 3Ps (Problem, Process, and Product) Model: A Claim Letter for a Defective Product

Problem

You are J.R. McCord, purchasing agent for People's Energy Company. On February 3, you ordered a box of four laser cartridges for your Sampson Model 25 printers at $69.35 each, plus $6.85 shipping and handling—total price of $284.25. The catalogue description for this cartridge (Part No. 02-8R01656) stated, "Fits Epson and Xerox printers and most compatibles." Since the Sampson is advertised as a Xerox clone printer, you assumed the cartridges would fit. When the order arrived, you discovered that the cartridges didn't fit your Sampson. Although the cartridge is the same shape, it is about 0.6 centimetres thicker and won't sit properly on the spindles.

You believe that your supplier's misleading advertising caused you to order the wrong model cartridge. You'd like the company to either refund the $284.25 you paid on its Invoice 95-076 or replace the cartridges with ones that do work with your printers. You'll be happy to return all four cartridges if the company will give you instructions for doing so.

Write your routine claim letter.

Process

a. What is the purpose of your letter?
b. Describe your audience.
c. Write the first sentence of your letter, in which you identify the problem. Strive for an overall tone of courtesy and confidence.
d. Using impersonal language, write the middle section of the letter, in which you tell specifically what went wrong and how you were inconvenienced by the problem.
e. Write the last paragraph of the letter, in which you identify the type of adjustment you expect and also perhaps mention some positive aspect of the company or its products.

Product

Revise, format, and proofread your letter, which should be addressed to the Customer Service Department of Nationwide Office Supply, Ottawa, ON, L9Z 2P5. Submit to your instructor both your responses to the process questions and your final letter.

3 Routine Request—Product Information   Luis St. Jean is a famous design house in France with annual sales of $1.2 billion in clothing, perfume, scarves, and other designer items. Each year it prepares more than 150 original designs for its seasonal collections. As head buyer for Cindy's, an upscale women's clothing store at West Edmonton Mall, you think you might like to begin offering LSJ's line of perfume. You need to know more about pricing, types of perfume offered, minimum ordering quantities, marketing assistance provided by LSJ, and the like. You'd also like to know if you can have exclusive marketing rights to LSJ perfumes in the Prairie region and whether you would have to carry LSJ's complete line (you don't think the most expensive perfumes would be big sellers).

CO1. Compose a routine request.

Write to Mr. Henri Vixier, License Supervisor, Luis St. Jean, 90513 Cergy, Pointoise Cedex, France, seeking answers to your questions.

4 Routine Request—Membership Information   Although your part-time job is only temporary while you finish university, your boss wants you to gain more experience in public speaking and has suggested that you join Toastmasters International, an organization devoted to helping its members practice and improve their public-speaking skills. You are interested in determining whether your town has a local chapter and, if so, the time and place of meetings, the amount of annual dues, and so on.

Locate the Toastmasters International homepage on the Internet and find an email address. Compose an email message, asking several specific pertinent questions. Email a copy of your message to your instructor. Follow your instructor's direction regarding whether to mail your message to Toastmasters.

5 Routine Request—Letter of Recommendation   As part of your application papers for a one-semester internship at CIBC, you are asked to include a letter of recommendation from one of your business professors. You made a good grade in MGT 382:Wage and Salary Administration, which you took three semesters ago from Dr. Dennis Thavinet in the management department at your institution. You liked the course so well that you missed class only twice (for good reasons). Although you were not one of the most vocal members in class, Dr. Thavinet did commend you for your group project. CIBC wants to know especially about your ability to work well with others.

Compose an email message to Dr. Thavinet, asking for a letter of recommendation. You would like him to respond within one week.

6 Routine Request—Product Information   Choose an advertisement from a newspaper or magazine for a product or service about which you have some interest. The ad probably does not have sufficient space to provide all the information you need to make an intelligent purchase decision. Write to the company (if necessary, locate its address using one of the directories available in your library or on the Internet), asking at least three questions about the product. Be sure to mention where you learned about the product. Try to encourage a prompt response.

Attach a copy of the ad to your letter and submit both to your instructor. Your instructor may ask you to mail the letter so that the class can later compare the types of responses received from different companies.

7 **Internet Exercise**   Web sites often provide an easy, pre-addressed form for visitors to use when submitting email messages, and MGD Computers is no exception. Visit MGD Computers' Web site (at www.mgd.ca) and follow the links to "Contact Us" on the bottom of the page. Then follow the "Education Sales" link to see how to contact the company by email. The dean wants to know how the PCs are shipped to the school, how much shipping costs are, and how students can buy on credit. Draft a routine request for this information that you can paste into MGD's pre-addressed email form.

8 **Routine Request—Seeking Day-Care Space**   Family Daycare Centre operates several daycare centres in the Greater Toronto Area. The director of the organization has hired you as the facilities manager. Because the organization is planning to expand its operations into other provinces, you decide to write national real estate firms requesting information about potential rental properties. Your first letter will go to J. Barnicke Limited (401 Bay St., Suite 2500, Toronto, ON Canada M5H 2Y4). What is the major idea you want to express in your letter? How much detail will you need from J. Barnicke Limited? Will you need to explain your request or add any details? How should you close this letter? Using your knowledge of routine requests, draft this message (make up any details you need).

CO2. **Compose a routine reply.**

9 **Routine Reply—Fashion Show**   You are Yolanda Davis, a fashion design instructor at Columbia College of Design. You have received a letter from Greg Bunker, a fashion merchandizing teacher at Sir Winston Churchill High School in Saskatoon, Saskatchewan.

Greg has asked about the possibility of having a provincial fashion show prior to the national fashion show in May. Greg is wondering if you would be willing to host seven high schools from Saskatchewan at your campus in Regina. Greg believes that most of the schools would be bringing between 10 and 15 students to the competition. They want to hold the contest on Friday, March 12, 20—. They would like to begin at 9 a.m. and hope to be finished by noon.

You are excited to host the high school students because you think it will be good exposure for Columbia College. You can host the schools on that day. You have made arrangements for several classrooms from 9 a.m. to noon. Schools should have their students at the Pace Building, Room 145, to register. Registration is from 8:00 to 8:30 a.m. You will need to charge the schools $50 each to cover your expenses.

Write a letter to Greg letting him know the good news and the details of the event. His title is Fashion Merchandising Instructor and his address is Sir Winston Churchill High School, 455 Riel Ave, Saskatoon, SK, S7L 3K9.

10 **Routine Reply—Comedian on Board**   You are the director of entertainment for a cruise ship, the *Sea Princess*. You are always looking for new acts to book on your cruises. Yesterday, you received a letter from Barbara Greensburg, manager of Canuck Entertainment Inc., who requested that you book one of her clients, Frank Nadon.

Frank is a young comedian from Montreal who has appeared in local comedy clubs in Montreal and the surrounding area. He has received great reviews for these shows. Frank also recently finished a university campus tour, which, according to Barbara, was very successful.

Barbara is now trying to get Frank a "gig" for a few weeks in May. You have made a few calls to promoters in Montreal and found that Frank is very good. You would like to meet with him and Barbara to discuss the possibility of having him perform on some of your cruises.

Write a letter to Barbara inviting her and Frank to come to Vancouver, British Columbia on March 15 for a visit. If things work out, you have two cruises that you could book him on during the month of May.

11 **Routine Response—Product Information**   As the business manager for Maison Richard, a 200-seat restaurant in Saint John's, you received an inquiry from Chris Shearing, 1926 Second Avenue, Vancouver, BC, V3E 5P2. She had some questions about the fish served in your restaurant. Here are her questions and the answers:

a. *Are the salmon you serve in your restaurant wild or farmed?* They are farmed, which helps ensure consistent quality at a reasonable price.
b. *Are the fish fed antibiotics or pesticides?* No, the feed is free of antibiotics unless there is a specific concern for the health of the fish, in which case antibiotics may be prescribed by a veterinarian. If necessary, sea lice may be treated with SLICE®, a drug designed to remove the lice within two to four weeks.

Ms. Shearing is a well-known nutritionist and promoter of natural foods, and you want to present your case as positively as possible to avoid the loss of her goodwill and any negative publicity that might result. Respond to her letter, supplying whatever other appropriate information you feel is reasonable. For further information go to the Web site www.salmonfarmers.org.

12 **Routine Response—Form Letter**   You are the executive producer for *The Sherry Show,* a popular syndicated morning talk show on public television featuring Sherry Baker as host. The show features interviews and panel discussions on a wide variety of current topics.

Because Sherry takes questions and comments from the audience, it is important to have a full house each day. When the show started two years ago, you had trouble filling the 150-seat studio. Now, however, you get more ticket requests than you can accommodate. Anyone wanting a ticket must write at least four months ahead and can request no more than four tickets (which are free). The show tapes from 9:30 until 11 a.m. Monday through Friday each week. Tickets are for reserved seats, but any seats not occupied by 9 a.m. are released on a first-come, first-served basis. Studio doors close promptly at 9:15 each morning and do not reopen until the show ends at 11 a.m. Children under age 12 are not admitted.

Write a form letter telling people how to order tickets and conveying other needed information. The letter will be sent to anyone who requests ticket information.

13 Work-Team Communication—Routine Response   You are a member of the Presidents' Council, an organization made up of the presidents of each student organization on campus. You just received a memorandum from Dr. Robin H. Hill, Vice President, Student Affairs, wanting to know what types of social projects the student organizations on campus have been engaged in during the past year. The dean must report to the board of trustees on the important role played by student organizations—both in the life of the university and community and in the development of student leadership and social skills. She wants to include such information as student-run programs on drug and alcohol abuse, community service, and fundraising.

Working in groups of four, identify and summarize the types of social projects that student organizations at your institution have completed this year. Then organize and synthesize your findings into a one-page memo to Dr. Hill. After writing your first draft, have each member review and comment on the draft. Then revise as needed and submit. Use only factual data for this assignment.

CO**3.** **Compose a routine claim.**

14 Routine Claim—Pump Order Mix Up   Assume the role of Uriah Castleton, purchasing agent for Western Electric in Calgary, Alberta. You recently placed an order (Purchase Order No. 44-0987) for 12 Model 2500 air conditioning pumps (Part No. 2500-89712) from ACE Supply Inc. in Edmonton.

When the pumps arrived, you noticed you had received more than 12 pumps, and they were not Model 2500. ACE had accidentally sent 25 Model 1200 pumps. Although you could sell the Model 1200 pumps, you already have plenty of them in stock. What you really need is the Model 2500 pumps.

Write a letter to Brent Sewell, the shipping manager at ACE Supply Inc., requesting that they ship the 12 Model 2500 pumps quickly because you only have three more left in stock. Also ask what his plans are for your returning the 25 Model 1200 pumps. Enclose a copy of your purchase order. The address for ACE Supply is P.O. Box 2238, Edmonton, AB, T5S 1B2.

15 Claim Letter—Inaccurate Reporting   As the marketing manager for ReSolve, a basic computer spreadsheet program for Windows, you were pleased that your product was reviewed in the current issue of *Computing Canada*. The review praised your product for its "lightning-fast speed and convenient user interface." You were not pleased, however, that your product was downgraded because it lacked high-level graphics capability. The reviewer compared ReSolve with full-featured spreadsheet programs costing, on average, $200 more than your program. No wonder, then, that your program rated 6.6 out of 10, coming in third out of the five programs reviewed. If your program had been compared with similar low-level programs, you feel certain that ReSolve would have easily come out on top.

Although you do not want to get the magazine upset with your company (Software Entrepreneurs, Inc.), you do feel that it should compare apples with apples and should conduct another review of your program. Write to Roberta J. Horton, the magazine's review editor, at 757 Carlaw Street, Toronto, ON, M4K 1T6.

16 Claim Letter—Poor Service   As the owner of Parker Central, a small plumbing business, you try to instill in all your employees a customer-first attitude. Therefore, you were quite put off by your own treatment yesterday (July 13) at the hands of the receptionist at Englehard Investment Service. You showed up 20 minutes early for your 2:30 p.m. appointment with Jack Nutley, an investment counsellor with the firm. You were meeting with him for the first time to discuss setting up an employee pension plan for your 20 employees.

To begin with, the receptionist ignored you for at least five minutes until she finished the last paragraph of a document she was typing. Then, after finding out who you wanted to see, she did not even call Jack's office to announce your arrival until 2:30 p.m. Finally, you learned that Jack had just become ill and had to go to the doctor. So you wasted half an afternoon and were also insulted by the receptionist's rude treatment.

You decide to write to Jack Nutley about the receptionist's office behaviour. Your claim is for better service in the future. You want him to know that if you are going to continue to be treated in such a manner, you have no interest in doing business with his firm. Write the claim letter (Englehard Investment Service, 505 Main Street, Kirkland Lake, ON, P2N 4M7).

17 **Routine Claim—No More Level Billing**   Your employer, Clearwater Fisheries, imports and bones fish for resale to hotels and food markets. When you were hired as office manager two years ago, you suggested that the Saint John company avoid the surprise of unusually high monthly utility bills by requesting year-round level billing. With this system, the utility (NB Power) divides the total year's anticipated energy usage by 12 so that each month's bill is approximately the same. This arrangement worked well until April. Then Clearwater started working with Anergen Corp., a local firm that transforms biodegradable materials—such as fish bones and fat—into energy. Because Anergen now uses Clearwater's by-products to produce electricity and natural gas, you called the utility in early April and asked to switch back to monthly billing.

When you opened the May invoice this morning, you noticed that the utility was still using level billing. The usage detail reflected far lower consumption of both electricity and gas, as you expected, but the bill was for the same amount as in April. You decide to bring this matter to the attention of NB Power's customer service department. Write to them at 75 King Cres., Saint John, NB, E2H 9R5.

18 **Routine Adjustment—Something Is Fishy**   Assume the role of Fredrick Samuelson, operator of Samuelson's Catering Service. You recently catered a holiday luncheon for Jones, Wilson, and Associates, a law firm in Hamilton, ON.

CO4. Compose a routine adjustment.

You worked with Karen Ahmed-Ashton, one of the administrative assistants, on the details of the meal. Karen had ordered salmon for the entrée. However, your supplier was unable to provide enough fresh salmon to serve the 250-plus guests who were invited to the luncheon. You became aware of the shortage of salmon at the last minute, so you made a decision to substitute halibut for the salmon. You were unable to get in touch with Karen before the luncheon to clear the substitution.

The luncheon was well received by the 265 people who attended. You received many compliments on the quality of the food. You billed Karen $18.95 per person for the meal—the same price you would have charged for the salmon. Now, three days later you receive a letter from Karen asking that $2 per plate be deducted because you substituted halibut for the salmon.

You value the company's business, and the substitution was made without her approval, so you decide to make the adjustment. Write to Karen explaining the reason for the substitution. Enclose a cheque for $530. Add other details to complete the letter. Send the letter to Ms. Karen Ahmed-Ashton, Administrative Assistant, Jones, Wilson, and Associates at 900 Brock St., Hamilton, ON, L8G 3K8.

19 **Adjustment Letter—Company at Fault**   Assume the role of customer service representative at Nationwide Office Supply (see Exercise 2). You've received Mr. McCord's letter. You've done some background investigation and have learned that what the customer said is true—the Sampson Model 25 *is* a Xerox clone and your catalogue does state that this cartridge fits Xerox printers and most compatibles. The problem came about because the Model 25, Sampson's newest model, was introduced shortly after your catalogue went to press. This model's spindle is slightly shorter than previous Sampson models.

Unfortunately, you do not carry in your inventory a cartridge that will fit the Sampson Model 25. The customer should return the case COD, marking on the address label "Return Authorization 95-076R." In the meantime, you've authorized a refund of $284.25; Mr. McCord should receive the check within ten days. Convey this information to Mr. McCord at 919 Harvey St., Sunderland, ON L0C 8M9.

20 **Adjustment Letter—Customer at Fault**   Assume the role of customer service representative at Nationwide Office Supply (see Exercises 2 and 19). You've done some background investigation and have learned that Mr. McCord was somewhat mistaken in stating that the Sampson Model 25 is a Xerox clone. What Sampson advertises instead is that the Model 25 uses the same character set as Xerox printers; this means that all fonts available from Xerox can also be downloaded to the Model 25. Sampson neither states nor implies that Xerox-compatible cartridges or other supplies will fit its machines.

Because the customer made an innocent mistake and you will be able to re-sell the unused cartridges, you decide to honour his claim anyway. He should return the case prepaid, marking on the address label "Return Authorization 95-076R." In the meantime, you're shipping him four cartridges (Part No. 02-9R32732) that *will* work on the Model 25; he can expect to receive them within 10 days. You're also enclosing your summer catalogue.

21 **Adjustment Letter—Form Letter**   As the new review editor at *Computing Canada* (see Exercise 15), you've already come to expect that whenever products are panned in your magazine, you can expect a negative reaction from the developers. You're happy to hear from them, however, because they sometimes bring to light additional information that your readers will find helpful. Unless the review contained a factual error, your policy is to publish the letters in the "Feedback" column in a future issue. (In this particular instance, you compared ReSolve with the full-featured spreadsheets because that is exactly how Software Entrepreneurs, Inc., advertises the program.)

You review most major software products once yearly in your state-of-the-art computer labs, using criteria established by your readers. Write a form letter that you can send to product developers who write to complain about the review of their products, giving them this information.

22 **Adjustment Letter—Form Letter**   Assume the role of fulfillment representative at Paperbacks by Post, a book club that automatically mails members a selected paperback every month unless they send back a postcard declining the shipment. Although the system works well most of the time, occasionally a member receives a book even after returning the refusal postcard. In such cases, your company asks the member to take the parcel to the post office, which will return it at company expense. You also cancel the invoice and send the member a discount coupon toward future selections.

Write a form letter that you can send to members who complain about receiving an unwanted shipment. Advise them to act promptly, posting returns no later than two weeks after receipt.

23 **Goodwill Message—Great Teacher, Honoured Guest**   As mayor of Vulcan, Alberta, you want to congratulate Elizabeth Mortensen for being named Elementary Teacher of the Year for the province of Alberta. Elizabeth has been teaching at the local elementary school for 15 years and has been one of the best teachers in the fourth grade for all of those years.

She has developed innovative teaching methods for teaching science and math and has also introduced some new safety programes for the children at the school. She has made a big difference in the lives of many young people in your community. You want to recognize her many contributions to the town's young people by having her as the guest of honour at the Vulcan Recognition Dinner in June.

Write a letter congratulating Ms. Mortensen on her Teacher-of-the-Year award and invite her to attend the recognition dinner as the guest of honour. Her address is 112 Moritmer Ave., Vulcan, AB T0L 7K4.

CO5. **Compose a goodwill message.**

24 **Goodwill Letter—Appreciation**   Think of a recent speech you have heard and enjoyed—perhaps by a speaker at a student organization meeting, a speaker sponsored by your institution, a guest speaker in class, or some similar presentation. If necessary, do some research to locate a correct mailing address for this person. Then write this person a letter of appreciation, letting him or her know how much you enjoyed and benefited from his or her remarks. (If you have not heard a speech you enjoyed lately, write a former professor, expressing appreciation for what you learned in class.) Use only actual data for this assignment.

continuing
case 6

The Case of the Missing Briefcase

It was Friday afternoon and Paul Yu was determined to take care of all pending correspondence before leaving for the weekend. On Tuesday, he had received a memo from Maurice Potts, a Northern Lights sales representative, that said in part:

Last week I made a sales presentation to Albertville Electronics and carried two briefcases with me—my regular case plus a second case filled with handouts and brochures.

At the conclusion of my presentation, I distributed the handouts and brochures, picked up my regular briefcase and left—completely forgetting about my second case. When I discovered the following morning what had happened, I immediately called Albertville Electronics, but it has been unable to locate the missing case.

This leather briefcase was two months old and cost $287.50 (see the attached sales slip). Since the Northern Lights policy manual states that employees will be reimbursed for all reasonable costs of carrying out their assigned duties, may I please be reimbursed for the $287.50 lost briefcase.

Paul had been thinking about this situation all week; he had even discussed it with Marc Kaplan, but Marc told him to make whatever decision he thought reasonable. On the one hand, Maurice is a good sales representative, and the policy manual does contain the exact sentence Maurice quoted. On the other hand, Paul does not feel that NL should be responsible for such obvious mistakes as this; assuming responsibility for such mistakes would not only be expensive but also might encourage padded expense accounts.

Finally, Paul decides to do two things. First, he'll write a memo to the sales staff, interpreting more fully company policy. Policy 14.2 is entitled *Reimbursement of Expenses,* and Paragraph 14.2.b states, "With the approval of their supervisors, employees will be reimbursed for all reasonable costs of carrying out their assigned duties." Paul wants the sales staff to know that in the future he intends to interpret this policy to mean that any personal property that is stolen will be reimbursed at its present value (not its replacement value) if reasonable care has been taken to secure such property, if the incident is reported within three days, and if the value of the property can be determined. Lost or damaged personal property will normally not be reimbursed, no matter what the reason. Any sales representative may, of course, appeal Paul's decisions to the vice-president of marketing.

Second, because the present policy may not have been sufficiently clear, Paul will write a memo to Maurice and agree to reimburse him $287.50 for the briefcase. He'll also enclose a copy of the new policy memo he is sending out to the sales staff.

Critical Thinking

1. How reasonable was Maurice Potts's claim? Was the intent of the policy clear? Should Paul have reimbursed him? Why or why not?

2. How reasonable is Paul's interpretation of the company policy?

After losing his second briefcase, Maurice Potts holds fast to his remaining case. He believes he should be reimbursed for the $287.50 cost of the briefcase he left behind.

Writing Projects

3. Compose the two documents that Paul intends to write: the memo to the sales staff and the memo to Maurice Potts. Format them in an appropriate style.

Retype the following press release from Northern Lights, correcting any punctuation problems according to the rules introduced in LAB 3 on page 541.

Tivoli Industries new illuminated step lights are designed to illuminate and define step edges with a soft, glowing light. Their non-skid surface assures a secure footing while providing necessary illumination for stairways.

5   The LampPaks cardboard container is designed for shipping spent fluorescent tubes from the end-user back to an authorized hazardous waste disposal site. The product was introduced for one reason Environment Canada now requires that everyones fluorescent tubes be disposed of in accordance with strict regulations. The LampPak can hold up to 64 standard

10   tubes a package for tubes smaller than 30 centimetres is also available. The cartons are shipped flat, thereby saving on shipping costs and storage space.

Bruck has introduced the Shou (which means long life), a lighting system with specially designed fixtures that feature curves and flowing shapes. According to a recent article in Industrial Interior Design, "The unity of hand-

15   crafted cased glass . . . creates ambient illumination that complements contemporary interior designs.

Finally, Verilux, a 40 year old fluorescent manufacturer has developed a sunlight simulator used by people with seasonal affective disorder, commonly known as the winter blues. The light is a self-contained tube that

20   produces flicker free light with almost no UV radiation or electromagnetic field.

7

Persuasive Messages

communication
OBJECTIVES

After you have finished this chapter, you should be able to

1. Compose a persuasive message promoting an idea.

2. Compose a persuasive message requesting a favour.

3. Compose a persuasive claim.

4. Compose a sales letter.

5. Compose a collection letter.

What's it like to write for an audience of thousands of employees spread across Canada and the US, with offices around the world? Communicating with an international audience of employees and clients is just one of the responsibilities handled by Martha Durdin, Managing Director of Marketing, Communications and Client Strategy for BMO Capital Markets. Part of BMO Financial Group, one of the largest banks in North America, BMO has offices around the world and total assets of over $312 billion.

A veteran of BMO, Durdin has seen business communication change significantly over the last decade, particularly with the introduction of text messaging devices and other forms of electronic communication. And with these changes, she has had to learn new strategies to keep her communication effective. "People's attention spans are shorter," she argues, "so we rely much more heavily on bullet points and callouts when delivering important messages," such as sales presentations. "Our emails need to be concise, without any unnecessary charts or visuals, so they can be easily read on BlackBerrys," she adds.

Durdin has also seen a shift away from traditional paper-based persuasive messages—particularly memos—towards much heavier reliance on electronic communication, such as email, PowerPoint, and online newsletters. With this shift, people's tolerance for lengthy messages has decreased while the sheer number of messages sent and received has increased significantly—up to 300 emails per day for some employees. To

an insider's perspective

MARTHA DURDIN
Managing Director of Marketing, Communications and Client Strategy for BMO Capital Markets

220

address these new challenges, Durdin pays as much attention to the medium as she does to the message. "When writing emails, to increase readability, we pay a lot of attention to the subject line and the source. The more senior the communicator, the more likely the email will be read. If we want people to pay attention to it, we tend to focus on the source," she says.

Elaborating on the importance of choosing an appropriate medium, she adds, "We are very targeted in our communications. When writing to CEOs or CFOs, who tend to be older, we know they'll be more receptive to paper documents, such as letters. When writing to traders, who tend to be younger and prefer electronic communication, we never use paper."

Not only do persuasive messages require the appropriate choice of medium, she argues, they also require careful attention to style and tone. "So much of our internal communication is around change management," says Durdin. "We insist on using simple, clear language while emphasizing the positive." Such positives include providing sufficient context, discussing business objectives, and stressing the impact on people, departments, or divisions. In short, Durdin ensures her messages focus on reader benefits.

Durdin further stresses that good communicators must clearly know their purpose before putting together a document or presentation. She sees each message as a "story" and insists that "when structuring the story you need to think about what you want the reader to take home. You need to fully understand the objectives of your communication."

For sales presentations conducted on PowerPoint (or "decks," in industry parlance), Durdin teaches her staff to tell the story on more than one level. "We spend a lot of time training our sales force how to use decks with straplines." (Straplines are lines at the bottom of the slide that summarize its content.) "Good straplines tell the whole story without the reader having to look at each slide," she adds. So while the slides themselves contain the background detail and the proofpoints, such as graphs and charts, the strapline tells a parallel story but in much abbreviated form. "Straplines give you the ability to take the listener through the document on two different levels" she emphasizes.

So what does a 20-year veteran of corporate communications see as the most important element in persuasive communication? "Know your purpose, know your audience, tailor your message to your audience, keep it simple, and then be very clear on how you articulate that message."

"Choose a vehicle that's appropriate to the purpose of your communication and ensure the content is relevant to your audience."

■ Planning the Persuasive Message

Persuasion is the process of motivating someone to take a specific action or to support a particular idea. Persuasion motivates someone to believe something or to do something that he or she would not otherwise have done. Every day many people try to persuade you to do certain things or to believe certain ideas. Likewise, you have many opportunities to persuade others each day.

As a business person, you will also need to persuade others to do as you want. You may need to persuade a superior to adopt a certain proposal, a supplier to refund the purchase price of a defective product, or a potential customer to buy your product or service. In a sense, *all* business communication involves persuasion. Even if your primary purpose is to inform, you still want your reader to accept your perspective and to believe the information you present.

The essence of persuasion is overcoming initial resistance. The reader may resist your efforts for any number of reasons. Your proposal may require the reader to spend time or money—at the very least, you're asking for his or her time to *read* your message. Or the reader may have had bad experiences in the past with similar requests or may hold opinions that predispose him or her against your request.

Persuasion is necessary when the other person initially resists your efforts.

Your job in writing a persuasive message, then, is to talk your readers into something, to convince them that your point of view is the most appropriate one. You'll have the best chance of succeeding if you tailor your message to your audience, provide your readers with reasons they will find convincing, and anticipate and deflect or disarm their objections. Such tailor-made writing requires careful planning; you need to define your purpose clearly and analyze your audience.

Once you've thought carefully about your message's purpose and audience, you'll also need to consider which strategies will be most effective at persuading your reader to accept—or "buy into"—your argument. Indeed, learning to write persuasively is really about learning to put together a convincing argument. Recall our discussion of ethos, pathos, and logos in Chapter 3, which are the essence of effective argumentation.

Applying logos by developing a sound, logical argument and supplying sufficient support through facts, examples, and expert opinion is the most effective form of persuasion in most cases. Whether you are writing to convince a supervisor to purchase a new piece of office equipment, to request a colleague to host a seminar, to convince a retailer to refund your money, or to sell mutual funds to a potential investor, convincing your reader that saying "yes" simply makes good sense is likely your most powerful argument. However, pathos—appealing to the emotions of the reader—also plays an important role in many business situations. Writing an appeal for a charitable donation may involve a logical argument, but it will more likely rely on appealing to the reader's empathy for those in need. Finally, building ethos (or credibility) must be done explicitly—through demonstrating expertise and earning your reader's respect—but it also must be done implicitly through your style and tone; writing clearly, concisely, and correctly while emphasizing the positive and maintaining a sincere, confident tone all contribute greatly to building your ethos. The more credible a writer is viewed by a reader, the more likely the reader is to be persuaded by the message. As we discuss the various kinds of persuasive messages throughout this chapter, we'll revisit these strategies and consider how all three contribute to your overall argument.

Purpose

The purpose of a persuasive message is to motivate the reader to agree with you or to do as you ask. Unless you are clear about the specific results you wish to achieve, you won't be able to plan an effective strategy that will achieve your goals.

Decide specifically what you want the reader to do as a result of your message.

Suppose, for example, you want to convince your superior to adopt a complex proposal. The purpose of your memo might be to persuade your superior to either (1) adopt your proposal, (2) approve a pilot test of the proposal, or (3) schedule a meeting where you can present your proposal in person and answer any questions. Achieving any one of these three goals may require a different strategy. Similarly, if you're writing a sales letter, you must determine whether your purpose is to actually make a sale, to get the reader to request more information, or to schedule a sales call. Again, your specific goal determines your strategy.

Knowing your purpose lets you know what kind of information to include in your persuasive message. "Knowledge is power" and never is this saying truer than when writing persuasive messages. To write effectively about an idea or product, you must know the idea or product intimately. If you're promoting an idea, consider all of the ramifications of your proposal.

- Are there competing proposals that should be considered?

- What are the implications for the organization (and for you) if your proposal is adopted and it *fails?*

- How does your proposal fit in with the existing plans and direction of the organization?

If you're promoting a product, how is the product made, marketed, operated, and maintained? You also need to learn this same information about your competition's products so you can determine the major differences between yours and theirs.

Audience Analysis

Once you've established your purpose, you need to consider how best to connect that purpose with the needs and desires of your chosen audience. Recall our discussion in Chapter 3 about the kinds of questions you should ask about your audience.

"I can't tell you what a pleasure and a privilege it is to teach such a bright-looking group of individuals."

By permission of Leigh Rubin and Creators Syndicate, Inc.

How Much Does Your Reader Already Know and How Will He or She React?
Answering these questions allows you to determine the level of detail, evidence, and background information you should include. Not enough detail will fail to persuade an audience, while too much may discourage them from even finishing the message. If your reader is predisposed to react negatively to a message, then where one or two reasons might ordinarily suffice, you will need to give more. Such initial resistance also calls for more objective, verifiable evidence (logos) than if the reader were initially neutral. You also need to learn why the reader is resistant so that you can tailor your arguments to overcome those specific objections.

How Will Your Proposal Affect the Reader? If the reader is being asked to commit resources (time or money), discuss the rewards for doing so. If the reader is being asked to endorse some proposal, provide enough specific information to enable the reader to make an informed decision. The reader wants to know "What's in it for me?" *You* are already convinced of the wisdom of your proposal. Your job is to let the reader know the benefits of doing as you ask.

To be persuasive, you must present *specific, believable* evidence and a sound argument. However, a common mistake is to simply describe the features of the product or list the advantages of doing as you ask. Instead, put yourself in the reader's place. Discuss how the reader will benefit from your proposal. Emphasize the *reader* rather than the product or idea you're promoting.

communication snapshot 6

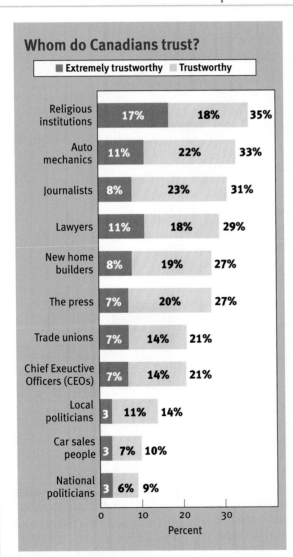

NOT: The Society of Management Accountants of Canada would like you to speak to us on the topic of expensing versus capitalizing assets.

BUT: Speaking to the Society of Management Accountants of Canada would enable you to present your firm's views on the controversial topic of expensing versus capitalizing assets.

Sometimes your readers won't benefit *directly* from doing as you ask. If you are trying to entice your employees to contribute to the United Way, for example, it would be difficult to discuss direct reader benefits. In such situations, discuss the *indirect* benefits of reader participation; for example, show how someone other than you, the solicitor of the funds, will benefit. Such indirect benefits often focus more on pathos—appealing to the reader's emotions—than logos.

> Your contribution will enable inner-city youngsters, many of whom have never even been outside the city of Winnipeg, to see pandas living and thriving in their natural habitat.

What is Unique about Your Reader? The marketing industry spends billions of dollars studying consumer behaviour—their ultimate goal being to find out as much as possible about the unique interests, desires, and concerns of consumers. Traditionally, market research has focused on demographics (age, gender, race, and other quantitative details). Today, more sophisticated research methods and technological advances allow marketers to narrow their target market much more precisely, focusing on psychographics (values, beliefs, lifestyles, and other more qualitative details) and specific consumer behaviour. If you've ever pur-

Source: Ipsos-Reid survey for *Reader's Digest.* January 22, 2003. www.acpa.ca/press_news/2003/trust.pdf. Accessed February 4, 2006.

chased a product online, for example, you may have noticed that the site tracks your purchases, creates a profile of your tastes, and makes recommendations for other items in which you may be interested. What such technology allows marketers to do is find unique information about each member of its market and tailor its message to the tastes of each individual.

In short, if you can find something unique about your audience, your task becomes much easier—and the more detailed and specific your understanding is, the better. Identifying unique characteristics of your audience is easy when you know the reader well or when you have access to specific information about your reader; it becomes more difficult when communicating with large audiences or with someone you don't know at all. The less familiar you are with your readers, the more time and effort you will have to expend analyzing them before writing the message. Generic messages—those that try to connect with virtually everyone—risk connecting with no one at all.

What is Your Credibility with the Reader?   The more trustworthy you are, the more trustworthy your message will appear; and the better your audience knows and trusts you, the less time you need to spend building your credibility. If you're writing to someone whom you don't know at all, care must be taken in gaining the reader's trust and respect. Credibility comes from many sources. You may be perceived as credible by virtue of the position you hold or by virtue of being a well-known authority (see, for example, Communication Snapshot 6). Or you may achieve credibility for your proposal by supplying convincing evidence, such as facts and statistics that can be verified.

Suppose, for example, you have worked in an advertising production department and have extensive experience with colour reproduction. If you are writing a memo to a colleague suggesting that certain photos will not reproduce clearly and should therefore be replaced, you probably don't need to explain your expertise. Your colleague is likely to believe you. But if you are writing a letter to the photographer, who does not know you, you would probably want to discuss past incidents that lead you to conclude the photos should be replaced.

The text below is a modified version of an actual email message sent to clients of a travel agency. Can you discern the purpose of the message? How well does the author establish credibility with the intended audience and address their specific needs?

Last week Western Airlines announced a financial decision that will drastically impact both you, the consumer, as well as the travel industry. I took the liberty to attach a copy of the official press release from Vacation Star's head office regarding their position on this matter.

This unilateral and draconian measure is a direct threat to travel agencies and consumers, especially if other airline companies also looking to grab greater profits follow the move. It is clear that Western Airlines, and those who follow this shameless bid to grab greater profits, is trying to reduce travel industry service levels while increasing the overall costs to the consumer.

It is outrageous that the battle for increased shareholder returns is being waged at the expense of consumers and travel agents. If you share our concerns regarding this latest unnecessary profit grab attempt, please stand with Vacation Star in opposing this greedy airline.

Matt Bledsoe,
Regional Manager, Vacation Star Travel Agency

First, the author fails to clearly communicate his purpose. While it's clear how the writer *feels* about the topic, it's not at all clear what the writer's purpose is. Is the purpose simply to get readers as angry as he is? If so, does it succeed? Or is the purpose to get readers to take a specific course of action? If so, what should that course of action be and how should it be undertaken? Second, the author fails to address the needs of his audience, who know nothing about the topic—a recent "financial decision" from Western Airlines. In failing to give the reader enough detail and background information to actually understand the writer's concerns and the implications on their own travel needs, the email simply leaves the reader bewildered.

Third, the author fails to anticipate and direct the reader's reaction to the message. Initial resistance to the message is probably quite low—the email has come from a source the reader will recognize, and the message appeals to the reader's fear of rising airfare. However, the lack of sufficient background detail, the lack of specific evidence, and the emotionally charged tone may actually increase the reader's resistance to the message. The writer has also assumed his audience is already predisposed to mistrust the airline industry, and he is hoping to touch on that nerve by relying on emotional language. This may be true of some of his audience, but it's more likely that the unique quality his readers share is the simple desire to get good service and good value. Aren't these the main reasons people seek the services of travel agencies? His message should therefore focus on their need to hear how the financial decision of Western Airlines will affect service and price.

Finally, how well does the Vacation Star email earn reader trust? The writer of the email, since he already has a professional relationship with his audience, assumes readers already respect his opinion and will therefore react to the news the same

As subjects watch a series of commercials, researchers at the Brain Sciences Institute in Melbourne, Australia, monitor a dozen different regions of the brain to see if they are forming emotional attachments to products.

way he has. This may be true if this were an email sent from one colleague or friend to another, but this particular message is a mass mailout to Vacation Star clients, who don't have a close enough relationship with the writer to simply be told how to feel about something—they need to be persuaded, not just by the content of the message but also by the credibility of the writer.

In summary, the more you know about your audience, the better you'll be able to promote the features of your idea or product as satisfying a *specific* need of your audience—and the more persuasive your message will be. As a final example, suppose you're promoting a line of men's shoes. You don't know your readers personally, but you do know enough about them to distinguish their unique interests. You should therefore stress different features, depending on your audience.

Young executive:	stylish . . . comes in various shades of black and brown . . . a perfect accessory to your business wardrobe
Mid-career executive:	perfect detailing . . . 12-hour comfort . . . stays sharp-looking through days of travel
Retired executive:	economical . . . comfortable . . . a no-nonsense type of shoe

The point to remember is to know your audience and to personalize your message to best meet its needs and interests. Use the "you" attitude to achieve the results you want. When sending a form letter to perhaps thousands of readers, your approach cannot, of necessity, be as personal. Nevertheless, you should still strive to make the approach as personal as possible.

■ Organizing a Persuasive Request

A persuasive request seeks to motivate the reader to accept your idea (rather than to buy your product). The purpose of your message and your knowledge of the reader will help determine the content of your message and the sequence in which you discuss each topic.

Determining How to Start the Message

In the past, it was common practice to organize *all* persuasive messages by using an indirect organizational plan—presenting the rationale first, followed by the major idea (the request for action)—and this plan is still used for many persuasive messages. However, writers today should determine which organizational plan (direct or indirect) will help them better achieve their objectives.

Direct Plan—Present the Major Idea First   Most superiors prefer to have messages from their subordinates organized in the direct style introduced in Chapter 6. Thus, when writing persuasive messages that travel up the organization, you should generally present the main idea (your recommendation) first, followed by the supporting evidence. The direct organizational plan saves time and immediately satisfies the reader's curiosity about your purpose. To get readers to accept your proposal when using the direct plan, present your recommendation along with the criteria or brief rationale in the first paragraph.

Prefer the direct plan when writing persuasive messages to your superior.

NOT: I recommend we hold our Ottawa sales meeting at the Chateau Laurier Hotel.

BUT: I have evaluated three hotels as possible meeting sites for our Ottawa sales conference and recommend we meet at the Chateau Laurier Hotel. As discussed below, the Chateau Laurier is centrally located, has the best meeting facilities, and fits within our budget.

In general, prefer the direct organizational plan for persuasive messages when any of the following conditions apply:

■ You are writing to superiors within the organization.

■ Your audience is predisposed to listen objectively to your request.

■ The proposal does not require strong persuasion (that is, there are no major obstacles present).

■ The proposal is long or complex (a reader may become impatient if your main point is buried in a long report).

■ You know that your reader prefers the direct approach.

Indirect Plan—Gain the Reader's Attention First   Unfortunately, many times your readers will initially resist your suggestions. Your job then is to explain the merits of your proposal and show how the reader will benefit from doing as you ask. Because a reluctant reader is more likely to agree to an idea *after* he or she understands its merits, your plan of organization is to convince the reader before asking for action.

Charitable organizations spend much of their time trying to persuade potential donors to support worthy causes. Here, University of Guelph students get involved in the screening of *Willie Wonka and the Chocolate Factory* as a fundraiser for World Vision's African relief.

Thus, you should use the indirect organizational plan when writing to subordinates, when strong persuasion is needed, or when you know that your reader prefers the indirect plan. When using the indirect plan, you delay asking for action until after you've presented your reasons.

A subject line that does not disclose your recommendation should be used in persuasive letters and emails. Don't announce your purpose immediately, but rather, lead up to it gradually.

NOT: SUBJECT: Proposal to Sell the Roper Division (too specific)

NOT: SUBJECT: Proposal (too general)

BUT: SUBJECT: Analysis of Roper Division Profitability

The first test of a good opening sentence in a persuasive request is whether it is interesting enough to catch and keep the reader's attention. It won't matter how much evidence you have marshalled to support your case if the recipient does not bother to continue reading carefully after the first sentence.

Various approaches for getting attention include opening your message with a rhetorical question, an interesting fact, a startling statement, a compliment to the reader, an endorsement or quote from an expert, a specific benefit, or a description of a problem (for which the rest of the message will provide the solution).

A **rhetorical question** is asked strictly to get the reader thinking about the topic of your message; a literal answer is not expected. Of course, questions with obvious answers are not effective motivators for further reading and, in fact, may insult the reader's intelligence. Similarly, yes-or-no questions rarely make good lead-ins because pondering an answer doesn't require much thought.

NOT: How would you like to save our department $7500 yearly?

BUT: What do you think the labour costs are for changing just one light bulb? $10? $25? More?

NOT: Did you know that the Kingston Community Fund is more than 70 years old?

BUT: What do Don Cherry and the Kingston Community Fund have in common?

Sometimes an unusual fact or unexpected statement will draw the reader into the message. At other times, you might want to select some statement about which the reader and writer will agree—to immediately establish some common ground.

Our company spent more money on janitorial service last year than on research and development.

A five-year-old boy taught me an important lesson last week.

Automotive News calls your six-year/100 000-kilometre warranty the best in the business (opening for a persuasive claim letter).

Northern Cruises will make you feel utterly insignificant (opening for a letter promoting breathtaking sights of an Alaskan cruise).

Particularly for sales letters or persuasive requests, starting the message by pointing out a problem for which you have the solution can be effective. (Consider how often election campaigns rely on this approach.) Because the problem-solution approach to persuasive writing plays on people's fears or concerns, it can be extremely effective. It can also be risky.

> We spent $162.50 to have Imagemaster develop the 32 transparencies we used in last month's purchasing managers' seminar. We could have printed them on the Lexcraft for less than $60—with same-day service.

The opening statement must be relevant.

Your opening statement must also be relevant to the purpose of your message. If it is too far off the topic or misleads the reader, you risk losing goodwill, and the reader may simply stop reading. At the very least, the reader will feel confused or deceived, making persuasion more difficult.

Keep your opening statement short. Often an opening paragraph of just one sentence will make the message inviting to read. Few readers have the patience to wade through a long introduction to figure out the purpose of the message. In summary, make the opening for a persuasive message written in the indirect organizational plan interesting, relevant, and short. The purpose is to make sure your reader gets to the body of your message.

Creating Interest and Justifying Your Request

Regardless of whether your opening is written in a direct or indirect style, you must now begin the process of convincing the reader that your request is reasonable. This process may require several paragraphs of discussion, depending on how much evidence will be needed to convince the reader. Because it takes more space to state *why* something should be done than simply to state *that* it should be done, persuasive requests are typically longer than other types of messages.

Provide convincing evidence and use a resonable tone.

To convince your readers, you must be objective, specific, logical, and reasonable. Avoid emotionalism, obvious flattery, insincerity, and exaggeration. Let your evidence carry the weight of your argument.

> **NOT:** Locating our plant in Summerside instead of in Kelowna would result in considerable savings.
>
> **BUT:** Locating our plant in Summerside instead of in Kelowna would result in annual savings of nearly $175 000, as shown in Table 3.
>
> **NOT:** Why should it take a thousand phone calls to convince your computer to credit my account for $38.50?
>
> **BUT:** Even after five phone calls over the past three weeks, I find that $38.50 has still not been credited to my account.

The type of evidence you present depends, of course, on the circumstances. The usual types of evidence are these:

- *Facts and statistics: Facts* are objective statements whose truth can be verified; *statistics* are facts consisting of numbers. Both must be relevant and accurate. For example, statistics that were accurate five years ago may no longer be accurate today. Avoid, however, overwhelming the reader with statistical data. Instead, highlight a few key statistics—for emphasis.

- *Expert opinion:* Testimony from authorities on the topic might be presented if their input is relevant and, if necessary, you can supply the experts' credentials.

Expert opinion is especially persuasive to readers who don't recognize you as an authority on the subject.

■ *Examples:* Specific cases or incidents used to illustrate the point under discussion should be relevant, representative, and complete.

Present the benefits (either direct or indirect) that will accompany the adoption of your proposal, and provide enough background and objective evidence to enable the reader to make an informed decision.

Overcoming Obstacles

Ignoring any obvious obstacles to granting your request would provide the reader a ready excuse to refuse your request. Assume, for example, that you're trying to persuade a supplier to provide an in-store demonstrator of the firm's products—even though you know it's against the supplier's company policy to do so. If you ignore this factor, you're simply inviting the reader to respond that company policy prohibits granting your request. Instead, your strategy should be to show that *even considering such an obstacle,* your request is still reasonable, perhaps as follows:

> Last year we sold 356 of your Golden Microwave ovens. We believe the extensive publicity our sale will generate justifies your temporarily setting aside company policy and providing an in-store demonstrator. The ease of use and the actual cooked results that your representative will be able to display are sure to increase the sales of your microwaves.

If you're asking someone to speak to a professional organization but are unable to provide an honorarium, emphasize the free publicity the speaker will receive and the impact that the speaker's remarks will have on the audience. If you're asking for confidential information, discuss how you will treat it as such. If you're asking for a large donation, explain how payment can be made on the instalment plan or by payroll deduction and point out the tax-deductible feature of the donation.

Even though you must address the major obstacles, do *not* emphasize them. Subordinate this discussion by devoting relatively little space to it, by dealing with obstacles in the same sentence as a reader benefit, or by putting the discussion in the middle of a paragraph. Regardless of how you do it, show the reader that you're aware of the obvious obstacles and that despite them, your proposal still has merit.

Subordinate your discussion of major obstacles.

Motivating Action

Although your request has been stated (direct organizational plan) or implied (indirect organizational plan) earlier, give a direct statement of the request late in the message—after most of the background information and reader benefits have been thoroughly covered. Make the specific action that you want taken clear and easy. For example, if the reader agrees to do as you ask, how is he or she to let you know? Will a phone call suffice, or is a written reply necessary? If a phone call is adequate, have you provided a phone number? If you're asking for a favour that requires a written response, have you included a stamped, addressed envelope?

Ask for the desired action in a confident tone. If your request or proposal is reasonable, there is no need to apologize, and you surely do not want to supply the reader with excuses for refusing. Take whatever steps you can to ensure a prompt reply.

NOT: I know you're a busy person, but I would appreciate your completing this questionnaire.

Note the indirect benefit implied.

BUT: So that this information will be available for the financial managers attending our fall conference, I would appreciate your returning the questionnaire by May 15.

NOT: If you agree this proposal is worthwhile, please let me know by June 1.

Note the motivation for a prompt reply.

BUT: To enable us to have this plan in place before the opening of our new branch on June 1, simply initial this memo and return it to me.

Checklist 8 on page 233 summarizes guidelines to use in writing persuasive requests. Although you will not be able to use all these suggestions in each persuasive request, you should use them as an overall framework for structuring your persuasive message.

■ Common Types of Persuasive Requests

CO1. Compose a persuasive message promoting an idea.

In many ways, writing a persuasive request is more difficult than writing a sales letter because reader benefits are not always obvious in persuasive requests. This section provides specific strategies and examples for selling an idea, requesting a favour, and writing a persuasive claim letter.

Selling an Idea

You will have many opportunities to use your education and experience to help solve problems faced by your organization. On the job you will frequently write messages proposing one alternative over another, suggesting a new procedure, or in some other way recommending some course of action. Organize such messages logically, showing what the problem is, how you intend to solve the problem, and why your solution is sound. Write in an objective style and provide evidence to support your claims.

The memo in Model 7 on page 234 illustrates the selling of an idea. In this case, a marketing supervisor for an auto-parts supplier is asking the vice-president to reassign parking spaces to give preference to those employees driving Ford products. Because the memo is written to his superior, the writer uses a direct organizational style.

Requesting a Favour

CO2. Compose a persuasive message requesting a favour.

It has often been said that the wheels of industry are greased with favours. The giving and receiving of favours makes success more likely and makes life in general more agreeable.

Favours require persuasion because the reader gets nothing tangible in return.

A request for a favour differs from a routine request in that routine requests are granted almost automatically, whereas favours require persuasion. For example, asking a colleague to trade places with you on the program for the monthly managers' meeting might be considered a routine request. Asking the same colleague to prepare and give your presentation for you would more likely be a favour, requiring some persuasion.

✓checklist 8

Persuasive Requests

Determine How to Start the Message

✓ **Direct Plan**—Use a direct organizational plan when writing to superiors, when your audience is predisposed to listen objectively to your request, when the proposal does not require strong persuasion, when the proposal is long or complex, or when you know your reader prefers the direct approach. Present the recommendation, along with the criteria or brief rationale, in the first paragraph.

✓ **Indirect Plan**—Use an indirect organizational plan when writing to subordinates, when strong persuasion is needed, or when you know your reader prefers the indirect approach. Start by gaining the reader's attention.

■ Make the first sentence motivate the reader to continue reading. Use, for example, a rhetorical question, unusual fact, unexpected statement, or common-ground statement.

■ Keep the opening paragraph short (often just one sentence), relevant to the message, and, when appropriate, related to a reader benefit.

Create Interest and Justify Your Request

✓ Devote the major part of your message to justifying your request. Give enough background and evidence to enable the reader to make an informed decision.

✓ Use facts and statistics, expert opinion, and examples to support your proposal. Ensure that the evidence is accurate, relevant, representative, and complete.

✓ Use an objective, logical, reasonable, and sincere tone. Avoid obvious flattery, emotionalism, and exaggeration.

✓ Present the evidence in terms of either direct or indirect reader benefits.

Minimize Obstacles

✓ Do not ignore obstacles or any negative aspects of your request. Instead, show that even considering them, your request is still reasonable.

✓ Subordinate the discussion of obstacles by position and amount of space devoted to the topic.

Ask Confidently for Action

✓ State (or restate) the specific request late in the message—after most of the benefits have been discussed.

✓ Make the desired action clear and easy for the reader, use a confident tone, do not apologize, and do not supply excuses.

✓ End on a forward-looking note, continuing to stress reader benefits.

Although friends and close colleagues often do each other favours as a matter of course, many times in business the granting of a favour might not be so automatic—especially if you don't know the person to whom you're writing. In such situations, you will want to begin your request with an attention-getter and stress the reader benefits from granting the favour.

Favours require persuasion because the reader gets nothing tangible in return.

Discuss at least one reader benefit before making your request. Explain why the favour is being asked and continue to show how the reader (or someone else) will benefit from the favour. Keep a positive, confident tone throughout, and make the action to be taken clear and easy.

Often the favour is requested because the reader is an expert on some topic. If that is the case, you may legitimately make a complimentary remark about the reader. Make sure, however, that your compliment sounds sincere. Readers are rightfully suspicious, for example, when they read in a form letter that they have been

For a sincere tone, make any complimentary comments unique to the reader.

model 7

PERSUASIVE REQUEST—SELLING AN IDEA

This persuasive memo uses the direct plan because the memo travels up the organization.

Begins by introducing the recommendation, along with a brief rationale.

Provides a smooth transition to the necessary background information. Cites statistics and external testimony for credibility.

Repeats the recommendation after presenting most of the rationale.

Neutralizes an obvious obstacle.

Closes on a positive, confident note; motivates prompt action.

NEWTON
Electrical
Systems

+ — + — + — + — + — + — + — + — + — + — + — + — + — + — + — + —
Serving the automotive industry for more than 50 years

1 **MEMO TO:**   Elliott Lamborn, Vice President

   FROM: Jenson J. Peterson, Marketing Supervisor

   DATE: April 3, 20—

   SUBJECT: Proposal to Reassign Employee Parking Lots

As one way of showing our support for the Ford Motor Company, which accounts for nearly half of our annual sales, I propose that the employee parking lots nearest our headquarters be restricted to use by owners of Ford vehicles.

2 During their frequent visits to our headquarters, Ford personnel must pass the employee parking lot. When they do, they will see that approximately 70 percent of our employees drive vehicles manufactured by competitors of Ford. In fact, a Ford purchasing agent asked me last week, "How can you expect us to support you if you don't support us?"

The purpose of this memo, then, is to seek approval to have our nearby employee parking lot restricted to use by Ford vehicles. The maintenance department estimates that it will need four weeks and about $500 to make the needed signs.

Our labour contract requires union approval of any changes in working conditions. However, Sally Marsh, our shop steward, has told me that she would be willing to consider this matter—especially if similar restrictions are imposed on the executive parking lot.

3 Since our next managers' meeting is on May 8-10, I look forward to being able to announce the new plan to them. By approving this change, Newton will be sending a powerful positive message to our visitors: Our employees believe in the products we sell.

JJP

Grammar and Mechanics Notes

1 Because of its more readable format, writers often prefer a standard memo format for persuasive messages—even when email is available. Often, the memo is sent as an attachment to an email message.

2 *70 percent:* Use figures and the word "percent" in business correspondence.

3 *managers' meeting:* Place the apostrophe *after* the *s* to form the possessive of a plural noun (*managers*).

specifically chosen to participate in some project. ("Me and how many thousands of others?" they might wonder.) On the other hand, such a compliment in a letter that is obviously personally typed and signed has much more credibility.

The most important factor to remember in asking for a favour has to do with the favour itself rather than with the writing process. Keep your request reasonable. Don't ask someone else to do something that you can or should do for yourself.

Figure 7.1 on page 236 illustrates how *not* to write an effective persuasive request. Model 8 on page 237, a revised version of the ineffective example, illustrates the guidelines discussed previously for writing an effective persuasive request. The reader and writer do not know each other, which makes persuasion a little more challenging and calls for an indirect organizational plan. Reader benefits (the opportunity to promote the reader's firm and the flattering prospect of being the centre of attention) are included.

Writing a Persuasive Claim

As discussed in Chapter 6, most claim letters are routine letters and should be written using a direct plan of organization—stating the problem early in the letter. Because it is to the company's benefit to keep its customers happy, most reasonable claims are settled to the customer's satisfaction. Therefore, persuasion is not ordinarily necessary.

CO3. Compose a persuasive claim.

Suppose, however, that you wrote a routine claim letter and the company, for some reason, denied your claim. If you still feel that your original claim is legitimate, you might then write a *persuasive* claim letter—using all the techniques discussed earlier in this chapter for writing persuasive requests. Or assume that your new photocopier broke three days after the warranty period expired. The company is not legally obligated to honour your claim, but you may decide to try to persuade it to do so anyway.

Showing anger in your persuasive claim letter is counterproductive, even if the company turns down your original claim. The goal of your letter is not to vent your anger but to solve a problem. And that is more likely to happen when a calm atmosphere prevails.

Avoid showing anger.

As in a routine claim letter, you will need to explain in sufficient detail precisely what the problem is, how it came about, and how you want the reader to solve the problem. Use a calm, objective, courteous tone, avoiding anger and exaggeration. Although similar in some respects to a routine claim letter, the persuasive claim differs in two important ways: it has an attention-getting opening and it presents more evidence.

Attention-Getting Opening   Recall that you begin a routine claim letter by stating the problem. This type of opening would not be wise for a persuasive claim because the reader may conclude the claim is unreasonable until he or she reads your rationale.

NOT: Would you please repair my Minolta 203 copier without charge, even though the 90-day warranty expired last week.

figure7.1
An Ineffective Persuasive Request

January 15, 20—

Ms. Tanya Porrat, Editor
Autoimmune Diseases Monthly
1800 Ten Hills Road, Suite B
Halifax, NS B3H 1P0

Dear Ms. Porrat

Subject: Request for You to Speak at the Multiple Sclerosis Congress

I have a favour to ask—a rather large one, I'm afraid. Having served as editor of a professional journal myself, I know how busy editors are, but I was wondering if you would be willing to fly to Victoria, BC, on April 25 and speak at the closing banquet of our annual Multiple Sclerosis Congress.

The problem, of course, is that as a non-profit association, we cannot afford to pay you an honorarium. I trust that this won't be a problem for you. We would, however, be willing to reimburse you for air travel and hotel accommodations.

Our conference attendants would benefit tremendously from your vast knowledge of multiple sclerosis, so we're really hoping you'll say yes. Just let me know your decision by March 3 in case we have to make other arrangements.

Please call me if you have any questions.

Cordially

May Lyon

May Lyon, Banquet Chair

Uses a subject line that is too specific

Begins by directly asking for the favour, using me-attitude language.

Omits important information (such as: Who will be attending the conference? How many attendees? How long will the presentation be?). Identifies the obstacle in a selfish manner—without including any reasons to minimize the obstacle.

Gives a deadline for answering—without providing any rationale.

Closes with a cliché.

BUT: We took a chance and lost! We bet that the Minolta 203 we purchased from you 96 days ago would prove to be as reliable as the other ten Minoltas our firm uses.

The original opening is counterproductive, providing a ready excuse for denying the claim. The revised version holds off making the request until enough background information has been provided. Note also the personal relationship the writer is beginning to establish with the reader in the revised version—disclosing not only that the company owns ten other Minolta copiers but also that the other copiers have all been very reliable. Such an understanding tone will make the reader more likely to grant the request.

PERSUASIVE REQUEST—ASKING FAVOUR

This persuasive request uses the indirect plan because the writer does not know the reader personally and because strong persuasion needed.

January 21, 20—

1   Ms. Tanya Porrat, Editor
Autoimmune Diseases Monthly
1800 Ten Hills Road, Suite B
Halifax, NS B3H 1P0

Dear Ms. Porrat

Subject: Program Planning for the Multiple Sclerosis Congress

2   "The average person has about 1 chance in 1000 of developing MS." Your comment in a recent interview in *The Daily News* made me sit up and think.

Your knack for exploring little-known facts like that would certainly be of keen interest to those attending our annual congress in Victoria, BC, on April 23-25. As the keynote speaker at the banquet at the Empress Hotel on April 25, you would be able to present your ideas on current initiatives to the 200 people present. You would, of course, be our guest for the banquet, which begins at 7 p.m. Your 45-minute presentation would begin at about 8:30 p.m.

We will reimburse you for air travel and hotel accommodations. Although our non-profit association is unable to offer an honorarium, we do offer you an opportunity to introduce your journal and to present your ideas to representatives of major autoimmune groups in the country.

3   We'd like to announce your presentation in our next newsletter, which goes to press on March 3. Won't you please call to let me know you can come. We'll have a large, enthusiastic audience of medical researchers waiting to hear you.

Cordially

May Lyon

May Lyon, Banquet Chair

4

Opens by quoting the reader, thus complimenting her.

Intimates the request; provides the necessary background information.

Subordinates a potential obstacle by putting it in the dependent clause of a sentence.

Closes with a restatement of reader benefit.

Grammar and Mechanics Notes

1 To increase readability, do not italicize publication titles in addresses.

2 *The Daily News:* Italicize the titles of separately published works, such as newspapers, magazines, and books.

3 *you can come.:* Use a period after a courteous request.

4 Do not include reference initials if the letter writer also types the letter.

More Evidence   Because your claim is either non-routine or has been rejected once, you will need to present as much convincing evidence as possible. Explain fully the basis for your claim; then request a specific adjustment.

Model 9 on page 239 illustrates these guidelines for writing a persuasive claim letter.

In a courteous manner, provide complete details.

■ Writing a Sales Letter

CO4. **Compose a sales letter.**

Small-business owners often write their own sales letters.

The heart of most business is sales—selling a product or service. Much of a company's sales effort is accomplished through the writing of effective sales letters—either individual letters for individual sales or form letters for large-scale sales.

In large companies, the writing of sales letters is centred in the advertising department and is a highly specialized task performed by advertising copywriters and marketing consultants. Within a few years after graduation, however, a growing number of college students opt to own their own businesses. These start-up companies are typically quite small, with only a few employees.

In such a situation, the company must mount an aggressive sales effort to develop business, but the company is typically too small to hire a full-time copywriter or marketing consultant. Thus, the owner usually ends up writing these sales letters, which are vital to the ongoing health of the firm. So no matter where you intend to work, the chances are that at some point you will need to write sales letters.

The indirect organizational plan is used for sales letters. It is sometimes called the *AIDA* plan, because you first gain the reader's *attention,* then create *interest* in and *desire* for the benefits of your product, and finally motivate *action.*

Selecting a Central Selling Theme

Your first step is to become thoroughly familiar with your product, its competition, and your intended audience. Then, you must select a **central selling theme** for your letter. Most products have numerous features that you will want to introduce and discuss. For your letter to make a real impact, however, you need to have a single theme running through your letter—a major reader benefit that you introduce early and emphasize throughout the letter. One noted copywriting consultant calls this principle a basic law of direct-mail advertising and labels it $E^2 = 0$, meaning that when you try to emphasize *everything,* you end up emphasizing *nothing.*[1]

It would be unrealistic to expect your reader to remember five different features that you mention about your product. In any case, you have only a short time to make a lasting impression on your reader. Use that time wisely to emphasize what you think is the most compelling benefit from owning your product. Two means of achieving this emphasis are *position* and *repetition.* Introduce your central selling theme early (in the opening sentence if possible), and keep referring to it throughout the letter.

Gaining the Reader's Attention

Review the earlier section on gaining the reader's attention when writing persuasive requests.

A reply to a request for product information from a potential customer is called a **solicited sales letter.** An **unsolicited sales letter,** on the other hand, is a letter promoting a firm's products that is mailed to potential customers who have not expressed any interest in the product. (Unsolicited sales letters are also called *prospecting letters.* Some recipients, of course, call them *junk mail.*)

PERSUASIVE CLAIM

This persuasive claim letter uses the indirect plan: the writer does not personally know the reader and thus cannot expect the claim to be granted automatically.

Begins on a warm and relevant note.

Provides a smooth transition from the opening sentence.

Provides the necessary background information.

Tells exactly what the problem is in a neutral, courteous tone.

Provides a rationale for granting the claim; asks confidently for specific action; mentions the reader benefit of keeping a satisfied customer.

June 18, 20—

Customer Service Supervisor
Western Air
P.O. Box 619616
Edmonton, AB T5X 2N8

Dear Customer Services Supervisor:

1   I think you will agree that a relaxing 90-minute flight on Western Air is more enjoyable than a gruelling six-hour automobile trip. Yet, on June 2, my wife and I found ourselves doing just that—driving from Calgary, Alberta, to Kelowna, British Columbia—in the middle of the night and in the company of three tired children.

2   We had made reservations on Western Flight 126 a month earlier. When we arrived at the airport, we were told that Flight 126 had been cancelled. Your gate agent (Ms. Nixon) had graciously rebooked us on the next available flight, leaving at 9:45 the next morning.

Since the purpose of our trip was to attend a family wedding on June 3, we had no choice but to cancel our rebooked flight and to drive to Kelowna instead. When we tried to turn in our tickets for a refund, Ms. Nixon informed us that because the flight had been cancelled due to inclement weather, she would be unable to credit my American Express charge card.

3   As a frequent flier on Western, I've often experienced the "Welcome Aboard!" feeling that is the basis for your current advertising; and I believe you will want to extend that same taken-care-of feeling to your ticket operations as well. Please credit my American Express charge card (No. 4102 817 171) for the $1680 cost of the five tickets, thus putting out the welcome mat again for my family.

Sincerely,

Oliver J. Arbin

Oliver J. Arbin
4   518 Thompson Street
Calgary, AB T2B 1J7

Grammar and Mechanics Notes

1 *just that—driving:* To insert a dash, type two hyphens (--) with no space before or after. The word processing program automatically converts two hyphens into a printed dash.

2 *rebooked:* Write most *re-* words solid—without a hyphen.

3 *taken-care-of feeling:* Hyphenate a compound adjective that comes before a noun.

4 For personal business letters on plain paper, type your address below your name.

Because most sales letters are unsolicited, you have only a line or two in which to grab the reader's attention. Unless a sales letter is addressed to the reader personally and is obviously not a form letter, the reader is likely to just skim it—either out of curiosity or because the opening sentence was especially intriguing.

Most readers will scan the opening, of even a form letter, perhaps just to learn what product is being promoted. If you can capture their attention in these first few lines, they may continue reading. Otherwise, all your efforts will have been wasted. The following types of opening sentences have proven effective for sales letters.

Technique	Example
Rhetorical question	What is the difference between extravagance and luxury? (*promoting a high-priced car*)
Thought-provoking statement	Most of what we had to say about business this morning was unprintable! (*promoting an early morning television news program*)
Unusual fact	If your family is typical, you will wash one ton of laundry this year. (*promoting a laundry detergent*)
Current event	The new Arrow assembly plant will bring 1700 new families to White Rock within three years. (*promoting a real estate company*)
Anecdote	During six years of college, the one experience that helped me the most did not even occur in the classroom. (*promoting a weekly business magazine*)
Direct challenge	Drop the enclosed Pointer pen on the floor, writing tip first, and then sign your name with it. (*promoting a no-blot ballpoint pen*)

Many attention-getting openings consist of a one-sentence paragraph.

As in persuasive requests, the opening of a sales letter should be interesting, short, and original. When possible, incorporate the central selling theme into your opening; and avoid irrelevant, obvious, or timeworn statements.

If you have received an inquiry from a potential customer about your product, you know that the person is already at least mildly interested in the product. Therefore, when you write solicited sales letters, an attention-getting opening is not as crucial. In such a situation, you might begin by expressing appreciation for the customer's inquiry and then start introducing the central selling theme.

Creating Interest and Building Desire

If your opening sentence is directly related to your product, the transition to the discussion of features and reader benefits will be smooth and logical. Make sure that the first sentence of the following paragraph relates directly to the idea introduced in your opening sentence. Unrelated ideas will make the reader pause and feel puzzled. Consider the following example. The first paragraph presents a

communication snapshot 7

Direct Mail Marketing

- 89% of Canadians open direct mail if it comes from a company they know.
- 86% open it if it looks intriguing or interesting.
- 84% open it if it has their name on it.
- 79% open it if it has their address.
- 66% open it if it has a postage stamp.
- 52% open it if it mentions a free draw.

Source: "Canada Post Survey," *Marketing.* Toronto: Nov 14, 2005, Vol. 110, Iss. 37, p. S4.

What May You Say in a Sales Letter?

In Canada, the *Competition Act* regulates trade and commerce, including what can and cannot be said about a product or service. At the provincial level, there are also statutes that regulate fair trading practices.

May I say our product is the best on the market?
Yes. You may legally express an opinion about a product or service; this is called "puffery". You may not, however, misrepresent a product or service, either by expressing an opinion that is intentionally misleading or by making a claim about the product that is untrue.

Can I compare my product or service to that of my competition?
Yes. But if your comparisons are inaccurate or misleading, they are illegal. Slander is an unfair or untrue oral statement made about a competitor; libel is such a statement made in writing. Product disparagement is a deceptive claim about a competitor's product. When such statements can be interpreted as damaging to a competitor's reputation, then legal action is warranted.

Can I charge any price I want for a product or service?
Yes. But you cannot charge a price considered to grossly exceed the price at which similar goods or services are readily available without informing the consumer of the difference in price and the reason for the difference. You also cannot charge a price greater than an advertised price unless you've taken action to correct the misleading advertisement.

Can I offer a "limited time" low price?
Yes. As long as you make reasonable quantities of the product available at that price or you make it clear that quantities are limited. Advertising a reduced price for a product that you don't actually supply and then promoting a more expensive product to the consumer is known as "bait and switch" selling, which is illegal.

Can I offer a "prize" to promote a product or service?
Yes. But it is illegal to then ask the winner to pay money or incur a cost in order to claim the prize. You are also required, in the case of a contest or raffle, to disclose the number of prizes available and the chances of winning. You must also be careful that your contest doesn't fall under the Canadian *Criminal Code*'s definition of gambling. The *Criminal Code* defines gambling as having three essential elements: "a valuable prize, the selection of a winner by chance, and a fee or consideration paid by participants." To avoid a contest being considered gambling, promoters will often require that a skill testing question be answered correctly before a prize can be claimed. They will also allow "free participation" in the contest to ensure the contest cannot be considered to be charging a fee for participation.

short, relevant attention getter, but the first sentence of the second paragraph abruptly changes direction, risking reader confusion about the message's purpose.

Attention getter: If you're like most Royal Bank customers, the demands on your time are growing, even at home.

NOT: **First sentence of second paragraph:** The Royal Bank Visa Classic offers solid value.

To improve the transition between the attention getter and the next paragraph, the writer should pick up a word, phrase, or theme from the attention getter and then refer to it—or even expand upon it—in the second paragraph.

Attention getter: If you're like most Royal Bank customers, the demands on your time are growing, even at home.

BUT: **First sentence of second paragraph:** That's why we've made it faster and easier than ever to acquire one of the most convenient credit cards around—the Royal Bank Visa Classic.

Interpreting Features   The major part of your letter (typically, several paragraphs) will probably be devoted to creating interest and building desire for your product. You should not only describe the product and its features but, more important, *interpret* these features by showing specifically how each will benefit the reader. Make the reader—not the product—the subject of most of your sentences.

Marketers refer to the benefit a user receives from a product or service as the **derived benefit.** As Charles Revson, founder of the Revlon cosmetics company, once said, "In our factory we make lipstick; in our advertising we sell hope."[2]

Devote several paragraphs to interpreting the product's features.

NOT: The JT Laser II prints at the speed of ten pages per minute.

BUT: After pressing the print key, you'll barely have time to reach over and retrieve the page from the bin. The JT Laser II's print speed of ten pages per minute is twice that of the typical printer.

NOT: Masco binoculars zoom from 3 to 12 power.

BUT: With Masco binoculars, you can look a ruby-throated hummingbird squarely in the eye at 100 metres and see it blink.

Although emphasizing the derived benefit rather than product features is generally the preferred strategy, two situations call for emphasizing product features instead: when promoting a product to experts and when promoting expensive equipment. For example, if the car you're promoting to sports car enthusiasts achieves a maximum torque of 330 ft-lb at 3000 rpm or produces 345 hp at 5500 rpm, tell the reader that. You would sound condescending trying to interpret to such experts what this means.

Using Vivid Language   Use action verbs when talking about the product's features and benefits. Within reason, use colourful adjectives and adverbs, being careful, however, to avoid a hard-sell approach. Finally, to convey a dynamic image, use positive language, stressing what your product *is,* rather than what it is *not.*

NOT: The paper tray is designed to hold 200 sheets.

BUT: The paper tray holds 200 sheets—enough to last the busy executive a full week without reloading.

NOT: The Terminator snowblower is not one of those lightweight models.

BUT: The Terminator's 4.5 hp engine is 50 percent more powerful than the standard 3.0 hp engine used in most snowblowers.

Maintain credibility by providing specific facts and figures.

Using Objective, Ethical Language   To be convincing, you must present specific, objective evidence. Simply saying that a product is great is not enough. You must provide evidence to show *why* or *how* the product is great. Here is where you'll use all the data you gathered before you started to write. Avoid generalities, unsupported superlatives and claims, and too many or too strong adjectives and adverbs.

Positive statements by independent agencies lend powerful support.

NOT: At $1595, the Sherwood moped is the best buy on the market.

BUT: The May 2004 *Independent Consumer* rated the $1595 Sherwood moped the year's best buy.

NOT: We know you will enjoy the convenience of our Bread Baker.

BUT: Our Bread Baker comes with one feature we don't think you'll ever use: a 30-day, no-questions-asked return policy.

Although the law allows you to promote your product aggressively, there are certain legal and ethical constraints under which you will want to operate. The guidelines provided in Spotlight 15, "What May You Say in a Sales Letter?," on page 241, apply to Canadian fair trading and competition practices. When operating in the international environment, you should follow local laws and customs.

Focusing on the Central Selling Theme   The recurring theme of your letter should be the one feature that sets your product apart from the competition and that satisfies a specific need or desire. If your reader remembers nothing else about your product, this one feature is what you want him or her to remember. Whenever possible, unify the features under one umbrella theme—whether the theme is convenience, ease of use, flexibility, price, or some other distinguishing characteristic around which you can build your case. Introduce this umbrella theme early in the message (often in your attention getter); reiterate and expand upon this theme in the body paragraphs by tying, as much as possible, the various features of your product into the umbrella theme; and refer to this theme again in the closing paragraph.

Discussing and fully interpreting the various features may take a considerable amount of space, and some readers may be unwilling to read through a long sales letter. By focusing on a central selling theme and demonstrating how each feature satisfies a specific need or desire, you increase the likelihood the message will be read through to the end and, more importantly, you leave the reader with a simple and clear reason to respond favourably to your request. Ultimately, the test of an effective sales letter is the number of sales it generates—*not* the number of people who read the letter.

> *Focus on the one feature that sets your product apart.*

Mentioning Price   If price is your central selling theme, introduce it early and emphasize it often. In most cases, however, price is not the central selling theme and should therefore be subordinated. Introduce the price late in the message, after most of the advantages of owning the product have been discussed. To subordinate price, mention it in a long complex or compound sentence, perhaps in a sentence that also mentions a reader benefit.

You'll consider the $250 cost of this spreadsheet seminar repaid in full the very next time your boss asks you to revise the quarterly sales budget—on a Friday afternoon!

Sometimes it is helpful to present the price in terms of small units.

The Royal Bank Visa Classic offers solid value. You'll receive many advantages for the low annual fee of $12…that's only $1 a month for unlimited transactions! Or, of you prefer, you can pay just 15 cents per transaction.

> *Use techniques of subordination when mentioning price.*

Another approach is to compare the price of your product to that of a familiar object—"about what you'd pay for your morning newspaper or cup of coffee."

Referring to Enclosures   Often, some of the features of a product or service are best displayed in a brochure that you can enclose with the sales letter. Subordinate your reference to the enclosure, and refer to some specific item in the enclosure to increase the likelihood of its being read.

NOT: I have enclosed a sales brochure on this product.

BUT: Note the porcelain robin's detailed colouring on the actual-size photograph on page 2 of the enclosed brochure.

NOT: I have enclosed a blank order form for your convenience.

BUT: Use the enclosed blank order form to send us your request today. Within three weeks, you will be enjoying this museum-quality sculpture in your own home.

Motivating Action

Push confidently, but gently, for prompt action.

Although the purpose of your letter should be apparent right from the start, delay making your specific request until late in the letter—after you have created interest and built desire for the product. Then state the specific action you want.

If the desired action is an actual sale, make taking action easy by including a toll-free number, enclosing a blank order form, accepting credit cards, and the like. For high-priced items, it would be unreasonable to expect to make an actual sale by mail. Probably no one has read a sales letter promoting a new automobile and then phoned in an order for the car. For such items, your goal is to get the reader to take just a small step toward purchasing—sending for more information, stopping by the dealer for a demonstration, or asking a sales representative to call. Again, make the next step easy for the reader.

Provide an incentive for prompt action by, for example, offering a gift to the first 100 people who respond or stressing the need to buy early while there is still a good selection, before the holiday rush, or during the three-day sale. Make your push for action *gently,* however. Any tactic that smacks of high-pressure selling at this point is likely to increase reader resistance.

Use confident language when asking for action, avoiding such hesitant phrases as "If you want to save money" or "I hope you agree that this product will save you time." When asking the reader to part with money, it is always a good idea to mention a reader benefit in the same sentence.

NOT: Hurry! Hurry! Hurry! These sale prices won't be in effect long.

NOT: If you agree that this ice cream maker will make your summers more enjoyable, you can place your order by telephone.

BUT: To have your Jiffy Ice Cream Maker available for use during the upcoming Canada Day weekend, simply call our toll-free number today.

Consider putting an important marketing point in a postscript (P.S.). Some marketing studies have shown that a postscript notation is the most-often-read part of a sales letter.[3] It can be as long or as short as needed, but it should contain new and interesting information.

P.S. If you stop in for a demonstration before May 1, you'll walk out with a free box of colour transparencies (retail value $21.95)—just for trying Up Front, the new presentation software program by Acme Products.

✓checklist 9

Sales Letters

Prepare

✓ Learn as much as possible about the product, the competition, and the audience.

✓ Select a central selling theme—your product's most distinguishing feature.

Gain the Reader's Attention

✓ Make your opening brief, interesting, and original. Avoid obvious, misleading, and irrelevant statements.

✓ Use any of these opening techniques: rhetorical question, thought-provoking statement, unusual fact, current event, anecdote, direct challenge, or some similar attention-getting device.

✓ Introduce (or at least lead up to) the central selling theme in the opening.

✓ If the letter is in response to a customer inquiry, begin by expressing appreciation for the inquiry and then introduce the central selling theme.

Create Interest and Build Desire

✓ Make the introduction of the product follow naturally from the attention-getter.

✓ *Interpret* the features of the product; instead of just describing the features, show how the reader will benefit from each feature. Let the reader picture owning, using, and enjoying the product.

✓ Use action-packed, positive, and objective language. Provide convincing evidence to support your claims—specific facts and figures, independent product reviews, endorsements, and so on.

✓ Continue to stress the central selling theme throughout.

✓ Subordinate price (unless price is the central selling theme). State price in small terms, in a long sentence, or in a sentence that also talks about benefits.

Motivate Action

✓ Make the desired action clear and easy to take.

✓ Ask confidently, avoiding the hesitant "If you'd like to" or "I hope you agree that."

✓ Encourage prompt action (but avoid a hard-sell approach).

✓ End your letter with a reminder of a reader benefit.

These guidelines for writing an effective sales letter are illustrated in Model 10 on page 246 and summarized in Checklist 9. As always, the test of the effectiveness of a message is whether it achieves its goal. Use whatever information you have available (especially in terms of audience analysis) to help your letter achieve its goal.

■ Collecting Money that is Due

The primary purpose of collection messages is to collect past-due accounts. The secondary purpose is to retain the debtor's goodwill. The collection process usually begins with mailing the monthly statement, and the vast majority of accounts are paid by the due date. For those that are not, companies often use a three-stage series of messages: reminder, appeal, and ultimatum (more than one message may be sent at any one of these strategies). Keep in mind that provincial consumer protection

CO5. **Compose a collection letter.**

model 10

SALES LETTER

Starts with a rhetorical question.

Introduces need for safety and security as the central selling theme.

Presents specific evidence and discusses it in terms of reader benefits.

Emphasizes *you* instead of the product in most sentences.

Subordinates price in a long sentence that also discusses benefits.

Makes the desired action clear and easy; ends with a reader benefit.

Success Home & Hardware
4047 Queens Street
Calgary, AL T25 IX5

1

2   Dear Homeowner:

Do you view your home as an investment or as your castle? Is it primarily a tax write-off or a place of refuge?

Most of us view our homes as places where we can feel safe from outside intrusions. Thus, we feel threatened by government statistics showing that 3 percent of all Canadian households were burglarized last year. How can we protect ourselves?

Today, there's a simple and dependable alarm that protects up to 700 square metres. Just plug in the Safescan Home Alarm System and turn the key. You then have 30 seconds to leave and 15 seconds to switch off the alarm once you return.

3   Worried that your dog might trigger the alarm? Safescan screens out normal sounds like crying babies, outside traffic, and rain. But hostile noises like breaking glass and splintering wood trigger the alarm. The 105-decibel siren is loud enough to alert neighbours and to drive away even the most determined burglar.

What if a smart burglar disconnects the electricity to your home or pulls the plug? Built-in batteries assure that Safescan operates through power failures, and batteries recharge automatically. Best of all, installation is easy. Simply mount the 1.8-kilogram unit on a wall, and plug it in. Nothing could be faster. Finally, there is a $259 home alarm that you can trust; and the one-year warranty and ten-day return policy ensure your complete satisfaction.

Last year, more than a quarter million burglaries occurred in Canada, but you can now tip the odds back in your favour. To order the Safescan Home Alarm System, stop by your nearest Success Home and Hardware. Within minutes, Safescan can be guarding your home, giving you peace of mind.

Sincerely yours,

Jeffrey Parret

Jeffrey Parret
National Sales Manager

Grammar and Mechanics Notes

1 In general, omit the date and inside address in form sales letters. Subject lines are also frequently omitted.

2 *Dear Homeowner:* Note the generic salutation.

3 *crying babies, outside traffic, and:* Separate items in a series by commas.

acts and/or privacy acts place limits on how you may go about collecting a debt. These laws should be consulted before you proceed.

For all collection letters:

1. Ensure that the information is accurate and that your message follows all provincial laws regarding collection practices.
2. Adopt a tone of reasonableness and helpfulness; avoid anger.
3. Send letters promptly and—if payment doesn't result—at systematic intervals, so that the debt is never out of the reader's mind.
4. In every letter include the reader's account number, the amount owed, and a pre-stamped, addressed envelope.

Reminder Stage

Early letters are gentle reminders that a bill has not been paid and that the reader fully intends to pay. You may wish to assume the bill is in the mail, but lost or delayed. Or, you could assume that this has been merely an oversight on the side of the customer. The tone should be positive throughout, and the letter should be short and direct, and treated as a routine matter.

The Opening　The opening of a reminder letter should state the status of the reader's account. Remind the reader that payment was due, and that the account is now overdue by the appropriate length of time.

> This is just a quick reminder that your account with us is 60 days past due.

The Explanation　In the explanation, you should briefly review the account history, stating the amount, when it was due, and even what it was for. You may include some benefits here as well, and keep the tone positive.

> On September 30, 2005, you purchased $1345.97 of building supplies from our Regina store, which were charged to your account. The amount was due on November 1, 2005, but we have not yet received payment. While this is probably just an oversight, payment by the end of this month will ensure that no interest accrues on the account.

The Closing　In the closing, urge the reader to act by making the action easy. You may also wish to give a personal contact number in case the reader has any questions.

> You can take care of this by calling 1-888-6767 or by using the postage paid envelope we've included with this reminder. We look forward to doing business with you again in the future.

Appeal Stage

At the appeal stage, you must ask for payment more assertively and work to persuade the reader that he or she must pay. You could educate the reader on credit ratings and how these are endangered by late and missing payments, or you could appeal to the reader's morals or ethics. Use the indirect form and a central appeal, with reader benefits and positive language. Keep the tone neutral, not accusatory, because if the reader feels accused, then he or she will be more likely to continue delaying payment.

The Opening   In the opening, you should gain the reader's attention to ensure that the letter is read. Recall that the reader has received an earlier letter from you and knows the status of his or her account. Consider appealing to the reader's pride, ethics, or even self-interest.

> Knowing that you are up-to-date on all your payments can give you a big sense of accomplishment. (pride)

> Just like any building, a business relationship needs a strong foundation. (ethics)

> Clearing up all your outstanding debts can help ensure that when you need a personal loan, a mortgage, or even a small-business loan, you'll be able to count on us. (self-interest)

The Explanation   In the explanation, you should again review the client's account history, keeping the tone as positive as possible. Include further benefits of keeping a good credit rating with the company. Show what you have done for the client in the past, and ask if there is any way you can help the client to rectify this matter.

> As of today, your payment for $1345.97 of building supplies you purchased on September 30, 2005, from our Regina store has not been received. As a business person yourself, you can understand our concern that this payment be received as early as possible.

> As one of our valued small-business customers, you have been able to take advantage of our large volume discounts, early opening hours, and convenient payment plan. To continue offering you these services, we would like to help you to rectify this matter.

The Closing   The closing should stress the need for prompt action and, again, make taking action easy.

> Please send us the full payment of $1574.79 (which includes the 1.17 percent interest charge) today, or contact me personally at 888-6767 to arrange a convenient payment schedule.

Final Letters

In final letters, assume that the reader has no intention of paying. This should be a direct letter explaining exactly what you will do if the bill is not paid. The letter's tone should still remain relatively neutral, but the letter must demand payment and provide a clear deadline. Overall, ensuring payment is more important here than maintaining goodwill. Check the provincial regulations on debt collecting to see just what you cannot and can include in this kind of letter.

The Opening   The opening restates the facts with a firmer tone. You do not need to use persuasive strategies here in order to get the reader interested in the letter. Let the details speak for themselves and keep a firm but neutral tone.

> On September 30, 2005, you purchased $1345.97 of building supplies from our Edmonton store. We have not yet received payment.

The Explanation   In the explanation, outline the steps you have taken thus far, and state the next step to be taken as clearly as possible, while still retaining the neutral tone.

Summary

When writing to superiors, use a direct writing style, giving the proposal or recommendation, along with the criteria or a brief rationale, in the first paragraph. For most other persuasive messages, prefer an indirect writing style. First gain the reader's attention by using an opening paragraph that is relevant, interesting, and short. For persuasive requests promoting an idea, devote the majority of the message to discussing the merits of your proposal and showing specifically how your proposal meets some need of the reader. Provide evidence that is accurate, relevant, representative, and complete. Discuss and minimize any obstacles to your proposal.

co1. Compose a persuasive message promoting an idea.

Begin your request with an attention-getter and stress the reader benefits from granting the favour. Discuss at least one reader benefit before making your request, and show how someone other than you will benefit from the favour. Keep a positive tone throughout, and make the action clear and easy.

co2. Compose a persuasive message requesting a favour.

Write persuasive claims in the indirect organization, beginning with an attention-getting opening. Use a calm, objective, courteous tone, avoiding anger and exaggeration. Explain in detail the problem, and provide objective evidence to persuade the reader to grant the claim.

co3. Compose a persuasive claim.

For sales letters, introduce a central selling theme early and build on it throughout the message. Devote most of the message to showing how the reader will specifically benefit from owning the product. Subordinate the price, unless price is the central selling theme.

co4. Compose a sales letter.

For collection letters, consider a three-stage appeal. Begin with a polite reminder. Maintain a positive tone throughout, keep the letter short and direct, and treat it as a routine matter. At the appeal stage, use the indirect form and stress reader benefits and positive language. Keep the tone neutral and avoid accusing the reader, which may provoke further delays. At the ultimatum stage maintain a neutral tone, but demand payment and provide a clear deadline.

co5. Compose a collection letter.

Key Terms

You should now be able to define the following terms in your own words and give an original example of each.

central selling theme (238)

rhetorical question (229)

derived benefit (242)

solicited sales letter (238)

persuasion (222)

unsolicited sales letter (238)

Exercises

1 **The 3Ps (Problem, Process, and Product) Model: Communication Applications at BMO Capital Markets**   Before Martha Durdin's sales team conducts a sales presentation to potential corporate clients, they carefully investigate their client's needs. Most important to the team is that they establish credibility, emphasize client benefits, and leave the audience with a clear and memorable story about why they should become a BMO Capital Markets client.

Problem

You are an associate with BMO Capital Markets. After going with Martha Durdin to visit a potential client, you need to draft your very first PowerPoint presentation, which you will present to the client in two weeks. You have learned that the client is particularly interested in acquiring a small winery to supplement her range of red wines. You need to introduce the client to a small winery that produces a pinot wine, well respected among wine connoisseurs, that might be receptive to being acquired by a larger winery. You also need to help the client understand how she could finance this acquisition and the impact of the additional sales revenue on her bottom line.

Process

a. Describe your audience.
b. Should you use a direct or indirect organizational plan for this presentation? Why?
c. What are the three messages you want to communicate to this client?
d. In what order should they be delivered?
e. What points should you include in the body of the presentation?
f. Write an opening that is attention-getting, relevant, and introduces your central selling theme.
g. What action do you want the audience to take?
h. Prepare a summary page that motivates your audience to take the desired action.

Product

Using your knowledge of persuasive messages, draft a series of PowerPoint slides for this sales presentation, inventing any reasonable data needed to complete this assignment.

CO1. Compose a persuasive message promoting an idea.

2 The 3Ps (Problem, Process, and Product) Model: A Persuasive Message—Selling an Idea

Problem

You are O.B. Presley, a sales representative for Midland Medical Supplies. Like most of the other 38 Midland reps, you are on the road three or four days a week, promoting your products to hospitals, clinics, and physicians in general practice. Three years ago, Midland purchased 3.6-kilogram laptop computers for all sales reps. These computers simplified your job immensely, especially in terms of filing call reports. Each evening in your hotel room, you keyboard the report, detailing to whom you spoke, their experiences with your products, what features they'd like to see changed, and the like. You then submit these reports, along with actual orders, electronically to headquarters via the computer's built-in modem.

It occurs to you that you could be more productive by replacing your bulky laptop with a notebook computer and portable printer. That way, whenever a customer wanted a specification sheet for a new product, you could electronically retrieve the information from the company's mainframe computer and print it on the spot for the customer. You're sure you'd get additional sales as a result.

The specific system you're interested in is the Apple MacBook, a lightweight, notebook computer with Bluetooth technology, 1 GB of RAM and a 120-GB hard drive. The system, which includes a portable inkjet printer, sells for $2199 and weighs just 2.5 kilograms. The only problem is that you don't know what to do with your present laptop computer. There's not much demand for used laptops, especially for a three-year-old, 3.6-kilogram machine. Still, you think the MacBooks would be a good investment for all sales reps. Send an email or memo to Charles J. Redding, national sales manager, trying to sell him on the idea.

Process

a. Describe your audience.
b. Should you use a direct or indirect organizational plan? Why?
c. Write the opening sentence of your memo.
d. List the reasons you might discuss for your proposal—including any reader benefits associated with each reason.
e. What is an obstacle that might prevent you from achieving your objective?
f. Write a sentence that addresses this obstacle (subordinate this discussion).
g. Write the last paragraph of your email or memo, in which you state (or restate) your request. Make taking action easy for the reader, ask confidently, and end on a forward-looking note.

Product

Draft, revise, format, and proofread your message. If necessary, go to Apple's Web site for further details about the computer. Then submit both your responses to the process questions and your revised memo to your instructor.

3 Routine Request—Helping a Friend   You are the plant manager of the Monterey Manufacturing Company in Montreal. You manufacture automotive ball bearings. Currently you have 125 employees. One of your employees, Francis Benoit, has been diagnosed with lung cancer.

Francis is well known and well liked at the plant, but his illness has kept him out of work for over two months, and he has exhausted all of his sick leave. His doctor believes he will probably be out of work for at least three more months. You want to encourage your employees to donate sick leave time to Francis. Employees can donate up to five days sick leave each. No one is required to participate, but anyone who can should give at least a few hours of sick leave.

To donate sick leave time to Francis, employees must fill out a form in the Human Resource Management department. Forms must be submitted before the end of the month for accounting purposes. Any unused hours and days will return to those who have donated on a proportional basis.

Write a memo, to be included in the company's electronic newsletter, encouraging the employees to donate time to Francis.

4 Gold Doesn't Always Glitter   For the last few years your union has been negotiating an incentive bonus plan for the employees at the Fremont Gold Extraction plant in Yellowknife, North West Territories. The plan was designed to compensate employees based on their productivity and would be given as a bonus at the end of the year based on the company's profitability.

Finally you, as the union representative, got the company to agree to the plan. At first the plan appeared a success. Projections showed that some employees would earn bonuses of up to $5000. The production rates had increased dramatically, and everyone seemed to be happy with the arrangement.

Now in the second half of the year, because of the increased production, the price of gold is taking a "nose dive." Although the plan seemed like a good idea, it needs to be reworked. You know the workers are expecting bonuses, but you want them to vote to rescind the plan. Not getting the bonus this year will hurt, but they need to have a plan that will consistently reward them for their efforts.

Write an email to the employees persuading them to vote to rescind the negotiated incentive bonus plan. The vote will be from 6 to 8 p.m. in the union hall on Tuesday, September 1, 20—.

5 **Watch What You Say!**   Is it just you or is profanity now being used everywhere— even in the workplace? Although you're no prude, as the store manager for DVDs Plus, you want to avoid creating a hostile work environment and also ensure that your employees project a positive image for the organization (and for themselves). Write an email to your sales staff encouraging them to clean up their language.

6 **Building Co-op Programs**   Students in your construction management program are struggling to find good-paying jobs after graduation. You are determined to resolve the issue. You have seen effective co-op programs offered in other schools, and you believe that a co-op program would be a great way for your students who are approaching graduation to get some very valuable hands-on experience in their chosen fields.

Your experience with such programs has been that once the student works with a company and the company spends time training the student, the company is more likely to hire him or her later. You also believe that some of the construction firms in the area could benefit from the innovative techniques your students are learning in the classroom.

You are proposing a program that would allow your students to get a 12-week paid co-op with local construction companies. The first two weeks would give the student an overview of the company's operation. For the last ten weeks, the student would receive specialized training in a particular area. Students would be paid one-half of the rate of an entry-level employee.

As the job placement director of your school in rural Manitoba, write a letter to Cleo S. Johnson, the owner of Johnson and Sons Construction, at 45 John Street, Eloy, MB R0H 5P9. Persuade him to accept an intern from your school for a 12-week assignment.

Selling an Idea—Indirect Organizational Plan   Refer to Exercise 2. Assume that you (O. B. Presley) are relatively new on the job and have not yet earned the trust of the national sales manager. In addition, you know that Redding is not a big fan of technology. Therefore, you decide to write your memo using an indirect organizational plan. Write the memo.

Selling an Idea—Oversized Dressing Rooms   You are Robert Kilcline, a merchandising manager at Nordstrom, Inc., a fine clothing store in Ottawa.

Your firm has decided to open a new store in Fashion Square Mall, an upscale department store. Retail space is quite expensive in this mall (nearly 50 percent more expensive than at your other locations), so Nordstrom facility engineers are trying to make every inch of space count.

Despite the costs, you feel that to be competitive in this mall, you will have to offer superior customer service. You already offer a no-questions-asked return policy, abundant inventory to ensure a complete selection of sizes and colours, and a harpist who performs on the main floor from 11 a.m. until 2 p.m. daily. But you think that the new store should also have oversized dressing rooms—ones large enough to hold a comfortable chair, garment rack, and adjustable three-sided mirrors. You want your customers to be able to make their selections in comfort.

You estimate that adding the furnishings and additional 3 square metres per dressing room in the new store will add $18 500 to the construction costs, plus $155 to the monthly lease. Present your ideas in an email to your boss, Rebecca Wiebe, executive vice-president.

9 Internet Exercise   Many businesses—on and off the Internet—use persuasive messages for both sales and non-sales purposes. Consider the situation at DoubleClick, a company that places advertisements for clients on various websites. Visit the firm's site (at www.doubleclick.com) and follow the link to review its privacy policy, especially the section about cookies and how to opt out. Then find and follow the link that discusses how consumers can opt out of DoubleClick's customized advertising program. Now assume the role of DoubleClick's Web master. Draft an email message intended to persuade consumers to reverse their opt-out decisions and continue allowing DoubleClick to send them customized advertising messages.

10 Conference Speaker   You are planning a conference for your professional organization. A good friend from your university days at Acadia, Virginia Jackson, is a highly regarded motivational speaker. You want to get her to be the keynote speaker for your annual conference, which will be held in Halifax, on Friday, October 22, 20—. You would not be able to pay her normal speaking fee of $2000, but you could cover her airfare and lodging.

CO2. Compose a persuasive message requesting a favour.

Although you were quite close in university, you have not visited in several years. The last time you did speak to her, she indicated that she would enjoy getting together with you and some other friends in the area. You could arrange to have her fly to Halifax on Thursday and leave on Sunday morning. Her speech would be from 10 to 11 a.m. on Friday. You and some of her other friends could spend time on Thursday and Saturday renewing old acquaintances.

Write a letter to Virginia at 1250 Whitney Lane in Ottawa, ON K2P 1C3, inviting her to come to Nova Scotia to visit and be the keynote speaker at the conference.

11 Requesting a Favour—Field Trip   You are David Pearson, owner and manager of Jack 'n Jill Preschool. During the next few weeks, you will be discussing food and nutrition with the youngsters; and you want to end the unit by having the children walk to the nearby Salad Haven, take a tour of the kitchens, and then make their own salads for lunch from the restaurant's popular salad bar. Of course, each family would pay for its child's meal. In fact, to help make the visit easier, you'll collect the money beforehand and pay the cashier for everyone at once. You will ask several parents to come with you to help supervise the 23 children, ages three through five, although they will probably need some extra help from the salad-bar attendants. You can come any day during the week of October 10–14. Provincial regulations require that the children eat lunch between

11 a.m. and 12:30 p.m. Write to Donna Jo Luse (Manager, Salad Haven, 75 Lakeshore Bld., Peachland, BC V0H 4K8) asking for permission to make the field trip.

12 Requesting a Favour—Celebrity Donation   Coming out of the movie theatre after watching the Academy Award–winning movie *Rocky Mountain Adventure,* starring Robert Forte, you suddenly have an idea. As executive director of the Wilderness Fund, you've been searching for an unusual raffle prize for your upcoming fundraiser. You wonder whether you could persuade Robert Forte to donate some item used in this popular movie (perhaps a stage prop or costume item) for the raffle. The Wilderness Fund is an 8000-member non-profit agency dedicated to preserving forest lands—the very type of lands photographed so beautifully in Forte's latest movie. Write to the actor at Century Studios, 467 Eastern Ave., Toronto, ON M5K 9G4.

13 Persuasive Request—Sidestepping a Digital Ban   The dean of your university recently read a news article describing how students can use pagers, cellphones, and hand-held computers to share answers during classroom exams. According to the article, one-third of students in a recent survey said they've cheated during tests, and half said they've cheated on written assignments. As a result, the dean issued a statement forbidding students from having or using electronic hand-held devices in class when working on tests and projects.

Your sister is about to give birth to twins, and you've pleaded with your instructors to relax the ban on cellphones for the next three weeks so that you can take the call if it comes during a test. The instructors, however, need the dean's permission to make such an exception. Now you must submit a written request for the dean's consideration. Should you use the direct or indirect plan? Why? How can you justify your request? What obstacles can you anticipate—and how can you overcome them? Based on your knowledge of persuasive requests, write a letter to the dean (making up the details for this assignment).

CO3. Compose a persuasive claim.

14 Writing a Persuasive Claim—Azaleas   You are Vera Malcolm, the facilities manager for the City of Saint John. In preparation for the recent dedication of your new hydroelectric plant, you spruced up the grounds near the viewing stand. As part of the stage decorations, you ordered ten potted azaleas at $28.50 each (plus $10.50 shipping) from Jackson-Parsons Nurseries (5 Fleming Road, Summerside, PE C1N 3K9 on June 3. The bushes were guaranteed to arrive in show condition—ready to burst into bloom within three days—or your money would be cheerfully refunded.

The plants arrived in healthy condition but were in their final days (perhaps hours) of flowering—certainly in no shape to display at the dedication. You decided, instead, to plant the azaleas as part of your permanent landscaping. Because the plants arrived only three days before the dedication, you had to purchase substitute azaleas from the local florist—at a much higher price. In fact, you ended up paying $436 for the florist plants—$140.50 more than the Jackson-Parsons price. You feel that the nursery was responsible for your having to incur the additional expenditure. Write a letter asking Jackson-Parsons to reimburse your company for the $140.50.

15 Writing a Persuasive Claim—Fans in the Stands   Assume the role of the ticket manager for the Victoria Angels Rookie League baseball team. You are looking for sponsors to be featured at your minor league baseball games. You also want to put fans in the stands and get youngsters interested in baseball.

You are planning a promotion that will allow local merchants to purchase tickets that would be donated to underprivileged children. The promotion involves businesses donating $500 worth of tickets (100 tickets) in exchange for being the featured sponsor at one of the Angels games. The company donating the tickets would be featured during the seventh-inning stretch. The children who received the tickets would also be featured and would receive a visit from Charlie the Wonder Whale—the Angels' mascot.

This promotion would be good for the children, it would be good for your fan base, and it would be good for the businesses that would get some positive publicity. Write a letter to the president of Allred's Sporting Goods, John N. Allred, encouraging him to be a featured sponsor at one of your games in August. His address is 95 Empire Street, Victoria, BC V8X 6M2.

16 Writing a Persuasive Claim—Ripped Suit After a hurried taxi ride from Pearson International Airport to the Marriott Marquis Hotel on May 15, you barely made it to your 2 p.m. appointment. You did not realize until you sat down at the conference table that you had ripped the pants of your $450 suit on an exposed spring in the taxi seat. The next day, your tailor tells you there is no way to repair the rip invisibly, so the suit is, in effect, now useless. Since you've owned the suit for a year, you don't expect the taxi company to reimburse you for $450, but you do think reimbursement of $200 is reasonable. From your taxi receipt, you learn that you took Taxi 1145 belonging to Hog Town Taxi (2215 Carlaw Ave., Toronto, ON M4R 8P3). Since this is a personal claim, write your letter on plain paper, using your own return address.

17 Writing a Persuasive Claim—Lemon SUV As the new owner of a sports utility vehicle, you were expecting to head into the backcountry for some camping and fishing trips. You purchased the SUV three months ago from Howard Williams, the owner of Big Willie's Auto. You paid $20 500 for the two-year-old SUV. Mr. Williams offered you a 12-month, 20 000 kilometre extended warranty for $1000, which you decided to purchase.

When you purchased the vehicle, it had 68 353 kilometres on the odometer; now it shows only 72 339 kilometres. You have driven it fewer than 5000 kilometres. It has been in the shop on two occasions in the three months. The first time you took it off-road, you had problems and had to have it towed back to town. The problem seems to be with the vehicle's transmission. So far, Mr. Williams has paid for the towing, $50, and transmission repair bills of $587.50; but you are getting tired of the continual problems with this "lemon."

Although the warranty does not cover the installation of a new transmission, you want Mr. Williams to pay for one. You have a friend who will install a new one for only $850—other shops have quoted $1800 to do the job. This will give you some peace of mind and eliminate the every-other-month trip to the repair shop. This would also restore your confidence in Mr. Williams as a fair business person. This will also help him because at the current rate, he will probably pay more for transmission repairs under the warranty than the $1150. Your friend will guarantee the new transmission for 24 months, so Mr. Williams would be off the hook for transmission repairs.

Write to Mr. Williams at Big Willie's Auto, 567 King Street, Windsor ON N8X 3E6, persuading him to pay the $850 for installation of a new transmission.

CO**4.** **Compose a sales letter.**

18 **Selling a Product—Work Boots**   As sales manager for Industrial Footwear, Inc., send a form sales letter advertising your Durham work boot to 3000 members of Local 147 of the Building Trades Union. Local 147 is made up primarily of construction workers on high-rise buildings in Vancouver.

The Durham is a 20-centimetre, waterproof, insulated boot, made of oil-tanned cowhide. It exceeds the guidelines for steel-toe protection issued by the Canadian Standards Association (CSA). The Durham has an all-rubber heel that provides firm footing, and its steel shanks provide additional support for arches and heels. It comes in whole sizes 7–13 in black or brown at a price of $79, plus $4.50 shipping. The price is guaranteed for the next 30 days. There is a one-year, no-questions-asked warranty.

Select a suitable salutation for your form letter and omit the date and inside address. The purpose of the letter is to motivate readers to order the boots by using the enclosed order form or by calling your toll-free order number, 800-555-2993.

19 **Writing a Solicited Sales Letter—Real Estate**   As a realtor in the local franchise of National Home Sales, you receive a letter from Ms. Edith Willis (58 Schooner Street, Lunenburg, NS B0J 7L2). Her letter states, in part,

I am a single mother of two young children who is being transferred to your town and wish to purchase a three-bedroom condominium in a nice area in the price range of $200 000 to $250 000. I would be able to make a maximum down payment of $25 000. Would you please write me, letting me know whether you have any property available that would fit my needs.

Although the housing market in your small town is tight, you do have a condominium available that might suit her needs. It has three bedrooms plus a finished basement, is air-conditioned (important in your part of the country), and is four years old. The neighbourhood elementary school is considered the best in town; the only drawback is that the condominium is next door to a large but attractive apartment building. The home is listed for $219 900.

Send Ms. Willis a photograph and fact sheet on the listing. The purpose of your letter is to encourage her to phone you at 602-555-3459 to make an appointment to visit your office so that you can personally show her this and perhaps other properties you have available.

20 **Work-team Communication—Pushing Snacks**   Assume the role of Randy Escobedo, vice-president of marketing for Krisbee Snax, a mid-sized snack food manufacturer in central Ontario. Your company is introducing a new snack food. The snack food industry is very competitive; and you believe your best chance to introduce the new product, Krisbee Korns, is to get grocery stores to feature the tasty, low-fat snacks on their end-of-aisle displays. Your company has a good reputation for quality snacks, and this new product promises to be a top seller. However, most grocery stores reserve the end-of-aisle display space for the bigger food companies in the industry.

You are willing to offer a sizeable discount (50 percent) in the price you charge retailers for the new product in exchange for this prime location in their stores during the month of November. Retailers who feature your new product can purchase 500-gram bags of Krisbee Korns for only $2.25—half the normal selling price. These bags have a suggested retail price for $4.59, so the mark-up would be more than 200 percent. In addition to this promotional allowance, you also plan a big advertising campaign for this new product, which should increase their sales even more.

Write a letter to Ms. Betty Eagleston, corporate buyer for the Allen's Food grocery store chain, persuading her to feature Krisbee Korns on the end-of-aisle displays in Allen's Food stores during the month of November. Write to her at the corporate headquarters located at 457 Coy Avenue, Barrie, ON L4N 3W9.

21 Selling a Service—Small Business   While studying for your bar exams, you decide to start a part-time business delivering singing telegrams throughout the Kingston area. For a flat fee of $150, you'll personally deliver a greeting card and sing any song (in good taste) of the customer's choice—using either the actual wording of the song or special lyrics composed by the customer. You promote your company (Musical Messages) for birthdays, anniversaries, graduations, promotions, and other special occasions.

Send a form letter to a random sample of Kingston residents, promoting your service. The purpose of your letter is to persuade the reader to call you at 613-555-9831 to order a singing telegram. Orders must be prepaid (no credit cards), and you require seven days' notice.

22 Form Letter—Selling for Charity   As the director of fundraising for the Buckeye Bread Basket, a British Columbia charity that buys food for people in need, you are starting a new program. You plan to sell holiday greeting cards to raise money for your annual Thanksgiving Day dinner. This year, more than 400 needy people (including singles and families) are expected to attend the dinner. A Vancouver artist created the original water colour scene on the cards, which come in boxes of 10, with green envelopes. People who buy the cards are able to take a tax deduction for their donations; the money from the sale of a single box can feed a family of four on Thanksgiving.

Write a form letter that will persuade people to order your cards. The price is $12 per box, plus $1 postage and handling, and orders can be placed using the enclosed form and return envelope.

23 Writing a Sales Letter—Making Dough from Organic Bread   You are a marketing consultant hired by Todd's Organic Garden Breads, which makes a variety of healthy, whole-wheat, eight-grain, sunflower-seed, and poppy-seed breads. Todd Lleras, who founded the Ottawa bakery after a successful career as a model, learned the business under the direction of a master baker. Although his fresh, organic breads retail for about 30 percent more than ordinary breads, Lleras has seen a steady rise in demand for his products. You believe that consumers and store executives alike are attracted by the company's colourful packaging and promotions, which feature the photogenic founder and his infant daughter.

Lleras originally sold his breads through small health-food outlets, but then was able to get his breads onto the shelves of Wild Oats and other health-food supermarkets. Now the company is moving into a larger baking facility and needs to expand its sales to mainstream supermarkets and gourmet specialty shops. You've done some research and believe that the breads would sell well at Dean & Deluca, a gourmet food retailer that operates upscale stores, cafés, and a catalogue division. Lleras asks you to draft a sales letter on his behalf to Dean & Deluca's president, John B. Richards (985 MacDonald Blvd., Kingston, ON K7P 3S9). What central selling theme will you use? How will you capture the reader's attention in this unsolicited letter? What features and benefits will you emphasize? How will you motivate action? Write this letter, using your knowledge of persuasive messages and supplying any specifics you need to complete this assignment.

co5. Compose a collection letter.

24 **Write a Collection Letter—Bringing in the Sheaves**   As the owner of a small but thriving lawn maintenance company, you recently started issuing credit to your preferred customers, which allows them to carry balances owing for up to three months. Customers are not charged interest over this period but are required to pay their balance in full every three months One of your customers, Barry Monroe, has used your services for three years, and has recently begun taking advantage of the full three-month credit period before paying off his balance. Unfortunately, Mr. Monroe missed his last payment, and you've not heard from him since—he owes your company $458.00 for lawn maintenance performed weekly over the summer. Mr. Monroe is now five months in arrears, and you're becoming concerned that you may not be able to collect payment. Last month, you sent a reminder letter but received no response. You've now decided to send him an appeal letter following the guidelines discussed in this chapter. Address your letter to Barry Monroe, 5867 Canada Street, Vancouver, BC V5N 2K7.

continuing case 7

Flying High at Northern Lights

Diana, Jean, and Larry were analyzing the quarterly expense report. "Look at line item 415," Diana said. "Air-travel expenses have increased 28 percent from last year. Is there any room for savings there?"

"Jean and I were discussing that earlier," Larry said. "I think we should begin requiring our people to join all the frequent-flyer programs so that after they fly 20 000 to 30 000 miles on any one airline, they get a free ticket. Then we should require them to use that free ticket the next time they have to take a business trip for us."

"I disagree," Jean said. "To begin with, there's no easy way to enforce the requirement. Who's going to keep track of how many miles each person flies on each airline and when a free flight coupon is due that person? It would make us appear to be Big Brother, looking over their shoulders all the time.

"In addition, our people put in long hours on the road. If they can get a free ticket and occasionally are able to take their spouses along with them, what's the big deal? They're happier and probably end up doing a better job for us."

"Still," Larry countered, "company resources were used to purchase the original tickets, so logically the free tickets belong to the company. And why should our people who travel get free tickets, compliments of the company, when those who don't travel do not get free tickets?"

Jean was ready with a counter argument, but Diana put an end to the discussion: "Both of you think about the matter some more and let me have a memo by next week giving me your position. Then I'll decide."

Should Northern Lights or its travelling employees receive the benefit of frequent-flyer miles earned while travelling on company business?

Critical Thinking

1. Jot down all the reasons you can for and against Larry's proposition—including any reasons that might not have been discussed at the meeting. What are the benefits associated with each reason? Has this topic been covered on the Internet?

Writing Projects

2. Assume the role of Larry. Write a memo to Diana trying to persuade her to begin requiring employees to use their frequent-flyer miles toward business travel. Knowing that Jean will be writing a memo arguing the opposing viewpoint—that employees should be able to use their free airline tickets for personal use—try to counteract her possible arguments.

3. Now assume the role of Jean. Write a memo to Diana arguing for the status quo. Try to anticipate and counteract Larry's likely arguments.

LABtest 7

Retype the following news item, correcting any grammar errors according to the rules introduced in LAB 4 on page 549.

With 14,000 professionals registered, Lightfair International has won its bet that Niagara Falls would be a good location for its trade show for architectural lighting. Not only is Niagara Falls one of the top trade show cities in the world. But its streets simply shimmer with billions of bright lights. This

5   show is the biggest of the two international lighting shows planned this year. In fact, if it wasn't for the competing smaller regional shows, this would be the largest lighting show ever held.

The conference program at this and similar shows offer light designers and architects a chance to earn continuing education credits. None of the

10   sessions are to be repeated, and neither tape recorders nor videotaping are allowed in any session.

One highlight of the show is a presentation by Luc Lafortune, lighting director for the Cirque du Soleil, Lightfair also has organized a group trip to see the Cirque du Soleil's latest show. Lafortune is always a lively speaker;

15   and at last year's show, it was him who provided a look at the challenges of lighting the dangerous feats of circus performers.

There are, for the first time, one session featuring lighting designers who will address the issues of adapting theatrical fixtures for permanent installations. Walt Disney Imagineering is also providing a look at lighting for

20   their themed environments.

Lighting designers Charles Stone from London and Rogier Heide from Amsterdam takes a look into the crystal ball of lighting for a preview of the future. Stone and him will also answer audience questions. Finally, the great Paul Gregory himself talks about project management in a global market.

Bad-News Messages

communication
OBJECTIVES

fter you have finished this
hapter, you should be able to

- Compose a message that
  rejects an idea.

- Compose a message that
  refuses a favour.

- Compose a message that
  refuses a claim.

- Compose an announcement
  that conveys bad news.

I n February 2006, Nortel Calgary announced to employees a delay in the divestiture of its Calgary Operations division. This was the third delay in two years. The senior leadership team was concerned about how the additional delay would affect employee morale and retention. Sandra Falconi, Nortel Calgary's Communications Manager, worked with the senior leadership team to plan and implement a strategic, two-way communication plan to ensure all employees clearly understood what was happening.

an insider's
perspective

SANDRA FALCONI
Communications Manager,
Nortel Calgary

Their plan, briefly described below, illustrates what Falconi calls an integrated approach to organizational communication, whereby all written and oral communication is supported by behaviours and actions. In addition to ensuring words and actions are consistent, Falconi believes strongly that organizations should foster a culture that values open and effective communication everyday: "Effective communication during the good times lays a foundation of trust for sustaining the organization through difficult times."

Falconi stresses that, when facing the need to deliver bad news, organizations should first focus primarily on formal communication, spending considerable time drafting written documents and planning meetings. While it is important to plan and deliver consistent messages formally, Falconi also emphasizes that it's just as important to be aware of the semi-formal and informal communication that is taking place: "The best way to do this is by engaging employees in two-way dialogue whenever possible to determine what they are hearing and what it means to them." This is exactly how

Nortel Calgary approached the divestiture delay. Not only were formal meetings planned, but employees were given opportunities to provide feedback, both through formal surveys and through an anonymous "rumour board."

When planning any important message, Falconi first carefully examines her purpose and audience, "clearly defining the issue, and articulating it in a language that your target audiences understand." Falconi and the leadership team considered a number of questions when preparing for the formal divestiture delay announcement to employees: What could be disclosed about the factors that led to the delay? What was the most effective way to reach the various employee groups? What information would these employee groups want to know?

Then, based on their answers to these questions, the team identified a number of key messages. After agreeing upon their content, the team determined which media would be most effective at accomplishing their purpose. In addition to a news release and a question-and-answer document developed by Nortel's corporate headquarters, a brief PowerPoint presentation was developed locally.

On the day of the announcement, Nortel Calgary's senior leader invited all managers to a meeting scheduled at the same time the external announcement was taking place. The PowerPoint slides were presented, and managers were given an opportunity to ask questions face to face. Managers were then asked to meet with their respective teams within the next two days to present the PowerPoint charts and provide an opportunity for dialogue. Immediately following the managers' meeting, the senior leader led an all-staff meeting to informally (no charts) announce the delay to all employees.

Falconi and her team then wanted to ensure employees had the opportunity to respond to the news formally, via an online survey. With an announcement as significant as this one, Falconi believes seeking feedback to ensure the message is understood is imperative: "Overall, satisfaction with the meetings was very high, and the comments provided an opportunity to identify any gaps in messaging."

Finally, recognizing the power of grapevine communication, Falconi and her team set up a rumour board to allow employees the opportunity to ask any questions or provide any feedback informally and anonymously. Rumour board questions and comments were tracked and used to further identify any potential gaps in understanding.

Ultimately, the various strategies Falconi and her team employed in communicating the news led to a smooth divestiture of the Nortel Calgary manufacturing operations. Falconi concludes, "Electronic surveys and several group interviews indicated that employees clearly understood the factors affecting the delay. However, the real indicators of success were that employees achieved a successful transition and there was no significant change in attrition prior to the transition, which took place on May 9th, 2006."

> *"Successfully delivering bad news to employees requires more than well-crafted speeches and written messages."*

■ Planning the Bad-News Message

At some point in our lives we have all probably been both the senders and the recipients of bad news. And just as most people find it difficult to accept bad news, they also find it difficult to convey bad news. Therefore, like persuasive messages, bad-news messages require careful planning.

How you write your messages won't change the news you have to convey, but it may determine whether your reader accepts your decision as reasonable—or goes away mad. As noted in Chapter 7, every message can be considered a persuasive message. This idea is especially true for bad-news messages, where you must persuade the reader of the reasonableness of your decision. Note, for example, the persuasive tone of the bad-news message written by Gary Larson, creator of "The Far Side" comic strip, shown in Spotlight 16, "Whose Idea Was This?" on page 268.

Your purpose in writing a bad-news message is twofold: first, to say "no" or to convey bad news, and second, to retain the reader's goodwill. To accomplish these goals, you must communicate your message politely, clearly, and firmly. And you must show the reader that you've seriously considered the matter. Because convincing the reader to accept your reasoning requires many of the persuasive techniques discussed in the previous chapter, it's best to consider conveying bad news as simply another, perhaps trickier, form of persuasive writing.

Your objectives are to convey the bad news and retain the reader's goodwill.

Sometimes you can achieve your purpose better with a phone call or personal visit than with a written message. A phone call is often appropriate when the reader will not be personally disappointed in the outcome, and a personal visit is often called for when you are giving a subordinate negative news of considerable consequence. Frequently, though, a written message is most appropriate because it lets you control more carefully the wording, sequence, and pace of the ideas presented. In addition, it provides a permanent record of what was communicated. As with all business communication, your choice of medium should be determined by your purpose and the needs of your audience. If, for example, a customer has emailed you with a request you must refuse, you'll likely respond through email; if you must inform an employee that he or she has been passed over for a promotion, you'd likely deliver this news in person, perhaps followed up by a written document.

For bad news internal to the organization, "the dilemma confronting a manager in conveying bad news is to balance efficiency of communication with sensitivity to its impact".[1] Indeed, the choice of medium for such messages may be as important as the message itself. According to over 200 organizations surveyed by the International Association of Business Communicators in 2005, email is the primary vehicle used to deliver bad news.[2] And according to a research study reported in *Information Systems Research Journal*, delivering bad news by email rather than in person or by phone helps ensure a more accurate and complete message.[3] The authors hypothesize that the reason is what has been called "the Mum Effect"—that is, because communicating bad news is difficult, the messenger often delays, distorts, or incompletely communicates the needed information. Because of the greater anonymity of email, messengers may be more forthcoming when they can deliver an unpopular message via email. (See Spotlight 18 on Law and Ethics on page 288 for some guidance on choosing an appropriate medium for varying degrees of bad news.)

Not only is the medium important, the timing is as well. As shown in Communication Snapshot 8, most business respondents to one survey felt that Fridays are the best day for communicating bad news.

Whose Idea Was This?

Gary Larson is a syndicated cartoonist whose "The Far Side" cartoon strip has been published in more than 17 languages and has appeared in 1900 newspapers worldwide. When Larson found that his cartoons were being displayed and distributed (illegally) on numerous Web sites, he knew he had to do something. Not only were he and his publishers losing money from the unauthorized distribution of his artwork, but Larson had also lost control of where and how his creative work appeared.

Of course, Larson could have simply had his lawyers issue a "cease-and-desist" order to the Net offenders. Because he wanted a more personal touch, however, he set about composing a letter that sought to persuade his fans to stop distributing his work without permission. The letter that he ultimately sent was thus both a persuasive letter and a bad-news letter. Here is his letter in its entirety. Judge for yourself how effective it is:[4]

To Whom It May Concern:

I'm walking a fine line here. On the one hand, I confess to finding it quite flattering that some of my fans have created Web sites displaying and/or distributing my work on the Internet, and on the other, I'm struggling to find the words that convincingly but sensitively persuade these "Far Side" enthusiasts to "cease and desist" before they have to read these words from some lawyer.

What impact this unauthorized use has had (and is having) in tangible terms is, naturally, of great concern to my publishers and therefore to me—but it's not the focus of this letter. My effort here is to try and speak to the intangible impact, the emotional cost to me personally, of seeing my work collected, digitized, and offered up in cyberspace beyond my control.

Years ago, I was having lunch one day with the cartoonist Richard Guindon, and the subject came up of how

Organizing to Suit Your Audience

The reader's needs, expectations, and personality—as well as the writer's relationship with the reader—will largely determine the content and organization of a bad-news message. Thus you need to put yourself in the place of the reader.

To decide whether to use the direct or the indirect plan for refusing a request, check the sender's original message. If the original message was written in the direct style, the sender may have considered it a routine request, and you would be safe in answering in the direct style. If the original message was written in the indirect style, the sender probably considered it a persuasive request, and you should consider answering in the indirect style. (However, messages written to one's superior are typically written in the direct style, regardless of whether the reader considers the original request routine or persuasive.)

For example, an email message telling employees that the company cafeteria will be closed for one day to permit installation of new equipment can be written directly and in a paragraph or two. A message telling employees that the company cafeteria will be closed permanently and that employees will now have to go outside for lunch (and pay higher prices) would require more explanation and should probably be written in the indirect style.

Direct Plan—Present the Bad News Immediately   As discussed in Chapter 6, many requests are routine; the writer simply wants a yes-or-no decision and wants to hear it in a direct manner. Similarly, if an announcement of bad news is not likely to generate an emotional response from the reader, you should use a direct approach.

neither one of us ever solicited or accepted ideas from others. But until Richard summed it up quite neatly, I never really understood my own aversion to doing this: "It's like having someone else write in your diary," he said. And how true that statement rang with me. In effect, we drew cartoons that we hoped would be entertaining or, at the very least, not boring; but regardless, they would always come from an intensely personal, and therefore original, perspective.

To attempt to be "funny" is a very scary, risk-laden proposition. (Ask any stand-up comic who has ever "bombed" on stage.) But if there was ever an axiom to follow in this business, it would be this: Be honest to yourself and—most important—respect your audience. So, in a nutshell (probably an unfortunate choice of words for me), I ask only that this respect be returned, and the way for anyone to do that is to please, please refrain from putting "The Far Side" out on the Internet. These cartoons are my "children" of sorts, and like a parent I'm concerned

about where they go at night without telling me. And seeing them at someone's website is like getting the call at 2 a.m. that goes, "Uh, Dad, you're not going to like this much, but guess where I am."

I hope my explanation helps you to understand the importance this has for me personally and why I'm making this request.

Please send my "kids" home. I'll be eternally grateful.

Most respectfully,
Gary Larson

Did the letter achieve its objective? Log on to the Internet and search for "The Far Side." How many private sites still display one of Larson's cartoons? (By the way, Larson's letter is reprinted here with the permission of Gary Larson and FarWorks, Inc.)

The direct plan for bad-news messages is basically the same plan used for routine messages discussed in Chapter 6: present the major idea (the bad news) up front. To help readers accept your decision when using the direct plan, present a brief rationale along with the bad news in the first paragraph.

NOT: The annual company picnic originally scheduled for August 3 at Riverside Park has been cancelled.

BUT: Because ongoing construction at Riverside Park might present safety hazards to our employees and their families, the annual company picnic originally scheduled for August 3 has been cancelled.

As usual, state the message in language as positive as possible, while still maintaining honesty.

NOT: Our departmental compliance report will be late next month. (*too blunt*)

NOT: I am pleased to announce that our departmental compliance report will be submitted on March 15. (*too positive*)

BUT: The extra time required to resolve the Bowden refinery problem means that our departmental compliance report will be submitted on March 15 rather than on March 1.

communication snapshot 8

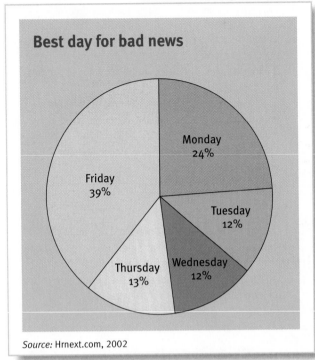

Best day for bad news

- Monday 24%
- Tuesday 12%
- Wednesday 12%
- Thursday 13%
- Friday 39%

Source: Hrnext.com, 2002

Prefer the direct organizational plan for communicating bad news to your superior.

Direct messages are not necessarily shorter than indirect messages.

Then follow with any needed explanation and a friendly closing. The direct organizational plan should be used under the following circumstances:

- The bad news involves a small, insignificant matter and can be considered routine. If the reader is not likely to be emotionally involved and thus not seriously disappointed by the decision, use the direct approach.

- The reader prefers directness. Superiors typically prefer that *all* messages from subordinates be written in the direct style.

- The reader expects a "no" response. For example, mid-career job applicants know that job offers at their level are typically made by phone and job rejections by letter. Thus, upon receiving a letter from the prospective employer, the applicant expects a "no" response; under these circumstances, delaying the inevitable only causes ill will and makes the writer look less than forthright.

- The writer wants to emphasize the negative news. Suppose that you have already refused a request once and the reader writes a second time. Under these circumstances, a forceful "no" might be in order. Or consider the situation where negative information is to be included in a form letter—perhaps as an insert in a monthly statement. Because the reader might otherwise discard or only skim an "unimportant-looking" message, you should consider placing the bad news up front—where it will be noticed.

A message organized according to a direct plan is not necessarily any shorter than one organized according to an indirect plan. Both types of message may contain the same basic information but simply in a different order. For example, assume that the program chairman of the Downtown Marketing Club has written to ask you to be the luncheon speaker at its March 8 meeting, but because of a prior commitment, you must decline. If you have a close relationship with the reader, you might choose the direct approach, as follows:

Except for the fact that I'll be in Mexico on March 8, I would have enjoyed speaking to the Downtown Marketing Club. As you know, Hansdorf Industries is opening an outlet in Nogales, and I'll be there March 7–14 interviewing marketing representatives and setting up sales territories.

If, however, you find yourself in need of a speaker during the summer months, please keep me in mind. My travel schedule thus far is quite light during June, July, and August.

As a long-time member of the Downtown Marketing Club, I've enjoyed and benefited from the luncheon speakers the club sponsors each month. Best wishes, Roger, for a successful year as program chairperson. (*114 words*)

Being forthright and up front about bad news is generally the best tactic. Many observers feel that if Martha Stewart had simply admitted the details of her phone call with stockbroker Peter Bacanovic, the entire incident would never had made headlines nor have had such serious repercussions on her company, Martha Stewart Living Omnimedia.

Now assume the same situation, except that you do not know the reader. This time, you might choose the indirect approach, as follows:

> As a long-time member of the Downtown Marketing Club, I've enjoyed and benefited from the luncheon speakers the club sponsors each month. Monica Foote's December talk on the pitfalls of international marketing was especially interesting and helpful.
>
> As you may have read in the newspaper, Hansdorf Industries is opening an outlet in Nogales, Mexico, and I'll be there March 7–14 interviewing marketing representatives and setting up sales territories. Thus, you will need to select another speaker for your March 8 meeting.
>
> If you find yourself in need of a speaker during the summer months, Mr. Caine, please keep me in mind. My travel schedule thus far is quite light during June, July, and August. (*113 words*)

Complex situations typically call for an indirect organizational pattern and require more explanation than simpler situations.

Direct messages are often shorter than indirect messages only because the direct plan is often used for *simpler* situations, which require little explanation and background information.

Indirect Plan—Buffer the Bad News

Because the preceding conditions are not true for many bad-news situations, you will often want to use an indirect plan. The indirect organizational plan should be used in the following circumstances:

- The reader is not expecting the bad news and will react emotionally to the message. Since the reader is emotionally involved, giving the bad news in the opening paragraph is risky, as the reader may stop reading before getting to the explanation. And since your goal is not only to be clear but also to provide a satisfying explanation, delaying the bad news until after the explanation is provided increases your chance of maintaining the reader's goodwill.

- The reader prefers the indirect approach. If you know the reader personally, you may be able to discern his or her preference for receiving bad news. If you don't know your reader, you may be able to discern such preference by reviewing past correspondence. If, for example, the reader's previous correspondence was written in a more indirect style, then your response should also be indirect. There are also cultural preferences for how bad news is delivered and received that, wherever possible, should be accounted for. Asian cultures, for example, have a more indirect communication style in general than do North American cultures. The following rejection letter, from a Chinese economics journal to a British journalist, would be unheard of in North America.

We have read your manuscript with boundless delight. If we were to publish your paper, it would be impossible for us to publish any work of lower standard. And as it is unthinkable that in the next thousand years we shall see its equal, we are, to our regret, compelled to return your divine composition, and to beg you a thousand times to overlook our short sight and timidity.[5]

With the indirect approach, you present the reasons first, then the negative news. This approach emphasizes the *reasons* for the bad news, rather than the bad news itself.

Suppose, for example, a subordinate expects a "yes" answer upon receiving your email message. Putting the negative news in the first sentence might be too harsh and emphatic, and your decision might sound unreasonable until the reader has heard the rationale. In such a situation, you should begin with a neutral and relevant statement—one that helps establish or strengthen the reader–writer relationship. Such a statement serves as a **buffer** between the reader and the bad news that will follow.

These are the characteristics of an effective opening buffer for bad-news messages:

A buffer lessens the impact of bad news.

1. It is *neutral*. To serve as a true buffer, the opening must not convey the negative news immediately. On the other hand, guard against implying that the request will be *granted*, thus building up the reader for a big letdown.

   NOT NEUTRAL: Stores like Parker Brothers benefit from our policy of not providing in-store demonstrators for our line of microwave ovens.

   MISLEADING: Your tenth-anniversary sale would be a great opportunity for us to promote our products.

A buffer should be neutral, relevant, supportive, interesting, and short.

2. It is *relevant*. The danger with starting too far from the topic is that the reader might not recognize that the letter is in response to his or her request. In addition, an irrelevant opening seems to avoid the issue, thus sounding insincere or self-serving. To show relevance and to personalize the opening, you might include some reference to the reader's letter in your first sentence. A relevant opening provides a smooth transition to the reasons that follow.

Relevant buffers provide a smooth transition to the discussion of reasons.

   IRRELEVANT: Our new apartment-sized microwave oven means that young couples, retirees, and students can enjoy the convenience of microwave cooking.

3. It is *supportive*. The purpose of the opening is to help establish compatibility between reader and writer. If the opening is controversial or seems to lecture the reader, it will not achieve its purpose.

UNSUPPORTIVE: You must realize how expensive it would be to supply an in-house demonstrator for anniversary sales such as yours.

4. It is *interesting.* Although buffer openings are not substitutes for the strong attention-getters that are used in persuasive messages, they should nevertheless be interesting enough to motivate the recipient to continue reading. Therefore, avoid giving obvious information.

OBVIOUS: We have received your letter requesting an in-store demonstrator for your upcoming tenth-anniversary sale.

5. Finally, it is *short.* Readers get impatient if they have to wait too long to get to the major point of the message.

TOO LONG: As you may remember, for many years we provided in-store demonstrators for our line of microwave ovens. We were happy to do this because we felt that customers needed to see the spectacular results of our new browning element, which made microwave food look as if it had just come from a regular oven. We discontinued this practice five years ago because . . .

DILBERT

Recall the earlier situation, introduced in Chapter 7, in which the owner of an appliance store wrote one of its suppliers, asking the supplier to provide an in-store demonstrator of the firm's products (even though it was against the company's policy to do so). In Chapter 7, we assumed the role of the appliance store owner and wrote a persuasive message. Now let's assume the role of the supplier, who, for good business reasons, must refuse the request. Because we're writing to a good customer, we decide to use an indirect plan. We might effectively start our message by using any of the following types of buffers:

Buffer Type	Example
Agreement	We both recognize the promotional possibilities that often accompany big anniversary sales such as yours.
Appreciation	Thanks for letting us know of your success in selling our microwaves. (*Avoid, however, thanking the reader for asking you to do something that you're going to refuse to do; such expressions of appreciation sound insincere.*)

Compliment	Congratulations on having served the community of Greenville for ten years.
Facts	Three-fourths of our distributors who held anniversary sales last year reported at least a 6 percent increase in annual sales of our home products.
General principle	We believe in furnishing our distributors a wide range of support in promoting our products.
Good news	Our upcoming 20 percent-off sale will be heavily advertised and will likely provide increased traffic for your February anniversary sale.
Understanding	I wish to assure you of our desire to help make your anniversary sale successful.

Ethical communicators use a buffer *not* in an attempt to manipulate or confuse the reader but in a sincere effort to help the reader accept the disappointing information in an objective manner.

Justifying Your Decision

Focus on the reasons for the refusal rather than on the refusal itself.

Presumably, you reached your negative decision by analyzing all the relevant information. Whether you began in a direct or an indirect manner, now explain your analysis to help convince the reader that your decision is reasonable. The major part of your message should thus focus on the reasons rather than on the bad news itself.

For routine bad-news messages (that is, those written in a direct approach), the reasons can probably be stated concisely and matter-of-factly. Indirectly written messages, however, require more careful planning—because the stakes are typically greater.

Provide a smooth transition from the opening buffer and present the reasons honestly and convincingly. If possible, explain how the reasons benefit the reader or, at least, benefit someone other than your organization. Here are some examples:

- Refusing to exchange a worn garment might enable you to offer better-quality merchandise to your customers.

- Raising the price of your product might enable you to switch to non-polluting energy for manufacturing it.

- Refusing to provide copies of company documents might protect the confidentiality of customer transactions.

Presenting reader benefits keeps your decision from sounding selfish. Sometimes, however, granting the request is simply not in the company's best interests. In such situations, don't "manufacture" reader benefits; instead, just provide whatever short explanation you can and let it go at that.

Because this data would be of strategic importance to our competitors, we treat the information as confidential. Similar information about our entire industry, however, is collected in the annual Canadian *Census of Manufacturers*. These census reports are available in most public and university libraries and online.

Show the reader that your decision was a *business* decision, not a personal one. Show that the request was taken seriously, and don't hide behind company policy. If

spotlight17
ON LAW AND ETHICS

Ten Reasons to Consult Your Lawyer

Because email, memos, letters, and corporate communications may be used as evidence against you or your organization in a court of law, it is often wise to check with a lawyer to make sure that what you write doesn't violate provincial or federal law. You should consult legal counsel when a document that you have written:

1. Commits you to a legally binding contract.
2. Commits you to a warranty or guarantee of a product or service.
3. Makes an advertising claim.
4. Amends or modifies corporate policy.
5. Requests documents from another lawyer.
6. Makes a statement to an insurance adjuster, the police, or a government agency.
7. Reports an accident involving a product, service, or employee.
8. Concerns the termination of an employee.
9. Concerns workers' compensation or insurance matters.
10. Concerns any product or process that will affect the environment.

the policy is a sound one, it was established for good reasons; therefore, explain the rationale for the policy.

NOT: Company policy prohibits our providing an in-store demonstrator for your tenth-anniversary sale.

BUT: A survey of our dealers three years ago indicated they felt the space taken up by in-store demonstrators and the resulting traffic problems were not worth the effort; they were also concerned about the legal liability of having someone cooking in their stores.

The reasons justifying your decision should take up the major part of the message, but be concise or your readers may become impatient. Do not belabour a point and do not provide more background than is necessary. If you have several reasons for refusing a request, present the strongest ones first—where they will receive the most emphasis. If possible, avoid mentioning any weak reasons. If the reader feels he or she can effectively rebut even one of your arguments, you're simply raising false hopes and inviting needless correspondence. Finally, be aware of the ethical and legal aspects of your decisions and your justification of your decisions (see Spotlight 17, "Ten Reasons to Consult Your Lawyer," above).

Giving the Bad News

The bad news is communicated up front in directly written messages. Even in an indirectly written message, if you have done a convincing job of explaining the reasons, the bad news itself will come as no surprise; the decision will appear logical and reasonable—indeed the *only* logical and reasonable decision that could have been made under the circumstances.

To retain the reader's goodwill, state the bad news in positive or neutral language, stressing what you *are* able to do rather than what you are not able to do. Avoid, for example, such words and phrases as "cannot," "are not able to," "impossible,"

The reader should be able to infer the bad news before it is presented.

While executives are given wide leeway in promoting their companies and products, laws require that bad news regarding financial operations must be openly and fully disclosed. Canadian-born Bernard Ebbers, the former chief executive officer at WorldCom, is shown here exiting Manhattan Federal Court following his sentencing for fraud.

"unfortunately," "sorry," and "must refuse." To subordinate the bad news, put it in the middle of a paragraph, and include in the same sentence (or immediately afterward) additional discussion of reasons.

> In response to these dealer concerns, we eliminated in-store demonstrations and now advertise exclusively in the print media. Doing so has enabled us to begin featuring a two-page spread in each major Sunday newspaper, including your local paper, the *Greenville Courier.*

When using the indirect plan, phrase the bad news in impersonal language, avoiding the use of *you* and *your*. The objective is to distance the reader from the bad news so that it will not be perceived as a personal rejection. So as not to point out the bad news that lies ahead, avoid using "but" and "however" to introduce it. The fact is, most readers won't remember what was written before the "but"—only what was written after it.

You do not need to apologize for making a rational business decision.

Resist any temptation to apologize for a decision that's based on sound logic. You may reasonably assume that if the reader were faced with the same options and had the same information available, he or she would act in a similar way. There is no reason to apologize for any reasonable business decision.

In some situations, the refusal can be implied, making a direct statement of refusal unnecessary. But don't be evasive. If you think a positive, subordinated refusal might be misunderstood, go ahead and state it directly. However, even under these circumstances, you should use impersonal language and include reader benefits.

Closing on a Pleasant Note

Any refusal, even when handled skillfully, has negative overtones. Therefore, you need to end your message on a more pleasant note. Avoid statements such as those listed here.

Problem to Avoid	Example of Problem
Apologizing	Again, I am sorry that we were unable to grant this request.
Anticipating problems	If you run into any other problems, please write me directly.
Inviting needless communication	If you have any further questions, please let me know.
Referring again to bad news	Although we are unable to supply an in-store demonstrator, we do wish you much success in your tenth-anniversary sale.
Repeating a cliché	If we can be of any further help, please don't hesitate to call on us.
Revealing doubt	I trust that you now understand why we made this decision.
Sounding selfish	Don't forget to feature Golden microwaves prominently in your anniversary display.

Make your closing original, friendly, and positive by using any of the following techniques. Avoid referring again to the bad news.

Do not refer to the bad news in the closing.

Technique	Example
Best wishes	Best wishes for success with your tenth-anniversary sale. We have certainly enjoyed our ten-year relationship with Parker Brothers and look forward to continuing to serve your needs in the future.
Counterproposal	To provide increased publicity for your tenth-anniversary sale, we would be happy to include a special 5- by 15-centimetre boxed notice of your sale in the *Greenville Courier* edition of our ad on Sunday, February 8. Just send us your camera-ready copy by January 26.
Other sources of help	A dealer in British Columbia switched from using in-store demonstrators to showing a video continuously during his microwave sale. He used the ten-minute film *Twenty-Minute Dinners with Pizzazz* (available for

$45 from the Microwave Research Institute, P.O. Box 800, Surrey BC V2K 1P9) and reported a favorable reaction from customers.

Resale or subtle sales promotion

You can be sure that the new Golden Mini-Micro we're introducing in January will draw many customers to your store during your anniversary sale.

To sound sincere and helpful, make your ending original. If you provide a counterproposal or offer other sources of help, provide all information the reader needs to follow through. If you include sales promotion, make it subtle and reader-oriented.

In short, the last idea the reader hears from you should be positive, friendly, and helpful. Checklist 10 on page 279 summarizes guidelines for writing bad-news letters. The remainder of this chapter discusses strategies for writing bad-news replies and bad-news announcements.

Close the letter on a positive, friendly, helpful note.

■ Bad-News Replies

Despite the skill with which a persuasive message is written, circumstances of which the reader is unaware may require a negative response. Your organization's well-being (and your own) may depend on the skill with which you are able to refuse a request and still maintain the goodwill of the reader.

Rejecting an Idea

CO1. **Compose a message that rejects an idea.**

One of the more challenging bad-news messages to write is one that rejects someone's idea or proposal. Put yourself in the role of the person making the suggestion. He or she has probably spent a considerable amount of time in developing the idea, studying its feasibility, perhaps doing some research, and, of course, writing the original persuasive message.

Consider, for example, the persuasive memo presented in Model 7 on page 234, in which Jenson Peterson tries to persuade Elliott Lamborn to restrict the nearest parking lots to Ford vehicles. Peterson obviously thinks his idea has merit. He went to the trouble of having his staff count the number of non-Ford vehicles in the lots, getting a cost estimate for making the change, and contacting the union representative to get the union's position. Finally, he organized all of his information into an effectively written memo.

Having invested that much time and energy in the proposal, Peterson probably feels quite strongly that his proposal is valid, and he likely expects Lamborn to approve it. If—or in this case *when*—his proposal is rejected, Peterson will be surprised and disappointed.

Organize to Suit Your Audience   Because Lamborn is Peterson's superior, he could send Peterson a directly written memo saying in effect, "I have considered your proposal and must reject it." But Peterson is obviously intelligent and enterprising, and Lamborn does not want to discourage future initiatives on his part. As with all such bad-news replies, then, Lamborn's twin objectives are to refuse the proposal and retain Peterson's goodwill. Given the amount of effort Peterson has

✔checklist 10

Bad-News Messages

Determine How to Start the Message

✔ **Direct Plan**—Use a direct organizational plan when the bad news is insignificant, the reader prefers directness (such as your superior) or expects a "no" response, or the writer wants to emphasize the bad news. Present the bad news (see "Give the Bad News" at right), along with a brief rationale, in the first paragraph.

✔ **Indirect Plan**—Use an indirect organizational plan when writing to subordinates, customers, readers who prefer the indirect plan, or readers you don't know. Start by buffering the bad news, following these guidelines:

- Remember the purpose: to establish a common ground with the reader.

- Select an opening statement that is neutral, relevant, supportive, interesting, and short.

- Consider establishing a point of agreement, expressing appreciation, giving a sincere compliment, presenting a fact or general principle, giving good news, or showing understanding.

- Provide a smooth transition from the buffer to the reasons that follow.

Justify Your Decision

✔ If possible, stress reasons that benefit someone other than yourself.

✔ State reasons in positive language.

✔ Avoid relying on "company policy"; instead, explain the reason behind the policy.

✔ State reasons concisely to avoid reader impatience. Do not over-explain.

✔ Present the strongest reasons first; avoid discussing weak reasons.

Give the Bad News

✔ If using the indirect plan, consider subordinating the bad news by putting it in the middle of a paragraph and including additional discussion of reasons.

✔ Present the bad news as a logical outcome of the reasons given.

✔ State the bad news in positive and impersonal language. Avoid terms such as *cannot* and *you*.

✔ Do not apologize.

✔ Make the refusal definite—by implication if appropriate; otherwise, by stating it directly.

Close on a Positive Note

✔ Make your closing original, friendly, positive, and defer from mentioning the bad news again.

✔ Consider expressing best wishes, offering a counter-proposal, suggesting other sources of help, or building in resale or subtle sales promotion.

✔ Avoid anticipating problems, apologizing, inviting needless communication, referring to the bad news, repeating a cliché, revealing doubt, or sounding selfish.

---

put into this project, Lamborn's response will be most effective if written in the indirect pattern. This pattern will let Lamborn gradually lead his subordinate into agreeing that the proposal is not in the best interests of the firm.

Determine How to Start Your Message   In using the indirect plan, Lamborn will need to start with an effective buffer, one that's neutral, relevant, supportive, interesting and short:

NOT: Your memo of April 3 focused on the automobile habits of our employees, but you are mistaken on several points.

> **BUT:** Your April 3 memo certainly enlightened me about the automobile preferences of our employees. I had no idea that our workers drive such a variety of models.

Justify Your Decision and Give the Bad News   To be successful, Lamborn has an educating job to do. He must give Peterson the reasons for the rejection, reasons of which Peterson is probably unaware. He must also show that he recognizes Peterson's proposal as carefully considered and that the rejection is based on business—not personal—considerations.

> **NOT:** I personally drive a foreign-made automobile, as do many others within the company. To insist that prime parking spots be restricted to Ford vehicles will create a great deal of strife among employees, not to mention a logistical nightmare.

> **BUT:** The increasing popularity of foreign-made vehicles recently led management to conclude that we should consider taking advantage of this expanding market. President Wrede has appointed a task force to determine how we might also promote our electrical systems to Asian automakers, as well as to Ford.

After presenting Peterson with his reasons, Lamborn may not need to explicitly state the bad news at all: the rejection may be implied within the explanation itself. Implied rejections, if worded poorly, however, risk leaving the reader bewildered.

> **NOT:** While I like your suggestion, I must base my decision on the changing driving habits of our employees. Thanks anyway.

> **BUT:** Because our own employees are driving foreign-made vehicles in increasing numbers, any proposal for changing parking arrangements will need to take this into account.

Alternatively, it may be necessary to state the rejection explicitly to avoid ambiguity or confusion. In either case, Lamborn will want to maintain a positive tone and use impersonal language.

> **NOT:** Thus, I have decided not to restrict parking spots to Ford vehicles.

> **BUT:** Thus, our firm will benefit from the continuing presence of these cars in all our lots.

Close on a Pleasant Note   Obviously, Peterson has put time and effort into this initiative, and it's in Lamborn's—and the company's—best interest to applaud his efforts and encourage his loyalty. To encourage such initiative in the future, Lamborn may wish to suggest a compromise or alternative course of action. He'll need to ensure that whatever he suggests, it is reasonable and attractive to Peterson.

> **NOT:** Would you please contact the Ford representative who suggested this and explain to him why the idea is a poor one.

> **BUT:** Would you please develop some type of awareness campaign (such as a bumper sticker for employee cars that contain a Newton electrical system) that shows our employees support the products we sell.

Lamborn's complete memo rejecting Peterson's proposal is shown in Model 11 on page 282. Although we label this memo a bad-news message, actually it is also a *persuasive* message. Like all bad-news messages, the memo seeks to persuade the reader that the writer's position is reasonable.

Refusing a Favour

Many favours are asked and granted almost automatically. Doing routine favours for others in the organization shows a cooperative spirit, and a spirit of reciprocity often prevails—we recognize that the person asking us for a favour today may be the person from whom we'll need a favour next week. Sometimes, however, for business or personal reasons, we are not able to accommodate the other person and must decline an invitation or a request for a favour.

The type of message written to refuse a favour depends on the particular circumstances. Occasionally, someone asks a "big" favour—perhaps one involving a major investment of time or resources. In that case, the person has probably written a thoughtful, reasoned message trying to persuade you to do as he or she asks. If you must refuse such a significant request, you should probably present your refusal indirectly, following the guidelines given earlier.

Most requests for favours, however, are routine, and a routine request should receive a routine response—that is, a response written in the direct organizational plan. A colleague asking you to attend a meeting in her place, a superior asking you to serve on a committee, or a business associate inviting you to lunch is not going to be deeply disappointed if you decline. The writer probably has not spent a great deal of energy composing the request; the main thing he or she wants to know from you is "yes" or "no."

In such situations, give your refusal in the first paragraph, but avoid curtness and coldness. Courtesy demands that you buffer the bad news somewhat and that you at least give a quick, reasonable rationale for declining. Although the refusal itself might not lose the reader's goodwill, a poorly written refusal message might! The email message in Model 12 on page 283 declines a request to serve on a corporate committee and is written using a direct plan.

Assume for a moment, however, that Peter Gates had decided, instead, that his best strategy would be to write the message (Model 12) in the indirect pattern, explaining his rationale before refusing. His opening buffer might then have been as follows:

> Like you, I believe our new Executive-in-Residence program will prove to be effective for both the University of Alberta and the executives who participate.

Refusing a Claim

The indirect plan is almost always used when refusing an adjustment request because the reader (a dissatisfied customer) is emotionally involved in the situation. The customer is already upset by the failure of the product to live up to expectations. If you refuse the claim immediately, you risk losing the customer's goodwill. And, as noted previously, every dissatisfied customer tells nine or ten people about the bad experience and they, in turn, each tell four or five others. Clearly, you want to avoid the ripple effect of such situations.

Determine How to Start Your Message   The tone of your refusal must convey respect and consideration for the customer—even when the customer is at fault. To

CO2. Compose a message that refuses a favour.

When refusing routine requests, give the refusal in the first paragraph.

CO3. Compose a message that refuses a claim.

Use impersonal, neutral language to explain the basis for the refusal.

model11

BAD-NEWS REPLY— REJECTING AN IDEA

This memo responds to the persuasive request in Model 7 (see page 234).

Uses a neutrally worded subject line.

Starts with a supportive buffer; the second sentence provides a smooth transition to the reason.

Begins discussing the reason.

Presents the refusal using positive and impersonal language.

Closes on a forward-looking, off-the-topic note.

**NEWTON
Electrical
Systems**

Serving the automotive industry for more than 50 years

MEMO TO: Jenson J. Peterson, Marketing Supervisor

FROM: Elliott Lamborn, Vice President   *EL*

DATE: April 15, 20—

SUBJECT: Employee Parking Lot Proposal

Your April 3 memo certainly enlightened me about the automobile preferences of our employees. I had no idea that our workers drive such a variety of models.

The increasing popularity of foreign-made vehicles recently led management to conclude that we should consider taking advantage of this expanding market. President Wrede has appointed a task force to determine how we might also promote our electrical systems to Asian automakers, as well as to Ford.

Our successful push into the international automotive market will mean that many of the foreign-made vehicles our employees drive will, in fact, be supplied with Newton Electrical Systems components. Thus, our firm will benefit from the continuing presence of these cars in all our lots.

1   Your memo got me to thinking, Jenson, that we might be missing an opportunity to promote our products to headquarters visitors. Would you please develop some type of awareness campaign (such as a bumper sticker for employee cars that contain a Newton electrical system) that shows our employees support the products we sell. I would appreciate having a memo from you with your ideas by May 3 so that I

2   might include this project in next year's marketing campaign.

amp

Grammar and Mechanics Notes

1 *thinking, Jenson, that:* Set off nouns of direct address (*Jenson*) with commas.

2 *year's:* Use apostrophe plus s to form the possessive of a singular noun (*year*).

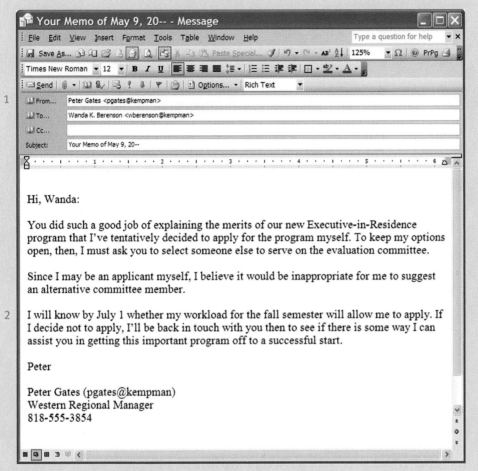

**BAD-NEWS REPLY—
REFUSING A FAVOUR**

Gives a quick reason,
immediately followed by
the refusal.

Provides additional details.

Closes on a helpful note.

Grammar and Mechanics Notes

1 Most email programs will automatically insert the From: line in the header.

2 *July 1 whether:* Do not use a comma after an incomplete date.

separate the reader from the refusal, begin with a buffer, using one of the techniques presented earlier (for example, showing understanding).

NOT: Smart travellers understand the limits of their luggage.

BUT: Frequent travellers like you depend on luggage that "can take it"— luggage that will hold up for many years under normal use.

Justify Your Decision and Give the Bad News

When explaining the reasons for denying the claim, do not accuse or lecture the reader. At the same time, however, don't appear to accept responsibility for the problem if the customer is at fault. In impersonal, neutral language, explain why the claim is being denied.

NOT: The reason the handles ripped off your Sebastian luggage is that you overloaded it. The tag on the luggage clearly states that you should use the luggage only for clothing, to a maximum of 18 kilograms. However, our engineers concluded that you had put at least 30 kilograms of items in the luggage.

BUT: On receiving your piece of Sebastian luggage, we sent it to our testing department. The engineers there found stretch marks on the leather and a frayed nylon stitching cord. They concluded that such wear could have been caused only by contents weighing substantially more than the 18-kilogram maximum weight that is stated on the luggage tag. Such use is beyond the "normal wear and tear" covered in our warranty.

Note that in the second example, the pronoun *you* is not used at all when discussing the bad news. By using third-person pronouns and the passive voice, the example avoids directly accusing the reader of misusing the product. The actual refusal, given in the last sentence, is conveyed in neutral language.

Close on a Pleasant Note

As with other bad-news messages, close on a friendly, forward-looking note. If you can offer a compromise, it will take the sting out of the rejection and show the customer that you are reasonable. It will also help the customer save face. Be careful, however, that your offer does not imply any assumption of responsibility on your part. The compromise can either come before or be part of the closing.

An offer of a compromise, however small, helps retain the reader's goodwill.

Although we replace luggage only when it is damaged in normal use, our repair shop tells me the damaged handle can easily be replaced. We would be happy to do so for $39.50, including return shipping. If you will simply initial this letter and return it to us in the enclosed, addressed envelope, we will return your repaired luggage within four weeks.

Somewhere in your letter you might also include a subtle pitch for resale. The customer has had a negative experience with your product. If you want your reader to continue to be a customer, you might restate some of the benefits that led him or her to buy the product in the first place. But use this technique carefully; a strong pitch may simply annoy an already unhappy customer.

Consider the persuasive request written by Oliver Arbin presented in Model 9 on page 239. Mr. Arbin, as you may remember, was upset that his family's flight to

figure8.1
**An Ineffective
Bad-News Message**

June 27, 20—   **Western Air**
                                              3929 Spring Ave.
                                           Winnipeg, MB R3D 3J9

Mr. Oliver J. Arbin
518 Thompson Street
Calgary, AB T2B 1J7

Dear Mr. Arbin

Subject: Denial of Your Claim of June 18, 20—

Although we were certainly sorry to learn of your troubles with Western Air,
I'm afraid that we won't be able to refund your money. Let me explain why.

Flight 126 was scheduled to depart at 8 p.m. and was canceled at 7:10 p.m. because
of inclement weather. If you and your family had remained in the boarding area as
requested, you would have been rebooked on Flight 3321, which arrived in Kelowna
just 75 minutes later than your scheduled flight. Company policy forbids our
refunding money when a flight is canceled because of inclement weather.

Although I'm sorry we could not help you this time, Mr. Arbin, I hope you will call
upon us in the future when your travel plans take you to one of the 200 cities
Western Air is proud to serve. Please let me know if you have any questions
about this matter.

Sincerely

Madelyn Masarani

Madelyn Masarani
Service Representative

eta

Uses a direct, negative subject line.

Begins by apologizing, giving the bad news first (where it is emphasized), and using personal language.

Uses an accusatory tone; hides behind company policy without explaining the reason for the policy.

Repeats the apology (thereby emphasizing the negative aspects), sounds insincere in its sales promotion, and ends with a cliché.

Kelowna was cancelled and that they were thus forced to make an eight-hour drive instead. He wanted a refund of $1680, the cost of his five non-refundable tickets. It appears, on further investigation, that Mr. Arbin was not completely forthright.

How might the company respond to Mr. Arbin under these circumstances? Figure 8.1 above illustrates how *not* to write an effective bad-news message. Model 13 on the next page, a revised version of the ineffective example, illustrates the guidelines discussed earlier for writing an effective bad-news message.

model13

**BAD-NEWS REPLY—
REFUSING A CLAIM**

*This letter responds to the
persuasive claim in Model 9
on page 239.*

**Opens on an agreeable and
relevant note.**

**Begins the explanation;
presents the refusal in
impersonal language.**

**Closes on a helpful note;
assumes that the reader
will continue to fly on
Western Air.**

Western Air
3929 Spring Ave.
Winnipeg, MB R3D 3J9

June 27, 20—

Mr. Oliver J. Arbin
518 Thompson Street
Calgary, AB T2B 1J7

1   Dear Mr. Arbin

Subject: Further Information About Flight 126

We make no money when our customers are forced to take long trips by car rather
than by flying Western Air; and when that happens, we want to find out why.

A review of the June 2 log of the aborted Flight 126 shows that it was scheduled to
depart at 8 p.m. and was cancelled at 7:10 p.m. because of inclement weather.
2   Passengers were asked to remain in the boarding area; those who did were rebooked
on Flight 3321, which departed at 9:15 p.m. Flight 3321 arrived in Kelowna, at
10:40 p.m., just 75 minutes later than the scheduled arrival of Flight 126. Given
these circumstances, the ticket agent was correct in disallowing any refund on non-
refundable tickets.

Because you indicated that you're a frequent traveller on Western, I've asked our
scheduling department to add you to the mailing list to receive a complimentary subscription to our quarterly flight schedule. A copy of the current schedule is enclosed.
From now on, you'll be sure to know exactly when every Western flight arrives at
and departs from Calgary International Airport.

Sincerely

Madelyn Masarani
Service Representative

eta
3   Enclosure

Grammar and Mechanics Notes

1 Insert no punctuation after the salutation and complimentary closing when using
open punctuation.

2 *boarding area;* Use a semicolon to separate two closely related independent clauses not
connected by a conjunction.

3 Use an enclosure notation to alert the recipient to look for some inserted material.

■ Bad-News Announcements

The previous section discussed strategies for writing negative replies. Often, however, the bad news we have to present involves a new situation; that is, it is not in response to another message. And quite often, these messages go to a large audience, as, for example, when you're announcing a major price increase or new rules and regulations. Such announcements may be either internal (addressed to employees) or external (addressed to customers, news media, stockholders, and the like). Interestingly, according an IABC survey in 2005, only 11 percent of the organizations felt they delivered bad news "very successfully", while just over 80 percent felt they delivered bad news either "pretty successfully" or only "somewhat successfully."[6]

As with other bad-news messages, you must decide whether to use the direct or the indirect plan of organization. Be guided by the effect the bad news will have on the recipients and on your relationship with them.

It is also important, particularly in announcing bad news to employees, to choose an appropriate medium. See Spotlight 18 on Law and Ethics on page 288 for some guidance on choosing an appropriate medium for varying degrees of bad news.

co4. Compose an announcement that conveys bad news.

Bad-news announcements are not in response to any request.

Bad News About Normal Operations

Assume that management has decided a price increase of 10 percent is justified on the Danforth cabin tent you manufacture. This price increase requires that you notify your order department, your wholesalers, and, finally, a special retail customer.

To notify the order department of the price change (a routine matter), you would probably send a memo or email message like this one, written in the direct pattern:

> Effective March 1, the regular price of our Danforth cabin tent (Item R-885) changes from $149.99 to $164.99, an increase of 10 percent. Any order postmarked before March 1 should be billed at the lower price, regardless of when the order is actually shipped.
>
> The new price will be shown in our spring catalogue, and a notice is being sent immediately to all wholesalers. If you receive orders postmarked after March 1 but showing the old price, please notify the wholesaler before filling the order.

The preceding message reflects the fact that the price increase will have minor negative consequences to the order department. Therefore, the news is given directly—in the first sentence—followed by the details. Because the person receiving this memorandum will not be personally disappointed in the news, you don't need to explain the price increase.

However, you also need to notify your wholesalers of this price increase. How will they react? They probably will not be personally disappointed because price increases are common in business and come as no surprise; thus a direct message is called for. But wholesalers *do* have a choice about where to buy tents for resale, so you need to justify your price increase.

If the reader will not be disappointed, present the bad news directly.

> Because of the prolonged strike in South African mines, we now must purchase the chrome used in our Danforth cabin tent elsewhere at a higher cost. Thus, effective March 1, the regular price of the Danforth tent (Item R-885) will change from $149.99 to $164.99.
>
> As a courtesy to our wholesalers, however, we are billing any orders postmarked prior to March 1 at the old price of $149.99. Use the enclosed form or call our toll-free

A reason may be presented first—even in a message written in a direct pattern.

spotlight18
ON LAW AND ETHICS

Choosing the Right Medium for Delivering Bad News to Subordinates

Recent research, conducted by Peter Timmerman and Wayne Harrison, for the *Journal of Business Communication* sheds some light on how best to deliver bad news to subordinates, whether the news affects numerous people, as in major layoff announcements or a takeover of the company, or simply one individual, as in a firing or a failed application for a promotion. Here is a summary of their findings.[7]

A key concern, particularly when announcing news that will potentially cause significant upheaval within the organization, is that of sensitivity: sensitivity to the recipients' interpersonal needs (the need to feel valued and cared for by the sender), and sensitivity to the recipients' informational needs (the need to know "Why?" or "Why me?"). Another concern, and one that often conflicts with the need for sensitivity, is that the information be delivered efficiently; that is, at a minimum of cost (both time and money) and with a minimum of follow-up communication to address concerns and clarify misunderstandings.

To address the tension between the need for sensitivity and efficiency, the authors suggest four considerations in determining the most appropriate medium for delivering bad news to subordinates. They also divide the types of media available on a declining scale from rich to lean. Rich media (such as face-to-face communication or the telephone) are more personal and allow for multiple channels (vocal cues, gestures, tone of voice, etc). Lean media (such as memos and email) are less personal but more efficient in that they allow the sender to more carefully construct and control the message. In order from richest to leanest, here are some commonly used media in delivering bad news:

1. Individual meeting
2. Phone conversation
3. Group meeting
4. Videoconference
5. Letter
6. Email
7. Group email

Four Considerations in Choosing a Medium

With the above media in mind, what follows are four considerations in determining what level of media richness may be appropriate. The authors suggest each consideration be given a score of either 0 or 1. If your final tally approaches 4, then a richer, more personal, medium should be used. If your final tally approaches 0, then a leaner, more efficient medium should be used.

Outcome Severity. Consider how severe the outcome will be perceived from the recipient's perspective. (What may seem an insignificant matter to a manager may be seen quite differently by an employee.) The greater the severity of the outcome, the greater will be the potential disappointment of the recipient. And the greater the potential disappointment, the greater is the need for a medium that allows for rich non-verbal cues, such as an individual meeting or a phone conversation.

If the outcome may be considered severe from your recipient's perspective, give this consideration a score of 1.

Explanation Complexity. Written communication allows the reader to read and reread the message at his or her own pace, which may be important when an explanation is complex. However, written communication does not allow for immediate questions and clarifications or any form of dialogue. When complex explanations are necessary, the authors actually propose that two media be

number (800-555-9843) to place your order for what *Canadian Camper* calls the "sock-it-to-me" tent.

Note how the bad news is cushioned by (1) presenting the reason first—a reason that is clearly beyond your control; (2) selling at the old price until March 1; and (3) including resale in the closing paragraph.

used: a richer medium such as a face-to-face meeting first, followed by a more detailed message using a leaner medium, such as a letter or memo.

If the bad news requires a complex explanation to ensure sensitivity to the recipient's informational needs, give this consideration a score of 1.

Explanation Type. Some forms of bad news result from external circumstances, such as an economic downturn, that are beyond the control of management. So the type of explanation required focuses on describing these external circumstances and demonstrating their negative effects on the company. (The authors refer to these as *causal* explanations.)

Other forms of bad news result from decisions made by management intended for the good of the company and/or the employees. So the type of explanation required focuses on demonstrating how the bad news isn't as bad as it seems (known as reframing) and may ultimately be for everyone's own good. (The authors refer to these as *ideological* explanations.)

Still other forms of bad news are, unfortunately, the result of bad decisions. The type of explanation required typically involves an apology and will centre around improving the negative perception the recipients may have of the sender. (The authors refer to these as *penitential* explanations.)

Studies have shown that causal explanations are actually more convincing to employees than other forms of explanations and therefore don't require as rich a medium. And because causal explanations require a detailed, logical argument, a written account may better meet a recipient's informational needs than an oral one. Finally, even though external circumstances have caused the bad news, recipients may still have a tendency to "shoot the messenger." A written explanation allows senders to more carefully deflect unwarranted criticism that may be aimed their way.

Ideological or penitential explanations, on the other hand, generally require dialogue so that the bad news can be reframed and, where necessary, a sincere apology be given. Greater sensitivity to the reader's interpersonal needs demands that these forms of explanations rely on a richer medium.

If the explanation is anything other than causal, give this consideration a score of 1.

Relationship Quality. If the sender has the trust of the recipients when delivering bad news, the job is that much easier. If trust must be earned while delivering the bad news, the job becomes more difficult and a richer medium must be chosen.

If the explanation is delivered to recipients who do not trust the sender, give this consideration a score of 1.

Finally, tally your score. The closer you score to 4, the richer the medium required; the closer to 0, the leaner the medium required.

A Final Consideration

As the deliverer of bad news, your own level of comfort with a chosen medium is also important. People are generally more comfortable delivering bad news through written communication which is a leaner medium than the various forms of oral communication. And while it may seem prudent to choose the richest medium possible when delivering bad news, keep in mind that richer media are less efficient, and therefore usually more expensive. Moreover, "using too rich a medium is not only inefficient but may cause the employee to wonder why the manager took such care in communicating a seemingly minor negative outcome. Provoking such speculation may not be in the manager's or organization's interest."[8]

Finally, you need to write a third message about the price increase. For the past two years, you have had an exclusive marketing agreement with the Association for Backpackers and Campers. It promotes the Danforth cabin tent in each issue of *Field News,* its quarterly magazine, at no cost to you in exchange for you offering ABC members the wholesale price of $149.99 (instead of the retail price, which is about 35 percent higher).

ABC selected the Danforth tent because of its quality *and* because of this attractive price arrangement, and you want to make sure that your price increase does not endanger this relationship. Thus, you write an indirect-pattern letter, in which your major emphasis is on the reasons, not the results.

> The popularity of the Danforth cabin tent that you feature in each issue of *Field News* is based partly on our exclusive use of a chrome frame. Chrome is twice as strong as aluminum, yet weighs about the same.
>
> Because of the prolonged strike in South African mines, we were faced with the choice of either switching to aluminum or securing the needed chrome elsewhere at a higher cost. We elected to continue using chrome in our tent. While this decision will increase the wholesale price of the Danforth cabin tent (Item R-885) from $149.99 to $164.99, maintaining the quality and strength you have come to expect of this product is our number one concern.
>
> The Danforth tent promotion in the spring issue of *Field News* should be changed to reflect this new price. Since the spring issue usually arrives the last week of February, we will bill any orders postmarked before March 1 at the lower price of $149.99.
>
> We have enjoyed the opportunity to serve ABC members and extend best wishes to your organization for another successful year of providing such valuable service to American backpackers and campers.

If the reader must be persuaded of the reasonableness of your decision, use the indirect approach.

Explain thoroughly the basis for your decision.

Another situation that calls for indirect organization is one in which a change in organizational policy will adversely affect employees. It is just as important, of course, to retain the goodwill of employees as it is to retain that of customers. Acceptance of a new policy depends not only on the reasons for the policy but also on the skill with which the reasons are communicated. An example of such a situation is shown in Model 14 on page 291.

When dealing with issues that are of such personal interest to the reader, don't hurry your discussion. Take as much space as necessary to show the reader that your decision was not made in haste, that you considered all options, and that the reader's interests were taken into account.

Note, especially, the use of personal and impersonal language throughout the memo in Model 14. When discussing insurance programs that will be retained (third paragraph), *you* and *your* are used extensively. When discussing the program that will be dropped (fourth paragraph), impersonal language is used instead. The purpose is to closely associate the readers with the good news and to separate them from the bad news. Such deliberate use of language does not manipulate the reader; it simply uses good human relations to bring the reader to an understanding and appreciation of the writer's position.

Bad News About the Organization

If your organization is experiencing serious problems, your employees, customers, and stockholders should hear the news from you—not from newspaper accounts or through the grapevine. For extremely serious problems that receive widespread attention (for example, product recalls, unexpected operating deficits, or legal problems), the company's public relations department will probably issue a news release. Common subjects of bad news announcements that may significantly affect the organization include mergers and acquisitions, changes in senior leadership, site facility and plant closings, legal issues, outsourcing, and market shifts.[9]

GENERAL BAD-NEWS ANNOUNCEMENT

TO: All Employees

FROM: Mary Louis Lytle, Vice President *MLL*

DATE: July 8, 20—

1   **RE:**   Change in Insurance Coverage

2   Thanks to you, President Adams will announce a 13 percent increase in sales for the year that ended June 30. Six of the seven divisions met or exceeded their sales quotas for the year. What an example of the company spirit!

Our pleasure at the 13 percent increase in sales is somewhat tempered by a corresponding increase in expenditures. In studying the reasons for this increase, we found that fringe benefits, especially insurance, were the largest factor. Dental insurance costs increased 23 percent last year and have risen 58 percent in the past three years.

To continue providing needed coverage for our employees and their families and still hold down costs, we've analyzed the use and cost of each benefit. Last year 89 percent of you used your dental insurance. Clearly, this benefit is important to you and, therefore, to us. Similarly, although only 6 percent used your long-term disability insurance last year, protecting our employees financially during extended absences from work remains a top priority for us.

On the other hand, only 9 percent of you used extended health care insurance for services such as chiropractics and optometry last year; yet extended health insurance represented 19 percent of our total insurance costs. With this in mind, it appears the funds now being used for extended health care for a small minority of our employees can better be used to pay the escalating costs of dental and long-term disability coverage for all of our employees. Thus, effective January 1, all company-paid insurance programs will include only dental and long-term disability coverage. All requests for reimbursement for dental bills submitted on or before December 31 will be paid at the normal rates.

3   The Benefits Office will hold an open forum on July 28 from 2 to 3 p.m. in the auditorium to solicit your views on all areas of employee benefits. Please come prepared with questions and comments. Your input will enable us to continue to provide our family of employees the kind of protection and options they deserve.

ama

Uses a neutral subject line.

Begins with a compliment.

Provides a smooth transition to the explanation; uses figures for believability.

Uses the overall welfare of all employees as the reader benefit; presents the good news before the bad.

Implies that fairness demands a change; subordinates the bad news in the middle of a long paragraph.

Closes by discussing a different, but related, topic.

Grammar and Mechanics Notes

1 You may use *RE:* instead of *SUBJECT:* in the memo heading.

2 *President Adams:* Capitalize a title that is used before a name.

3 *3 p.m.:* Use figures to express time; type the abbreviation *p.m.* in lowercase letters, with no space after the internal period.

A 2005 survey by the International Association of Business Communicators produced some enlightening statistics on just how well businesses actually deliver bad news to employees: just under 50 percent of respondents believed their organization was only somewhat or not at all successful in delivering bad news. The same survey revealed that, counter to what most experts advise, email was the primary vehicle for delivering such news.[10] According to many communication experts, extremely bad news should be delivered by the organization's leader face to face (see the Spotlight 18 on Law and Ethics). The face-to-face meeting should also be followed up by additional written material such as intranet postings of email messages.[11]

Show that the situation is receiving top-management attention.

However the initial bad news is delivered, often some type of correspondence is also necessary. For example, owners of recalled products must be notified, customers must be notified if an impending strike will affect delivery dates, and employees must be notified if they will be affected by plant closings or layoffs. To show that these situations are receiving attention from top management, such messages should generally come from a high-level official.

If the situation about which you are writing has news value, assume that your communication may find its way to a reporter's desk. Thus, make sure not only that the overall tone of the letter is appropriate but also that individual sentences of the letter cannot be misinterpreted if they are lifted out of context.

Write in such a way as not to be misinterpreted.

Throughout your message, choose each word with care. In general, avoid using words with negative connotations and emphasize those with positive connotations. Effective communication techniques can help you control the emphasis, subordination, and tone of your *own* message; however, you cannot do so for a news item that quotes individual parts of your message. For example, note the following misinterpretation, in a published news item, of a sentence from a company president's letter.

President's actual statement:	Unlike several other firms in the area, we have always had a strict policy of not allowing any digging in residential areas. In fact, all our excavation sites are at least 3.2 kilometres from any paved road and are well marked by 3-metre signs. Because these sites are so isolated, our company does not require fences around these sites.
News item:	Although other drilling companies in the area erect 2.5-metre fences around their excavation sites, AllCana President Robert Leach admitted in a letter to stockholders yesterday that "our company does not require fences around these sites."

The last sentence of the president's statement would have been more effective had it been worded in positive, impersonal language.

> Fences are unnecessary in such isolated sites and, in fact, can cause safety hazards of their own. For example, . . .

If the reader has already learned about the situation from other sources, your best strategy is to use a direct organizational pattern. In a spirit of helpfulness and forthrightness, confirm the bad news quickly and begin immediately to provide the necessary information to help the reader understand the situation. For example,

> As you entered the building this morning, you may have seen the evidence of a burglary last night. The purpose of this memo is to let you know exactly what happened and to outline steps we are taking to ensure the continued safety of our employees who work during evening hours.

If the reader is hearing the news for the first time, your best strategy is to use the indirect pattern, using a buffer opening and stressing the most positive aspects of the situation (in this case, the steps you're taking to prevent a recurrence of the problem).

> Employees in our data-entry and maintenance departments who work at night perform a valuable service for Martin Company, and their safety and well-being are of prime concern to us. In that spirit, I would like to discuss with you several steps we are taking as a result of . . .

Model 15 on page 294 shows a letter written to alert customers to the possibility of a demonstration outside the site of a meeting announcing a new product. By showing a respectful attitude toward the demonstrators and by avoiding emotional language, the writer is able to convey the bad news with a minimum of fuss. And the fact that each customer received a personally typed letter from the president is in itself reassuring.

This letter also illustrates another common aspect of bad-news messages: occasionally, you may have to defend positions with which you personally disagree. Your disagreement may be strategic (it's not a smart move at this time) or philosophical (we shouldn't be selling and promoting this product). The issue, of course, goes much deeper than communicating. If you and your organization's philosophies consistently do not mesh, you might be happier finding employment in a more compatible environment. If you decide to stay, however, you may be required to defend any legal and ethical position the organization decides to take.

Being a part of the management team sometimes requires that you support decisions with which you personally disagree.

model15

BAD-NEWS ANNOUNCEMENT— PERSONAL LETTER

A personal letter from the president draws the needed attention.

Uses sales promotion for the opening buffer.

Presents the company in a favourable light by using a reasoned and even-handed approach.

Treats the news of the expected demonstrations (the bad news) objectively and unemotionally.

Closes with additional sales promotion and reader benefits.

PACIFIC LABORATORIES   *A LIFE-LABS COMPANY*

1   November 8, 20—

Ms. Michele Loftis
Planning Department
Crosslanes Pharmacies
1842 Lesage Blvd.
Victoria, BC V8S 6U5

Dear Ms. Loftis:

The breakthrough in over-the-counter birth control that Pacific Laboratories will announce at 3 p.m. on December 5 at the Park Inn will present a very substantial marketing opportunity for Crosslanes Pharmacies. I'm pleased you can be with us for the announcement.

Like many scientific breakthroughs, our new product is generating quite a bit of media interest. Already, 12 newspapers and television stations have requested permission to cover this announcement. We welcome such coverage and believe that an
2   open discussion will lead to more informed decisions by consumers.

In the same spirit, we have taken no steps to prevent any demonstrations outside the Park Inn on that day. It is likely that some pro-life and anti-abortion groups will march and distribute leaflets. So long as they do so peacefully, they are perfectly within their rights. We also are within our rights to hold a meeting without disruption, and there will be adequate security personnel on hand to ensure that everything runs smoothly. We do ask that you bring your original invitation (or this letter) to
3   identify yourself.

We look forward to showing off the efforts of five years of research by our staff. The safety, convenience, and price of this product will make it a very popular item on your pharmacy shelves.

Sincerely,

Stephen Lynch

Stephen Lynch, President

12 Baldwin Street • Vancouver, BC V6T 9V8 • (604)555-2389

Grammar and Mechanics Notes

1 Begin the date and closing lines at the centre point when using a modified block style of letter.

2 *coverage and:* Do not insert a comma before the conjunction (*and*) because what follows is not an independent clause.

3 *runs smoothly:* Use an adverb (*smoothly*) instead of an adjective (*smooth*) to modify a verb.

The **3Ps**

Problem, Process, Product

A BAD-NEWS MESSAGE

Problem

You are a facilities manager for Canadian Western Natural Gas (CWNG). CWNG recently constructed a new administrative building on a 5-acre lot, and you've landscaped the unused 4 acres with lighted walkways, fountains, and ponds for employees to enjoy during their lunch hours and before and after work. Your lovely campus-like site is one of the few such locations within the city limits.

Joan Bradley, the mayor of your city, is running for re-election. She has written to you asking permission to hold a campaign fundraiser on your grounds on July 7 from 8 p.m. until midnight. This event will be for "heavy" contributors; as many as 150 people, each paying $500, are expected. Her re-election committee will take care of all catering, security, and cleanup.

You do not want to become involved in this event for numerous reasons. Write to the mayor (The Honourable Joan Bradley, Mayor of Calgary) and decline her request.

Process

1. Describe your primary audience.
   - Very important person (don't want to offend her)
   - Holds political views different from my own
   - Possibility of her losing the election (don't want to appear to be backing a loser)

2. Describe your secondary audience.
   - The 150 big contributors (What will be their reaction to my refusal?)
   - The other candidates (do not wish to offend anyone who might become the next mayor)

3. Brainstorm: List as many reasons as you can why you might refuse her request. Then, after you've come up with several, determine which one will be most effective. Underline that reason.
   - Other sites in the city offering a more suitable environment for the event
   - Would have to provide the same favour for every other candidate
   - Possible harm to lawn, plants, and animals
   - Company policy that prohibits outside use

4. Write your buffer opening—neutral, relevant, supportive, interesting, and short.

   Thank you for your kind comments about our lovely grounds. Our staff has been able to create an environment in which plants and animals not normally found in the foothills are able to thrive.

5. Now skip to the actual refusal itself. Write the statement in which you refuse the request—making it positive, subordinated, and unselfish.

   To protect this delicate environment, we restrict the use of these grounds to company employees.

6. Write the closing for your letter—original, friendly, off the topic of the refusal, and positive. *Suggestions:* best wishes, counterproposal, other sources of help, or subtle resale.

   As an alternative, may I suggest the beautiful grounds at the Inglewood Bird Sanctuary. They were designed with a Southern Alberta motif by Larry Miller, the designer for our grounds.

**Canadian Western
Natural Gas**
710 Wonderland Rd.
London, ON N6C 4E9

May 20, 20—

The Honorable Joan Bradley
Mayor of Calgary
Calgary City Hall

Dear Mayor Bradley:

Thank you for your kind comments about our lovely grounds. Our staff has been able
to create an environment here in which plants and animals not normally found in the
foothills are able to thrive.

For example, after much effort, we have finally been able to attract a family of Eastern
Bluebirds to our site. At this very moment, the female is sitting on three eggs, and
members of our staff unobtrusively check on her progress each day.

Similar efforts have resulted in the successful introduction of beautiful but sensitive
flowers, shrubs, and marsh grasses. To protect this delicate environment, we restrict
the use of these grounds to company employees, many of whom have contributed
ideas, plants, and time in developing the grounds.

As an alternative, may I suggest the beautiful grounds at the Inglewood Bird Sanctuary. They were designed with a Southern Alberta motif by Larry Miller, who designed
our grounds. Various public events have been held there without damage to the environment. Susan Siebold, their executive director (555-9832), is the person to contact
about using IBS's facilities.

Sincerely,

J. W. Hudson
Facilities Manager

tma

■ Summary

When writing a bad-news message, your goal is to convey the bad news and, at the same time, keep the reader's goodwill. A direct organizational plan is recommended when you are writing to superiors, when the bad news involves a small, insignificant matter, or when you want to emphasize the bad news. When using the direct plan, state the bad news in positive language in the first paragraph, perhaps preceded or followed by a short buffer or a reason for the decision. Then present the explanation or reasons, and close on a friendly and positive note.

When writing to subordinates, customers, or people you don't know, you should generally use an indirect plan. This approach begins with a buffer—a neutral and relevant statement that helps establish or strengthen the reader–writer relationship. Then follows the explanation of or reasons for the bad news. The reasons should be logical and, when possible, should identify a reader benefit. The bad news should be subordinated, using positive and impersonal language; apologies are not necessary. The closing should be friendly, positive, and off the topic.

CO1. **Compose a message that rejects an idea.**

When rejecting someone's idea, tact is especially important, inasmuch as the person presenting the idea is probably strongly convinced of its merits. Devote most of your message to presenting reasons for the rejection, reasons of which the reader is probably unaware. Show that the proposal was carefully considered and that the rejection is based on business, not personal, beliefs.

CO2. **Compose a message that refuses a favour.**

Most requests for favours are routine and should receive a routine response, that is, a response written in the direct organizational plan. Give your refusal in the first paragraph, but avoid curtness or coldness. Provide a quick, reasonable rationale for declining.

CO3. **Compose a message that refuses a claim.**

Use the indirect plan when refusing an adjustment request. The tone of your refusal must convey respect and consideration for the customer, even when the customer is at fault. When explaining the reasons for denying the claim, do not accuse or lecture the reader. Close on a friendly, forward-looking note.

CO4. **Compose a message that conveys bad news.**

Announcements of bad news may be either internal (addressed to employees) or external (addressed to those outside the organization). If the bad news will have little effect on the reader, use a direct organizational plan. If the reader will be personally affected by the announcement, use an indirect pattern, with a buffer opening and stress any positive aspects of the situation (that is, the steps you're taking to resolve the situation).

■ Key Term

You should be able to define the following term in your own words and give an original example.

buffer (272)

■ Exercises

1 The 3Ps (Problem, Process, and Product) Model: Communication Applications at Nortel   Taking the employees' perspective helps Sandra Falconi craft bad-news messages when there is a problem to announce. The company is diligent about keeping employees informed about any problems as soon as it is possible to do so. This open disclosure policy allows Falconi and her colleagues to minimize the possibility of a negative reaction to bad news.

Problem

Imagine that Nortel is announcing a series of layoffs following an unprofitable quarter. As a Nortel communication specialist, you have been asked by the general manager to draft a memo to all employees, which will be one of the communication tools used to deliver this announcement. Though the number of layoffs is small and local to your plant, the announcement has the potential to affect employee morale and attract further negative media attention.

Process

a. Describe your audience.
b. Should you use a direct or indirect organizational memo for this announcement? Why?
c. Write your buffer opening, bearing in mind the need to retain Nortel's goodwill internally and externally despite the news.
d. What points should you make in discussing the reason for this layoff?
e. Write the closing of your memo, striving for a positive, supportive tone.

Product

Using your knowledge of bad news messages, draft this memo, which will be sent to all employees.

2 Rejecting an Idea—Job Too Big   You are the owner of AMX Construction in Saskatoon, Saskatchewan. You are putting together a proposal for a construction loan to build the Eagle's Nest apartments, a 100-unit apartment complex in Saskatoon. You will be the general contractor on the project, and you have accepted bids from subcontractors for the plumbing work on the apartments.

CO1. Compose a message that rejects an idea.

You reviewed the bids very carefully and narrowed the field of 15 to two bidders. The second lowest bid was from a plumbing firm in Regina. This firm specializes in plumbing for large apartment complexes. You have worked with them before, and their work is good.

The lowest bidder was Alpine Plumbing from Fort Saskatchewan. You have worked with Alpine before; and although their work was also good, the company took longer than expected to complete jobs. Alpine Plumbing is a small firm with only three plumbers. They usually work on small complexes of between 20 and 30 units and have never tackled a job this big.

You are concerned that Alpine wouldn't be able to meet the deadlines you have proposed. Therefore, you elect to go with the company from Regina rather than Alpine. You would be willing to work with Alpine Plumbing again on smaller jobs, but you believe that the Regina firm with its ten plumbers is better suited to get this job done on schedule.

Write a letter to Mr. Alex Gephardt, General Manager, Alpine Plumbing, 608 Cool Air, Fort Saskatchewan, Alberta T8L 2N6.

3 **Refusing an Application—Bad Times for Raising Ostriches**   Cyndi Fallis is 28 years old and a real estate agent. She and her husband have purchased a small 50-acre farm just outside of Teulon, Manitoba. She grew up in the area and wants to try her hand at raising ostriches.

Yesterday, she applied to Canada West Bank for a loan to purchase two breeding pairs. She hopes to raise the chicks and sell them for a profit. Cyndi has the land to accommodate the ostriches, and her flexible schedule selling real estate allows her time to feed and care for the birds. She also has a good credit history and good references. However, she has had no experience raising ostriches.

Because the ostrich industry is quite easy to get into, there has been a glut of farms in the area, reducing prices and making it difficult to find buyers for breeding stock. Moreover, the market for ostrich meat has not developed as quickly as anticipated. As a result, several farmers have quit the ostrich business in recent years.

Now is not a good time for someone with limited experience to try to get into this industry. Write a letter to Cyndi, at 2505 Peavy Road, Teulon, Manitoba R8N 0Y4, denying her loan application for purchasing the breeding stock. She might be a good loan candidate for some other investment.

4 **Refusing a Request—No Home-and-Home Schedule**   You are the Women's Athletic Director of McGill University in Montreal. Paula Trembley, an acquaintance whom you met 15 years ago at the University of New Brunswick, is now the women's athletic director for Western Canada University College in Medicine Hat. She has written to you inquiring about the possibility of scheduling a home-and-home women's basketball series between the two schools.

She has suggested that they would be willing to play on your home court next year, and they would host you the following year. Western Canada University College (WCUC) has only recently transformed from a two-year community college and it is not considered a fully accredited university. Nor is it a member of Canadian Interuniversity Sport (CIS), an organization to which McGill and many other universities belong.

While you love the idea of a trip across Canada to play WCUC, you are concerned that scheduling a home-and-home tournament against them could risk violating CIS regulations. You would be willing to play WCUC on a home-and-home basis once they have been granted admission into CIS.

Write a letter to Ms. Trembley letting her know that you are unwilling to play them on a home-and-home basis at this time. Her address is 11819 Flamingo Rd., Medicine Hat, AB T1A 8E6.

5 **Refusing an Idea—Oversized Dressing Rooms**   You are Rebecca Wiebe (see Exercise 8 of Chapter 7), and you certainly appreciate Robert Kilcline's memo recommending oversized dressing rooms for your new store in Fashion Square Mall. Robert has always been very customer-conscious, a trait you try to instill and nurture in all your employees.

After checking with the facility planner for the new store, you find that the Fashion Square Mall management has only a certain amount of space available for your store. Thus, any space taken up by the dressing rooms would have to be at the expense of the public store areas.

Write a memo to Robert, giving him this information. Perhaps he can suggest other ways to enhance customer service.

6 **Refusing Business—Hotel Reservation** You are the manager of the Elk Mountain Lodge, a 100-room hotel in Banff, Alberta, that caters to business people. You've received a reservation from the University of Winnipeg chapter of ACE (Advancing Canadian Entrepreneurship) to rent 24 double rooms during their reading break (February 21-28). They have offered to send a $1000 deposit to guarantee the rooms if necessary.

As a member of ACE yourself, you know that these future entrepreneurs are responsible students who would cause no problems. You also recognize that when these students graduate and start their own businesses (as you've done), they are the very type of people you hope will use your hotel. However, because of previous bad experiences, you now have a strict policy against accepting reservations from student groups. Write to the ACE treasurer, Scott Kumar, 2040 Bayonne, Winnipeg, Manitoba R3B 2A9 conveying this information.

7 **Rejecting an Idea—Getting Around a Long Wait** You're new to the management staff of Cedar Point, a new amusement park in Kelowna, British Columbia. Cedar Point is renowned for its seven roller coasters and dozens of other exciting rides. Each ride can accommodate many people at once, so the lines don't stand still for very long. Even so, on summer holidays and weekends, the wait for Cedar Point's most popular rides, such as the Millennium Force roller coaster, can be lengthy. In fact, when *National Post* reporters sampled the midday waiting time at parks around Canada, they wound up standing for an hour in the line for the two-minute Millennium Force ride. At the other end of the spectrum, the reporters waited only 11 minutes or less to jump on rides at Paramount Canada's Wonderland near Toronto.

Your boss, Cedar Point's top operational officer, has asked all employees to submit ideas for a system that would make the wait less onerous for customers. One employee suggests that parents with strollers be allowed to go to the front of the line, on the theory that this policy reduces the likelihood of noisy scenes with fussy youngsters. You believe that other customers would resent this system; you also don't believe that it would dramatically affect either the wait or customers' perceptions of it. With your boss's approval, you decide to reject this idea. What is your goal in writing this bad-news memo? What organizational pattern will you use? Write this memo, using your knowledge of bad-news replies (creating any details you need).

8 **No Magic** Today you received in the mail a letter you have come to expect. The letter is from Olivia Frances, a close personal friend in Saint John's, Newfoundland. Olivia has been the chairperson of NHP, a non-profit organization that helps raise money for the local children's hospital.

Because of your national reputation as a magician and your friendship with Olivia, you have been invited for several years in a row to do a magic show at the organization's annual conference. The magic show has been a big moneymaker for the hospital, and you have enjoyed volunteering your time to help such a worthy cause and to help a dear friend.

However, this year you have a prior family commitment and must deny your friend's request to do the magic show. Write a personal letter to Olivia letting her know the bad news. However, you know a friend who might volunteer to do a comedy show. Olivia's address is 10034 Big Sky Drive, St. John's, Newfoundland A1C 5H5.

CO**2.** Compose a message that refuses a favour.

9 Refusing a Favour—Summer Internship   Assume the role of vice-president of operations for Kolour Kosmetics, a small manufacturer in Hamilton, Ontario. One of your colleagues from the local chamber of commerce, Dr. Andrea T. Mazzi, has written asking whether your firm can provide a summer internship in your department for her son Peter, a second-year college student who is interested in a manufacturing career. Kolour Kosmetics has no provisions for temporary summer employees and does not currently operate an internship program. Further, the factory shuts down for a two-week vacation every July.

Write Dr. Mazzi (5 Windbriar Ct., Hamilton, Ontario L8P 4Y5) to let her know this information. Perhaps there are other ways that her son can gain first-hand experience in manufacturing during the summer.

10 Refusing a Favour—Field Trip   You are Donna Jo Luse and you have received the letter written by David Pearson (see Exercise 11 of Chapter 7). Lunch is, of course, your busiest time, and no one has the time then (or the patience) to provide a tour of the kitchens and help 23 youngsters make their salads. Perhaps, instead, they could come for a tour and snack mid-morning or mid-afternoon. Write to Mr. Pearson (Jack 'n Jill Preschool, 14 Marie Dr., Peachland, BC V0H 4K8), refusing his request.

11 Declining an Invitation—Dinner   You are the purchasing manager at your firm and have received an email message from Barbara Sorrels, one of your firm's major suppliers. She will be in town on October 13 and would like to take you out to dinner that evening. However, you have an early morning flight on October 14 to Quebec City and will need to pack and make last-minute preparations on the evening of the 13th. Write an email to Ms. Sorrels (bsorrels@canada.com), declining her invitation.

12 Declining an Invitation—Public Speaking   You are Tanya Porrat, editor of *Autoimmune Diseases Monthly*. You just received an invitation from May Lyon to speak as the keynote speaker at the annual Multiple Sclerosis Congress (see Model 8 on page 237). In the past, you frequently accepted such invitations. However, your medical journal is in the process of being purchased by Triton Medical Research Group, and for the time being you have new rules to follow: you cannot speak in public until the sale is complete. Because you are unsure of the final date, you are refusing all speaking engagements until October. Tell this to Lyon in a letter.

CO3. Compose a message that refuses a claim.

13 Refusing a Claim—No Refund   Once again, assume you are the fulfillment representative at Paperbacks by Post (see Exercise 22 of Chapter 6). Robert Luongo has written to request that you take back a book he received three months ago. The problem is not the book itself, which he read and enjoyed, but the value for the money. He complains that the book is too short (162 pages) to justify the amount he paid ($10.95). Luongo wants his money back, and he also wants the book club to refund the cost of shipping the book back.

This is the fourth time in five months that Luongo has returned a book. Each time he had a different complaint—once he didn't like the cover illustration, another time he found the language offensive—and you agreed to send him his refunds. At this point, however, you believe that he is simply reading the books and then making up an excuse to avoid paying for them. You decide not to refund his money on this occasion (the number of pages and price of the book were both clearly noted in the announcement Luongo received before the book was shipped). You also decide to cancel his membership. Write him a letter (1729 Honeysuckle, Vancouver, BC V5Y 1V4) to let him know your decisions.

14 **Refusing a Claim—Azaleas**   You are a customer service representative for Jackson-Parsons Nurseries and have received the letter written by Vera Malcolm (see Exercise 14 of Chapter 7). Jackson-Parsons goes to great expense to use only the highest-quality patented stock and to pack each order in dampened sphagnum moss. However, there is no way that any nursery can control the care that plants receive on reaching their destination. Your obligation in this matter clearly ended when Ms. Malcolm did not notify you of the problem immediately. If she had, you would have cheerfully refunded her money. But evidently the azaleas are now thriving where they were planted, and you feel you have no further obligation. Tell this to Ms. Malcolm in a letter (City of Saint John, 101 Market Street, Saint John, NB E1C 5H5.

15 **Internet Exercise**   Online auctions are increasingly popular, but not every transaction ends satisfactorily for both buyer and seller. That's why the auction site eBay posts written guidelines alerting consumers that they, not eBay, are responsible for safe trading. View these guidelines by following the "User Agreement" link at eBay (at www.ebay.com). Now assume the role of customer service representative at eBay. You have received an email message from a buyer who misunderstood the description of an item she just purchased at auction—and she wants eBay to get her money back. Using the information in the User Agreement (and making up any reasonable details you need), draft an email response breaking the bad news that the buyer is responsible for requesting additional information, understanding the terms of the auction, and communicating with the seller to resolve misunderstandings.

16 **Work-team Communication—A Slow Economy—No Bonus**   You are the manager of a fitness equipment manufacturing plant called Muscles Galore located in Edmonston, New Brunswick. The plant has been in operation for seven years. Over the years your employees have been very productive, and sales have been high. Therefore, Muscles Galore has been able to give generous holiday bonuses (usually more than $1000) to all of its employees for the last five years.

CO4. Compose a message that conveys bad news.

This year, however, because of a slow economy, you will not be able to offer the holiday bonus. Although the workers have been very productive, fitness equipment sales are down about 15 percent from last year. Your projections indicate that the economy is recovering, and sales should be up about 20 percent next year. If the projections are accurate, you should be able to offer the bonus again next year.

Write a memo to your employees letting them know the bad news. Add any additional details to make your message complete.

17 **Bad-News Announcement—Mad Cow Disease—No Beef**   You represent Triple M Meats in Medicine Hat, Alberta. As a meat packing plant, you supply meat to wholesalers throughout the country. Blue Ribbon Meats of Morden, Manitoba, has a standing order for 100 sides of beef to be delivered every week. Normally, filling this order is not a problem; however, because of new restrictions brought about because of the mad cow disease scare, you are going to have to make changes in your processing procedure. Starting March 1, 20—, your plant will be closed for two weeks to upgrade your facilities to allow for the new processing procedure. Blue Ribbon Meats has been a steady customer for over 20 years. You want to keep them as a customer, but you will not be able to fill its orders for beef from March 1 through March 14. You will still be able to fill orders for pork products. Write a letter to Mr. Larry Stokers, President of Blue Ribbon Meats, 928 Pinecrest, Morden, MB R6M 1V3. Let him know the bad news, but try to keep his business. Add additional details to complete the letter.

18 Bad-News Announcement—No Renewal   Assume the role of Gene Harley, the leasing manager of Northern Plaza. You have decided not to renew the lease of T-shirts Plus, which operates a tiny T-shirt decorating outlet in the mall. Three times in the past 13 months, the store's employees have left their heat-transfer machinery switched on after closing. Each time, the smoke activated the mall's smoke alarms and brought the fire department to the mall during the late-night hours. Although no damage has occurred, your insurance agent warns that the mall's rates will rise if this situation continues.

The lease that T-shirts Plus signed five years ago specifies that either party can decide not to renew. All that is required is written notification to the other party at least 90 days in advance of the yearly anniversary of the contract date. By writing this week, you will be providing adequate notice. Convey this information to the store's manager, Henry D. Curtis (at Northern Plaza, Brook Parkway North, Cranbrook, BC V1C 2Z3).

19 Bad-News Announcement—Moving to Ottawa—No Help at Thanksgiving   You own Kitco Inc., a small financial consulting firm in Pickering, Ontario. For the last 12 years, some of your employees have voluntarily prepared and served a Thanksgiving meal at St. Benedict's homeless shelter in nearby Toronto. You paid for the turkeys, hams, and other trimmings to feed the 100–150 people; your employees cooked the food at their homes and served the meal at a local church. This meal has been greatly appreciated by the St. Benedict staff and anticipated by the poor and homeless people in the area. However, you are closing your office in Pickering and moving to Ottawa in early October; therefore, no one from your company will be available to prepare and serve the meal. You have enjoyed your partnership with the homeless shelter, and you plan to continue the tradition in Ottawa. Although you cannot prepare and serve the meal, you would be willing to donate $250 to the shelter to cover the cost of buying the food. Write a letter to Pastor Sullivan O'Malley, giving him the bad news. The address of the shelter is St. Benedict Parish, 704 N. Pearl St., Toronto, ON M5X 1J2.

20 Bad-News Announcement—No Party   Nobody likes a party more than Edgar Dunkirk, the president of Rockabilly Enterprises. In the early days, the company's holiday parties were legendary for their splendid food arrangements and outstanding entertainment (featuring the label's popular singing stars). Employees performed elaborate skits and competed for valuable prizes that included colour television sets and DVD players. These days, however, sales of the company's country and rockabilly recordings are down. In fact, Dunkirk recently had to lay off 150 of the company's 350 employees, the most severe austerity measure in the company's history.

Because so many employees had to be let go, including some who had helped Dunkirk found the company a decade ago, the president has decided that a lavish party would be inappropriate. He has therefore cancelled the traditional holiday party. As Dunkirk's vice-president of personnel, you must prepare a memo conveying this information to Rockabilly's employees.

21   Bad-News Announcement—Fringe Benefits   When your organization moved to its new building in Vancouver three years ago, you negotiated a contract with the Universal Self-Parking garage a half-block away to provide free parking to all employees at Grade Level 11 or above. Your rationale was that these managerial employees often work long hours and that convenient, free parking was a justifiable fringe benefit.

Universal has just notified you that when your contract expires in three months, the monthly fee will increase by 15 percent. Given the state of the economy and your organization's declining profits, you feel that not only can you not afford the 15 percent increase but you must, reluctantly, discontinue the free parking altogether.

Therefore, beginning January 1, all employees must locate and pay for their own parking. Your organization continues to promote ride sharing; and the receptionist has copies of the city bus schedule—a bus stops a block from your building. Write a memo to these managerial employees giving them the information.

22   Bad-News Announcement—Product Recall   You have received two reports that users of your ten-stitch portable sewing machine, Sew-Now, have been injured when the needle broke off while sewing. One person was sewing lined denim and the other was sewing drapery fabric—neither of which should have been used on this small machine. Fortunately, neither injury was serious. Although your firm accepts no responsibility for these injuries, you decide to recall all Sew-Now machines to have a stronger needle installed.

Owners should take their machines to the store where they purchased them. These stores have been notified and already have a supply of the replacement needles. The needle can be replaced while the customer waits. Alternatively, users can ship their machines to you prepaid (Central Sewing Machines, 329 Ash Lane, Niagara Falls, ON L2E 6X5). Other than shipping, there is no cost to the user.

Prepare a form letter that will go out to the 1750 Sew-Now purchasers. Customers can call your toll-free number (800-555-9821) if they have questions.

23   Bad-News Announcement—From Free to Fee   Supermart's e-commerce division, SuperShopper.ca, had a great idea for promoting its online shopping site: offer Internet access to Supermart shoppers. After attracting two million users, however, the company decided that providing entirely free, unlimited Internet access was too costly. First, the company tried a two-tiered plan, offering 12 hours of free access every month with an option to choose 100 hours of access for $8.95. Within a few months, the company—under pressure to improve efficiencies and become profitable—decided to do away with all free service. Under the new arrangement, customers who signed up for Internet access before September 1 will pay a discounted rate of $9.95 for their first three months, then pay the full $18.95 per month after that.

As director of customer service for SuperShopper.ca, it is your responsibility to notify all Internet access customers of this change. Will you use the direct or indirect organization plan? What kind of buffer will be most effective in this situation? How can you justify the company's change? How can you close your message on a positive note? Using your knowledge of bad-news messages, draft this email announcement.

continuing
case 8

NORTHERN LIGHTS

No Such Thing as a Free Flight

Diana has now received the memos she requested from Jean and Larry regarding the frequent-flyer program (see Continuing Case 7 in Chapter 7). She has thought about the issue quite a bit and discussed it with Marc, Tom, and Dave.

It seems to her that Larry has the more convincing argument: Company funds *were* used to purchase the tickets; therefore, the company logically owns the free tickets its employees earned. In addition, allowing travelling employees to keep their free tickets in effect amounts to an additional fringe benefit that equally hard-working non-travelling employees do not receive. So Diana decides to begin requiring NL employees to use their frequent-flyer free tickets for business travel rather than personal travel.

Diana must now decide whether Larry or Jean presented the more compelling argument regarding the use of frequent-flyer miles at Northern Lights.

Now she needs to write to Jean and Larry to communicate her decision. Larry, of course, will be pleased; Jean will be extremely disappointed—not only because she believes her position to be correct but because she will feel threatened by being turned down by her superior. Jean was promoted to her present position only several months ago and is still a little unsure of her abilities.

Diana also needs to issue a policy memo to all employees outlining the new program. The system will have to operate on trust; she does not intend to act as "Big Brother," policing the program and verifying mileage. Each employee will be required to join the frequent-flyer program for any airline he or she uses in connection with business travel. Employees can use different versions of their names if they also have a frequent-flyer number for their non-business travel.

The expense report form will be revised to include a check-off question that asks if their frequent-flyer mileage for the flight was recorded. The clerk who makes all flight reservations will be instructed to ask each manager requesting tickets if he or she has accumulated enough miles on any airline to receive a free flight. Other details can be worked out.

Although many employees, especially those in marketing and R&D who travel extensively, will be upset, Diana is confident her decision is reasonable and in the best interests of Northern Lights.

Critical Thinking

1. Should Diana send Jean and Larry a joint memo or separate memos? Why?

Writing Projects

2. Write the needed memos: to Jean and Larry (either a joint memo or separate memos, depending on your response to Question 1) and to the staff.

3. Assume that Northern Lights employees do *not* travel extensively and that Diana's memo outlining the new restrictions will be considered a routine policy announcement. Write a second version of this memo to the staff using the direct pattern.

LABtest 8

Retype the following news item, correcting any mechanical errors (including misspellings) according to the rules introduced in LAB 5 on page 554.

A major educational campaign is under way to prommote dimming, even though most designers are not using flourescent lamps with a dimming range as low as eight percent. 2 recent developments, however, have broadened the range of possibilities for designers—compact fluorescent lamps and

5   electronic ballasts.

The national dimming institute, made up of leading electrical mfrs, seeks to increase awareness of the benefits of lighting controls. The group's education 101 program has released a C.D.R.O.M. that will be widely distributed.

Advanced Lighting Concepts started the group. In a recent Illuminating

10   Engineering Society newsletter artical entitled "I am dim," Dr Steve Purdy, 1 of the group's founders and the company's Director of Sales, noted, "we intend for this new organization to mount a national educational outreach program."

Meetings have been schedualed for different regions of the country, espe-

15   cially in the east, to inform the design community about the many options available.

9

Understanding Reports

As a link between the brand team—the people who develop and prepare the market for AstraZeneca's cardiovascular drugs—and the corporation's senior leadership, Anne Cobuzzi regularly plans and writes reports for different audiences. AstraZeneca is a $19 billion, London-based pharmaceutical company with more than 60,000 employees worldwide. In addition to cardiovascular drugs, the company offers medications to treat cancer, asthma, hypertension, high cholesterol, and other conditions.

Cobuzzi's first step in planning any report is to identify the audience and the purpose. "Once I know my audience, and I know whether this report will help them make a decision, provide them with information, or request their guidance, I have a direction," she says. Knowing the audience also helps her determine how much detail to include in the report. For top managers, Cobuzzi will summarize key points in the body of the report and then put all the supporting data in the appendix. Although she avoids reiterating information for readers who are knowledgeable about the topic, she also is aware that some readers may need the report's context and relevance explained. She often consults with colleagues when considering how much background to include because, she says, "having people who can give you that fresh perspective is very helpful."

In the exacting world of pharmaceuticals, facts and figures must be very precise. Cobuzzi gathers data from a variety of sources and takes particular care to ensure that her sources are recent, reliable, and meaningful to each audience. Depending on the report, she will plan and draft the body, then collaborate with other AstraZeneca experts who comment on the draft and write additional sections. In addition, she stresses the importance of examining every report for accuracy, logic, and proper organization. "If you can't challenge yourself," she suggests, "approach a colleague who is not involved in the report and say, 'Challenge me on this. Is this the right way to go? Have I convinced you?'"

Finally, Cobuzzi believes that business communicators sometimes concentrate too heavily on the end result of a report and miss some of the vital steps in between. Her advice: "Really plan the report by thinking it through, jotting down a number of ideas, deciding on a direction, and not getting bogged down by the ending. Once you've decided which direction to take, stay on that path, but don't be so rigid that you miss a good point."

"Plan the report by thinking it through, jotting down a number of ideas, deciding on a direction, and not getting bogged down by the ending."

■ Who Reads and Writes Reports?

CO1. Understand the importance of business reports to organizations.

Consider the following routine informational needs of management and other human resources in a large, complex, and perhaps multinational organization:

- A sales manager at headquarters uses information provided by the field representatives to make sales projections.

- A vice-president asks subordinates to gather and analyze information needed to make an operational decision.

- A human resources supervisor relies on the firm's legal staff to interpret government requirements for completing a compliance report.

- A manager prepares a proposal for the company to bid on a government project.

- An administrator informs all subordinates about a new company policy on hiring temporary personnel.

A wide variety of reports helps managers solve problems.

These common situations show why a wide variety of reports have become such a basic part of the typical management information system (MIS) of the contemporary organization. Because constraints are imposed by geography, time, and technical expertise, most managers often rely on others to provide the information, analysis, and recommendations they need for making decisions and solving problems. Reports travel upward, downward, and laterally within the organization, so reading and writing reports is a typical part of nearly every manager's duties.

Reports can range from a fill-in form to a one-page letter or memo to a multi-volume manuscript. For our purposes, we define a *business report* as an orderly and objective presentation of information that helps in decision making and problem solving. Note the different parts of our definition.

- The report must be *orderly* so that the reader can locate the needed information quickly.

- It must be *objective* because the reader will use the report to make decisions that affect the health and welfare of the organization.

- It must present *information*—facts, data. Where subjective judgments are required, as in drawing conclusions and making recommendations, they must be presented ethically and be based squarely on the information presented in the report.

- Finally, the report must aid in *decision making* and *problem solving*. There is a practical, "need-to-know" dimension in business reports that is sometimes missing in scientific and academic reports. Business reports must provide the specific information that management and other personnel need to make a decision or solve a problem. This goal should be uppermost in the writer's mind during all phases of the reporting process.

■ Characteristics of Business Reports

CO2. Describe the common characteristics of business reports.

To better understand your role as a reporter of business information, consider the following four characteristics of business reports:

- Reports vary widely—in length, complexity, formality, and format.

- The quality of the report process affects the quality of the product.

- Accuracy is the most important trait of a report.

- Reports are often collaborative efforts.

Reports Vary Widely

There is no such document as a standard report—in length, complexity, formality, or format. The sales representative who spends five minutes completing a half-page call report showing which customers were contacted has completed a report. Likewise, the team of designers, engineers, and marketing personnel who spend six months preparing a six-volume proposal to submit to the Ministry of Transportation has completed a report. The typical report lies somewhere in between. One analysis of 383 actual business reports found that 36 percent were one page, 37 percent were two to three pages, and 27 percent were four or more pages long.[1]

The typical business report is one to three pages long and written in narrative format.

Most reports are written using a standard narrative (manuscript) format, but reports may also be in the form of letters, memos, email, or pre-printed forms. In addition to the body, a report may include such preliminary (prefatory) parts as a cover letter, title page, table of contents, and executive summary. Supplemental parts may include a list of references, appendixes, and an index.

Although reports may be either oral or written, most important reports are written; even most oral reports are written initially. In other words, many reports are first written and then presented orally. Having the report available in written format is important for several reasons: (1) the written report provides a permanent record; (2) it can be read and reread as needed; and (3) the reader can control the pace—rereading the complex parts, marking the important points, and skipping some sections.

The Quality of the Process Affects the Quality of the Product

Writing a report involves much more than "writing a report." As contradictory as this statement might seem, consider a fairly routine report assignment—determining whether to recommend the purchase of the Brand A, B, or C computer projection system for your organization's conference room. Before you can begin to write your recommendation, you must do your homework. At a minimum, you must (1) determine which technical features are most important to the users of the machines; (2) evaluate each brand in terms of these features; (3) compare the brands on such characteristics as cost, maintenance, reliability, and ease of use; and (4) draw a conclusion about which brand to recommend.

A report may be well written and still contain faulty data.

If at any step you make a mistake, your report will be worse than useless; it will contain errors that the reader will in turn rely on to make a decision. Suppose you interviewed only two of the 50 managers who will be using the new system. The needs of these two managers may not be typical of the needs of the other 48. Or suppose you failed to consider the amount of downtime required by each brand. Regardless of its features, no machine can meet the needs of its users when it is inoperable.

As such situations show, your report itself (the end product of your efforts) can be well written and well designed, with appropriate charts and tables; yet if the

GRANTLAND®

process by which the information was gathered and analyzed was defective, erroneous, or incomplete, the report will be also. The final product can be only as good as the weakest link in the chain of events leading up to the report.

As indicated in Checklist 11 on page 313, the reporting process involves planning, data gathering and analysis, and writing. The two major components of the planning stage—defining the purpose of the report and analyzing the audience—will be covered later in this chapter. The other steps are discussed in the subsequent chapters.

Accuracy Is the Most Important Trait

Your most important job is to ensure that the information you transmit is correct.

No report weakness—including making major grammatical mistakes, misspelling the name of the report reader, or missing the deadline for submitting the report—is as serious as communicating inaccurate information. It's a basic tenet of management that bad information leads to bad decisions. And in such situations, the bearer of the "bad" news will surely suffer the consequences.

Suppose that while conducting the research for the computer projection system report, you inadvertently noted that the bulbs for Brand A had a 100-hour life when, in fact, they have a 300-hour life. If operating costs were a major criterion, your final recommendation might be incorrect because of this simple careless error. It doesn't even matter how the error occurred—whether you made it or the typist made it. You are responsible for the project, and the praise or criticism of the results of your efforts will fall on you.

To achieve accuracy, follow these guidelines:

1. *Report all relevant facts.* Errors of *omission* are just as serious as errors of *commission.* Don't mislead the reader by reporting just those facts that tend to support your position.

    NOT: During the two-year period of 2006 and 2007, our return on investment averaged 21 percent.

    BUT: Our return on investment was 34 percent in 2006 but 8 percent in 2007, for an average of 21 percent.

2. *Use emphasis and subordination appropriately.* Your goal is to help the reader see the relative importance of the points you discuss. If you honestly think a certain idea is of minor importance, subordinate it—regardless of whether

✔checklist 11

The Reporting Process

Planning

✔ Define the purpose of the report.

- Determine why the issue is important; what use will be made of the report; and what the time, resource, and length constraints are.
- Decide whether the purpose is to inform, analyze, or recommend.
- Using neutral language, construct a one-sentence problem statement, perhaps in question form.

✔ Define the audience for the report.

- Is the report for an internal or an external reader?
- Did the reader authorize the report or is it voluntary?
- What is the level of knowledge and interest of the reader?

Data Gathering and Analysis

✔ Determine what data will be required.

- Factor the problem statement into its component parts, perhaps stating each sub-problem as a question.
- Determine what data will be needed to answer each sub-problem.

✔ Decide which methods to use to collect the needed data.

- Ensure that any secondary data used is current, accurate, complete, free from bias and misinterpretation, and relevant.
- If secondary data is not available, determine the most efficient means of collecting the needed data.

✔ Collect the data.

- Ensure that all informational needs have been identified.
- Allot sufficient time to gather the needed data.
- Ensure that the collection methods will produce valid and reliable data.

✔ Compile the data in a systematic and logical form, organizing the information according to the sub-problems.

✔ Analyze each bit of data individually at first and then in conjunction with every other bit of data. Finally, look at all the data together to try to discern trends, contradictions, unexpected findings, areas for further investigation, and the like.

✔ Construct appropriate visual aids.

Writing

✔ Draft the report.

- Consider the needs of the reader and the nature of the problem.
- Determine the organization, length, formality, and format of the report.
- Make sure the report is clear, complete, objective, and credible.

✔ Revise the report for content, style, and correctness.

✔ Use generally accepted formatting conventions to format the report in an attractive, efficient, and effective style.

✔ Proofread to ensure that the report reflects the highest standards of scholarship, critical thinking, and care.

it reinforces or weakens your ultimate conclusion. Don't emphasize a point simply because it reinforces your position, and don't subordinate a point simply because it weakens your position.

3. *Give enough evidence to support your conclusions.* Make sure that your sources are accurate, reliable, and objective and that there is enough evidence to support your position. Sometimes your evidence (the data you gather) may be so sparse, or of such questionable quality, that you are unable to draw a valid conclusion. If so, simply present the findings and don't draw a conclusion.

Draw valid conclusions, if appropriate.

To give the reader confidence in your statements, discuss your procedures thoroughly and cite all your sources.

4. *Avoid letting personal biases and unfounded opinions influence your interpretation and presentation of the data.* Sometimes you will be asked to draw conclusions and to make recommendations, and such judgments inherently involve a certain amount of subjectivity. You must make a special effort to look at the data objectively and to base your conclusions solely on the data. Avoid letting your personal feelings influence the outcomes. Sometimes the use of a single word can unintentionally convey bias.

NOT: The accounting supervisor *claimed* the error was unintentional.

BUT: The accounting supervisor *stated* the error was unintentional.

Reports Are Often Collaborative Efforts

Complex reports require the talents of many people.

Short, informal reports are usually a one-person effort. Many recurring reports in an organization, however, are multiperson efforts. It is not likely, for example, that general management would ask a single person to study the feasibility of entering the generic-product market. Instead, a combination of talents would be needed— marketing, manufacturing, human resources, and the like.

Such joint efforts require well-defined organizational skills, time management, close coordination, and a genuine spirit of cooperation. Although more difficult to manage than individually written reports, team-written reports offer these advantages:

- They draw on the diverse experiences and talents of many members.
- They increase each manager's awareness of other viewpoints.
- They typically result in higher-quality output than might be the case if a single person worked alone on a complex assignment.
- They produce a final product in less time than would be possible otherwise.
- They help develop important networking contacts.
- They provide valuable experience in working with small groups.

■ Purposes of Reports

CO3. Analyze purpose and audience in developing business reports.

At the outset, you need to determine why you are writing the report. Business reports generally aim to inform, analyze, or recommend.

Informing

Informational reports present information without analyzing it.

Informational reports relate objectively the facts and events surrounding a particular situation. No attempt is made to analyze and interpret the data, draw conclusions, or recommend a course of action. Most periodic reports, as well as policies and procedures, are examples of informational reports. In most cases, these types of reports are the easiest to complete. The report writer's major interest is in presenting all of the relevant information objectively, accurately, and clearly, while refraining from including unsolicited analysis and recommendations.

Analyzing

One step in complexity above the informational report is the **analytical** report, which not only presents the information but also analyzes it. Data by itself may be meaningless; the information must be put into some context before readers can make use of it. As social forecaster John Naisbitt has remarked, "We are drowning in information, but starved for knowledge."[2]

Consider, for example, this informational statement: "Sales for the quarter ending June 30 were $780,000." Was this performance good or bad? We cannot possibly know unless the writer *analyzes* the information for us. Here are two possible interpretations of this statement:

> Sales for the quarter ending June 30 were $780,000, up 7 percent from the previous quarter. This strong showing was achieved despite an industry-wide slump and may be attributed to the new "Tell One—Sell One" campaign we introduced in January.

> Sales for the quarter ending June 30 were $780,000, a decline of 5.5 percent from the same quarter last year. All regions experienced a 3 percent to 5 percent increase except for the western region, which experienced an 18 percent decrease in sales. John Manilow, western regional manager, attributes his area's sharp drop in sales to the budgetary problems now being experienced by the provincial governments in Ontario and Quebec.

The report writer must be careful that any conclusions drawn are reasonable, valid, and fully supported by the data presented. Although the writer must attempt to avoid inserting his or her own biases or pre-existing opinions into the report, analysis and interpretation can never be completely objective. The report writer makes numerous decisions that call for subjective evaluations. Note the difference in effect of the following two statements, which contain the same information but in reversed order:

Original:

> Although it is too early to determine the effectiveness of Mundrake's efforts, he believes the steps he is taking will bring Limerick's absentee rate down to the industry average of 3.6 percent by December.

Reversed:

> Although Mundrake believes the steps he is taking will bring Limerick's absentee rate down to the industry average of 3.6 percent by December, it is too early to determine the effectiveness of his efforts.

The original order leaves a confident impression of the probable success of the steps taken, whereas the reversed order leaves a much more skeptical impression. Only the report writer can determine which version leaves the more accurate impression.

Recommending

Recommendation reports add the element of endorsing a specific course of action (see, for example, the feasibility report in Model 16). The writer presents the relevant information, interprets it, and then suggests a plan of attack. The important point is that you must let the *data* be the basis for any conclusions you draw and

Analytical reports interpret the information.

Recommendation reports propose a course of action.

model16

FEASIBILITY REPORT

This feasibility study is shown in memo format.

Begins by introducing the topic. This report uses the indirect pattern, saving the recommendations until the end.

Is organized according to the criteria used to solve the problem.

MEMO TO:	Ms. Jennifer McKinley
C.C.:	Board of Governors
FROM:	George Poulias, Marketing Director
DATE:	May 9, 20—
SUBJECT:	Response to your idea for advertising on Smart Cars

As was discussed in last month's Board of Governors' meeting, we are looking at innovative ways to advertise the College to the Calgary community and beyond, and your idea to invest in five Smart Cars with wrap-around advertising immediately caught the group's interest. I've looked into the possibility, more specifically its cost and effectiveness.

Wrapped Cars Get Noticed

Advertising on vehicles is getting more popular, and it is a good way to get your advertising noticed by the general public. From my research, I discovered that wrapped cars provide a three-dimensional, 360-degree, moving billboard. Unlike conventional billboards that are only seen by moving traffic for a few seconds, wrapped cars tend to be visible longer as drivers drive beside or behind them or see them parked in and around local businesses. Smart Cars contribute to this advantage still further, since they are already one of the most noticeable and unique vehicles on the road today.

The success of a wrapped vehicle's advertising seems to depend primarily on its "visibility" and uniqueness (which the Smart car definitely provides), but most advertisers rely on bigger vehicles, such as buses, trains, subway cars, Hummers, and vans. This does, however, work in our favour, since there are very few Smart Cars on the road, and I have seen none with a full advertising wrap.

Financing Is Within Our Means

The College currently has a yearly advertising budget of $500 000. With Smart Car advertising, we have two options:

model16

(CONTINUED)

2

1
- Base-level Smart Cars start at approximately $16 700 before GST, but my contact at the Hyatt Auto Gallery has assured me that they could drop the price to $15 000, GST included, making the total cost for a five-car fleet $75 000.
- The vehicles could also be leased at a guaranteed cost of $300.00 per month, per vehicle, for a total monthly payment of $1500. This may be a better choice.

2

The wrapping of the cars, a one-time cost, could be done by several Calgary companies: Speedpro Calgary, Mobile Installations, or Ads To Go, among a number of others. Each of the three companies quoted roughly the same price: ranging from $1800 to $2500.00, depending on the design and number of vehicles. Our overall cost would be a one-time payment of approximately $9000 to $12 500. And, since these wraps are completely removeable, they would not affect the leasing agreement.

3

We Can Reach Our Advertising Targets

Using a fleet of wrapped Smart Cars does meet our two main advertising targets for 2006-2007: 1) To compete directly and aggressively with University of Calgary for first-year students, and 2) To increase our visibility in the Calgary community.

The choice of Smart Cars and the suggested design of the wrap accomplish these two goals well. On the front and rear of the vehicle would appear our logo and name; on the passenger side, the words *Small Classes,* and on the driver's side, the words *Smart Choice.* Small classes are one of our main selling features. *Smart Choice* ties in with the vehicle itself, and putting the college's logo and name on the front and back (and quite possibly the roof) of the car make it very visible in all directions. The wrap would, of course, be in the school colours of royal blue and white.

Smart Cars Are a Smart Choice

The students, staff, and faculty I have surveyed were overwhelmingly in support of the idea and commented on its uniqueness. I propose we take the next step and implement this idea into next year's advertising campaign. I've included the survey results, cost analysis and breakdown, as well as brochures from Hyatt Auto Gallery, Speedpro, Mobile Installations, and Ads To Go, along with the prices we've been quoted, in the attached appendix.

Closes by making a recommendation based on the findings presented.

Grammar and Mechanics Notes

1 Hyphenate compound adjectives such as *base-level* and *first-year.*

2 Be sure that a complete sentence precedes a colon when introducing lists within a paragraph.

3 Be consistent in formatting report side headings; there is no one standard format (other than consistency). This report uses "talking" headings, which identify both the topic and the major conclusion of each section.

any recommendations you make. You want to analyze and present your data so that the truth, the whole truth, and nothing but the truth emerges. In other words, avoid the temptation of beginning with a preconceived idea and then marshalling and manipulating data to support it.

In a sense, your final recommendation is only the tip of the iceberg, but it is a very visible tip. The logic, clarity, and strength of your recommendation can have major implications for your career and for your organization's well-being.

■ Audience Analysis

The audience for a report—the reader or readers—is typically homogeneous. Many times, of course, the audience is one person; but even when it is not, the audience usually consists of people with similar levels of expertise, background knowledge, and the like. Thus, you can, and should, develop your report to take into account the needs of your reader. In doing so, you will need to consider the following elements.

Internal Versus External Audiences

Internal reports are generally less formal and contain less background information than external reports.

Internal reports are written for readers within the organization and are usually less formal than external reports, for which the reader might be a customer, potential customer, or government agency. Internal reports also typically require less background information and can safely use more technical vocabulary than external reports, which are often more sensitive to public relations issues.

Internal reports are also directional and are aimed at the writer's superiors, peers, or subordinates. The strategy used must be appropriate for the audience's position. For example, reports often have a costs-and-profits tone when directed to superiors, a conversational tone when directed to peers, and an emphatic tone when directed to subordinates.

Authorized Versus Voluntary Reports

Voluntary reports require more background information and more persuasion than authorized reports.

Authorized reports are written at the specific request of some higher authority. Thus, the reader has an inherent interest in the report. Voluntary reports, on the other hand, are prepared on the writer's own initiative. Therefore, the reader needs more background information and frequently more persuasive evidence than do readers of authorized reports.

Authorized reports may be either periodic or situational. Periodic reports are submitted on a recurring, systematic basis. Very often they are form reports, with space provided for specific items of information. Readers of periodic reports need little introductory or background information because of the report's recurring nature. Readers of situational, one-time reports, on the other hand, need more explanatory material because of the uniqueness of the situation.

Level of Knowledge and Interest

Gear the amount of information presented and the order in which it is presented to the needs of the reader.

Is the reader already familiar with your topic? Will he or she understand the terms used, or will you need to define them? If you have a heterogeneous audience for your report, striking an appropriate balance in level of detail given will require careful planning.

spotlight19
ACROSS CULTURES

Context in International Reports

Most business reports are written for a relatively homoge-neous audience. However, in the international arena the reader and writer often have different cultural viewpoints. The greater the amount of knowledge, perceptions, and attitudes the reader and writer share (that is, the higher the *context* of the communication exchange), the less important it is for report writers to directly express *every-thing* they wish to communicate. Conversely, the less the reader and writer have in common, the more they need to convey every nuance of their meaning explicitly through words; that is, the less they can assume to be implicitly understood.

Contexting can be categorized as either high or low. When report writers have considerable knowledge and experience in common with their readers, their reports are generally *highly contexted*. In highly contexted reports, what the writer chooses *not* to put into words is still essential to understanding the actual message intended. But the writer assumes that what is not said is actually *already understood*.

When report writers rely relatively little on shared knowledge and experience, their report is *low contexted*. As a result, in low-context exchanges more information must be explicitly stated than in high-context ones. Thus, low-context cultures tend to rely on *direct* communication;

they often consider the indirect pattern a waste of time or a strain on the receiver's patience. High-context cultures, on the other hand, tend to rely on *indirect* communication to smooth over interpersonal differences and to keep from losing face in a conflict situation. They often consider directness rude and offensive.

Importance of Context in Different Cultures

To a large extent, contexting is a culturally learned behav-iour, with the degree of context varying from culture to culture. As shown below, Germans and German-speaking Swiss tend to be low-context cultures (all important infor-mation is explicitly stated), whereas the Japanese, Arabic, and Latin American people tend to be high-context cultures (much important information is implicitly assumed).

As Stella Ting-Toomey has noted, "In the HCC [high-context culture] system, what is not said is sometimes more important than what is said. In contrast, in the LCC [low-context culture] system, words represent truth and power."

Competent communicators ensure that the degree of explicitness, the amount of detail, and the assumptions built into their reports match the context expectations of their audience.[3]

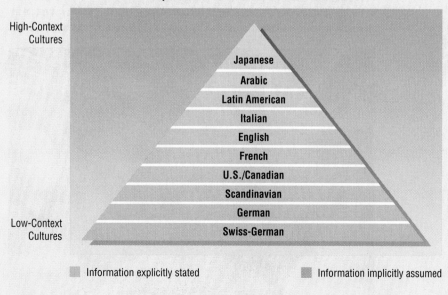

Importance of Context in Different Cultures

High-Context Cultures

- Japanese
- Arabic
- Latin American
- Italian
- English
- French
- U.S./Canadian
- Scandinavian
- German
- Swiss-German

Low-Context Cultures

Information explicitly stated   Information implicitly assumed

Most reports are written in the direct pattern, with the major conclusions and recommendations given up front (but see, however, Spotlight 19, "Context in International Reports," on page 319). This situation is especially true when you know the reader is interested in your project or is likely to agree with your opinions and judgments. Reports that make a recommendation with which the reader may disagree are often written in the indirect pattern because you want the reader to study the reasons first. The reader will be more likely to accept or at least consider the recommendation if he or she has first had an opportunity to study its rationale.

■ Common Types of Reports

CO4. Describe the common types of business reports.

Earlier we broadly categorized reports into information, analytical, and recommendation reports. These categories can be further broken into numerous types of reports, where each serves a specific purpose.

Periodic Reports

Three common types of periodic reports are routine management reports, compliance reports, and progress reports, all of which are considered **informational;** that is, they present all of the relevant information objectively, accurately, and clearly, while refraining from including unsolicited analysis and recommendations.

Routine Management Reports   Every organization requires its own set of recurring reports to provide the knowledge base from which decisions are made and problems are solved. Some of these routine management reports are statistical, consisting sometimes of just computer printouts; other management reports are primarily narrative. Routine management reports range from accounting, financial, and sales updates to various human resources and equipment reports.

At Motorola's Communication (or Comm) Sector, employees and managers brainstorm to develop improvements for two-way radios. This scene is typical in business where a combination of talents joins to produce a collaborative report.

Compliance Reports   Many government agencies, such as Human Resources Development Canada or Environment Canada, require companies to file reports showing that they are complying with regulations in such areas as affirmative action, contacts with foreign firms, labour relations, occupational safety, financial dealings, and environmental concerns. Completing these compliance reports is often mostly a matter of gathering the needed data and reporting the information honestly and completely. Typically, very little analysis of the data is required.

Progress Reports   Interim progress reports are often used to communicate the status of long-term projects. They are submitted periodically to management for internal projects, to the customer for external projects, and to the investor for an accounting of venture capital expenditures. Typically, these narrative reports (1) tell what has been accomplished since the last progress report; (2) document how well the project is adhering to the schedule and budget; (3) describe any problems encountered and how they were solved; and (4) outline future plans (see Model 17 on page 322).

Proposals

A **proposal** is an analytical report that seeks to persuade the reader to accept a suggested plan of action. Two common types of proposals in business are project proposals and research proposals.

Project Proposals   A manager may write a project proposal that, for example, seeks to persuade a potential customer to purchase goods or services from the writer's firm, persuade the federal government to locate a new research facility in the headquarters' city of the writer's firm, or persuade a foundation to fund a project to be undertaken by the writer's firm.

Proposals may be solicited or unsolicited. Government agencies and many large commercial firms routinely solicit proposals from potential suppliers. For example, the government might publish an RFP (request for proposal) stating its intention to purchase 5000 microcomputers, giving detailed specifications regarding the features it needs on these computers, and inviting prospective suppliers to bid on the project. Similarly, the computer manufacturer that submits the successful bid might itself publish an RFP to invite parts manufacturers to bid on supplying some component the manufacturer needs for these computers.

The unsolicited proposal differs from the solicited proposal in that the former typically requires more background information and more persuasion. Because the reader may not be familiar with the project, the writer must present more evidence to convince the reader of the merits of the proposal. (See Model 18 on page 324.)

Research Proposals   Because research is a cost to the organization in terms of personnel time and monetary expenses, superiors want to know what they will gain in return for expending these resources. Thus, a research proposal is a structured presentation of what you plan to do in research, why you plan to conduct the research, and how you plan to accomplish it. The proposal gives those concerned with your research effort an opportunity to evaluate your research approach. Every step of your proposal should be developed with extreme care. Once it has been accepted, any substantive changes you may wish to make must receive prior approval.

Research proposal formats vary depending on the desires and needs of those who will appraise your work. (See Model 19 on page 326.)

model17

PROGRESS REPORT

This progress report is submitted in memo format.

Begins by giving the purpose and an overall summary.

Identifies the work completed, in progress, and still to be done.

Uses enumerations to make the items stand out.

Uses first and second person pronouns (appropriate in a letter or memo report).

Identifies problems and needed decisions.

Closes on a goodwill note.

Holiday Books
1900 Regency Street
Fredericton, NB S3B 6N9

MEMO TO: Mr. Clarence Yeung, Manufacturing Department

FROM: Michel Bouchard, Project Manager

DATE: May 9, 20—

SUBJECT: Warehouse Status Report

This memo brings you up to date on the status of the construction of our new warehouse on Birmingham Street. As you will see, construction is on schedule and within budget, with no major problems foreseen.

Work Completed to Date: We have now completed the following jobs:
1. The foundation was poured on March 27.
2. The exterior of the building, including asphalt roofing and aluminum siding, was completed on April 23.

Work in Progress: The following work has been started but has not yet been completed:
1. The drywallers are installing the interior walls and partitions; they should be finished by the end of next week.
2. The plumbers have installed the necessary fixtures in the washrooms and are installing the Amana high-energy-efficient heating/cooling unit.

Work to Be Completed: From now until July 20, we will be completing these tasks:
1. The vinyl flooring will be installed by June 23.
2. The painters will paint the interior on July 1–3.
3. The city inspector and fire marshal will perform a final inspection on July 17.

Miscellaneous: The modular rack storage system was ordered on April 3 and should have been delivered two weeks ago. Our supplier assures me that the system will be delivered by May 12. If so, we should have no problems installing it on schedule.

By June 25, you will need to make a final colour selection for the interior walls. The plan calls for one colour.

We appreciate the opportunity to build this facility for you and are sure you will enjoy using it. I will provide you another update in June.

hwc

Holiday Books • 10 Argyle Street • Halifax, NS A5B 2T8

Grammar and Mechanics Notes

1 *exterior . . . was:* Ignore intervening words when establishing subject/verb agreement.

2 *been started but:* Do not insert a comma between parts of a compound predicate.

3 *partitions; they:* Connect two closely related independent clauses with a semicolon—not a comma.

4 Use your word processing program's enumeration or bullet feature to format lists automatically.

Effective collaborative writing requires tact, patience, and a spirit of cooperation—just a few of the many skills the team from *This Hour Has 22 Minutes* must employ as they write for their weekly program. The winner of numerous Gemini awards, *This Hour Has 22 Minutes* is a mock news program and sketch comedy show, filled with social and political satire.

Policies and Procedures

Policies are broad operating guidelines that govern the general direction and activities of an organization; **procedures** are the recommended methods or sequential steps to follow when performing a specific activity. Both types fall under the general category of informational reports. Thus, information about an organization's attitude toward promoting from within the firm would constitute a policy, and information about the steps to be taken to apply for a promotion would constitute a procedure. Policy statements are typically written by top management; procedures are typically written by the managers and supervisors who are involved in the day-to-day operation of the organization.

Policy   Policy reports (or statements) typically begin with a policy statement that justifies the need for a policy. Such justification should be general enough that the policy covers a broad range of situations but not so general that it has no real "teeth." Policy statements ensure that the reader knows exactly who is covered by the policy, what is required, and any other needed information. They also may include some discussion of how the reader, the organization, or *someone* benefits from this policy. Depending on the complexity and the scope of the policy, lawyers may be involved in their composition to ensure the legal ramifications of the policies have been adequately considered.

model18

PROJECT PROPOSAL

This solicited proposal seeks to persuade an organization to sponsor a workshop.

Begins by identifying the purpose of the letter.

Provides specific examples to show that a need exists.

Suggests a reasonable solution.

Tells exactly what the proposal should accomplish.

Words Ink
6090 Bank Street
Ottowa, ON K3P 5M7

September 16, 20—

Ms. Carolyn Soule, Employee Manager
335 Banff Avenue
Calgary, AB T2A 8H9

Dear Ms. Soule:

1 Subject: Proposal for an In-house Workshop on Business Writing

I enjoyed discussing with you the business writing workshops you intend to sponsor for the engineering staff at Evergreen National Corporation. As you requested, I am submitting this proposal to conduct a two-day workshop.

BACKGROUND

2 On September 4–5, I interviewed four engineers at your organization and analyzed samples of their writing. Your engineers are typical of many highly trained specialists who know exactly what they want to say but sometimes do not structure their communications in the most effective manner. Problems with audience analysis, organization, and overall writing style were especially apparent when they were communicating with non-specialists either inside or outside the organization.

3 Thus, I propose that you sponsor a two-day writing workshop that I will develop entitled "The Process of Business Writing." The workshop could be held during any two days between November 26 and December 10.

OBJECTIVES

The workshop would help your engineers achieve these objectives:

1. Specify the purpose of a message and perform an audience analysis.

2. Determine what information to include and in what order to present it.

3. Set an appropriate overall tone by using confident language, using appropriate emphasis and subordination, and stressing the "you" attitude.

4. Revise a draft for content, style, correctness, and readability.

5. Format written communications in an efficient standard format.

Grammar and Mechanics Notes

1 Leave one blank line before and after a subject line.

2 *highly trained specialists:* Do not hyphenate a compound modifier when the first word (an adverb) ends in *-ly.*

3 *Business Writing.":* Place the period inside the closing quotation marks.

2

model18

(CONTINUED)

PROCEDURES

The enclosed outline shows the coverage of the course. The workshop would require a meeting room with participants seated at tables, an overhead projector, and a chalkboard or some other writing surface. The program would be divided into four half-day segments, each lasting three hours. The first two hours would be devoted to discussing the topics listed, followed by a 15-minute break. The final hour would consist of group and individual writing assignments, with appropriate guidance, discussion, and feedback provided.

Provides enough details to enable the reader to understand what is planned.

4 My fee for teaching the two-day workshop would be $2000, plus expenses (including photocopying handouts, automobile mileage, and lunch on the workshop days). Your organization would be responsible for arranging and providing the morning and afternoon refreshments and lunch for the participants.

Discusses costs in an open and confident manner.

QUALIFICATIONS

I would be responsible for planning and conducting the workshop. As you can see from the enclosed data sheet, I've had 15 years of consulting experience in business communications and have spoken and written widely on the topic.

Highlights only the most relevant information from the enclosed data sheet.

SUMMARY

5 My experience in working with engineers has taught me that they recognize the value of effective business communications and are motivated to improve their writing skills. The course should help them become more effective communicators and more effective managers for Evergreen National Corporation.

Shows how the reader will benefit from doing as asked.

I wish you much success in your efforts to upgrade your staff's writing skills. Please call me at 403-571-8766 to let me know your reactions to this proposal.

Closes on a friendly, confident note.

6 Sincerely yours,

Ann Skarzinski

Ann Skarzinski, Executive Trainer

mje
Enclosures

Grammar and Mechanics Notes

4 *$2000:* Omit the decimal point and zeroes for even amounts of money. The metric system promotes the use of spaces, rather than commas, to separate large numbers. In some industries, such as accounting and financial services, the comma is preferred.

5 *engineers has:* Use the singular verb (*has*) because the subject is *experience,* not *engineers.*

6 *Sincerely yours,:* Capitalize only the first word of a complimentary closing.

model19

RESEARCH PROPOSAL

This research proposal is shown in manuscript format.

Uses a neutral, descriptive title.

Introduces the topic and establishes a need for the study.

Phrases the problem to be solved in question format.

Includes sub-problems that, taken together, will answer the problem statement.

EMPLOYEES' EVALUATION OF THE BENEFIT PROGRAM AT AEGON OIL AND GAS

A Research Proposal by Lyn O'Neal
January 23, 20—

1   Employee benefits are a rapidly growing and an increasingly important form of employee compensation for both profit and non-profit organizations. According to a recent study by the Human Resource Board of Canada, benefits now constitute 27
2   percent of all payroll costs, averaging $10 857 yearly for each employee.[1] As has been noted by two management consultants, "The success of employee benefit programs depends directly on whether employees need and understand the value of the benefits provided." [2] Thus, an organization's employee benefit program must be monitored and evaluated if it is to remain an effective recruitment and retention tool.

Aegon employs 2500 personnel, who have not received a cost-of-living increase in two years. Thus, employee salaries may not have kept pace with industry, and the company's benefits program may become more important in attracting and retaining good workers.

PROBLEM AND SCOPE

To help ensure that the benefit program is operating as effectively as possible, the following problem will be addressed in this study: What are the opinions of employees at Aegon Oil and Gas regarding their employee benefits? To answer this question, the following sub-problems will be addressed:

1. How knowledgeable are the employees about the benefit program?
2. What are the employees' opinions of the benefits presently available to them?
3. What benefits would the employees like to have added to the program?

---

[1] Enar Ignatio, "Can Flexible Benefits Promote Your Company?" *Personnel Quarterly*, Vol. 20, September 2006, p. 812.
3   [2] Ramon Adams and Seymour Stevens, *Personnel Administration*, All-State, Cambridge, MA, 2002, p. 483.

Grammar and Mechanics Notes

1 Like most research proposals, this one is written in third-person language. Note the absence of "I" and "you" pronouns.

2 When using the business-style citation method, use footnotes and include page numbers when citing statistics or a direct quotation. Omit page numbers if citing the entire work.

3 Format publications in italics; enclose parts of publications (such as article titles) in parentheses.

model19

2

This study attempts to determine employee preferences only. Whether employee preferences are economically feasible is not within the scope of this study. As used in this study, employee benefits (also called fringe benefits) means an employment benefit given in addition to one's wages or salary.

Identifies those parts of the problem the researcher has chosen *not* to investigate.

PROCEDURES

A random sample of 250 employees at Aegon Oil and Gas will be surveyed to answer the three sub-problems. In addition to the questionnaire data, personal interviews will be held with three benefits managers. The primary data provided by the survey and personal interviews will then be analyzed and compared with findings from secondary sources to determine the employees' opinions of the benefits program at Aegon.

Identifies the procedures needed to answer each sub-problem.

CONCLUSION

This information will be analyzed, and appropriate tables and charts will be developed. Conclusions will be drawn and recommendations made as appropriate to explain the employees' opinions about the benefit program at Aegon Oil and Gas.

Provides a sense of closure.

model20

PROCEDURE

A step-by-step outline of who (Actor) does what (Action) when temporary help is hired.

Uses a descriptive title.

Begins with the act that starts the process and ends with the final result.

Contains only essential information.

Details clearly and concisely what steps are necessary and in what order.

Maintains parallel structure (complete sentences are not necessary).

PROCEDURE FOR HIRING A TEMPORARY EMPLOYEE

Actor	Action
Requester	1. Requests a temporary employee with specialized skills by filling out Form 722, "Request for a Temporary Employee." 2. Secures manager's approval. 3. Sends four copies of Form 722 to labour analyst in Human Resources.
Labour Analyst	4. Checks overtime figures of regular employees in the department. 5. If satisfied that the specific people are necessary, checks budget. 6. If funds are available, approves Form 722, sends three copies to buyer of special services in Human Resources, and files the fourth copy.
Buyer of Special Services	7. Notifies outside temporary help contractor by phone and follows up the same day with a confirming letter or email. 8. Negotiates a mutually agreeable effective date. 9. Contacts Human Resources by phone, telling them of the number of people and the effective dates.
Human Resources	10. Notifies Security, Badges, and Gate Guards. 11. Returns one copy of Form 722 to the requester. 12. Provides a temporary ID.
Temporary Help Contractor	13. Furnishes assigned employee or employees with information on the job description, effective date, and the individual to whom to report.
Temporary Employee	14. Reports to receptionist one half-hour early on the effective date.

Grammar and Mechanics Note

The format used is optional. This procedure uses a play-script format that clearly specifies what role each person plays in the process.

Procedure   Procedural reports (which include user manuals and other forms of instructions) can be as simple as a memo detailing the procedures for filling out an expense report to as complex as a user manual for a new piece of software. Procedures take the reader step by step through a process, explaining, when necessary, what should *not* be done as well as what should be done. Complex procedures may be accompanied—or even dominated—by visuals to illustrate the procedure. Consider, for example, IKEA instructions for putting together a piece of furniture—they often contain no text at all, just easy-to-follow diagrams.

As procedures become more complex, they are typically written by specialists in a particular area who will work with technical writers experienced in the stylistic, organizational, and formatting requirements that ensure the procedures are both comprehensive and easy to follow. An example of a procedure is given in Model 20 (see page 328). Could you follow this procedure and get the desired results?

*word*wise

BY THE NUMBERS

- Forty is the only number that has its letters in alphabetical order.
- A *googol* is a 1 followed by 100 zeros.
- No number from one to nine hundred ninety-nine contains the letter a.
- The word *misunderstanding* contains at least 13 different words of 3 or more letters: *and, din, sun, tan, ding, erst, under, stand, sunder, standing, understand, understanding,* and *misunderstand.*

Situational Reports

In any organization, unique problems and opportunities appear that require one-time only reports. Such reports can fall into any of the three broad categories—informational, analytical, or recommendation. In their simplest form, situational reports might simply consist of a memo to a manager summarizing the results of a trip, conference, or course. Other, more complex, situations may call for information to be gathered and analyzed and for recommendations to be made. A *feasibility report,* for example, is used to assess whether a project is advisable and usually concludes with recommendations on whether the project should be pursued, revised, delayed, or scrapped. A *yardstick report* is an analytical report that assesses several alternative courses of action in solving a problem. The same set of criteria—or yardstick—is used to assess each course of action. Such criteria may include cost, durability, length of warranty, etc.

Situational reports are perhaps the most challenging for the report writer. Because they involve a unique event, the writer often has no previous reports to use as a guide; he or she must decide what types of information and how much information are needed and how best to organize and present the findings.

A sample situational report—a feasibility study—is shown in Model 16 (see page 316). The guidelines presented in the upcoming report chapters are especially applicable to situational reports because of the many decisions that surround these one-of-a-kind projects.

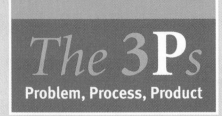

A PROJECT PROPOSAL

Problem

You and your colleagues who teach business communication at Red Valley College are interested in setting up a business writer's hotline—a telephone and email service that will provide answers to grammar, mechanics, and format questions from people who call in or write. You see it as a way of providing a much-needed service to local business people, as well as a way of providing positive public relations for your institution.

Each faculty member is willing to donate time to answer the phones and email, but you will need funds for telephone lines, answering machines, reference books, advertising, and the like. You decide to apply for a grant from the Lougheed Foundation to fund the project for one year. After that, if the hotline is successful, you will either reapply for funds or ask the Red Valley College administration to fund the continuing costs. For requests of less than $3000, the foundation requires a simple narrative report explaining and justifying the request.

Process

1. What is the background of the problem?

   Every writer has occasional questions about writing style but may not have a reference book or style manual available to answer the questions. We know there is a need for such a service because we frequently get calls from people on campus with these questions. Although several grammar hotlines operate nationally, none is available within a 500 kilometre radius of the college.

2. What will be the outcome of the project?

   A telephone and email service that will be available free of charge 24 hours a day to answer any question regarding business writing.

3. Describe the audience for this report and the implications for structuring your report.

   The Lougheed Foundation makes grants to non-profit organizations in the Northern Alberta area, mostly for small projects of less than $10 000 each. Because of the foundation's small size and personal orientation, a direct and personal (rather than scholarly) writing style should be used. As there is no reason to expect that the foundation holds a negative attitude toward this project, the proposal will be written in a direct pattern—the request for funds will be made at the beginning of the report.

4. Describe how the hotline will work.

   a. Questions phoned in will be recorded on an answering machine. Email questions can, of course, be sent at any time.

   b. A separate phone line will be installed.

   c. The faculty will agree on which books should serve as the standards of reference.

   d. The faculty will attempt to answer any reasonable question about grammar, mechanics, format, and the like, but will not review or edit anyone's writing and will not answer questions requiring extensive research.

5. What are the advantages of this project?

   a. Enhancing the college's reputation as an asset to the community.

   b. Providing a genuine service to business writers.

   c. Aiding business productivity by decreasing communication problems.

   d. Helping the business communication faculty members stay abreast of their fields.

6. What will the project cost?

   The faculty members will donate their time. Two copies of each of the reference books needed will cost $123.50. The telephone line will cost $61.30 monthly, and the long-distance charges for returning calls are estimated at $55 monthly. An answering machine costs $119.50. Monthly advertisements in the campus newspaper and in the local newspaper are estimated at $62.50.

7. What are the qualifications of those involved in this project?

   Each of the 12 faculty members has a doctoral degree and has taught business communication and related courses for an average of eight years.

Product

THE BUSINESS WRITER'S HOTLINE

A Proposal Submitted by Professor Steve Harland
Red Valley College
March 15, 20—

All business writers have occasional questions about writing style. Indeed, the business communication faculty at Red Valley College frequently receives calls asking questions about punctuation, subject-verb agreement, the correct format for business documents, and the like. Thus, the business communication faculty requests a grant of $2388.60 to establish and operate a Business Writer's Hotline for one year to benefit students, faculty, and staff, as well as the Northern Alberta community in general.

OUTCOME OF THE PROJECT

The project will fund the operation of a Business Writer's Hotline in which faculty members answer telephone and email inquires from business writers on the subject of grammar, mechanics, and format. The service will operate at no cost to users and will serve the following purposes:

1. Increase business productivity by lessening the chance that an error in writing will cause communication problems, delays, or even incorrect decisions.

2. Provide a service to business writers (including college students, faculty, staff, business people, and the general community) who presently have no convenient way of getting their questions answered.

3. Enhance the college's reputation as an asset to the local community.

PROCEDURES

Questions may be phoned in or emailed at any time. Questions phoned in will be recorded on an answering machine. While the school is in session, questions will be answered by the end of the following business day.

2

A dedicated telephone line will be installed. Faculty consultants will attempt to answer any reasonable question regarding grammar, mechanics (including punctuation and spelling), document format, and the like. They will not review or edit anyone's writing and will not be available to answer questions that require extensive research. Three books will serve as the standard references: *The Chicago Manual of Style, The Canadian Press Stylebook,* and the *Canadian Oxford Dictionary*.

The hotline will begin operating the first day of the school year and will continue for one year. A small ad announcing the availability of the service will be placed monthly in the *Valley Voice* and in the *Edmonton Journal*.

BUDGET

The following budget is projected for the first year of operation:

Purchase of two copies each of three reference books	$ 123.50
Purchase of one telephone-answering machine	119.50
Rental of one telephone line (12 mo. @ $61.30)	735.60
Long-distance charges (12 mo. estimated @ $55)	660.00
Newspaper advertisements (12 mo. @ $62.50)	750.00
Total	$ 2388.60

PERSONNEL QUALIFICATIONS

Each of the 12 faculty members who will act as a voluntary consultant has a doctoral degree and an average of eight years of experience teaching business communication and related courses. Thus, they have had much experience in answering the types of questions likely to be encountered.

SUMMARY

The establishment of a Business Writer's Hotline will increase the communication skills of the local community. The recurring yearly cost of $2145.60 is less than $10 per day and 40¢ per hour for the 45 weeks of 24-hour service. This cost is a small amount to pay for the benefits that will be provided.

◼ Summary

co1. Understand the importance of business reports to organizations.

co2. Describe the common characteristics of business reports.

co3. Analyze purpose and audience in developing business reports.

co4. Describe the common types of business reports.

Reports are central to decision making in most organizations. They vary widely in their complexity, their purpose, their level of formality and their audience. They also vary considerably in how they are authored—a simple trip report may be a brief memo from a staff member to a supervisor; a project proposal may be dozens or even hundreds of pages long and written by numerous authors.

Reports vary widely on their length, complexity, formality, and format; and they may be authored by one or several individuals. No matter what form reports take, accuracy is their most important trait.

Because the audience for a specific report is typically homogeneous, reports should be developed to take into account the reader's needs—in terms of level of knowledge and interest, internal versus external readers, and authorized versus voluntary reports.

The most common types of reports are periodic reports (including routine management, compliance, and progress reports), proposals, policies and procedures, and situational reports. The purpose of each type of report may be either to inform, to analyze, or to recommend.

◼ Key Terms

You should now be able to define the following terms in your own words and give an original example of each.

analytical (321)	procedure (323)
informational (320)	proposal (321)
policy (323)	recommendation (323)

◼ Exercises

1 **The 3Ps (Problem, Process, and Product) Model: Communication Applications at AstraZeneca.** As senior brand planning manager for AstraZeneca's cardio-vascular drugs, Anne Cobuzzi writes reports to keep corporate executives informed, to support management decision making, and to obtain management guidance about a particular issue. Depending on the report's purpose, audience, and content, she will draft the body, ask colleagues for feedback, and, if needed, ask internal experts to draft additional sections.

Problem

Cobuzzi has asked you, the assistant brand planning manager, to draft a brief report for top AstraZeneca executives. She wants you to compare sales of your cardiovascular drugs for the first half of this year with sales during the same period last year. This data will help company executives monitor sales patterns and determine whether results are as expected. Your research shows that sales were much stronger in the first quarter of this year than in the first quarter of last year. You also find that this year's second-quarter sales were lower than last year's second-quarter sales. This year's pattern is atypical: for the past five years, sales of your drugs have been stronger in the second quarter than in the first quarter. You will need another two weeks to determine whether this year's sales were affected by changes in promotional activities, competition, or another cause. Cobuzzi wants you to draft your report now and mention that you will file a second report after researching all the details.

Process

a. What is the purpose of this report?
b. Describe your audience.
c. What points will you cover and in what order?
d. Which point(s) should you emphasize? Why?
e. Compose the specific headings for this report.
f. Draft an opening paragraph to introduce the report and bring the highlights to your readers' attention.

Product

Using your knowledge of reports, prepare a short report in memorandum format, inventing any reasonable data you need to complete this assignment.

2 The 3Ps (Problem, Process, and Product) Model: A Proposal—Starting a Student-Run Business

Problem

You are the president of the Hospitality Services Association (HSA), a campus organization made up of students planning careers in hotel and motel management, tourism, and the like. You've just received a copy of a memo from the provost at your university addressed to the presidents of all campus organizations. The university is seeking proposals from student organizations to run a part-time business, tentatively named University Hosts (UH), which would provide local services and organize various events for campus visitors.

For example, when the admissions office lets UH know that a prospective student and his or her family will be visiting the campus, UH would immediately contact the family and offer to provide any reasonable service to help campus visitors enjoy their stay and receive a favourable impression of the institution. The service would be aimed at potential students and their families, alumni, donors, prospective faculty and staff members, and visiting legislators.

You feel that HSA would be the most logical organization to run this enterprise for the university. Your executive council has authorized you to submit a proposal to the provost. Personnel time (to be supplied by student members of HSA) would be billed at $15 per hour; a 10 percent surcharge would be added to the actual cost of all services provided (for example, tickets to campus or local events); automobile expenses would be billed at 22¢ per kilometre; and other charges would be billed at actual cost. Depending on the purpose of the campus visits, costs of the services would be billed either to the university or to the actual clients.

Process

a. What is the purpose of your report?
b. Describe your audience.
c. Is this a solicited or unsolicited proposal?
d. List the major advantages of this project and indicate how someone other than HSA will benefit from each advantage.
e. What costs are involved?

f. What qualifies HSA members to operate this business?

g. Will you request approval for this project at the beginning or end of your proposal? Why?

h. Compose an effective first sentence for your proposal.

i. What topics will you cover and in what order? Compose the specific headings for each topic.

Product

Prepare a three- to five-page typed proposal in memorandum format and submit it, along with your answers to the process questions, to your instructor. (You may invent any reasonable data needed.)

3 **Factoring Problems—Proposal Memo**　Write a proposal to your instructor seeking his or her approval of a topic and tentative content of an analytical report that could be prepared later in the semester. Submit the proposal as a one-page memo.

In the proposal, identify what has happened in the past to create the problem, the purpose of the report, the scope of the report, how you would gather data (both primary data and secondary data) regarding the topic, and a plan of action for completing the report. Select appropriate headings to identify the problem statement, report purpose, report scope, data collection process, and report timeline.

CO1. **Understand the importance of business reports to organizations.**

4 **Small Business—Reporting Needs**　Interview the owner/operator of a small business (with 10 to 50 employees) in your area. Determine the extent and types of reports written and received by employees in this firm. Write a memo report to your instructor summarizing your findings.

5 **Managing Reports—Large Business**　Interview the records manager at a large business in your area (personally or by phone). Determine what policies the organization follows to control reports, especially recurring reports, in terms of need, frequency, length, distribution, and the like. Write a memo to your instructor summarizing your findings.

6 **Managing Reports—Procedures**　Managers are often uncertain about how to go about discontinuing a recurring report that doesn't seem to be needed anymore. When does a report become obsolete? For example, several departments or managers at several levels may be simply accustomed to seeing a given report, even if they no longer need it, but there may be one manager who actually needs and uses the information in the report. You decide to prepare a procedure that describes the steps to take before discontinuing a recurring report. Consider both the writer's and the readers' needs for information. What can you do before distributing your procedure statement to determine whether it is reasonable and appropriate?

CO2. **Describe the common characteristics of business reports.**

7 **Work-team Communication—Report Characteristics**　Four types of business reports were identified in this chapter. Working in a group of three to five students, obtain a sample of three report types, perhaps from someone at the university or where you work. Analyze these reports for such factors as the following:

a. Purpose (to inform, analyze, or recommend)

b. Target audience

c. Length, format, and degree of formality
d. Clarity, completeness, and accuracy of the information
e. Authorship (individual or work-team)
f. Prefatory and supplemental elements

Write a two-page memo report to your instructor summarizing your findings.

8 Internet Activity In a group of three or four students, find and download a hard copy of a business report from the Internet. Try to get reports that are relatively short—fewer than 20 pages. Evaluate the report's effectiveness based on the principles covered in this chapter.

Answer the following question as you complete the evaluation: What type of report is it? What is the report's purpose? Who is the audience? Is the report formal or informal? Does it follow a direct or indirect plan? What are the report's strengths and weaknesses? How about content, spelling, grammar, punctuation, and other aspects of report writing? Does the report use primary and secondary data? Does the report appear to be written by one person or a group? What suggestions would you make to improve the quality of the report? Submit a memo to your instructor with your answers to the questions listed above and a copy of the report.

9 Audience Analysis—Market Research Your market research firm, National Collegiate Solutions, Inc. (NCSI), was recently hired by Archway Publications, a publisher of teen magazines. Edgar Martin, Archway's vice-president of marketing, hired you several months ago to analyze the market for a proposed monthly magazine geared toward college students. You've since completed your research (primarily interviews with students) and have analyzed your results. Now you are planning the final report of your findings, conclusions, and recommendations. Analyze your audience for this report. Is the audience internal or external? Is this a solicited or unsolicited report? What is the level of interest of the reader? Should you use a formal or informal style? Will you use a memo, letter, or manuscript format for this report? What organizational plan is appropriate? Prepare a one- to two-page summary of your answers to these questions.

co3. Analyze purpose and audience in developing business reports.

10 Progress Report—What Do You Already Know? You are serving on a school hiring committee. The committee is planning to interview three candidates who are interested in teaching at your school. As part of the interview process, the candidates have been asked to teach a section of the business communication class. The topic to be taught is writing business reports.

One of the candidates has asked for a report on what the class has already covered during the semester so he knows what has been covered previously. As the only student on the committee who is currently taking the class, you have been asked to prepare a short progress report of what has been covered in the class during the semester. Write a two-page report summarizing the material covered in Chapters 1–9 of the book.

Submit the report to your instructor for evaluation.

co4. Describe the common types of business reports.

11 Progress Report—Market Analysis Resume the role of director of National Collegiate Solutions, Inc.(see Exercise 9). Assume you are only part way through your initial research and have agreed to submit a progress report at the end of each month. It's April 30 (you started the project on April 5), so it's time to tell Martin what your firm has accomplished so far.

First, you developed an interview form to gather data on what college students like and dislike about the magazines currently available. After testing this interview form on 35 students to be sure the questions were clearly phrased, you made appropriate revisions and obtained Archway's approval of the final instrument. Then you began the lengthy process of conducting 50 face-to-face interviews on each of 12 campuses across the country. By April 29, you had scheduled and completed the 50 interviews on 3 campuses; you expect to schedule and complete the remainder of the interviews by June 1. All interviews are going according to schedule. You plan to submit a brief synopsis of your findings by June 6, and by June 20 you will submit a full report including conclusions and recommendations.

Using a letter format, write a progress report to Martin, whose company is located at 325 Zierer Blvd, Scarborough, ON M1V 3K9.

12 Work-team Communication—Situational Report   You are one member of a four-student team that has volunteered to look into the advantages and disadvantages of extending the university's library's hours the week before each long break and the final week of each term or semester. You have heard some students complain that the evening hours are too short; they would especially like to see the library open later during periods when most students are working on research papers, examinations, and projects. Of course, longer hours would have an effect on payroll, staff scheduling, and other aspects of the library's operation. Your team will examine the issues, report your findings, and suggest how the administration might proceed.

Team up with three other students to plan a situational report for your school's head of administrative services. Prepare a one- to two-page memo to your instructor indicating the purpose of your report, the audience, and the data that you will gather. Also list the issues you expect to examine. Will this situational report include recommendations? Why or why not?

13 Procedure—Giving Directions   As director of the student union at your institution, you frequently receive calls from for-profit and non-profit organizations inquiring about reserving a room for special meetings. Sometimes these organizations want food service such as a meal or refreshments, sometimes they want a cash bar, and at other times they simply want an attractive meeting room. Of course, they're also interested in the cost, availability of parking, use of audio-visual equipment, deadlines, forms that need to be completed, and the like.

Prepare a procedure that can be distributed to inquirers that will answer their most frequent questions and that will take them through the reservation process from initial inquiry through paying the final bill (if there is one). Use the actual practices in effect at your institution. Decide on an effective format for the written procedure report.

14 Policy—Using University Facilities   Refer to Exercise 13. Assume that your institution is establishing a policy that only non-profit organizations may reserve meeting rooms on campus and that reservations by any on-campus groups take precedence over those from off-campus groups. The reason for this policy is to avoid competing with local commercial establishments and to prevent overcrowding of campus facilities. Prepare a policy statement (University Policy No. 403) for the board of trustees to consider at its next meeting.

15 **Planning a Research Proposal**   If you were going to gather data to resolve each of the following problem situations, which factors would you consider to be the most important? Select at least three factors for each problem.

a. You are halfway through your university education and still undecided about what career path you should follow.
b. You are planning to get married in three months and need a place to live. You are wondering what considerations should be made in selecting the apartment.
c. You own a small convenience store. The store has been robbed twice in the last three months. You wonder what could be done to better protect against robberies.

The Copy Cat

Larry Haas has been surprised to learn when examining the quarterly departmental statements that photocopying costs have more than doubled from the previous quarter. In talking over the problem with others, he has learned that some workers photocopy nearly everything on their small departmental photocopier (there are five of these convenient, but relatively inefficient, copiers at headquarters) and other workers copy only small jobs on the departmental copiers and send larger jobs to the copy centre, one of the departments managed by Eric Fox.

Jobs that are too big or too complicated for even the copy centre to manage are sent to a local print shop. Some departments do the sending on their own; others rely on the copy centre to do it. Regardless of where the copying is done, the individual department is charged for the job. From a company point of view, however, Larry is interested in ensuring that each job is completed in the most cost-effective way possible.

An additional problem that Larry has discovered is that the company's lax attitude about using the departmental photocopiers may have given the erroneous impression that employees have permission to photocopy personal documents. He has heard of numerous instances regarding the copying of personal insurance forms, recipes, sports stories, and even kids' homework.

Northern Lights attempts to control photocopying costs by adopting appropriate policies and procedures.

In speaking with the manager of the copy centre, Larry learns that departmental copiers are designed for small jobs—no more than 30 copies of an original and no more than 20 originals per job. Any larger job should be sent to the copy centre, which will decide whether to do the job in-house or send it outside. Generally, the in-house centre handles one-colour jobs on 216 by 279 millimetre paper and up to 2000 copies. Any job requiring more copies, more than one colour, special binding, photographs, or the like is sent to the print shop.

Larry decides that a policy is needed on photocopying. Several specific procedures also need to be established to accomplish the legitimate photocopying efficiently.

Critical Thinking

1. Taking into account the absence of any formal organizational policy, what are the ethical implications of employees' copying personal insurance forms, recipes, sports stories, and the like on the office copier?

Writing Projects

2. Write a policy statement (General Guideline 72) on the topic of photocopying. You may assume any reasonable information needed.

3. Once a job is submitted to the copy centre, a procedure must be in place for deciding whether it's an in-house or outside job. Write a procedure that covers the situation from when the job reaches the copy centre until it is returned to the requester.

LABtest 9

Retype the following press release, correcting any word-usage problems according to the rules introduced in LAB 6 on page •••.

Unless you live in a glass house, you will need to throw switches, because lighting up your life is adviced for safety and vision. Depending on it's function, lighting serves as general illumination, task lighting, or accent lighting. Irregardless, in a good-designed plan, all three types must interact.

5   General illumination creates the principle seeing environment. If you notice any one groping around or tripping, if nobody seems to want to be in a room, or if a cite seems dull, then you're general lighting probably needs improvement.

When it was installed, task lighting should of been glare-free and directed to shine directly on the task area; i.e., reading lamps should be aimed at the

10   book, not at the reader. The reason is because task lighting prevents fatigue and eye strain.

In passed years, a fixture hanging on a chain over the coffee table was common. Today, these hanging lamps make a room look gloomy and flat, so its important to be an informed consumer.

15   You can buy fluorescent lighting in colours that are close to the affect of regular bulbs and that are easier on the eye than the old fluorescent lights. Try and avoid any kind of unshielded bare light bulbs. When planning recessed lights, be sure and give the builder a sample fixture so he may make the holes the correct size.

Collecting and Analyzing Data

an insider's
perspective

JERRY PAGE
Director, Western Region
and Northern Territories,
Statistics Canada

A s a 40-year veteran with Statistics Canada, few know as much about data collection—or Canadians—as Jerry Page. As a director for Statistics Canada, Page is responsible for gathering census data for the western region and the northern territories. Arguably the most important database in all of Canada, the census is used by governments, businesses, and non-profit organizations to make decisions ranging from the calculation of equalization payments to determining where to build schools or hospitals, to deciding where to move a manufacturing plant or head office. Conducted every five years, the census also provides comprehensive information vital to many of the country's programs. For example, the census is used to determine representation in the House of Commons and is the backbone of the population estimates program, which helps determine federal-provincial transfer payments.

Asked what he considers most important when collecting data, Page emphasizes that respecting Canadian's privacy is paramount. "The *Statistics Act* is committed to respecting the privacy of individuals," he stresses. "All personal information created, held or collected by Statistics Canada is protected by the *Privacy Act* and the *Statistics Act*."

A significant challenge Page and his team face when conducting the census is ensuring respondents understand the questions. "At Statistics Canada we maintain data quality through rigorous pretesting procedures for our questionnaires," Page adds. "Pretesting ensures that respondents understand and answer questions correctly."

341

Over the years, Page and his team have designed numerous strategies to overcome "under-coverage," another problem in data collection. From engaging celebrities such as Wayne Gretzky, Leslie Neilson, and George Fox to personally enumerating the people of the North, Page is both dogged and creative. His biggest challenge, and some of his proudest moments, continue to be collecting information from Canadians who are traditionally under-represented in the census data, such as First Nations people. Working tirelessly to remedy this, Page has recently succeeded in reducing the number of First Nations communities in Alberta who do not participate in the census from 12 in 2001 to only three.

For the 2006 census, Page and his team set their sights on another under-represented group (youth aged 18 to 24). "We're constantly faced with the question of how to boost census participation among young adults," says Page.[1] To remedy this problem, Page struck up a unique partnership with Ravinder Minhas, the 24-year-old owner of Calgary's Mountain Crest Brew Co.

"When they first asked me, I had to admit I knew very little about the census," said Minhas. "I initially thought it was a weird partnership, but now I know why it's important to get the message out to be counted."[2] Minhas finally agreed to a run of 25 000 six packs with special labels promoting the May 16, 2006, census. The "Census six-pack" features the Census logo and information about the Statistics Canada Web site. "Our message is for people to drink responsibly, but also to stand up and be counted," adds Page.[3]

Interestingly, when Minhas first went into business (with his sister Manjit) he didn't use census data to help him target his beer, saying he was a "naive young businessman." Now understanding the importance of the data, Minhas agrees that the 2006 results will help him better target his demographic when designing future marketing campaigns.[4]

When asked how well the promotion worked, Page concludes, "From a public relations point of view, it generated a lot of publicity and awareness. We will not know at this point whether the response rate increased for this target group. We would certainly do it again, as it was seen as non-bureaucratic, which is a plus when dealing with many Canadians who believe the government bureaucracy is out of touch."

Mahjit and Ravinder Minhas, Co-Presidents of Mountain Crest Brewing Company in Calgary.

"At Statistics Canada we maintain data quality through rigorous pretesting procedures for our questionnaires. Pretesting ensures that respondents understand and answer questions correctly."

■ What Data Is Already Available?

Before collecting any data, you must define the report purpose and analyze the intended audience. Then you must determine what data is needed to solve the problem. Sometimes the data you need will be in your mind or in documents you already have at hand, sometimes it will be in documents located elsewhere, and sometimes the data is not available at all but must be generated by you.

CO1. Evaluate the quality of data already available.

Start the data-collection phase by **factoring** your problem—that is, by breaking it down into its component parts so that you will know what data you need to collect. The easiest way to do this is to think about what questions you need to answer before you can solve the problem. The answers to these questions will ultimately provide the answer to the overall problem you're trying to solve, and the question topics may, in fact, ultimately serve as the major divisions of your report.

Research and report writing are a cost, just like other corporate expenses. Thus, you should use data-collection methods that will provide the needed data with the least expenditure of time and money but at the level of completeness, accuracy, and precision needed to solve your problem. There is a break-even point to data collection. You do not want to provide a $100 answer to a $5 question, but neither do you want to provide a $5 answer to a $100 question.

Common Types of Data

The two major types of data you will use are secondary and primary data. **Secondary data** is data collected by someone else for some other purpose; it may be published or unpublished. Published data includes any material that is widely disseminated, including the following:

- **World Wide Web** and other Internet resources

- Statistics Canada

- Journal, magazine, and newspaper articles. (*Note:* A *journal* is a scholarly periodical published by a professional association or a university, and a *magazine* is a commercial periodical published by a for-profit organization. Although the distinction is sometimes useful in evaluating secondary sources, the two terms are used interchangeably in this chapter to refer to any periodical publication.) These articles may be located in print format or may be retrieved from an electronic database.

- Books

- Brochures and pamphlets

- Technical reports

Unpublished secondary data includes any material that is not widely disseminated, including the following:

- Company records (such as financial records, personnel data, and previous correspondence and reports)

- Legal documents (such as court records and minutes of regulatory hearings)

- Personal records (such as diaries, receipts, and cheque book registers)

- Medical records

Primary data is collected by the researcher to solve the specific problem at hand. Because you are collecting the data yourself, you have more control over its accuracy, completeness, objectivity, and relevance. The three main methods of primary data collection are surveys (questionnaires, interviews, and telephone inquiries), observation, and experimentation.

Although secondary and primary data are both important sources for business reports, we usually start our data collection by reviewing the data that is already available. Not all report situations require collecting new (primary) data, but it would be unusual to write a report that did not use some type of secondary data.

Studying what is already known about a topic and what remains to be learned makes the reporting process more efficient because the report writer can then concentrate scarce resources on generating new information rather than rediscovering existing information. Also, studying secondary data can provide sources for additional information, suggest methods of primary research, or give clues for questionnaire items—that is, provide guidance for primary research. For these reasons, our discussion of data collection first focuses on secondary sources.

Secondary data is neither better nor worse than primary data; it's simply *different*. The source of the data is not as important as its quality and its relevance for your particular purpose. The major advantages of using secondary data are economic: using secondary data is less costly and less time-consuming than collecting primary data. The disadvantages relate not only to the availability of sufficient secondary data but also to the quality of the data that is available. Never use any data before you have evaluated its appropriateness for the intended purpose.

Evaluating Secondary Data

By definition, secondary data was gathered for some purpose other than your particular report needs. Therefore, the categories used, the population sampled, and the analyses reported might not be appropriate for your use. To determine the quality and relevance of secondary data, ask yourself the following questions about any secondary sources you're thinking about incorporating into your report.

Suspicious about the accuracy of Nestle Canada's claim that Canadians eat enough Smarties to circle the earth 350 times, a grade six class from Thunder Bay did the math. Multiplying the number of Smarties Canadians eat in a year (four billion) by the size of a single Smartie, the class discovered that four billion Smarties would only circle the earth once. Nestle has since changed its packaging.[5]

What Was the Purpose of the Study?

If the study was undertaken to genuinely find the answer to a question or problem, you can have more confidence about the accuracy and objectivity of the results than if, for example, the study was undertaken merely to prove a point. People seeking honest answers to honest questions are more likely to select their samples carefully, to ask clear and unbiased questions, and to analyze the data appropriately.

Be wary of secondary data if the researcher had a vested interest in the outcome of the study. For example, you would probably have more faith in a study extolling the merits of the Hubbard automobile that had been conducted by *Maclean's* than one conducted by Hubbard Motors, Inc.

How Was the Data Collected?   Were appropriate procedures used? Although you may not be an experienced researcher yourself, your reading of secondary data will likely alert you to certain standard research procedures that should be followed. For example, common sense should tell you that if you are interested in learning the reactions of all factory workers in your organization to a particular proposal, you would not gather data from just the newly hired workers. Likewise, if a questionnaire was sent to all the factory workers and only 10 percent responded, you would probably not be able to conclude that the opinions of these few respondents represented the views of all the workers.

How Was the Data Analyzed?   Different types of data lend themselves to different types of analyses. Sometimes the low number of responses to a particular question, or ambiguity in the question itself, prevents us from drawing any valid conclusions.

In some situations, even though the analysis was appropriate for the original study, it may not be appropriate for your particular purposes. For example, suppose you're interested in the reactions of teenagers and the only available secondary data used the category "younger than 21 years of age." You would not know whether the responses came mostly from those younger than 13 years old, those 13 to 19 years old (your target group), or those older than 19 years old.

How Consistent Is the Data with That from Other Studies?   When you find the same general conclusions in several independent sources, you can have greater confidence in the data. On the other hand, if four studies of a particular topic reached one conclusion and a fifth study reached an opposite conclusion, you would need to scrutinize the fifth study carefully before accepting its findings.

Avoid accepting something as true simply because you read it in print or saw it on the Internet. Because the reader of your report will be making decisions based on the data you present, take care that the data in your report is accurate.

How Old Is the Data?   Data that was true at the time it was collected might or might not be true today. A job-satisfaction study completed at your organization last year may have yielded accurate data then. But if in the meantime your organization has merged with another company, moved its headquarters, or been torn by a strike, the job-satisfaction data may have no relevance today. On the other hand, some data may still be accurate years after its collection. For example, a thorough study of the importance of universal health care to Canadians may have almost permanent validity.

Your data must pass these five tests, whether it comes from company records or printed sources on the Internet. Data that fails even one of these tests should probably be discarded and not used in your report. At the very least, such data requires extra scrutiny and perhaps extra explanation in the report itself if you do choose to use it.

■ Gathering Secondary Data

Before the widespread availability of the Internet and electronic databases, performing secondary research required a trip to a library and a search through the stacks. While physical—or hard-copy—materials such books, journals, magazines, and various reference materials still play an important role in secondary research,

CO2. Identify the major sources of electronic information.

much of the most current material—even many books—is now available electronically, some of it in electronic databases and some of it on the World Wide Web.

Searching Electronic Databases

An entire knowledge industry has evolved in which organizations store huge amounts of statistical, financial, and bibliographic information in the memory banks of their mainframe computers or on compact discs and then make this information available to users worldwide for a fee.

An **electronic database** is a computer-searchable collection of information on a general subject area, such as business, education, or psychology. Electronic databases are fast; you can typically collect more data electronically in a half-hour than would be possible in an entire day of conventional library research. They are available either on CD-ROM or online via computer network or Internet hookup. Public and post-secondary libraries usually provide free access to various electronic databases. The number and scope of the electronic databases subscribed to by a particular library will typically depend on the library's size and budget.

In addition, electronic databases are typically more current than printed databases; most are updated daily, weekly or monthly. Also, each contains several years' worth of citations, whereas manual indexes require searching through individual annual volumes and monthly supplements. Finally, electronic databases are extremely flexible. You can use different search terms, combine them, and modify your search at every step.

E-book databases offer the full text of books from select publishers and are generally available at most academic institutions. While e-book databases are still very much in their infancy, they will no doubt become more and more widespread in coming years. Even Google, through its "Google Book Search" initiative, is beginning to allow electronic searches of books. Presently, Google supplies digitized content (currently only sample pages, not entire books) from many publishers and research libraries (including samples from the entire collections of both Harvard and Oxford universities).

A word of caution about electronic databases—because of their flexibility, they can be cumbersome. Subtle variations in your search terms can yield radically different results, and each database may require slight variations in how search terms are entered. Patience and practice are necessary in refining your search to yield the results you need. If unfamiliar with a database, your best advice is to seek guidance from the librarian of the company or institution that subscribes to the database. A few minutes spent with a librarian can save you hours of hit-and-miss search attempts.

Moreover, each database tends to specialize in a particular subject and/or genre of documents, and some content of these databases overlaps. For example, the Canadian Business and Current Affairs database specializes in Canadian journals and newspapers, whereas the Canadian Newsstand database focuses primarily on newspapers, newswires, and news magazines. Between the two databases there is plenty of overlap, but there are also sources to be found on one that are not available on the other. Google has recently created subscription software, called Google Scholar, that provides a sort of "one-stop-shop" for electronic databases. If your company or institution subscribes to such software, a Google search may be the easiest and most comprehensive method of researching electronic sources—both on the web and in various databases. (Google Scholar, along with electronic databases, stock reports, and news reports are part of what's known as "the deep web," as they provide access to material not commonly found by conventional search methods.)

Although you may never write another academic report after graduating from college, you *will* continue to need to locate information—for business, political, or personal reasons. Computer-assisted information retrieval has now become so widely available, economical, and easy to use that it has emerged as a powerful tool for helping managers solve problems and make decisions.

Searching the Internet

The **Internet** is a vast information system that connects millions of computers worldwide, allowing them to exchange all types of information and to conduct many types of business transactions, such as online banking and shopping. While much of the information on the Internet is credible and reliable, always be cautious in relying too heavily on Internet research: the beauty and the danger of the Internet is that it's everyone's domain, so anyone can post information on a Web site regardless of the information's veracity. In the next section, we offer some guidelines for evaluating the quality of electronic sources.

Nobody "owns" the Internet; that is, there is no one governing authority that can make rules and impose order. Thus, it should not surprise you that the massive amount of information available on the Internet is not neatly and logically organized for easy search and retrieval. One "Internaut" describes the situation this way:

> Imagine yourself having a key to the door of a large library. Unfortunately, everyone else has a key also. Everyone has free access to put anything they want in the library, wherever they want to put it. To make matters worse, there is no librarian, there is no card catalog, no computerized index, no map, and no reference staff; so after people deposit materials, there is no structure to help others locate them. The Internet is like that library—a disorganized chaotic repository of information.[6]

Fortunately, a variety of search tools are available on the Internet to make accessing Internet resources if not painless, at least more pleasant and productive. The most dominant search tool on the Internet today is undoubtedly Google. (Indeed, "to Google" is now often used as a verb synonymous the act of researching the Internet.) Google is both a web directory and a search engine. Web directories are hyperlinked lists of Web sites, hierarchically organized into topical categories and subcategories. Virtually every library, government agency, non-profit group, and company will provide directories on their Web site with links to relevant material. Clicking your way through these lists will lead you to Web site links for the subject you're investigating. Use these directories when you need to find common information that can be easily classified. If you are looking for something very specific, try moving down through the general categories listed to reach a more specific category (in computer language, to "drill down"). In this way, you can narrow your search.

Unlike directories, which are put together by editors with an interest or expertise in a particular subject, search engines use automated software programs (called *web crawlers, robots,* or *spiders*) that roam the Web. When conducting a search for material with a search engine, the success of your search will depend on how skillfully you choose your keywords (or *search terms*). Remember that the computer makes a very literal search; it will find exactly what you ask for—and nothing more. If you use the search term *secretaries,* many search engines will not find citations for the words *secretary* or *secretarial.* Some engines have a feature known as *truncation,* which allows you to search for the root of a term. Thus, a search for *secre* would retrieve *secret, secretarial, secretaries, secretary, secretion,* and so on. You would then choose the entries appropriate for your purpose.

One of the most common mistakes people make is to use too few keywords in their searches or to use the wrong kinds of keywords. (Too many hits is just as unhelpful as too few hits.) Generally, try to identify three or four keywords—and use nouns. The only time you generally need to use adjectives or adverbs is if the term itself contains one—such as *World Wide Web* (and don't forget to put phrases in quotation marks).

Most engines also allow the use of logical search operators (called *Boolean logic*) in the keywords. There are four basic search operators—AND, OR, NOT, and NEAR—and as you can see, they are always typed in all capitals. The operators broaden or narrow searches as follows:

- AND identifies sources that contain both term 1 AND term 2; AND decreases the number of hits.

- OR identifies sources that contain either term 1 OR term 2; OR increases the number of hits.

- NOT excludes sources that contain the NOT term; NOT decreases the number of hits.

- NEAR identifies sources in which the two terms are within a given distance from each other; NEAR decreases the number of hits.

Placing quotation marks around a phrase requires the exact matching of a phrase. As in algebra, the operations inside parentheses are performed first, and most search engines read command lines from left to right. Thus, the search term *"heavy metal"* would eliminate the flagging of Web sites devoted to metals and ores, whereas *"metal" NOT "heavy metal"* would find *only* those sites devoted to metals and ores.

Evaluating the Quality of Electronic Information

CO3. Evaluate the quality of the electronic data you gather.

Anyone with access to the Internet can post pretty much anything that he or she wants online. Indeed there is currently much contention about whether stronger regulations over Internet content need to be in place. Currently there is very little legislation in Canada to control the content circulated on the Internet, and many argue that that is the way it should be. Criminal law (and specifically Bill C-15A, which became law in 2002) guards against the creation and circulation of child pornography on the Internet, and certainly existing hate crime and privacy legislation does apply to the Internet, but at present there are no regulations stipulating that information posted on the Internet has to be true, objective, intelligent, or politically correct (recall that there is no central authority for managing the Internet).

According to Donald T. Hawkins, editor-in-chief of *Information Science Abstracts,*

> Information does not gain or lose credibility simply by virtue of its format (print or electronic). However, because of the ephemeral, dynamic, and fluid nature of the Web and the lack of a review process, one must be much more cautious when evaluating information obtained from it than when evaluating information obtained from a peer-reviewed or scholarly journal.
>
> More stringent evaluation criteria should be used for Web-based sources than for print sources. Methods of evaluating print sources have evolved over many years and have stood the test of time. The Web . . . is constantly evolving.[7]

The range of informational quality on the Net is enormous. Information posted by governmental and educational institutions (typically, those sites that end in

".gov" or ".edu") is most often comprehensive, accurate, and up to date. Most pages sponsored by commercial organizations (typically, those sites that end in ".com") are also of high quality, as long as you recognize the profit incentive for these pages. Personal home pages and those sponsored by advocacy organizations should be evaluated especially carefully for accuracy, fairness, and coverage. The same is true for Usenet newsgroups and mailing lists.

The consequences of making decisions based on invalid data can range from minor inconvenience to receiving a failing grade in a class to jeopardizing the financial viability of your organization. You are responsible for the quality of the information you include in your correspondence, reports, and presentations. Avoid accepting something as fact just because you saw it on the Net. Evaluate your sources critically, using the questions in Checklist 12, "Evaluating the Quality of Internet Resources," as a guide.

■ Gathering Primary Data

Typically, your search begins with searching secondary sources. On many occasions, however, especially for very specific studies, the information available through secondary sources will be either inadequate or unavailable. In such a situation, you will probably need to collect primary data. As noted earlier, the three main methods of primary data collection are surveys (questionnaires, interviews, and telephone inquiries), observation, and experimentation.

Collecting Data Through Questionnaires

A **survey** is a data-collection method that gathers information through questionnaires, telephone or email inquiries, or interviews. The **questionnaire** (a written instrument containing questions designed to obtain information from the individual being surveyed) is the most frequently used method in business research. The researcher can economically get a representative sampling over a large geographical area. After all, it costs no more to mail a questionnaire across the country than across the street.

CO4. Develop an effective questionnaire and cover letter.

Also, the anonymity of a questionnaire increases the validity of some responses. Certain personal and economic data may be given more completely and honestly when the respondent remains unidentified. In addition, no interviewer is present to possibly bias the results. Finally, respondents can answer at a time convenient for them, which is not always the case with telephone or interview studies.

The big disadvantage of mail questionnaires is the low response rate, and those who do respond may not be representative (typical) of the population. Indeed, extensive research has shown that respondents tend to be better educated, have higher social status, are more intelligent, have higher need for social approval, and are more sociable than those who choose not to respond.[8] Thus, mail questionnaires should be used only under certain conditions:

- *When the desired information can be provided easily and quickly.* Questionnaires should contain mostly yes-or-no questions, check-off alternatives, or one- to two-word fill-in responses. People tend not to complete questionnaires that call for lengthy or complex responses.

- *When the target audience is homogeneous.* To ensure a high response rate, your study must interest the respondents and you must use language they understand.

✓checklist 12

Evaluating the Quality of Internet Resources[9]

Criterion 1: Authority

✓ Is it clear who sponsors the page and what the sponsor's purpose in maintaining the page is?

✓ Is it clear who wrote the material and what the author's qualifications for writing on this topic are?

✓ Is there a way of verifying the legitimacy of the page's sponsor; that is, is there a phone number or postal address to contact for more information?

✓ If the material is protected by copyright, is the name of the copyright holder given?

Criterion 2: Accuracy

✓ Are the sources for any factual information clearly listed so they can be verified in another source?

✓ Has the sponsor provided a link to outside sources (such as product reviews) that can be used to verify the sponsor's claims?

✓ Is the information free of grammatical, spelling, and other typographical errors? (These kinds of errors not only indicate a lack of quality control but can actually produce inaccuracies in information.)

✓ Are statistical data in graphs and charts clearly labelled and easy to read?

✓ Does anyone monitor the accuracy of the information being published?

Criterion 3: Objectivity

✓ For any given piece of information, is the sponsor's motivation for providing it clear?

✓ Is the information content clearly separated from any advertising or opinion content?

✓ Is the point of view of the sponsor presented in a clear manner, with well-supported arguments?

Criterion 4: Currency

✓ Are there dates on the page to indicate when the page was written, first placed on the Web, and last revised?

✓ Are there any other indications that the material is kept current?

✓ If the material is presented in graphs or charts, is it clearly stated when the data was gathered?

✓ Is there evidence that the page has been completed and is not still in the process of being developed?

It is difficult to construct a questionnaire that would be clearly and uniformly understood by people with widely differing interests, education, and socio-economic backgrounds.

■ *When sufficient time is available.* Three to four weeks is generally required from questionnaire mailing to final returns—including follow-ups of the non-respondents. (Emailing questionnaires, of course, requires less total time.) A telephone survey, on the other hand, can often be completed in one day.

Constructing the Questionnaire

The question should not yield clues to the "correct" answer.

Because the target audience's time is valuable, make sure that every question you ask is necessary—that it is essential to help you solve your problem and that you cannot acquire the information from other sources (such as through library or online

✔checklist 13

Questionnaires

Content

✔ Do not ask for information that is easily available elsewhere.

✔ Have a purpose for each question. Make sure that all questions directly help you to solve your problem. Avoid asking for unimportant or merely "interesting" information.

✔ Use precise wording so that no question can possibly be misunderstood. Use clear, simple language, and define any term that may be unfamiliar to the respondent or that you are using in a special way.

✔ Use neutrally worded questions and deal with only one topic per question. Avoid loaded, leading, or multi-faceted questions.

✔ Ensure that the response choices are both exhaustive and mutually exclusive (that is, that there is an appropriate response for everyone and that there are no overlapping categories).

✔ Be especially careful about asking sensitive questions, such as information about age, salary, or morals. Consider using broad categories for such questions (instead of narrow, more specific categories).

✔ Pilot-test your questionnaire on a few people to ensure that all questions function as intended. Revise as needed.

Organization

✔ Arrange the questions in some logical order. Group together all questions that deal with a particular topic. If your questionnaire is long, divide it into sections.

✔ Arrange the alternatives for each question in some logical order—such as numerical, chronological, or alphabetical.

✔ Give the questionnaire a descriptive title, provide whatever directions are necessary, and include your name and return address somewhere on the questionnaire.

Format

✔ Use an easy-to-answer format. Check-off questions draw the most responses and are easiest to answer and tabulate. Use free-response items only when absolutely necessary.

✔ To increase the likelihood that your target audience will cooperate and take your study seriously, ensure that your questionnaire has a professional appearance:

- Use a simple and attractive format, allowing for plenty of white (blank) space.

- Ensure that the questionnaire is free from errors in grammar, spelling, and style.

- Use a high-quality printer and make high-quality photocopies.

---

research). Guidelines for constructing a questionnaire are provided in Checklist 13. Some of the more important points are illustrated in the following paragraphs.

Your language must be clear, precise, and understandable so that the questionnaire yields valid and reliable data. Moreover, each question must be neutral (unbiased). Consider the following question:

Simply checking a broad range of figures might be less threatening than having to write in an exact figure.

NOT: Do you think our company should open an on-site child-care centre as a means of ensuring the welfare of our employees' small children?

___ yes
___ no

This wording of the question favours the "pro" side, thereby biasing the responses. A more neutral question is needed if valid responses are to result.

> **BUT:** Which one of the following possible additional fringe benefits would you most prefer?
>
> ___ a dental insurance plan
> ___ an on-site child-care centre
> ___ three personal-leave days annually
> ___ other (please specify: _____)

Note several things about the revised question. First, it is more neutral than the original version; no "right" answer is apparent. Second, the alternatives are arranged in alphabetical order. To avoid possibly biasing the responses, always arrange the alternatives in some logical order—alphabetical, numerical, chronological, or the like.

Finally, note that an "other" category is provided; it always goes last and is accompanied by the request to "please specify." Suppose the one fringe benefit that the vast majority of employees really wanted most was for the company to increase its pension contributions. If the "other" category were missing, the researcher would never learn that important information. Ensure that your categories are *exhaustive* (that is, that they include all possible alternatives) by including an "other" category if necessary. Also be certain that each question contains a single idea. Note the following question:

> **NOT:** Our company should spend less money on advertising and more money on research and development.
>
> ___ agree
> ___ disagree

Suppose the respondent believes that the company should spend more (or less) money on advertising and on research and development? How is he or she supposed to answer? The solution is to put each of the two ideas in a separate question. Finally, ensure that your categories are *mutually exclusive*—that is, that there are no overlapping categories.

> **NOT:** In your opinion, what is the major cause of high employee turnover?
>
> ___ lack of air-conditioning
> ___ non-competitive financial package
> ___ poor benefits package
> ___ poor working conditions
> ___ weak management

The problem with this item is that the "lack of air-conditioning" category overlaps with the "poor working conditions" category, and "non-competitive financial package" overlaps with "poor benefits package." And all four of these probably overlap with "weak management." Such intermingling of categories will thoroughly confuse the respondent and yield unreliable survey results.

Recognize that respondents may be hesitant to answer sensitive questions (regarding age, salary, morals, and the like). Even worse, they may deliberately provide *inaccurate* responses. When it is necessary to gather such data, ensure that the respondent understands that the questionnaire is anonymous (by prominently discussing that fact in the cover letter). Respondents tend to be more cooperative in answering such questions when broad categories are used. Accurate estimates provided by broad categories are preferable to precise data that is incorrect.

NOT: What is your annual gross salary? $ _____

BUT: Please check the category that best describes your annual salary:

      ___ Less than $25 000
      ___ $25 000–$40 000
      ___ $40 001–$70 000
      ___ More than $70 000

Note that the use of the number "$40 001" in the third category is necessary to avoid overlap with the figure "$40 000" in the second category; remember that the categories must be mutually exclusive.

Even experienced researchers find it difficult to spot ambiguities or other problems in their own questionnaires. If time permits, administer the draft questionnaire to a small sample of potential respondents and then revise it as necessary. At a minimum, ask a colleague to edit your instrument with a critical eye. The sample questionnaire shown in Model 21 (on pages 354–355) illustrates a variety of question types, along with clear directions and an efficient format.

Online Surveys

We've already discussed some of the limitations of conducting surveys via mail questionnaires, perhaps most significantly their low response rate. Mail surveys are also costly. A potential solution to these and other limitations of mail surveys is offered by the Internet. There are two main methods of administering surveys online: email surveys sent directly to your potential subjects, and web surveys, whereby the survey is hosted by a web page.[10] These online surveys can overcome many of the limitations of mail surveys, but they also present certain pitfalls. Researchers have identified the following advantages and disadvantages of using the Internet to conduct primary research:[11]

Advantages:

1. Online surveys are inexpensive and easy to set up. Numerous software programs, such as WebSurveyor and Inquisite, allow even inexperienced users to create their own surveys. Many survey companies, such as ClientSurveys.ca, can also be found on the Net, some which allow users to create their own simple survey for free.
2. Online surveys allow researchers to more easily target special groups (e.g., snowboarders, audiophiles, or car enthusiasts) through the use of newsgroups or mailing lists.
3. Once surveys are posted on a Web site, they run automatically and can generate data very quickly.
4. Web-based surveys allow for the inclusion of images, video, animation, and sound, which can enhance response rates.
5. Transcription errors are minimized as survey software can transfer data directly to a spreadsheet.
6. Response times (how quickly the surveys are completed) tend to be faster for online surveys than for conventional mail surveys. (As the sheer volume of unsolicited email sent around the world increases every year, however, some argue that *response rates*—i.e., the proportion of those contacted who actually respond—are dropping year after year.)

model21

QUESTIONNAIRE

Uses a descriptive title.

Provides clear directions.

Note the variety of response formats used.

Uses check-off responses for Questions 1–3.

Uses fill-in-the-blank responses for Question 4.

Uses a qualification (branching) response for Question 6.

Lists alternatives in logical order (alphabetically, here).

Provides clear directions and an example for the complex response in Question 8.

1   ## STUDENT USE OF COMPUTERS AT PEACE RIVER COMMUNITY COLLEGE

This survey is being conducted as part of a class research project. Please complete this questionnaire only if you (a) are a full-time first- or second-year student at PRCC, (b) attended PRCC last semester, and (c) have declared a major.

A. DESCRIPTIVE INFORMATION

2   1.   Grade level: 2.   Gender: 3.   Age:
         ___ first year   ___ female   ___ 20 or younger
         ___ second year   ___ male   ___ 21–24
                                                              ___ 25 or older

4.   Are you pursuing a professional or academic major?
     ___ professional *(Please write in the name of your major:* _____ *)*
     ___ academic *(Please write in the name of your major:* _____ *)*

5.   Faculty where major is located:
     ___ Arts and Sciences
     ___ Business
     ___ Education
     ___ Other *(Please specify:* _____ *)*

6.   Did you use a computer in a PRCC computer lab last semester?
     ___ yes   *(Please continue with Question 7.)*
     ___ no   *(Please disregard the following questions and return the questionnaire in the enclosed campus envelope to Matt Jones, Academic Affairs.)*

B. EXTENT OF COMPUTER USE

7.   Which on-campus computer labs were most convenient for completing your computer assignments? Please rank the labs from 1 *(most convenient)* to 4 *(least convenient)* by writing in the appropriate number in each blank. If you did not use a lab, leave that alternative blank.
     ___ business lab
     ___ dormitory lab
     ___ library lab
     ___ student centre lab

3   8.   Listed on the reverse side are different types of software. For each, first check the type of use you made of this software at any time during the previous semester. You may check both *Required* and *Personal* if appropriate. An example of personal use would be using a spreadsheet in a business assignment—if such use were not required. Then, if you used this software, check the total number of hours of use during the semester, including both in-class and out-of-class use.

Grammar and Mechanics Notes

1 Make the title and section heading stand out through the use of bold type and perhaps a larger font size.

2 If space is at a premium, you may group shorter questions on the same line (as in Questions 1–3).

3 Although not always possible (as illustrated here), try to avoid splitting a question between two pages.

model21

(CONTINUED)

8. *(continued)*

Software	Type of Use			Hrs. Used Per Semester		
	None	Required	Personal	<5	5–15	>15
Example: Games	——	——	——	——	——	——
Accounting/Financial	——	——	——	——	——	——
Database	——	——	——	——	——	——
Educational/Tutorial	——	——	——	——	——	——
Email	——	——	——	——	——	——
Graphics/Presentation	——	——	——	——	——	——
Internet	——	——	——	——	——	——
Programming	——	——	——	——	——	——
Spreadsheet	——	——	——	——	——	——
Word Processing	——	——	——	——	——	——
Other *(Please specify:*						
_____ *)*	——	——	——	——	——	——

4

C. OPINIONS

Please check whether you agree with, have no opinion about, or disagree with each of the following statements.

Uses attitude-scale responses for Questions 9–13, with both positive and negative statements.

	Agree	No Opinion	Disagree
9. I am receiving adequate training in the use of computers and software.	——	——	——
10. I have to wait an unreasonable length of time to get onto a computer in the lab.	——	——	——
11. The computer labs at PRCC are up to date.	——	——	——
12. Lab attendants are not very helpful.	——	——	——
13. Most instructors provide adequate instruction in the use of the software they require.	——	——	——

D. IMPROVEMENTS NEEDED

5 14. How could the university administration improve computer services at PRCC?

_____
_____
_____

Places the open-ended question last.

Thanks so much for your help. Please return the completed questionnaire in the enclosed campus envelope to Matt Jones, Academic Affairs.

Expresses appreciation and provides the name and address of the researcher.

Grammar and Mechanics Notes

4 Label different sections if the questionnaire is more than one or two pages long.

5 Provide sufficient space for the respondent to answer open-ended questions.

Disadvantages:

1. Certain groups—those with low levels of computer literacy or certain minority groups—may be disproportionately excluded from the Internet sample, which will then produce a distorted picture of the population. And, because the Internet does not penetrate the population as deeply as the telephone or mail service, a large proportion of the population may be inaccessible through online survey methods.

2. Because of its anonymity, the Internet poses greater risks that a participant will lie or make multiple submissions. Conversely, employees asked to respond to surveys posted on a company *Intranet* often fear for a lack of confidentiality and may thus sugar-coat their responses.[12]

3. Differently configured computer platforms and different connection speeds can lead to technical problems that can't be controlled by the researcher. Additionally, if the interface is not well designed—a common problem is the inability for participants to move forward and backward within a survey; another is the inability to save, exit, and then return to a survey—participants can be frustrated and exit the survey before it's completed.

4. Mailing lists of potential survey participants are notoriously inaccurate or outdated. One study identified 83 percent of mailing list members as "lurkers"—members who had never contributed anything to the group and thus did not fit the target market of the survey.[13] Moreover, long after participants have abandoned a mailing list, the list may continue its existence in cyberspace.

5. Unsolicited or unexpected email surveys—the online equivalent of a cold call—are often treated as spam and deleted. Or they are blocked by a server's firewall.

Keeping in mind the various pitfalls in conducting primary research online, the guidelines for creating online surveys are much the same as those we've provided for designing mail questionnaires. Perhaps the most significant precautions that must be taken for email surveys is preventing, as much as possible, the survey from being grouped in with other "junk" email, treated as spam, and discarded. For web-based surveys, the greatest challenge is ensuring the survey is well designed and therefore easy to complete. Here are some general suggestions for minimizing these obstacles.

- Be courteous. Send potential participants an invitation email, asking for their participation and striving to make the completion of the survey important to them, most notably by highlighting reader benefits and offering incentives.

- Personalize your email correspondence. Several studies have concluded that using a personalized salutation, as opposed to a generic one, can enhance response rates, particularly when inviting participation in a web survey. This guideline also holds true for mail surveys.

- Use caution in compiling your list of participants' email addresses. As noted earlier, these lists can be outdated and/or may not be representative of the population you wish to study.

- Consider the complexity and design of web surveys: the addition of graphics and sound can enhance response rates if done with care. However, overly complex designs can distract a participant from answering the questions, as well as slow download times, thus reducing response rates. With this in mind, it may be advisable to seek help from a professional when designing a web-based survey, particularly when the stakes are high, such as in performance appraisals or market research.

- Consult an expert to identify potential statistical errors. Sometimes the speed and ease with which web surveys can be designed and implemented leads to a false sense of their validity. Web surveys are still subject to the same errors that plague traditional surveys, such as sampling or measurement errors.

Writing the Cover Letter

Whether you choose to mail or email your surveys, or post them on a web page, you should include a cover letter or email, which discusses the purpose and procedures of the survey. A model cover letter is shown in Model 22 (on page 358). The cover letter should be written as a regular persuasive letter (see Chapter 7). Your job is to convince the reader that it's worth taking the time to complete the survey.

■ Collecting Data Through Interviews

Personal interviews are generally considered to be the most valid method of survey research. In a personal interview, the interviewer can probe, ask for clarification, clear up any misunderstandings immediately, ensure that all questions are answered completely, and pursue unexpected avenues. Thus, data resulting from an interview is often of a higher quality than data resulting from a questionnaire.

CO5. Conduct a data-gathering interview.

Personal interviews are most appropriate when in-depth information is desired. The interview permits open-ended questions and gives the respondent free rein to answer as he or she desires. Respondents are likely to *say* more than they will write. Research into topics such as motives, deeply held feelings, and complex issues simply does not lend itself to the objective questions that are found in most questionnaires.

Although expensive to conduct, personal interviews are appropriate for gathering in-depth or complex data.

There are, however, several problems with interviews. First, interview research is expensive; it is time-consuming to schedule the interviews, conduct them, and analyze the subjective data that flows from them. Also, in-depth interviewing requires specially trained and experienced interviewers.

Second, the interviewer can consciously or unconsciously bias the results—by not recording the answers exactly, for instance, or showing a favourable or unfavourable reaction to a response, or hurrying through parts of the interview. Different interviewers may experience the same situation and "see" different things. Thus, analyzing interview data is often more difficult than analyzing questionnaire data. The subjective nature of the data given and of the data received affects the validity of the research.

Finally, a personal interview is not appropriate for eliciting information of a sensitive nature. Questions about age, salary, personal beliefs, and the like should generally not be used in face-to-face questioning where anonymity is not possible. (The alert interviewer can, however, sometimes get an estimate of these variables by carefully observing the interviewee and his or her environment.)

In most situations, the sample for a questionnaire study is selected so that each member is typical of the population. However, interviewees are often selected for just the opposite reason: they may have *unique* expertise or experiences to share, and the data they provide will serve as "expert testimony" and not be tabulated and generalized to the population.

model 22

QUESTIONNAIRE COVER LETTER

This cover letter would accompany the questionnaire shown in Model 21.

Begins with a short attention-getter.

Provides a smooth transition to the purpose of the letter. Provides reasons for cooperating.

Makes the requested action easy to take.

Peace River Community College

100 COLLEGE DRIVE PEACE RIVER, AB T8S 4U9

February 8, 20—

1   Dear Fellow Student:

"Oh no—not another computer project!"

Have you ever felt this way during the first day of class when the instructor makes course assignments? Or, instead, do you sometimes wonder, "Why is the instructor making us do this project manually when it would be so much easier to do on a computer?"

2   Either way, here is your chance to provide administration with your views on student computer and software use at Peace River Community College. This research project is a class project for BEOA 249 (Business Communication), and the results will be shared with Dr. Dan Rulong, vice-president for academic computing.

3   If you are a full-time first- or second-year student, attended PRCC last semester, and have declared a major, please take five minutes to complete this questionnaire. Then simply return it by February 19 in the enclosed envelope. You'll be doing yourself and your fellow students a big favour.

Sincerely,

Matt Jones

Matt Jones, Project Leader
Academic Affairs

Enclosures

Grammar and Mechanics Notes

1 *Dear Fellow Student:* Use a generic salutation for form letters that are not individually prepared.

2 *on a computer?":* Position the question mark inside the closing quotation mark if the entire quoted matter is a question.

3 The word *questionnaire* contains two *ns* and one *r*.

Types of Questions

In most ways, your interview questions should follow the guidelines given in Checklist 13 on page 351 for questionnaire items; they should be clear and unbiased and deal with only one topic per question. However, because of the increased complexity of many interview topics, you now have other choices to make.

Open-ended Versus Closed Questions   Open-ended questions allow the interviewee flexibility in responding, whereas closed questions limit the subject matter of the response:

Open: What is your opinion of the NAFTA treaty?

Closed: How much of your firm's business is attributable to Canadian or Mexican sales?

Open questions expose the interviewee's priorities and frame of reference and may uncover information that the interviewer may never have thought to ask about. Interviewees like open questions because they are easy to answer (there is no wrong answer), and they give recognition to the interviewee—by letting him or her talk through ideas while the interviewer listens intently. The drawbacks to open questions are that they are time-consuming and the responses may be rambling, difficult to record, and difficult to tabulate later.

Closed questions save time and are very useful when you know exactly what type of information you want, when you intend to tabulate the responses, and when the responses don't require elaborate explanation by the interviewee. The amount of interview information that can be obtained by closed questions, however, is fairly restricted. After all, if all your questions lend themselves to the closed format, a questionnaire would probably yield just as valid results for much less expense.

In actual practice, the interviewer usually uses both open and closed questions, often following up a closed question with an open one.

Closed: Do you agree or disagree with the proposal?

Open: Why?

Closed: Will it have any effect on your own firm?

Open: In what way?

Direct Versus Indirect Questions   Most questions may be asked directly. In threatening or sensitive situations, however, you may want to resort to indirect questions, which are less threatening because they let the interviewee camouflage his or her response.

Direct: How would you evaluate your boss's people skills?

Indirect: How do you think most people in this department would evaluate your boss's people skills?

Conducting the Interview

As an interviewer, you must wear two hats—that of an observer and that of a participant. You participate by asking questions, but you must also analyze the responses to ensure that the interviewee is indeed answering the question asked and to determine whether follow-up questions are needed. Fulfilling this dual role requires concentration, preparation, and flexibility.

Use both open-ended and closed questions.

Listening in an interview involves much more than simply hearing what is being said.

To secure the greatest cooperation from interviewees, make them feel comfortable and important (they are!). The first few minutes of the interview are crucial for establishing rapport. Begin with a warm greeting; reintroduce yourself; and explain again the purpose of the interview, how the information will be used, and how much time will be required.

One of the barriers to effective listening during an interview is the need for note-taking. Keep note-taking to a minimum by using a small portable cassette recorder when possible. Always get permission first, assuring the interviewee that the purpose is to make certain that he or she is not misquoted and to let you give his or her responses your full attention. Keep the recorder out of sight (perhaps on the floor beside you) so that the interviewee is not constantly reminded that his or her remarks are being recorded. Test the recording level beforehand to ensure that the responses will be audible.

> *It is difficult to listen actively if you are busy taking notes.*

Always use an **interview guide**—a list of questions to ask, with suggested wording and possible follow-up questions. Mark off each question as it is asked and answered (don't assume that just because a question was asked, it was answered). Nothing is more embarrassing than repeating a question that has already been answered, and nothing is more frustrating than learning after the interview is over that you failed to ask an important question.

Provide smooth transitions when moving from topic to topic by using periodic summaries of what has been covered and previews of what will be covered next—for example,

> We've covered the start-up and initial funding for your firm. Next, I'd like to investigate any problems your firm experienced during its early years.

Follow up a point if the interviewee's response is inadequate in some way; for example, the interviewee may have consciously or unconsciously failed to answer all or part of a question, given inaccurate information, or given a response you did not understand completely. When the response needs amplification, you can probe by asking for more information, by asking for clarification, or simply by repeating the question.

Indicate when the interview is over—either by a direct statement or by such non-verbal gestures as putting your papers away or standing up. Experienced interviewers often end an interview by asking these two questions:

> Is there some question you think I should have asked that I didn't ask? *(to uncover unexpected information)*

> May I call you if I need to verify some information? *(to enable the checking of some fact or spelling or to ask a quick follow-up question)*

Leave the interviewee with a sense of accomplishment by quickly summarizing the important points you've gathered (to show that you've listened) or by restating how the information will be used. Finally, express appreciation once more for the time granted.

Although not nearly as common as surveys for business-related research, the use of human subjects for observation or experimentation can provide the researcher with much more detailed insight than can a simple survey. Focus groups—often used in marketing research—are one example where primary research involves actually observing and recording the reactions of participants. Whenever human subjects are involved in research they must sign a **consent form.** Such research, if conducted within a university, college, or any other publicly funded institution, must also pass the scrutiny of an ethics committee. A quick Internet search on consent forms produces dozens of reputable sources—particularly Canadian universities

spotlight20
ON LAW AND ETHICS

Consent Forms

Consent forms should be kept in equally direct and comprehensible language and must include the following:
1. the project title (as submitted to the Unit REB or the RMC Research Ethics Board)
2. the participant's name
3. a statement that this participant has read the Letter of Information and has had any questions answered to his/her satisfaction
4. a statement that the participant understands that s/he will be participating in [title of study], that s/he has been informed that her/his involvement consists of [procedures] which will be recorded by [recording device], that s/he understand that the purpose of the [study] is to [insert purpose]
5. a statement that the participant is aware that s/he can contact [researcher and the Unit REB or the RMC Resarch Ethics Board] with any question, concern or complaint that s/he has
6. a statement that the participant understands that her/his participation is voluntary and that s/he is free to withdraw at any time (if relevant add further specifics from point 5 above)
7. a statement that the participant has been assured that [insert provisions taken to maintain confidentiality]

Name:_____
Date: _____

Signature: _____

www.rmc.ca/academic/gradrech/ethics/information_and_consent_e.html

and colleges—that offer guidelines on how to construct consent forms. Spotlight 20 provides a sample set of guidelines from the Royal Military College of Canada.

■ Interpreting Data

At some point in the reporting process, you will have gathered enough data from your secondary and primary sources to enable you to solve your problem. (It is always possible, of course, that during data analysis and report writing you may find that you need additional information on a topic.)

Your job at this point, then, is to convert your raw data, which might be represented by your notes, photocopies of journal articles, completed questionnaires, audiotapes of interviews, Internet and computer printouts, and the like, into *information*—meaningful facts, statistics, and conclusions—that will help the reader of your report make a decision. In addition to interpreting your findings in narrative form, you will also likely prepare some **visual aids**—tables, charts, photographs, or other graphic materials—to aid comprehension and add interest. (The Reference Manual at the back of this book offers some specific guidelines in how to construct, integrate, and interpret the most common forms of visual aids.)

Data analysis is not a step that can be accomplished at one sitting. The more familiar you become with the data and the more you pore over it, the more different things you will see. Data analysis is usually the part of the report process that requires the most time as well as the most skill. The more insight you can provide the

CO6. Interpret the data for the report reader.

Determine the meaning of each finding by itself, in conjunction with each other finding, and in conjunction with all other findings.

reader about the *meaning* of the data you've collected and presented, the more help-ful your report will be.

When analyzing the data, you must first determine whether the data does, in fact, solve your problem. It would make no sense to prepare elaborate tables and other visual aids if your data is irrelevant, incomplete, or inaccurate. To help your-self make this initial evaluation of your data, assume for the sake of simplicity that you have gathered only three bits of information—a paraphrase from a secondary source, a chart you developed, and a computer printout, labelled Findings A, B, and C, respectively (see Figure 10.1). Now, you are ready to analyze this data, using the following process:

Step 1. Look at each piece of data in isolation. If Finding A were the only piece of data you collected, what would it mean in terms of solving the problem? What conclu-sions, if any, could you draw from this one bit of data? Follow the same process for Findings B and C, examining each in isolation, without considering any other data.

Step 2. Look at each piece of data in combination with the other bits. For example, by itself Finding A might lead to one conclusion, but when viewed in conjunction with B and C, it might take on a different shade of meaning. In other words, does adding Findings B and C to your data pool *reinforce* your initial conclusion? If so, you can use stronger language in drawing your conclusion. Or does it *weaken* your initial conclusion? If so, you might wish to qualify your conclusion with less certain lan-guage or refrain from drawing any conclusion at all.

Step 3. Synthesize all the information you've collected. When you consider all the facts and their relationships together, what do they mean? For example, if Findings A, B, and C all point in the same direction, you might be able to define a trend. More important, you must determine whether all the data taken together provide an accurate and complete answer to your problem statement. If so, you're then ready to begin the detailed analysis and presentation that will help the reader understand your findings. If not, you must backtrack and start the research process again.

Making Sense of the Data

As a report writer, you cannot simply present the raw data without interpreting it. Raw data, often presented in the form of tables and charts, helps to solve a problem,

figure**10.1**

The Three Steps in Interpreting Data

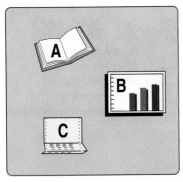
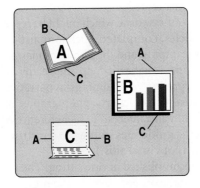

| Step 1 | Step 2 | Step 3 |
| Isolation | Context | Synthesis |

and the report writer must make the connection between that data and the solution to the problem. In the report narrative, you need not discuss *all* the data in the tables and charts; that would be boring and insulting to the reader's intelligence. But you must determine what you think the important implications of your data are, and then you must identify and discuss them for the reader.

What types of important points do you look for? Almost always, the most important finding is the overall response to a question. And almost always the category within the question that receives the largest response is the most important point. So discuss this question and this category first. Table 4 (presented as Figure 10.2, below) summarizes the results of a survey investigating the reputation of Apex Credit Union within the community. In Table 4, the major finding is this: four-fifths of the respondents believe that Apex Credit Union is an asset to their community. Note that if you give the exact figure given in the table (here, 80 percent), you can use less precise language in the narrative—"four-fifths" in this case, or in other cases "one in four," "a slight majority," and the like. Doing so helps you avoid presenting facts and figures too quickly. Pace your analysis because the reader will not be able to comprehend data that is presented too quickly or in too concentrated a format.

Once you've discussed the overall finding, begin discussing other details revealed by the data as necessary. Look for any of these features:

- Trends

- Unexpected findings

- Data that reinforces or contradicts other data

- Extreme values

- Data that raises questions

> Don't just present tables and figures. Interpret their important points. At a minimum, discuss the overall response and any important findings.

If these features are important, discuss them. In our example, there were no major differences in the responses by marital status, so you would probably not need to discuss them. However, you would need to discuss the big difference in responses between males and females. If possible, present data or draw any valid conclusions regarding the *reasons* for these differences.

Finally, point out the trend that is evident with regard to age: the older the respondent, the more positive the response. If it's important enough, you might display this trend in a graph for more visual effect.

Table 4. Response to Statement "Apex Company is an asset to our community." ($N = 271$; all figures in %)								
		Marital Status		**Sex**		**Age**		
	Total	**Married**	**Single**	**Male**	**Female**	**Under 21**	**21–50**	**Over 50**
Agree	80	82	77	83	57	69	77	90
No opinion	12	11	15	12	21	18	14	9
Disagree	8	7	8	5	22	13	9	1
Total	100	100	100	100	100	100	100	100

figure10.2

Simplified Table

CROCK

Sometimes you will want to include descriptive statistics (such as the mean, median, range, and standard deviation). At other times, the nature of your data will necessitate the use of inference (significance) testing—to determine whether the differences found in your sample data are also likely to exist in the general population. By now, you probably know more about the topic on which you're writing than the reader knows. Assist the reader, then, by pointing out the important implications, findings, and relationships of your data. Help your reader reach the same conclusions you have reached.

The Ethical Dimension

Everyone involved in the reporting situation has a responsibility to act in an ethical manner.

In gathering, analyzing, reporting, and disseminating data, everyone involved has both rights and obligations. For example, the researcher (1) has the right to expect that respondents will be truthful in their responses and (2) has an obligation not to deceive the respondent. Similarly, the organization that is paying for the research (1) has the right to expect that the researcher will provide valid and reliable information and (2) has an obligation not to misuse that data.

Emerging technology will no doubt provide even greater ethical dilemmas (see Spotlight 21, "When Is a Picture Not Worth a Thousand Words?"). If your research and corresponding report are to help solve problems and aid in decision making, all parties involved must use common sense, good judgment, goodwill, and an ethical mindset to make the project successful.

spotlight21
ON LAW AND ETHICS

When Is a Picture Not Worth a Thousand Words?

"Seeing is believing" may no longer be the case. Granted, commercial photographers have long used the airbrush to touch up portraits, wedding scenes, and advertising layouts, but only recently has the technology to manipulate photos come to the desktop computer. Today, any computer user, with the appropriate software, can electronically alter photographs—even to the extent that they no longer reflect reality. As you can see on page 365, for this Spotlight box the head of Marc Kaplan was put onto Dave's body. (The doctored photo is on the left.)

Doctored Photo   **Actual Photo**

It does not take a wide stretch of the imagination to ponder the ethical dilemmas report writers may soon face. Suppose, as an adjunct to your report on the status of a building project, you use a digital camera to take a photo of the partially completed building. The digital camera stores the image directly on a compact disc rather than on film. You pop the CD into your personal computer and view the image on the screen. You notice that a worker is standing next to the building, providing a distraction. So you use your software to digitally remove the worker from the image. Then you notice that the sign on the building, which contained a typographical error, had not been fixed when you took the photo (it has since been corrected). Should you digitally correct it on the photo? How about changing the colour of the building's exterior, which you plan to paint next week?

By allowing us to capture, store, and manipulate photographs, emerging computer technology is going to have an enormous impact on business communications.[14]

Another form of misleading visual is that of a graph or table that has not been constructed honestly. Perhaps the most common distortion in the design of graphs is the use of a misleading scale. The sample below illustrates two versions of a simple bar chart. Notice that the scale on the Y axis of the first version starts at $20 million, whereas the scale on the second version (correctly) starts at $0. In the first, it appears that the East region has experienced a profound increase in sales, while the West region's sales appear to be in sharp decline. Looking at the second version, however, you can see that, while the East is certainly enjoying increasing sales and the West is suffering decreasing sales, the proportional differences aren't nearly as significant as they appear.

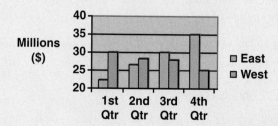

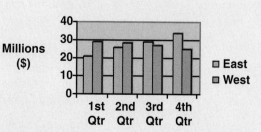

Two Versions of the Same Data

Problem, Process, Product

A QUESTIONNAIRE

Problem	You are Martha Halpern, assistant store manager for Just Pool Supplies, a small firm in Penticton, British Columbia. You have been asked by Joe Cox, store owner, to determine the feasibility of expanding into the spa supply business. To help yourself determine whether there is a sufficient demand for spa supplies, you decide to develop and administer a short questionnaire to potential customers.

Process	1. What is the purpose of your questionnaire?

To determine whether there are enough potential customers to make it profitable for us to expand into the spa supply business.

2. Who is your audience?

The theoretical population for my study would be all spa owners in Southern British Columbia. However, because our major business will still be pool supplies, I'll assume that most of my spa supply business would come from my present pool supply customers.

Thus, the real population for my survey will be the approximately 1500 existing customers that I have on my mailing list. I don't need to contact every customer, only a representative sample. I'll have my database program generate address labels for every fifth customer.

3. What information do you need from these customers?

   a. Whether they presently own a spa or intend to purchase one in the near future
   b. Where they typically purchase their spa supplies
   c. How much money they typically spend on spa supplies each year
   d. How satisfied they are with their suppliers
   e. What the likelihood is that they'd switch their spa supply business to us
   f. How many spa supply firms are located in the area

4. Is all this information necessary? Can any of it be secured elsewhere?

I can probably determine the number of spa supply firms and their volume of business from secondary data or from the local chamber of commerce, so I won't need to address that question (3f) in my survey. All of the other information is needed and none of it can be obtained elsewhere.

5. Do any of these questions ask for sensitive information, or are any of them difficult to answer?

No. The question asking about the amount of money spent on spa supplies depends a little on memory; because most people buy spa supplies only four or five times a year, however, respondents should be able to provide a fairly accurate estimate.

6. Is there any logical order to the questions in Item 3?

The question about spa ownership must come first, because respondents cannot answer the other questions unless they own a spa. In reviewing the other questions, I think the logical order appears to be a, c, b, d, and e.

7. Will the questionnaire require a cover letter?

Yes, because it will be mailed to the respondents, instead of being administered personally. I'll use my word processing program to generate a personalized form letter to each of the customers selected.

Product

JUST POOL SUPPLIES

P.O. Box 2277 Penticton BC V2A 2E1
(604) 555-0083

February 22, 20—

Mr. Frederic J. Diehl
Okanagan Estates
1876 Anderson Road
Summerland, BC V0H 6T8

Dear Mr. Diehl:

We miss you during the winter!

Although you're a frequent shopper at Just Pool Supplies during the summer months when you're using your pool, we miss having the opportunity to serve you during the rest of the year. Therefore, we're considering adding a complete line of spa supplies to our inventory.

Would you please help us make this decision by answering the enclosed five questions and then returning this form to us in the enclosed stamped envelope.

Thanks for sharing your views with us. We look forward to seeing you during our traditional Pool Party Sale in March.

Sincerely,

Martha Halpern
Assistant Manager

swm
Enclosures

Questionnaire

SPA SUPPLIES

1. Do you presently own a spa?
   ___ yes
   ___ no (Please skip the remaining questions and return this form to us
        in the enclosed envelope.)

2. Considering the number of times you purchased spa supplies last year and
   the average amount of each purchase, how much do you estimate you spent
   on spa supplies last year (include all types of purchases—chemicals, acces-
   sories, decorative items, and the like).
   ___ less than $100
   ___ $100–$300
   ___ $301–$500
   ___ more than $500

3. Where did you purchase <u>most</u> of your spa supplies last year? (Please check
   only one.)
   ___ at a general-merchandise store (e.g., Zellers or The Bay)
   ___ at a pool- or spa-supply store
   ___ from a mail-order firm
   ___ other (please specify: _____)

4. How satisfied were you with each of these factors at the store where you
   purchased most of your spa supplies?

Factor	Very Satisfied	Satisfied	Very Dissatisfied
Customer service	___	___	___
Hours of operation	___	___	___
Location of store	___	___	___
Prices	___	___	___
Quality of products	___	___	___
Quantity of products	___	___	___

5. If Just Pool Supplies were to sell spa supplies, how likely would you be to
   purchase most of your spa supplies there, assuming that the quality, selection, and pricing would be similar to those for its pool supplies?
   ___ very likely
   ___ somewhat likely
   ___ don't know
   ___ somewhat unlikely
   ___ very unlikely

*Thanks for your cooperation. Please return the completed questionnaire in the enclosed envelope
to Martha Halpern, Just Pool Supplies, P.O. Box 2277, Penticton, BC V2A 2E1.*

■ Summary

Secondary data is collected by others for their own specific purposes. Therefore, the researcher who wants to use secondary data for his or her own study must first evaluate it in terms of why and how the data was collected, how it was analyzed, how consistent the data is with that found in other studies, and how old the data is.

CO1. Evaluate the quality of data already available.

The two primary sources of electronic information are databases and the Internet. Databases typically require a subscription and allow the user access to numerous resources, including periodicals, journals, magazines, and even some books. Reference resources on the Internet include the World Wide Web, which contains pages of text, graphics, sound, and video, with hyperlinks that enable the reader to instantly jump to related topics. Electronic information can be located by using directories for browsing the Internet and search engines for searching for specific information. Use directories when the information you are seeking can be easily classified; otherwise, use one (or more) of the search engines. Use logical search operators (such as AND, OR, NOT, and NEAR) and phrases to make your search more efficient and productive.

CO2. Identify the major sources of electronic information.

Because the quality of the information on the Internet varies tremendously, you should seriously evaluate the information you receive before deciding whether to use it. Evaluate all information in terms of the authority of the writer and sponsoring organization and the accuracy, objectivity, and currency of the content.

CO3. Evaluate the quality of the electronic data you gather.

Primary data is collected by various survey methods—mainly questionnaires, telephone inquiries, and interviews. Mail questionnaires are an economical and convenient way to gather primary data when the desired information can be supplied easily and quickly. Care should be taken to ensure that all questions are necessary, clearly worded, complete, and unbiased. Email or web-based surveys overcome some of the limitations of mail surveys, namely high cost and slow response times. However, as with mail questionnaires, care must be taken when gathering primary data electronically to avoid some of the common pitfalls. Whatever method you use, the questions and their alternatives should be organized in a logical order, the directions should be clear, and the overall format should be attractive and efficient. The cover letter or email should be a persuasive message explaining why it is in the reader's interest to answer the survey.

CO4. Develop an effective questionnaire and cover letter.

Personal interviews are preferable to questionnaires when the information desired is complex or requires extensive explanation or elaboration. The interviewer must determine whether to use open-ended or closed questions and whether to use direct or indirect questions. The use of a cassette recorder will enable the interviewer to minimize note-taking, thereby enabling him or her to listen more attentively.

CO5. Conduct a data-gathering interview.

When analyzing your data, ensure that it actually solves your problem by first looking at each piece of data in isolation, then in combination with other bits of information. Finally synthesize the information you've collected to determine whether all the data taken together provide an accurate and complete answer to your problem statement. When making sense of the data for your reader, arrange the data in logical order, most often in order of descending value. Do not analyze every figure from the table in your narrative. Instead, interpret the important points from the table, pointing out the major findings, trends, contradictions, and the like. Avoid misrepresenting your information. The competent reporter of business information is an ethical reporter of business information.

CO6. Interpret the data for the report reader.

■ Key Terms

You should be able to define the following terms in your own words and give an original example of each.

consent form (360)   questionnaire (349)

electronic database (346)   secondary data (343)

factoring (343)   survey (349)

Internet (347)   visual aids (361)

interview guide (360)   World Wide Web (343)

primary data (344)

■ Exercises

1 The 3Ps (Problem, Process, and Product) Model: Communication Applications at Statistics Canada   Statistics Canada is constantly collecting and interpreting information from Canadians, as well as looking for ways to increase participation rates in various Statistics Canada surveys. Statistics Canada uses a variety of methods for collecting data from Canadians, including computer-assisted personal interviews (CAPI), computer-assisted telephone interviews (CATI), online questionnaires, and even traditional pen-and-paper questionnaires. Statistics Canada then compiles the results into a variety of formats, including reports, graphs, tables, and charts, to help users easily grasp the data's significance. (Users include various public and private sector researchers and decision makers, such as businesses, the media, unions, and numerous federal, provincial, and municipal agencies.)

Problem

As a summer intern with Statistics Canada, imagine that you've been asked to develop an online interactive questionnaire for gathering data from young Canadians about their use of electronic communication tools (email, text messaging, instant messaging, blogs, wikis, etc.). You will be developing the questionnaire with the goal of reaching youth aged 18 to 24, a group that is traditionally under-represented in this kind of data collection. The results will help Statistics Canada's clients better understand the role of electronic communication in shaping how young Canadians absorb, process, and exchange information.

Process

a. Brainstorm about possible questions. What specific information will each question uncover? What might the users of the survey be able to do as a result of knowing the answer to each question?

b. Choose the most appropriate questions and arrange them in a logical order.

c. Edit the wording of each question for clarity. Is every question bias-free? Does each deal with only one element?

d. Consider how to format each question for the respondents' convenience in answering. Which questions should be open-ended and which should be closed?

e. Should you revise or eliminate some questions or change some formats to speed up the survey and encourage more respondents to participate?

Product

Using your knowledge of data collection and analysis, prepare, format, and proofread a suitable questionnaire. Submit your questionnaire and the answers to these process questions to your instructor.

2 **Evaluate the Quality of Secondary Sources of Information**   Assume that you are starting a summer internship with Research in Motion (RIM). Your first assignment is to look for sources of information about the future of wireless technology (demand, growth, innovations, etc.) during the next few years. This information will be used to help RIM gauge product demand as well as identify potential marketing niches. Search your library's databases for two or three newspaper or magazine articles that discuss the future of wireless technology. Using the guidelines provided in this chapter, assess the quality of each of these secondary sources. Then draft an email message summarizing your findings for your supervisor, Cindy Roller.

CO1. Evaluate the quality of data already available.

3 **Evaluate Quality of Electronic Data**   The library at your college or university will subscribe to a number of electronic databases. Pick a current topic in business communications, such as electronic communications, strategic communications, or media richness theory. From a computer with access to your library's databases, find at least four articles on the same topic from four or more different databases. Read and then summarize each of the articles, submitting your findings in a two-page memorandum report to your instructor.

CO2. Identify the major sources of electronic information.

4 **The Quality of Internet Resources**   Select two Internet resources and evaluate them based on the four criteria—authority, accuracy, objectivity, and currency—from Checklist 12 on page 350. Submit copies of the resources and a brief summary of their quality to your instructor.

CO3. Evaluate the quality of the electronic data you gather.

5 **Questionable Internet Resources**   Pick a business-related topic. Do research for the topic on the Internet using the four basic search operators—AND, OR, NOT, and NEAR. Try to find misinformation regarding the topic. Make a copy of the questionable information and discuss why you believe the information is unreliable.

6 **A Questionnaire**   The dean of your school of business has asked you, as director of the Bureau of Business Research at your university, to survey typical businesses in your province that have hired your business graduates within the past five years. The purpose of the survey is to determine whether your business graduates have competent communication skills.

CO4. Develop an effective questionnaire and cover letter.

a. Brainstorm for ten minutes. List every possible question you might ask these businesses; don't worry at this point about the wording of the questions or their sequence.
b. Review your questions. Are all of them necessary? Can any of the information be secured elsewhere?
c. Edit your questions to ensure that they are clear and unbiased.
d. Arrange the questions in some logical order.

e. Where possible, format each question with check-off responses, arranging the responses in some logical order.

f. Do any of the questions ask for sensitive information, or are any of them difficult to answer? If so, how will you handle these questions?

g. What information, other than the questions themselves, should you include on the questionnaire?

h. Should you add a questionnaire cover letter?

Draft, revise, format, and proofread your questionnaire. Submit both your questionnaire and your answers to the process questions to your instructor.

7 **Seafood Restaurant Survey**   As the marketing vice president of Joey's Only Seafood Restaurant, the largest seafood restaurant chain in Canada, you are considering opening a new restaurant in Moncton, New Brunswick. You currently have 95 restaurants in Canada but have not yet opened any franchises in the Maritimes.

To determine the suitability of a Joey's Only franchise in Moncton, you are preparing a short survey to be completed by people living in the Moncton area. Your restaurant features a full seafood menu, specializing in fish and chips, and has also branched out into serving wraps, chicken, and ribs. You are a full-service restaurant with a family-style atmosphere. Your prices range from $8.99 for two pieces of fish and chips to $21.99 for a half-kilo crab dinner. Average price for a lunch or dinner would be around $12.50.

Working with a partner, prepare a short questionnaire to be completed by the residents of Moncton. You should have a title for your questionnaire and a brief introduction. Then ask six to ten appropriate questions that are clearly worded and unbiased. Put the questions in a logical sequence and make sure the options given are mutually exclusive and exhaustive. Submit the questionnaire to your instructor for evaluation.

8 **Seafood Restaurant Cover Letter**   Prepare a cover letter to introduce the questionnaire prepared for Exercise 7. The letter should encourage readers to complete the questionnaire and return it quickly in the stamped, addressed envelope. It should also lay some groundwork for establishing potential customers if the restaurant becomes a reality. If the demand is sufficient, a Joey's Only Seafood Restaurant could be coming soon.

9 **Exhaustive and Mutually Exclusive**   You are planning to open an ice cream parlour. You want to have a wide variety of flavours for your patrons to select from, so you are going to ask potential customers to identify their favourite flavours of ice cream.

a. Write a question that presents an exhaustive list of ice cream flavours.

You also want to know how much people are willing to pay for a single scoop of ice cream and a double scoop of ice cream.

b. Prepare questions that list the various price ranges people would be willing to pay for a single scoop of ice cream and a double scoop of ice cream. Make sure the questions are exhaustive and mutually exclusive.

Finally, you want to know what other ice cream novelty items your store should offer.

c. Write a question that gathers this information. The question should be exhaustive, and it should follow a logical sequence.

Make sure the options for each question are listed in an appropriate order.

10 **Work-team Communication—Questionnaire**   Assume that you have been asked to write a report on the feasibility of opening a frozen yogurt store in your town. As the student body at your institution would provide a major source of potential customers for your yogourt store, you decide to survey the students to gather relevant data. Working in a group of four or five, develop a two-page questionnaire and a cover letter that you will mail to a sample of these students.

Ensure that the content and appearance of the questionnaire follow the guidelines given in Checklist 13 (page 351). Pilot-test your questionnaire and cover letter on a small sample of students; then revise it as necessary and submit it to your instructor.

11 **Online Surveys**   By creating your questionnaire so that it can be read and completed online, you'll save time and mailing expenses. Navigate to a free online survey site (such as freeonlinesurveysonline.com), and reformat the questionnaire you developed in Exercise 10 for administering online. Your instructor may ask you to actually administer this questionnaire online by emailing it to selected students.

CO**5.** Conduct a data-gathering interview.

12 **Primary Data—Interview**   Refer to Exercise 10. You decide to get some first-hand information from the owner-manager of a premium ice cream or frozen yogourt store in your area (such as Dairy Queen, Baskin-Robbins, or I Can't Believe It's Yogurt).

Think of the type of information he or she might be able to provide that would help you solve your research problem. Then prepare an interview guide, listing questions in a logical order and noting possible follow-up questions.

Schedule an interview with the owner-manager and conduct the interview, recording it on tape. Write up your findings in a one- or two-page memo report to your instructor. Retain your tape of the interview until after this assignment has been returned to you.

13 **Internet Exercise**   Many research groups use online polling as one of their sources of information. The Environics Research Group, a Toronto-based research group with international affiliations, conducts quantitative and qualitative research for business and governments. Go to the Environics web page and participate in one of their online surveys (erg.environics.net/surveys/). As you complete the survey, reflect on the guidelines provided in this chapter for effective phrasing of questionnaires. Is the language clear, precise, and neutral? Do you feel the survey will yield valid and reliable data?

CO**6.** Interpret the data for the report reader.

14 **Making Sense of Data**   As a marriage counsellor, you have gathered the following statistics.

■ The average age at which women marry for the first time has increased by 1.5 years in the last decade.

■ The average age at which men marry for the first time has increased by 2.5 years in the last decade.

- The number of people getting married for the first time has dropped by 13 percent in the last decade.

- The number of divorces has increased by 22 percent in the last decade.

- The average number of years couples remain married has decreased by 2.8 years in the last decade.

- The number of people who were divorced more than once has increased 26 percent in the last decade.

- The number of women between the ages of 20 and 50 entering the workforce has increased by 12 percent in the last decade.

- The number of men between the ages of 20 and 50 entering the workforce has decreased by 8 percent.

- The amount of debt for married couples has increased by more than 31 percent (an all-time high) during the last decade.

This is a lot of data, but what does it all mean? In groups of five or six people, discuss possible answers to the following questions: What trends can be identified in the data? What could the trends mean? How do the pieces of data relate to each other? Could one factor be causing another? If so, which ones? Before drawing any conclusions, what additional information would be helpful? What kind of visual aid would be best for showing these changes in the last decade?

15 **Misrepresenting Data—Interpreting a Table**   The following sentences interpret the table in Figure 10.2 on page 363. Analyze each sentence to determine whether it represents the data in the table accurately.

a. Males and females alike believe Apex is an asset to the community.
b. More than one-fifth of the females (22 percent) did not respond.
c. Age and the generation gap bring about different beliefs.
d. Married males over age 50 had the most positive opinions.
e. Females disagree more than males—probably because most of the workers at Apex are male.
f. Female respondents tend to disagree with the statement.
g. Apex should be proud of the fact that four-fifths of the residents believe the company is an asset to the community.
h. Thirteen percent of the younger residents have doubts about whether Apex is an asset to the community.
i. More single than married residents didn't care or had no opinion about the topic.
j. Overall, the residents believe that 8 percent of the company is not an asset to the community.

16 **Misrepresenting Data—Use of Statistics**   Politicians, business people, and others love to quote statistics to support their viewpoints. Locate three news stories in which someone quotes statistics to support a particular case, then find an unbiased source that either confirms or refutes those statistics. Write a memo to your instructor discussing your findings. Include a photocopy of both the original news articles and your supporting statistics.

The Keyboard Strikes Back

The manufacturing facility in Winnipeg employs three data-entry operators who work full-time keyboarding production, personnel, and inventory data into a terminal. This data is then sent over telephone lines to the Northern Lights minicomputer, where it becomes part of the corporate database for financial, production, and personnel management.

As required by the labour agreement, in addition to a one-hour lunch period, these three operators receive two 15-minute breaks daily; they may take them at any convenient time, once in the morning and once in the afternoon. Otherwise, they generally work at their keyboards all day.

Last year, Arlene Berkowitz, one of the operators, was absent from work for two weeks for a condition diagnosed as carpal tunnel syndrome, a neuromuscular disorder of the tendons and tissue in the wrists caused by repeated hand motions. Her symptoms included a dull ache in the wrist and excruciating pain in the shoulder and neck. Her doctor treated her with anti-inflammatory medicine and a cortisone injection, and she has had no further problems. However, just last week a second data-entry operator experienced similar symptoms; her doctor diagnosed her ailment as "repeated-motion illness" or RSI (repetitive stress injury) and referred to it informally as the "VDT (video display terminal) disease."

Increasing automation requires contemporary companies like Northern Lights to address such ergonomic issues as carpal tunnel syndrome. Here, Arlene Berkowitz, a data-entry operator, wears wrist splints to ease the pain of this disability.

Because the company anticipates further automation in the future, with more data-entry operators to be hired, Jean Tate asked her assistant, Pat Robbins, to gather additional information on this condition. In fact, Jean wants Pat to survey all workers at NL who use a computer to determine the type and degree of their use and to identify any related health problems. Once the extent of the problem is known, she wants Pat to make any appropriate recommendations regarding the work environment—posture, furniture, work habits, rest breaks, and the like—that will alleviate this problem.

Critical Thinking

1. Assume the role of Pat Robbins. Define the problem of the report and then identify the component sub-parts (that is, *factor* the problem).

2. What are the ethical implications of this case?

Writing Projects

3. Search the appropriate sources and identify five relevant journal articles and five Internet resources on this topic. Photocopy or download each article and save the articles for a future assignment. Evaluate each article using the criteria given in this chapter; write a one-paragraph summary of your *evaluation* of each article. Make notes of these articles.

4. Develop an employee questionnaire that elicits the information requested by Jean, plus whatever additional information you believe would be helpful, based on your reading of the journal articles and Internet sources you located. In lieu of a cover letter, include a short introductory paragraph at the top of the questionnaire explaining the purpose of the study and giving any needed directions.

LABtest 10

Retype the following news item, correcting any grammar and mechanics errors according to the rules introduced in LABs 2–6 beginning on page 534.

Not too many years ago, computers were something of an office novelty, most office workers then performed one major visual task the reading of black characters printed on white paper laid flat or nearly flat on a desk.

5   Office workers now spend there days looking into a monitor who's screen is almost perpendicular to the desk. Some screens still display low-contrast green characters on a dark background. The higher the contrast, the easier faster and more accurately a worker can perform their visual tasks.

While the electric illumination produced by a buildings system may be

10 ideal for performing paper tasks they could create conditions inappropriate

for computer-based tasks. Managers must recognize that office lighting have many qualities but the differences aren't apparent in a cursory survey of the work area.

15   Glare creates visual discomfort.Which is often subtle, due to your eyes amazing ability to except relatively-poor viewing conditions. Tiny ocular muscles react to lighting and causes the eyes to adapt, minimizing viewing problems. Long term viewing problems however cause these muscles to become strained. These conditions can make the workplace far less hospitable, and can have a damaging affect on productivity and moral. In addition, a

20   productivity loss of one percent in a payroll of $1,000,000.00 costs the company $10000 annually.

11

Writing the Report

communication

OBJECTIVES

After you have finished this chapter, you should be able to

1. **Determine an appropriate report structure and organization.**

2. **Draft the report components.**

3. **Use an effective writing style.**

4. **Provide appropriate documentation when using someone else's work.**

5. **Revise, format, and proofread the report.**

When Kent Schroeder writes a report, it is meant not only to document an experience or inform colleagues, but also to play a key role in bettering the lives of those in the developing world. Schroeder is a freelance international development consultant. He has worked on projects that address such issues as AIDS in southern Africa, women's health in Nepal, homelessness in Zimbabwe, and agricultural development in the Caribbean and Tanzania. He's worked with a range of organizations—from nongovernmental organizations to post-secondary institutions to businesses—as a project manager, trainer, researcher, and evaluator.

Schroeder writes a variety of reports, including progress reports for donors who fund international projects, travel mission reports for colleagues, proposals for new projects, and programmatic reports for international partners. This type of reporting plays an important role in contributing to organizational learning, which leads to the development of better programming. "Reporting is sometimes seen as a necessary evil," says Schroeder. "But, ultimately, good reports should generate information and analysis that improve programming. Improved programming, in turn, betters the lives of those who are poor and marginalized."

Regardless of the type of report Schroeder writes, his primary focus is on describing the results of a project. In the past, international development reporting focused on inputs and activities: how much money was spent digging a new well, or how many people were trained in a new agricultural method. Beginning in the 1990s, however, donors began insisting on reports that emphasized the ultimate results of activities: how did people's health change with access to clean well water, or how did training in new agricultural methods generate higher incomes for poor farmers?

an insider's
perspective

KENT SCHROEDER
International Development
Consultant

The focus on results has implications for the structure of Schroeder's reports. Whether reporting on the progress of an existing project or proposing a new project, Schroeder always includes a discussion of the expected results of a project, outlines the activities that contribute to achieving these results, analyzes the challenges and risks in reaching these results and, in the case of existing projects, describes the actual results and any discrepancies from the expected results. All report components connect directly to project results. "Donors always want to see results as the centrepiece of any report," says Schroeder. "This is especially the case when those donors are governments who are accountable to their taxpayers."

One of Schroeder's recent reports is a proposal for a project to assist small businesses destroyed by the December 2004 tsunami in Sri Lanka. The report opens with an information page that provides the project name, organizations involved, and contact information of project managers. Next is the table of contents, list of acronyms used in the report, and executive summary. "The executive summary is perhaps the most important part of the document," says Schroeder. "As a brief overview of the entire project, it is the best way to grab the reader's attention. A poorly written executive summary will lose the reader's interest from the start." The executive summary is followed by a detailed description of the project, broken down into sections on expected results, proposed activities, potential risks to project success, and a proposed budget.

Schroeder's reports rarely use appendices or footnotes. "Only essential information should be included in reports and therefore should be a part of the main body of text," says Schroeder. In the rare cases when footnotes are necessary, he ensures that complete information and an accurate citation appear at the bottom of the same page.

Before submitting a report, Schroeder always tries to send a draft to a colleague for review. This is important to ensure there are no grammatical errors and to get input on the content of the report. In addition, as many of Schroeder's reports are read by partners in other countries, a review by a colleague can help identify any colloquial language or expressions that may not be understood by an international audience. It is critical for Schroeder to know his audience, especially when it is international. "Expressions we use in Canada may be new and confusing to people from other cultures, even if English is their first language," says Schroeder. "Ensuring your report is accessible to a culturally diverse audience is essential if it is to play a meaningful role in contributing to positive change in the developing world."

"The executive summary . . . is the best way to grab the reader's attention. A poorly written executive summary will lose the reader's interest from the start."

■ Planning

As we have seen throughout our study of business communication, the writing process consists of planning, drafting, revising, formatting, and proofreading. You follow this same process when writing a report.

Although much of the planning in the report process is, of necessity, done even before collecting the data, the written presentation of the results requires its own stage of planning. You need to make decisions about the structure of the report, the organization of the content, and the framework of the headings both before and as you write.

Determining the Report Structure

CO1. Determine an appropriate report structure and organization.

Most reports are formatted as manuscripts, memos, or letters.

The physical structure of the report and such general traits as complexity, degree of formality, and length depend on the audience for the report and the nature of the problem that the report addresses. The three most common formats for a report are manuscript, memorandum, and letter format.

Manuscript reports (see Models 26 through 34) are the most formal of the three. They are formatted in narrative (paragraph) style, with headings and subheadings separating the different sections. If the problem that the report addresses is complex and has serious consequences, the report will likely follow a manuscript format and a formal writing style. A formal writing style typically avoids the use of first- and second-person pronouns, such as *I* and *you*. In addition, the more formal the report, the more supplementary parts are included (such as a table of contents, executive summary, and appendix) and, therefore, the longer the report.

Memorandum and letter reports contain the standard correspondence parts (for example, lines identifying the names of the sender and receiver). They use a more informal writing style and may or may not contain headings and subheadings. Compare the informal, simple, and short report in memo format shown in Model 23 on page 381 to the more formal, complex, and long report in manuscript format shown (in abbreviated form) in Model 24 on page 382.

Organizing the Report Findings

A sculptor creating a statue of someone doesn't necessarily start at the head and work down to the feet in lock-step fashion. Instead, he or she may first create part of the torso, then part of the head, then another part of the torso, and so on. Likewise, a movie director may film segments of the movie out of narrative order. But in the end, both creations are put together in such a way as to show unity, order, logic, and beauty.

Similarly, you may have organized the collection and analysis of data in a way that suited the investigation of various subtopics of the problem. But now that it is time to put the results of your work together into a coherent written presentation, you may need a new organization, one that integrates the whole and takes into account what you have learned through your research.

Planning your written presentation to show unity, order, logic, and yes, even beauty, involves selecting an organizational basis for the findings (the data you've collected and analyzed) and developing an outline. You must decide in what order to present each piece of the puzzle and when to "spill the beans"; that is, when to

All Systems Go Company   FAX 604 390-1445
175 Granville St.
Vancouver, BC   VZN ZE6

MEMO TO: Marketing Manager

FROM: Barbara Novak, Sales Assistant

DATE: August 9, 20__

SUBJECT: Yellow Pages Advertising

I recommend we continue purchasing a quarter-page ad in the Yellow Pages. My recommendation is based on the fact that Yellow Pages advertising has produced more inquiries than any other method of advertising and has increased net profits.

1 **A Pilot Test Was Set Up**

2 On March 1, you asked me to conduct a three-month test of the effectiveness of Yellow Pages advertising. I subsequently purchased a quarter-page ad for the edition of the Yellow Pages that was distributed the week of June 2 to 6. For six weeks thereafter, we queried all telephone and walk-in customers to determine how they had learned about our company. I also compared the percentage of signed contracts resulting from each source. Precise before-and-after sales data could not be generated because of other factors that affected sales for each period (for example, time of year and other promotional campaigns).

Results Were Positive

My analysis of the data shows that 38 percent of the callers after June 2 to 6 first learned about our company from the Yellow Pages. The next highest source was referrals and repeat business, which accounted for 26 percent of the calls. In addition, 21 percent of the Yellow Pages inquiries resulted in signed contracts.

Advertising Should Be Continued

Based on the $358 monthly cost of our quarter-page ad, each dollar of ad cost is producing $3.77 in sales revenue and $0.983 toward product margin. These results clearly support the continuation of our Yellow Pages advertising. I would be happy to discuss the results of this research with you in more detail and to provide the supporting statistical data if you wish.

jco

model 23

INFORMAL MEMO REPORT

The memo format indicates the reader is someone from within the firm.

Uses a direct organizational style: the recommendation and conclusions are given first, followed by the supporting evidence.

Uses informal language: makes extensive use of first- and second-person pronouns such as *I, me, we,* and *you.*

Uses talking headings to reinforce the direct plan.

Does not include detailed statistical information but makes it available if needed.

Grammar and Mechanics Notes

1 Keep all same-level headings parallel. In this memo, all headings are in the passive voice.

2 Use first- and second-person pronouns such as *I* and *you* for most business documents, with the exception of some formal reports.

model24

FORMAL MANUSCRIPT REPORT (ABBREVIATED FORM)

1 **THE EFFECTIVENESS OF YELLOW PAGE ADVERTISING FOR ALL SYSTEMS GO COMPANY**

Barbara Novak, Sales Assistant

According to Mountain Bell, display advertising typically accounts for 55 percent of total sales for a firm in the moving business.[1] Thus, Hiram
2 Cooper, director of marketing, requested a three-month test be conducted of the effectiveness of Yellow Pages advertising for All Systems Go. This report describes the procedures used to gather the data and the results
3 obtained. Based on the data, a recommendation is made regarding the continuation of Yellow Pages advertising.

A quarter-page ad was purchased in the edition of the Mountain Bell Yellow Pages that was distributed the week of June 2 to 6. For the six-week period encompassing June 9 through July 17, all telephone and walk-in customers were queried to determine how they had learned about the company.

One delimitation of this study was that precise before-and-after sales data could not be generated because of other factors that affected sales for each period (for example, time of year and other promotional campaigns).

FINDINGS

The findings of this study are reported in terms of the sources of information for learning about All Systems Go, the amount of new business generated, and a cost-benefits comparison for Yellow Pages advertising.

Sources of Information

As shown in Table 1, 38 percent of the callers during the test period first learned about All Systems Go from the Yellow Pages display. The second highest score was referrals and repeat business, which together accounted for 26 percent of the calls. In addition, 21 percent of the Yellow Pages

[1]Joseph L. Dye <jldye@aol.com>, "Answers to Your Question," May 18, 2001, personal email.

Grammar and Mechanics Notes

1 Formal reports often include the report title and author's name at the top of the first page.

2 Avoid capitalizing position titles if they appear after the person's name: *Hiram Cooper, director of marketing.*

3 To avoid first-person references in formal reports, use the passive voice: *a recommendation is made.*

present your overall **conclusions** (the answers to the research questions raised in the introduction) and any recommendations you may wish to make.

As shown in Figure 11.1 on page 385, the four most common bases for organizing your findings are time, location, importance, and criteria. There are, of course, other patterns for organizing data; for example, you can move from the known to the unknown or from the simple to the complex. The purpose of the report (information, analysis, or recommendation), the nature of the problem, and your knowledge of the reader will help you select the organizational framework that will be most useful.

MAKE UP YOUR MIND!   *word*wise

An *"antagonym"* is a single word that has meanings that contradict each other. Examples:

Bound: Moving ("I was bound for Montreal") or unable to move ("I was bound to a post").
Buckle: To hold together ("Buckle your belt") or to fall apart ("to buckle under pressure").
Cut: Get in ("Cut in line") or to get out ("cut a class").
Replace: Take away ("replace the worn carpet") or put back ("replace the papers in the file").
Trim: To add things to ("trim a Christmas tree") or take pieces off ("trim your hair").

Time   The use of chronology, or time sequence, is appropriate for agendas, minutes of meetings, programs, many status reports, and similar projects. Discussing events in the order in which they occurred, or in the order in which they will or should occur, is an efficient way to organize many informational reports—those whose purpose is simply to inform.

Most reports are organized by time, location, importance, or criteria.

Despite its usefulness and simplicity, time sequence should not be overused. Because events occur one after another, chronology is often the most efficient way to record data, but it may not be the most efficient way to present that data to your readers. Assume, for example, that you are writing a progress report on a recruiting trip you made to four university campuses. Each day you interviewed candidates for the three positions you have open. The first passage, given in time sequence, requires too much work of the reader. The second version saves the reader time.

Organize your report chronologically only when it is important for the reader to know the sequence of events.

NOT: On Monday morning, I interviewed one candidate for the budget-analyst position and two candidates for the junior-accountant position. Then, in the afternoon, I interviewed two candidates for the asset-manager position and another for the budget-analyst position. Finally, on Tuesday, I interviewed another candidate for budget analyst and two for junior accountant.

BUT: On Monday and Tuesday, I interviewed three candidates for the budget-analyst position, four for the junior-accountant position, and two for the asset-manager position.

A blow-by-blow description is not necessarily the most efficient means of communicating information to the reader. Sometimes it forces the reader to do too much work. Organize your information in time sequence only when it is important for the reader to know the sequence in which events occurred.

Location   Like the use of time sequence, the use of location as the basis for organizing a report is often appropriate for simple informational reports. Discussing topics according to their geographical or physical location (for example, describing an office layout) may be the most efficient way to present the data. Again, however, be sure that such an organizational plan helps the reader process the information most efficiently and that it is not merely the easiest way for you to report the data. Decisions should be based on reader needs rather than on writer convenience.

Larry Page (left) and Sergey Brin founded the search firm Google in 1999. Today it earns roughly $1 billion a year and accounts for 48 percent of all Internet queries. Yet, according to them, their first business plan wasn't much more than a series of notes scribbled on a whiteboard.

The most logical organization for most analytical and recommendation reports is by criteria.

Importance   For the busy reader, the most efficient organizational plan may be to have the most important topic discussed first, followed in order by topics of decreasing importance. The reader then gets the major idea up front and can skim the less important information as desired or needed. This organizational plan is routinely used by newspapers, where the most important points are discussed in the lead paragraph.

For some types of reports, especially recommendation reports, the opposite plan might be used effectively. If you've analyzed four alternatives and will recommend the implementation of Alternative 4, you might first present each of the other alternatives in turn (starting with the least viable solution) and show why they're not feasible. Then, you save your "trump card" until last, thus making the alternative you are recommending the freshest in the reader's mind because it is the last one read. If you use this option, make sure that you effectively "slay all the dragons", except your own, so the reader will agree that your recommendation is the most logical one.

Criteria   For most analytical and recommendation reports, where the purpose is to analyze the data, draw conclusions, and possibly recommend a solution, the most logical arrangement is to organize the data by criteria. One of the important steps in the reporting process is to develop hypotheses regarding causes of or solutions for the problem you're exploring. This process requires factoring, or breaking down, your problem into its component sub-problems. These factors, or criteria, then, become the basis for organizing the report.

In Example D in Figure 11.1 on page 385, for instance, the three factors presented—professional training, work experience, and programming skills—are the bases on which you will evaluate each candidate. Thus, they should also form the bases for presenting the data. By focusing attention on the criteria, you help lead the reader to the same conclusion you reached. For this reason, organizing data by criteria is an especially effective organizational plan when the reader might be initially resistant to your recommendations.

If you're evaluating three sites for a new facility, for example, avoid the temptation to use the locations of these sites as the report headings. Such an organizational plan focuses attention on the sites themselves instead of on the criteria by which you evaluated them and on which you based your recommendations. Instead, use the criteria as the headings. Similarly, avoid using "advantages" and "disadvantages" as headings. Keep your reader in step with you by helping the reader focus on the same topics—the criteria—that you focused on during the research and analysis phases of your project

In actual practice, you might use a combination of these organizational plans. For instance, you might organize your first-level headings by criteria but your second-level headings in simple-to-complex order. Or you might organize your first-level headings by criteria but present these criteria in their order of importance. Competent communicators select an organizational plan with a view toward helping the reader comprehend and appreciate the information and viewpoints being presented in the most efficient manner possible.

figure **11.1**   **Four Methods of Organizing the Report Findings**

Example A	Example B	Example C	Example D
Time	Location	Importance	Criteria
Eastern Electronics: A Case Study	Renovation Needs	Progress on Automation Project	Evaluation of Applicants
1. Start-up of Firm: 1999 2. Rapid Expansion: 1999–2005 3. Industry-wide Slowdown: 2003 4. Retrenchment: 2004–2005 5. Return to Profitability: 2006	1. Expanding the Mailroom 2. Modernizing the Foyer 3. Installing a New HVAC System 4. Repaving the Parking Lot	1. Conversion on Budget 2. Schedule Revised by One Month 3. Branch Offices Added to Project 4. Software Programs Upgraded	1. Kurji Has Higher Level of Professional Training 2. Calvert Has More Work Experience 3. Nadon Has Stronger Programming Skills

Outlining the Report Findings

Although we've not used the term *outlining* thus far, whenever we've talked about organizing we've actually been talking about outlining as well. For example, early in the report process you factored your problem statement into its logical component sub-problems. Thus, your problem statement and sub-problems served as your first working outline.

Many business writers find it useful at this point in the report process to construct a more formal outline. A formal outline provides an orderly visual representation of the report, showing clearly which points are to be covered, in what order they are to be covered, and what the relationship of each is to the rest of the report. The purpose of the outline is to guide you, the writer, in structuring your report logically and efficiently. Consider it a working draft, subject to being revised as you compose the report.

The outline provides a concise visual picture of the structure of your report.

Use the working title of your report as the title of your outline. Then use uppercase roman numerals for the major headings, uppercase letters for first-level subheadings, Arabic numerals for second-level subheadings, and lowercase letters for third-level subheadings. Only rarely will you need to use all four levels of headings. Model 25 on page 387 shows an outline for a formal report.

As part of the process of developing a formal outline, you should compose the actual wording for your headings and decide how many headings you will need. Headings play an important role in helping to focus the reader's attention and in helping your report achieve unity and coherence, so plan them carefully, and revise them as needed as you work toward a final version of your report.

Talking Versus Generic Headings   **Talking headings** identify not only the topic of the section but also the major conclusion. For instance, Example C in Figure 11.1 above uses talking headings to indicate not only that the first section of the report is about the budget for the conversion but also that the conversion is proceeding on budget.

Use descriptive and parallel headings for unity and coherence.

Talking headings, which are typically used in newspapers and magazines, are often also useful for business reports, where they can serve as a preview or executive summary of the entire report. They are especially useful when directness is desired—the reader can simply skim the headings in the report (or in the table of contents) and get an overview of the topics covered and each topic's conclusions.

Generic headings, on the other hand, identify only the topic of the section, without giving the conclusion. Most formal reports and any report written in an indirect pattern would use generic headings, similar to the headings used for Examples A and B in Figure 11.1 and used throughout Model 25 on page 387.

Parallelism   As illustrated in Figure 11.1, you have wide leeway in selecting the formats of headings you wish to use in your report. Noun phrases are probably the most common form of heading, but you may also choose participial phrases, partial statements (in which a verb is missing—the kind often used in newspaper headlines), statements, or questions. Perhaps there are other forms you might choose as well.

Regardless of the form of heading you select, be consistent within each level of heading. If the first major heading (a first-level heading) is a noun phrase, all first-level headings should be noun phrases. If the first major heading is a talking heading, the others should be too. As you move from level to level, you may switch to another form of heading if it would be more appropriate. Again, however, the headings within the same level must be parallel.

Length and Number of Headings   Four to eight words is about the right length for most headings. Headings that are too long lose some of their effectiveness; the shorter the heading, the more emphasis it receives. Yet headings that are too short are ineffective because they do not convey enough meaning.

Use headings to break up a long report and refocus the reader's attention.

Similarly, choose an appropriate number of headings. Having too many headings weakens the unity of a report—they chop the report up too much, making it look more like an outline than a reasoned analysis. Having too few headings, however, confronts the reader with page after page of solid copy, without the chance to stop periodically and refocus attention on the topic.

In general, consider having at least one heading or visual aid to break up each single-spaced page or two consecutive, double-spaced pages. Make your report inviting to read.

Balance   Maintain a sense of balance within and among sections. It would be unusual to give one section of a report eight subsections (eight second-level headings) and give the following section none. Similarly, it would be unusual to have one section ten pages long and another section only half a page long. Also, ensure that the most important ideas appear in the highest levels of headings. If you're discussing four criteria for a topic, for example, all four should be in the same level of heading—presumably in first-level headings.

When you divide a section into subsections, it must have at least two subsections. You cannot logically have just one second-level heading within a section because when you divide something, it divides into more than one "piece."

Choosing an Overall Organizational Plan

In general, prefer the direct plan (conclusions and recommendations first) for most business reports.

After you've determined how to organize your findings, you will also need to determine where other components of the report will be placed, specifically your recommendations and conclusions. Recall our discussions about the direct and indirect plans for memo and letter writing. The direct plan presents your major idea first; the indirect plan presents the main idea only after some discussion or explanation has been provided. These two models also apply to report writing. Depending on

model25

REPORT OUTLINE
Uses the working title of the report as the outline title.

STAFF EVALUATION
OF THE BENEFIT PROGRAM
AT AEGON OIL AND GAS

Lynn O'Neal

1 I. INTRODUCTION

   A. Purpose and Scope
   B. Procedures

II. FINDINGS

2   A. Knowledge of Benefits
      1. Familiarity with Benefits
      2. Present Methods of Communication
         a. Formal Channels
         b. Informal Channels
      3. Preferred Methods of Communication
   B. Opinions of Present Benefits
      1. Importance of Benefits
      2. Satisfaction with Benefits
   C. Desirability of Additional Benefits

III. CONCLUSIONS AND RECOMMENDATIONS

   A. Summary of Key Findings
   B. Recommendations

APPENDIX

3   A. Cover Letter
    B. Questionnaire

Organizes the findings by criteria.

Contains at least two items each level of subdivision.

Uses parallel structure (noun phrases are used for each heading and subheading).

Grammar and Mechanics Notes

1 Align the roman numerals vertically on the page.
2 Type each entry in upper- and lowercase letters.
3 Identify each appendix item by letter.

your purpose and the needs of your audience, you may choose to put your conclusions and recommendations up front, before discussing your findings. Alternatively, you may choose to discuss your findings first, then present your conclusion and recommendations.

The conclusions answer the research questions raised in the introduction.

Academic reports and many business reports have traditionally presented the conclusions and recommendations of a study at the end of the report, the rationale being that conclusions cannot logically be drawn until the data has been presented and analyzed; similarly, recommendations cannot be made until conclusions have been drawn.

Although hard-and-fast rules cannot be given for when to use the direct and indirect organizational plans in reports, some guidance can be given. Generally, it is better to use the direct organizational plan (in which the conclusions and recommendations are presented at the beginning of the report) when:

- The reader prefers the direct plan for reports (as is typically the case when preparing a business report for your superior).

- The reader will be receptive to your conclusions and recommendations.

- The reader can evaluate the information in the report more efficiently if the conclusions and recommendations are given up front.

Similarly, the indirect plan (in which the evidence is presented first, followed by conclusions and recommendations) is more appropriate when:

- The reader prefers the indirect plan for reports.

- The reader will be initially uninterested in or resistant to the conclusions and recommendations.

- The topic is so complex that detailed explanations and discussions are needed for the conclusions and recommendations to be understood and accepted.

The decision isn't necessarily an either/or situation. Instead of putting all the conclusions and recommendations either first or last, you may choose to split them up, discussing each in the appropriate subsection of your report. Similarly, even though you write a report using an indirect plan, you may add an executive summary or letter of transmittal that communicates the conclusions and recommendations to the reader before the report itself has been read. Occasionally, reports will include the recommendations up front, right after the executive summary, but save the concluding remarks for the end of the report. (See Figure 11.2 on page 389.)

■ Drafting the Report Components

CO2. Draft the report components.

Although it is the last step of a long and sometimes complex process, the written presentation of your research is the only evidence your reader has of the effort you have invested in the project. The success or failure of all your work depends on this physical evidence. Prepare the written report carefully to bring out the full significance of your data and to help the reader reach a decision and solve a problem.

The final product—the written report—is the only evidence the reader has of your efforts.

Everything that you learned in Chapter 3 about the writing process applies directly to report writing—choosing a productive work environment; scheduling a reasonable block of time to devote to the drafting phase; letting ideas flow quickly during the drafting stage, without worrying about style, correctness, or format; and

figure11.2   **Formal Report Components**

Front Matter (also known as prefatory parts)

| Cover Page | Title Page | Letter or Memo of Transmittal | Table of Contents | List of Illustrations | Executive Summary |

Report Body (Indirect Plan)

| Introduction | Findings | Conclusions and Recommendations |

Report Body (Direct Plan)

| Conclusions and Recommendations | Introduction | Findings |

NOTE: Some readers may find this plan a little disorienting, as the report simply ends, without providing any clues that it's doing so, right after the findings. An alternative to this approach is the mixed plan illustrated below.

Report Body (Mixed Plan)

| Recommendations | Introduction | Findings | Conclusions |

Back Matter

| Appendices | Bibliography |

revising for content, style, correctness, and readability. However, because of their complexity, report writing requires several additional considerations as well.

The order in which you choose to draft each component of the report may vary somewhat from author to author. However, the most logical and efficient approach is probably as follows:

1. Write your findings first. Not only is this typically the longest and most complex section of the report, it also forms the backbone on which all other report components are built.

2. Write your conclusions and recommendations next. Sometimes these two sections are presented together under one heading, and sometimes they are treated as separate components. Whichever the case, these sections must flow logically from your findings and it therefore makes sense to write them immediately after completing your findings section.

3. Write the introduction. While it may seem logical to novice report writers to write the introduction first, as we'll learn later, part of the introduction's purpose is to preview the main topics or problems discussed in your findings. While your outline should give you a clear idea of what the main topics will be, occasionally they change as you draft and re-draft your findings. It's therefore more efficient to write the introduction only after the findings have been finalized.

4. Write the executive summary. As this is a condensed version of the report (the introduction, findings, conclusions, and recommendations), it must be written only after the body of the report is complete.

5. Finally, for manuscript reports, write the table of contents, the title page, and if appropriate, the transmittal document, the bibliography, and any required appendices.

Drafting the Supplementary Sections

The length, formality, and complexity of the report, as well as the needs of the reader, affect the number of report components that precede and follow the body of the report. Use as many of the various report components as will help you achieve your report objectives. (These components are discussed below, not necessarily in the order that they will be written, but in the order that they would typically appear in a formal manuscript report organized according to the indirect plan.)

Title Page　A title page is typically used for reports typed in manuscript (as opposed to letter or memorandum) format. It shows such information as the title of the report, the names (and often titles and departments) of the reader and writer, and the date the report was transmitted to the reader. Other information may be included at the writer's discretion. The information on the title page should be arranged attractively on the page. See Model 26 on page 391 for a sample layout.

Transmittal Document　Formal reports, and all reports that are not hand-delivered to the reader, should be accompanied by a **transmittal document** (see Model 27 on page 392). As its name implies, a transmittal document conveys the report to the reader. If the reader is outside the organization, you would use a transmittal letter; if the reader is within the organization, you would typically use a transmittal memo. Whether the report is written in formal or informal style, use a conversational, personal style of writing for the transmittal document.

Write the transmittal memo or letter in a direct pattern.

Because the completion of the report assignment is good news (whether the information it contains is good or bad news), use the direct organizational plan. Begin by actually transmitting the report. Briefly discuss any needed background information, and perhaps give an overview of the conclusions and recommendations of the report (unless you want the reader to read the evidence supporting these conclusions and recommendations first). Include any other information that will help the reader understand, appreciate, and make use of the information presented in the report. End with such goodwill features as an expression of appreciation for being

model26

TITLE PAGE

1   EVALUATION OF STAFF BENEFIT PROGRAM
AT THE AEGON OIL AND GAS

2

Prepared for

David Riggins
Director of Human Resources
Aegon Oil and Gas

Prepared by

Lynn O'Neal
3   Assistant Director of Human Resources
Aegon Oil and Gas

March 30, 20—

Sets the title centre, bold, and in capitals. Be sure the title itself is descriptive of the report's purpose.

Includes the name or names of the recipients, their titles, and their company or institution.

Includes the name or names of the authors, their title, and their company or institution.

Includes the date on which the report is transmitted.

Grammar and Mechanics Notes

1 Centre each section of the title page.

2 Include plenty of white space after each section to avoid a cramped appearance.

3 Set page margins to at least 2.5 cm.

model27

TRANSMITTAL MEMO

Uses letter or memo format.

Introduces the report.

Discusses briefly the report background and provides an overview of conclusions and recommendations.

Concludes with an expression of appreciation and willingness to provide further help.

MEMO TO:　David Riggins, Director of Human Resources

FROM:　Lynn O'Neal, Assistant Director of Human Resources

DATE:　March 30, 20—

SUBJECT:　Staff Employees' Evaluation of the Benefit Program at Aegon Oil and Gas

Here is the report on our staff benefit program that you requested on February 15.

1　The report shows that the staff is familiar with and values most of the benefits we offer. At the end of the report, I've made several recommendations regarding issuing individualized benefit statements annually and determining the usefulness of the automobile insurance benefit, the feasibility of offering compensation for unused sick leave, and the competitiveness of our retirement program.

2　I enjoyed working on this assignment, Dave, and learned quite a bit from my analysis that will help me during the upcoming labour negotiations. Please let me know if you have any questions about the report.

mek
3　Attachment

Grammar and Mechanics Notes

1 *the usefulness . . . , the feasibility . . . , the competitiveness . . .* : Ensure that items in a series are stated in parallel format.

2 *assignment, Dave,:* set off nouns of address with commas.

3 Use the term *Attachment* for memos rather than *Enclosure*

given the report assignment, an offer of willingness to discuss the report further, or perhaps an offer of assistance in the future.

The letter or memo may simply be transmitted along with the report, or it may be a part of the report. In the latter case, it is placed immediately after the title page but before the executive summary or table of contents.

Executive Summary   An **executive summary** is a condensed version of the body of the report (including introduction, findings, and any conclusions or recommendations). Although some readers may simply scan the report itself, most will read the executive summary carefully. Like the transmittal document, the executive summary is an optional component of the report. It is especially appropriate when the conclusions and recommendations will be welcomed by the reader, when the report is long, or when you know your reader appreciates having such information up front.

Because the purpose of the executive summary is to save the reader time, the summary should be short—generally no more than 10 percent of the length of the report. The summary should contain the same emphasis as the report itself and should be independent of the report; that is, a busy reader should be able to read the summary and understand the report's background, purpose, key findings, conclusions, and recommendations, without ever having to consult the report itself. Indeed, you should assume that the person reading the summary will not have a chance to read the report, so include as much useful information as possible. Use the same writing style for the summary as you used in the report. Position the summary immediately before the table of contents.

Because the executive summary must both be concise and provide a comprehensive summary of the document, it may be the most difficult of all the report components to write. Probably the most common error novice writers make when summarizing their findings is to simply *describe,* rather than actually summarize, them.

The report summary may be read more carefully than the report itself.

NOT: This report discusses Aegon staff's familiarity with their benefits.

BUT: At least three quarters of Aegon staff say they are familiar with all major benefits, except for long-term disability and auto insurance.

One strategy for writing the executive summary is to read each section of the report body in isolation and then draft a summary of the section in a few sentences. Do this for the introduction, for each main section within the findings, for the conclusion, and for the recommendations. Then, take each of your "mini" summaries and pull them together into unified paragraphs with strong transitions between ideas. If appropriate, you may also wish to include headings within the executive summary. In Model 28 on page 394, note that nothing new is added here that isn't discussed elsewhere in the report. Executive summaries, by definition, are redundant of the rest of the report.

Table of Contents   Long reports with many headings and subheadings usually benefit from a table of contents. The wording used in the headings in the table of contents must be identical to the wording used in the headings in the body of the report. Typically, only two or three levels of headings are included in the table of contents—even if more levels are used in the body of the report. The page numbers identify only the page on which the section heading appears, even though the section itself may comprise many pages. Obviously, the table of contents cannot be written until after the report has been typed. See Model 29 for a sample table of contents.

model 28

EXECUTIVE SUMMARY

1 PURPOSE AND BACKGROUND OF STUDY

This study seeks to examine the opinions of staff at Aegon Oil and Gas regarding their employee benefits. Specifically, the study examines how knowledgeable staff are regarding their benefits, how much value staff place on each of their benefits, and what benefits, if any, staff would like to add to their package.

2 From the list of 2489 staff members, a sample of 250 staff was surveyed, with a response rate of 82 percent. Personal interviews were also held with three benefits managers. The primary data was then compared with existing secondary data to determine staff's opinions about their benefits package.

KNOWLEDGE OF BENEFITS

The survey revealed that at least three-quarters of the staff are familiar with all major benefits, except for long-term disability insurance and auto insurance. Present formal channels of communicating benefits—which include brochures, the monthly newsletter, and new employee orientation programs—were considered by over half of the respondents to be reasonably effective. Informal channels for communicating benefits were considered less effective than formal ones and over 80 percent of respondents agreed that more resources should be put into communicating benefits via formal channels. Finally, over 60 percent said they would prefer an individualized benefit statement over the existing brochures.

SATISFACTION WITH BENEFITS

The overwhelming majority of respondents (92 percent) agreed that all of the existing benefits were important. Paid time off is considered the most important benefit, and auto insurance discounts the least. Current retirement benefits, while considered important, generated a high level of dissatisfaction. The majority of respondents (76 percent) would like to see compensation for unused sick leave added to the benefits package.

CONCLUSIONS AND RECOMMENDATIONS

The survey revealed that the existing benefits package is familiar to most employees and highly valued by all. The survey did reveal some areas of dissatisfaction, most notably the auto insurance benefit, as well as the desire for individualized benefits statements and some form of unused sick-leave compensation.

The following recommendations are based on these conclusions:

1. Determine the feasibility of generating annual individualized benefit statements.
2. Re-evaluate the auto insurance discount benefit and consider the feasibility of substituting compensation for unused sick leave for the auto insurance benefit.
3. Conduct a follow-up study to compare benefits at this company with those at other oil and gas companies.

ii

Grammar and Mechanics Notes

1 Consider including headings within the executive summary to identify major themes.

2 Maintain a semi-formal tone throughout the executive summary, and avoid first-person references.

CONTENTS

model29

TABLE OF CONTENTS

Uses leader lines.

Capitalizes first-level headings.

Indents second- and third-level headings.

Includes only page number on which each section heading appears.

Traditionally, prefatory report components are paginated in lower case Roman numerals.

Grammar and Mechanics Notes

1 Don't list the title page or the table of contents in the table of contents.

2 Ensure the phrasing of each heading in the table of contents is identical to the phrasing of each heading within the report.

3 Double-check the pagination of your final draft to ensure the page references in the table of contents remain accurate.

List of Illustrations   The list of illustrations should be considered a separate report component from the table of contents. In other words, like the table of contents, the list of illustrations should be given its own first-level heading. If there is sufficient room, you may choose to put your list of illustrations on the same page as your table of contents; if not put this on the next page. Model 30 on page 397 provides a typical layout for this component.

Introduction   The introduction sets the stage for understanding the findings that follow. In this section, present such information as the following:

The introduction presents the information the reader needs to make sense of the findings.

- *Background of the study.* Describe why the study is needed. Identify who authorized the study and why. Discuss what problem (or problems) the report is trying to solve and how the problem has evolved. You may also discuss the implications of the problem to the organization as a whole. Is the problem costing money? Is the problem leading to morale or turnover concerns? Is the problem limiting growth? (We are, of course, using the word "problem" loosely here. Often a report may be exploring an opportunity rather than solving a problem.)

- *Purpose and scope (including definition of terms, if needed).* In the background section, you will have identified the problem in fairly general terms. Here you want to be more specific about the goal (or goals) of this study. Are you seeking concrete solutions to a problem, or are you merely seeking to better understand a problem? Will you be making recommendations? Will this study somehow dovetail with other studies completed or currently underway? Is this just a preliminary study that will be followed by a more in-depth study later? In addition to defining the report's purpose, you should preview for your reader the key topics (or sub-problems) that are addressed in your findings. These key topics are known as the report's scope, and they let the reader know just how far-reaching your analysis is.

- *Limitations.* Readers not only want to know what is included in the study; they may also want to know what's excluded. If, for example, your report merely explores a problem but provides no specific recommendations—other than perhaps the need for further study—your reader should be made aware of this limitation before reading the report. You may think of your limitations as the boundaries of the report's coverage. No report can satisfy all readers, so out of courtesy you should alert those readers who may be expecting something more than what the report actually delivers. You may choose to discuss the report's limitations alongside your discussion of the report's scope: together these two sections inform readers both what *is* and what *is not* included in the report.

- *Procedures used to gather and analyze the data.* What methods have you used to gather your data? Is the report based primarily on primary data, such as surveys and interviews? Or have you incorporated secondary research that helps elucidate your findings or provides the basis for your recommendations? For research reports, your methodology may consist entirely of secondary sources. Depending on the complexity of your methodology, this section may actually be removed from the introduction and become the first—and largest—section of the report. (Lengthy methodology sections are more common in scientific and academic circles where a researcher's methods must be scrutinized for their validity.)

A sample introduction can be found in Model 31 on page 398.

LIST OF ILLUSTRATIONS

iv

model 30

LIST OF ILLUSTRATIONS

Gives the list of illustrations its own first-level heading.

Includes both the number and the title of each visual.

Groups all tables together and all figures together.

Grammar and Mechanics Notes

1 Ensure the title of each illustration listed here is identical to the title used in the report.

2 All illustrations with columns and rows should be identified as tables; all other illustrations should be identified as figures.

model 31

REPORT INTRODUCTION

Identifies significance of study and who authorized the report.

Writes in present, not future, tense whenever discussing the report document.

Identifies the general purpose of the report as well as the specific scope (sub-problems).

Discusses the limitations of the study.

Discusses the procedures used to gather the data. (Procedures are typically discussed using past tense and passive voice.)

Begins on page 1, using Arabic numerals.

1

INTRODUCTION

Employee benefits are a rapidly growing and an increasingly important form of employee compensation for both profit and non-profit organizations. According to a recent study by the Human Resource Board of Canada, benefits now constitute 27 percent of all payroll costs, averaging $10 857 yearly for each employee.[1] Thus, on the basis of cost alone, an organization's benefit program must be carefully monitored and evaluated.

To ensure that the benefit program for Aegon Oil and Gas's 2489 staff is operating as effectively as possible, David Riggins, director of personnel, authorized this report on February 15, 20—.

PURPOSE AND SCOPE

Specifically, the following problem is addressed in this study: What are the opinions of staff at Aegon Oil and Gas regarding their employee benefits? To answer this question, the following sub-problems are addressed, following which recommendations are made:

2
1. How knowledgeable are the employees about the benefit program?
2. What are the employees' opinions of the value of the benefits already available?
3. What benefits, if any, would the employees like to have added to the program?

This study attempts to determine employee preferences only. Whether or not employee preferences are economically feasible is not within the scope of this study. As used in this study, employee benefits (also called fringe benefits) means an employment benefit given in addition to one's wages or salary.

PROCEDURES

3
A list of the 2489 staff eligible for benefits was generated from the January 15 payroll run. Using a 10 percent systematic sample, 250 employees were selected for the survey. On March 3, each of these employees was sent the cover letter and questionnaire shown in Appendices A and B via inter-office mail. A total of 206 employees completed usable questionnaires, for a response rate of 82 percent.

In addition to the questionnaire data, personal interviews were held with three benefits managers. The primary data provided by the survey and personal interviews were then analyzed and compared with findings from secondary sources to determine employees' opinions of the benefits program at Aegon.

see p582   *Business Style?*

1

---

[1] Avril Lewis, *Compensation Planning 2007*. Human Resource Board of Canada, Spring 2006, pp. 20–25.

Grammar and Mechanics Notes

1 Centre the first-level headings in bold and all capitals. Type second-level headings in bold at the left margin. (Capitalization is optional.)

2 In a single-spaced report, single space numbered and bulleted lists if every item comprises a single line. Otherwise, single space lines within an item but double space between items.

3 Be consistent in using either the word "percent" or the percent sign (%). Regardless, use figures for the actual percentage.

Findings   The findings of the study represent the major contribution of the report and make up the largest section of the report. Discuss and interpret any relevant primary and secondary data you gathered. Organize this section using one of the plans discussed earlier (for example, by time, location, importance, or, more frequently, criteria). Using objective language, present the information clearly, concisely, and accurately.

Don't just present your findings; analyze and interpret them for the reader.

Many reports will display numerical information as illustrations in the form of tables and figures (such as bar, line, or pie charts). The information in any illustration should be self-explanatory; that is, readers should understand it without having to refer to the text. Nevertheless, all tables and figures must be mentioned and explained in the text so that the text, too, is self-explanatory. All text references should be by number (for example, "as shown in Table 4")—never by a phrase such as "shown below," because the table or figure might actually appear at the top of the following page.

Summarize the important information from the illustration (see Model 32 on page 400). Give enough interpretation to help the reader comprehend the table or figure, but don't repeat all the information it contains. Discussing illustrated information in the narrative *emphasizes* that information, so discuss only what merits such emphasis.

For all primary and secondary data, point out important items, implications, trends, contradictions, unexpected findings, similarities and differences, and the like. Use emphasis, subordination, preview, summary, and transition to make the report read clearly and smoothly. Avoid presenting facts and figures so fast that the reader is overwhelmed with data. Keep the reader's needs and desires uppermost in mind as you organize, present, and discuss the information. For an excerpt from a findings section, including samples of illustrations, see Model 32.

Conclusions and Recommendations   Once you've decided how to organize the findings of your study, you must decide how to present the conclusions and any recommendations that have resulted from these findings. The differences among findings, conclusions, and recommendations can be illustrated by the following examples:

Findings lead to conclusions; conclusions lead to recommendations.

Finding: The computer monitor sometimes goes blank during operation.
Conclusion: The computer is broken.
Recommendation: We should repair the computer before May 3, when payroll processing begins.

Finding: Our East Coast branch has lost money four out of the past five years.
Conclusion: Our East Coast branch is not profitable.
Recommendation: We should close our East Coast branch.

While all reports will have some form of concluding remarks, not all reports contain recommendations, and not all reports require a summary at the end of the document. If your report only analyzes the information presented and does not make recommendations, your final section may be entitled "Conclusions," "Summary," or "Summary and Conclusions." Moreover, if your report includes an executive summary at the beginning, there is no need to provide another detailed summary at the end. Instead, merely offer a very general overview of your key findings and some concluding remarks, perhaps reminding the reader of the importance of the document, and, if relevant, discussing what elements of your findings deserve further study.

model32

REPORT FINDINGS

Offers a brief preview of the major topics that follow.

Uses headings to introduce topics and subtopics.

Introduces and discusses first subtopic: its context, its importance, and its implications to reader.

Introduces figures and tables by number.

FINDINGS

For a benefit program to achieve its goals, employees must be aware of the benefits provided. Thus, the first section that follows discusses the employees' familiarity with their benefits, as well as the effectiveness of Aegon's present method of communicating benefits and those methods that employees would prefer. An effective benefit package must also include benefits that are relevant to employee needs. Thus, the employees' opinions of the importance of and their satisfaction with each benefit offered are discussed next. The section concludes with a discussion of those benefits employees would like to see added to the package at Aegon.

KNOWLEDGE OF BENEFITS

One study has shown that employees' satisfaction with benefits is directly correlated with their knowledge of such benefits.[2] Thus, an indication of the staff's level of familiarity with their benefits and suggestions for improving communication were solicited.

FAMILIARITY WITH BENEFITS

Numerous methods are presently being used to communicate fringe benefits to employees. According to Lewis Rigby, our Human Resources Manager, every new employee in the company views a 30-minute video entitled "In Addition to Your Salary" as part of the new-employee orientation. Also, the major benefits are explained during one-on-one counselling on the first day of orientation.

The staff were asked to rate their level of familiarity with each benefit. As shown in Table 1, most staff believe that most benefits have been adequately communicated to them. At least three-quarters of the staff are familiar with all major benefits except for the long-term disability insurance, which is familiar only to a slight majority, and auto insurance, which is familiar only to one-third of respondents.

3

[2]Donna Jean Egan and Annette Kantelzoglou (eds.), *Human Resources.* Varsity Books, New Haven, CT, 2005.

model32

(CONTINUED)

1   **TABLE 1. LEVEL OF FAMILIARITY WITH BENEFIT PROGRAM**

Benefit	Level of Familiarity (%)				
	Familiar	Unfamiliar	Undecided	No Response	Total
Sick leave	94	4	1	1	100
Vacation	94	4	1	1	100
Paid holidays	92	4	3	1	100
Extended medical insurance	90	7	2	0	100
Life insurance	84	10	5	1	100
Retirement	84	11	4	1	100
Long-term disability insurance	55	33	12	1	100
Auto insurance	36	57	6	15	100

At least four-fifths of the employees are familiar with all major benefits except for long-term disability insurance, which is familiar to only a slight majority. The low level of knowledge about auto insurance (36 percent familiarity) may be explained by the fact that this benefit started just six weeks before the survey was taken.

In general, benefit familiarity is not related to length of employment at Aegon. Most employees are familiar with most benefits regardless of their length of employment. However, as shown in Figure 1, the only benefit for which this is not true is life insurance. The longer a person has been employed at Aegon, the more likely he or she is to know about this benefit.

2   **FIGURE 1. KNOWLEDGE OF LIFE INSURANCE BENEFITS**

3

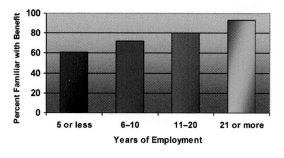

4

Uses visuals to enhance readability.

Provides evidence for any conclusions drawn; interprets that evidence in light of report's purpose.

Gives each visual a number, a meaningful title, and clear, helpful labels.

Grammar and Mechanics Notes

1 Position tables and charts immediately after the paragraph that introduces them, whenever possible.

2 Label charts as "figures" and number them independently of table numbers.

3 If a display does not fit completely at the bottom of the page, continue with the text to the bottom of the page and then place the display at the top of the following page.

If you have no executive summary at the beginning of the report, do provide a reasonably detailed summary of all your key findings at the end, just before presenting your conclusions and recommendations. Repeating the main points or arguments immediately before presenting the conclusions and recommendations reinforces the reasonableness of those conclusions and recommendations. To avoid monotony when summarizing, use wording that is different from the original presentation.

Finally, if your report is to contain recommendations, you may choose to separate the conclusions (and/or summary) and the recommendations, or you may group them together under one heading. Whatever the case, ensure that the conclusions stem directly from your findings and that the recommendations stem directly from the conclusions. Provide ample evidence to support all your conclusions and recommendations. Finally, keep in mind that if your report is to contain an executive summary, your recommendations will also be summarized there, although typically not in as much detail as in the recommendations section. An example of the conclusion and recommendations sections of a report is shown in Model 33 on page 403.

An appendix might include supplementary reference material not important enough to go in the body of the report.

Appendix   The appendix is an optional report component that contains supplementary information or documents. For example, in an appendix you might include a copy of the questionnaire and cover letter used to collect data, supplementary tables, forms, or computer printouts that might be helpful to the reader but that are not important enough to include in the body of the report. Label each appendix separately, by letter—for example, "Appendix A: Cover Letter" and "Appendix B: Questionnaire." In the body of the report, refer by letter to any items placed in an appendix. Refer to Model 22 from Chapter 10 on page 358.

References   The reference list contains the complete record of any secondary sources cited in the report. Different disciplines use different formats for citing these references; whichever you choose, be consistent and include enough information so that the reader can easily locate any source if he or she wants to do so. See Model 34 on page 404 for a sample.

A good indication of a report writer's scholarship is the accuracy of the reference list—in terms of both content and format—so proofread this part of your report carefully. The reference list is the very last section of the report.

▪ Developing an Effective Writing Style

CO3. Use an effective writing style.

You can enhance the effectiveness of your written reports by paying attention to your writing style.

Tone

Regardless of the structure of your report, the writing style used is typically more objective and less conversational than, for example, the style of an informal memorandum. Avoid colloquial expressions, attempts at humour, subjectivity, bias, and exaggeration.

NOT: The company *hit the jackpot* with its new MRP program.

BUT: The new MRP program saved the company $125 000 the first year.

model33

CONCLUSIONS AND RECOMMENDATIONS

CONCLUSIONS

1 Nationwide, employee benefits now account for more than a third of all payroll costs. Thus, on the basis of cost alone, an organization's benefit program must be carefully monitored and evaluated.

The problem in this study was to determine the opinions of the nearly 2500 staff employees at Aegon Oil and Gas regarding the employee benefit program. The findings show that staff at Aegon Oil and Gas are extremely knowledgeable about all benefits except long-term disability and automobile insurance; however, a majority would prefer to have an individualized benefit statement instead of the brochures now used to explain the benefit program. They consider paid time off the most important benefit and automobile insurance the least important. A majority are satisfied with all benefits, although retirement benefits generated substantial dissatisfaction. The only additional benefit desired by a majority of the employees is compensation for unused sick leave.

RECOMMENDATIONS

The following recommendations, as well as the findings of this study, should help Aegon's executive team ensure that its benefit program is accomplishing its stated objectives of attracting and retaining high-quality employees and meeting their needs once employed:

1. Distribute this report to all HR managers at Aegon and meet to discuss its findings and recommendations. If this meeting were held within the next month, the necessary follow-up studies could begin soon enough to allow the required changes to be implemented at the start of the next fiscal year.

2

2. Determine the feasibility of generating an annual individualized benefit statement for each staff employee. This will require a follow-up study of similarly sized companies within the oil and gas industry who currently engage in this practice.

3 3. Re-evaluate the attractiveness of the automobile insurance benefit in one year to determine employees' knowledge about, use of, and desire for this benefit. Consider the feasibility of substituting compensation for unused sick leave for the automobile insurance benefit. Again, a study of other companies in the oil and gas industry should provide some insight.

4. Conduct a follow-up study of the retirement benefits at Aegon to determine how competitive they are with those offered by comparable companies.

13

Reminds reader of the importance of the study.

Provides a general overview of the key findings. (A more detailed summary is provided in the executive summary.)

Introduces list of recommendations, reminding reader of their importance.

Enumerates each recommendation. If chronology is important, list each action in the order that it should be performed.

Provides specific actions reader should take to solve the problems identified in the report.

Grammar and Mechanics Notes

1 Note the use of the present tense when summarizing the findings.
2 Leave a blank line between multi-line numbered items.
3 Begin each recommendation with a verb.

model34

REFERENCES

When using APA style, call the bibliography "References."

Put the entries in alphabetical order.

Note the use of lower-case lettering for titles under APA style.

Staff Benefit Program 18

References

1   Abbey Petroleum Industries. (2006). *2005 annual report.* San Francisco: Author.

Adams, J. B. (2005). *Compensation systems.* Boston: Brunswick Press.

Adhams, R., & Stevens, S. (2000). *Personnel management.* Cambridge, MA:
        All-State.

Directory of business and financial services. (2005). New York: Corporate Libraries
        Association.

Ivarson, A., Jr. (2005, September 29). Creating your benefit plan: A primer. *Business
        Month, 75,* 19–31.

Let employees determine their own benefits. (2006, January 12). *Manhattan Times,*
        p. C17.

Market research. (2006). In *The encyclopedia of business* (2nd ed., Vol. 2,
        pp. 436–441). Cleveland, OH: Collins.

National Institute of Mental Health. (2005). *Who pays the piper? Ten years of passing
        the buck* (DHHS Publication No. ADM 82-1195). Washington, DC: U.S.
        Government Printing Office.

Preminger, L. (Executive Producer). (2006, August 5). *The WKVX-TV evening news*
        [Television broadcast]. Los Angeles: Valhalla Broadcasting Co.

Quincy, D. J. (2004, November 13). Maxwell announces new health benefit. New
        York: Maxwell. Retrieved January 14, 2005, from
2   http://www.maxcorp.com/NEWS/2004/f93500.html

Salary survey of service industries. (n.d.). Retrieved July 8, 2006, from BizInfo data-
        base, http://www.bizinfo.com/census.gov/ind.lib/tab-0315.html

Young, L. (2004, June 3). Training doesn't always last. Message posted to
        http://groups.yahoo.com/group/personnel/message/51

18

Grammar and Mechanics Notes

1 Italicize titles of books, journals and magazines.

2 Include the URL and the date accessed for any material borrowed from the Internet.

NOT: He *claimed* that half of his projects involved name-brand advertising.

BUT: He stated that half of his projects involved name-brand advertising.

Pronouns

For most business reports, the use of first- and second-person pronouns is not only acceptable but also quite helpful for achieving an effective writing style. Formal language, however, focuses attention on the information being conveyed instead of on the writer; therefore, reports written in the formal style should use third-person pronouns and avoid using *I, we,* and *you.*

You can avoid the awkward substitution, "the writer," by recasting the sentence. Most often, it is evident that the writer is the person doing the action communicated.

Informal: I recommend that the project be cancelled.

Awkward: The writer recommends that the project be cancelled.

Formal: The project should be cancelled.

Using the passive voice is a common device for avoiding the use of *I* in formal reports, but doing so weakens the impact. Instead, recast the sentence to avoid undue use of the passive voice.

Informal: I interviewed Jan Smith.

Passive: Jan Smith was interviewed.

Formal: In a personal interview, Jan Smith stated . . .

You will probably also want to avoid using *he* as a generic pronoun when referring to an unidentified person. Chapter 5 discusses many ways to avoid such discriminatory language.

> First- and second-person pronouns can be used appropriately in most business reports.

Verb Tense

Use the verb tense (past, present, or future) that is appropriate at the time the reader *reads* the report—not necessarily at the time that you *wrote* the report. Use past tense to describe procedures and to describe the findings of other studies already completed, but use present tense for conclusions from those studies.

When possible, use the stronger present tense to present the data from your study. The rationale for doing so is that we assume our findings continue to be true; thus, the use of the present tense is justified. (If we cannot assume the continuing truth of any findings, we should probably not use them in the study.)

> Verb tenses should reflect the reader's (not the writer's) time frame.

NOT: These findings *will be discussed* later in this report.

BUT: These findings *are discussed* later in the report. (*But:* These findings *were discussed* earlier in this report.)

NOT: Three-fourths of the managers *believed* quality circles *were* effective at the plant.

BUT: Three-fourths of the managers *believe* that quality circles *are* effective at the plant.

Procedure: Nearly 500 people *responded* to this survey.

Finding: Only 11 percent of the managers *received* any specific training on the new procedure. *(The event happened in the past.)*

Conclusion: Most managers *do not receive* any specific training on the new procedures.

Emphasis and Subordination

Only rarely does all of the data consistently point to one conclusion. More likely, you will have a mixed bag of data from which you will have to evaluate the relative merits of each point. For your report to achieve its objective, the reader must evaluate the importance of each point in the same way that you did. At the very least, your reader must be *aware* of the importance you attached to each point. Therefore, you should employ the emphasis and subordination techniques learned in Chapter 5 when discussing your findings.

By (a) making sure that the amount of space devoted to a topic reflects the importance of that topic, (b) carefully positioning your major ideas, and (c) using language that directly tells what is more and less important, you can help ensure that you and your reader have the same perspective when your reader analyzes the data.

Use emphasis and subordination ethically—not to pressure the reader.

Use emphasis and subordination to let the reader know what you consider most and least important—but *not* to unduly sway the reader. If the data honestly leads to a strong, definite conclusion, then by all means make your conclusion strong and definite. But if the data permits only a tentative conclusion, then say so.

Coherence

One of the difficulties of writing any long document—especially when the document is drafted in sections and then put together—is making the finished product read smoothly and coherently, like a unified presentation rather than a cut-and-paste job. The problem is even greater for team-written reports (see "Team Writing" on page 43 of Chapter 2).

Use previews, summaries and transitions to achieve coherence and unity.

One effective way to achieve coherence in a report is to use previews, summaries, and transitions regularly. At the beginning of each major section, preview what is discussed in that section. At the conclusion of each section, summarize what was presented and provide a smooth transition to the next topic. For long sections, the preview, summary, and transition might each be a separate paragraph; for short sections, a sentence might suffice.

Note how preview, summary, and transition are used in the following example of a report section opening and closing.

Training of System Users

The training program can be evaluated in terms of the opinions of the users and in terms of the cost of training in relation to the cost of the system itself. . . . *(After this topic preview, several paragraphs follow that discuss the opinions of the users and the cost of the training program.)*

Even though a slight majority of users now feel competent in using the system, the training provided falls far short of the 20 percent of total system cost recommended by experts. This low level of training may have affected the precision of the data generated by the MRP system. *(The first sentence contains the summary of this section; the second, the transition to the next.)*

Don't depend on your heading structure for coherence. Your report should read smoothly and coherently without the headings. Avoid repeating the exact words of the heading in the subsequent narrative, and avoid using the heading as part of the narrative.

NOT: **THE TWO DEPARTMENTS SHOULD BE MERGED.** The reason is that there is a duplication of services.

NOT: **THE TWO DEPARTMENTS SHOULD BE MERGED.** The two departments should be merged. The reason is that there is a duplication of services.

BUT: **THE TWO DEPARTMENTS SHOULD BE MERGED.** Merging the two departments would eliminate the duplication of services.

Always introduce a topic before dividing it into subtopics. Thus, you should never have one heading following another without some intervening text. (The exception to this guideline is that the heading "Introduction" may be used immediately after the report title or subtitle.) Preview for the reader how the topic will be divided before you actually make the division.

Paraphrasing Versus Direct Quotation

When including the ideas of another person in your report, avoid the temptation to become lazy and simply repeat everything in the author's exact words. It is unlikely that the problem you're trying to solve and the problem discussed by the author mesh exactly. More than likely, you'll need to take bits and pieces of information from numerous sources and integrate them into a context appropriate for your specific purposes.

A **paraphrase** is a summary or restatement of a passage in your own words. A **direct quotation**, on the other hand, contains the exact words of another. Use direct quotations (always enclosed in quotation marks) only for definitions or for text that is so precise, clear, or otherwise noteworthy that it cannot be improved on. Most of your references to secondary data should be in the form of paraphrases. Paraphrasing involves more than just rearranging the words or leaving out a word or two. It requires, instead, that you understand the writer's idea and then restate it in your own language.

CO4. Provide appropriate documentation when using someone else's work.

Use direct quotations sparingly.

Documenting Your Sources

Documentation is the identification of sources by giving credit to another person, either in the text or in the reference list, for using his or her words or ideas. You may, of course, use the words and ideas of others, provided such use is properly documented; in fact, for many business reports such secondary information may be the *only* data you use. You must, however, provide appropriate documentation whenever you quote, paraphrase, or summarize someone else's work (see Spotlight 26, "Who Said So?" on page 408).

Plagiarism is the use of another person's words or ideas without giving proper credit. Writings are considered the writer's legal property; someone else who wrongfully uses such property is guilty of theft. Plagiarism, therefore, carries stiff

Who Said So?

Jay Leno, in his book *Leading with My Chin,* tells a humorous story about himself on the old Dinah Shore television show. The only problem is that the incident didn't happen to Leno but to a fellow comedian. When questioned later about the incident, Leno said he liked the story so much that he paid the comedian $1000 for the right to publish it as his own.

Plagiarism is a potential problem for anyone who communicates. Consider, for example, these other recent incidents:

- In 2006, Little, Brown and Company cancelled a six-figure book deal and pulled the novel *How Opal Mehta Got Kissed, Got Wild, and Got a Life* by 19-year-old Harvard University student Kaavya Viswanathan, after it was revealed that her novel contained passages similar to Meg Cabot's 2000 novel *The Princess Diaries,* as well as similarities to Sophie Kinsella's book *Can You Keep a Secret?*

  In Cabot's novel, this passage appears on page 12: "There isn't a single inch of me that hasn't been pinched, cut, filed, painted, sloughed, blown dry, or moisturized. . . . Because I don't look a thing like Mia Thermopolis. Mia Thermopolis never had fingernails. Mia Thermopolis never had blond highlights."

  In Viswanathan's book, page 59 reads: "Every inch of me had been cut, filed, steamed, exfoliated, polished, painted, or moisturized. I didn't look a thing like Opal Mehta. Opal Mehta didn't own five pairs of shoes so expensive they could have been traded in for a small sailboat."[1]

- In 2004, Ralph Klein, then Premier of Alberta, was accused of plagiarism for failing to properly cite Internet sources he'd used in writing a report on Chilean history. Athabasca University, where Klein was taking distance courses, investigated the matter and cleared Klein of the charges, citing the errors as minor and unintentional. The incident prompted many universities to re-examine, and in some cases toughen, their policies covering plagiarism.

penalties. In the classroom, the penalty ranges from failure in a course to expulsion from school. On the job, the penalty for plagiarism ranges from loss of credibility to loss of employment.

Provide a reference citation for material that came from others, unless that material is common knowledge or can be verified easily.

What Needs to Be Documented   Except as noted here, all material in your report that comes from secondary sources must be documented; that is, enough information about the original source must be given to enable the reader to locate the source if he or she so desires. If the secondary source is published (for example, a journal article), the documentation should appear as a reference citation. If the source is unpublished, sufficient documentation can generally be given in the narrative, making a formal citation unnecessary, as in these examples:

> According to Board Policy 91-18b, all position vacancies above the level of C-3 must be posted internally at least two weeks prior to being advertised.

> The contractor's letter of May 23, 2003, stated, "We agree to modify Blueprint 3884 by widening the southeast entrance from 3 metres to 4 metres for a total additional charge of $273.50."

- The *Wall Street Journal* reported that almost half of one of the best-selling business books in history, *The One-Minute Manager,* was lifted nearly verbatim by the authors without attribution from another writer's *Wall Street Journal* article.

- The head of the Harvard University psychiatric hospital resigned when it was found he had committed plagiarism in four papers he had published.

- The director of a university law school resigned immediately after admitting he used "substantial unattributed quotations" in a law review article.

- In *Pacific Rim Trade,* a book published by the American Management Association, the writers stated that Lakewood Industries in Minnesota sells the most chopsticks in Japan. *Forbes* magazine investigated and found that the company doesn't sell the most chopsticks in Japan, never did, and never will—because it went bankrupt trying to perfect a technique for manufacturing chopsticks.

Cite and Check Your Sources

To avoid problems of dishonesty, always cite your secondary sources of information. You can, of course, go too far and provide excessive documentation. Such a practice not only is distracting but also leaves the impression that the writer is not an original thinker. As an example of excessive documentation, a study of criminal procedure published in the *Georgetown Law Journal* was accompanied by 3917 footnotes!

In addition to citing your sources, you should also verify any information you include in a report, regardless of who said it. For example, despite widespread belief to the contrary,

- Voltaire never said, "I disapprove of what you say, but I will defend to the death your right to say it."

- Leo Durocher never said, "Nice guys finish last."

- W.C. Fields never said, "Anybody who hates children and dogs can't be all bad."

- James Cagney never used the line "You dirty rat" in any of his movies. Nor did Humphrey Bogart ever say the line "Play it again, Sam."

- Sherlock Holmes never uttered "Elementary, my dear Watson" in any of Arthur Conan Doyle's novels.

Give Credit Where Credit Is Due

As a competent communicator, you must give appropriate credit to your sources and ensure the accuracy of your data. Make certain that you have answered completely and fairly the question "Who said so?" Your organization's reputation and welfare—not to mention your own—demand no less.[2]

Occasionally, enough information can be given in the narrative so that a formal citation is unnecessary even for published sources. This format is most appropriate when only one or two sources are used in a report.

Widmark made this very argument in a guest editorial entitled "Here We Go Again" in the May 4, 2002, *National Post* (p. A12).

After a study has been cited once, it may be mentioned again in continuous discussion on the same page or even on the next pages without further citation if no ambiguity results. If several pages intervene or if ambiguity might result, the citation should be given again.

What Does Not Need to Be Documented   The use of two types of material by others does not need to be documented: (1) facts that are common knowledge to the readers of your report and (2) facts that can be verified easily.

Dell Computer is a large manufacturer of microcomputers.

The TSE closed at 10 506 on November 8.

But such statements as "Sales of the original Dell computer were disappointing" and "Only 4000 Dell computers were sold last year" would need to be documented. If in doubt about whether you need to document, provide the citation.

Forms of Documentation   The three major forms for documenting the ideas, information, and quotations of other people in a report are endnotes, footnotes, and author-date references (see the Reference Manual at the back of this text for examples and formatting conventions). Let the nature of the report and the needs of the reader dictate the documentation method used. Regardless of the method you select, ensure that the citations are accurate, complete, and consistently formatted and that your bibliography format is consistent with your documentation format.

1. *Endnotes:* The endnote format uses superscript (raised) numbers to identify secondary sources in the text and then provides the actual citations in a numbered list entitled "Notes" at the end of the report. The endnotes are numbered consecutively throughout the report. Some readers prefer the endnote format because it avoids the clutter of footnotes and because it's easy to use.

   In the past, using endnotes for a long or complex report was somewhat risky because of the possibility of introducing errors when revising text. Every time text with a reference was inserted, deleted, or moved, all following endnote references in the text and in the list at the back of the report had to be renumbered. Today, however, word processors have an endnote feature that automatically numbers and keeps track of endnote references. Still, some readers prefer one of the other formats because endnotes provide no clues in the text regarding the source.

2. *Footnotes:* For years, footnotes were the traditional method of citing sources, especially in academic reports. A bibliographic footnote provides the complete reference at the bottom of the page on which the citation occurs in the text. Thus, a reader interested in exploring the source does not have to turn to the back of the report. Today's word processors can format footnotes almost painlessly—automatically numbering and positioning each note correctly. Some readers, however, find the presence of footnotes on the text page distracting.

The author-date format is preferred by many users of business reports.

3. *Author-Date Format:* Some business report readers prefer the author-date format of documentation, regarding the method as a reasonable compromise between endnotes (which provide *no* reference information on the text page) and footnotes (which provide *all* the reference information on the text page). In the author-date format, the writer inserts at an appropriate point in the text the last name of the author and the year of publication in parentheses. Complete bibliographic information is then included in the Notes or References section at the end of the report.

Distortion by Omission

Do not use quotations out of context.

It would be unethical to leave an inaccurate impression, even when what you do report is true. Sins of *omission* are as serious as sins of *commission*. Distortion by omission can occur when using quotations out of context, when omitting certain relevant background information, or when including only the most extreme or most interesting data.

It would be inappropriate, for example, to quote extensively from a survey that was conducted 15 years ago without first establishing for the reader that the findings are still valid. Likewise, it would be inappropriate to quote a finding from one study and not discuss the fact that four similar studies reached opposite conclusions.

Be especially careful to quote and paraphrase accurately from interview sources. Provide enough information to ensure that the passage reflects the interviewee's *intention*. Here are examples of possible distortions:

Original Quotation:	"I think the Lancelot is an excellent car for anyone who does not need to worry about fuel economy."
Distortion:	Johnson stated that the Lancelot "is an excellent car."
Worse Distortion:	Johnson stated that the Lancelot "is an excellent car for anyone."

■ Revising

Once you have produced a first draft of your report, put it away for a few days. Doing so will enable you to view the draft with a fresh perspective and perhaps find a more effective means of communicating your ideas to the reader. Don't try to correct all problems in one review. Instead, look at this process as having three steps—revising first for content, then for style, and finally for correctness.

Revise first for content. Make sure you've included sufficient information to support each point, that you've included no extraneous information (regardless of how interesting it might be or how hard you worked to gather the information), that all information is accurate, and that the information is presented in an efficient and logical sequence. Keep the purpose of the report and the reader's needs and desires in mind as you review for content

Once you're satisfied with the content of the report, revise for style (refer to Checklist 5 on page 172). Ensure that your writing is clear and that you have used short, simple, vigorous, and concise words. Check to see whether you have used a variety of sentence types and have relied on active and passive voice appropriately. Do your paragraphs have unity and coherence, and are they of reasonable length? Have you maintained an overall tone of confidence, courtesy, sincerity, and objectivity? Finally, review your draft to ensure that you have used non-discriminatory language and appropriate emphasis and subordination.

After you're confident about the content and style of your draft, revise once more for correctness. This revision step, known as *editing*, identifies and resolves any problems with grammar, spelling, punctuation, and word usage—the topics covered in the LABs in the Reference Manual at the back of this text. (See Communication Snapshot 9 on page 412 for information about which writing distractions executives consider most serious.) Do not risk losing credibility with the reader by careless English usage. If possible, have a colleague review your draft to catch any errors you may have overlooked.

CO5. Revise, format, and proofread the report.

Adopt a consistent, logical format, keeping the needs of the reader in mind.

■ Formatting

The physical format of your report (font, type size, margins, spacing, and the like) depends to a certain extent on the length and complexity of the report and the

communication snapshot 9

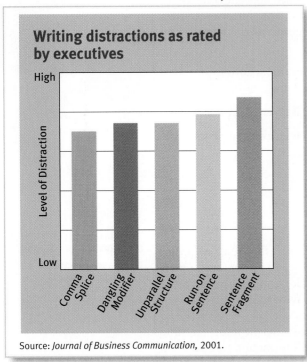

Writing distractions as rated by executives

Level of Distraction — High / Low

Comma Splice · Dangling Modifier · Unparallel Structure · Run-on Sentence · Sentence Fragment

Source: *Journal of Business Communication*, 2001.

format preferred by either the organization or the reader. Whatever your readers' preferences and your "house rules" regarding format, one of your main goals in putting together any business document is to build and retain credibility with your audience. Do not underestimate the importance of a clean, professional looking, readable report on your and your organization's credibility. Additionally, do not underestimate the time it takes to accomplish this goal. Novice writers too often leave considerations over format until just hours before a report is due. This is a mistake. Leave yourself at least a day to finalize the format of your report, after all other revisions have been completed. The formatting stage often takes several iterations to get right, as format changes in one part of the report often have a "domino effect" on the format of other parts of the report.

When formatting, your main considerations are those covered under Effective Page Design on page 167 of Chapter 5. In addition to reviewing those guidelines, pay particular attention to the format of your headings, which we discuss below.

Formatting Headings

We've already discussed the difference between talking and generic headings, on page 385. We've also offered some guidelines on how to ensure headings are parallel, balanced, and of reasonable length and number. Model 35 on page 413 offers some further guidelines on the formatting of headings.

The number of levels of headings used will vary from report to report. Memo reports may have only first-level subheadings, with no part titles or other headings. Long reports may have as many as four levels of headings. One standard format for the various levels is given here. Recognize, however, that the format presented here is only one of several that might be used.

Consistency and readability are your major goals. For example, be sure that all of your first-level headings are formatted consistently; if they are not, the reader may not be able to tell which headings are superior or subordinate to other headings. Regardless of the format used, make sure the reader can instantly tell which are major headings and which are minor headings. You can differentiate among headings by using different fonts, font sizes, styles (such as bold or italic), and horizontal alignment.

"Richard, let's have a talk about margins and report lengths."

5-cm top margin

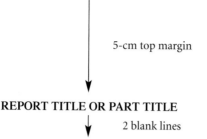

REPORT TITLE OR PART TITLE

2 blank lines

Using a slightly larger font size than used for the body of the report, centre a part title (for example, "Introduction" or "References") in all capitals and in bold on a new page, leaving a 5-cm top margin. Double-space titles of two or more lines, using an inverted pyramid style (the first line longer). Leave two blank lines below the part title.

2 blank lines

FIRST-LEVEL SUBHEADING

1 blank line

Using the same font size as that used in the body of the report, bold first-level subheadings. (If flush left, the headings may be in capitals; if centred, lower-case letters are preferred to better distinguish first-level subheadings from report and part titles.) Leave two blank lines above and one blank line below the heading.

2 blank lines

Second-Level Subheading

1 blank line

Begin the second-level subheading at the left margin. Use bold type and capitalize the first letter of the first and last words and all other words except articles, prepositions with four or fewer letters, and conjunctions. Leave two blank lines above and one blank line below the heading.

2 blank lines

Third-Level Subheading. Begin third-level subheadings at the left margin. Bold and italicize the heading. Capitalize the first letter of major words, as described above. Leave two blank lines above the heading and a period and one space after the subheading. Begin typing the text on the same line.

Source: Journal of Business Communication, 2001.

model35

FORMATTING HEADINGS

Part titles introduce major sections of the report.

First-level subheadings may be in all caps or lower case.

Third-level subheadings are frequently italicized.

Incorporating Illustrations

The Reference Manual at the back of this text provides both examples and guidelines for the design and integration of various illustrations, such as graphs and tables. As you are finalizing your report format, use the following checklist to ensure your illustrations are effectively introduced and presented.

1. Are all illustrations directly relevant to the discussion? If an illustration merely contains supplemental information, it should be placed in an appendix.
2. Has each illustration been introduced by number *before* it appears? Use phrasing such as:

   > As shown in Table 1, report headings can take two forms: talking and generic.

3. Does each illustration have a title and a number?
4. Is each illustration clearly labelled so its meaning is readily apparent to the reader?
5. Is each illustration surrounded by sufficient white space?
6. Have you avoided splitting an illustration between two pages? If not enough space is available on the page for the display, continue with the narrative to the bottom of the page and then place the display at the very top of the following page.
7. Are all illustrations correctly documented? The source of each borrowed illustration should be identified directly beneath the illustration.

■ Proofreading

First impressions are important. Even before reading the first line of your report, the reader will have formed an initial impression of the report—and of *you*. Make this impression a positive one by ensuring that the report carries with it a professional appearance.

After making all your revisions and formatting the various pages, give each page one final proofread. Check closely for typographical errors. Check for appearance. Have you arranged the pages in correct order and stapled them neatly? If you're submitting a photocopy, are all the copies legible and of even brightness? Is each page free of wrinkles and smudges?

Do not risk destroying your credibility by failing to proofread carefully.

Ensure that in moving passages about, you did not inadvertently delete a line or two or repeat a passage. Run spell check a final time after making all changes. (Remember, however, that spell check will not locate an incorrect word that is spelled correctly.) If you have a grammar software program, evaluate your writing electronically. The grammar check will check for use of passive voice, sentence length, misuse of words, unmatched punctuation (for example, an opening parenthesis not followed by a closing parenthesis), and readability. Use every aid at your disposal to ensure that your report reflects the highest standards of scholarship, critical thinking, and care.

In short, let your pride of authorship show through in every facet of your report. Appearances and details count. Review your entire document to ensure that you can answer "yes" to every question contained in Checklist 14.

Reviewing Your Report Draft

Front Matter

✔ Does the title page include an accurate, honest, descriptive title, the name(s) of the recipient, the author's name, and the date?

✔ Does the transmittal document provide a courteous, appreciative introduction to the report?

✔ Is the executive summary short, descriptive, and in proportion to the report itself?

✔ Is the table of contents accurate, with correct page numbers and wording that is identical to that used in the report headings?

✔ Does the list of illustrations include table or figure numbers for each visual? Does it include a title for each visual, worded identically to the wording used in the report?

Introduction

✔ Is the research problem or the purpose of the study stated clearly and accurately?

✔ Are the scope and limitations of the study identified?

✔ Are all technical terms, or any terms used in a special way, defined?

✔ Are the procedures discussed in sufficient detail?

Findings

✔ Is the data analyzed completely, accurately, and appropriately?

✔ Is the analysis free of bias and misrepresentation?

✔ Is the data *interpreted* (its importance and implications discussed) rather than just presented?

✔ Are all calculations correct?

✔ Is all relevant data included and all irrelevant data excluded?

✔ Are visual aids correct, needed, clear, appropriately sized and positioned, and correctly labelled?

✔ Is any appended material properly labelled and referred to in the body of the report?

✔ Is the reference list accurate, complete, and appropriately formatted?

Writing Style and Format

✔ Does the overall report take into account the needs and desires of the reader?

✔ Is the material appropriately organized?

✔ Are the headings descriptive, parallel, and appropriate in number?

✔ Are emphasis and subordination used effectively?

✔ Does each major section contain a preview, summary, and transition?

✔ Has proper verb tense been used throughout?

✔ Has an appropriate level of formality been used?

✔ Are all references to secondary sources properly documented?

✔ Is each needed report component included and in an appropriate format?

✔ Is the length of the report appropriate?

✔ Are the paragraphs of an appropriate length?

✔ Have the principles of document design been followed to enhance the report's effectiveness?

✔ Is the report free from spelling, grammar, and punctuation errors?

✔ Does the overall report provide a positive first impression and reflect care, neatness, and scholarship?

Summary, Conclusions, and Recommendations

✔ Is the wording used in the summary different from that used earlier to present the data initially?

✔ Are the conclusions drawn supported by ample, credible evidence?

✔ Do the conclusions answer the questions or issues raised in the introduction?

✔ Are the recommendations reasonable in light of the conclusions?

✔ Does the report end with a sense of completion and convey an impression that the project is important?

Back Matter

✔ Is your bibliography accurate, complete, and appropriately formatted?

✔ Is any appended material properly labelled and referred to in the body of the report?

The **3Ps**
Problem, Process, Product

A SECTION OF A REPORT

Problem

You are a manager at a software development house that publishes communication software for the HAL and Pear microcomputers. Together, these two computers account for about 90 percent of the business market. In 2006, you were asked to survey users of communication software—a repeat of a similar study you undertook in 2001.

You conducted the survey using the same questionnaire and same procedures from the 2001 study. Now you've gathered the data, along with the comparable data collected in 2001, and have organized it roughly into draft tables, one of which is shown in Figure 11.3. You're now ready to put this table into final report format and analyze its contents.

FIGURE 11.3   Draft Table

Q. From what source did you obtain your last software program?												
	2001						**2006**					
	Total		**HAL**		**Pear**		**Total**		**HAL**		**Pear**	
Source	N	%	N	%	N	%	N	%	N	%	N	%
Online	28	21.2	24	26.1	4	10.0	60	41.1	25	30.9	35	53.9
Mail-order company	3	2.3	2	2.2	1	2.5	4	2.7	2	2.5	2	3.1
Retail outlet	70	53.0	46	50.0	24	60.0	63	43.2	44	54.3	19	29.2
Software publisher	9	6.8	4	4.3	5	12.5	10	6.8	4	4.9	6	9.2
Unauthorized copy	21	15.9	15	16.3	6	15.0	6	4.1	3	3.7	3	4.6
Other	1	.8	1	1.1	0	0.0	3	2.1	3	3.7	0	0.0
Total	132	100.0	92	100.0	40	100.0	146	100.0	81	100.0	65	100.0

1. **Table Format**

a. Examine the format of your draft table—the arrangement of columns and rows. Should you change anything for the final table?

   First, the year columns (2001 and 2006) should be transposed. The new data is more important than the old data, so putting it first will emphasize it.

   Second, the rows need to be rearranged. They're now in alphabetical order but should be rearranged in descending order according to the first amount column—the 2006 total column. Doing this will put the most important data first in the table.

b. Assuming that you will have many tables in your final report, is there some way to condense the information in this table without undue loss of precision or detail?

   Although the number of respondents is important, the readers of my report will be much more interested in the percentages. Therefore, I'll give only the total number of respondents for each column and put that figure immediately under each column heading.

   Also, I see immediately that very few people obtained their software from mail-order companies either in 2001 or 2006, so I'll combine that category with the "Other" category.

   These changes are shown in Figure 11.4.

FIGURE 11.4   Draft Report Table

Source	2006			2001		
	Total (*N* = 146)	HAL (*N* = 81)	Pear (*N* = 65)	Total (*N* = 132)	HAL (*N* = 92)	Pear (*N* = 40)
Retail outlet	43	54	29	53	50	60
Online	41	31	54	21	26	10
Software publisher	7	5	9	7	4	13
Unauthorized copy	4	3	5	16	17	15
Other	5	7	3	3	3	2
Total	100	100	100	100	100	100

2. **Table Interpretation**

a. Study the table in Figure 11.4. If you had space to make only one statement about this table, what would it be?

   Retail outlets and online companies are equally important sources for obtaining software, together accounting for more than four-fifths of all sources.

b. What other 2006 data should you discuss in your narrative?

> HAL and Pear users obtain their software in different ways: the majority of HAL users obtain theirs from retail outlets, whereas the majority of Pear users obtain theirs from online firms.

c. What should you point out in comparing 2006 data with 2001 data?

> The market share for retail outlets decreased by almost 20 percent from 2001 to 2006, whereas the market share for online companies almost doubled, increasing by 95 percent.
>
> Also, the use of unauthorized copies appears to be decreasing (although the actual figures are probably somewhat higher than these self-reported figures).

3. **Report Writing**

a. Develop an effective talking heading and an effective generic heading for this section of the report. Which one will you use?

> *Talking Heading:* **ONLINE ORDERS CATCHING UP WITH RETAIL SALES**
>
> *Generic Heading:* **SOURCES OF SOFTWARE PURCHASES**
>
> Because I do not know personally the readers of the report and their preferences, I'll make the conservative choice and use a generic heading.

b. Compose an effective topic (preview) sentence for this section.

> Respondents were asked to indicate the source of the last software program they purchased.

c. Where will you position the table for this section?

> At the end of the first paragraph that refers to the table.

d. What verb tense will you use in this section?

> Past tense for the procedures; present tense for the findings.

e. Assume that the next report section discusses the cost of software. Compose an effective summary/transition sentence for this section of the report.

> Perhaps the increasing reliance on online purchases is one reason that the cost of communication software has decreased since 2001.

SOURCES OF SOFTWARE PURCHASES

Respondents were asked to indicate the source of the last software program they purchased. As shown in Table 8, retail outlets and online companies are now equally important sources for obtaining software, together accounting for more than four-fifths of all sources. HAL and Pear users obtain their software in different ways: the majority of HAL users obtain theirs from retail outlets, whereas the majority of Pear users obtain theirs online.

TABLE 8. SOURCE OF LAST SOFTWARE PROGRAM
(In Percentages)

Source	2006			2001		
	Total (N = 146)	HAL (N = 81)	Pear (N = 65)	Total (N = 132)	HAL (N = 92)	Pear (N = 40)
Retail outlet	43	54	29	53	50	60
Online	41	31	54	21	26	10
Software publisher	7	5	9	7	4	13
Unauthorized copy	4	3	5	16	17	15
Other	5	7	3	3	3	2
Total	100	100	100	100	100	100

Retail outlets have decreased in popularity (down 10 percent) since 2001, whereas online sources have dramatically increased in popularity (up 20 percent). Also, the use of unauthorized copies appears to be decreasing (although the actual figure is probably somewhat higher than these self-reported figures).

Perhaps the increasing reliance on online purchases is one reason that the cost of communication software has declined since 2001.

COST OF SOFTWARE

■ Summary

co1. Determine an appropriate report structure and organization.

The most common report formats are manuscript (for formal reports) and letter or memorandum (for informal reports). The most common plans for organizing the findings of a study are by time, location, importance, and criteria. Conclusions should be presented at the beginning of the report unless the reader prefers the indirect plan, the reader will not be receptive toward the conclusions, or the topic is complex. Report headings should be composed carefully—in terms of their type, parallelism, length, and number.

co2. Draft the report body and supplementary pages.

The body of the report consists of the introduction, findings (the major component of the report), and, as needed, the summary, conclusions, and recommendations. Long, formal reports might also require such supplementary components as a title page, transmittal document, executive summary, table of contents, appendix, and reference list.

co3. Use an effective writing style.

Use an objective writing style, appropriate pronouns, and verb tenses that reflect the reader's time frame (rather than the writer's). Use emphasis and subordination techniques to help alert the reader to what you consider important; and use preview, summary, and transitional devices to help maintain coherence.

co4. Provide appropriate documentation when using someone else's work.

Use direct quotations sparingly; most references to secondary data should be paraphrases. Provide appropriate documentation whenever you quote, paraphrase, or summarize someone else's work by using endnotes, footnotes, or the author-date method of citation. Do not omit important, relevant information from the report.

co5. Revise, format, and proofread the report.

Delay revising the report until a few days after completing the first draft. Revise in three distinct steps: first for content, then for style, and finally for correctness. The report's format should enhance the report's appearance and readability and should be based on the organization's and reader's preferences. Unless directed otherwise, follow generally accepted formatting guidelines for margins, report headings, and pagination. Use a simple, consistent design and make generous use of white space. After all revisions and formatting have been completed, give each page one final proofreading. Make sure the final report reflects the highest standards of scholarship, critical thinking, and pride of authorship.

■ Key Terms

You should be able to define the following terms in your own words and give an original example of each.

conclusions (383)

direct quotation (407)

documentation (407)

executive summary (393)

generic heading (386)

paraphrase (407)

plagiarism (407)

talking heading (385)

transmittal document (390)

■ Exercises

1 **The 3Ps (Problem, Process, and Product) Model: Communication Applications in International Development**   When Kent Schroeder writes a report about an international development project, he goes beyond the bare facts and figures. He documents the nature of activities and the results these activities generate that improve the lives of people in the developing world. Before Schroeder begins to draft any report, he starts by analyzing his audience, selecting an appropriate report structure, and organizing his points in a logical order. No report leaves his office without being proofread to catch the tiniest error.

Problem

As a colleague of Schroeder's working on an agricultural project in Africa, you coordinate the recruitment of Canadian technical experts. These technical experts travel to Africa for short assignments to provide expertise and training to project personnel. Over the last year, six technical experts have undertaken assignments for the project. The individual mission reports written by each technical expert indicate that these assignments were very successful. Given this success, you want to recommend to the project management team that the number of technical experts be increased in the following year. As you sit down at your computer to write a recommendation report for the project management team, which includes both Canadians and Africans, you look again at the six mission reports you received from the technical experts.

Process

a. What is the purpose of your report?
b. Describe your audience.
c. What data will you include in your report?
d. Will you use talking or generic headings? Why?
e. Will you use a transmittal letter or memo? Why?

Product

Using your knowledge of reports, research and prepare this two-page report in memorandum format.

2 **Constructing Tables**   Next year Broadway Productions will move its headquarters from Toronto to Mississauga, Ontario, in the building where Golden Horseshoe Bank occupies the first floor. The bank hopes to secure many Broadway Productions employees as customers and has conducted a survey to determine their banking habits. The handwritten figures on the questionnaire in Figure 11.5 show the number of respondents who checked each alternative.

All exercises require the application of all five chapter objectives shown at the beginning of this chapter.

a. Is a table needed to present the information in Question 1?
b. Would any cross-tabulation analyses help readers understand the data in this questionnaire? Explain.
c. Construct a table that presents the important information from Question 4 of the questionnaire in a logical, helpful, and efficient manner. Give the table an appropriate title and arrange it in final report format.

figure11.5
Survey Results

BROADWAY PRODUCTIONS SURVEY

1. Do you currently have an account at Golden Horseshoe Bank?
   58 yes
   170 no

2. At which of the following institutions do you currently have an account?
   (Please check all that apply.)
   201 commercial bank
   52 employee credit union
   75 savings and loan association
   6 other (please specify: _____)
   18 none

3. In terms of convenience, which one of the following bank locations do you consider
   most important in selecting your main bank?
   70 near home
   102 near office
   12 near shopping
   31 on way to and from work
   13 other (please specify: _____)

4. How important do you consider each of the following banking services?

	Very Important	Somewhat Important	Not Important
Bank credit card	88	132	8
Check-guarantee card	74	32	122
Convenient ATM machines	143	56	29
Drive-in service	148	47	33
Free checking	219	9	0
Overdraft privileges	20	187	21
Personal banker	40	32	156
Telephone transfer	6	20	202
Trust department	13	45	170

5. If you have changed banks within the past three years, what was the major reason
   for the change?
   33 relocation of residence
   4 relocation of bank
   18 dissatisfaction with bank service
   7 other (please specify: _____)

   *Thank you so much for your cooperation. Please return this questionnaire in the enclosed envelope to Customer
   Service Department, Golden Horseshoe Bank, P.O. Box 1086, Mississauga, ON, L5L 6T8.*

3 **A Report Section**   Review Exercise 2c. You have constructed your report table
and analyzed the data. Now you are ready to write this section of the report.

   a. Compose an effective talking heading and an effective generic heading for
      this section of the report. Which one will you use?
   b. Compose an effective topic sentence for this section.
   c. Compose the sentence that contains your recommendation.
   d. Assume that the next section of the report discusses reasons for changing
      banks. Compose an effective summary/transition sentence for this section
      of the report.

Prepare this section of your report (one to three paragraphs). Include the table in the appropriate position. Submit both your report section and your responses to the process activities to your instructor.

4 **Organizing the Report—Outlining**   Using the method of outlining discussed in the chapter, develop an outline of this chapter using the headings and sub-headings.

5 **Report Section—Secondary Statistical Data Furnished**   You are the vice-president of marketing for Excelsior Organics, a small manufacturer of natural consumer products, located in Oshawa, Ontario. Although your firm currently manufactures only soap, toothpaste, and various household cleaners, you have the capability of manufacturing numerous different types of small, inexpensive products. The CEO of your firm has asked you to prepare an extensive report on the feasibility of Excelsior's entering the international market.

One strategy that you're considering is the possibility of becoming a supplier of natural products for a large multinational company. As part of your research, you have located data on the world's 100 largest public companies (see Figure 11.6). You are interested, first, in the non-banking firms in this group that have the largest sales, and, second, in the percentage change in sales from the previous year. (You are not interested in market value and profit data because they are too much affected by extraneous market conditions that are irrelevant to your purposes, and you are not interested in banks, mortgage companies, and holding companies because they would not be potential purchasers of your products.)

Compose the section of your report that presents and discusses this data. Include a table of the 25 largest firms (in terms of sales) that meet your criteria. Discuss the data in terms of the largest companies, their countries of origin, changes in sales from the previous year, and similar factors. Format the section in appropriate report format (beginning with page 5 of your report), provide an effective heading for this section, a topic sentence, summary, and transition to the next section, which discusses the largest companies in terms of the major products they sell.

6 **Supplementary Sections—Going International**   Resume the role of vice-president of marketing for Excelsior (see Exercise 5). Your report to Victor Trillingham, Excelsior's CEO, needs several supplementary sections.

a. Assuming that the report will be submitted tomorrow, prepare a title page.
b. Using the data you analyzed in Exercise 5, draw conclusions and make recommendations. Then write a transmittal memo to accompany this report. Include brief statements of your conclusions and recommendations.
c. Decide whether you need an appendix; if so, note what it should contain.

7 **Short Memorandum Report—New Analysis**   Excelsior's CEO has read your report (see Exercise 6). He would like the data on the 25 companies you identified as potential purchasers analyzed from a different perspective: he wants you to group the companies according to the country in which they are based. Put the data into a table and, from your findings, draw conclusions about the geographic concentration of prospects. Write a brief memorandum report to the CEO; include your table and your conclusion.

figure 11.6 The World's 100 Largest Public Companies

Ranked by market value as of August 29, 2003, as determined by The Wall Street Journal Market Data Group (in millions of U.S. dollars at Dec. 31, 2002, exchange rates; percentage changes based on home currencies)

RANK 2003	RANK 2002	COMPANY (COUNTRY)	MARKET VALUE	FISCAL 2002 SALES*	PERCENT CHANGE FROM 2001	FISCAL 2002 PROFIT*	PERCENT CHANGE FROM 2001
1	1	General Electric (U.S.)	$294,206	$130,732	4%	$15,133	7%
2	2	Microsoft (U.S.)	283,576	32,187	13	9,993	28
3	3	Wal-Mart Stores (U.S.)	259,501	244,524	12	8,039	21
4	4	Exxon Mobil (U.S.)	251,813	204,506	-4	11,011	-27
5	5	Pfizer (U.S.)	236,203	32,373	12	9,459	21
6	8	Citigroup (U.S.)	222,849	92,556	-7	15,276	8
7	21	Intel (U.S.)	187,003	26,764	1	3,117	141
8	9	American International Group (U.S.)	155,382	67,482	9	5,519	3
9	10	Royal Dutch/Shell (Netherlands/U.K.)	154,194	235,598	83	9,419	-13
10	7	BP (U.K.)	151,431	178,721	3	6,845	4
11	6	Johnson & Johnson (U.S.)	147,194	36,298	12	6,597	16
12	16	International Business Machines (U.S.)	141,713	81,186	-2	3,579	-54
13	19	HSBC Holdings (U.K.)	137,526	44,365	-18	6,239	25
14	28	Cisco Systems (U.S.)	134,409	18,878	0	3,578	89
15	25	NTT DoCoMo (Japan)	128,766	40,479	3	1,789	N.A.
16	23	Vodafone Group (U.K.)	124,425	48,949	33	-15,823	N.A.
17	17	Bank of America (U.S.)	118,613	46,724	-12	9,249	36
18	12	GlaxoSmithKline (U.K.)	114,811	34,183	4	6,309	28
19	13	Procter & Gamble (U.S.)	112,858	43,377	8	5,186	19
20	15	Merck (U.S.)	112,834	51,790	9	7,150	-2
21	11	Coca-Cola (U.S.)	107,201	19,564	12	3,050	-23
22	20	Total (France)	105,437	107,554	-3	6,232	-22
23	14	Novartis (Switzerland)	99,873	23,453	2	5,292	4
24	22	Toyota Motor (Japan)	99,429	130,479	9	6,321	35
25	17	Berkshire Hathaway (U.S.)	98,255	41,970	12	4,286	439
26	29	Verizon Communications (U.S.)	96,368	67,625	1	4,079	949
27	24	Nestle (Switzerland)	87,872	64,515	5	5,473	13
28	46	Amgen (U.S.)	84,232	5,523	10	-1,392	N.A.
29	27	Wells Fargo (U.S.)	83,990	28,790	1	5,430	59
30	40	Dell Computer (U.S.)	83,803	35,404	14	2,122	70
31	26	Altria Group (U.S.)	83,464	80,408	-1	11,102	30
32	37	Nokia (Finland)	78,458	31,484	-4	3,546	54
33	30	ChevronTexaco (U.S.)	77,891	98,691	-5	1,132	-71
34	34	PepsiCo (U.S.)	76,525	25,112	7	3,313	24
35	38	Eli Lilly (U.S.)	74,738	11,078	-4	2,708	-4
36	32	SBC Communications (U.S.)	74,671	43,138	-6	5,653	-19
37	39	Home Depot (U.S.)	73,891	58,247	9	3,664	20
38	33	Viacom (U.S.)	72,953	24,606	6	2,207	N.A.
39	53	Roche Holding (Switzerland)	72,562	21,509	2	-2,913	N.A.
40	44	Royal Bank of Scotland (U.K.)	71,808	35,678	0	3,176	6
41	31	United Parcel Service (U.S.)	70,628	31,272	3	3,254	84
42	50	AOL Time Warner (U.S.)	70,219	40,961	10	-44,461	N.A.
43	45	Nippon Telegraph & Telephone (Japan)	70,048	91,942	-1	1,964	N.A.
44	73	J.P. Morgan Chase (U.S.)	69,461	25,283	-3	1,612	-1
45	48	UBS (Switzerland)	67,766	48,914	-21	2,558	-29
46	61	Oracle (U.S.)	67,005	9,475	-2	2,307	4
47	47	AstraZeneca (U.K.)	65,896	17,841	10	2,836	-2
48	–	Comcast (U.S.)	65,380	12,460	27	-274	N.A.
49	42	Fannie Mae (U.S.)	63,483	52,901	4	4,520	-21
50	36	Abbott Laboratories (U.S.)	62,907	17,685	9	2,794	80
51	79	Hewlett-Packard (U.S.)	$60,785	$56,588	25%	$ -923	N.A.
52	43	ENI (Italy)	60,478	50,265	-2	4,818	-41%
53	49	Medtronic (U.S.)	60,234	7,665	20	1,600	63
54	84	Deutsche Telekom (Germany)	59,935	56,314	11	-25,789	N.A.
55	77	Telefonica (Spain)	59,540	29,801	-9	-5,850	N.A.
56	65	American Express (U.S.)	58,790	23,807	5	2,671	104
57	62	Wyeth (U.S.)	56,782	14,584	4	4,447	95
58	57	Wachovia (U.S.)	56,699	23,591	5	3,560	121
59	75	Samsung Electronics (South Korea)	55,843	50,216	28	5,946	131
60	60	3M (U.S.)	55,565	16,332	8	1,974	38
61	41	Unilever (Netherlands/U.K.)	55,458	50,630	-6	2,233	16
62	–	France Telecom (France)	55,357	48,910	8	-16,109	N.A.
63	99	Siemens (Germany)	55,153	88,124	-3	2,724	24
64	76	Morgan Stanley (U.S.)	52,967	32,242	-26	2,988	-16
65	35	Kraft Foods (U.S.)	51,450	29,723	3	3,394	80
66	56	China Mobile (Hong Kong)	50,571	14,630	28	3,726	17
67	–	Merrill Lynch (U.S.)	49,851	28,253	-27	2,475	363
68	55	Bristol-Myers Squibb (U.S.)	49,143	18,119	1	2,066	-57
69	87	Nissan Motor (Japan)	48,412	57,477	10	4,168	33
70	71	Barclays (U.K.)	47,677	28,515	-8	3,594	-10
71	52	L'Oreal (France)	47,001	14,987	4	1,475	18
72	85	BellSouth (U.S.)	46,540	22,440	-7	2,708	5
73	59	Bank One (U.S.)	45,791	22,171	-10	3,295	25
74	81	U.S. Bancorp (U.S.)	45,755	15,422	-6	3,326	95
75	–	Orange (France)	44,682	17,920	13	664	N.A.
76	–	BNP Paribas (France)	44,651	47,668	-17	3,456	-18
77	78	DuPont (U.S.)	44,440	24,006	-3	-1,103	N.A.
78	58	Anheuser-Busch (U.S.)	43,002	13,566	5	1,934	13
79	90	Lowe's (U.S.)	42,695	26,491	20	1,471	44
80	80	BHP Billiton (Australia/U.K.)	42,465	17,506	15	1,920	3
81	83	HBOS (U.K.)	41,937	32,700	5	3,088	31
82	–	Canon (Japan)	41,841	24,748	1	1,605	16
83	97	Walt Disney (U.S.)	41,839	25,329	1	1,236	930
84	88	Telstra (Australia)	41,825	12,141	-27	1,926	-6
85	92	Goldman Sachs (U.S.)	41,554	22,854	-27	2,114	-8
86	–	Texas Instruments (U.S.)	41,243	8,383	2	-344	N.A.
87	67	Sanofi-Synthelabo (France)	41,183	7,812	15	1,845	11
88	–	Tyco International (Bermuda)	41,061	35,590	5	-9,180	N.A.
89	–	News Corporation (Australia)	40,865	16,801	3	1,015	N.A.
90	–	Grupo Santander Central Hispano (Spain)	40,693	30,225	-18	2,357	-10
91	–	Genentech (U.S.)	40,506	2,719	23	64	-58
92	69	Honda Motor (Japan)	39,590	67,097	8	3,591	18
93	–	Taiwan Semiconductor (Taiwan)	39,552	4,684	29	624	49
94	73	ING Group (Netherlands)	38,997	94,582	0	4,698	-2
95	64	Aventis (France)	38,845	21,630	-10	2,198	39
96	86	DaimlerChrysler (Germany)	38,588	156,898	-2	5,115	N.A.
97	–	SAP (Germany)	37,812	7,775	1	527	-13
98	–	Telecom Italia Mobile (Italy)	37,790	11,398	6	1,222	23
99	96	ConocoPhillips (U.S.)	37,743	57,224	-14	-295	N.A.
100	–	United Technologies (U.S.)	37,548	27,980	2	2,234	15

N.A.=Not applicable

*March 31, 2002, results are used for Japanese companies

†Figures reflect the July 2002 acquisition of Immunex

NOTE: Rank calculated for Royal Dutch/Shell Group by combining market value of the Netherlands' Royal Dutch Petroleum and Britain's Shell Transport & Trading. Rank calculated for Unilever by combining market value of Netherlands' Unilever NV. and Britain's Unilever PLC. Rank calculated for BHP Billiton by combining market value of Australia's BHP Billiton Ltd. and Britain's BHP Billiton PLC.

Source: "Wall Street Journal Reports", World Business. August 29, 2003.

8 **Secondary Data—International Competition** Excelsior CEO Victor Trillingham (see Exercises 5, 6, and 7) is concerned about the international activities of The Body Shop, which competes with Excelsior in Canada and would be a formidable rival in international markets. Conduct secondary research on the Internet to uncover the answers to Trillingham's questions.

a. In how many countries does The Body Shop sell its products? List the countries.
b. What percentage of The Body Shop's overall sales are made outside Canada?
c. What companies (if any) has The Body Shop acquired during the past 12 months?
d. What major new consumer products has The Body Shop introduced in Canada during the past 12 months?

Using talking headings, outline an informational report in manuscript format to present your findings. Prepare visual aids to convey the answers to Questions 8a and b. Include a reference list of secondary sources used in your research. Then draft a transmittal memorandum to Trillingham (assume that the report will be submitted next Monday).

9 **Short Formal Report—Primary and Secondary Statistical Data Furnished** North Star is a producer of consumer products with annual sales of $847.2 million. Its focus is currently in Eastern and Central Canada. It has 4.5 percent of the consumer market for its six consumer products (soap, deodorant, ammonia, chili, canned ham, and frozen vegetables).

On July 8 of this year, Paul Trembley, sales manager, asked you, a product manager, to study the feasibility of North Star entering the generic-products market. Generic products are products that do not have brand names but instead carry a plain generic label, such as "Paper Towels." Generic products are typically not advertised; they involve less packaging, less processing, and cheaper ingredients than brand names; and they compete both with private brands (those distributed solely by individual store chains such as Sobeys and Loblaws) and with national brands (those available for sale at all grocery stores and advertised nationally). At the present time, North Star produces only national brands.

Paul specifically asked you *not* to explore whether North Star had the necessary plant capacity. He wanted you only to provide up-to-date information on the generic market in general and to explore likely consumer acceptance of generic brands for the products that North Star produces. He is quite interested in learning the results of your research.

In August you conducted a mail survey of 1500 consumers in the four provinces (Nova Scotia, New Brunswick, Ontario, and Quebec) that constitute your largest market. Responses were received from 832 consumers to the following questions; responses are provided for all 832 consumers and for the 237 largest consumers (those who indicated that they did 51 percent to 100 percent of their household shopping):

Have you purchased a food generic product (such as canned fruit or vegetables) in the last month?

All consumers: 36 percent yes, 64 percent no
Largest consumers: 29 percent yes, 71 percent no

Was this the first time you had purchased a food generic product?

All consumers: 18 percent yes, 82 percent no
Largest consumers: 20 percent yes, 80 percent no

Have you purchased a non-food generic product (such as paper towels or soap) in the last month?

All consumers: 60 percent yes, 40 percent no
Largest consumers: 59 percent yes, 41 percent no

Was this the first time you had purchased a non-food generic product?

All consumers: 5 percent yes, 95 percent no
Largest consumers: 7 percent yes, 93 percent no

If you could save at least 30 percent by purchasing a generic brand rather than a national brand, would you purchase a generic brand of any of the following products?

Bar of soap: 43 percent yes, 57 percent no, 0 percent don't use this product
Deodorant: 31 percent yes, 67 percent no, 2 percent don't use this product
Ammonia: 80 percent yes, 10 percent no, 10 percent don't use this product
Chili: 34 percent yes, 52 percent no, 14 percent don't use this product
Canned ham: 19 percent yes, 44 percent no, 37 percent don't use this product
Frozen vegetables: 54 percent yes, 30 percent no, 16 percent don't use this product

You also asked the local North Star sales representatives to audit 20 randomly selected chain supermarkets in each of these four provinces in August. Personal observation showed that 39 of the stores stocked generic brands, 37 of these 39 stocked 100 or more generic items, and 15 had separate generic-product sections. All but 3 of the 60 stores stocked all six products that North Star produces.

In gathering your data, you also made the following notes from three secondary sources:

1. *Hammond's Market Reports,* Gary, IN, 2006, pp. 1027–1030: This annual index lists various information for more than 2000 consumer products. The percentages of market share for the six products North Star produces are as follows:

	2000	2003	2006
Generic brands	1.5%	2.6%	7.3%
Private labels	31.6%	30.7%	27.8%
National brands	66.9%	66.7%	64.9%

2. Carolyn Green. *Canadian Grocer.* Toronto: Oct 2005. Vol. 119, Iss. 8; p. 22 (5 pages)

   a. Generic brands are typically priced 30 percent to 50 percent below national brands (p. 31).
   b. Consumers require a 36 percent saving on a bar of soap and 40 percent savings on deodorant to motivate them to switch to a generic (p. 32).
   c. Consumer awareness of generics has tripled since 1978 (p. 33).
   d. "The easiest way to become a no-name store is to ignore no-name brands" (direct quotation from p. 33).

e. Many leading brand manufacturers feel compelled to produce the lower-profit generic brands because either the market has grown too big to ignore or the inroads generic brands have made on their own brands have left them with idle capacity (p. 35).

3. Edward J. Rauch and Pamela G. McCleary, "National Brands to Play a Bit Part in the Future," *Grocery Business*, Fall 2004, pp. 118–120.

   a. Eight out of ten food-chain officers believe their costs will rise more than their prices this year (p. 118).
   b. Generics are now available in 84 percent of the stores nationwide and account for about 4 percent of the store space (p. 118).
   c. "Supermarket executives foresee a drop in shelf space allocated to brand products and an increase in the space allocated to generics and private labels. Many experts predict that supermarkets will ultimately carry no more than the top two brands in a category plus a private label and a generic label" (direct quotation from p. 119).
   d. Today, 37 percent of the grocery stores have switched from paper bags to the less expensive plastic bags for packaging customer purchases, even though the plastic bags are non-biodegradable (p. 119).
   e. Starting from nearly zero in 1977, generics have acquired 7 percent of the $75 billion grocery market. Many observers predict they will go up to 25 percent within the next five years (p. 120).

Analyze the data, prepare whatever visual aids would be helpful, and then write a formal report for Trembley. Include any supplementary report pages you think would be helpful.

10 Short Memorandum Report—Findings, Conclusions, and Recommendations
The National Council of Welfare (NCW) is a citizens' advisory body to the Minister of Social Development Canada on matters of concern to low-income Canadians. It is concerned about rising levels of social inequality among Canadians. It has conducted a study to look into this matter. It has gathered, among other findings, the following statistics:

a. In 2003, there were 4 917 000 poor people living in Canada, 1 201 000 of whom were children.
b. In 2004, 1.7 million Canadian children, women, and men relied on welfare.
c. In 2004, two-parent families with children on welfare in Nova Scotia, Ontario, Saskatchewan, Alberta, and British Columbia, and the three territories, had lower total incomes in 2004 than in 1999.[3]

Working in groups of two or three, draw conclusions about these findings and, based on additional research, make recommendations as to what should or should not be done to deal with the NCW's concerns .

Share your conclusions and recommendations with the rest of the class. Are the other groups' conclusions and recommendations similar or different? What additional information, if any, would have been helpful? What are the differences between conclusions and recommendations?

11 **Work-team Communication—Long Formal Report Requiring Additional Research**
Assume that your group of four has been asked by Jim Miller, executive vice-president of Jefferson Industries, to write an exploratory report on the feasibility of Jefferson's opening a frozen yogourt store in Niagara-on-the-Lake, Ontario. If the preliminary data your group gathers warrants further exploration of this project, a professional venture-consultant group will be hired to conduct an in-depth "dollars-and-cents" study. Your job, then, is to recommend whether such an expensive follow-up study is warranted. Assume that Jefferson has the financial resources to support such a venture if it looks promising.

You can immediately think of several areas you'll want to explore: the general market outlook for frozen yogourt stores, the demographic makeup of Niagara-on-the-Lake, the local economic climate, franchise opportunities in the industry, and the like. Undoubtedly, other topics (or criteria) will surface as you brainstorm the problem.

Working as a group, carry through the entire research process for this project—planning the study, collecting the data, organizing and analyzing the data, and writing the report.

Write the body of the report using formal language, organize the study by criteria, and place the conclusions and recommendations at the end. Include a title page, transmittal memo (addressed to James H. Miller), executive summary, table of contents, and reference list (use the author-date method of citation).

Regardless of how your group decides to divide up the work, everyone should review and comment on the draft of the final report. If different members write different components, edit as needed to ensure that the report reads smoothly and coherently.

12 **Documenting Using Endnotes**   Assume you are writing a report and have used the following secondary sources.

> An article written by John J. Richer on pages 45–48 of the April 2, 20—, edition of *Sports Weekly* entitled "The Big Profit Breakdown."
> A quotation by Scott Taylor from an article entitled "Winter Olympics—Boom or Bust" on page A2, column 1, of the April 17, 20—, edition of the *Fredericton Gleaner.*
> Statistics from page 233 in a book entitled *How to Win at the Service Game* written by James Michaels in 20— and published by Ammiden Publishing in Toronto.
> A quote from an interview conducted with T. Winkle Toewes, a professor of economics at the University of Winnipeg, conducted on March 31, 20—.

Using these sources of information and the examples shown in Section B (see pages 582–586), prepare the bibliography for your report.

For Exercises 13–16, follow the desires of your instructor (the audience) in terms of length, format, degree of formality, number of report components, and the like.

13 **Secondary Data—The Female Manager**   Using the appropriate business indexes (print or computer), identify three women who are presidents or CEOs of companies listed on the Toronto Stock Exchange. Provide information on their backgrounds. Did they make it to the top by rising through the ranks, by starting the firm, by taking over from another family member, or by following some other path?

Analyze the effectiveness of these three individuals. How profitable are the firms they head in relation to others in the industry? Are their firms more or less profitable now than when they assumed the top job? Finally, try to uncover data regarding their management styles—how they see their role, how they relate to their employees, what problems they've experienced, and the like.

From your study of these three individuals, are there any valid conclusions you can draw? Write a report objectively presenting and analyzing the information you've gathered.

14 Secondary Data—Keyboarding Skills You are the director of training for a telecommunications firm located in Pickering, Ontario. Your superior, Charles R. Underwood, personnel manager, is concerned that many of the firm's 2000 white-collar employees use their computers for hours each day but still do not know how to touch-keyboard. He believes the hunt-and-peck method is inefficient and increases the possibility of making errors when inputting data, thus lowering its reliability.

He has asked you to recommend a software program that teaches the user how to type. He is specifically interested in a program that is IBM-compatible, is geared to adults, is educationally sound, and can be learned on an individual basis without an instructor present.

Identify and evaluate three to five keyboarding software programs that meet these criteria, and write a report recommending the best one to Underwood. Justify your choice.

15 Primary Data—Career Choices Explore a career position in which you are interested. Determine the job outlook, present level of employment, salary trends, typical duties, working conditions, educational or experience requirements, and the like. If possible, interview someone holding this position to gain first-hand impressions. Then write your findings in a report to your instructor. Include at least five secondary sources and at least one table or visual aid in your report.

16 Primary Data—Intercultural Dimensions To what extent does network and cable television accurately portray members of cultural, ethnic, and racial minorities? To what extent are they portrayed at all during prime time (8 p.m. to 11 p.m.)? In what types of roles are they shown, and what is their relationship with non-minority characters? As assistant to the director of public relations of the National Minority Alliance, you are interested in such questions.

Locate and review at least three journal articles on this topic. Then develop a definition of the term *minority*. Randomly select and view at least ten prime-time television shows, and develop a form for recording the needed data on minority representation in these shows. As part of your research, compare the proportion of minority members in this country with their representation on prime-time television. Integrate your primary and secondary data into a report. Use objective language, being careful to present ample data to support any conclusions or recommendations you may make.

17 Primary Data—Student Living Arrangements Darlene Anderson, a real estate developer and president of Anderson and Associates, is exploring the feasibility of building a large student-apartment complex on a lot her firm owns two blocks from campus. Even though the city planning commission believes there is already enough student housing, Anderson thinks she can succeed if she addresses specific problems of present housing. She has asked you, her executive assistant, to survey students to determine their views of off-campus living.

Specifically, she wants you to develop a ranked listing of the most important attributes of student housing. How important to students are such criteria as price, location (access to campus, shopping, public transportation, and the like), space and layout, furnishings (furnished versus unfurnished), social activities, parking, pets policy, and the like?

In addition, the architect has drawn a plan that features the following options: private hotel-like rooms (sleeping and sitting area and private bath but no kitchen); private one-room efficiency apartments; one-bedroom two-person apartments; and four-bedroom four-person apartments. Which of these arrangements would students most likely rent, given their present economic situation? Would another alternative be more appealing to them?

Develop a questionnaire and administer it to a sample of students. Then analyze the data and write a report for Anderson.

18 **Proofreading—Selling Business on Business Software**   Assume that the following passage is part of an informational report that you have prepared. Proofread it carefully for spelling errors, misused words, and grammar errors. Rewrite the passage showing the correction you made.

> Our lawyers have reviewed the wording of the contacts you sent us. They're advice is to accept provisions 1 thru 8 and 11 thorough 15. The remainder of the provisions (9 and 10) require farther negotiation.
>
> The number of people we want to include in these talks has not yet been determined. We do expect, however, to have fewer people involved now then in our proceeding meetings.
>
> Marcia Nash, our chief legal council, will be your principal contact during these negotiations. Please telephone her at 555-7376 to sit a mutually beneficial time for us too meet early next month. We are eager to settle this matter soon.

continuing case 11

Reporting—A Pain in the Wrist

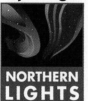

Review the Continuing Case account at the end of Chapter 10, in which Jean Tate asked Pat Robbins to write a report on carpal tunnel syndrome, a neuromuscular wrist ailment caused by repeated hand motions as in typing.

Now, administer the questionnaire you developed in Chapter 10 to a sample of at least 30 clerical workers at your institution, where you work, or at some other office. For the purposes of this assignment, assume that the responses you receive were actually those from Northern Lights clerical workers. Then analyze the questionnaire data carefully. Construct whatever tables and charts would be helpful to the reader.

Critical Thinking

1. Considering the findings from your questionnaire and the secondary sources you checked, what does all this information mean in terms of your problem statement?

2. For each sub-problem you specified (see Chapter 10), what conclusion can you draw? In view of each of these individual conclusions, what overall conclusion is merited? In view of your individual and overall conclusions, what recommendations are appropriate?

Writing Project

3. Prepare a recommendation report in manuscript format for Tate. Use formal language for the body of the report, organize the study by criteria, and place the conclusions and recommendations at the end. Include a title page, transmittal memo, executive summary, table of contents, abstract, appendix (copy of the questionnaire), and reference list (use the author-date method of citation).

Pat analyzes the results of secondary research, primary data, and Internet searching to draft her recommendation report on carpal tunnel syndrome.

LABtest 11

Retype the following news item, correcting any grammar and mechanics errors according to the rules introduced in LABs 2–6 beginning on page 534.

Even on the brightest of evenings navigating your garden can be a challenge at best. At worst, the cause of a nasty spill. Today, alot of people are discovering the benifits of low voltage lighting as an economical effective and energy-efficient source of exterior lighting.

5   Many Lighting Systems are sold in kits for do-it-yourself installation, many folks who would'nt otherwise fool with an electrical outlet is now installing a lighting system.

Essentially, there is only 3 basic types of fixtures spot lighting, path lighting, and general lighting. Spot lighting consist of a floodlight that is

10   used to direct light to a specific location so as to illuminate a tree, decorative

shrub, or architectural element of the homes exterior. Path lighting and accent lighting is the most popular styles used by homeowners' today.

One aspect of design that deserves creative ideas are the maximum distance that the wire will travel. The further the wire travels, the more the voltage drops. Which, in turn, creates a drop in illumination. To avoid this condition experts advice using several wires of varying lengths.

Some transformers are equiped with a photoelectric cell that automatically turn the lights on and off. Another poplar accessory is a dimmer to control the lights' intensity.

12

Business Presentations

After you have finished this chapter, you should be able to

1. Describe the important role that business presentations play in the organization.

2. Plan a presentation by determining its purpose, analyzing the audience, and deciding the timing and method of delivery.

3. Write a presentation by collecting the data and organizing it in a logical format.

4. Plan a team presentation.

5. Plan other types of business presentations.

6. Incorporate visual aids and audience handouts to enhance business presentations.

7. Practice and deliver a business presentation.

Martin and Farah Perelmuter founded Speakers' Spotlight in 1995, and the husband-and-wife team can now boast a roster of over 400 speakers from around the world. The company represents such notable Canadians as the Hon. Adrienne Clarkson, Justin J.P. Trudeau, the Rt. Hon. Joe Clark, David Suzuki, Michael "Pinball" Clemons, Ron MacLean, Rubin "Hurricane" Carter, Stephen Lewis, Jessica Holmes, and Ron James. Speakers' Spotlight now has offices in Toronto, Vancouver, and Calgary and was recently

an insider's
perspective

MARTIN AND FARAH PERELMUTER
President (Martin) and CEO (Farah) of
Speakers' Spotlight

ranked by *Profit* magazine as one of Canada's fastest growing companies. Farah has also appeared on *Profit* magazine's Canada's Top 100 list of Women Entrepreneurs.

Running a company that represents such a large and diverse group of professional speakers—*and* observing literally thousands of presentations over the last decade—has taught the couple more than a little about what it takes to succeed as a public speaker. When asked what distinguishes the best speakers from the mediocre ones, Martin stresses that "Speakers who succeed must be able to meet the changing expectations of their audiences."[1]

Of course, meeting your audience's expectations means going beyond just delivering the content. "I believe that an outstanding presentation is educational, entertaining and inspiring," Martin emphasizes. "If the audience is inspired to take what they've learned and then act on it, the presentation will have a much greater likelihood of making a positive impact."

433

One of Martin's favourite speakers, Stephen Lewis, regularly concludes his presentations with a call to action. When speaking to the Canadian Association of Supply Chain & Logistics Management, recalls Martin, Lewis challenged his audience to use their collective knowledge and expertise to help solve some of the complex problems and issues he discussed in his presentation. The association subsequently established Logisticians Without Borders/Logisticiens Sans Frontiers to serve the international community. "I believe that this should be the ultimate goal of any presentation—to impact how the audience members think and feel about the presentation topic, *and* to provide the impetus to take action and make a positive change," adds Martin.

Farah stresses that the best speakers are those who can take a topic their audience may be unfamiliar with and link it to their own needs. Few, for example, can directly relate to the experiences of Roberta Bondar, the first Canadian woman to fly into space, or Cassie Campbell, Olympic gold medal winner. But these speakers "relate their stories back to the needs of the audience." Farah cites goal setting as an example. "They would describe the necessity to set goals, whether you climb a mountain, fly in space or are trying to increase your sales."

As for delivery, Farah emphasizes the importance of using visuals properly and sticking to the allotted time. "The audience should be focused on the speaker, not the screen. Choose visuals that enhance your point with as few words as possible." Exuding confidence is also key, Farah adds. "When you start off your presentation, don't apologize that you aren't a 'professional speaker'. As long as you look confident, your audience will believe you know what you're doing! The more you do it, the more you really will feel comfortable."

Martin downplays the importance of flashy performances, noting that "there is a big difference between Canada and the United States, where there is an increasing emphasis on flash and sizzle."[3] He believes that, at least for Canadians, content still trumps style. "An effective presentation doesn't have to be a performance,"[4] says Martin, who adds, "I think Canadian audiences still want to be entertained but they want more substance."[5] When giving advice to speakers, Martin always stresses that they go with whatever they most feel comfortable with. "Content is obviously critically important, but I'm also a big believer that if people are enjoying themselves and having fun, they will be much more open to learning and embracing new ideas." Martin again turns to Stephen Lewis for an example: "It's partly a gift he has with the spoken word but he is very comfortable being who he is and speaking his mind. His speaking style reflects his personality."[6]

"An effective presentation doesn't have to be a performance."[2]

One of the couple's favourite anecdotes—one that nicely underscores the differences between Canadian and American audiences—comes from a Canadian speaker who was presenting to an American audience in California. The speaker began his presentation by saying, "There is one very big difference between speaking to a Canadian audience and speaking to an American audience." The speaker then began his presentation, only to be interrupted almost immediately by an audience member who yelled, "Hey! What's the difference?" The speaker responded, "That's the difference!"

■ The Role of Business Presentations

Anyone who plans a career in sales, training, or education expects to make many oral presentations to customers, employees, or students each week. What you may not realize, though, is that just about *everyone* in business will probably give at least one major presentation and many smaller ones each year to customers, superiors, subordinates, or colleagues—not to mention presentations for various volunteer groups, such as homeowners' boards or community hockey associations.

The costs of ineffective presentations are immense. With many managers earning six-figure salaries, a presentation that discusses ideas incompletely and inefficiently wastes time and money. Sales are lost, vital information is not communicated, training programs fail, policies are not implemented, and profits fall.

Technology is undoubtedly changing the physical characteristics of oral presentations in business—for example, by making it possible to present via videotape, interactive television, or the Internet rather than in person. Competent communicators recognize, however, that the compelling effects of verbal and non-verbal communication strategies that are possible in oral presentations will continue to make them a critical communication competency in the contemporary business organization.

CO1. Describe the important role that business presentations play in the organization.

Almost everyone in business is required to give a presentation occasionally.

The Process of Making a Business Presentation

As you will remember, we followed a specific process when learning to communicate business information in written form; the process consisted of planning, drafting, revising, formatting, and finally proofreading the written document. We follow a similar logical process for making an oral presentation.

1. *Planning:* Determining the purpose of the presentation, analyzing the audience, and deciding the timing and method of delivery.
2. *Organizing:* Collecting the data and arranging it in a logical order.
3. *Developing visual aids:* Selecting the appropriate type, number, and content of visual aids.
4. *Practicing:* Rehearsing by simulating the actual presentation conditions as closely as possible.
5. *Delivering:* Dressing appropriately, maintaining friendly eye contact, speaking in an effective manner, and answering questions confidently.

The presentation process requires planning, organizing, developing visual aids, practicing, and delivering the presentation.

■ Planning the Presentation

When assigned the task of making a business presentation, your first impulse might be to sit down at your desk or computer and begin writing. Resist the temptation. As in written communications, several important steps precede the actual writing. These steps involve determining the purpose of the presentation, analyzing the audience, planning the timing of the presentation, and selecting a delivery method.

In addition to helping you decide what to include in your presentation, these planning tasks will give you important information about the degree of formality appropriate for the situation. The more formal the presentation, the more time you'll devote to the project. In general, complex topics or proposals with "high

CO2. Plan a presentation by determining its purpose, analyzing the audience, and deciding the timing and method of delivery.

stakes" demand more formal presentations—with well-planned visuals, a carefully thought-out organizational plan, and extensive research. Likewise, the larger the audience and the greater the audience's opposition to your ideas, the more formal the presentation should be. A presentation you will deliver more than once is likely to be more formal than a one-time speech, as is a presentation on a complex topic.

Purpose

Keeping your purpose uppermost in mind helps you decide what information to include and what to omit, in what order to present this information, and which points to emphasize and subordinate. (See Communication Snapshot 10 for a look at the most popular topics of professional speakers.)

Most business presentations have one of these four purposes:

> Most presentations seek to report, explain, persuade, or motivate.

- *Reporting:* Updating the audience on some project or event.

- *Explaining:* Detailing how to carry out a procedure or how to operate a new piece of equipment.

- *Persuading:* Convincing the listeners to purchase something or to accept an idea you're presenting.

- *Motivating:* Inspiring the listeners to take some action.

Assume, for example, that you have been asked to make a short oral presentation on the topic of absenteeism at the Fremont Manufacturing Plant. If you're speaking to the management committee, your purpose would be to *report* the results of your research. Using a logical organization, you would discuss the effects of the problem on productivity, its causes, and possible solutions.

If you're speaking to the union personnel, however, your purpose might be to *motivate* the employees to reduce their absenteeism. You might then briefly discuss the extent of the problem, devote your major efforts to showing how the employees ultimately benefit from lower absenteeism, and finally introduce a monthly recognition program.

After your presentation is over, your purpose provides a criterion—the *only* important criterion—by which to judge the success of your presentation. In other words, did the management committee understand the results of your research? Were the union members motivated to reduce their absenteeism? No matter how well or how poorly you spoke and no matter how impressive or ineffective your visual aids, the important question is whether you accomplished your purpose.

Audience Analysis

In addition to identifying such demographic factors as the size, age, and organizational status of

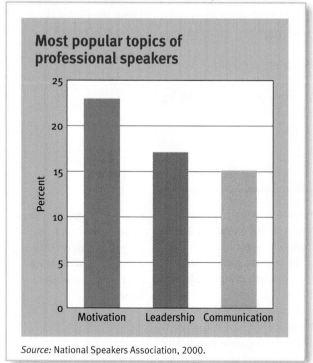

communication snapshot 10

Most popular topics of professional speakers

Source: National Speakers Association, 2000.

your audience, you will also need to determine their level of knowledge about your topic and their psychological needs (values, attitudes, and beliefs). These factors provide clues to everything from the overall content, tone, and types of examples you should use to the types of questions to expect and even the way you should dress.

Analyze the audience in terms of demographics, level of knowledge, and psychological needs.

The principles by which you analyze your audience are the same as those we discussed in the chapters on writing letters, memos, and reports. How much does your audience already know about the subject? What is your relationship to the audience? How will they benefit from the material? How high is their resistance to you or your message? What is unique about your audience? Consider the effect of your message on your audience and your credibility with them. The key is to put yourself in your audience's place so that you can anticipate their questions and reactions.

In terms of receptivity to your message, you can expect your audience to fall into one of the following categories: receptive, neutral, unreceptive.

Receptive Audiences   Audiences are typically receptive to a message for one or both of the following reasons:

1. the speaker has credibility with the audience (either because the speaker is known and liked by the audience or because the speaker has a favourable reputation); or
2. the content of the presentation is appealing to the audience.

In either case, the job of preparing for a presentation is somewhat simplified when presenting to a receptive audience. You don't have to put as much effort into gaining credibility (although you do need to ensure you maintain it), and you don't have to start by convincing the audience that listening to the message is worth their time— they've already decided that it is. The advantages of delivering to a receptive audience include these:

Here, Justin Trudeau gives a speech to high school students about the youth program, Katimavik, in Toronto.

■ You can take more risks. While your presentation should follow a predetermined structure, you can be more spontaneous with a receptive audience. Sometimes, the interests of the audience will influence the direction your presentation will take.

■ You can be less formal. Receptive audiences tend to appreciate a more casual, interactive, and conversational presentation style. This can even extend to how you dress: business casual versus business formal.

■ You can depend more on stories and humour. All audiences are receptive to stories, if told well. Receptive audiences allow you to tell more personal anecdotes, rely more on humour, even self-deprecation, and even solicit examples from your audience.

■ You can usually count on audience participation. Receptive audiences aren't necessarily going to have more questions, but they are more likely to share their own experiences and engage the speaker in discussion. If you have an exercise prepared, receptive audiences are generally eager to participate.

The main hazard of preparing to present to a receptive audience is overestimating their receptivity to your topic. Always expect to have some in the audience who need more convincing: anticipate these points of resistance and be prepared to address them. Finally, be wary of being overly casual if you already know your audience. You're taking up their valuable time, and they expect to be rewarded with an engaging, meaningful presentation.

Neutral and Unreceptive Audiences

With neutral audiences, you are speaking to individuals who have yet to make up their minds about you or your topic. They need some convincing. With unreceptive audiences, you are speaking to individuals who have already made up their minds about you or your topic—they disagree with or even disapprove of you and/or what you are going to say. Indeed, the only significant difference between the two types of audiences is the degree to which they need convincing. Thus, for both types of audiences you will have to put more effort into establishing your own credibility and into gaining the audience's favour. Here are some guidelines for winning over a less than receptive audience:

- Grab their attention. Later we will discuss the specific components of a good introduction. One of the goals of any introduction is to get your audience interested in the topic. With neutral audiences, just gaining their curiosity is often enough—tell an interesting story, cite a startling statistic, point out something they may not have considered before. With highly resistant audiences, consider focusing on a concrete benefit such as improved productivity, reduced costs, or increased revenues. Be sure to provide convincing evidence of how these benefits can be realized. Avoid exaggeration or obsequiousness, however. A highly resistant audience is already expecting "smoke and mirrors", so be sure your evidence is well researched, well organized, and convincing.

- Address potential obstacles early. Anticipate the primary reasons why your audience may not be receptive: they don't know and therefore don't yet trust you; they've had a bad experience that's made them skeptical about you or your subject matter; there is a high cost (time or money) to their adopting your ideas; they see you as unqualified to be speaking about a certain matter; they are sharply polarized over an issue and see you as "one of them;" they are busy and are attending the presentation against their will; or they are simply fatigued by the sheer number of presentations they attend over the course of the year. Whatever you perceive as the biggest point of resistance should be addressed early and often. Providing examples, telling stories, citing statistics, stressing reader benefits, offering expert endorsements—all of these can help you overcome initial resistance.

- Maintain confident body language. Particularly when presenting to a resistant audience, you're likely to be a little nervous. Disarming them with a confident presence can go a long way in breaking down their resistance. Maintain eye contact, carefully control the pace of your delivery, use precise, controlled hand gestures, stand up straight and face your audience, and speak clearly and loudly. All of these guidelines should be applied to every presentation, but pay particular attention to them when facing a resistant audience. It's also a good idea to dress more formally than you might with a receptive audience, even to the point of dressing a little more formally than your audience members.

- Show, don't tell. Receptive audiences can usually be relied upon to take your word for it when you're making a claim about a product or course of action. Not so with resistant or even neutral audiences. Never expect them to implicitly accept any claim you make; provide evidence for everything. This usually means spending more time putting together visuals, gathering examples, and researching statistics. Letting the evidence speak for itself is particularly wise when presenting to an audience that doesn't trust you. When presenting evidence, do so using objective, unemotional language.

- Maintain a more formal structure and delivery style. Until you've gained your audience's trust, they're not likely to respond well to humour, especially if they perceive your humour as evidence that you're not taking them seriously. Moreover, a loose or indiscernible structure will further alienate such an audience. Keep the structure simple (generally three or four main points), be efficient, tell them how much of their time you'll need, and end the presentation when you said you would.

See Figure 12.1 for an illustration of how the structure and style of a presentation may differ depending on your purpose and the needs of your audience. In the first slide, the intended audience is the management committee, who may expect a formal presentation with a focus on the bottom line. In the second slide, the intended audience consists of the union members who, as a more heterogeneous group, may appreciate a less formal, more conversational presentation.

Delivery Method

At some point during your planning, you must decide on the method of delivery—that is, will you memorize your speech, read it, or speak from notes? Your choice will be determined by the answers to such questions as, how long is your talk; how complex is the content; how formal is the presentation; and, with what method (or combination of methods) are you most comfortable?

figure**12.1** **The Audience and Purpose Determine the Content**

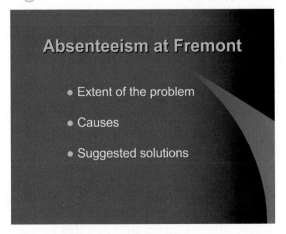

Audience: Management Committee
Purpose: Reporting

OR

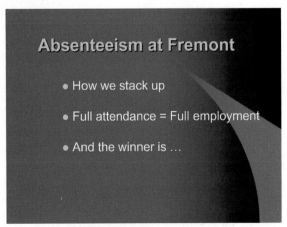

Audience: Union Members
Purpose: Motivating

Impromptu or Extemporaneous Speaking.   Occasionally, you may be called upon to present to a group without having been given the opportunity to prepare— you may be asked to give a summary of a project at a meeting, or perhaps to offer an impromptu toast at a wedding, for example. Impromptu speaking, by definition, precludes any formal planning, but you can often take a few seconds to gather your main points and mentally put them into order before beginning. A quick mental plan helps you avoid the two most common pitfalls of impromptu speaking— freezing up or rambling on.

Once you've decided on your key points, stand up, establish eye contact with your audience, and discuss each point in as much detail as necessary. Since you generally don't have the benefit of visual aids, avoid thrusting your hands in your pockets or clutching the podium or table. Instead, emphasize and augment your message through hand gestures and appropriate facial expressions. When finished, indicate that you are done, and if appropriate thank your audience. Then sit down.

If you truly have no warning and not even a minute to prepare, stay calm. You would not have been called on unless you had something positive to contribute. Remember that the audience knows you are giving impromptu remarks, so they won't expect you to demonstrate the same polish as a person who is giving a prepared presentation.

Obviously, impromptu speaking comes easier for some than others, and doing it well takes practice. Taking advantage of any opportunity that arises to speak publicly, even if just for a few seconds, will help you build the confidence you need to excel when asked to speak without notice.

Memorizing   Unless a presentation is short and significant, memorizing an entire speech is risky, not to mention time-consuming. You always run the risk (a very real one if you're nervous) of forgetting your lines and perhaps ruining your entire presentation. In addition, memorized presentations often sound mechanical and do not let you adapt the material to the needs of the audience. However, memorizing the first or last section of your presentation, a telling quotation, or a humorous story may be extremely effective for presenting a key part of your talk.

Reading   Reading speeches is quite common in academic and scientific settings, where a professor or researcher might be asked to read a paper at a professional conference. Writing out a speech and reading from the prepared text is helpful if you're dealing with a highly complex or technical topic, if the subject is controversial (making a statement to the press, for example), or if you have a lot of information to present in a short time. Such delivery is *not* recommended for most business settings because the presenter's eyes are typically focused too much on the paper and not enough on the audience and because spontaneity and flexibility are lost. After all, if the speech is going to be read word for word, why not just duplicate and distribute it to the audience for them to read at their leisure?

Of the four common methods of presentation (impromptu speaking, memorizing, reading, and speaking from notes), the last is the most common for business presentations.

Speaking from Notes   By far the most common (and generally the most effective) method for delivering business presentations is speaking from prepared notes, such as an outline. The notes contain key phrases rather than complete sentences, and you compose the exact wording as you speak. Although you may occasionally stumble in choosing a word, the spontaneous, conversational quality and the close audience rapport that result are generally superior to those of other presentation methods. The notes help ensure that you will cover all the material and cover it in a logical order; yet this method provides enough flexibility that you can adapt your remarks in reaction to verbal and non-verbal cues from the audience.

The specific content and format of the notes is not important; choose whatever works best for you. Some people use a formal outline on full sheets of paper; others prefer notes jotted on index cards. What gets put on your notes is up to you, but unless you actually intend to read the presentation, as described above, it is generally advisable *not* to write your notes in full sentences. Novice speakers will often write full-sentence notes as a crutch to help them with their nervousness, thinking they'll only read from them if they get stuck. What often happens is that they end up reading them word for word, pausing only occasionally to look up at their audience. When they look back down, they often struggle to find the sentence where they left off and then stumble around for a moment while they regain their bearings. Aware that they are starting to struggle, they become more nervous and focus even harder on their notes, forgetting their audience altogether. The presentation ends up being a stilted and jumbled mess.

Instead, rehearse the material well so you are comfortable speaking about it without notes. Then write key words and phrases on index cards as a guide to keep you organized while you present the material. Sometimes, it may also be helpful to insert delivery cues, indicating when to pause, smile, make a gesture, display a visual aid, slow down, and the like.

Some speakers start off by writing out the entire speech and then practice extensively from the prepared script. Only after they are thoroughly familiar with their verbatim script do they condense it into an outline and then speak from the outline. Most experienced speakers work directly from notes right from the beginning. Whatever method you use, the key to a successful delivery is practice, practice, practice.

Whether you use full sheets or index cards, be sure to number each page (in case the pages are dropped). For ease in moving from sheet to sheet or card to card, write on just one side and do not staple. Typed copy is better than handwritten copy and large type is better than small type. Type your notes in standard upper- and lower-case letters rather than in all capitals, which are more difficult to read because all the letters are the same size. Model 36 on page 442 provides examples of two techniques.

Use larger type and upper and lower case letters for outline notes.

■ Organizing the Presentation

For most presentations, the best way to begin is simply to brainstorm: write down every point you can think of that might be included in your presentation. Don't worry about the order or format—just get it all down. During the next several days, carry a pen and some paper with you so that you can jot down random thoughts as they occur—during a meeting, at lunch, going to and from work, or in the evening at home.

CO3. Write a presentation by collecting the data and organizing it in a logical format.

Later, separate your notes into three categories: opening, body, and ending. As you begin to analyze and organize your material, you may find that you need additional information. You may need to retrieve records from files, consult with a colleague, visit your corporate or local library to fill in the gaps, or perhaps go online to retrieve data from the World Wide Web.

The Opening

The purpose of the opening is to capture the interest of your audience, and the first 90 seconds of your presentation are crucial. The audience will be observing every

Your opening should introduce the topic, identify the purpose, and preview the presentation.

model36

PREPARING SPEAKING NOTES

Full-sentence notes (not advisable unless your intent is to read them word for word).

1

> There are several ways to organize a presentation. (Slides 1–3). They include the chronological plan, the cause/effect/solution plan, the order of importance plan, and the criteria plan.
>
> The chronological plan treats the content as if it were the plot in a story, with a clear beginning, middle, and end.....
>
> The problem-solution plan works well with persuasive presentations, where the audience needs to be convinced that whatever solution your are positing is the answer to a serious problem that will only grow worse if not addressed.

Point-form notes (more conversational, easier to follow).

> Four Organizational Plans (Slides 1–3):
>
> • Chronological
>   – compare to story

2

> • Problem-Solution
>   – good for persuasive messages

3

> • Order of Importance
>   – good for complex arguments

Grammar and Mechanics Notes

1 When constructing full-sentence notes, put no more than one or two sentences in a paragraph.

2 When constructing point-form notes, ensure plenty of white space between bullet points.

3 Whichever format you choose, use a large type size to enhance readability.

detail about you—your dress, posture, facial features, and voice qualities, as well as what you're actually saying—for clues about you and your topic, and they will be making preliminary judgments accordingly.

Begin immediately to establish rapport and build a relationship with your audience—not just for the duration of your presentation but for the long term. If you're making a proposal, you need not only the audience's attention during your presentation but also their cooperation later to implement your proposal. Because the opening is so crucial, many professionals write out the entire opening and practice it until they are extremely familiar with it.

The kind of opening that will be effective depends on your topic, how well you know the audience, and how well they know you. If, for example, you're giving a status report on a project about which you've reported before, you can immediately announce your main points (for example, that the project is on schedule and proceeding as planned) and then go to the body of your remarks. If, however, you're presenting a new proposal to your superiors, you'll first have to introduce the topic and provide background information.

Spreading her money knowledge, Jacquette Timmons, president and CEO of Sterling Investment Management Inc., conducts a "Meet Your Money" workshop. She spices her presentations with hard data. According to her, "The numbers reveal the facts, the facts tell a story, and the story gives clues about what to do next."

If most of the listeners don't know you, you'll have to gain their attention with a creative opening. The following types of attention-getting openings have proven successful for business presentations; the examples given are for a presentation to union employees on the topic of absenteeism.

- *Quote a well-known person:* "Comedian Woody Allen once noted that 90 percent of the job is just showing up."

- *Ask a question:* "If we were able to cut our absenteeism rate by half during the coming six months, exactly how much do you think that would mean for each of us in our end-of-year bonus cheques?"

- *Present a hypothetical situation:* "Assume that as you were leaving home this morning to put in a full day at work, your son came up to you and said he was too tired to go to school because he had stayed up so late last night watching *Wrestle Mania*. What would be your reaction?"

- *Relate an appropriate anecdote, story, joke, or personal experience:* "George, a friend of mine who had recently changed jobs, happened to meet his former boss and asked her whom she had hired to fill his vacancy. 'George,' his former boss said, 'when you left, you didn't *leave* any vacancy!' Perhaps the reason George didn't leave any vacancy was that . . ."

- *Give a startling fact:* "During the next 24 hours, Canadian industry will lose $136 million because of absenteeism."

- *Use a dramatic prop or visual aid:* (holding up a paper clip) "What do you think is the *true* cost of this paper clip to our company?"

Effective openings include a quotation, question, hypothetical situation, story, startling fact, or visual aid.

Don't apologize or make excuses (for example, "I wish I had had more time to prepare my remarks today" or "I'm not really much of a speaker"). The audience may agree with you! At any rate, you'll turn them off immediately and weaken your credibility.

Your opening should lead into the body of your presentation by previewing your remarks: "Today, I'll cover four main points. First, . . ." Let the audience know the scope and limitations of your remarks. For example, if you're discussing the pros and cons of a plant closing from a strictly dollars-and-cents standpoint, advise the audience immediately that your analysis does not include political or human relations considerations. If you don't first define the scope of your remarks, you may invite needless questions and second-guessing during your presentation.

For most business presentations, let the audience know up front what you expect of them. Are you simply presenting information for them to absorb, or will the audience be expected to react to your remarks? Are you asking for their endorsement, their resources, their help, or what? Let the audience know what their role will be so that they can then place your remarks in perspective.

The Body

The body of your presentation conveys the real content. Here you'll develop the points you introduced in the opening, giving background information, specific evidence, examples, implications, consequences, and other needed information.

Organize the body logically, according to your topic and audience needs.

Choose a Logical Sequence   Just as you do when writing a letter or report, choose an organizational plan that suits your purpose and your audience's needs. The most commonly used organizational plans are these:

- *Criteria:* Introduce each criterion in turn and show how well each alternative meets that criterion (typically used for presenting proposals).

- *Direct sequence:* Give the major conclusions first, followed by the supporting details (typically used for presenting routine information).

- *Indirect sequence:* Present the reasons first, followed by the major conclusion (typically used for persuasive presentations).

- *Chronology:* Present the points in the order in which they occurred (typically used in status reports or when reporting on some event).

- *Cause/effect/solution:* Present the sources and consequences of some problem and then pose a solution.

- *Order of importance:* Arrange the points in order of importance and then pose each point as a question and answer it (an effective way of ensuring that the audience can follow your arguments).

- *Elimination of alternatives:* List all alternatives and then gradually eliminate each one until only one option remains—the one you're recommending.

Whatever organizational plan you choose, make sure that your audience knows at the outset where you're going and is able to follow your organization. In a written document, signposts such as headings tell the reader how the parts fit together. In an oral presentation, you must compensate for the lack of such aids by using frequent and clear transitions that tell your listeners where you are. Pace your presentation of data so that you do not lose your audience.

Establish Your Credibility   Convince the listener that you've done a thorough job of collecting and analyzing the data and that your points are reasonable. Support your arguments with credible evidence—statistics, actual experiences, examples, and support from experts. Use objective language; let the data—not exaggeration or emotion—persuade the audience. Be guided by the same principles you use when writing a persuasive letter or report.

Avoid saturating your presentation with so many facts and figures that your audience won't be able to absorb them. Regardless of their relevance, statistics will not strengthen your presentation if the audience is unable to digest all the data. A more effective tactic is to prepare handouts of detailed statistical data to distribute for review at a later time.

Address Negative Information   It would be unusual if *all* the data you've collected and analyzed support your proposal. (If that were the case, persuasion would not be needed.) What should you do, then, about negative information, which, if presented, might weaken your argument? You cannot simply ignore negative information. To do so would surely open up a host of questions and subsequent doubts that would seriously weaken your position.

Think about your own analysis of the data. Despite the negative information, you still concluded that your solution has merit. Your tactic, then, is to present all the important information—pro and con—and to show through your analysis and discussion that your recommendations are still valid, in spite of the disadvantages and drawbacks. Use the techniques you learned in Chapter 5 about emphasis and subordination to let your listeners know which points you considered major and which you considered minor.

Although you should discuss the important negative points, you may safely omit discussing minor ones. You must, however, be prepared to discuss these minor negative points if any questions about them arise at the conclusion of your presentation.

Use Transitions   Unlike the written word, where headings, paragraphs, and even punctuation help the reader see clearly where ideas begin and end, oral presentations rely on your voice and your non-verbal cues (and your visual aids, where appropriate) to help the audience follow the discussion. For this reason, transitional cues are even more important in presentations than in written material.

A common transitional technique is to preview what you're about to say for each section within the body of the presentation—not just in the introduction. When

Do not ignore negative information.

DILBERT

© Scott Adams/Dist. by United Features Syndicate, Inc.

doing so, try to be as concrete as possible to give the audience a kind of mental outline for each section:

NOT: And now I'm going to talk about résumé format.

BUT: For the next 10 minutes, I'd like to discuss the importance of page layout, headings, type size, and font to ensure a professional looking résumé.

Once you've previewed a topic, use repetition and transitional words to allow the audience to see where you are within each section:

"Now that we've covered headings, I'd like to discuss page layout, specifically the use of margins and white space."

OR

"Not only can the appropriate use of white space enhance the readability of a résumé, so too can your choice of type size and font."

Finally, and particularly for complex information, offer a brief summary of your main points within a section before proceeding to the next section. The summary will often include a preview of the next section:

"Now that we've discussed the importance of page layout, headings, type size, and font, I'd like to demonstrate how to use vigorous language in describing your skills and job functions."

The Ending

Finish on a strong, upbeat note, leaving your audience with a clear and simple message.

The ending of your presentation is your last opportunity to achieve your objective. Don't waste it. A presentation without a strong ending is like a joke without a punch line.

Your closing should summarize the main points of your presentation, especially if it has been a long one. Even if the members of your audience have had an easy time following the structure of your talk, they won't necessarily remember all your important points. Let the audience know the significance of what you've said. Draw conclusions, make recommendations, or outline the next steps to take. Leave the audience with a clear and simple message.

If you wish to allow time for the audience to ask questions, avoid leaving this until the very end. Many a presentation has fizzled out as the speaker solicited questions from the audience, received none, and thus concluded, "Well, I guess I'm done then." Instead, inform the audience that you are about to conclude and that you'd first like to give them an opportunity to ask questions. This way, you still control how the presentation ends. When soliciting questions, guide the audience into considering specific questions.

NOT: Are there any questions?

BUT: Would anyone like further clarification on any of the three topics I've covered today: the current problems with our benefits plan, the recommendations for improving the plan, or the costs of expanding the plan?

Some experts suggest that when presenting to highly resistant (even hostile) audiences, you may wish to avoid soliciting questions. This may occasionally be sound advice, but it's not always realistic, and it runs the risk of making you look like you're avoiding tough questions. The keys to answering questions from a hostile audience are to be well prepared and anticipate the kinds of questions you might receive; to avoid sounding defensive by maintaining a neutral, unemotional tone; and to maintain confident body language. Obviously, all of these suggestions are easier said than done, and even well-seasoned presenters do not always handle hostile audiences well. If presenting as a team (see our discussion on page 448), you can also appoint one member as the moderator to act as a neutral, diplomatic voice between those posing and those answering the questions.

To add punch to your ending, you may want to use one of the same techniques discussed for opening a presentation. You might tell a story, make a personal appeal, or issue a challenge. However, resist the temptation to end with a quotation. It won't sound dramatic enough. Besides, you want your listeners to remember *your* words and thoughts—not someone else's. Also avoid fading out with a weak "That's about all I have to say" or "I see that our time is running out."

After you've developed some experience in giving presentations, you will be able to judge fairly accurately how long to spend on each point so as to finish on time. Until then, practice your presentation with a stopwatch. If necessary, insert reminders at critical points in your notes indicating where you should be at what point in time. Avoid having to drop important sections or rush through the conclusion of your presentation because you misjudged your timing.

Because your audience will remember best what they hear last, think of your ending as one of the most important parts of your presentation. Finish on a strong, upbeat note. Also remember that no one ever lost any friends by finishing a minute or two ahead of schedule. As Toastmasters International puts it, "Get up, speak up, shut up, and sit down."

Even veterans of the public stage don't always handle hostile audiences well. While generally congenial with the press, former Prime Minister Jean Chrétien once physically lashed out at a reporter, grabbing him around the neck.

The Use of Humour in Business Presentations

Memory research indicates that when ideas are presented with humour, the audience not only is able to recall more details of the presentation but also is able to retain the information longer.[7]

Use humour if it is appropriate and you are adept at telling humorous stories.

Most of us are not capable of being a Rick Mercer, even if we wanted to be. If you know you do not tell humorous stories well, the moment you're in front of an audience is not the time to try to rectify that situation. Both you and your audience will suffer. If, however, you feel that you can use humour effectively, doing so might add just the appropriate touch to your presentation.

Jokes, puns, satire, and especially amusing real-life incidents are just a few examples of humour, all of which serve to form a bond between speaker and audience. Humour can be used anywhere in a presentation—in the opening to get attention, in the body to add interest, or in the closing to drive home a point. Humour should be avoided, of course, if the topic is very serious or has negative consequences for the audience.

Personalize an amusing story to make it relate more directly to your topic.

If you tell an amusing story, it must always be appropriate to the situation and in good taste. Never tell an off-colour or sexist joke; never use offensive language; never single out an ethnic, racial, or religious group; and never use a dialect or foreign accent in telling a story. Such tactics are always in bad taste. The best stories are directed at you; they show that you are human and can laugh at yourself.

Before telling a humorous story, make sure you understand it and think it's funny. Then personalize it for your own style of speaking and for the particular situation. Avoid beginning jokes by saying, "I heard a funny story the other day about . . ." A major element of humour is surprise, so don't warn the audience a joke is coming. If you do, they're mentally preparing for a funny punch line, and you may disappoint them. If, on the other hand, you're already halfway into the story before the audience even realizes it's a joke, your chances of success are greater.

Resist the temptation to laugh at your own stories. A slight smile is more effective. Wait for the (hoped-for) laughter to subside; then continue your presentation by relating the punch line to the topic at hand.

Regardless of your expertise as a joke teller, do not use humour too frequently. Humour is a means to an end—not an end in itself. When all is said and done, you don't want your audience to remember that you were funny. You want them to remember that what you had to say was important and made sense.

■ Work-Team Presentations

CO**4.** **Plan a team presentation.**

Work-team presentations are common strategies for communicating about complex projects. For example, when presenting the organization's marketing plan to management or when updating the five-year plan, it is unlikely that any one person will have the expertise or time to prepare the entire presentation. Instead, a cooperative effort will be most effective.

Work-team presentations, whether written or oral, require extensive planning, close coordination, and a measure of maturity and goodwill. If you are responsible for coordinating such efforts, allow enough time and assign responsibilities on the basis of individual talents and time constraints.

Your major criterion for assigning responsibilities is the division of duties that will result in the most effective presentation. Tap into each member's strengths. Some members may be better at collecting and analyzing the information to be presented, others may be better at developing the visual aids, and others may be better at delivering the presentation. Does any work-team member have a knack for telling good stories or connecting with strangers? Maybe he or she should begin the presentation. Or pick a "diplomat" to moderate the question-and-answer session.

Make individual assignments for a team presentation based on individual strengths and preferences.

Everyone need not share equally in each aspect of the project. As coordinator, you should ensure that all efforts are recognized publicly and equally during the actual presentation, regardless of how much "podium time" is assigned to each person.

The Role of the Team Leader

Every team needs a leader—someone who will assume overall responsibility for the project. The team leader should be organized, knowledgeable about the topic, and well liked and respected by the rest of the team.

The effective team leader will lead the group in developing a cohesive strategy for the entire presentation and preparing a tentative schedule. Delay dividing up individual responsibilities until all team members are aware of and support the basic framework for the presentation. Assigning roles too early in the process is, in fact, one of the most common problems encountered with team presentations.

The team leader will want to give each member a written assignment of his or her responsibilities for content, visual aids, audience handouts, deadlines, rehearsals, and the like. In setting deadlines, work backward from the presentation date—not forward from the starting date.

Achieving Coherence

Just as people have different writing styles, so also they have different speaking styles. You must ensure that your overall presentation has coherence and unity—that is, that it sounds as if it were prepared and given by one individual. Thus, the group members should decide beforehand the most appropriate tone, format, organization, style for visual aids, manner of dress, method of handling questions, and similar factors that will help the presentation flow smoothly from topic to topic and from speaker to speaker.

Make your team presentation look as though it were prepared and given by a single person.

If using PowerPoint or some other presentation software, use a presentation template (either one that comes with your software package or one developed by your team) to maintain a consistent "look-and-feel" across everyone's slides. These templates define backgrounds and colours, slide heading formats, and font styles and sizes. Someone must also monitor for semantic consistency—both in the visual aids and in the verbal portion. Do you refer to people by first and last names, last names only, or a personal title and last name? Do you refer to your visual aids as charts, slides, overheads, graphics, or something else? If an unfamiliar term is used, ensure that the first person using the term (and only the first person) defines it.

Practicing the Team Presentation

A full-scale rehearsal—in the room where the presentation will be made and using all visual aids—is crucial for work-team presentations. If possible, videotape this rehearsal for later analysis by the entire group. Schedule your final practice session early enough that you will have time to make any changes needed—and then to run through the presentation once more, if necessary.

Critiquing the performance of a colleague requires tact, empathy, and goodwill; accepting such feedback requires grace and maturity. For the entire presentation to succeed, each individual element must succeed. If it does, each contributor shares in the success and any rewards that may result.

If dividing up the team parts prematurely is the most common problem of team presentations, then surely the failure to plan and coordinate introductions and transitions is the second most frequently encountered problem. Will the first speaker introduce all team members at the beginning, or will speakers introduce themselves as they get up to speak? To improve transitions between topics and between speakers, it's often wise to have each speaker introduce both the next speaker *and* the next topic before the next speaker moves into the centre stage.

NOT: "And that concludes my part of the presentation."

BUT: "And now Nancy will speak to you about the importance of starting a retirement plan *before* graduating from university."

If a question comes up during the presentation that you know a team member will answer during a subsequent segment, avoid stealing the team member's thunder. Instead, respond that "Alice will be covering that very point in a few minutes." If a question is asked of the group itself, the team leader should determine who will answer it. Refrain from adding to another member's response unless what you have to contribute is truly an important point not covered in the original answer.

Consider yourself on stage during the entire team presentation—no matter who is presenting. If you're on the sidelines, stand straight, pay attention to the presenter (even though you may have heard the content a dozen times), and try to read the audience for non-verbal signs of confusion, boredom, disagreement, and the like. Be aware that even though the audience's attention will primarily be focused on the speaker, fidgeting or bored expressions by those on the sidelines will be noticed, and such negative non-verbal cues will elicit similar responses from the audience.

Another consideration you should address during the rehearsal is where each member will stand. Obviously, the speaker should be centre stage, but the number of speakers and the room layout will dictate where the rest of the team should stand. Be sure the distance each team member stands from the speaker and from each other appears natural to the audience. If members appear to be hiding way in the corner or crowding the speaker or each other, the audience will notice.

Finally, one of the dangers of presenting as a team is if the presentation ends up being a series of loosely connected individual presentations, rather than a coherent team effort. Although it takes more planning and rehearsing, strive to transition between speakers often. This adds some energy to the presentation and, provided the transitions are strong, strengthens its coherence. Depending on how dynamic you wish the presentation to be, you may even wish to share the stage with another presenter and keep the transitions between speakers really short—one to two minutes. Some presenters even engage in a rehearsed banter or dialogue with each other as an alternative to the standard lecture style. This method takes some confidence and a lot of practice, but if done properly, it works well at keeping the audience engaged.

■ Other Business Presentations

CO5. Plan other types of business presentations.

In the standard types of business presentations discussed so far, you, the presenter, are the star of the show: you present information that is necessary to conduct the business of the organization, and you prepare your presentation carefully. Occasionally, however, you may be asked to participate in other types of presentations—ones in which you act as a supporting player. Such situations include making introductions, and making or receiving special recognitions.

Introductions

If you're the host of a presentation given by someone else, your actions can set the stage for a successful performance, which reflects well on both the speaker and the host. Make sure that you request background information about the speaker ahead of time, including correct pronunciations for all proper names. Also, communicate to the speaker the audience needs and interests, the nature of the expected presentation, its preferred length, the type of physical accommodations, and the like.

Briefly introduce the speaker, keeping the emphasis on the speaker and his or her qualifications.

When introducing someone, remember that the speaker is the main event—not you. All of your remarks should be directed at welcoming the speaker and establishing his or her qualifications to speak on the topic being addressed. Avoid inserting your own opinions about the topic or speaking for too long, thereby cutting into the speaker's time.

Select from the speaker's data sheet those accomplishments that are particularly relevant to the current topic, add any personal asides such as hobbies or family information to show the speaker as a human being, and conclude with a statement such as "We're honoured to have with us Ms. Jane Doe, who will now speak on the topic of . . . Ms. Doe." Lead the applause as the speaker rises; then step back from the podium and welcome the speaker with a handshake.

After the presentation, return to the podium and extend your appreciation to the person once again with another handshake and some brief remarks about the importance and relevance of the speaker's comments. Also, lead the question-and-answer session if one is planned, and be prepared to ask the first question in case no one in the audience wants to go first. At the conclusion, extend a sincere "thank you" to the speaker.

If you are responsible for seating and introducing a head table, you and the speaker should be seated on opposite sides of the podium, with the speaker sitting at the immediate left as you face the audience and you, as master of ceremonies, sitting at the immediate right side of the podium. When making the introductions, indicate whether each person should stand when introduced or remain seated, and ask the audience to hold any applause until everyone has been introduced. Then introduce each person, making a few appropriate remarks about each. Proceed from your extreme right to the podium and then from your extreme left to the podium.

Introduce the head table, beginning from the speaker's extreme right to the podium and then from the extreme left to the podium.

Give similar types and amounts of information about each person and ensure that all names are pronounced correctly. Be consistent in identifying each person—all first names or all personal titles and last names. When you get to the speaker, introduce him or her in a similar manner, indicating that a more complete introduction will follow. Lead the applause when all members of the head table have been introduced.

Special Recognitions

When presenting an award or recognizing someone for special achievement, first provide some background about the award—its history and criteria for selection. Then discuss the award winner's accomplishments, emphasizing those most relevant to the award. Under such happy circumstances, extensive praise is appropriate. Lead the applause as the recipient rises.

When accepting an honour, show genuine appreciation and graciously thank those responsible for the award. You may briefly thank people who helped you in your accomplishments, but do not bore the audience by thanking a long list of individuals who may be unknown to the audience.

■ Visual Aids for Business Presentations

Today's audiences are accustomed to multimedia events that bombard the senses. They often assume that any formal presentation must be accompanied by some visual element, whether it is a flipchart, overhead transparency, PowerPoint slide, film, DVD, or actual model.

CO6. Incorporate visual aids and audience handouts to enhance business presentations.

Use visual aids to enhance audience interest and comprehension and to help tell your story.

Visual aids are relatively simple to create and help the audience understand the presentation, especially if it includes complex or statistical material. A University of Pennsylvania study found that presenters who used visual aids successfully persuaded 67 percent of their audience, whereas those who did not use such aids persuaded only 50 percent of their audience. In addition, meetings in which visual aids were used were 28 percent shorter than those that lacked such aids. Similarly, a University of Minnesota study found that the use of graphics increased a presenter's persuasiveness by 43 percent. Presenters who used visual aids were also perceived as being more professional, better prepared, and more interesting than those who didn't use visual aids.[8] (For an indication of how much your sense of sight contributes to your knowledge, see Communication Snapshot 11.)

Preparing Visual Aids

Visual aids should be used only when needed and should be simple, readable, and of high quality.

Avoid overusing visual aids. Novice presenters sometimes use them as a crutch. Such overuse keeps the emphasis on the visual aid rather than on the presenter. Use visual aids only when they will help the audience grasp an important point, and remove them when they're no longer needed. One or two relevant, helpful visual aids are better than an entire armload of irrelevant ones—no matter how attractive they are.

Practice using your visual aids smoothly and effectively.

One of the most common mistakes presenters make in developing visual aids is to simply photocopy tables or illustrations from reports, printouts, or journals and project them on a screen. Print graphics usually contain far too much information to serve effectively as presentation graphics. Using print graphics in a presentation will often do more to hinder your presentation than to help it.

As a general rule, each slide or transparency should contain no more than 40 characters per line, no more than six or seven lines per visual, and no more than three columns of data (think of your slide as a highway billboard rather than a memo). Use upper- and lowercase letters (rather than all capitals) in a large, simple typeface with plenty of white (empty) space. Use bulleted lists to show a group of related items that have no specific order and numbered lists to show related items in a specific order. Figure 12.2 demonstrates the best placement of text on slides.

Establish a colour scheme and stay with it for all your visual aids; that is, use the same background colour for each slide or transparency. For handouts and overheads, use dark type on a light background; for slides, use light type on a dark background.

If you do not keep your visual aids clear and simple, your audience can easily become overwhelmed, with their attention drawn to the technology rather than to the content. As always, seek to *express*—not to *impress*. With visual aids, less is more. In his book *PowerPoint Is Evil*, Yale professor Edward R. Tufte makes the point that "the PowerPoint style routinely disrupts, domi-

communication snapshot 11

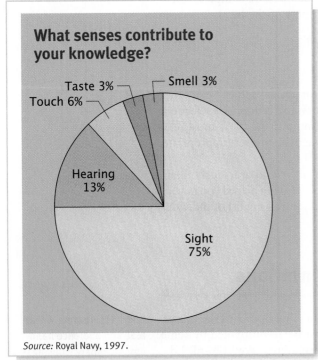

What senses contribute to your knowledge?

Taste 3%
Touch 6%
Smell 3%
Hearing 13%
Sight 75%

Source: Royal Navy, 1997.

figure12.2 **Placing Text Within Presentation Slides**

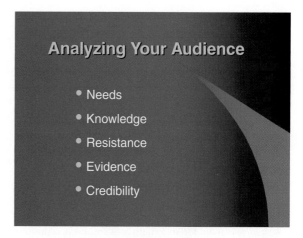

Avoid text-heavy slides   Keep text to a minimum

nates, and trivializes content." And according to Joan Detz, speaker, trainer, and author of *How to Write and Give a Speech:*[9]

> A successful presentation has little to do with technical wizardry. The single biggest mistake I see is overusing technology. Most of the time, visuals are used as a security blanket for people who haven't thought through a presentation. It's easier to have an audience look at a slide or other visual rather than at you.

See Spotlight 23 on Technology on page 454–455 for a discussion of some of the pros and cons of PowerPoint.

Transparencies

Figure 12.3 on page 456 compares features of the most common types of visual aids. Inexpensive, easy-to-produce, and simple-to-update transparencies for overhead projection can be used without darkening the room and while you face the audience. Thus, your audience can see to take notes, and you can maintain eye contact with them. Thanks to presentation software, overhead transparencies easily take advantage of colour, designed fonts, charts, artwork, and pre-planned layouts (called *templates*). The availability and low cost of computer projectors, combined with growing sales of notebook computers, however, has brought a significant drop in the use of transparencies in recent years.

Electronic Presentations

Today, electronic presentations are the newest medium for visual aids. They consist of slides or video shown directly from a computer and projected onto a screen via a projector. The most common software for electronic presentation is PowerPoint by Microsoft. Electronic presentations enable you to easily add multimedia effects to your presentation—if doing so helps you tell your story more effectively. You could, for example, show a short video, move text across the screen, or play background

Electronic presentations are fast becoming the method of choice for business presenters.

The Perils of PowerPoint

Presentation aids have been around for many decades, but surely no other piece of presentation technology has caused more controversy than PowerPoint. Much has been written on the subject, some sources with heavily derisive titles such as *PowerPoint is Evil, The Misuse of PowerPoint, The Trouble with PowerPoint, Where's the Power? What's the Point,* and *Ban it Now! Friends Don't Let Friends Use PowerPoint.*

Because the technology is inexpensive, relatively easy to use, and ubiquitous—Microsoft estimates that this software is used for 30 million presentations around the globe every day[10]—too many business presentations are dominated by poorly planned and poorly utilized Power-Point slides. Some corporations, like 3M, have strongly discouraged the use of PowerPoint in their meetings. PowerPoint is not, of course, problematic by definition. Like any piece of presentation equipment or software, PowerPoint can be a powerful tool if used effectively. Before offering some guidelines on how to do so, it's worth reviewing what some of its critics have to say.

J. Keller, in the article, *The Power of PowerPoint* writes:

[PowerPoint] squeezes ideas into a preconceived format, organizing and condensing not only your material but—inevitably it seems—your way of thinking about and looking at the material. A complicated, nuanced issue invariably is reduced to headings and bullets. And if that doesn't stultify your thinking about a subject, it may have that effect upon your audience—which is at the mercy of your presentation.[11]

Cornelius B. Pratt, in *The Misuse of PowerPoint,* argues that although PowerPoint is a useful tool, it is often mis-used as the presenter "habitually invokes more of his or her audiences' reading—not listening—skills. A presenter expects 'listeners' to 'multi-task,' rather than to focus on what the presenter has to offer."[12] In short, presenters often rely on the audience to do the work during the presentation so they don't have to. And it's easy to understand why. If given the choice between spending a couple

of hours putting together a few PowerPoint slides and then clicking through them in front of an audience or spending a few minutes delivering an engaging, insight-ful, and interesting presentation where the audience is focused on you, not the screen, many would choose the former every time.

In addition to allowing—even preferring—the Power-Point slides to take over the presentation, many presenters design the slides poorly, including too many words on a slide, using busy or inappropriate backgrounds, in-corporating distracting "bells and whistles" such as ex-cessive animation or sound, and relying on far too many slides.[13] On top of this, frequent equipment problems or poor knowledge of the technology often leaves the audi-ence waiting, with increasing impatience, as the presenter fumbles around trying to figure out what's wrong, some-times culminating in a plea for help from anyone in the audience who knows something about the technology.

Here are some suggestions to help you avoid falling into the many traps that PowerPoint sets:

Preparation

- Take advantage of what PowerPoint does best: it's great at providing visual information such as photo-graphs, charts, or diagrams, and it also allows you to easily insert video clips. It's much less effective at presenting text-heavy information, as the audience ends up reading the slides, rather than listening to the presenter.[14]

- When inserting visuals, keep charts, tables, and dia-grams fairly simple, and avoid the tired clip art of too many presentations. It's easy to find fresh, relevant images on Google or elsewhere and insert them into your presentation. And never include anything just because you think it looks cool; if a visual doesn't fur-ther your discussion, discard it.

- Unless appropriate for your topic, don't let multimedia elements such as music or video clips overwhelm your presentation. (Some suggest avoiding them altogether.)

If you do choose to use them, one or two brief clips have far more impact than a barrage of images and sound.

- Keep the content of each slide to a minimum. Pratt suggests using the "triple-seven" rule: no more than seven bullets, no more than seven words per bullet, and no more than seven lines of text (including the title) per bulleted slide. (Some suggest even fewer bullets and fewer lines of text). If text is not presented in bulleted form, keep the number of lines to no more than three.[15]

- When writing bullet points, stay away from complete sentences; stick to words or phrases, and avoid including explanatory details on your slides. As the presenter, take responsibility for fleshing out your bullets through explanation, anecdote, or example; don't rely on your slides to do this for you. (Compare Slides 1 and 2 in Figure 12.2. Slide 2 has only five lines of text, uses words, rather than sentences, is far easier to read, and requires the presenter to provide the explanatory details.)

- Keep the number of slides to a minimum. Pratt suggests using only about one text-based slide for every five minutes of presentation time. That amounts to only about six slides for a half-hour presentation—far fewer than most practitioners of PowerPoint generally include. You may, of course, include other slides that present visual information, such as discussed above.[16]

- Choose your font and colour schemes to maximize readability. According to one Microsoft Office specialist, research has shown that yellow text on a dark blue background is most visible.[17] Also keep in mind that the colours you select when designing your slides don't always look the same on the screen, so always review the slideshow on a screen before you present. Avoid excessive use of colours, generally no more than four in an entire presentation. Finally, choose *sans serif* fonts, as you should when designing headings in a written document, and use a minimum of a 32-point type size.

- Consider using PowerPoint's "Notes" function to write out your speaking notes underneath each slide; then print them off as an alternative to the standard index cards. This helps you better integrate the material on each slide with what you plan to say.

Presentation

- Avoid using PowerPoint from start to finish. Think of PowerPoint as being akin to a highlighter pen: it draws attention to important features and helps the reader form a mental outline of the material. Highlighting everything is meaningless and fatiguing; so too is the continuous use of PowerPoint from introduction through conclusion. At set points in the presentation, blacken the screen by hitting the "B" key or by using the picture mute function on the projector, if available. This draws the audience's attention back to where it belongs—the speaker. This also helps you re-establish rapport, tell a story, address questions, and move about more freely without worrying if everyone can see the screen. Using a remote also allows to you move around the stage when you are referring to your slides.

- Display each bullet point one at a time. This keeps the audience, who read much faster than you can speak, from getting ahead of you.[18] PowerPoint's animation feature makes this easy. As you load each phrase, avoid accompanying them with sound effects. These add unwanted external noise, serve no meaningful purpose, and often distract the audience.

- Don't read from your slides. PowerPoint is not a teleprompter; your eyes should be focused on the audience, and occasionally on your notes, not on the screen behind you. Besides, if you're using PowerPoint correctly, there shouldn't be much to read. The details should be in your head and in your speaking notes.

PowerPoint, if used well, can add energy and polish to your presentation. If handled poorly, PowerPoint deadens the presentation and makes the audience wish you'd just mailed them the information and not wasted their time.

figure12.3

Criteria for Selecting Visual Aids

Criteria	Electronic presentations	Transparencies	35-mm slides	Films	Videotape	Flipcharts	Handouts
Quality	Good	Good	Excellent	Excellent	Excellent	Poor	Good
Cost	Moderate	Low	Moderate	High	High	Low	Low
Ease of use	Difficult	Easy	Moderate	Moderate	Easy	Easy	Easy
Ease of preparation	Easy	Easy	Moderate	Difficult	Difficult	Easy	Easy
Ease of updating	Easy	Easy	Moderate	Difficult	Difficult	N/A	Easy
Degrees of formality	Formal	Either	Formal	Either	Either	Informal	Either
Adaptability to audience size	Moderate	Excellent	Excellent	Excellent	Moderate	Poor	Moderate
Dependence on equipment	High	Moderate	Moderate	Moderate	Moderate	Low	None

sound effects. Electronic slide presentations offer greater flexibility than traditional slide presentations do, but their use also requires high-powered projectors to obtain the best results.

When giving an electronic presentation, follow these guidelines:

When showing slides, be sure to avoid walking in front of the projector. Also, avoid including too much information on each slide.

- Check colours for accuracy. If precise colour matching is important (for example, with the colour of your corporate logo), ensure that the colour projected on the computer on which you designed the presentation matches the colour shown on the projection system on which you will display it.

- Keep special effects simple. Elaborate or random transition effects, for example, are distracting. Nevertheless, consider using builds to reveal one bullet point at a time; doing so helps focus the audience's attention. Avoid sound effects unless absolutely essential for understanding.

- Disable any screen savers and energy-saving automatic shut-down features of your computer. You don't want your screen to begin displaying a screen saver or to go blank in the middle of your presentation.

- Be seen and heard. Stand on the left side from the audience's point of view—in the light and away from the computer—using a remote mouse if necessary. Make sure that you're still easily visible when the projection screen is dark.

Even the best visual aid will not be effective if it is not used properly during the presentation or if the equipment doesn't work. Using equipment smoothly does not come naturally; it takes practice and a keen awareness of audience needs, especially when using a slide or overhead projector. Ensure that the image is readable from every seat and that neither you nor the projector blocks anyone's view (see Figure 12.4).

figure12.4
Positioning the Projector Correctly

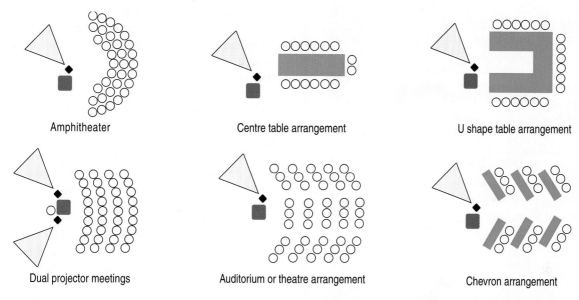

Amphitheater   Centre table arrangement   U shape table arrangement

Dual projector meetings   Auditorium or theatre arrangement   Chevron arrangement

■ Handouts

Audience handouts—printed copies of notes, tables, or illustrations—are often important in helping the audience follow a presentation. They are a standard part of most business presentations because they provide a review and new information for the audience long after your presentation is over. In addition, they represent a permanent record of the major points of the presentation and reduce or eliminate the need for note taking. Handouts are especially helpful when you are dealing with complex information such as detailed statistical tables, which would be ineffective if projected as a slide or transparency.

Handouts may, of course, contain miniature versions of the slides containing the most important points of your presentation. As a rule, however, you should avoid including them all. It's also much better if you can annotate each slide you do include. Include additional information that would not fit on the projected slide—examples, details, background data, summaries, more complete charts, or sources of extra information. Keep the content simple, concise, and to the point. Avoid padding with irrelevant information.

Organize your handout topics in the sequence in which you present them. Use a generous number of headings, and number the pages so that you can easily refer your audience to the section you're presenting. Also, provide plenty of white space—both as a design element for readability and as space for note taking. If a high-quality colour printer or copier is available, use colour within reason—for the cover page, headings, charts, and the like—but not for body type, which should be black on a white background.

Provide good photocopies, avoiding off-centre, smudged, grey, or faint copies. Retype a document that is unattractive or difficult to read or that contains non-essential information. Use a legible font—at least 12 points in size—to facilitate reading in a

Audience handouts supplement your oral information, provide space for note taking, and represent a permanent record of your presentation.

communication snapshot 12

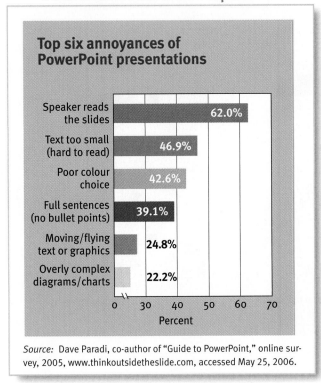

Top six annoyances of PowerPoint presentations

	Percent
Speaker reads the slides	62.0%
Text too small (hard to read)	46.9%
Poor colour choice	42.6%
Full sentences (no bullet points)	39.1%
Moving/flying text or graphics	24.8%
Overly complex diagrams/charts	22.2%

Source: Dave Paradi, co-author of "Guide to PowerPoint," online survey, 2005, www.thinkoutsidetheslide.com, accessed May 25, 2006.

The content and purpose of your handout determine when it should be distributed.

somewhat darkened room during an audiovisual presentation.

You must decide the most effective time to distribute your handout—before, during, or after your presentation. Some handouts contain complex data or extensive information that should be read before your presentation as a framework for understanding your remarks (for example, a complex proposal). In that case, send the handout to the audience members prior to their arrival for the presentation. In a cover letter, tell them the purpose of the handout and ask them to read it before attending your presentation. Obviously, you must then ensure that you do not merely repeat the information in the handout during your presentation.

You should distribute your handout immediately before the presentation if you will be referring to material in it as you speak. Ensure that the audience members have time to browse the material before the session starts so that you will have their complete attention when you begin speaking. Many audience members prefer to have the handout available during the presentation as a handy means of taking notes. In this scenario, your message will be reinforced three times—once when you present it, once when the audience views your handout, and again when they take notes.

Finally, if your handout merely summarizes your message, you may decide to distribute it immediately after your presentation—to ensure that you have the audience's complete attention during your remarks. Do, however, tell the audience that you intend to do so to prevent them from taking unnecessary notes.

■ Practicing and Delivering the Presentation

CO7. Practice and deliver a business presentation.

Begin practicing by simulating the conditions of the meeting room as closely as possible. Always practice standing, with your notes at the same level and angle as at a podium, and use any visual aids that will be a part of your presentation.

Videotaping your rehearsal can help you review and modify your voice qualities, gestures, and speech content. Remember that 55 percent of your credibility with an audience comes from your body language, 38 percent comes from your voice qualities, and only 7 percent comes from the actual words you use.[19] Play back the video recording several times, paying attention to your voice qualities (especially speed and pitch), pauses, grouping of words and phrases, and pronunciation.

For important presentations, plan on a minimum of three run-throughs. The first run-through should focus on continuity (does everything you say make sense when you say it aloud?) and approximate timing. If necessary, cut out a key point so that you have time for a solid, well-rehearsed, and non-rushed summary and conclusion. Your second and third run-throughs should focus on polishing your delivery, including transitions between speakers (if doing a team presentation), vocal qualities such as volume and intonation, and gestures. For each run-through, record how much time it takes on each section of your outline. Schedule your practice sessions far enough ahead of time to allow you to make any needed changes. Start small and add on later. Your first run-through should probably be private, or perhaps with one close colleague in attendance to give feedback. Then, when you're satisfied, move up to the next step.

By your final run-through, you should be familiar enough with your message that a few notes or a graphic will keep you on track. Practice the most important parts (introduction, summary of key points, conclusion) as many times as possible.

Body Language and Vocal Cues

Experts suggest that "nonverbal cues carry approximately two-thirds of the communicative nature of a message."[20] And since effective communication is the primary goal of any business presentation, it's worth having someone observe and comment on your non-verbal behaviour at the rehearsal stage. Interestingly, when students are asked to view their own video recorded presentations and comment on their delivery, the overwhelming majority are somewhat surprised to see nonverbal signals they had no idea they were sending. While it's difficult to eliminate undesirable non-verbal mannerisms (we all have bad habits), you should try to identify the most distracting ones and minimize them as best you can. It's also difficult to adopt new non-verbal behaviours that may improve your delivery, so be realistic about how many changes you wish to make. You may wish to just work on two or three behaviours to start with and gradually attend to others as you become more confident. Here is a list of some of the more important non-verbal considerations when conducting business presentations.

Style and Tone   With rare exceptions, the language of oral presentations should be relatively simple and conversational. Most people understand intuitively what is meant by a "conversational style"—it's simply the style we all use when having a relaxed, informal conversation. Achieving a conversational style when delivering a presentation can be trickier, however. Here are some tips that will help you relax and sound more conversational:

- Maintain eye contact. This is the single most important piece of advice experts give to would-be public speakers, and it's worth repeating often. You should know your presentation well enough that you can maintain eye contact easily with your audience, taking care to include members in all corners of the room. Lock in on one person and maintain eye contact for at least three seconds—or until you have completed a thought. If you're looking at individuals within the audience, you will unconsciously adopt a more conversational style.

- Stick to relatively simple sentence structures. Long, complex sentences that work well on paper can sound stuffy and formal when spoken aloud.

- Think of yourself as having a conversation with your audience, not lecturing to them. This is why we advise not using full-sentence notes, which make it impossible to sound conversational.

- If appropriate, ask a question or two early in the presentation. Your questions may be rhetorical, which don't require the audience to actually respond, or they can be actual solicitations for audience input. The most common error when asking rhetorical questions is the failure to pause long enough for the audience to consider them. Be sure to wait two or three seconds after asking a rhetorical question to let it sink in. An advantage of asking real questions—those to which you expect audience members to respond—is that the presentation quickly begins to feel more like a dialogue (i.e., a conversation) than a monologue. This also tends to "loosen up" the speaker by taking a little of the attention off him or her at the outset.

- Use contractions freely. We do so in everyday speech, so there's no reason not to when giving a presentation.

- Avoid the use of words that you wouldn't use in ordinary speech or that you may have trouble pronouncing.

- Insert conversational words and phrases such as "by the way," "obviously," "after all," and "let's face it."[21] These little asides or interjections mimic a one-to-one conversation, the tone for which you're striving.

- Use humour. We've already discussed the appropriateness of humour in presentations. Occasionally laughing at ourselves or even gently poking fun at our audience further contributes to the conversational feel of a presentation.

As noted earlier, a conversational style isn't appropriate for every presentation. Formal proposals or presentations presented to senior executives, bank officers, or venture capitalists would typically be more scripted, more formal, and less conversational. But most audiences, even in formal settings, appreciate the warmth of a conversation. The degree to which you apply the above suggestions must ultimately be left up to good judgment and experience.

Voice   Expert presenters go beyond just clearly communicating the information; they bring it to life. And the most important tool you have to animate a presentation is your own voice. Here are some specific guidelines for helping you use your voice effectively:

- If you are speaking to a very large room, you will typically not need a microphone. You will, however, need to increase your volume beyond the level of a normal conversation. Have someone sit at the back of the room during your rehearsal, turn on the projector or any other presentation device that might emit noise, then adjust your volume so that person can hear you easily. Keep in mind that during the actual presentation, there will be more people and more noise, so it's crucial your volume is adequate.

- For interest and to fit the situation, vary your volume. Decreases in volume in the middle of an example or anecdote forces your audience to lean in and pay attention, while sudden (and unexpected) increases in volume create intensity (and jolt anyone who might be losing focus).

Speak in a conversational tone—but slightly slower.

- Speak at a slightly slower rate than normally used in conversation, but vary your rate of speaking, slowing down when presenting important or complex information and speeding up when summarizing. Slowing down also adds dramatic tension to a story, while speeding up enhances the story's climax.

- Use periodic pauses to emphasize important points, waiting two or three seconds before speaking again.

■ Avoid peppering your speech with vocal ticks such as "um," "ahh," "like," "okay," and "you know." It's difficult to eliminate these entirely, but listening to a recording of yourself can help you identify those to which you are most prone. Remember that you need not fill every bit of air space with noise. Rather than preceding a sentence with "um" or "ah," force yourself to be silent for a second while considering what to say next.

■ Lower your pitch. Speaking at the lower end of your natural register not only helps your voice carry better, it also enhances your credibility. Deep voices tend to command attention.

■ Vary your pitch. We've all experienced that dreaded monotone of the very worst presentations. An unvaried pitch tends to come from one of two places: nervousness or a naturally flat speaking style. Nervousness can be tackled in a number of ways, many of which are discussed on page 463. But the most important thing you can do to combat nervousness is to prepare; plan your presentation carefully and rehearse it well. Harder to combat is a natural tendency toward a monotone voice. Try recording a few minutes of your presentation and just listening to (not watching) it. If you tend to be monotone, whether naturally or through nervousness, you'll hear it right away. Then practice the same few minutes of the presentation, consciously varying both your pitch and your volume. Do this a few times until your recorded voice sounds more dynamic.

Gestures, Postures, and Use of Space   Almost as important as your voice is how you use the rest of your body to emphasize and illustrate the content of your presentation. We all have a certain amount of nervous energy, which if channelled appropriately, can actually improve our delivery. Unfortunately, some of us allow the nervous energy to "leak out" through fidgeting, pacing, foot shuffling, and the like. Instead of allowing this nervous energy to control you, learn to consciously channel it through the deliberate use of gestures, postures, and space.

■ Use hand and arm gestures to add interest and emphasis. Most people, even if they don't realize it, do "speak with their hands" to at least some degree, especially when standing. Some keep their gestures small and their hands close to their body; others prefer broad and animated gestures. Whatever your preference, be sure your gestures are appropriate and appear natural. Some argue that one-handed gestures are more effective and less distracting than two-handed ones, but this depends entirely on how comfortable the speaker appears when using gestures. Again, viewing a video of yourself presenting can help you identify what appears natural to you.

Use appropriate gestures if you are comfortable doing so.

■ Keep your hands out of your pockets and above your waist. While it's certainly not wrong to occasionally put a hand in your pocket while presenting, it's never a good idea to keep your hands in your pockets the entire time. Doing so can make you appear a little too relaxed, even disengaged from your audience. While rehearsing, practice keeping your hands in front of your body and above your waist; this forces you to gesture as you speak. If you find yourself fidgeting, try holding your notes or even a pen in one hand while speaking. Be careful, however, not to start tapping or clicking the pen or shuffling your notes, which can be extremely distracting.

■ Establish an anchor. Position your body on the left side of the room (the left side from the audience's point of view) when speaking in English, which reads from left to right. With this setup, the audience looks toward the left to view the speaker, glances slightly to the right to begin reading the visual aid, and then moves back left to the speaker again.

- Avoid "gluing" yourself to your anchor. Observe how often the camera angle changes next time you're watching the news. Producers do this with the understanding that the attention span of viewers is limited and that frequent changes in the viewing angle helps keep the audience engaged. Your anchor is the place you will continually return to, but unless speaking from behind a lectern, try occasionally taking a few steps away from your anchor, pausing to speak from that new position, returning to the anchor, and then stepping out in a different direction. As you become more comfortable with this technique, you may try stepping forward into the middle of the audience for a brief moment, before returning to your anchor. This is a great way to establish and maintain rapport with your audience. When moving about the room, be careful not to block your audience's view of your visual aids.

- Practice smiling occasionally, standing tall and naturally, with the body balanced on both feet. Your voice and demeanour should reflect professionalism, enthusiasm, and self-confidence.

- Avoid annoying and distracting mannerisms and gestures, such as jingling coins or keys in your pocket; coughing or clearing your throat excessively; wildly waving your hands; gripping the lectern tightly; nervously swaying or pacing; or playing with jewellery, pens, or paper clips. All of these mannerisms are a result of nervous energy escaping in undesirable ways. Channelling this energy, using the guidelines suggested here, will help you minimize these distractions.

Dress   Your clothing is a part of the message you communicate to your audience, so dress appropriately—in comfortable and businesslike attire. Different clothes give us different energy levels, and if you can feel it, so can your audience. Follow these guidelines:[22]

Dress comfortably—just slightly dressier than your audience.

- Dress just slightly better than the audience; the audience will be complimented by your efforts.

- Make sure your shoes are the same colour or darker than the hemline of your pants or skirt.

- Consider wearing long sleeves when presenting. They project authority and a higher level of professionalism and respect. Short sleeves create a more casual appearance.

- Ensure that the tip of a man's tie hits the middle of his belt buckle.

- Be aware that the higher the stage, the shorter a woman's skirt will appear. The best skirt length is mid-knee for women of short or medium height and a few centimetres below mid-knee for taller women.

Handling Nervousness

According to author Mark Twain, "There are two types of speakers—those who are nervous and those who are liars." For some people, making a presentation is accompanied by such symptoms as gasping for air; feeling faint or nauseated ("butterflies in the stomach"); having shaking hands or legs and sweaty palms; feeling the heart beat rapidly and loudly; or speaking too rapidly and in a high-pitched voice.

If you've ever experienced any of these symptoms, take comfort in the fact that you're not alone. Fear of giving a speech is the number one fear of many Canadians. Fortunately, behaviour-modification experts have found that of the full range of anxiety disorders, people can most predictably overcome their fear of public speaking.[23]

Recognize that you have been asked to make a presentation because someone obviously thinks you have something important to say. You should feel complimented. Unless you are an exceptionally good or exceptionally bad speaker, the audience will more likely remember *what* you say rather than how you say it. Most of us fall somewhere between these two extremes as presenters. Here are a few guidelines for reducing nervousness:

- The best way to minimize any lingering anxiety is to over-prepare. For the anxious presenter, there is no such thing as over-practice. The more familiar you are with the content of your speech and the more trial runs you've made, the better you'll be able to concentrate on your delivery once you're actually in front of the group. Plan a strong introduction, and rehearse it well, even to the point of memorizing the first few lines. Even highly anxious speakers start to relax after the first minute or two, and a strong, well-rehearsed start will get you through the most anxious moments.

- Visit the room beforehand. Ideally, you'll have had a chance to rehearse in the room in which you'll be presenting. If not, visit the room a day or even a few hours beforehand. When you actually get up to present, you'll feel you're on familiar ground. If appropriate, you may also find it helpful to be in the room a few minutes before your audience arrives, giving you a chance to greet some of them as they walk in. Because they are walking into your territory, rather than the other way around, you'll have a sense of "home-ice advantage," which can further boost your confidence.

- Practice mental imagery. Several times before your big presentation, sit in a comfortable position, close your eyes, and visualize yourself giving your speech. Picture yourself speaking confidently, loudly, and clearly in an assured voice. If you can imagine yourself giving a successful speech, you will be able to do so.

- Before your presentation, take a short walk to relax your body. While waiting for your presentation to begin, let your arms drop loosely by your sides and shake your wrists gently, all the while breathing deeply several times. As you begin to speak, look for friendly faces in the crowd, and concentrate on them initially.

- If you're particularly nervous, remind yourself that you never look as nervous as you may feel. As much as you may feel like your hands are shaking and your heart is pounding, the audience can't see this. Moreover, unless you're speaking to a hostile audience, they're not looking for evidence of nervousness or weakness. They want and expect you to do well, and you should too. With this in mind, avoid announcing that you're nervous. This cues the audience to look for signs of nervousness rather than pay attention. It also draws your own attention away from your task.

- Just before the presentation, practice relaxation exercises. Take a deep breath and hold it for a few seconds; then let it out slowly. This helps to slow your heart rate and avoid the "panting" that some people get when they are particularly nervous. If you're worried about trembling hands, try clenching your hands as tight

To avoid anxiety, practice, develop a positive attitude, and concentrate on friendly faces.

as you can, holding them tight for a few seconds, and relaxing. Do this several times until your hands begin to relax.

- Have a glass of water handy. One of the more common results of nervousness is a dry mouth. Unlike an increased heart rate or trembling hands, a dry mouth can actually disrupt your speech. Most often a glass of water is available to speakers, but bring your own just in case. Even when water is available, too often people fail to take advantage of it. No one will mind, and few will even notice, if you pause for a second to have a drink.

Finally, the professional who is anxious about speaking in public should consider taking a public speaking course or joining Toastmasters International, the world's oldest and largest non-profit educational organization. The purpose of Toastmasters is to improve the speaking skills of its members. Members meet weekly or monthly and deliver prepared speeches, evaluate one another's oral presentations, give impromptu talks, develop their listening skills, conduct meetings, and learn parliamentary procedure.

The homepage for Toastmasters International is found at www.toastmasters.org.

Answering Questions

One advantage of oral presentations over written reports is the opportunity to engage in two-way communication. The question-and-answer session is a vital part of your presentation; plan for it accordingly.

Normally, you should announce at the beginning of your presentation that you will be happy to answer any questions when you're through. Holding questions until near the end helps you avoid being interrupted and losing your train of thought or possibly running out of time and not being able to complete your prepared remarks. Also, there is always the possibility that the listener's question will be answered later in the course of your presentation.

The exception to a questions-near-the-end policy is when your topic is so complex that a listener's question must be answered immediately if he or she is to follow the rest of the presentation. Another exception is informal (and generally small) meetings, where questions and comments naturally occur throughout the presentation.

As you prepare your presentation, anticipate what questions you might expect from the audience. Make a list of them and think through possible answers. If necessary, make notes to refer to while answering. If your list of questions is very long, you should probably consider revising your presentation to incorporate some of the answers into your prepared remarks.

Plan your answers to possible questions ahead of time.

Always listen carefully to the question; repeat it, if necessary, for the benefit of the entire audience; and look at the entire audience as you answer—not just at the questioner. Treat each questioner with unfailing courtesy. If the question is antagonistic, be firm but fair and polite.

If you don't know the answer to a question, freely say so and promise to have the answer within a specific period. Then write down the question (and the name of the questioner) to remind yourself to find the answer later. Do not risk embarrassing another member of the audience by referring the question to him or her.

If your call for questions results in absolute silence, you may conclude either that you did a superb job of explaining your topic or that no one wishes to be the first to ask a question. If you suspect the latter, to break the ice, you might start the questions yourself, by saying something like, "One question I'm frequently asked that might interest you is. . . ." Or you may ask the program chair ahead of time to be prepared to ask the first question if no one in the audience begins.

✔checklist 15

The Oral Presentation Process

Planning

✔ Determine whether an oral presentation will be more effective than a written report.

✔ Determine your purpose: What response do you want from your audience?

✔ Analyze your audience in terms of demographic factors, level of knowledge, and psychological needs.

✔ If possible, schedule the presentation at an appropriate time.

✔ Select an appropriate delivery method.

Organizing

✔ Brainstorm by writing down every point you think you might cover.

✔ Separate your notes into the opening, body, and ending. Gather additional information if needed.

✔ Write an effective opening that introduces the topic, discusses the points you'll cover, and tells the audience what you hope will happen as a result of your presentation.

✔ In the body, develop your points fully, giving background data, evidence, and examples.

■ Organize the points logically.

■ To maintain credibility, discuss any major negative points and be prepared to discuss any minor ones.

■ Pace the presentation of data to avoid presenting facts and figures too quickly.

■ Finish on a strong, upbeat note.

✔ Use humour only when appropriate and only if you are effective at telling amusing stories.

✔ Ensure that your visual aids are needed, simple, easily readable, and of the highest quality.

✔ Ensure that your audience handout contains useful and new information and is attractive and readable.

Practicing

✔ Rehearse your presentation extensively, simulating the actual speaking conditions and using your visual aids.

✔ Use simple language and short sentences, with frequent preview, summary, transition, and repetition.

✔ Stand tall and naturally, and speak in a loud, clear, enthusiastic, and friendly voice. Vary the rate and volume of your voice.

✔ Use correct diction and appropriate gestures.

Delivering

✔ Dress appropriately—in comfortable, businesslike, conservative clothing.

✔ If needed, use a microphone effectively.

✔ Maintain eye contact with the audience, including all corners of the room in your gaze.

✔ To avoid anxiety, practice extensively, develop a positive attitude, and concentrate on the friendly faces in the audience.

✔ Plan your answers to possible questions ahead of time. Listen to each question carefully and address your answer to the entire audience.

As we've discussed earlier, save some closing remarks for the very end, after you've addressed questions. You want to end your presentation on a high note and, because you can never be sure what kind of questions your going to get, if any, save some interesting memorable remarks for the closing of the presentation.

The 3Ps
Problem, Process, Product

A BUSINESS PRESENTATION

You are Matt Kromer, an information specialist at Lewis & Smith, a large import/export firm in Vancouver. Your company publishes three major external documents—a quarterly customer newsletter, a semi-annual catalogue, and an annual report. All three are currently prepared by an outside printing company. However, the decision was recently made to switch to some form of in-house publishing for these publications.

Your superior asked you to research the question of whether your firm should use word processing or desktop publishing software to create these documents. Considering the importance of these external documents, you have been asked to make a formal 20-minute presentation of your findings and recommendations to the firm's administrative committee.

1. What is the purpose of your presentation?

   To present the findings from my research, to recommend a type of software program, and to persuade the audience that my recommendations are sound.

2. Describe your audience.

   The administrative committee consists of the five managers (including my superior) who report to the vice-president for administration. I have met them all, but with the exception of my own superior, I do not know any of them well.

   Their role will be to make the final decision regarding which type of software program to use. Once that decision has been made, the actual users will decide which brand to purchase. Four of the five managers are casual users of word processing software. They've all likely heard of desktop publishing but have never used it.

3. What type of presentation will be most appropriate?

   This will be a normal business presentation to a small audience, so I'll speak from notes and use slides. Because I have only 20 minutes to present, I'll hold off answering questions until the end—to make sure I have enough time to cover the needed information.

4. What kind of data have you collected for your presentation?

    I studied each publication's formatting requirements, analyzed the features of the most popular word processing (Microsoft Word) and desktop publishing (Adobe PageMaker) programs, and spoke with a colleague from a firm that recently began publishing its documents in-house.
        On the basis of the criteria of cost, ease of use, and features, I'll recommend the use of word processing software to publish our three documents.

5. How will you organize the data?

    First, I'll present the background information. Then, I could organize my research data by presenting the advantages and disadvantages of each type of program. However, I think it would be more effective to organize my findings by criteria instead; that is, I will show how each program rates in terms of cost, ease of use, and features.

6. Outline an effective opening section for your presentation.

    a. Introduction: "Freedom of the Press" (Computer software now gives us the freedom to publish our own documents at lower cost and with greater flexibility.)

    b. Purpose: to recommend whether to use WP or DTP software

    c. Organization: by criteria (cost, ease of use, and features)

    d. Audience role: to make the final decision

7. How will you handle negative information?

    Although I'm recommending word processing software, the desktop publishing program has more features. However, I'll show that (a) we don't necessarily need those features and (b) those features make the program more difficult to learn.

Product

Provides identifying information in the opening—in case of loss or for future reference.

Uses an attention-getting opening that is written verbatim for a stress-free start.

Uses the opening to give the purpose, preview the topics, and identify the audience's role.

Alerts the audience to prevent interrupting questions and unnecessary note taking.

Marks the slide references for easy identification.

SELECTING DESKTOP PUBLISHING SOFTWARE
Presented to the Administrative Committee
Matt Kromer, 10/3/—

I. OPENING

A. I'd like to talk to you today about <u>freedom of the press</u>—specifically about our recent decision to switch to in-house publishing. And though our publications won't be completely "free," desktop publishing <u>will</u> provide us with more flexibility—at a greatly reduced price.

B. <u>Purpose</u>: To recommend whether to use word processing or desktop publishing software to publish our company newsletter, catalog, and annual report.

<u>SLIDE 1—FREEDOM OF THE PRESS</u>

C. <u>Preview</u>:
    1. Background information
    2. Criteria for decision:
       a. Cost
       b. Ease of use
       c. Features
    3. My recommendation

D. <u>Your Job</u>: Make final decision.
    Will <u>not</u> have to decide which brand of software.

E. Will take questions at the end.
    Will distribute handout.

II. BODY

<u>SLIDE 2—PUBLICATIONS</u>

A. <u>Background</u>:

Grammar and Mechanics Notes

Type the outline in large upper and lower case letters, either on individual note cards or on full sheets of paper. Leave plenty of white space between sections so that you can easily find your place.

1. 3 major external documents; all have strategic marketing value:

   a. Newsletter *(Show copy)*: The Forum
      — 2000 copies quarterly
      — 8 pp. 1-color (black) on ivory stock, with brown masthead
      — Photos and line art

   b. Catalog *(Show copy)*:
      — 4000 copies semiannually
      — 36–44 pp.
      — 1-color (black) interior with 4-color cover

   c. Annual Report *(Show copy)*:
      — 1500 copies annually
      — 24–28 pp.
      — 1-color (blue) interior on gray stock with 4-color cover

2. All 3 presently published by Medallion Printing Company

3. Research:

   a. Analyzed each pub. to determine formatting reqs.

   b. Analyzed features of Microsoft Word, the WP program we now support, and Adobe PageMaker, the most popular DTP program.

   c. Spoke with Paula Henning from Crown Busch.
      Her co. began producing documents in-house using DTP last year.

B. Criteria:

SLIDE 3—COST COMPARISON

1. Cost:

   a. Either program will require:
      (1) One flatbed scanner and software: $375
      (2) One digital camera: $475

   b. Microsoft Word: $175—But we already own.

   c. Adobe PageMaker: $495—Have to buy.

Makes a note to hold up copies of documents.

Discusses research procedures to help establish credibility.

Organizes the main part of the speech body by the criteria used for making the decision.

Grammar and Mechanics Notes

You do not have to write your presentation notes in parallel format; no one will see them but you. You may need complete sentences to jog your memory for some parts, but keep these to a minimum. Use only partial sentences, individual words, or abbreviations for most of your speaking notes.

Presents both positive and negative information and discusses the importance and implications of each feature.

        d. <u>Conclusion</u>: PageMaker costs $495 more than Microsoft Word.

    2. <u>Ease of Use</u>:

        a. <u>Microsoft Word</u>:
           (1) Operators already know how to use.
           (2) ½-day seminar to teach advanced features—$500

        b. <u>Adobe PageMaker</u>:
           (1) Difficult to learn because of adv. features
           (2) Danger of forgetting—used infrequently
           (3) 2-day seminar needed—$2000

        c. Conclusion: Word costs $1500 less than PageMaker.

SLIDE 4—FEATURE COMPARISON

Underline important points for easy referral. Use columns when needed for easy reference.

    3. <u>Features</u>:

a. Font flexibility	Both have.
b. Column feature	Both have.
c. Import/manipulate graphics	PM has more options.
d. Color separations	PM has; Word doesn't. Don't need now; maybe in future.
e. Predesigned templates	Both have; PM better.
f. Ease of revisions	Important criterion Both have; easier in Word.

III. CLOSING

SLIDE 5—RECOMMENDATION

Puts the final recommendation and the rationale on a slide—for emphasis.

  A. <u>Recommendation</u>: Microsoft Word

    1. Cheaper (by $1500)

    2. Easier to use/less training needed

    3. Has all the features we presently need

SLIDE 6—SCHEDULE

B. Schedule:

Today	Make software decision
November	Purchase and install hardware and software
December	Conduct user training
January	Begin producing 3 docs. in-house

HANDOUT—SELECTING DESKTOP PUBLISHING SOFTWARE

C. Questions regarding two programs or recommendations.

D. Conclusion:

Our entry into DTP is an exciting project because it gives us greater control over our publications at less cost. In addition, DTP will open up opportunities for even more publishing projects in the future to help us better fulfill our corporate mission.

NOTES *(to be taken during presentation)*

Closes by giving the recommendation and telling what happens next. Ends on a confident, forward-looking note.

Follows presentation with a question-and-answer session.

Leaves room for taking notes during question-and-answer session.

Grammar and Mechanics Notes

If you plan to give the conclusion verbatim, as this speaker has, double-space the concluding sentences. *Note:* You would no doubt have to insert some last-minute handwritten changes in your final outline prior to actually giving the presentation.

■ Summary

CO1. Describe the important role that business presentations play in the organization.

Oral business presentations are a vital part of the contemporary organization because they provide immediate feedback, give the presenter full control of the situation, and require less audience effort than do written presentations. However, oral presentations are also impermanent and expensive, and the speaker-controlled pace means that some people in the audience may not be able to keep up with the flow of information. Managers need to develop their presentation skills so as to take advantage of these strengths and to minimize these weaknesses.

CO2. Plan a presentation by determining its purpose, analyzing the audience, and deciding the timing and method of delivery.

Planning the presentation requires determining the purpose, analyzing the audience, and planning the timing and method of presentation appropriate for the situation. Organizing the presentation requires developing an effective opening, developing each point logically in the middle, and closing on a strong, confident note.

CO3. Write a presentation by collecting the data and organizing it in a logical format.

Use your opening remarks to capture the interest of your audience and build rapport. In the body, choose a logical sequence and deal effectively with any negative information. At the end, summarize your main points and outline the next steps to be taken. At any point in your presentation, you may use humour if it is appropriate to the situation.

CO4. Plan a team presentation.

When making a work-team presentation, allow enough time to prepare, assign responsibilities on the basis of individual talents, and rehearse sufficiently to ensure that the overall presentation has coherence and unity.

CO5. Plan other types of business presentations.

Other common types of business presentations include introductions and special recognitions. Plan for and practice these so that you can make coherent, effective remarks as appropriate.

CO6. Incorporate visual aids and audience handouts to enhance business presentations.

Visual aids are a component of most business presentations. Although overhead transparencies and 35-mm slides were traditionally the format of choice, today presenters are making electronic presentations, with the slides or video being shown directly from a computer connected to a projector. Regardless of the format used, your visual aids should be relevant, simple, easily readable, and of high quality.

Audience handouts can supplement the oral information presented, provide space for audience note taking, and represent a permanent record of your presentation. Distribute the handout prior to the presentation if the audience needs to read the information beforehand, during the presentation if you will be referring to the handout during your remarks, or afterward if the handout simply contains a recap of what you presented.

CO7. Practice and deliver a business presentation.

Practice your presentation as much as necessary. Speak in a conversational tone, but at a slightly slower rate than normal. Use appropriate arm and hand gestures, but avoid annoying and distracting mannerisms and gestures.

When actually delivering your presentation, dress appropriately, speak in a clear and confident manner, and maintain eye contact with the audience. If needed, follow the recommended techniques for dealing with nervousness. Plan answers to possible questions and determine beforehand when you will take questions.

Finally, evaluate your performance afterward to ensure that your presentation skills improve with each opportunity to speak. Try to determine what worked well and what worked not so well.

■ Exercises

1 **The 3Ps (Problem, Process, and Product) Model: Communication Applications at Speakers' Spotlight**   As the owners of Canada's most innovative speakers' bureau, Martin and Farah Perelmuter host dozens of presentations every year. While they emphasize the importance of content over style, they recognize the role that visual aids play in helping communicate information clearly and in reinforcing key points. Visual aids also provide simple but vivid word pictures to help audiences grasp complex issues and technical concepts.

Problem

Occasionally Martin or Farah is required to give speeches of their own, whether it's introducing one of the many speakers on the Speakers' Spotlight roster or marketing their services to would-be clients. Assume you are helping Farah plan a presentation to the Halifax Chamber of Commerce, focusing on the important role that professional speakers play in bringing publicity and business to a city or region. As Farah's assistant, you are in charge of researching this presentation and developing the visual aids. You learn that the seminar organizers expect an audience of 100 and have allotted 20 minutes for this presentation, which will take place in the ballroom of a nearby hotel. Now you have to get to work on the visual aids for this speech.

Process

a. What is the purpose of your presentation?
b. Describe your audience.
c. What type of visual aids are most appropriate, given the presentation length, the audience, the information to be conveyed, and the speaker's preferences?
d. If you decide to prepare handouts for Farah, when do you recommend that she distribute them?

Product

Using your knowledge of presentations, prepare rough drafts of the visual aids you will provide for Farah's speech, creating any details you need to complete this assignment.

2 **The 3Ps (Problem, Process, and Product) Model: A Proposal Presentation**

Problem

Review Exercise 2 of Chapter 9 (pages 335–336), in which the Hospitality Services Association at your university proposes to start University Hosts, a business that would provide hospitality services for campus visitors. Assume that you have been given ten minutes to present your proposal orally to the President's Council at your institution.

Process

a. What is the purpose of your presentation?
b. Describe your audience.
c. What type of delivery would be most appropriate—reading, memorizing, or speaking from notes?

d. Because of the importance of both the topic and the audience, you decide to write in full your opening remarks. Write a one- to one-and-a-half-minute opening section for your presentation. Include an attention-getter.

e. Outline the topics you will discuss and the order in which you will discuss them. Be sure to include reader benefits.

f. Write a one- to one-and-a-half-minute closing section for your presentation.

g. Prepare rough drafts of the slides you will use for your presentation.

Product

Prepare a complete presentation outline, including where the slides will be used.

CO1. Describe the important role that business presentations play in the organization.

3 Understanding the Role of Business Presentations Interview two business people in your community who hold positions in your area of interest to learn more about their experiences in making oral presentations. Write a memorandum to your instructor summarizing what you've learned. You may want to ask such questions as the following:

a. How important has the ability to make effective oral presentations been to your career?

b. What kinds of oral presentations do you make in and out of the office, and how often?

c. How do you typically prepare for oral presentations?

CO2. Plan a presentation by determining its purpose, analyzing the audience, and deciding the timing and method of delivery.

4 The Opening This chapter lists six types of effective openings for an oral presentation—quotation, question, hypothetical situation, story, startling fact, or visual aid. Select two of these methods and develop effective openings for the same oral presentation. Plan your presentation: first, describe your purpose for the presentation; second, perform an audience analysis by identifying the demographics, the knowledge level, and the psychological needs of a potential audience; third, prepare two effective openings for your presentation and explain why you selected these types.

5 Planning a Presentation You decided at the last minute to apply to the graduate school at your institution to work toward an MBA. Even though you have a 3.4 GPA (on a 4.0 scale), you were denied admission because you had not taken the GMAT, which is a prerequisite for admission. You have, however, been given ten minutes to appear before the Graduate Council to try to convince them to grant you a temporary waiver of this requirement and permit you to enrol in graduate classes next term, during which time you will take the GMAT. The Graduate Council consists of the director of the MBA program and two senior faculty members, one of whom is your business communication professor.

a. What is the purpose of your presentation?

b. What do you know or what can you surmise about your audience that might help you prepare a more effective presentation?

c. What considerations affect the timing of your presentation?

d. What method of delivery should you use?

CO3. Write a presentation by collecting the data and organizing it in a logical format.

6 Presenting Research Data Review the analytical or recommendation report you prepared in Chapter 11. Assume that you have been given 15 minutes to present the important information from your written report to a committee of your superiors who will not have an opportunity to read the written report. Write your presentation notes, using either full sheets of paper or note cards.

7 **Presentation Notes**   Prepare a three-minute oral presentation on the business topic of your choice. First, write out the complete presentation. Next, select several excerpts of the complete script to be used as notes for your presentation. Then, prepare an outline of notes for your presentation. Submit all three versions of the presentation to your instructor for evaluation.

8 **Self-Presentation**   A big part of any company's success is the ability to sell its goods or services. As a new sales associate in Pinkston Inc., you have been asked to work with other new sales associates to improve your selling skills. You are to prepare a three-minute oral presentation in which you attempt to sell yourself as a product to a group of buyers. The buyers will be members of your class. You will be placed in groups of five or six people, and each person will have three minutes to sell him- or herself to the other group members.

The other group members will evaluate the seller using an evaluation sheet that will rate him or her in eight areas: (1) effectiveness of opening, (2) ability to hold buyers' interest, (3) appropriateness of eye contact, (4) logical sequence of presentation, (5) quality of voice, (6) clear identification of talents and skills, (7) motivational level of buyers, and (8) overall impression of the presentation. You will be evaluated in each area as being Poor, Fair, Good, or Excellent.

To prepare for your sales presentation, you might refer to the following steps:

a. List at least three skills and/or talents you have (e.g., playing the guitar, playing tennis, and reciting the alphabet backward in less than 10 seconds).
b. Turn your skills and talents into buyer benefits.
c. Prepare an outline that identifies talents and skills you will be selling, and why these benefits would appeal to your buyers.

9 **Presenting to an International Audience**   The West Coast manager of Honda has approached your school of business about the possibility of sending 30 of its Japanese managers to your institution to pursue a three-month intensive course in written and oral business communication. The purpose of the course is to make the Japanese managers better able to interact with their North American counterparts.

You, as the assistant provost at your institution, have been asked to give a six- to eight-minute presentation to the four Japanese executives who will decide whether to fund this program at your institution. The purpose of your presentation is to convince them to select your school.

Because of the care with which you will want to select your wording for this international audience and because of the high stakes involved, you decide to prepare a full script of your presentation (approximately 1000 words).

10 **Business Presentation Role Play**   Prepare a data sheet and a two-minute speech (using note cards) on the business topic of your choice. Then form into groups of six or seven to make up the head table. A few minutes before starting, randomly select roles to be played: host, head table guests (with professional titles), and a guest speaker. The rest of the class will serve as the audience.

The person selected to be the host should quickly obtain and review the data sheet of the speaker and the professional titles and names of the people at the head table. Then the host should seat the members of the head table in their chairs. The host should next introduce the people at the head table—including the speaker. At that point, the speaker should give his or her two-minute speech. After the speech is finished, the host should present the speaker with a token of appreciation.

Next, a member of the audience should be selected for an award such as employee of the year, and he or she should be invited to the podium by the host to receive the award and to make a short impromptu acceptance speech. Roles can be changed to allow others to be host, guests at the head table, speaker, or employee of the year. Have everyone submit his or her notes for the two-minute speech, whether or not he or she actually spoke.

co4. Plan a team presentation.

11 Work-team Presentation   Divide into teams of four or five students. Your instructor will assign you to either the pro or the con side of one of the following topics:

- Drug testing should be mandatory for all employees.

- All forms of smoking should be banned completely from the workplace—including outside the building.

- Employers should provide flex-time (flexible working hours) for all office employees.

- Employers should provide on-site child-care facilities for the preschool children of their employees.

- Employees who deal extensively with the public should be required to wear a company uniform.

- Employers should have the right to hire the most qualified employees without regard to affirmative action guidelines.

Assume that your employee group has been asked to present its views to a management committee that will make the final decision regarding your topic. The presentations will be given as follows:

a. Each side (beginning with the pro side) will have eight minutes to present its views.
b. Each side will then have three minutes to confer.
c. Each side (beginning with the con side) will deliver a two-minute rebuttal—to refute the arguments and answer the issues raised by the other side.
d. Each side (beginning with the pro side) will give a one-minute summary.
e. The management committee (the rest of the class) will then vote by secret ballot regarding which side (pro or con) presented its case more effectively.

Gather whatever data you think will be helpful to your case, organize it, divide up the speaking roles as you deem best, and prepare speaker notes. (*Hint:* It might be helpful to gather information on both the pro and the con sides of the issue in preparation for the rebuttal session, which will be given impromptu.)

co5. Plan other types of business presentations.

12 Impromptu Presentation   Your instructor will randomly call on members of the class to come to the front of the room and give a one-minute impromptu presentation on a topic that he or she selects from the following list. As you give your presentation, be aware of the time limits and your body language. Recognize that the audience doesn't expect a polished spur-of-the-moment presentation, but do your best, recognizing that surprises like this one occasionally happen in business.

a. How I feel about giving impromptu presentations
b. My career plans after college
c. My most embarrassing experience on a date
d. My opinion of Microsoft
e. The college course I enjoyed most
f. The cost of college
g. What bugs me about email
h. What I like (or dislike) about the current Prime Minister of Canada
i. What I've learned from the Internet
j. Where I grew up
k. Why I do (or do not) live on campus
l. Why I enjoy (or dislike) team projects

13 Presenting and Accepting an Honour   Your instructor will divide you into two-member teams for this exercise. By a flip of the coin, determine which one of you has just been named Business Student of the Month for this month and will be recognized at the business faculty meeting next week. Prepare a one-minute acceptance of this award. The other student should assume the role of president of the business faculty and prepare to present the Business Student of the Month award. Prepare a one- or two-minute introduction.

14 Visual Aids   You are the owner of a mid-sized company. You have 25 agents who travel throughout the country making presentations to small groups of people (10 to 20) regarding retirement programs. Many of your agents have been weak in their presentations. You are concerned that they need to improve their oral presentations because their presentations seem to be a little stale.

CO6. Incorporate visual aids and audience handouts to enhance business presentations.

Your agents have been making their own visual aids—most of them have used only flipcharts and transparencies. Needless to say, the visuals are not very professionally done; they probably hurt more than they help. You are going to hold a one-day seminar with your agents to work on their oral presentation skills.

One of the things you plan to cover in the seminar is the use of visual aids in oral presentations. Using the information shown in Figure 12.3 on page 456, develop one or more visual aids to illustrate to your agents the criteria for selecting visual aids. You will be presenting in a typical classroom that is able to accommodate all 25 agents.

15 Planning the Visual Element   You are the trainer for an in-house survey course in effective advertising techniques that is being offered to franchise owners of your Mexican fast-food chain. As part of the course, you are scheduled to present a 30-minute session on writing effective sales letters. You decide to use the sales letter section of Chapter 7 in this text (beginning on page 238) as the basis for your presentation. Prepare four to six slides that you might use for your presentation to the 25 participants in the course. Submit full-sized colour copies of the transparencies to your instructor.

16 Planning the Audience Handout   Refer to Exercise 15, in which you prepared slides for your presentation on writing effective sales letters. Using the techniques discussed in this chapter, prepare a handout that not only highlights the important points of your presentation but also provides useful supplementary information.

co7. **Practice and deliver a business presentation.**

17 Stage Fright   Working in groups of three or four, develop at least three slides for an electronic presentation on how to overcome stage fright. The presentation would be to ten people in a small boardroom. Use the Internet and other outside sources as well as information from the textbook for your slides. Remember to use an appropriate background colour and to keep the special effects simple. Submit the slides to your instructor for evaluation.

continuing
case 12

NORTHERN
LIGHTS

Pat's staff helps her plan how to organize her presentation to the executive committee at Northern Lights.

The Typists Who Lost Their Touch

Review the Continuing Case presented at the ends of Chapters 10 and 11. As you recall, in response to increasing sick-leave among data-entry personnel, Jean Tate asked Pat Robbins to write a report on carpal tunnel syndrome, a neuromuscular wrist injury caused by repeated hand motions such as those used in typing.

Assume the role of Pat Robbins. You have now been asked to present the results of your research in a 20-minute session to the executive committee, composed of Dave Kaplan and the three vice-presidents. This occasion is your first opportunity to speak to this high-ranking group, and the speech is on a topic about which you developed strong feelings over the past few months as you researched the topic in depth.

Critical Thinking

1. Analyze your audience. Specifically, what do you know (or what can you learn) about each of the executive committee members that will affect your presentation?

2. How will your strong feelings about this topic affect your presentation—either positively or negatively?

Speaking/Writing Projects

If you did not conduct any primary research for this project, base your presentation on secondary data.

3. Write your presentation notes, using either full sheets of paper or note cards.

LABtest 12

Retype the following letter, correcting any grammar and mechanics errors according to the rules introduced in LABs 2–6 beginning on page 534.

Dear Ms. Allison:

During your remodelling planning think about the amount of natural light in each room the use you make of the room, and the layout of it's furniture. Then consider what quality of light you need and where you need it—bright
5 economical fluorescent tubes or low level standard bulbs.

A combination of different lighting types give enormous variety. Spotlights or a ceiling pendant are quite affective. You will also need atmospheric lighting, don't however overdo levels of light. You don't want to feel as if your living in a lamp shop; and if their are too many lights pointed down-
10 ward, a room can feel flat. In addition fluorescent strips are unflattering in bathrooms, go for tungsten bulbs instead.

Flexibility is everything so always choose the easy solution. Which is generally also the most economical solution.

Thank you Ms. Allison for this opportunity to introduce some of
15 northern lights quality products. Please stop by our showroom any weekday from eight a.m. until five p.m. for help in "lighting up your life.

Sincerly,

13

Employment Communication

After you have finished this chapter, you should be able to

1. **Determine the appropriate length, content and format for your résumé.**

2. **Compose solicited and unsolicited job application letters.**

3. **Conduct yourself appropriately during an employment interview.**

4. **Complete the communication tasks needed after the employment interview.**

As President of Workopolis, Patrick Sullivan is responsible for the vision and business strategy behind Canada's leading provider of recruitment and job-search solutions, including workopolis.com and workopolisCampus.com. Workopolis has offices in Vancouver, Calgary, Guelph, Toronto, Ottawa and Montreal. Among his many roles, Sullivan provides advice to job seekers and employers through interviews, speaking engagements, and appearances on workopolis TV.

an insider's
perspective

PATRICK SULLIVAN
President, Workopolis

Particularly in a booming job market, efficiency is key, stresses Sullivan. And much of that efficiency can be gained through carefully targeted résumés and well written job postings: "Job-seekers need to be careful to only apply for jobs they have the right qualifications and skills for."[1] Moreover, Sullivan argues that "employers can help make the hiring process more efficient by clearly listing the specific qualifications and skills they are looking for in their job postings. That's the key to finding the right employees."[2]

Sullivan further urges job seekers to be strategic in their search: "It's better to be at the top of the résumé pile for one job, rather than at the bottom of the pile for three others. It's quality not quantity that will help land the job."[3]

Sullivan encourages students to clearly state their career objectives as well as the particular job position they are seeking. Furthermore, job seekers should tailor each résumé and cover letter so as to emphasize skills appropriate to the job. "The résumé and cover letter provide a good opportunity for students to show prospective employers they're keen and have done their homework on the company," Sullivan explains. "The best way to do this is to include material that relates directly back to the specific job, the company or the industry."

For those students whose work experience is limited, Sullivan suggests they include school projects and part-time or summer jobs on their résumé, with an emphasis on skills and accomplishments rather than job duties. Sullivan also believes strongly in the importance of carefully proofreading both the résumé and cover letter. One workopolis news release puts an even finer point on the matter: "Even one error can mean the difference between the circular file and the interview pile."[4]

As part of Sullivan's efforts to stay attuned to the ever-changing workplace, workopolis.com conducts periodic online surveys, seeking input from both employers and job seekers. One interesting finding of their 2006 survey is that Canadians' priorities are changing—family now being more important than careers for the majority of respondents. "There's been a significant shift in what matters to Canadian job seekers—family has replaced career development as our number one life priority," he says. "Smart employers will recognize this shift and create a workplace that allows people to nurture both their personal and professional lives."[5]

Another result of the survey revealed that Canadians are placing a higher and higher emphasis on work–life balance, an important reminder to employers struggling to motivate and retain good employees. "Employers need to understand what keeps their employees happy and motivated at work," says Sullivan. "No matter what the job, people want positive feedback and suitable financial compensation. Improving retention can be as simple as listening to staff needs and acting accordingly."[6]

"It's better to be at the top of the résumé pile for one job, rather than at the bottom of the pile for three others. It's quality not quantity that will help land the job."

■ Preparing Your Résumé

CO1. Determine the appropriate length, format, and content for your résumé.

> Communication skills play an important role in the job campaign.

> The purpose of a résumé is to get you a job interview—not to get you a job.

A **résumé** is a brief record of one's personal history and qualifications that is typically prepared by an applicant for a job. The emphasis in the résumé should be on the future rather than on the past: you must show how your education and work experience have prepared you for future jobs—specifically, the job for which you are applying.

Right from the start, be realistic about the purpose of your résumé. Few people are actually hired on the basis of their résumés alone. (However, many people are *rejected* because of their poorly written or poorly presented résumés.) Instead, applicants are generally hired on the basis of their performance during one or more job interviews.

Thus, the purpose of the résumé is to get you an interview, and the purpose of the interview is to get you a job. Remember, however, that the résumé and accompanying application letter (cover letter) are crucial in advancing you beyond the mass of initial applicants and into the much smaller group of potential candidates invited to an interview.

Résumé Length

Traditionally, the advice given to applicants for entry-level positions was to keep your résumé to one page. The rationale behind this advice is sound: recruiters typically spend less than 30 seconds looking at each résumé during their initial screening to pare down the perhaps hundreds of applications for a position into a manageable number to study in more detail.[7] The problem with limiting your résumé to one page, however, is that you risk selling yourself short. With few exceptions, most applicants, even those fresh out of college or university, have sufficient relevant education, work experience, volunteer experience, transferable skills, interests, and activities to easily fill out a two-page résumé. And since most applicants will send a two-page résumé, regardless of advice they may have been given to the contrary, one-page résumés risk making you look under-qualified by comparison. One study done for the *Journal of Business Communication* suggests that many "recruiters may *claim* to prefer one-page résumés when in actual practice they *choose* to interview candidates with two-page résumés."[8] (Indeed, for more senior positions and in certain industries, it's not uncommon to find résumés that are three or more pages long.)

Keep in mind that in a 30-second scan, the employer may only initially look at the first page. This is why it's so important to target a résumé effectively, putting your strongest qualifications on the first page. Typically, this is accomplished by including a skills summary near the top of the first page, which provides the reader with a quick snapshot of your strongest qualifications. If recruiters like what they see, they'll return to your résumé for a more thorough look after their initial culling of under-qualified candidates.

As with all business documents, knowing your audience's preferences will help significantly in determining both appropriate length and content. Consulting your college or university's career centre is a good first step in determining if there are industry preferences for résumé length. If unsure of your reader's preferences, we recommend you default to a two-page résumé for most entry- and mid-level positions.

Résumé Styles

There are three common styles of résumés: chronological, functional (or skills based), and combination). Each serves a slightly different function. You should chose carefully which style of résumé best suits your unique combination of skills and experience as it relates to the requirements of the position you seek.

■ *Chronological:* In a chronological arrangement, you organize your experience by date, describing your most recent position first and working backward. This format is most appropriate when you have had a strong continuing work history and your work has been related to your objective (i.e., to the position you seek). (See Model 37, page 484.) Chronological résumés are less effective for people seeking new positions for which they have little or no track record. Nor are they appropriate for those with blemishes or large gaps in their work history; this style of résumé will only enhance these. If you are a new graduate, with little or no relevant work experience, you should consider one of the other two styles.

■ *Functional (or skills based):* In a functional arrangement, you organize your experience by type of function performed (such as *supervision* or *budgeting*) or by transferable skills developed (such as *human relations* or *communication skills*). Then, under each function or skill, are specific examples (evidence), as illustrated in Model 38 on page 486. Because your various functions and skills are handled in detail in this section, you include no details under your work history section, other than the position held, names of employers, and dates of employment.

 Functional résumés are most appropriate when you're changing industries, moving into an entirely different line of work, or re-entering the work force after a long period of unemployment, because they emphasize your skills rather than your employment history and let you show how these skills have broad applicability to other jobs.

 The functional résumé is also well suited to new graduates with little relevant work experience, as it allows you to draw relevant competencies from your education, work experience, volunteer experience, and even recreational experience (such as sports or music) and highlight them all in one place.

■ *Combination:* A combination résumé incorporates elements of both the chronological and the functional résumé. It includes a more detailed skills section than does a chronological résumé (but not typically as detailed as in a functional résumé) and it includes brief descriptions of your duties and associated accomplishments within the work history section, as illustrated in Model 39 on page 488. Combination résumés work well for people with some relevant work experience but without a long or proven track record. They also work well for new graduates who possess some relevant part-time or summer work experience.

> *Regardless of which type of organizational pattern you use, provide complete information about your work history.*

Résumé Content

Fortunately, perhaps, there is no such thing as a standard résumé; each is as individual as the person it represents. We've already discussed the differences among chronological, functional, and combination résumés. Although each style treats certain components of the résumé differently, there are still standard parts of every résumé—those parts recruiters expect and need to see to make valid judgments.

model 37

RÉSUMÉ IN CHRONOLOGICAL FORMAT

Aurelia is using this résumé to apply for a part-time position for which she is well qualified: both her education and work experience are relevant. As a result, she has chosen to submit a chronological résumé. The position requires some post-secondary education and is flexible enough that she can remain at university while working.

Provides specific enough objective to be meaningful.

Places education before work experience because some post-secondary is a minimum qualification.

2913 40th Avenue
Edmonton, Alberta
Home: (780) 599-1253
Cell: (780) 222-1234
achow@sympatico.ca

1

AURELIA CHOW

OBJECTIVE

A part-time position processing expenses and completing report verifications and royalty calculations for ABC Ltd, a leading oil and gas company.

2 **SKILLS SUMMARY**

- Well-developed team work and leadership skills exemplified by receiving an 'A' on a marketing research group project involving a local financial firm
- Excellent interpersonal and communications skills revealed through participation as a council member of a Calgary-based non-profit group; commended for important input
- Effective time management and organizational skills as evidenced by balancing full-time studies, part-time work, and community involvement
- Practical experience with Microsoft Office (Excel, Word, PowerPoint), Personal Taxprep 2004, and ACCPAC Version 6.1
- Exceptional problem-solving and conflict resolution skills demonstrated by resolving a variety of customer concerns with diplomacy and confidence
- Strong work ethic demonstrated by consistently exceeding daily targets at current job
- Strong understanding of accounting systems and processes from part-time job and school

EDUCATION

UNIVERSITY OF ALBERTA
Edmonton, AB
2005–Present

Bachelor of Business Administration Degree Program (Accounting)
(Expected graduation December 2008)
- Courses completed include Advanced Financial and Management Accounting, Personal and Corporate Income Tax, Audit, and International Finance
- Listed on Dean's Honour Roll, 2005 (3.75/4.00 GPA)

MOUNT ROYAL COLLEGE
Calgary, AB
2003–2005

Business Administration Diploma (Marketing Management)
Graduated April 2006

EMPLOYMENT EXPERIENCE

3 **XYZ CANADIAN COMPANY LTD.**
Calgary, AB
2005–2006

Junior Operations Accountant (Part-time)
- Gained practical knowledge of several software applications utilized in the oil and gas industry, including Qbyte, Accumap, PetroLab, QBLM, CS Explorer, and JIBLink
- Maintained positive relationships with internal and external partners by clarifying queries and resolving potential disputes

Grammar and Mechanics Notes

1 The name is formatted in larger type for emphasis.

2 The major section headings are parallel in format and in wording.

3 Dates and places of employment are formatted in a column for ease of reading.

page 2 of 2

AURELIA CHOW • (780) 599-1253

model37

(CONTINUED)

EMPLOYMENT EXPERIENCE
(continued)

CLEARTEL
Calgary, AB
2003–2005

Customer Service Associate—Major Telecom Accounts (Part-time)
- Exercised and improved communication skills by finding creative solutions for customers with varying backgrounds, personalities, and expectations
- Demonstrated excellent conflict resolution skills when concerns were raised by customers
- Developed self-reliance while working with minimal/no supervision
- Produced effective results by consistently exceeding daily sales targets

LAKE ALBERTA HOCKEY SCHOOL
Calgary, AB
2001–2003

Skating Program Manager
- Developed organizational skills by allocating ice time, and scheduling staff, and program
- Gained experience with marketing different hockey and ice-skating classes to the community
- Demonstrated strong communication skills while dealing with staff, parents, coaches, children, and concession workers
- Enhanced customer service skills through direct customer contact

LAKE ALBERTA HOCKEY SCHOOL
Calgary, AB
1996–2001

Counselor & On-ice Instructor
- Displayed effective team skills with co-workers as well as children of all ages
- Developed problem-solving skills while answering parents' and players' questions

Uses action words like *developed* and *enhanced*; uses incomplete sentences to emphasize the action words and to conserve space.

COMMUNITY INVOLVEMENT
- Special Olympics, Calgary Region—Volunteer
- Calgary Stampeders Football Club—Promotions Assistant
- Calgary Non-profit Society—Council Member
- Canada Revenue Agency—2005 Community Volunteer Income Tax Program

Provides additional data to enhance her credentials.

INTERESTS AND ACTIVITIES

I enjoy travelling and learning new languages (Spanish). I am also interested in continued leadership development and am coaching a women's recreational hockey league this term. I am also an avid golfer and tennis player, and I enjoy mountain biking.

Omits actual names and addresses of references.

References available on request

model38

RÉSUMÉ IN FUNCTIONAL FORMAT

Aurelia is using a functional résumé to apply for a marketing/management position in the non-profit sector. She has chosen this format because, while neither her education nor work experience is directly related to the job, she does have the skills outlined in the job ad.

Includes several skill areas in skills summary and expands on each with bulleted statements.

Bulleted statements detail both skills and accomplishments and provide concrete evidence.

Relates each listed item directly to the desired job.

Provides specific evidence to support each skill.

Weaves work experiences, education, and extra-curricular activities into the skill statements.

AURELIA CHOW

1 **OBJECTIVE**

To coordinate and manage volunteer recruitment, training, and assignments for the Special Olympics tournaments, special events, and other activities and make Special Olympics programs more visible in Calgary.

SKILLS

2 **MANAGEMENT/LEADERSHIP**
- Elected project leader on marketing research group project involving a local financial firm. Project received an A
- Captained university college hockey team for two years, winning the divisional championship in final year as captain
- Oversaw account department operations on several occasions while management was away
- Managed programs and staff for two years at Lake Alberta Hockey School
- Demonstrated strong organizational skills while allocating ice-time and scheduling staff and programs at Alberta Hockey School

COMMUNICATION
- Proficient in Spanish and competent in French
- Communicate effectively with a diverse group of people as demonstrated by my work history
- Awarded first prize and runner-up in two case competitions, each requiring a 20-minute presentation to a panel of judges
- Excellent interpersonal and communications skills revealed through participation as a Council Member of a Calgary-based non-profit group; commended for important input
- Excelled in the completion of two courses in business communications while at university: developed strong presentation skills and the ability to write clearly, concisely, and persuasively in a variety of genre
- Provided creative solutions to the often conflicting needs of a diverse group of customers in the telecommunications industry and while program manager

3 - Liaised with concession staff, customers, parents, and children at Lake Alberta Hockey School

MARKETING
- Helped promote Special Olympics through community out-reach fairs, radio spots, and newspaper advertisements
- Consistently exceeded daily sales targets in the challenging field of phone sales
- Promoted new skating programs to existing customers and within community
- Helped create several new marketing campaigns for the Calgary Stampeders Football Club as assistant to promoter
- Ran a highly successful sport-drink-cooler promotion to encourage Stampeders' season tickets sales

2913 40th AVENUE, EDMONTON, ALBERTA • (780) 599-1253 CELL: (780) 222-1234 • ACHOW@SYMPATICO.CA

Grammar and Mechanics Notes

1 Putting the major headings along the side and indenting the sub-headings opens up the résumé, providing more white space.

2 Bullets, rather than asterisks, further enhance readability and give the résumé a professional appearance.

3 More white space is left *between* different sections than within sections (to clearly separate each section).

AURELIA CHOW • (780) 599-1253 • Page 2 of 2

model38

(CONTINUED)

EDUCATION

UNIVERSITY OF ALBERTA **Edmonton, AB** 2005–Present	**Bachelor of Applied Business Administration Degree** • Expected graduation, 2008 • Enlisted on Dean's HonoUr Roll, 2005 (3.75/4.00 GPA)
MOUNT ROYAL **Calgary AB** 2003–2005	**Business Administration Diploma** **(Marketing Management)** • Completed courses in market research, professional selling, e-commerce • Won second in business plan competition

EMPLOYMENT EXPERIENCE

Includes only the employer, position title and dates of each position.

XYZ CANADIAN **COMPANY LTD.**	Junior Operations Accountant Calgary, AB 2005–Present
CLEARTEL	Customer Service Associate – Major Telecom Accounts (Part-Time) Calgary, AB 2003–2005
LAKE ALBERTA **HOCKEY SCHOOL**	Skating Program Manager Calgary, AB 2001–2003

COMMUNITY INVOLVEMENT

• Special Olympics, Calgary Region—Volunteer
• Calgary Stampeders Football Club—Promotions Assistant
• Calgary Non-profit Society—Council Member
• Canada Revenue Agency—2005 Community Volunteer Income Tax Program

INTERESTS AND ACTIVITIES

I enjoy travelling and learning new languages. I am also interested in continued leadership development and am coaching a women's recreational hockey league this term. I am also an avid golfer and tennis player, and I enjoy mountain biking.

References available on request

model 39

RÉSUMÉ IN COMBINATION FORMAT

Aurelia is using the combination résumé to apply for an assistant supervisory position within an office at a marketing agency. Because she is majoring in accounting, her degree is not her strongest qualification, and little of her work experience is directly relevant. She'll use a combination résumé to highlight her most relevant skill sets and also to retain some detail under her past positions, since some of them required similar skills.

Includes three skill areas in skills summary and expands on each with bulleted statements.

Bulleted statements detail both skills and accomplishments and provide concrete evidence.

Relates each listed item directly to the desired job.

Provides specific evidence to support each skill.

Weaves work experiences, education, and extracurricular activities into the skill statements.

AURELIA CHOW

1   **OBJECTIVE**

Assistant to the Vice-President, conducting presentations for clients and overseeing the office functions of the Marketing Department of ABC Textiles Inc.

2   **SKILLS SUMMARY**

Leadership
- Elected project leader on marketing research group project involving a local financial firm. Project received an A
- Managed programs and staff for two years at Lake Alberta Hockey School
- Captained university college hockey team for two years, winning the divisional championship in final year as captain

Communication
- Won first-prize and runner-up in two case competitions, each requiring a 20-minute presentation to a panel of judges
- Demonstrated excellent interpersonal and communications skills while participating as a Council Member of a Calgary-based non-profit group; commended for important input
- Excelled in the completion of two courses in business communications while at university: developed strong presentation skills and the ability to write clearly, concisely, and persuasively in a variety of genre
- Provided creative solutions to the often conflicting needs of a diverse group of customers in the telecommunications industry
- Liaised with concession staff, customers, parents, and children while program manager at an ice rink

Computer Software
- Practical experience with Microsoft Office (Excel, Word, PowerPoint), Personal Taxprep 2004, and ACCPAC Version 6.1
- Proficient in several software applications utilized in the oil and gas industry, including Qbyte, Accumap, PetroLab, QBLM, CS Explorer, and JIBLink

EDUCATION

UNIVERSITY OF ALBERTA **Edmonton, AB** 2005–Present	**Bachelor of Applied Business Administration Degree** • Expected graduation, 2008 • Enlisted on Dean's Honour Roll, 2005 (3.75/4.00 GPA)
MOUNT ROYAL **Calgary AB** 2005–Present	**Business Administration Diploma** **(Marketing Management)** • Completed courses in market research, professional selling, e-commerce • Won second in business plan competition

2913 40TH AVENUE, EDMONTON, ALBERTA • (780) 599-1253 CELL: (780) 222-1234 • ACHOW@SYMPATICO.CA

Grammar and Mechanics Notes

1 Objectives should clearly identify what you can do for your prospective employer.

2 Using upper case letters for major headings and lower case for subheadings is another way to distinguish the various sections within the résumé.

3   AURELIA CHOW • (780) 599-1253 • Page 2 of 2

EMPLOYMENT EXPERIENCE

XYZ CANADIAN COMPANY LTD. Calgary AB 2005–Present	**Junior Operations Accountant** • Performed report verifications and royalty calculations, and processed capital, revenue, royalty and expense amounts • Entrusted with overseeing the department operations on several occasions while management was away
CLEARTEL Calgary AB 2003–2005	**Customer Service Associate—Major Telecom Accounts (Part-time)** • Provided creative solutions for customers with varying backgrounds, personalities, and expectations • Dealt with customers' concerns and questions • Worked with minimal/no supervision • Produced effective results by consistently exceeding daily sales targets
LAKE ALBERTA HOCKEY SCHOOL Calgary AB 2001–2003	**Skating Program Manager** • Allocated ice-time and scheduled staff and programs • Marketed different hockey and ice-skating classes to the community • Communicated with and liaised between staff, parents, coaches, children, and concession workers
LAKE ALBERTA HOCKEY SCOOL Calgary AB 1996–2001	**Counselor & On-ice Instructor** • Displayed effective team skills with co-workers as well as children of all ages

COMMUNITY INVOLVEMENT

• Special Olympics, Calgary Region—Volunteer
• Calgary Stampeders Football Club—Promotions Assistant
• Calgary Non-profit Society—Council Member
• Canada Revenue Agency—2005 Community Volunteer Income Tax Program

INTERESTS AND ACTIVITIES

I enjoy travelling and learning new languages (Spanish). I am also interested in continued leadership development and am coaching a women's recreational hockey league this term. I am also an avid golfer and tennis player, and I enjoy mountain biking.

References available on request

Includes brief descriptions of duties under each position and highlights some key accomplishments.

Grammar and Mechanics Notes

3 Including identifying information such as your name and phone number on the second page ensures you can be contacted if the employer misplaces your first page.

These are the most commonly included résumé components:

- Name, address, and telephone number

- Objective or career profile

- Relevant aptitudes and skills (These should be brief for chronological résumés and much more detailed on functional and combination résumés.)

- University major, degree or program, name of university, and date of graduation

- Jobs held, employing company or companies (but not complete mailing addresses or the names of your supervisors), dates of employment, and descriptions of skills, accomplishments, and duties

- References (included, if required, or a promise to make them available)

Other components you should consider including are:

- Volunteer experience or community involvement

- Accomplishments or awards that may not fit under the experience or education sections

- Additional training, such as second languages, specialized computer training, WHIMIS or CPR

- Interests and activities

Similarly, information you should *not* include on a résumé is anything that could be used as a basis for discrimination: religion, ethnicity, age, gender, photograph, and marital status. The standard and optional parts of the résumé are discussed here in the order in which they typically appear on the reverse chronological résumé of a recent (or soon-to-be) college or university graduate.

Identifying Information   It doesn't do any good to impress a recruiter if he or she cannot locate you easily to schedule an interview; therefore, your name and complete contact information are crucial. Include both your home and cell phone numbers, with area codes, as well as your email address. And be sure your email address, like everything else on the résumé, enhances your credibility. (In other words, lose that old Hotmail address: "BeerMan@Hotmail.com" will stop most recruiters from even looking at the rest of the résumé.)

Your name should be the very first item on the résumé, arranged attractively at the top. Use whatever form you typically use for signing your name (for example, with or without initials). Give your complete name, avoiding nicknames, and do not use a personal title such as *Mr.* or *Ms.*

If you will soon be changing your address (as from a college address to a home address), include both, along with the relevant dates for each. If you are away from your telephone most of the day and no one is at home to answer it and take a message, you would be wise to secure voice mail or an answering machine (and make sure your recorded message is businesslike). The important point is to be available for contact.

Since most résumés in Canada are more than one page, include your name and phone number as a header on your second (and any subsequent) page. That way, if your first page goes missing after being received by the recruiter, you can still be contacted and given the opportunity to re-submit your whole résumé.

Job Objective or Career Summary   An objective is a one- to two-line statement clarifying the work you seek. One expert describes objectives as simply "What I'm offering to do in exchange for a paycheque."[9] Of course, what you are offering to do should match closely with what you are capable of doing, so avoid focusing on the skills or credentials you hope to possess at some point in the future. An objective should focus on what you can do now.

While objectives are typically used by new graduates or people changing careers, a career summary is used by those with experience who are seeking employment in the same field. Workopolis.com describes them this way: "A career summary highlights your background and provides a brief overview of your most important qualifications, skills, and/or professional experience."

Few components of a résumé receive such mixed reviews as objectives. According to one expert, only about half of those Canadian employers she interviewed like to see an objective.[10] When pressed as to why, most agree that it's not the presence of an objective that bothers them, it's that most objectives are so vague and poorly written as to be meaningless.

Avoid vague or generic objectives like the following:

NOT: "A position that offers both a challenge and an opportunity for growth."

"Challenging position in a progressive organization."

"A responsible position that lets me use my education and experience and that provides opportunities for increased responsibilities."

The problem with such goals is not that they're unworthy objectives; they are *very* worthwhile. That is why everyone—perhaps including the recruiter—wants such positions. The problem is that such vague, high-flown goals don't help the recruiter find a suitable position for *you*. They waste valuable space on your résumé.

For your objective to help you, it must be specific enough to be useful to the prospective employer. A good formula for writing objectives is as follows:

Doing what (specific work tasks) *for/with whom* (type of industry, client group, area of company).[11]

The work tasks themselves should be carefully gleaned from the job ad or job description. Once written, the objective then becomes a sort of thesis statement for the rest of the résumé. Everything in the résumé should be consistent with your objective and should seek to demonstrate that you can do those tasks that you've identified in your objective. Some experts also advise the inclusion of a future goal, such as the attainment of a credential or a more senior position within the industry. If you choose to include a future goal, be sure it's consistent with your employer's needs—you don't want to leave the impression that this position is just a brief stop over before you get the job you *really* want.

Here are some examples of effective objectives:

OBJECTIVE: "Position as project supervisor within the home construction industry."

"Program manager, focusing on corporate training, within the telecommunications sector."

"Volunteer coordinator for the Ottawa Drop-in Centre."

"Part-time clerical position in the oil and gas industry, assisting management with word processing, filing, and phone duties."

"Assistant to the Director of International Operations, focusing on Pacific Rim expansion opportunities."

"Position as a personal consultant in the financial services industry, providing financial planning and insurance services while working toward a CFP designation."

If you are seeking work in the same field for which you have considerable experience, a career summary may be more appropriate than an objective. Workopolis.com offers these guidelines in writing career summaries. Start with a short phrase describing your profession, then add two or three additional statements relating to the following: the breadth or depth of your skills; the unique combination of skills you possess; your innovative approach to work; the range of environments in which you have experience; your history of awards, promotions or commendations; your special or well documented accomplishments in the field. Finally, conclude with a sentence that describes your objective.

Here's an example of an effective career summary:

An MBA with over ten year's experience as a marketing manager, overseeing numerous research projects and marketing initiatives for Canada's largest marketing firm. Successfully brought over a dozen separate clients from relative obscurity to industry-wide recognition as *the* market leaders in their respective brands. Seeking position as Market Research Manager at Ipsos North America.

Summary of Qualifications　　Often called "Highlights", "Key Qualifications", or "Skills Summary," this section serves a similar function to an executive summary in a report: it offers a quick snapshot of the most important information in the résumé, most notably, your strongest qualifications for the specific position being targeted. Although this section typically appears near the top of your first page, since it summarizes other parts of the résumé, you will want to write it last. Again, you should glean what you can from the job ad or job description before writing your summary to ensure your summary and the recruiter's requirements closely match. Be sure that anything you include here is specific and verifiable. Avoid such vague claims as the following:

- Excellent communication skills

- A team player

- Strong managerial and organizational skills

Instead, dig out the most relevant competencies, credentials and accomplishments found elsewhere on the résumé (typically your education, work experience, and volunteer experience sections) and describe them using concrete language in anywhere from three to six bullet points. (If you're using a career summary, you may wish to omit this section; otherwise, we recommend you include it.) A new graduate seeking a supervisory position requiring strong organizational, interpersonal, and team work skills, as well as the ability to work well under pressure, might write the following summary of qualifications:

- Possess strong interpersonal skills and the ability to work under pressure: served up to 12 tables at a time with efficiency and courtesy in a busy family restaurant.

- Excel in a team environment: in capstone marketing course at university, took lead role in researching, writing, and presenting term report, for which the group received an A.

- Apply excellent organizational skills as a volunteer with the Mustard Seed: responsible for coordinating the needs of kitchen and front line staff while ensuring each client is treated efficiently and with dignity.

- Four years' experience in supervisory positions within both the restaurant and retail industries.

- Effective time management skills evidenced by balancing full-time studies, part-time employment, weekly community involvement, and participation on a sports team through all four years of university.

The examples above are written as they would appear in a chronological résumé. If you are writing a combination or functional résumé, you'll need to group your skills or functions under broad categories that reflect the needs of the position to which you're applying: communication, accounting, marketing, leadership, and the like. Then include several bulleted entries under each category. Remember, with a combination résumé, your work experience section provides only a few details about your duties and accomplishments, so your skills must be covered in detail in your summary of qualifications. The same holds true for a functional résumé, but more so, as the work experience section of a functional résumé provides no details about the positions you've held.

One criticism regarding the inclusion of a summary is that it's redundant: it describes skills and accomplishments that are detailed in other parts of the résumé. This is only partially true. A summary may pick up details found elsewhere on the résumé, but by highlighting your key qualifications all in one place, it offers a sort of "big picture" image for your reader of how your unique combination of experience, education, skills, and accomplishments qualify you for the position. The summary also allows you to describe skills (such as time management) that may only be implied elsewhere in the résumé.

To avoid repetition when writing your summary, be sure to use different phrasing than you've used elsewhere and try to include some details that don't appear elsewhere, as illustrated in the résumé examples on pages 484–489.

Education   Allow the job ad or description to determine whether your education or work experience section appears first. For most recent graduates with little relevant work experience, your degree or diploma is probably more important to your reader than your experience. However, if your work experience has been extensive, fairly high level, or directly related to your objective, you'll want to describe your work experience before your education.

List the title of your degree, diploma, or program; the formal name of your college or university and its location, if needed; your major and (if applicable) minor; and your expected date of graduation (month and year).

List your grade-point average if it will set you apart from the competition (generally, at least a 3.0 on a 4.0 scale). If you've made the dean's list or have financed any substantial portion of your post-secondary expenses through part-time work, savings, or scholarships, mention that. Unless your course of study provided distinctive experiences that uniquely qualify you for the job, avoid including a lengthy list of courses. Some advise applicants to include their high school diploma on the résumé up until they've completed a more advanced diploma or degree, then to drop high school off the résumé.

Finally, consider including, either here or in a new section, other relevant training or education you may have received, again in reverse chronological order. If you've completed some additional training in sales, computers, or languages, or have taken some graduate-level courses, these are usually worth mentioning. Additionally, if you attended a post-secondary institution, but did not complete a credential, you can still include it in your education section. Simply identify your program and/or major and the years you attended. (At the interview, be prepared to address your reasons for not completing the credential.)

Show how your work experience qualifies you for the type of job for which you are applying.

Work Experience   Particularly since tuition costs have risen dramatically in Canada since the late 80s (according to Statistics Canada, almost 10 percent per year throughout the 1990s), many students have chosen to work at least part-time while attending university or college. While working and attending school may not be the best recipe for academic success, the benefit has been that many students now graduate with considerable work experience, some of it highly relevant to their anticipated careers. Because of this highly competitive environment, you'll want to spend considerable time developing the experience section of your résumé to ensure your application is competitive. If your work experience has been directly related to your objective, consider putting it ahead of the education section, where it will receive more emphasis. (If you are writing a functional résumé, you may ignore what we say here, since you'll not be including any details within your work experience section.)

While some positions require a very specific set of skills (e.g., experience doing accounts payable and receivable or knowledge of specific computer programs), many positions, particularly those at the entry level, require candidates to possess a broad set of transferable skills, rather than specific technical skills—skills such as fundraising, conducting research, supervising, selling, serving, writing, organizing, and so on.

Begin developing this section by considering, for each position you've held, not just the duties you performed but also how well you performed them, what specific accomplishments you achieved while performing them, and what skills you were required to demonstrate to complete those duties successfully. Remember, skills and accomplishments are not the same as duties. The duties of a restaurant server are to take orders, deliver food, clean tables, and the like. But the skills and accomplishments associated with these duties are of much more interest to employers—working well under pressure; handling customer concerns with tact and efficiency; coordinating the demands of customers, kitchen staff, and other servers; exceeding sales quotas; being entrusted with managerial responsibilities; winning employee of the month; and the like.

In describing your work experience, do so in light of the position being applied for; in other words each description should directly support the objective at the top of the résumé. Because each position requires a different combination of skills and experience, you should rewrite these descriptions every time you apply for a new position.

The key to writing effective work experience descriptions is to adhere to the rule of "show me, don't tell me." Saying you performed supervisory duties, for example, isn't enough; demonstrate your supervisory skills through concrete qualifiers that answer questions such as how much; how often; how well; to what degree; for whom; with whom; in what context and with what result. When possible, ensure credibility by giving numbers or dollar amounts.

Complete sentences are not necessary. Instead, start your descriptions with action verbs, using present tense for current duties and past tense for previous duties or accomplishments. (When describing skills, always use present tense.) Avoid using pronouns such as *I* or *my*. The I is understood; this is your résumé. Here are some examples:

NOT: Dealt with customers

BUT: Recognized for excellent customer service at the highest volume branch

NOT: Assisted the manager

BUT: Researched and booked hotels and meeting rooms for conferences; coordinated arrivals, departures and accommodations for 500 participants

NOT: Supervised staff

BUT: Recruited, trained, and mentored up to 20 restaurant staff, including interviewing, conducting performance reviews, and scheduling

NOT: Sold merchandise

BUT: Exceeded sales quotas in every month of employment, contributing to a 30 percent gain in yearly revenues

NOT: Was responsible for a large sales territory

BUT: Managed sales territory for Northern B.C.; increased sales 13 percent during first full year

NOT: Worked as a clerk in the cashier's office

BUT: Balanced the cash register every day; was the only part-time employee entrusted to make nightly cash deposits

NOT: Worked as a bouncer at a local bar

BUT: Maintained order at Nick's Side-Door Saloon; learned first-hand the importance of compromise and negotiation in solving problems

NOT: Worked as a volunteer for Art Reach

BUT: Personally sold more than $1000 worth of tickets to annual benefit dance; introduced an "Each one, reach one" membership drive that increased membership every year during my three-year term as membership chairperson

Put some careful thought into the opening verb of each of these descriptions. Avoid weak verbs such as *attempted, endeavoured, hoped,* and *tried,* or vague verbs such as *dealt* or *worked.*

Concrete verbs such as the following make your work experience come alive:

Use concrete, achievement-oriented words to describe your experience.

accomplished	analyzed	arranged	balanced
achieved	applied	assisted	budgeted
administered	approved	authorized	built

constructed	diagnosed	maintained	reported
contracted	directed	managed	researched
controlled	edited	marketed	revised
changed	established	modified	scheduled
collected	evaluated	motivated	screened
communicated	forecast	negotiated	secured
completed	generated	operated	simplified
conceived	guided	ordered	sold
concluded	handled	organized	studied
conducted	hired	oversaw	supervised
consolidated	implemented	planned	taught
coordinated	increased	prepared	trained
created	instituted	presented	transformed
delegated	interviewed	presided	updated
designed	introduced	produced	wrote
determined	investigated	purchased	
developed	led	recommended	

Stress specific accomplishments directly related to the desired job.

If you have little or no actual work experience, show how your involvement with professional, social, or civic organizations has helped you develop skills that are transferable to the workplace. Volunteer work, for example, can help develop valuable skills in time management, working with groups, handling money, speaking, accepting responsibility, and the like. In addition, most schools offer internships in which a student receives course credit and close supervision while holding down a temporary job.

Work experience need not be restricted to paid positions.

Other Relevant Information   If you have special skills or experiences that might give you an edge over the competition (such as knowledge of a foreign language, extensive travel experience, or Web page-creation competence), list them on your résumé. Although employers assume that graduates today have competence in word processing, you should specify any other particular software skills you possess.

Include any honours or recognitions that have relevance to the job you're seeking. Memberships in business-related organizations demonstrate your commitment to your profession, and you should list them if space permits. Likewise, involvement in volunteer, civic, and other extracurricular activities gives evidence of a well-rounded individual and reflects your values and commitment.

If you have performed any volunteer work, be sure to include this on your résumé. Not only does including volunteer work reveal a commitment to giving back to the community, it also allows you to further describe relevant skills and accomplishments. Indeed, some new graduates may find their volunteer work has provided them with stronger relevant experience than has their paid employment. (If this is the case, a combination or functional résumé is your best bet.) As in your work experience section, be sure to target your description of your volunteer experience—duties, skills, and accomplishments—to the position being sought. If your volunteer experience hasn't contributed to your qualifications, you may choose to exclude it, or simply list, rather than describe, your various volunteer activities.

The inclusion of hobbies or special interests is an area of some debate. Many experts discourage including such information, arguing that it robs you of precious résumé space that should be reserved for more relevant, work related, information. Others feel this is one area of the résumé that gives them a peek at an applicant's character. Susan Hodkinson, Director of Human Resources at Toronto law firm, Goodman and Carr, offers this opinion: "I look for well-rounded people who are involved in activities for their own pleasure, and/or for the betterment of the community." She further adds that, "This section provides a good jumping-off point in the interview, as people are comfortable talking about their interests and why and how they got involved."[12]

If you choose to include hobbies or special interests on your résumé, be sure they contribute to your goal: convincing the recruiter that you're a good fit within the organization. An applicant seeking a data entry position that requires hour after hour of solitary work would be wise not to emphasize that all his or her favourite hobbies are highly social activities, such as team sports, playing in a band, and hosting large dinner parties.

References   A **reference** is a person who has agreed to provide information to a prospective employer regarding a job applicant's fitness for a job. As a general rule, the names and addresses of references need not be included on the résumé itself. Instead, give a general statement that references are available. This policy ensures that you will be contacted before your references are called. The exception to this practice is if you are specifically requested to include the names of references or if your references are likely to be known by the person reading the résumé; in this case, list their names.

Your references should be professional references rather than character references. The best ones are employers, especially your present employer. University professors with whom you have had a close and successful relationship are also valuable references. When asking for references, be prepared to sign a waiver stating that you forgo your right to see the recommendation or that you won't claim that a reference prevented you from getting a job. Many firms are becoming reluctant to authorize their managers to provide reference letters because of the possibility of being sued.

When putting together your reference list, to be carried with you to the interview, be sure to contact each referee, reminding them that you're including their name as a reference and that they will likely be contacted by the employer. After the interview it's a good idea to phone your referees again to give them as much information as possible about the position and its requirements. This allows your referees to better target their response when the employer calls. On your reference list include the person's name, title, company's name and address, and a phone number where he or she can be reached during business hours.

Résumé Format

Choose a simple, easy-to-read typeface. *Sans serif* fonts, in bold, work well for headings, while *serif* fonts work well for text. (If you prefer to use just one font, serif fonts, such as Times New Roman, are easier to read than sans serif fonts.) And avoid reducing the type size to squeeze more detail onto a page: an 11- or 12-point type size for text, and a slightly larger type size for headings, is preferred. Although not a hard-and-fast rule, consider using upper case, bold lettering for headings and lower

As space permits, include other information that uniquely qualifies you for the type of position for which you're applying.

The names of references are generally not included on the résumé.

case for everything else. Finally, avoid the temptation to use a lot of "special effects" just because they're available on your computer. One or two font styles in one or two different sizes should be enough. Figure 13.1 below illustrates an effective format.

The overall page layout can take many variations, but to ensure maximum readability keep the format simple, with lots of white space. The illustration in Figure 13.1 employs a split-column format, whereby the headings and the dates of education or employment are put in the first (imaginary) column and all other information is put in the second column. (This format, because it leaves a lot of unused space in the left margin, can pose a problem for applicants with a lot of experience who still wish to keep their résumé to two pages. Never let the format dictate the content; find a format that's appropriate for you.)

Some sources recommend using your word processor's résumé template as a starting point. While these templates offer a neat infrastructure on which to build, résumés based on such templates are, unfortunately, easily recognizable by many recruiters. At best, such résumés blend in too readily with many of the others sitting on the recruiter's desk; at worst, template-based résumés make the applicant look unoriginal, poorly versed in word-processing skills, and even lazy. Such templates also tend to be inflexible, forcing your content into a structure that may be unsuitable to your needs.

Finally, your résumé and application letter must be 100 percent free from error—in content, spelling, grammar, and format. Ninety-nine percent accuracy is simply not good enough when seeking a job. One survey of executives of large companies showed that fully 80 percent of them had decided against interviewing a job seeker simply because of poor grammar, spelling, or punctuation in his or her résumé.[13] Don't write, as one job applicant did, "Education: Advanced Curses in Accounting," or as another did, "I have an obsession for detail; I make sure that I cross my *is* and dot my *ts*." Show right from the start that you're the type of person who takes pride in your work.

figure13.1 **Formatting Your Résumé**

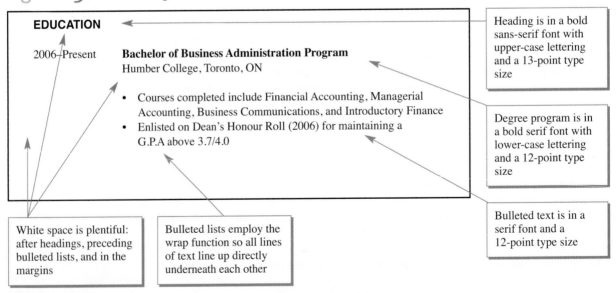

EDUCATION

2006–Present   **Bachelor of Business Administration Program**
               Humber College, Toronto, ON

- Courses completed include Financial Accounting, Managerial Accounting, Business Communications, and Introductory Finance
- Enlisted on Dean's Honour Roll (2006) for maintaining a G.P.A above 3.7/4.0

Heading is in a bold sans-serif font with upper-case lettering and a 13-point type size

Degree program is in a bold serif font with lower-case lettering and a 12-point type size

Bulleted text is in a serif font and a 12-point type size

White space is plentiful: after headings, preceding bulleted lists, and in the margins

Bulleted lists employ the wrap function so all lines of text line up directly underneath each other

Electronic Résumés

An **electronic résumé** is a résumé that is stored in a computer database, typically a job site, designed to help manage and initially screen job applicants. The five most popular Canadian sites are Workopolis.com, Monster.ca, CareerClick.com, JobShark.ca, and HotJobs.ca. Such sites allow you to either upload your résumé or fill in a form.

Electronic résumés provide many benefits—both to the recruiter and to the job seeker:

- The job seeker's résumé is potentially available to a large number of employers.

- The job seeker may be considered for positions of which he or she wasn't even aware.

- The initial screening is done by a bias-free computer.

- Employers are relieved of the drudgery of having to manually screen and acknowledge résumés.

- A focused search can be conducted quickly.

- Information is always available until the individual résumé is purged from the system (often in six months).

Submitting an electronic résumé makes you available to more people and for more positions.

When jobs need to be filled, a recruiter will log onto his or her private account and select a number of criteria. These could include where you live, how recently your résumé has been updated, the highest level of education you've received, etc. More importantly, the criteria will also include key words and phrases, such as *accounts payable, sales, finance,* or *supervisor.* The computer then searches the database and prints out a list of candidates with the most keyword matches. A person picks it up from there, manually studying each selected résumé to determine whom to invite for an interview. (So far, electronic tools alter only the screening, not the selection, process. People are still hired by people.)

Using appropriate key words is essential in an electronic résumé.

Content Guidelines for Electronic Résumés   Two strategies are essential for getting your résumé included in the list of those to be considered further. First, update your résumé regularly, even daily. The computer generates the lists of résumés starting with those most recently updated. Such revisions need not be substantial—even adding and then removing a space and then clicking "revise" or "submit" may suffice.[14] Second, only those résumés with the relevant keywords will be selected, so building appropriate keywords into your résumé is essential.

Keywords are the descriptive terms that employers search for when trying to fill a position. They are the words and phrases employers believe best summarize the characteristics that they are seeking in candidates for particular jobs, such as college degree, foreign language skills, job titles, specific job skills, software packages, or the names of competitors for whom applicants may have worked. Other examples of keywords include *human resources manager, Windows XP, teamwork,* or *ISO 9000.*

Here are some guidelines to ensure your résumé is "computer-friendly" and to maximize the chance that your résumé will be picked by the computer for further review by humans:

1. Think "nouns" instead of "verbs" (users rarely search for verbs). Use concrete words rather than vague descriptions. Include industry-specific descriptive nouns that characterize your skills accurately and that people in your field

Prefer nouns for describing your work experience.

use and commonly look for. (Browse other online résumés, newspaper ads, and industry publications to see what terms are currently being used.)

2. Put keywords in proper context, weaving them throughout your résumé. (This strategy is considered a more polished and sophisticated approach than listing them in a block at the beginning of the résumé.)

3. Use a variety of different words to describe your skills, and don't overuse important words. In most searches, each word counts once, no matter how many times it is used.

Format Guidelines for Electronic Résumés   Not only do electronic résumés require you to make changes to the content of your paper-based résumé, they also require a much simpler format. The following guidelines will ensure that your résumé is in a format that can be scanned and transmitted accurately as an email message. (See Model 40 on page 501 for a sample of an electronic résumé.)

1. Save your traditionally formatted résumé as a text-only file; most word processors allow you to save a file in ASCII format, which has a file name with a .txt extension.

2. Reopen the text file and make any needed changes to your résumé (see the remaining guidelines). Make sure you always save the document as a text file—not as a word processing document.

3. To ensure accurate reading by computer software, make the format as plain as possible. Do not change typefaces, justification, margins, tabs, font sizes, and the like; do not insert underlines, bold, or italic; and do not use horizontal or vertical rules, graphics, boxes, tables, or columns. None of these will show up in a scan of a text file.

4. Use a line length of no more than 70 characters per line. Because you can't change margins in a text file, press Enter at the ends of lines if necessary.

5. Do not divide (hyphenate) words at the end of a line.

6. Change bullets to asterisks (*) or plus (+) signs at the beginning of the line; then insert spaces at the beginning of run-over lines to make all lines of a bulleted paragraph begin at the same point.

7. Use capitalization to make headings stand out.

8. If responding via email, use the job title or noted reference number as the subject of your message. Always send the résumé in the body of the email message. Don't assume that you can attach a word-processed document to an email message; it may or may not be readable.

9. Whenever you update your résumé, remember to update both versions.

10. Because your résumé is going to look very bland in plain text, stripped of all formatting, consider adding a sentence such as this one to the end of your posted résumé: "An attractive and fully formatted hard-copy version of this résumé is available upon request."

If you are posting your résumé on your own Web page, use an online HTML (or XML) résumé. (See Model 41 on page 502 for a sample.) Many providers, such as Yahoo! Geocities, will host your home page for free or little cost. (To locate other Web sites with free Web space hosting, log on to freewebspace.net.)

HTML résumés offer these advantages:

HTML résumés send a subtle message about your online skills.

■ Potential employers can access your résumé at any time. Assume, for example, you're talking to a potential employer who expresses an interest in your qualifications. You can simply refer him or her to your Web address for instant reviewing.

```
COMPUTER SKILLS
    * Microsoft Word, PowerPoint, and Excel
    * Microsoft Publisher
    * Print Shop
    * All aspects of Internet research

REFERENCES
    Available on request

NOTE
    A fully formatted hard-copy version of this resume
    is available upon request
```

model 40

ELECTRONIC RÉSUMÉ

Includes notice of availability of a fully formatted version.

```
HEIDI MCDONALD
103 Queen Street,
Fredericton, NB E3N 1N4
506-839-4392
aswan@yahoo.com

OBJECTIVE
    Position as Health Coach, applying community
    health, organizational, and communication skills to
    help people improve their health and lifestyles

SKILLS SUMMARY
    * Certification First Aid and CPR
    * Experienced in patient appraisals and health
      program design
    * Strong communication skills developed while
      working with diverse groups of clientele in the
      healthcare field
    * Work well under pressure: prioritize and organize
      quickly and efficiently, as evidenced while
      responding to the urgent demands of nurses and
      physicians within a busy healthcare facility

EDUCATION
    Bachelor of Science Degree, University of New
    Brunswick, June 06
    * Major: Community Health
    * GPA: 3.8 in major on 4.0 scale

EXPERIENCE
    Volunteer Instructor, Canadian Red Cross,
    Fredericton, NB,
    July 06-Present
    * Taught First Aid and CPR
    * Adapted instructional material to individual
      learning styles
```

Begins with name at the top, followed immediately by addresses (both an email address and a home address).

Emphasizes, where possible, nouns as keywords.

Grammar and Mechanics Notes

Only ASCII characters are used; all text is one size with no special formatting other than capitalization of headings; no rules, graphics, columns, tables, and the like are used. Vertical line spaces (Enter key) and horizontal spacing (space bar) show relationship of parts. Lists are formatted with asterisks instead of bullets.

model41

HTML RÉSUMÉ

Provides appropriate identification information in an attractive heading.

Allows the reader to view, download, and print the résumé in different formats.

Provides links to make it easy to navigate the page.

Links to a copy of her transcript for viewing courses taken and grades.

Heidi McDonald   *506-839-4392*
103 Queen Street, Fredericton, NB E3N 1N4   aswan@yahoo.com

1

[MS Word Version]   [Scannable Plain-Text Version]   [PDF Version]

▶ Education

▶ Experience

▶ Certifications

▶ Computer Skills

▶ References

▶ Contact me

OBJECTIVE

Position as Health Coach, applying community health, organizational, and communication skills to help people improve their health and lifestyles

SKILLS SUMMARY

- Certification First Aid and CPR
- Experienced in patient appraisals and health program design
- Strong communication skills developed while working with diverse groups of clientele in the healthcare field
- Work well under pressure: prioritize and organize quickly and efficiently, as evidenced while responding to the urgent demands of nurses and physicians within a busy healthcare facility

2

EDUCATION

Bachelor of Science Degree, University of New Brunswick, June 06
- Major: Community Health
- GPA: 3.8 in major on 4.0 scale [Transcript]

EXPERIENCE

Volunteer Instructor, Canadian Red Cross, Fredericton, NB, July 06–Present
- Taught First Aid and CPR
- Exposed to individual learning styles

Assistant Pool Manager, Fredericton, NB, May 05–Aug 05
- Assisted the manager with everyday duties of running a community swimming pool
- Applied first-aid skills as needed

Grammar and Mechanics Notes

1 Use colour—but in moderation; ensure that your web page projects a professional image.

2 Avoid the tendency to include a photograph of yourself on your Web page.

Heidi McDonald • 506-839-4392 • aswan@yahoo.com

model41

(CONTINUED)

EXPERIENCE (continued)

Intern, Health Centre, Ottawa, ON, Sep 04–Dec 04
- Developed and presented PowerPoint health programs
- Produced resource folders to be used as supplemental material in existing programs
- Assisted in conducting corporate health appraisals

Nursing Assistant, Saint John Regional Hospital, NB, Jan 03–Aug 04
- Assisted physicians and nurses in performing medical exams and charting
- Wrote Procedures Handbook for the staff

CERTIFICATIONS
- First Aid and CPR Instructor
- Professional Rescuer Instructor

COMPUTER SKILLS
- Microsoft Word, PowerPoint, and Excel (Ver. 2003)
- Microsoft Publisher
- Print Shop
- All aspects of Internet research

REFERENCES

Available on request

CONTACT ME

Please contact me by email at aswan@yahoo.com or by phone at 506-839-4362

Created on April 3, 2006
Last updated on April 21, 2006

Return to Top • Education • Experience
Certifications • Computer Skills • References

Contains underlined links throughout the page that bring up copies of the actual documents for viewing.

Provides links to a sample of her report-writing skills.

Provides links to actual copies of the certification documents.

Shows the currency of the information.

Repeats the navigation links.

3

4

Grammar and Mechanics Notes

3 Do not underline any part of your Web page. Save underlining to indicate links.

4 Leave plenty of white space and make your section headings stand out.

- You can include hypertext links to work samples you've completed. For example, instead of merely saying that you wrote extensive reports in your job or that you have top-level communication skills, you can prove it by providing links to actual documents you have created.

- You can highlight your creativity because the online language provides enough formatting options to enable you to produce a very attractive page (your HTML résumé also provides evidence of your technical expertise).

Because you can never be sure how your résumé will be treated, you should prepare two résumés—one for the computer to read and one for people to read. When mailing a résumé, you may wish to include both versions, making note of that fact in your cover letter. Differences between the two versions concern both content and format.

Because your résumé is about you, it is perhaps the most personal business document you'll ever write. Use everything you know about successful communication techniques to ensure that you tell your story in the most effective manner possible. After you're satisfied with the content and arrangement of your résumé, proofread your document carefully and have several others proofread it also. Then have it printed on high-quality white or off-white 216 by 279 mm paper, and turn your attention to your cover letters.

The guidelines for developing a résumé are summarized in Checklist 16 on page 505.

■ Writing Job Application Letters

CO2. Compose solicited and unsolicited job application letters.

A résumé itself is all that is generally needed to secure an interview with an on-campus recruiter. However, you will likely not want to limit your job search to those employers that interview on campus. Campus recruiters typically represent large organizations or regional employers. Thus, if you want to work in a smaller organization or in a distant location, you will need to contact those organizations by writing application letters.

An **application letter** communicates to the prospective employer your interest in and qualifications for a position within the organization. The letter is also called a *cover letter*, because it introduces (or "covers") the major points in your résumé, which you should include with the application letter. A **solicited application letter** is written in response to an advertised vacancy, whereas an **unsolicited application letter** (also called a *prospecting letter*) is written to an organization that has not advertised a vacancy.

Use the application letter, which is often your first contact with the potential employer, to personalize your qualifications for one specific job.

Because the application letter is the first thing the employer will read about you, it is of crucial importance. Make sure the letter is formatted appropriately, looks attractive, and is free from typographical, spelling, and grammatical errors. Don't forget to sign the letter and enclose a copy of your résumé (or perhaps both versions—formatted and plain-text).

Your cover letter is a sales letter—you're selling your qualifications to the prospective employer. You should use the same persuasive techniques you learned earlier: provide specific evidence, stress reader benefits, avoid exaggeration, and show confidence in the quality of your product.

An application letter should be no longer than one page. Let's examine each part of a typical letter. Model 42 (on page 507) shows a solicited application letter, written to accompany the résumé presented in Model 37. (An unsolicited application letter appears in the 3Ps model on page 520.)

✔checklist 16

Résumés

Length and Format

✔ Use a two-page résumé when applying for most entry-level positions.

✔ Use a simple format, with lots of white space and short blocks of text. By means of type size, indenting, bullets, boldface, and the like, show which parts are subordinate to other parts.

✔ Print your résumé on standard-sized (216 by 279 mm), good-quality, white or off-white (cream or ivory) paper.

✔ Make sure the finished document looks professional, attractive, and conservative, and that it is 100 percent error-free.

Content

✔ Type your complete name without a personal title at the top of the document (omit the word *résumé*), followed by an address, a daytime phone number, and an email address.

✔ Include a one-sentence objective that follows this formula: *doing what* (specific work tasks) *for/with whom* (type of industry, client group, area of company).

✔ Include a summary of qualifications that highlights your relevant skills, experience, and accomplishments.

✔ Decide whether your education or work experience is your stronger qualification, and list it first. For education, list the title of your degree, the name of your university or college and its location, your major and minor, and your expected date of graduation (month and year). List your grade-point average if it is impressive and any academic honours. Avoid long lists of courses that are part of the normal preparation for your desired position.

✔ For work experience, determine whether to use a chronological (most recent job first), functional (list of competencies and skills developed), or combination organizational pattern. For whichever you choose, stress those duties or skills that are transferable to the new position. Use short phrases and action verbs, and provide specific evidence of the results you achieved.

✔ Include any additional information (such as special skills, professional affiliations, and willingness to travel or relocate) that will help to distinguish you from the competition. Avoid including such personal information as age, gender, ethnicity, religion, disabilities, or marital status.

✔ Provide a statement that references are available on request.

✔ Throughout, highlight your strengths and minimize any weaknesses, but always tell the truth.

Electronic Résumés

✔ In general, describe your qualifications and experiences in terms of nouns rather than verbs. Weave these keywords throughout your résumé—do not list them in a block at the beginning of the résumé.

✔ Save the electronic résumé in plain ASCII text.

✔ Use a line length of no more than 70 characters—manually press the Enter key if necessary.

✔ Include a note at the end of your text résumé that a fully formatted version is available upon request.

Address and Salutation

Your letter should be addressed to an individual rather than to an organization or department. Remember, the more hands your letter must go through before it reaches the right person, the more chance for something to go wrong. Ideally, your letter should be addressed to the person who will actually interview you and who will likely be your supervisor if you get the job.

If you do not know enough about the prospective employer to know the name of the appropriate person (the decision maker), you have probably not gathered enough data. If necessary, call the organization to make sure you have the right name—including the correct spelling—and position title. In your salutation, use a courtesy title (such as *Mr.* or *Ms.*) along with the person's last name. If you do know the person's name but are unsure of his or her gender, you may use both their first and last name in the salutation and drop the courtesy title. (This approach does make the salutation less personal, so avoid doing this unless absolutely necessary.)

Some job vacancy ads are blind ads; they do not identify the hiring company by name and provide only a box number address, often in care of the newspaper or magazine that contains the ad. In such a situation, you (and all others responding to that ad) have no choice but to address your letter to the newspaper and to use a generic salutation, such as "Dear Human Resources Manager." (Alternatively you can use an attention line, such as "Attention: Human Resources.") Insert a subject line to identify immediately the purpose of this important message.

Opening

Use the direct organizational plan for writing a solicited application letter.

The opening paragraph of a solicited application letter is fairly straightforward. Because the organization has advertised an opening, it is eager to receive quality applications, so use a direct organization: state (or imply) the reason for your letter, identify the particular position for which you're applying, and indicate how you learned about the opening. Keep in mind that a cover letter, like any sales letter, must be written from the assumption that your reader has a number of alternatives on how to spend his or her time and resources. Making the reader guess about what position you're applying for is not only discourteous, it's poor strategy.

Moreover, your opening should make the reader want to read further, so it's a good idea to offer a short preview of your qualifications right in the opening. Gear your opening to the job and to the specific organization. For positions that are widely perceived to be somewhat conservative (such as in finance, accounting, and banking), use a restrained opening. For more creative work (like sales, advertising, and public relations), you might start out on a more imaginative note. Here are two examples:

Conservative:

Mr. Adam Storkel, manager of your King Street branch, has suggested that I submit my qualifications for the position of assistant loan officer, as advertised in last week's *Kingston Whig Standard.* I have four years of customer service experience in the banking industry and have recently completed a bachelor of business administration degree.

Creative:

If quality is Job 1 at Ford, then Job 2 must surely be communicating that message effectively to the public. My degree in journalism and work experience at the Kintzell Agency will enable me to help you achieve that objective. The enclosed résumé further describes my qualifications for the position of advertising copywriter posted in the June issue of *Automotive Age.*

For unsolicited application letters, you must first get the reader's attention. You can gain that attention most easily by talking about the company rather than about yourself. One effective strategy is to show that you know something about the

JOB APPLICATION LETTER

This model is an example of a solicited application letter; it accompanies the résumé in Model 37 on page 484.

Begins by identifying the job position and the source of advertising.

Emphasizes a qualification that might distinguish her from other applicants.

Relates her work experience to the specific needs of the employer.

Provides a telephone number (may be done either in the body of the letter or in the last line of the address block).

March 13, 20—

Mr. David Norman, Partner
Klein & Lougheed
205 5th Avenue SW
Calgary, AB T2P 4B9

1 Dear Mr. Norman:

2 My work experience in accounting, coupled with my ongoing education in the Bachelor of Business Administration Program at the University of Alberta, has prepared me for the part-time junior accounting position you advertised in the March 9 *Edmonton Journal*.

3 In addition to completing required courses in accounting and management information systems as part of my accounting major, I've also completed an elective course in production accounting. This course focused on some of the unique accounting needs of the oil and gas industry and provided me with the skills required to perform accurate and timely royalty calculations. Moreover, my experience at XYZ Canadian has given me experience with several of the software programs you require for this position, including Accumap, PetroLab, and QBLM.

Your job posting seeks candidates who possess both strong technical and strong people skills. My technical training and experience in accounting is supplemented by work experience as a customer service associate, which has allowed me to develop strong communication skills, the ability to resolve conflicts, and the ability to take charge of situations where creative solutions are needed quickly. Indeed, my supervisor at Telecom frequently called upon me to mediate when conflicts arose between sales staff within this highly competitive, commission-sales environment.

4 After you have reviewed the enclosed resume, I would appreciate the opportunity to discuss with you in person why my combination of technical training, relevant accounting experience, and excellent people skills well match the needs of this position. I can be reached at (780) 222-1234 after 3 p.m. daily.

Sincerely,

Aurelia Chow
2913 40th Avenue
Edmonton, AB T24 1Z7
achow@sympatico.ca

Grammar and Mechanics Notes

1 This letter is formatted in modified-block style with standard punctuation (colon after the salutation and comma after the complimentary closing).

2 *Edmonton Journal:* Italicize the names of newspapers.

3 *accounting and management information systems:* Do not capitalize the names of university courses unless they include a proper noun.

4 *résumé:* This word may also properly be written without the accent marks: resume.

organization—its recent projects, awards, changes in personnel, and the like—and then show how you can contribute to the corporate effort.

Now that Palliser Furniture has expanded operations to Mexico, can you use a marketing graduate who speaks fluent Spanish and who knows the culture of the region?

Make the opening short, original, interesting, and reader-oriented.

Your opening should be short, interesting, and reader-oriented. Avoid tired openings such as "This is to apply for . . ." or "Please consider this letter my application for . . ." Maintain an air of formality. Don't address the reader by a first name and don't try to be cute. Avoid such attention-grabbing (but unsuccessful) stunts as sending a worn, once-white running shoe with the note "Now that I have one foot in the door, I hope you'll let me get the other one in" or writing the application letter beginning at the bottom of the page and working upward (to indicate a willingness to start at the bottom and work one's way up). Such gimmicks send a non-verbal message to the reader that the applicant may be trying to deflect attention from a weak résumé.

Body

Don't repeat all the information from the résumé.

In two to three paragraphs, highlight your strongest qualifications and show how they can benefit the employer. Emphasize how you aim to contribute to the organization by discussing previous accomplishments relevant to the position sought—these should include accomplishments from your past and present employment, as well as your volunteer and educational experiences. In addition, discuss relevant skills. As always, show—don't tell; that is, provide specific, credible evidence to support your statements, using wording different from that used in the résumé. Tell an anecdote about yourself ("For example, recently I . . ."). Your discussion should reflect modest confidence rather than a hard-sell approach. Avoid starting too many sentences with *I*, and insert the occasional *you* and *your* in the letter while stressing reader benefits.

NOT: I am an effective supervisor.

BUT: Supervising a staff of five counter clerks has given me the leadership skills your front line requires.

NOT: I am an accurate person.

BUT: In my two years of experience as a student secretary, none of the letters, memorandums, and reports I typed was ever returned with a typographical error marked.

NOT: I took a course in business communication.

BUT: The communication strategies I learned in my business communication course will enable me to uphold your reputation as the industry leader in customer satisfaction.

Refer the reader to the enclosed résumé. Subordinate the reference to the résumé, and emphasize instead what the résumé contains.

NOT: I am enclosing a copy of my résumé for your review.

BUT: As detailed in the enclosed résumé, my extensive work experience in records management has prepared me to help you "take charge of this paperwork jungle," as headlined in your classified ad.

Closing

You are not likely to get what you do not ask for, so close by asking for a personal interview. Indicate flexibility regarding scheduling and location. Provide your phone number and email address, either in the last paragraph or immediately below your name and address in the closing lines. And don't forget to thank your reader for his or her time.

Politely ask for an interview.

> After you have reviewed my qualifications, I would appreciate your letting me know when we can meet to discuss further my employment with Ontario Power. You can reach me by phone at (905)564-8723 or by email at LynnTruss@Canada.com. Thank you for the opportunity to compete for this position.

OR

> I will call your office next week to see if we can arrange a meeting at your convenience to discuss my qualifications for working as a financial analyst with your organization. Thank you for reviewing my application.

Use a standard complimentary closing (such as "Sincerely"), leave enough space to sign the letter, and then type your name, address, phone number, and email address. Even though you may be sending out many application letters at the same time, take care with each individual letter. You never know which one will be the one that actually gets you an interview. Sign your name neatly in blue or black ink, fold each letter and accompanying résumé neatly, and mail.

The guidelines for writing an application letter are summarized in Checklist 17.

✔checklist 17

Job Application Letters

✔ Use your job application letter to show how the qualifications listed in your résumé have prepared you for the specific job for which you're applying.

✔ If possible, address your letter to the individual in the organization who will interview you if you're successful.

✔ When applying for an advertised opening, begin by stating (or implying) the reason for the letter, identify the position for which you're applying, tell how you learned about the opening, and offer a brief preview of your qualifications.

✔ When writing an unsolicited application letter, first gain the reader's attention by showing that you are familiar with the company and can make a unique contribution to its efforts.

✔ In two to three paragraphs, highlight your strongest qualifications and relate them directly to the needs of the specific position for which you're applying. Refer the reader to the enclosed résumé.

✔ Treat your letter as a persuasive sales letter: provide specific evidence, stress reader benefits, incorporate the *you* attitude, avoid exaggeration, and show confidence in the quality of your product.

✔ Close by tactfully asking for an interview and thanking the reader for his or her time.

✔ Maintain an air of formality throughout the letter. Avoid cuteness.

✔ Make sure the finished document presents a professional, attractive, and conservative appearance and that it is 100 percent error-free.

■ Preparing for a Job Interview

CO3. Conduct yourself appropriately during an employment interview.

Consider the employment interview as a sales presentation. Just as any good sales representative would never attempt to walk into a potential customer's office without having a thorough knowledge of the product, neither should you. You are both the product and the product promoter, so do your homework—both on yourself and on the potential customer.

Researching the Organization

Learn as much as you can about the organization—your possible future employer.

As a result of having developed your résumé and written your application letters, you have probably done enough general homework on yourself. You are likely to have a reasonably accurate picture of who you are and what you want out of your career. Now is the time to zero in on the organization.

It is no exaggeration to say that you should learn everything you possibly can about the organization. Research the specific organization in depth, using the research techniques you developed in Chapter 10. If you're a student, the best place to start is your career services department—they have plenty of resources available free to students. Also, search the current business periodical indexes and go online to learn what has been happening recently with the company. Many libraries maintain copies of the annual reports from large companies. Study these or other sources for current product information, profitability, plans for the future, and the like. Learn about the company's products and services, its history, the names of its officers, what the business press has to say about the organization, its recent stock activity, financial health, corporate structure, and the like.

Relate what you discover about the individual company to what you've learned about competing companies and about the industry in general. By trying to fit what you've learned into the broader perspective of the industry, you will be able to discuss matters more intelligently during your interview instead of just having a bunch of jumbled facts at your disposal.

If you're interviewing at a governmental agency, determine its role, recent funding levels, recent activities, spending legislation affecting the agency, and the extent to which being on the "right" side (that is, the official side) of a political question matters. If you're interviewing for a teaching position at an educational institution, determine the range of course offerings, types of students, conditions of the facilities and equipment, professionalism of the staff, and funding levels. In short, every tidbit of information you can learn about your prospective employer will help you make the most appropriate career decision.

DILBERT

© Scott Adams/Dist. by United Features Syndicate, Inc.

spotlight24
ON LAW AND ETHICS

The Ethical Dimensions of the Job Campaign

Most recruiters have heard the story about the job applicant who, when told that he was overqualified for a position, pleaded in vain, "But I lied about my credentials." When constructing your résumé and application letter, when completing an application form, and when answering questions during an interview, you will constantly have to make judgments about what to divulge and what to omit. Everyone would agree that outright lying is unethical (and clearly illegal as well). But when is hedging or omitting negative information about yourself simply being smart, and when is it unethical?

The Ethics of Constructing a Résumé

Recruiters believe that the problem they call "résumé inflation" has increased in recent years, and plenty of research backs them up. One survey of executives found that 26 percent of them reported hiring employees during the previous year who had misrepresented their qualifications, education, or salary history. By far, the most frequent transgression is misrepresenting one's qualifications.

Acting ethically does not, of course, require that you emphasize every little problem that has occurred in your past. Indeed, one study showed that the majority of *Fortune* 500 human resources directors agree with the statement "Interviewees should stress their strengths and not mention their weaknesses unless the interviewer asks for information in an area of weakness."

Recognize, however, that some employers have a standard policy of terminating all employees who are found to have falsely represented their qualifications on their résumés. Generally, the employer must show evidence that the employee intentionally misrepresented his or her qualifications so as to fraudulently secure a job. Claiming to have a university degree when, in fact, one does not would likely be grounds for termination, whereas an unintentional mistake in the dates of previous employment would probably not be.

The Ethics of Accepting a Position

For some applicants, another ethical dilemma occurs when they receive a second, perhaps more attractive, job offer after having already accepted a prior offer. Most professionals believe that such a situation should not present a dilemma. A job acceptance is a promise that the applicant is expected to keep. The hiring organization has made many decisions based on the applicant's acceptance, not the least of which was to notify all other candidates that the job had been filled. Reneging on the commitment to the employer not only puts the applicant in a bad light (and don't underestimate the power of the network in spreading such information) but also puts the applicant's school in a bad light.

If you're unsure about whether to accept a job offer, ask for a time extension. Once you've made your decision, however, stick to it and have no regrets. If you decide to accept the job, immediately notify all other employers that you are withdrawing from further consideration. If you decide to decline the job, move on to your next interviews without looking back. Learn to live with your decisions.[15]

You will use this information as a resource to help you understand and discuss topics with some familiarity during the interview. No one is impressed by the interviewee who, out of the blue, spouts, "I see your stock went up 5½ points last week." However, in response to the interviewer's comment about the company's recent announcement of a new product line, it would be quite appropriate to respond, "That must have been the reason your stock jumped so high last week."

In short, bring up such information only if it flows naturally into the conversation. Even if you're never able to discuss some of the information you've gathered, the knowledge itself will still provide perspective in helping you to make a reasonable decision if a job offer is extended.

Avoid "showing off" your knowledge of the organization.

The Legal Dimensions of the Job Campaign[16]

Human rights guidelines for employment interview questions are clear: applicants for employment may be asked to divulge only information which has relevance to the position applied for. Employers, by law, must focus only on gathering relevant information to decide if the applicant is able to perform the functions of the position.

I applied for a job and was told I will be hired if I take a lie-detector test. Must I take this test?

Lie detector tests are very uncommon in Canada, and they should be administered only if deemed directly relevant to the needs of the position, such as law enforcement. While requiring a lie detector test is not specifically prohibited, employers would be expected to have a "reasonable" argument for doing so.

The computer firm where I want to work requires all job applicants to take a psychological test as part of the application process. Is this legal?

Yes. Aptitude, personality, and psychological tests are legal as long as the results are accurate, are deemed as essential to identifying certain personality characteristics to seek (or avoid), and do not tend to eliminate anyone on the basis of gender, age, race, religion, or national origin.

I work full-time and have been offered a dream job by another employer—if I can start the new job immediately. Do I have to give my current employer a certain number of days' notice?

Provincial and employment standards will differ on the specifics. According to the Alberta Provincial Employment Standards Code, an employee is required to provide an employer with sufficient notice of termination—one week, if the employee has been employed by the employer for more than three months but less than two years, or two weeks, if the employee has been employed by the employer for two years or more.

An employer is also required to provide an employee with sufficient notice of termination. However, this notice does not have to be fulfilled by a period of time; it could instead be fulfilled by a cash payment (i.e., an employer can "pay out" an employee in lieu of notice and have

the employee leave immediately). Be aware that some companies may have specific termination requirements outlined in a policy or Collective Agreement.

I'm an older student who will be applying for positions along with much younger ones. Can the interviewer ask my age?

No, age discrimination contravenes both federal and provincial human rights legislation. Exceptions would be made for jobs requiring a minimum age (e.g., serving drinks in a bar). If you're worried about the possible impact of your age, you might wish to volunteer certain information to allay the interviewer's concerns—mentioning some vigorous physical activity you regularly engage in, for example.

What types of information may not be asked for on an application form or during a job interview?

- Race, ancestry, religious beliefs, or place of origin (including origin of a surname or place of birth); however, you may be asked to prove that you have legal authorization to work in Canada.

- Gender, age, or family information (including marital status, plans for marriage or children, number of children or their ages, child-care arrangements, spouse's occupation, roommate arrangements, and home ownership). Some employers will ask, typically at the end of the interview, whether there is any reason why you may not be able to fulfill the duties as expected.

- Disabilities, either physical or mental (unless based on a bona fide occupational requirement).

- Arrests (you may, however, be asked about convictions for serious offences related to the position—e.g., driving record for a courier job).

How should I respond to an illegal question during a job interview?

The best response, assuming you want to continue to be considered for the position, may be to deflect the question by focusing on how you can contribute to the job. For example, if you were asked about your plans to have children in the immediate future, you might respond, "I assure you that I'm fully committed to my career and to making a real contribution to the organization for which I work." Or you may respond by saying you don't believe such questions are relevant to your ability to do the job, or by asking the interviewer to explain the relevance of the question.

Another option is to speak with the company's Human Resources Department (assuming they have one) or interviewer's supervisor after the interview. Often, employers do not ask illegal questions on purpose, but do so in oversight or due to a lack of interview experience or expertise.

Finally, you could file a complaint with the provincial Human Rights Commission.

NOTE: Legislation governing employment standards, including what can and cannot be asked in an interview, exists at both the federal and provincial levels. "The jurisdiction of the provincial and federal governments arises from the *Constitution Act, 1867,* sections 91 and 92. Judicial interpretation of these sections gives provincial legislatures major jurisdiction, with federal authority limited to a narrow field."[17] Answers to the above questions are thus broadly interpreted and may not apply to every part of the country.

Preparing for Questions

As you review your own qualifications and the needs of the position sought, start a list of potential questions. Some of the questions will require fairly straightforward elaboration of your qualifications, as detailed on your résumé. Be prepared to flesh these out, offering specific anecdotes of how you demonstrated a skill or aptitude in a past position.

More difficult questions are those that focus on your limitations to do the job. Anticipate these. Write up a list of all your limitations: lack of direct experience, lack of a required educational credential, little work history, periods of inactivity in your work or educational history, and the like. Then prepare honest, convincing explanations for the limitation, as well as convincing arguments on how you plan to overcome these limitations, how you've overcome similar limitations in past positions, or how your existing strengths make up for these limitations.

There are several kinds of questions interviewers commonly ask: behaviour-based (sometimes called BDI, for Behavioural Descriptive Interview), theoretical, open-ended, and closed-ended. Behaviour-based questions are designed to encourage candidates to provide examples of how they've behaved in the past—rather than discuss how they intend to behave in the future, which is the purpose of theoretical questions. (The rationale behind behaviour-based questions is that past behaviour is a good predictor of future performance.) These interviews are carefully structured, and each candidate is typically asked the same set of questions. Responses may then be scored for later comparison of candidates.

Practice your response to typical interview questions.

Open-ended questions allow the candidate to interpret the question as he or she sees fit. A question such as "How are you qualified?" or "Why should I hire you" allows the candidate the freedom to answer in a number of ways. When answering such questions, tailor your answer to the needs of the position and the organization. Finally, closed questions may be used to confirm or clarify information you've offered on the résumé or cover letter.

Occasionally, interviewers may pose questions you didn't anticipate and for which there is seemingly no "right" answer. ("Are you competitive?" is a good example.) The strategy to use in such a circumstance is to keep the desired job firmly in mind and to formulate each answer—no matter what the question—so as to highlight your ability to perform the desired job competently. You don't have

Answer each question honestly, but in a way that highlights your qualifications.

to accept each question as asked. You can ask the interviewer to be more specific or to rephrase the question. Doing so not only will provide guidance for answering the question but will give you a few additional moments to prepare your response.

Preparing Your Own Questions

Ensure that any relevant questions you may have are answered during the interview.

During the course of the interview, many of the questions you may have about the organization or the job will probably be answered. However, an interview is a two-way conversation, so it is legitimate for you to pose relevant questions at appropriate moments. Prepare these questions beforehand—three to five is sufficient.

Questions such as the following will provide useful information on which to base a decision if a job is offered:

- How would you describe a typical day on the job?
- What is the first task or problem that would need my attention?
- Why is this position vacant?
- Can you describe the environment and values here?
- How is an employee evaluated and promoted?
- What types of training are available?
- What are your expectations of new employees?
- What are the organization's plans for the future?
- To whom would I report? Would anyone report to me?
- What are the advancement opportunities for this position?
- Can I clarify anything more about my skills, education, or experience?
- When do you expect to make a decision on the successful candidate?

Each of these questions not only secures needed information to help you make a decision but also sends a positive non-verbal message to the interviewer that you are interested in this position as a long-term commitment. Do not, however, ask so many questions that the roles of the interviewer and the interviewee become blurred, and avoid putting the interviewer on the spot.

Avoid appearing to be overly concerned about salary.

Finally, avoid asking about salary and fringe benefits during the initial interview. There will be plenty of time for such questions later, after you've convinced the organization that you're the person it wants. In terms of planning, however, you should know ahead of time the market value of the position for which you're applying. Check the classified ads, reports collected by your college career service, and library and Internet sources to learn what a reasonable salary figure for your position would be.

Types of Interviews

Most interviews follow a general three-stage structure—rapport building, information exchange, and closing—but the specifics of each interview can vary quite widely. Here's a brief overview of the kinds of interviews you might encounter.[18]

Telephone Interview   These are often used to pre-screen candidates before a more formal face-to face interview is conducted. Treat these as you would any other interview: be on time, be prepared, smile, and be professional. (And be sure you are uninterrupted during the interview.) Occasionally, unarranged interviews are used to assess how well a candidate handles unexpected situations. If you suddenly find yourself in an unexpected phone interview, ask the interviewer for a moment to close the door and grab your résumé and a pen.

Personal Interview   Personal interviews are conducted one on one and are usually conducted by the department manager or a member of the human resources department. These are common for entry-level positions.

Panel Interview   Becoming more and more common, the interview is conducted by a panel of two or more interviewers. Frequently one of the members of the panel will be from human resources, in addition to a department manager, and occasionally some potential work peers.

Group Interview   These interviews will interview two or more candidates at the same time. Occasionally the candidates will be invited to discuss topics or work together on a task.

Stress Interview   For positions that require workers to operate under stressful conditions, a stress interview is designed to see how each candidate manages stressful situations. Barbara Simmons, a career counsellor at George Brown College, offers these examples of stress inducing interview tactics:[19] A mildly stressful question might be something like, "With your lack of a university degree, what makes you think you're qualified for this position?" More stressful still are statements that blatantly criticize the candidate, like, "You don't seem nearly assertive enough to handle this kind of position" or, "That was a terrible answer, the worst I've heard." Long silences on behalf of the interviewers can also be used to induce stress and to see how well a candidate initiates conversation. If you find yourself in a stress interview, remind yourself the purpose of the tactic: don't let yourself be intimidated, remain calm, and think before you speak.

■ Communicating After the Interview

Immediately after the interview, make some notes about the kinds of questions asked and anything you learned about the position that you may not have known before. This will help you in any future interviews or phone calls that may precede a job offer. Also, conduct a self-appraisal of your performance. Try to recall each question that was asked and evaluate your response. If you're not satisfied with one of your responses, take the time to formulate a more effective answer. Chances are that you will be asked a similar question in the future.

CO4. Complete the communication tasks needed after the employment interview.

Also re-evaluate your résumé. Were any questions asked during the interview that indicated some confusion about your qualifications? Does some section need to be revised or some information added or deleted?

Determine too whether you can improve your application letter on the basis of your interview experience. Were the qualifications you discussed in your letter the

✔checklist 18

Employment Interviews

Preparing for an Employment Interview

✔ Before going on an employment interview, learn everything you can about the organization.

✔ Practice answering common interview questions and prepare questions of your own to ask.

✔ Select appropriate clothing to wear.

✔ Control your nervousness by being well prepared, well equipped, and on time.

Conducting Yourself During the Interview

✔ Throughout the interview, be aware of the non-verbal signals you are communicating through your body language.

✔ Answer each question completely and accurately, always trying to relate your qualifications to the specific needs of the desired job.

✔ Whether you are interviewed by one person or a group of people, you will likely be evaluated on your education and experience, mental qualities, manner and personal traits, and general appearance.

Communicating After the Interview

✔ Immediately following the interview, critique your performance, your résumé, and your application letter.

✔ Send a thank-you note or email message to the interviewer.

ones that seemed to impress the interviewers the most? Were these qualifications discussed in terms of how they would benefit the organization? Did you provide specific evidence to support your claims?

You should also take the time to send the interviewer (or interviewers) a short thank-you note or email message as a gesture of courtesy and to reaffirm your interest in the job. The interviewer, who probably devoted quite a bit of time to you before, during, and after the interview session, deserves to have his or her efforts on your behalf acknowledged.

Reiterate your interest in the position and, if relevant, cite something from the interview that you are particularly excited about. If there was anything asked at the interview that you'd like to restate more clearly, you can also do that here, but avoid a lengthy letter attempting to resell yourself. Close on a hopeful, forward-looking note.

Recognize that your thank-you note may or may not have any effect on the hiring decision. Most decisions to offer the candidate a job or to invite him or her back for another round of interviewing are made the day of the interview, often during the interview itself. Thus, your thank-you note may arrive after the decision, good or bad, has been made.

Your note might sound similar to the following:

Thank you for the opportunity to interview for the position of EDP specialist yesterday. I very much enjoyed meeting you and Arlene Worthington and learning more about the position and about Klein & Lougheed.

I especially appreciated the opportunity to observe the long-range planning meeting yesterday afternoon and to learn of your firm's plans for increasing your consulting practice with non-profit agencies. My experience working in city government leads me to believe that non-profit agencies can benefit greatly from your expertise.

Again, thank you for taking the time to visit with me yesterday. I look forward to hearing from you.

Your thank-you note should be short and may be either typed or handwritten. Consider it a routine message that should be written in a direct organizational pattern. If you have not heard from the interviewer by the deadline date he or she gave you for making a decision, telephone or email the interviewer for a status report. If no decision has been made, your inquiry will keep your name and your interest in the position in the interviewer's mind. If someone else has been selected, you need to know so that you can continue your job search. The steps of the interview process are summarized in Checklist 18.

Send a short thank-you note immediately after the interview.

AN APPLICATION LETTER

Problem

You are Ray Arnold, a human resource major at McGill University. You have analyzed your interests, strengths and weaknesses, and preferred lifestyle and have decided you would like to work in some area of human resources for a firm on the West Coast with an environmental focus. Because you attend a school in the East, you decide not to limit your job search to on-campus interviewing.

In your research you learned that Ballard Power Systems, Inc., has recently been awarded a $23-million contract by the federal government to develop eco-friendly technology for the public transit sector. Ballard, which is headquartered in Burnaby, British Columbia, also has offices in the US and Germany.

You decide to write to Ballard to see whether it might have an opening for someone with your qualifications. You will, of course, include a copy of your résumé with your letter. The following is a brief summary of your qualifications (add other details as necessary):

- Major in Human Resources; minor in psychology
- As an extracurricular activity, was president of the Eco Club on campus and successfully lobbied for a comprehensive recycling program at McGill University and for a switch to hybrid-powered vehicles for their fleet of maintenance trucks
- While at university, worked part time for RBC as a customer service representative and most recently as a supervisor; received three promotions in four years

Send your letter to Ms. Phyllis Morrison, Assistant Director of Human Resources, Ballard Power Systems, Inc., 4343 North Fraser Way, Burnaby, BC V5J 5J9.

Process

1. Will this letter be a solicited or unsolicited (prospecting) letter?

   Unsolicited—I don't know whether Ballard has an opening.

2. Write an opening paragraph for your letter that gets attention and that relates your skills to Ballard's needs. Make sure the purpose of your letter is made clear in your opening paragraph.

   Ballard's recently accepted proposal to the federal government estimated that you would be adding up to 300 new staff for the City Transit Project. With this dramatic increase in personnel, do you have an opening in your human resources department for a university graduate with a major in human resources and a minor in psychology?

3. Compare your education with Ballard's likely requirements. What will help you stand out from the competition?

   ▪ It's somewhat unusual for a human resources major to have a psychology minor.

   ▪ My course work in my major and minor were pretty standard, so there's no need to list individual courses.

   ▪ My involvement in an environmental club on campus reveals a familiarity with and passion for alternative sources of energy.

4. Compare your work experiences with Ballard's likely requirements. What qualifications from your résumé should you highlight in your letter?

   ▪ The interpersonal and human relations skills developed as a customer service representative will be an important asset as a human resource specialist.

   ▪ Written and oral communications skills developed through work and extracurricular activities will enable me to communicate effectively with a diverse workforce.

5. What other qualifications should you mention?

   My degree in human resources, combined with my diverse experience as both an employee and an administrator, will help me look at each issue from the perspective of both management and labour.

6. Write the sentence in which you request the interview.

   I would welcome the opportunity to come to Burnaby to discuss with you the role I might play in helping Ballard efficiently manage its growing human resource needs.

Product

Begins with an attention-getting opening that relates the writer's skills to the needs of the company.

Shows how the writer's unique qualifications will benefit the company.

Provides specific evidence to support his claims: *shows* rather than *tells*.

Gives the reader the option of phoning the applicant or having him phone her.

1   McGill University
845 Sherbrooke St. W.
Montreal, Quebec, H3A 2T5
February 7, 20—

Ms. Phyllis Morrison
Assistant Human Resources Director
Ballard Power Systems, Inc.
4343 North Fraser Way, Burnaby, BC V5J 5J9

2   Dear Ms. Morrison

Ballard's recent proposal to the federal government estimated that you would be adding up to 300 new positions for the City Transit Project. With this increase in personnel, will you have an opening in your human resources department for a recent university graduate with a major in human resources and a minor in psychology?

3

My combination of course work in business and liberal arts will enable me to approach each issue from both a management and a behavioural point of view. Further, my degree in human resources, combined with my diverse experience as both an employee and an administrator, will help me look at each issue from the perspective of both management and labour.

On the job, dealing successfully with customers' overdrawn accounts, bank computer errors, and delayed-deposit recording has taught me the value of active listening and has provided me experience in explaining and justifying the company's position. And as a supervisor of up to 20 full- and part-time customer service representatives, I've learned how to recruit, train, motivate, and discipline a diverse group of individuals. My writing skills, as well as my passion for alternative sources of energy, were gained during my term as president of the Eco Club at McGill University. The Students' Association recognized our club as having the most significant impact on the university community of any club on campus. As detailed on the enclosed résumé, these communication and human relations skills will help me to interact and communicate effectively with Ballard employees at all levels and at widely dispersed locations.

I would welcome the opportunity to come to Burnaby to discuss with you the role I might play in helping Ballard efficiently manage its growing human resource needs. I will call your office on February 21, or you may call me at any time after 2 p.m. (EST) daily at 514-398-4455.

Sincerely

Raymond J. Arnold

Raymond J. Arnold

Enclosure

Grammar and Mechanics Notes

1 In a personal business letter, the writer's return address may be typed above the date (as shown here) or below the sender's name in the closing.

2 This letter is formatted in block style, with all lines beginning at the left margin, and in open punctuation style, with no punctuation after the salutation and complimentary closing.

3 *major in human resources:* Do not capitalize the names of college majors and minors.

■ Summary

One of the most important communication tasks you will ever face is securing a rewarding and worthwhile job. The job-seeking campaign thus requires considerable time, effort, and thought.

The purpose of your résumé is to get you a job interview. Strive for a two-page document, typed in a simple, readable format on a computer and output on a laser printer. Include your name, address, phone number, objective, summary of qualifications, information about your education and work experience, and special aptitudes and skills. Include other information only if it will help distinguish you favourably from the other applicants. Use either a chronological, functional, or combination organization for your skills and work experience, and stress those skills and experiences that can be transferred to the job you want. Consider formatting an electronic version of your résumé for emailing or computer scanning. This version should be in plain text, with no special formatting.

co1. Determine the appropriate length, content, and format for your résumé.

You should tailor each résumé to the specific position sought, as well as compose an application letter that discusses how your education and work experience qualify you, offering examples where relevant. If possible, address your letter to the person who will interview you for the job. When writing a solicited application letter, begin by stating the reason for your letter, identify the position for which you're applying, and tell how you learned about the position. When writing an unsolicited letter, first gain the reader's attention. Then use the body of your letter to highlight one or two of your strongest qualifications, relating them to the needs of the position for which you're applying. Close by politely asking for an interview.

co2. Compose solicited and unsolicited job application letters.

If your application efforts are successful, you will be invited to come for an interview. To succeed at the interview phase of the job campaign, prepare for the interview and conduct yourself appropriately during the interview. Be prepared to ask some questions of your own.

co3. Conduct yourself appropriately during an employment interview.

After the interview is over, evaluate your performance and resolve to do better the next time. Also evaluate your résumé and cover letter and revise them if necessary. Finally, take the time to write a thank-you note to express appreciation to the courtesies extended to you.

co4. Complete the communication tasks needed after the employment interview.

■ Key Terms

You should be able to define the following terms in your own words and give an original example of each.

application letter (504)   résumé (482)

electronic résumé (499)   solicited application letter (504)

reference (497)   unsolicited application letter (504)

■ Exercises

1 **The 3Ps (Problem, Process, and Product) Model: Communication Applications at workopolis.com**   When Patrick Sullivan and his colleagues need to fill an open position at Workopolis, they use keywords to search through the huge workopolis.com résumé database for candidates with the appropriate education and experience. During interviews, Sullivan asks open-ended questions so candidates can talk about strengths and interests beyond the basic facts on their résumés. He also expects candidates to ask creative questions about the company, the position, or his role as president of Workopolis.

Problem

Imagine that you are getting ready to apply to Workopolis for a full-time job in human resources, marketing, information technology, or another functional area. In preparation, you need to find out more about Workopolis and its industry. This research will help you understand the company's direction and its employment needs, both immediate and long-term, so you can tailor your résumé accordingly and ask relevant questions during an interview.

Process

a. What kinds of job opportunities with Workopolis are you interested in researching?
b. Visit the Workopolis Web site (at www.workopolis.com) and search for company information. What industry is Workopolis in, and what is its strategy? Who are its customers? Where are its offices?
c. How do your skills and personal interests match up with what you have learned about Workopolis?
d. Look at the types of open positions that Workopolis wants to fill. Are your education and work experience appropriate for the positions that interest you? What other qualifications do you need to apply for the most promising positions?

Product

Using your knowledge of employment communication, write a brief analysis of Workopolis and one open position that you find interesting. Mention details that will help you customize your résumé for this job and prepare for a personal interview with Patrick Sullivan.

CO1. **Determine the appropriate length, content, and format for your résumé.**

2 **The 3Ps (Problem, Process, and Product) Model: Developing A Résumé— Getting to Know You**

Problem

Assume that you are beginning your last term of university before graduating. Using factual data from your own education, work experience, and so on (include any data that you expect to be true at the time of your graduation), prepare a résumé in an effective format.

Process

a. How will you word your name at the top of your résumé—for example, with or without any initials? (Remember *not* to include a personal title before your name.)

b. What is your mailing address? If you will be changing addresses during the job search, include both addresses, along with the effective dates of each.

c. What is your daytime phone number? When can you typically be reached at this number? What is your email address?

d. For what type of position are you searching? Prepare an effective one-sentence job objective—one that is neither too general nor too specific.

e. What is the title of your degree; the name of your university; the location of the university; your major and minor; and your expected date of graduation (month and year)?

f. What is your grade-point average overall and in your major? Is either one high enough to be considered a personal selling point?

g. Have you received any academic honours throughout your collegiate years, such as scholarships or being named to the dean's list? If so, list them.

h. Did you take any elective courses (courses that most applicants for this position probably did *not* take) that might be especially helpful in this position? If so, list them.

i. List in reverse chronological order (most recent job first) the following information for each job you've held during your college years: job title, organizational name, location (city and province), inclusive dates of employment, and full- or part-time status. Describe your specific duties in each position, stressing those duties that helped prepare you for your job objective. Use short phrases, beginning each duty or responsibility with one of the action verbs on pages 495–496 and showing, where possible, specific evidence of the results you achieved.

j. Will your education or your work experience be more likely to impress the recruiter?

k. What additional information might you include, such as special skills, professional affiliations, offices held, or willingness to relocate or travel?

l. What key qualifications do you need to highlight at the beginning of the résumé? Look at the job ad or description; then summarize your most relevant skills, aptitudes, and qualifications in three or more bullet points.

m. Are your reference letters on file at your school's placement office? If so, provide the office name, address, and phone number. (If not, include a statement such as "References available on request" at the bottom of your résumé.)

Product

Using the preceding information, draft, revise, format, and then proofread your résumé. Then prepare an electronic version of this résumé for computer scanning. Submit both of your résumés and your responses to the process questions to your instructor.

3 Objectives   Working in groups of three or four, come up with 20 to 25 jobs that group members might consider. From the list of jobs, select four and write an appropriate objective for that job. Compare your objectives with those of the other group members. Do your objectives clearly identify what specific work tasks you can do and for whom? Evaluate the job objectives of the other group members. How do they compare to yours?

4 Internet Exercise   Electronic résumés are an increasingly important part of the job search. Point your browser to Rebecca Smith's eRésumés and Resources

Web site and look at her erésumé gallery (at www.erésumés.com), which features a number of creative examples of electronic résumés. Review one of the creative résumés, and then return to the erésumé gallery to view an electronic résumé selected from the listing of individuals' résumés. How do these résumés differ? Which do you think would be more attractive to an employer? Why? What ideas can you glean from these examples that would be appropriate and effective for your own résumé?

5 Reference List   You have been scheduled for a job interview for an entry-level position with Stay Fit Gym. As part of the interview process, you have been asked to bring a list of references. Prepare a reference sheet with the names, professional titles, addresses, email addresses, and phone numbers for at least four people who could recommend you for employment. This should be an actual list of references (real people) that could be left after your interview. Assume your instructor is the interviewer. Submit the reference sheet to him or her for evaluation.

CO2. Compose solicited and unsolicited job application letters.

6 Application Letter Project   This project consists of writing both a solicited and an unsolicited application letter. Prepare each letter in an appropriate format and on appropriate paper. Include a copy of your résumé with each letter. Submit each letter to your instructor folded and inserted into a correctly addressed envelope (don't forget to sign your letter).

a. Identify a large prospective employer—one that has not advertised for an opening in your field. Using one of the résumés you developed earlier, write an unsolicited application letter.

b. For various reasons, you might not secure a position directly related to your college or university major. In such a situation, it is especially important to be able to show how your qualifications (no matter what they are) match the needs of the employer. Using your own background, apply for the following position, which was advertised in last Sunday's *Toronto Star*: MANAGER-TRAINEE POSITION. Bombardier is looking for recent college graduates to enter its management-trainee program in preparation for an exciting career in one of the diversified companies that make up Bombardier. Excellent beginning salary and benefits, good working conditions, and a company that cares about you. (Reply to Box 385-G in care of this newspaper.)

7 Job Application Letters—Looking for a Spring Internship   You're looking for an internship where you can work part-time from February to May during your final university semester. One of your friends at the University of Saskatchewan has mentioned that Carnegie Learning hires interns throughout the year. Through research, you find out that Carnegie Learning makes math software for use by elementary school, junior high, and high school students. Interns get involved in product development and many other projects. Although you're not a math or education major, your friend says that the company is most interested in interns who are willing to test new programs and handle other tasks that regular employees simply don't have enough time to tackle.

You decide to apply for an internship at Carnegie Learning. Browse the company's Web site at www.carnegielearning.com, reading about its products and its employment needs. Then draft a job application letter in which you highlight your qualifications and ask to be considered for an internship in the spring. As far as possible, base this letter on your actual educational background and work qualifications, but stress your interest in Carnegie Learning's industry and products.

8 **Interview Evaluation**   You are employed by EverGreen Inc., a plant nursery, in Antigonish, Nova Scotia. You and two other people in the human resource department have been asked to prepare an interview evaluation form to be used for hiring new employees. Based on what you have learned regarding interviewing skills, develop a form that could be used to rate applicants' interviewing skills.

CO3. Conduct yourself appropriately during an employment interview.

9 **Researching the Employer**   Refer to Exercise 6. Assume that Bombardier has invited you to interview for the manager-trainee position. Research this company prior to your interview. Prepare a two-page, double-spaced report on your findings. You will concentrate, of course, on that information most likely to help you during the interview. As you're conducting your research, some questions are likely to occur to you that you'll want to get answered during the interview. Prepare a list of these questions and attach it as an appendix to your report.

10 **Work-team Communication—Mock Interviews**   This project uses information collected as part of Exercise 9. Divide into groups of six students. Draw straws to determine which three members will be interviewers and which three will be job applicants. Both groups now have homework to do. The interviewers must get together to plan their interview strategy (10 to 12 minutes for each candidate); and the applicants, working individually, must prepare for this interview.

The interviews will be conducted in front of the entire class, with each participant dressed appropriately. On the designated day, the three interviewers as a group will interview each of the three job applicants in turn (while the other two are out of the room). Given the short length of each interview, the applicant should refrain from asking any questions of his or her own, except to clarify the meaning of an interviewer's question.

After each round of interviews, the class as a whole will vote for the most effective interviewer and interviewee.

11 **Thank-You Letters—Pedalling Toward Employment**   As your friends interview for jobs with investment banking firms and corporate giants, you decide on a different career path: retailing. You recently bought a Rocky Mountain mountain bike at Zane's Cycles. You were impressed by the store's huge selection, knowledgeable salespeople, and customer service culture. Customers can have their bikes adjusted or repaired for free, and the prices they pay are guaranteed to be the lowest available. Zane's also operates a highly successful business selling bikes to businesses that give the cycles away as rewards for sales performance and other achievements. This operation suggests that there are other opportunities beyond the retail side of the business. Another reason Zane's seems so appealing is that the founder, Chris Zane, lets his staff run the day-to-day operation—which means that managers have the responsibility and authority to do their jobs as they see fit.

You sent an unsolicited job application letter and résumé to the store's human resources director, asking about a management trainee position. After

CO4. Complete the communication tasks needed after the employment interview.

going through an initial interview with two human resource experts, you're called back for a second interview. This time, you meet directly with Chris Zane to hear his vision for the store and his expectations for new managers. As soon as you get home, you turn on your computer to write a brief but professional thank-you note. What should you say in this letter? Should you send a printed letter or an email message? Should you communicate with the human resources director at this time, even though you didn't see him during your second interview? Using your knowledge of employment communication, draft this thank-you note (making up appropriate details if needed).

continuing case 13

"Help Wanted"

When Diana Coleman accepted the position of vice president of administration at Northern Lights, she knew that she would have to work closely with Marc Kaplan, vice-president of marketing. Diana had originally believed that the differences in their personalities, attitudes, and political biases would be outweighed by their commitment to Northern Lights. The subtle tensions between Diana and Marc have begun to escalate lately, however, and Diana is tired of working in that atmosphere.

Diana is savvy enough to recognize that she is highly marketable and that many organizations would be eager to create a position for her even if they had no advertised openings. She is interested in finding a position in information management at a large organization located in a metropolitan area. She is free to relocate anywhere in the country. She would like to become associated with a progressive organization, preferably one whose top-level officers are active in social and political causes. An organization with other women in prominent executive positions who could serve as her mentors would be especially attractive.

Note: Although you already know quite a bit about Diana, you may assume any additional, reasonable information you need to complete this project.

Diana contemplates working for a large, progressive organization with an activist social agenda.

Critical Thinking

1. Is Diana making the right decision in leaving? Why or why not?

2. Review what you know about Diana—both from the background information contained in the Appendix to Chapter 1 and from the case studies in previous chapters. Develop a list of short phrases that describe her. What implication might each of these characteristics have for choosing a suitable new work environment?

Writing Project

3. Locate three organizations that would be top prospects for Diana to explore for a career move. Identify the

organizations for Diana in terms of the criteria just discussed. Present a balanced view of the organizations, incorporating both positive and negative information. Finally, provide the name, address, and phone number of an appropriate person for Diana to contact. Organize your information in a logical manner, and present it as a letter report to Diana.

LABtest 13

Retype the following news release, correcting any grammar and mechanics errors according to the rules introduced in LABs 2–6 beginning on page 534. Be especially alert for misused punctuation and misspellings.

Of all the elements that effect the ambiance of a room;

none are more important then lighting. Beyond it's mood enhancing

qualities good-lighting is essential for safety reading and

spotlighting points of interest, and for such basics as cleaning.

5 Many people associate chandeleirs with elegant hotels or

old, movie palaces. But many dinning rooms need a fixture over

the table, it may be brass and glass, or metal.

In contrast to chandeliers, pendant's are hanging lights.

that represent one of todays' hottest lighting styles. Because

10 their small, it can be placed over object's without overpowering

it. In small spaces such as entries, or above-kitchen islands or

counters, glass shades add punch. Its shapes are intresting.

If classical designs are you're favourite, there are many

time less designs. Classic designs can be used like contemporary

15 fixtures. They add elegance as they preform task lighting. In

an other part of the room, maybe a carved fixture with 6 candle

lights covered with silk shades with a scalloped, trim.

Shades incidently, also play a key role in the story. With

their high's and low's, pendant lights, and shades are given us

20 alot to look up too.

Reference Manual

■ LAB 1: Parts of Speech

We use words, of course, to communicate. Of the hundreds of thousands of words in an unabridged dictionary, each can be classified as one of just eight parts of speech: noun, pronoun, verb, adjective, adverb, preposition, conjunction, or interjection. These eight parts of speech are illustrated in the sentence below:

| Interjection | Pronoun | Adverb | Verb | Preposition | Adjective | Noun | Conjunction | Noun |

Oh, I eagerly waited for new computers and printers.

Many words can act as different parts of speech, depending on how they are used in a sentence. (A *sentence* is a group of words that contains a subject and predicate and that expresses a complete thought.)

Consider, for example, the different parts of speech played by the word *following*:

We agree to do the *following. (noun)*
I was only *following* orders. *(verb)*
We met the *following* day. *(adjective)*
Following his remarks, he sat down. *(preposition)*

All words do not serve more than one function, but many do. Following is a brief introduction to the eight parts of speech.

1.1 Nouns   A *noun* is a word that *names* something—for example, a person, place, thing, or idea:

Person:	employee, Mr. Watkins
Place:	office, Winnipeg
Thing:	animal, computer
Idea:	concentration, impatience, week, typing

The words in italics in the following sentences are all nouns.

Roger promoted his *idea* to the *vice president* on *Wednesday.*
Word processing is just one of the *skills* you'll need as a *temp.*
How much does one *litre* of *water* weigh on our bathroom *scales?*
The animal *doctor* treated my *animal* well in *Vancouver.*

If you were asked to give an example of a noun, you would probably think of a *concrete noun*—that is, a *physical* object that you can see, hear, feel, taste, or smell. An *abstract noun,* on the other hand, names a quality or concept and not something physical.

Concrete Noun	*Abstract Noun*
book	success
stapler	patience

computer	skills
dictionary	loyalty

A *common noun,* as its name suggests, is the name of a *general* person, place, thing, or idea. If you want to give the name of a *specific* person, place, thing, or idea, you would use a *proper noun.* Proper nouns are always capitalized.

Common Noun	*Proper Noun*
man	Lon Adams
city	Montreal
car	Corvette
religion	Judaism

A *singular noun* names one person, place, thing, or idea. A *plural noun* names more than one.

Singular Noun	*Plural Noun*
Smith	Smiths
watch	watches
computer	computers
victory	victories

1.2 Pronouns   A *pronoun* is a word used in place of a noun. Consider the following sentence:

> *Anna* went to *Anna's* kitchen and made *Anna's* favorite dessert because *Anna* was going to a party with *Anna's* friends.

The noun *Anna* is used five times in this awkward sentence. A smoother, less monotonous version of the sentence substitutes pronouns for all but the first *Anna:*

> Anna went to *her* kitchen and made *her* favourite dessert because *she* was going to a party with *her* friends.

The words in italics in the following sentences are pronouns. The nouns to which they refer are underlined:

> <u>Mary</u> thought *she* might get the promotion.
>
> *None* of the <u>speakers</u> were interesting.
>
> <u>Juan</u> forgot to bring *his* slides.

1.3 Verbs   A *verb* is a word (or group of words) that expresses either action or a state of being. The first kind of verb is called an *action verb;* the second kind is known as a *linking verb.* Without a verb, you have no sentence because the verb makes a statement about the subject.

Most verbs express action of some sort—either physical or mental—as indicated by the words in italics in the following sentences:

> Courtland *planted* his garden while Carol *pulled* weeds.
>
> I *solved* my problems as I *baked* bread.
>
> Jeremy *decided* he should *call* a meeting.

A small (but important) group of verbs do not express action. Instead, they simply link the subject with words that describe it. The most common linking verbs are forms of the verb *to be,* such as *is, am, are, was, were,* and *will.* Other forms of linking verbs involve the senses, such as *feels, looks, smells, sounds,* and *tastes.* The following words in italics are verbs (note that verbs can comprise one or more words):

Rosemary *was* angry because Dennis *looked* impatient.

If Lauren *is having* a party, I *should have been* invited.

Jason *had* already *seen* the report.

1.4 Adjectives   You can make sentences consisting of only nouns or pronouns and verbs (such as "Dogs bark."), but most of the time you'll need to add other parts of speech to make the meaning of the sentence clearer or more complete. An *adjective* is a word that modifies a noun or pronoun. Adjectives answer questions about the nouns or pronouns they describe, such as *how many?, what kind?,* and *which one? (Articles* are a special group of adjectives that include the words *a, an,* and *the.)*

As shown by the words in italics in the following sentences, adjectives may come before or after the nouns or pronouns they modify:

Seventeen applicants took the *typing* test.

The interview was *short,* but *comprehensive.*

She took the *last* plane and landed at a *small Mexican* airport.

1.5 Adverbs   An *adverb* is a word that modifies a verb (usually), an adjective, or another adverb. Adverbs often answer the questions *when?, where?, how?,* or *to what extent?* The words in italics in the following sentences are adverbs:

Please perform the procedure *now. (When?)*

Put the papers *here. (Where?)*

Alice performed *brilliantly. (How?)*

I am *almost* finished. *(To what extent?)*

The *exceedingly* expensive car was *very carefully* protected.

In the last sentence, the adverb *exceedingly* modifies the adjective *expensive* (how expensive?) and the adverb *very* modifies the adverb *carefully* (how carefully?).

Many (but, by no means, all) adverbs end in *–ly,* such as *loudly, quickly, really,* and *carefully.* However, not all words that end in *–ly* are adverbs; for example, *friendly, stately,* and *ugly* are all adjectives.

1.6 Prepositions   A *preposition* is a word (such as *to, for, from, of,* and *with*) that shows the relationship between a noun or pronoun and some other word in the sentence. The noun or pronoun following the preposition is called the *object* of the preposition, and the entire group of words is called a *prepositional phrase.* In the following sentences, the preposition is shown in italics; the entire prepositional phrase is underlined:

The ceremony occurred *on the covered bridge.*
The ceremony occurred *under the covered bridge.*
Marsha talked *with* Mr. Hines.
Marsha talked *about* Mr. Hines.

1.7 Conjunctions   A *conjunction* is a word (such as *and, or,* or *but*) that joins words or groups of words. For example, in the sentence "Ari and Alice are brokers," the conjunction *and* connects the two nouns *Ari* and *Alice.* In the following sentences, the conjunction is shown in italics; the words it joins are underlined:

Francesca *or* Teresa will attend the conference. (*joins two nouns*)
Howard spoke quietly *and* deliberately. (*joins two adverbs*)
Harriet tripped *but* caught her balance. (*joins two verbs*)

1.8 Interjections   An *interjection* is a word that expresses strong emotions. Interjections are used more often in oral communication than in written communication. If an interjection stands alone, it is followed by an exclamation point. If it is a part of the sentence, it is followed by a comma. You should not be surprised to learn that some words can serve as interjections in some sentences and as other parts of speech in other sentences. In the following sentences, the interjection is shown in italics:

Good! I'm glad to learn that the new employee does good work.
Oh! I didn't mean to startle you.
My, I wouldn't do that.
Gosh, that was an exhausting exercise. *Whew!*

APPLICATION

Note: For all LAB application exercises, first photocopy the exercise and then complete the exercise on the photocopied pages.

DIRECTIONS Label each part of speech in Sentences 1–8 with the abbreviation shown below.

adjective	*adj.*
adverb	*adv.*
conjunction	*conj.*
interjection	*interj.*
noun	*n.*
preposition	*prep.*
pronoun	*pron.*
verb	*v.*

1. Oh, don't tell me I missed my flight.

2. My, your new chair is comfortable.

3. When I received your package, I was relieved. Whew!

4. Gosh! I could not believe the depth of the raging water in the river.

5. When the quail and her chicks came into the yard, the hen carefully

   checked the area for predators.

6. Alas! By the time he received her report, the decision had been made.

7. I was disappointed we missed your input to the decision-making process,

   but I hope you can meet the deadline next time.

8. Valerie Renoir, the major conference speaker, was delayed at Pearson and

   did not arrive at the hall until 2 p.m.

■ LAB 2: Punctuation—Commas

Punctuation serves as a roadmap to help guide the reader through the twists and turns of your message—pointing out what is important (italics or underscores), subordinate (commas), copied from another source (quotation marks), explained further (colon), considered as a unit (hyphens), and the like. Sometimes correct punctuation is absolutely essential for comprehension. Consider, for example, the different meanings of the following sentences, depending on the punctuation:

What's the latest, Dope?
What's the latest dope?

The social secretary called the guests names as they arrived.
The social secretary called the guests' names as they arrived.

Our new model comes in red, green and brown, and white.
Our new model comes in red, green, and brown and white.

The play ended, happily.
The play ended happily.

A clever dog knows it's master.
A clever dog knows its master.

We must still play Montreal, which tied Edmonton, and Vancouver.
We must still play Montreal, which tied Edmonton and Vancouver.

"Medics Help Dog Bite Victim"
"Medics Help Dog-Bite Victim"

The comma rules presented in LAB 2 and the other punctuation rules presented in LAB 3 do not cover every possible situation; comprehensive style manuals, for example, routinely present more than 100 rules for using the comma rather than just the 12 rules presented here. These rules cover the most frequent uses of punctuation in business writing. Learn them—because you will be using them frequently.

Commas are used to connect ideas and to set off elements within a sentence. When typing, leave one space after a comma. Many writers use commas inappropriately. No matter how long the sentence, make sure you have a legitimate reason before inserting a comma.

COMMAS USED *BETWEEN* EXPRESSIONS

Three types of expressions (an expression is words or groups of words) typically require commas between them: independent clauses, consecutive adjectives, and items in a series.

2.1 Independent Clauses   Use a comma between two independent clauses   *, ind*
joined by a coordinate conjunction (unless both clauses are short and closely related).

> Mr. Karas discussed last month's performance, and Ms. Daniels presented the sales projections.
> The meeting was running late, but Mr. Mears was in no hurry to adjourn.
> *But:* The firm hadn't paid and John was angry.

The major coordinate conjunctions are *and, but, or,* and *nor.* An independent clause is a subject-predicate combination that can stand alone as a complete sentence.

Do not confuse two independent clauses joined by a coordinate conjunction and a comma with a compound predicate, whose verbs are not separated by a comma. *Hint:* Cover up the conjunction with your pencil. If what's on both sides of your pencil could stand alone as complete sentences, a comma is needed.

No comma:	Mrs. Ames had read the report_but had not discussed it with her colleagues. (*"Had not discussed it with her colleagues" is not an independent clause; it lacks a subject.*)

> *Comma:*   Mrs. Ames had read the report, but she had not discussed it with her colleagues.

, adj   **2.2 Adjacent Adjectives**   Use a comma between two adjacent adjectives that modify the same noun.

> He was an aggressive, unpleasant manager.
>
> *But:* He was an aggressive_and unpleasant manager. *(The two adjectives are not adjacent; they are separated by the conjunction "and.")*

Do not use a comma if the first adjective modifies the combined idea of the second adjective plus the noun. *Hint:* Mentally insert the word "and" between the two consecutive adjectives. If it does not make sense, do not use a comma.

> Please order a new bulletin board for the executive_conference room.

Do not use a comma between the last adjective and the noun.

> Wednesday, was a long, hot, humid_day.

, ser   **2.3 Items in a Series**   Use a comma between each item in a series of three or more. Do not use a comma after the last item in the series.

> The committee may meet on Wednesday, Thursday, or Friday_of next week.
>
> Carl wrote the questionnaire, Anna distributed the forms, and Tim tabulated the results_for our survey on employee satisfaction.

Some style manuals indicate that the last comma before the conjunction is optional. However, to avoid ambiguity in business writing, you should insert this comma.

> *Not:* We were served salads, macaroni and cheese and crackers.
>
> *But:* We were served salads, macaroni and cheese, and crackers.
>
> *Or:* We were served salads, macaroni, and cheese and crackers.

COMMAS USED *AFTER* EXPRESSIONS

Two types of expressions typically require commas after them: introductory expressions and complimentary closings in letters.

, intro   **2.4 Introductory Expressions**   Use a comma after an introductory expression. An *introductory expression* is a word, phrase, or clause that comes before the subject and verb of the independent clause. When the same expression occurs at the end of the sentence, no comma is used.

> No, the status report is not ready. *(introductory word)*
>
> Of course, you are not required to sign the petition. *(introductory phrase)*
>
> When the status report is ready, I shall call you. *(introductory clause)*
>
> *But:* I shall call you when the status report is ready.

Do not use a comma between the subject and verb—no matter how long or complex the subject is.

To finish that boring and time-consuming task in time for the monthly sales meeting_was a major challenge.

The effort to bring all of our products into compliance with ISO standards and to be eligible for sales in Common Market countries_required a full year of detailed planning.

2.5 Complimentary Closing   Use a comma after the complimentary closing of a business letter formatted in the standard punctuation style.

, clos

Sincerely,	Cordially yours,
Yours truly,	With warm regards,

With standard punctuation, a colon follows the salutation (such as "Dear Ms. Jones:" and a comma follows the complimentary closing. With open punctuation, no punctuation follows either the salutation or complimentary closing.

COMMAS USED *BEFORE* AND *AFTER* EXPRESSIONS

Numerous types of expressions typically require commas before *and* after them. Of course, if the expression comes at the beginning of a sentence, use a comma only after the expression; if it comes at the end of a sentence, use a comma only before it.

2.6 Nonrestrictive Expressions   Use commas before and after a nonrestrictive expression. A *restrictive expression* is one that limits (restricts) the meaning of the noun or pronoun that it follows and is, therefore, essential to complete the basic meaning of the sentence. A *nonrestrictive expression,* on the other hand, may be omitted without changing the basic meaning of the sentence.

, nonr

Restrictive:	Anyone *with some experience* should apply for the position. (*"with some experience" restricts which "anyone" should apply.*)
Non-restrictive:	Anne Cosgrave, *a clerk with extensive experience,* should apply for the position. (Because Anne Cosgrave can be only one person, the phrase "a clerk with extensive experience" does not serve to further restrict the noun and is, therefore, not essential to the meaning of the sentence.)
Restrictive:	Only the papers *left on the conference table* are missing. (identifies which papers are missing)
Non-restrictive:	Lever Brothers, *one of our best customers,* is expanding in Europe. ("One of our best customers" could be omitted without changing the basic meaning of the sentence.)
Restrictive:	Ellis, *using a great deal of tact,* disagreed with her.
Non-restrictive:	The manager *using a great deal of tact* was Ellis.

An *appositive* is a noun or noun phrase that identifies another noun or pronoun that comes immediately before it. If the appositive is nonrestrictive, insert commas before and after the appositive.

| *Restrictive:* | The word *plagiarism* strikes fear into the heart of many. ("Plagiarism" is an appositive that identifies which word.) |
| *Non-restrictive:* | Mr. Bayrami, *president of the corporation*, is planning to resign. ("President of the corporation" is an appositive that provides additional, but nonessential, information about Mr. Bayrami.) |

, inter   **2.7 Interrupting Expressions**   Use commas before and after an interrupting expression. An *interrupting expression* breaks the normal flow of a sentence. Common examples are *in addition, as a result, therefore, in summary, on the other hand, however, unfortunately,* and *as a matter of fact*—when these expressions come in the middle of the sentence.

> You may, of course, cancel your subscription at any time.
>
> One suggestion, for example, was to undertake a leveraged buyout.
>
> I believe it was John, not Nancy, who raised the question.
>
> It is still not too late to make the change, is it?
>
> Anna's present salary, you must admit, is not in line with those of other network managers.
>
> *But:* You must admit_Anna's present salary is not in line with those of other network managers.

If the expression does not interrupt the normal flow of the sentence, do not use a comma.

> There is no doubt that you are qualified for the position.
>
> *But:* There is, no doubt, a good explanation for his actions.

, date   **2.8 Dates**   Use commas before and after the year when it follows the month and day. Do not use a comma after a partial date or when the date is formatted in day-month-year order. If the name of the day precedes the date, also use a comma *after* the name of the day.

> The note is due on May 31, 2007, at 5 p.m.
>
> *But:* The note is due on May 31 at 5 p.m.
>
> *But:* The note is due in May 2007.
>
> *But:* The note is due on 31 May 2007 at 5 p.m.
>
> Let's plan to meet on Wednesday, December 15, 2007, for our year-end review.

, place   **2.9 Places**   Use commas before and after a state or country that follows a city and between elements of an address in narrative writing.

> The sales conference will be held in Windsor, Ontario, in May.
>
> Our business agent is located in Brussels, Belgium, in the P.O.M. Building.
>
> You may contact her at 500 Beaufort Drive, Edmonton, AB T5X 8G4. *(Note that there is no comma between the provincial abbreviation and the postal code.)*

2.10 Direct Address   Use commas before and after a name used in direct   *, dir ad*
address. A name is used in *direct address* when the writer speaks directly to (that is,
directly addresses) another person.

> Thank you, Ms. Cross, for bringing the matter to our attention.
> Ladies and gentlemen, we appreciate your attending our session today.

2.11 Direct Quotation   Use commas before and after a direct quotation in a   *, quote*
sentence.

> The president said, "You have nothing to fear," and then changed the subject.
> "I assure you," the human resources director said, "that no positions will be
>   terminated."

If the quotation is a question, use a question mark instead of a comma.

> "How many have applied?" she asked.

APPLICATION

DIRECTIONS   Insert any needed commas in the following sentences. Above each comma,
indicate the reason for the comma. If the sentence needs no commas, leave it blank.

Example: As a matter of fact, you may tell her yourself.
                                  intro

1. A comma comes between two adjacent adjectives that modify the same noun

   but do not use a comma if the first adjective modifies the combined idea of

   the second adjective and the noun.

2. Stephen generated questions and I supplied responses.

3. At the request of your accountant we are summarizing all charitable deduc-

   tions in a new format.

4. By asking the right questions we gained all the pertinent information we

   needed.

5. Everyone please use the door in the rear of the hall.

6. His bid for the party leadership was successful this time.

7. I disagree with Beverly but do feel some change in policy is needed.

8. I feel as a matter of fact that the proposed legislation will fall short of the

   required votes.

9. Ethan will prepare the presentation graphics and let you know when they are ready.

10. Determining purpose analyzing the audience and making content and organization decisions are critical planning steps.

11. It is appropriate I believe to make a preliminary announcement about the new position.

12. A goodwill message is prompt direct sincere specific and brief.

13. Look this decision affects me as much as it does you.

14. The teacher using one of her favourite techniques prompted the student into action.

15. Subordinate bad news by using the direct plan by avoiding negative terms and by presenting the news after the reasons are given.

16. My favourite destination is Victoria British Columbia.

17. The team presented a well-planned logical scenario to explain the company's status.

18. Evan plans to conclude his investigation and explain the results by Friday but would not promise a written report until Tuesday.

19. We appreciate your business.

Sincerely

Jason P. Smith

20. Those instructors who were from eastern schools were anxious to see the results of the study completed in Fredericton.

21. A group of teachers from Ontario attended the conference this year.

22. Our next training session will be located in Whistler British Columbia sometime in the spring.

23. The next meeting of our professional organization will be held in the winter not in the spring.

24. The brochure states "Satisfaction guaranteed or your money back."

25. The department meeting you will note will be held every other Monday.

26. This assignment is due on April 20 which is one week before the end of the semester.

27. I need the cabinets installed by the week before my family arrives.

28. To qualify for promotion will require recommendations and long hours of preparation.

29. To qualify for promotion you will need recommendations from previous managers.

30. To earn an award for outstanding sales is an achievable goal for Mary.

31. To earn an award for outstanding sales Mary must set intermittent goals that are attainable.

32. Dave was promoted in his job by working hard.

33. Harriet's sister was born on June 6 1957, in Uxbridge Ontario.

34. Ted could paint the house himself or he could hire a professional to do the job.

35. I am telling you Esther that your report has been misplaced.

■ LAB 3: Punctuation—Other Marks

HYPHENS

Hyphens are used to form some compound adjectives, to link some prefixes to root words (such as *quasi-public*), and to divide words at the ends of lines. When typing, do not leave a space before or after a regular hyphen. Likewise, do not use a hyphen with a space before and after to substitute for a dash. Make a dash by typing two hyphens with no space before, between, or after. Most word processing programs automatically reformat two hyphens into a printed dash.

3.1 Compound Adjective   Hyphenate a compound adjective that comes *before* a noun (unless the adjective is a proper noun or unless the first word is an adverb ending in *-ly*).

> We hired a first-class management team.
> *But:* Our new management team is first_class.
> The long-term outlook for our investments is excellent.
> *But:* We intend to hold our investments for the long_term.
> *But:* The General_Motors warranty received high ratings.
> *But:* Alice presented a poorly_conceived proposal.

Note: Don't confuse compound adjectives (which are generally temporary combinations) with compound nouns (which are generally well-established concepts). Compound nouns (such as *Social Security, life insurance, word processing,* and *high school*) are not hyphenated when used as adjectives that come before a noun; thus, use *income_tax form, real_estate agent, public_relations firm,* and *data_processing centre.*

3.2 Numbers   Hyphenate fractions and compound numbers 21 through 99 when they are spelled out.

> Nearly three-fourths of our new applicants were unqualified.
> Seventy-two orders were processed incorrectly last week.

SEMICOLONS

Semicolons are used to show where elements in a sentence are separated. The separation is stronger than a comma but not as strong as a period. When typing, leave one space after a semicolon and begin the following word with a lowercase letter.

; comma   **3.3 Independent Clauses with Commas**   If a misreading might otherwise occur, use a semicolon (instead of a comma) to separate independent clauses that contain internal commas. Make sure that the semicolon is inserted *between* the independent clauses—not *within* one of the clauses.

> *Confusing:* I ordered juice, toast, and bacon, and eggs, toast, and sausage were sent instead.
> *Clear:* I ordered juice, toast, and bacon; and eggs, toast, and sausage were sent instead.
> *But:* Although high-quality paper was used, the photocopy machine still jammed, and neither of us knew how to repair it. *(no misreading likely to occur)*

; no conj   **3.4 Independent Clauses Without a Conjunction**   Use a semicolon between independent clauses that are not connected by a coordinate conjunction (such as *and, but, or,* or *nor*). You have already learned to use a comma before coordinate

conjunctions when they connect independent clauses. This rule applies to independent clauses *not* connected by a conjunction.

> The president was eager to proceed with the plans; the board still had some reservations.
>
> *But:* The president was eager to proceed with the plans, but the board still had some reservations. *(Use a comma instead of a semicolon if the clauses are joined by a coordinate conjunction.)*
>
> Bannon Corporation exceeded its sales goal this quarter; furthermore, it rang up its highest net profit ever.
>
> *But:* Bannon Corporation exceeded its sales goal this quarter, and, furthermore, it rang up its highest net profit ever. *(Use a comma instead of a semicolon if the clauses are joined by a coordinate conjunction.)*

3.5 Series with Internal Commas Use a semicolon after each item in a series   *; ser*
if any of the items already contain a comma. Normally, we separate items in a series with commas. However, if any of those items already contain a comma, we need a stronger mark (semicolon) between the items.

> The human resources department will be interviewing in Vancouver, British Columbia; Calgary, Alberta; and Winnipeg, Manitoba, for the new position.
>
> Among the guests were Henry Halston, our attorney; Lisa Hart-Wilder; and Edith Grimes, our new controller.

COLONS

A colon is used after an independent clause that introduces explanatory material and after the salutation of a business letter that uses the standard punctuation style. When typing, leave one space after a colon; do not begin the following word with a capital letter unless it begins a quoted sentence.

3.6 Explanatory Material Use a colon to introduce explanatory material that   *: exp*
is preceded by an independent clause.

> His directions were as follows: turn right and proceed to the third house on the left.
>
> I now have openings on the following dates: January 18, 19, and 20.
>
> Just remember this: you may need a reference from her in the future.
>
> The fall trade show offers the following advantages: inexpensive show space, abundant traffic, and free press publicity.

Expressions commonly used to introduce explanatory material are *the following, as follows, this,* and *these.* Make sure the clause preceding the explanatory material can stand alone as a complete sentence. Do not place a colon after a verb or a preposition that introduces a listing.

> *Not:* My responsibilities were: opening the mail, sorting it, and delivering it to each department.

But: My responsibilities were opening the mail, sorting it, and delivering it to each department.

: salut 3.7 Salutations   Use a colon after the salutation of a business letter that uses the standard punctuation style.

Dear Ms. Havelchek: Ladies and Gentlemen: Dear Lee:

Never use a comma after the salutation in a business letter. (A comma is appropriate only in a personal letter.) With standard punctuation, a colon follows the salutation and a comma follows the complimentary closing. With *open* punctuation, no punctuation follows the salutation or complimentary closing.

APOSTROPHES

Apostrophes are used to show that letters have been omitted (as in contractions) and to show possession. When typing, do not space before or after an apostrophe (unless a space after is needed before another word).

Remember this helpful hint: Whenever a noun ending in *s* is followed by another noun, the first noun is probably a possessive, requiring an apostrophe. However, if the first noun *describes* rather than establishes ownership, no apostrophe is used.

Bernie's department *(shows ownership; therefore, an apostrophe)*

the sales department *(describes; therefore, no apostrophe)*

' sing 3.8 Singular Nouns   To form the possessive of a singular noun, add an apostrophe plus *s.*

my accountant's fee	a child's toy
the company's stock	Ellen's choice
Alzheimer's disease	Mr. and Mrs. Dye's home
a year's time	the boss's contract
Ms. Morris's office	Liz's promotion
Gil Hodges's record	Carl Bissett Jr.'s birthday

' plur + s 3.9 Plural Nouns Ending in S   To form the possessive of a plural noun that ends in *s* (that is, most plural nouns), add an apostrophe only.

our accountants' fees	both companies' stock
the Dyes' home	two years' time

' plur – s 3.10 Plural Nouns Not Ending in S   To form the possessive of a plural noun that does not end in *s*, add an apostrophe plus *s* (just as you would for singular nouns).

the children's hour	the men's room
The alumni's contribution	

Hint: To avoid confusion in forming the possessive of plural nouns, first form the plural; then apply the appropriate rule.

Singular	*Plural*	*Plural Possessive*
employee	employees	employees' bonuses
hero	heroes	heroes' welcome
Mr. and Mrs. Lake	the Lakes	the Lakes' home
lady	ladies	ladies' clothing

3.11 Pronouns   To form the possessive of an indefinite pronoun, add an apostrophe plus *s*. Do not use an apostrophe to form the possessive of personal pronouns.   *' pro*

It is *someone's* responsibility
But: The responsibility is *theirs.*

I will review *everybody's* figures.
But: The bank will review *its* figures.

Note: Examples of indefinite possessive pronouns are *anybody's, everyone's, no one's, nobody's, one's,* and *somebody's.* Examples of personal possessive pronouns are *hers, his, its, ours, theirs,* and *yours.* Do not confuse the possessive pronouns *its, theirs,* and *whose* with the contractions *it's, there's,* and *who's.*

It's time to put litter in *its* place.
There's no reason to take *theirs.*
Who's determining *whose* jobs will be eliminated?

3.12 Gerunds   Use the possessive form for a noun or pronoun that comes before a gerund. (A gerund is the *–ing* form of a verb used as a noun.)   *' ger*

Garth questioned *Karen's* leaving so soon.
Stockholders' raising so many questions delayed the adjournment.
Mr. Matsumoto knew Karl and objected to *his* going to the meeting.

PERIODS

Periods are used at the ends of declarative sentences and polite requests and in abbreviations. When typing, leave one space after a period (or any other punctuation mark).

3.13 Polite Requests   Use a period after a polite request. Consider a statement a polite request if you expect the reader to respond by *acting* rather than by giving a yes-or-no answer.   *. req*

Would you please sign the form on page 2.
May I please have the report by Friday.
But: Would you be willing to take on this assignment? *(This sentence is a real question, requiring a question mark. You expect the reader to respond by saying "yes" or "no.")*

QUOTATION MARKS

Quotation marks are used around direct quotations, titles of some publications and conferences, and special terms. Type the closing quotation mark after a period or comma but before a colon or semicolon. Type the closing quotation mark after a question mark or exclamation point if the quoted material itself is a question or an exclamation; otherwise, type it before the question mark or exclamation. Capitalize the first word of a quotation that begins a sentence.

"quote   **3.14 Direct Quotation**   Use quotation marks around a direct quotation—that is, around the exact words of a person.

> "When we return on Thursday," Luis said, "we need to meet with you."
>
> *But:* Luis said that when we return on Thursday, we need to meet with you. *(no quotation marks needed in an indirect quotation)*
>
> Did Helen say, "He will represent us"?
>
> Helen asked, "Will he represent us?"

"term   **3.15 Term**   Use quotation marks around a term to clarify its meaning or to show that it is being used in a special way.

> Net income after taxes is known as "the bottom line"; that's what's important around here.
>
> The job title changed from "chairman" to "chief executive officer."
>
> The president misused the word "effect" in last night's press conference.

"title   **3.16 Title**   Use quotation marks around the title of a newspaper or magazine article, chapter in a book, report, conference, and similar items.

> Read the article entitled "Wall Street Recovery."
>
> Chapter 4, "Market Segmentation," of *Industrial Marketing* is of special interest.
>
> The theme of this year's sales conference is "Quality Sells."
>
> The report "Common Carriers" shows the extent of the transportation problems.

Note: The titles of *complete* published works are shown in italics (see below). The titles of *parts* of published works and most other titles are enclosed in quotation marks.

ITALICS (OR UNDERLINING)

Before the advent of word processing software, underlining was used to emphasize words or indicate certain titles. Today, the use of italics is preferred for these functions.

Title   **3.17 Titles**   Italicize the title of a book, magazine, newspaper, and other *complete* published works.

> Roger's newest book, *All That Glitters,* was reviewed in *The Globe and Mail* and in the *National Post.*

The cover story in last week's *Maclean's* magazine was "Is the Economic Expansion Over?"

ELLIPSES

An ellipsis is an omission. Three periods, with one space before and after each, are used to show that something has been left out of a quotation. Four periods (the sentence period plus the three ellipsis periods) indicate the omission of the last part of a quoted sentence, the first part of the next sentence, or a whole sentence or paragraph. Here is an example:

Complete Quotation:

The average age of our homebuyers has risen from 29.6 years in 1998 to 31.5 years today. This increase is partly due to the rising cost of new home mortgages. Adjustable-rate mortgages now account for 20% of all our new mortgages.

Shortened Quotation:

The average age of our homebuyers has risen . . . to 31.5 years today. . . . Adjustable-rate mortgages now account for 20% of all our new mortgages.

Note: The typing sequence for the first ellipsis is *space period space period space period space.* The sequence for the second ellipsis is *period space period space period space period space.*

3.18 Omission   Use ellipsis periods to indicate that one or more words have been omitted from quoted material.

According to *Business Week,* "A continuing protest could shut down . . . Pemex, which brought in 34% of Mexico's dollar income last year."

APPLICATION

DIRECTIONS   Insert any needed punctuation (including commas) in the following sentences. Underline any expression that should be italicized. Above each mark of punctuation, indicate the reason for the punctuation. If the sentence needs no punctuation, leave it blank.

Example: We received our money's worth.

1. Bernice tried to use the new software but she had trouble with the computer.

2. James Johnsons raising the expectations for promotion was hotly debated.

3. The short term goal of the department was improvement in software utilization.

4. It was a poorly designed office.

5. Approximately one half of the orders came from Regina Saskatchewan.

6. Bertram preferred soda hamburgers and fries but iced tea, hot dogs and onion rings were served instead.

7. The classes started on time the school was entirely on schedule.

8. Did you met Sally Henley our manager Paul Krause and Gina South our attorney?

9. Remember this the best recommendation is a job well done.

10. Dear Mr. Weatherby

11. Did you get the total from the sales department?

12. Jason s boss will distribute the new guidelines for his department.

13. Within two years time the neighbourhood will double in size.

14. Locking the door to the department was someones responsibility.

15. Madelyns guiding the discussion was a departure from the regular procedure.

16. Would you please sort these responses for me

17. The teacher said The samples you submitted were excellent.

18. Would you believe he misspelled the word their in his report?

19. The article entitled Technology for Fitness should be required reading.

20. Maclean's magazine features a person of the year each December.

21. I want her to know she is a highly respected employee.

22. Its a good thing the meeting was rescheduled.

23. If the tickets sell we will tell Mrs. Zimfer she will take it from there.

24. The hotels guests thought the conference rooms temperatures were too cold.

25. They were watching the demonstration nevertheless they didn't understand the last section.

26. Can we keep this off the record?

27. You will receive the materials tomorrow but stop by today to see Alberto our corporate trainer for a quick preview.

28. I can do this for you either on December 5 2005 or January 13 2006.

29. This is a once in a lifetime opportunity for our employees families.

30. Mr. Henry will see you after the meeting Mr. Perez will not be available.

■ LAB 4: Grammar

Suppose the vice president of your organization asked you, a systems analyst, to try to locate a troublesome problem in a computer spreadsheet. After some sharp detective work, you finally resolved the problem and wrote a memo to the vice president saying, "John and myself discovered that one of the formulas were incorrect, so I asked he to revise it."

Instantly, you've turned what should have been a "good-news" opportunity for you into, at best, a "mixed-news" situation. The vice president will be pleased that you've uncovered the bug in the program but will probably focus entirely too much attention on your poor grammar skills.

Grammar refers to the rules for combining words into sentences. The most frequent grammar problems faced by business writers are discussed below. Learn these common rules well so that your use of grammar will not present a communication barrier in the message you're trying to convey.

COMPLETE SENTENCES

4.1 Fragment   Avoid sentence fragments.

NOT: He had always wanted to be a marketing representative. Because he liked to interact with people.

BUT: He had always wanted to be a marketing representative because he liked to interact with people.

Note: A fragment is a part of a sentence that is incorrectly punctuated as a complete sentence. Each sentence must contain a complete thought.

DRABBLE

4.2 Run-on Sentences   Avoid run-on sentences.

NOT: Karen Raines is a hard worker she even frequently works through lunch.

NOT: Karen Raines is a hard worker, she even frequently works through lunch.

BUT: Karen Raines is a hard worker; she even frequently works through lunch.

OR: Karen Raines is a hard worker. She even frequently works through lunch.

Note: A run-on sentence is two independent clauses run together without any punctuation between them or with only a comma between them (the latter error is called a *comma splice*).

MODIFIERS (ADJECTIVES AND ADVERBS)

An adjective modifies a noun or pronoun; an adverb modifies a verb, an adjective, or another adverb.

4.3 Modifiers   Use a comparative adjective or adverb (*-er, more,* or *less*) to refer to two persons, places, or things and a superlative adjective or adverb (*-est, most,* or *least*) to refer to more than two.

The Datascan is the fast**er** of the two machines.
The XR-75 is the slow**est** of all the machines.

Rose Marie is the **less** qualified of the two applicants.
Rose Marie is the **least** qualified of the three applicants.

Note: Do not use double comparisons, such as "more faster."

AGREEMENT (SUBJECT/VERB/PRONOUN)

Agreement refers to correspondence in number between related subjects, verbs, and pronouns. All must be singular if they refer to one, plural if they refer to more than one.

4.4 Agreement   Use a singular verb or pronoun with a singular subject and a plural verb or pronoun with a plural subject.

The four **workers have** a photocopy of **their** assignments.
Roger's **wife was** quite late for **her** appointment.
Mr. Tibbetts and Mrs. Downs plan to forgo **their** bonuses.
Included in this envelope **are a contract and an affidavit.**

Note: This is the general rule; variations are discussed below. In the first sentence, the plural subject (*workers*) requires a plural verb (*have*) and a plural pronoun (*their*). In the second sentence, the singular subject (*wife*) requires a singular verb (*was*) and a singular pronoun (*her*). In the third sentence, the plural subject (*Mr. Tibbetts and Ms. Downs*) requires a plural verb (*plan*) and a plural pronoun (*their*). In the last sentence, the subject is *a contract and an affidavit*—not *envelope.*

4.5 Company Names   Treat company names as singular.

NOT: Bickley and Bates **has** paid for **its** last order. **They** are ready to reorder.

BUT: Bickley and Bates **has** paid for **its** last order. **It** is now ready to reorder.

4.6 Expletives   In sentences that begin with an expletive, the true subject follows the verb. Use *is* or *are,* as appropriate.

There **is** no **reason** for his behaviour.

There **are** many **reasons** for his behaviour.

Note: An expletive is an expression such as *there is, there are, here is,* and *here are* that comes at the beginning of a clause or sentence. Because the topic of a sentence that begins with an expletive is not immediately apparent, such sentences should be used sparingly in business writing.

4.7 Intervening Words   Disregard any words that come between the subject and verb when establishing agreement. See, however, Rule 4.8 regarding special treatment of certain pronouns.

Only **one** of the mechanics **guarantees his** work. (not *their work*)

The **appearance** of the workers, not their competence, **was** being questioned.

The **secretary,** as well as the clerks, **was** late filing **her** form. (not *their forms*)

Note: First determine the subject; then make the verb agree. Other intervening words that do not affect the number of the verb are *together with, rather than, accompanied by, in addition to,* and *except.*

4.8 Pronouns   Some pronouns (*anybody, each, either, everybody, everyone, much, neither, no one, nobody,* and *one*) are always singular. Other pronouns (*all, any, more, most, none,* and *some*) may be singular or plural, depending on the noun to which they refer.

Each of the labourers **has** a different view of **his or her** job.

Neither of the models **is** doing **her** job well.

Everybody is required to take **his or her** turn at the booth. (not *their turn*)

All the **pie has** been eaten.   **None** of the **work is** finished.

All the **cookies have** been eaten.   **None** of the **workers are** finished.

4.9 Subject Nearer to Verb   If two subjects are joined by correlative conjunctions (*or, either/or, nor, neither/nor,* or *not only/but also*), the verb and any pronoun should agree with the subject that is nearer to the verb.

Either Robert or **Harold is** at **his** desk.

Neither the receptionist nor the **operators were** able to finish **their** tasks.

Not only the actress but also the **dancer has** to practice **her** routine.

The tellers or the **clerks have** to balance **their** cash drawers before leaving.

Note: The first noun in this type of construction may be disregarded when determining whether the verb should be singular or plural. Pay special attention to using the correct pronoun; do not use the plural pronoun *their* unless the subject and verb are plural. Note that subjects joined by *and* or *both/and* are always plural: *Both* **the actress and the dancer have** to practice **their** routines.

4.10 Subjunctive Mood   Verbs in the subjunctive mood require the plural form, even when the subject is singular.

> I wish the situation **were** reversed.
>
> If I **were** you, I would not mention the matter.

Note: Verbs in the subjunctive mood refer to conditions that are impossible or improbable.

CASE

Case refers to the form of a pronoun and indicates its use in a sentence. There are three cases: nominative, objective, and possessive. (Possessive-case pronouns are covered under "Apostrophes" in the section on punctuation in LAB 3.) Reflexive pronouns, which end in *-self* or *-selves,* refer to nouns or other pronouns.

4.11 Nominative Case   Use nominative pronouns (*I, he, she, we, they, who, whoever*) as subjects of a sentence or clause and with the verb *to be.*

> The customer representative and **he** are furnishing the figures. (**he** *is furnishing*)
>
> Mrs. Quigley asked if Oscar and **I** were ready to begin. (**I** *was ready to begin*)
>
> **We** old-timers can provide some background. (**we** *can provide*)
>
> It was **she** who agreed to the proposal. (**she** *agreed*)
>
> **Who** is chairing the meeting? (**he** *is chairing*)
>
> Mr. Lentzner wanted to know **who** was responsible. (**she** *was responsible*)
>
> Anna is the type of person **who** can be depended upon. (**she** *can be depended upon*)

Note: If you have trouble determining which pronoun to use, ignore the plural subject or substitute another pronoun. See the reworded clauses in parentheses above.

4.12 Objective Case   Use objective pronouns (*me, him, her, us, them, whom, whomever*) as objects in a sentence, clause, or phrase.

> Thomas sent a fax to Mr. Baird and **me.** (*sent a fax to* **me**)
>
> This policy applies to Eric and **her.** (*applies to* **her**)
>
> Joe asked **us** old-timers to provide some background. (*Joe asked* **us** *to provide*)
>
> The work was assigned to **her** and me. (*the work was assigned to* **me**)
>
> To **whom** shall we mail the specifications? (*mail them to* **him**)
>
> Anna is the type of person **whom** we can depend upon. (*we can depend upon* **her**)

Note: For *who/whom* constructions, if *he* or *she* can be substituted, *who* is the correct choice; if *him* or *her* can be substituted, *whom* is the correct choice. Remember: *who-he, whom-him.* The difference is apparent in the final examples shown here and under "Nominative Case," Rule 4.11: **who** *can be depended upon* versus **whom** *we can depend upon.*

4.13 Reflexive Pronouns   Use reflexive pronouns (*myself, yourself, himself, herself, itself, ourselves, yourselves,* or *themselves*) to refer to or emphasize a noun or pronoun *that has already been named.* Do not use reflexive pronouns to *substitute for* nominative or objective pronouns.

> I **myself** have some doubts about the proposal.
> You should see the exhibit **yourself.**

> **NOT:**   Virginia and **myself** will take care of the details.
> **BUT:**   Virginia and **I** will take care of the details.

> **NOT:**   Mary Louise administered the test to Thomas and **myself.**
> **BUT:**   Mary Louise administered the test to Thomas and **me.**

APPLICATION

DIRECTIONS   Select the correct words or words in parentheses.

1. (Who/Whom) is your favorite new chef? Laura Buraston, who along with Frederico Fox, (are/is) new chefs in Toronto. Some of my friends (has/have) eaten at their restaurants. Laura, they say, is the (better/best) of the two.

2. Merchant Associates is presenting (its/it's/their/there) seminar in Quebec City. The associates will work with seven or eight participants in developing (their/there) portfolios. Not only Dr. Merchant, but also his associates (is/are) willing to mentor faculty members. Dr. Merchant asked all participants to acknowledge the invitation with written responses to (he/him).

3. If I (was/were) you, I would be (more/most) helpful with organizing the conference. You can work directly with Sandra and (me/myself). After all, Sandra knows that it was (I/me) (who/whom) made key contacts. This opportunity is open to the type of person (who/whom) we can depend on.

4. The report on sales volume (is/are) finally on my desk. (Us/We) managers may be somewhat apprehensive about these reports, but sales results tend to predict (who/whom) can be depended upon.

5. Not only the lawyer but also the manager (was/were) able to attend the conference on ethics. Everybody in the firm (is/are) trying to participate as a way to improve (their/his or her) performance. Each of the employees (is/are) eager to attend the next session.

6. There (was/were) several students in the class (who/whom) challenged whether each of the assignments (was/were) comparable in complexity. The professor asked (us/we) group leaders to evaluate the student's concerns.

7. Neither the professors nor the dean (was/were) able to meet Dr. Phyllis Hart, the conference speaker, at the airport. In fact, neither of the professors (was/were) able to pick him up at the hotel either. However, Dean Dye, as well as two other professors, (is/are) escorting him to the banquet.

8. Martin's and Jay's groups are the (more quicker/most quicker/quicker/quickest) in the class. Jay's group is the (more slow/most slow/slower/slowest) of these two groups. In any case, all of the jobs (has/have) been submitted for both groups.

9. (Who/Whom) will you ask to participate in the evaluation process? If I (was/were) you I'd consider Hillary. While Jane is the (more/most) competent software expert we have available, Hillary is the type of team player (who/whom) can provide the leadership we need.

10. I wish it (was/were) possible for Jim and (I/me/myself) to see both Marty and Alex in (his/their) last performance this season. Jim and (I/me/myself) have always had a gathering in our home after they finished. Watching their reactions to the reviewers' comments as they were given (is/are) exciting, but as we are leaving too, it remains to be seen (who/whom) will assume that function next year.

DIRECTIONS   Revise the following paragraph to eliminate any fragments and run-on sentences.

FunTimes by Travel Log is a prepaid vacation program designed with families in mind. Club owners have permanent usage rights in a continually growing system of outstanding resorts. Unlike the traditional time-share plans. Members may select any of the club resorts as a destination with optional access to other resorts through exchange programs, the owners may select additional vacation sites, both in the United States and internationally. The membership fee entitles an owner to a fixed number of points each year, up to three years' worth can be accumulated so a selected vacation can be upgraded or lengthened. Future points can be "borrowed" for use on a current vacation. Reservations may be made up to 13 months in advance these features make this plan an economical and flexible way to create family vacation memories.

■ LAB 5: Mechanics

Writing mechanics refer to those elements in communication that are evident only in written form: abbreviations, capitalization, number expression, spelling, and word division. (Punctuation, also a form of writing mechanics, was covered in LABs 2 and 3.) While creating a first draft, you need not be too concerned about the mechanics of your writing. However, you should be especially alert during the editing and proofreading stages to follow these common rules.

ABBREVIATIONS

Use abbreviations sparingly in narrative writing; many abbreviations are appropriate only in technical writing, statistical material, and tables. Consult a dictionary for the correct form for abbreviations, and follow the rule "When in doubt, write it out." When typing, do not space within abbreviations except to separate each initial of a person's name. Leave one space after an abbreviation unless another mark of punctuation follows immediately.

5.1 Not Abbreviated In narrative writing, do not abbreviate common nouns (such as *acct., assoc., bldg., co., dept., misc.,* and *pkg.*) or the names of cities, states (except in addresses), months, and days of the week.

5.2 With Periods Use periods to indicate many abbreviations.

No.	8 a.m.	4 m.
Dr. M. L. Peterson	P.O. Box 45	e.g.

5.3 Without Periods Write some abbreviations in all capitals, with no periods—including all two-letter provincial abbreviations used in addresses with postal codes.

CPA	CPP	ON
TWA	UNESCO	OK

Note: Use two-letter provincial abbreviations in bibliographic citations.

CAPITALIZATION

The function of capitalization is to emphasize words or to show their importance. For example, the first word of a sentence is capitalized to emphasize that a new sentence has begun.

5.4 Compass Point Capitalize a compass point that designates a definite region or that is part of an official name. (Do not capitalize compass points used as directions.)

Margot lives in the **S**outh.

Our display window faces **w**est.

Is **E**ast Orange in **W**est Virginia?

5.5 Letter Part Capitalize the first word and any proper nouns in the salutation and complimentary closing of a business letter.

Dear **Mr. S**mith:	Sincerely yours,
Dear **Mr.** and **Mrs. A**mes:	Yours truly,

5.6 Noun Plus Number   Capitalize a noun followed by a number or letter (except for page and size numbers).

Table 3	**p**age 79
Flight 1062	**s**ize 8D

5.7 Position Title   Capitalize an official position title that comes before a personal name, unless the personal name is an appositive set off by commas. Do not capitalize a position title used alone.

Vice **P**resident Alfredo Tenegco	Shirley Wilhite, **d**ean,
our **p**resident, Joanne Rathburn,	The **c**hief **e**xecutive **o**fficer retired.

5.8 Proper Noun   Capitalize proper nouns and adjectives derived from proper nouns. Do not capitalize articles, conjunctions, and prepositions of four or fewer letters (for example, *a, an, the, and, of,* and *with*). The names of the seasons and the names of generic school courses are not proper nouns and are not capitalized.

Xerox copier	Queen's University (*but:* the university)
Quebec **C**ity (*but:* the **c**ity)	the **M**exican border
the Fourth of July	Friday, March 3,
CN Tower	Bank of Commerce
First-Class Storage Company	Margaret Adams-White
business **c**ommunication	the **w**inter holidays

5.9 Quotation   Capitalize the first word of a quoted sentence. (Do not capitalize the first word of an indirect quotation.)

According to Hall, "**T**he goal of quality control is specified uniform quality."

Hall thinks we should work toward "**s**pecified uniform quality."

Hall said that **u**niform quality is the goal.

5.10 Title   In a published title, capitalize the first and last words, the first word after a colon or dash, and all other words except articles, conjunctions, and prepositions of three or fewer letters.

"**A** Word to the Wise"

Pricing Strategies: The Link With Reality

NUMBERS

Authorities do not agree on a single style for expressing numbers—whether to spell out a number in words or to write it in figures. The following guidelines apply to typical business writing. (The alternative is to use a *formal* style, in which all numbers that can be expressed in one or two words are spelled out.) When typing numbers in figures, separate tens of thousands, millions, and billions with a space; and leave a space between a whole-number figure and its fraction unless the fraction is a character on the keyboard. (Many disciplines, such as accounting and finance, prefer commas rather than spaces as separators in large numbers.)

5.11 General   Spell out numbers for zero through ten and use figures for 11 and higher.

the first three pages	ten complaints
18 photocopies	5376 stockholders

Note: Follow this rule only when none of the following special rules apply.

5.12 Figures   Use figures for

- dates (Use the endings *-st, -d, -rd,* or *-th* only when the day precedes the month.)
- all numbers if two or more *related* numbers both above and below ten are used in the same sentence
- measurements—such as time, money, distance, weight, and percentage. Be consistent in using either the word *percent* or the symbol *%*.
- mixed numbers

May 9 (or the 9th of May)	10 kilometres
4 men and 18 women	*But:* The **18** women had **four** cars.
$6	5 p.m. (or 5 o'clock)
5 percent (or 5%)	6½
	But: 6 3/18

5.13 Words   Spell out

- a number used as the first word of a sentence
- the smaller number when two numbers come together
- fractions
- the words *million* and *billion* in even numbers

Thirty-two people attended.	nearly two-thirds of them
three 37-cent stamps	150 two-page brochures
37 million	$4.8 billion

Note: When fractions and the numbers 21 through 99 are spelled out, they should be hyphenated.

SPELLING

Correct spelling is essential to effective communication. A misspelled word can distract the reader, cause misunderstanding, and send a negative message about the writer's competence. Because of the many variations in the spelling of English words, no spelling guidelines are foolproof; there are exceptions to every spelling rule. The five rules that follow, however, may be safely applied in most business writing situations. Learning them will save you the time of looking up many words in a dictionary.

5.14 Doubling a Final Consonant   If the last syllable of a root word is stressed, double the final consonant when adding a suffix.

Last Syllable Stressed		Last Syllable Not Stressed	
prefer	preferring	happen	happening
control	controlling	differ	differed
occur	occurrence		

5.15 One-Syllable Words   If a one-syllable word ends in a consonant preceded by a single vowel, double the final consonant before a suffix starting with a vowel.

Suffix Starting with Vowel		Suffix Starting with Consonant	
ship	shipper	ship	shipment
drop	dropped	glad	gladness
bag	baggage	bad	badly

5.16 Final *E*   If a final *e* is preceded by a consonant, drop the *e* before a suffix starting with a vowel.

Suffix Starting with Vowel		Suffix Starting with Consonant	
come	coming	hope	hopeful
use	usable	manage	management
sincere	sincerity	sincere	sincerely

Note: Words ending in *ce* or *ge* usually retain the *e* before a suffix starting with a vowel: *noticeable, advantageous.*

5.17 Final *Y*   If a final *y* is preceded by a consonant, change *y* to *i* before any suffix except one starting with *i.*

Most Suffixes		Suffix Starting with i	
company	companies	try	trying
ordinary	ordinarily	forty	fortyish
hurry	hurried		

5.18 *EI* and *IE* Words   Remember the rhyme:

Use *i* before *e*	believe	yield
Except after *c*	receive	deceit
Or when sounded like *a*	freight	their
As in *neighbour* and *weigh.*		

WORD AND PARAGRAPH DIVISION

When possible, avoid dividing words at the end of a line, because word divisions tend to slow down or even confuse a reader (for example, *rear- range* for *rearrange* or *read- just* for *readjust*). However, when necessary to avoid grossly uneven right margins, use the following rules. Most word processing software programs have a hyphenation feature that automatically divides words to make a more even right margin; you can change these word divisions manually if necessary. When you are typing, do not space before a hyphen.

5.19 Compound Word   Divide a compound word either after the hyphen or where the two words join to make a solid compound.

   self- service   free- way   battle- field

5.20 Division Point   Leave at least two letters on the upper line and carry at least three letters to the next line.

   ex- treme   typ- ing

5.21 Not Divided   Do not divide a one-syllable word, contraction, or abbreviation.

straight   shouldn't
UNESCO   approx.

5.22 Syllables   Divide words only between syllables.

   per- sonnel   knowl- edge

Note: When in doubt about where a syllable ends, consult a dictionary.

5.23 Web Addresses   If necessary, break an online address (either an email address or a webpage address) *before* (but never after) a dot (.), single slash (/), double slash (//), hyphen (-), underscore (_), *at* symbol (@), or any other mark of punctuation. Do not insert a hyphen within an online address to signify an end-of-line break.

   For further information, check out this online source: http://college.hmco.com /business/ober/Sources/.

5.24 Paragraphs   If it is necessary to divide a paragraph between two pages, leave at least two lines of the paragraph at the bottom of the first page and carry forward at least two lines to the top of the next page. Do not divide a three-line paragraph.

APPLICATION

DIRECTIONS Rewrite the following paragraphs so that all words and numbers are expressed correctly. Do not change the wording in any sentences.

1. 100 of our elementary students will receive passes to Holly's Heartland Amusement Park today. Mrs. freda t. albertson, principal, indicated students from every grade were randomly selected to receive the free passes. The students represent about a 1/5 of the school's population.

2. As of Sept. 1ˢᵗ, nearly 34 of our parents have attended at least one learning style orientation seminar. The School Psychologist, John Sibilsky, summarized the response of the participants and reported a favourable evaluation by ninety-six parents.

3. The Athletes for Freedom participants sponsored 12 2-hour presentations in a 3-week period. The last stop was east St. Louis, before the long ride home.

4. As reported on Page 2 of today's newspaper, the price of a barrel of oil has continued to climb. According to premier Donald allan, the price is 1 12 times higher than last year.

5. This month's issue of Maclean's magazine reports an interview with justin lake who said, "Service to our country is measured by many things, but a gift of time is one of the more significant." Our employees gave a total of two-hundred-ninety-five hours.

DIRECTIONS Correct the one misspelling in each line.

1. preferring	controlling	occurence
2. shipper	droped	baggage
3. totalling	badly	shipment
4. differred	happening	gladness
5. sincerity	sincerly	noticeable
6. trying	fortyish	ordinarly
7. deceit	yeild	believe
8. advantagous	hopeful	companies
9. changeable	boundary	arguement
10. catagory	apparent	criticize
11. recommend	accomodate	weird
12. plausable	indispensable	allotted
13. camouflage	innocence	seperately
14. nickle	miniature	embarrassing
15. liaison	exhilarated	inadvertant

DIRECTIONS Write the following words, inserting a hyphen or blank space at the first correct division point. If a word cannot be divided, write it without a hyphen.

Examples: mis-spelled
              thought

1. freeway	chairperson	level
2. express	exploitation	right

3. MADD   soared   solitary
4. wouldn't   mayor-elect   reliance
5. agree   recourse   Ohio
6. www.homemadesimple.com/newsletter/index.shtml
7. Saddlebrooke_tripticket@yahoo.com

■ LAB 6: Word Usage

The following words and phrases are often used incorrectly in everyday speech and in business writing. Learn to use them correctly to help achieve your communication goals.

In some cases in the following list, one word is often confused with another similar word; in other cases, the structure of our language requires that certain words be used only in certain ways. Because of space, only brief and incomplete definitions are given here. Consult a dictionary for more complete or additional meanings.

6.1 Accept/Except   *Accept* means "to agree to"; *except* means "with the exclusion of."

I will **accept** all the recommendations **except** the last one.

6.2 Advice/Advise   *Advice* is a noun meaning "counsel"; *advise* is a verb meaning "to recommend."

If I ask for her **advice,** she may **advise** me to quit.

6.3 Affect/Effect   *Affect* is most often used as a verb meaning "to influence" or "to change"; *effect* is most often used as a noun meaning "result" or "impression."

The legislation may **affect** sales but should have no **effect** on gross margin.

6.4 All Right/Alright   Use *all right.* (*Alright* is considered substandard.)

The arrangement is **all right** (not *alright*) with me.

6.5 A Lot/Alot   Use *a lot.* (*Alot* is considered substandard.)

We used **a lot** (not *alot*) of overtime on the project.

6.6 Among/Between   Use *among* when referring to three or more; use *between* when referring to two.

Among the three candidates was one manager who divided his time **between** London and Toronto.

6.7 Amount/Number   Use *amount* to refer to money or to things that cannot be counted; use *number* to refer to things that can be counted.

> The **amount** of consumer interest was measured by the **number** of coupons returned.

6.8 Anxious/Eager   Use *anxious* only if great concern or worry is involved.

> Jon was **eager** to get the new car although he was **anxious** about making such high payments.

6.9 Any One/Anyone   Spell as two words when followed by *of;* spell as one word when the accent is on *any.*

> **Anyone** is allowed to attend **any one** of the sessions.

> **Between**   See *Among/Between.*

6.10 Can/May   *Can* indicates ability; *may* indicates permission.

> I **can** finish the project on time if I **may** hire an additional secretary.

6.11 Cite/Sight/Site   *Cite* means "to quote" or "to mention"; *sight* is either a verb meaning "to look at" or a noun meaning "something seen"; *site* is most often a noun meaning "location."

> The **sight** of the high-rise building on the **site** of the old battlefield reminded Monica to **cite** several other examples to the commission members.

6.12 Complement/Compliment   *Complement* means "to complete" or "something that completes"; *compliment* means "to praise" or "words of praise."

> I must **compliment** you on the new model, which will **complement** our line.

6.13 Could of/Could've   Use *could've* (or *could have*). (*Could of* is incorrect.)

> We **could've** (not *could of*) prevented that loss had we been more alert.

6.14 Different from/Different than   Use *different from.* (*Different than* is considered substandard.)

> Your computer is **different from** (not *different than*) mine.

6.15 Each Other/One Another   Use *each other* when referring to two; use *one another* when referring to three or more.

> The two workers helped **each other,** but their three visitors would not even look at **one another.**

Eager   See *Anxious/Eager.*

Effect   See *Affect/Effect.*

6.16 e.g./i.e.   The abbreviation *e.g.* means "for example"; *i.e.* means "that is." Use *i.e.* to introduce a restatement or explanation of a preceding expression. Both abbreviations, like the expressions for which they stand, are followed by commas. (Many writers prefer the full English terms to the abbreviations because they are clearer.)

The proposal has merit; **e.g.,** it is economical, forward-looking, and timely.

Or: The proposal has merit; for example, it is economical, forward-looking, and timely.

Unfortunately, it is also a hot potato; **i.e.,** it will generate unfavorable publicity.

Or: Unfortunately, it is also a hot potato; that is, it will generate unfavorable publicity.

6.17 Eminent/Imminent   *Eminent* means "well-known"; *imminent* means "about to happen."

The arrival of the **eminent** scientist from Russia is **imminent.**

6.18 Enthused/Enthusiastic   Use *enthusiastic.* (*Enthused* is considered substandard.)

I have become quite **enthusiastic** (not *enthused*) about the possibilities.

Except   See *Accept/Except.*

6.19 Farther/Further   *Farther* refers to distance; *further* refers to extent or degree.

We drove 10 kilometres **farther** while we discussed the matter **further.**

6.20 Fewer/Less   Use *fewer* to refer to things that can be counted; use *less* to refer to money or to things that cannot be counted.

Alvin worked **fewer** hours at the exhibit and therefore generated **less** interest.

Further   See *Farther/Further.*

6.21 Good/Well   *Good* is an adjective; *well* is an adverb or (with reference to health) an adjective.

Joe does a **good** job and performs **well** on tests, even when he does not feel **well.**

i.e.   See *e.g./i.e.*

Imminent   See *Eminent/Imminent.*

6.22 Imply/Infer   *Imply* means "to hint" or "to suggest"; *infer* means "to draw a conclusion." Speakers and writers *imply;* readers and listeners *infer.*

> The president **implied** that changes will be forthcoming; I **inferred** from his tone of voice that these changes will not be pleasant.

6.23 Irregardless/Regardless   Use *regardless.* (*Irregardless* is considered substandard.)

> He wants to proceed, **regardless** (not *irregardless*) of the costs.

6.24 Its/It's   *Its* is a possessive pronoun; *it's* is a contraction for "it is."

> **It's** time to let the department increase **its** budget.

6.25 Lay/Lie   *Lay* (principal forms: *lay, laid, laid, laying*) means "to put" and requires an object to complete its meaning; *lie* (principal forms: *lie, lay, lain, lying*) means "to rest."

> Please **lay** the supplies on the shelf.   I **lie** on the couch after lunch each day.
> I **laid** the folders in the drawer.   The report **lay** on his desk yesterday.
> She had **laid** the notes on her desk.   The job has **lain** untouched for a week.

> **Less**   See *Fewer/Less.*

> **Lie**   See *Lay/Lie.*

6.26 Loose/Lose   *Loose* means "not fastened"; *lose* means "to be unable to find."

> Do not **lose** the **loose** change in your pocket.

> **May**   See *Can/May.*

> **Number**   See *Amount/Number.*

> **One Another**   See *Each Other/One Another.*

6.27 Passed/Past   *Passed* is a verb (the past tense or past participle of *pass,* meaning "to move on or by"); *past* is an adjective, adverb, or preposition meaning "earlier."

> The committee **passed** the no-confidence motion at a **past** meeting.

6.28 Percent/Percentage   With figures, use *percent;* without figures, use *percentage.*

> We took a commission of 6 **percent** (or 6%), which was a lower **percentage** than last year.

6.29 Personal/Personnel   *Personal* means "private" or "belonging to one individual"; *personnel* means "employees."

I used my **personal** time to draft a memo to all **personnel.**

6.30 Principal/Principle   *Principal* means "primary" (adjective) or "sum of money" (noun); *principle* means "rule" or "law."

The guiding **principle** is fair play, and the **principal** means of achieving it is a code of ethics.

6.31 Real/Really   *Real* is an adjective; *really* is an adverb. Do not use *real* to modify another adjective.

She was **really** (not *real*) proud that her necklace contained **real** pearls.

6.32 Reason Is Because/Reason Is That   Use *reason is that.* (*Reason is because* is considered substandard.)

The **reason** for such low attendance **is that** (not *is because*) the weather was stormy.

> **Regardless**   See *Irregardless/Regardless.*

6.33 Same   Do not use *same* to refer to a previously mentioned item. Use *it* or some other wording instead.

We have received your order and will ship **it** (not *same*) in three days.

6.34 Set/Sit   *Set* (principal forms: *set, set, set, setting*) means "to place"; *sit* (principal forms: *sit, sat, sat, sitting*) means "to be seated."

Please **set** your papers on the table.	Please **sit** in the chair.
She **set** the computer on the desk.	She **sat** in the first-class section.
I have **set** the computer there before.	I had not **sat** there before.

6.35 Should of/Should've   Use *should've* (or *should have*). (*Should of* is incorrect.)

We **should've** (not *should of*) been more careful.

> **Sight**   See *Cite/Sight/Site.*

> **Sit**   See *Set/Sit.*

> **Site**   See *Cite/Sight/Site.*

6.36 Stationary/Stationery   *Stationary* means "remaining in one place"; *stationery* is writing paper.

I used my personal **stationery** to write them to ask whether the minicomputer should remain **stationary.**

6.37 Sure/Surely   *Sure* is an adjective; *surely* is an adverb. Do not use *sure* to modify another adjective.

I'm **surely** (not *sure*) glad that she is running and feel **sure** that she will be nominated.

6.38 Sure and/Sure to   Use *sure to.* (*Sure and* is considered substandard.)

Be **sure to** (not *sure and*) attend the meeting.

6.39 Their/There/They're   *Their* means "belonging to them"; *there* means "in that place"; and *they're* is a contraction for "they are."

They're too busy with **their** reports to be **there** for the hearing.

6.40 Theirs/There's   *Theirs* is a possessive pronoun; *there's* is a contraction for "there is."

We finished our meal but **there's** no time for them to finish **theirs.**

They're   See *Their/There/They're.*

6.41 Try and/Try to   Use *try to.* (*Try and* is considered substandard.)

Please **try to** (not *try and*) attend the meeting.

Well   See *Good/Well.*

6.42 Whose/Who's   *Whose* is a possessive pronoun; *who's* is a contraction for "who is."

Who's going to let us know **whose** turn it is to make coffee?

6.43 Your/You're   *Your* means "belonging to you"; *you're* is a contraction for "you are."

You're going to present **your** report first.

APPLICATION

DIRECTIONS Select the correct words in parentheses.

1. I will (accept/except) your (advice/advise), but the (affect/effect) of doing

so may bring (alot/a lot) of change.

2. The seminar was (all right/alright), but (among/between) Jamie and me, most participants were (anxious/eager) to complete the training.

3. The (amount/number) of political activity generated (fewer/less) interest than anticipated.

4. (Any one/Anyone) of the students (may/can) apply that (principal/principle) if (theirs/there's) time.

5. The first (sight/cite/site) for the new office (could of/could've) (complimented/ complemented) the surrounding community, mainly because it is (different from/different than) the typical building.

6. The program will succeed; (e.g./i.e.), it is positive, forward-looking, and cost effective.

7. The group members supported (each other/one another) and were enthused/ enthusiastic) about their presentation.

8. The CEO (implied/inferred) that arrangements with an (eminent/imminent) scientist have been finalized, and (irregardless/regardless) of the number who are invited, we will be included.

9. How much (farther/further) can we pursue this if (its/it's) not (passed/past) on through regular channels?

10. Please (lay/lie) your (loose/lose) change on the dresser and I'll be (real/ really) pleased.

11. You (should of/should've) taken advantage of the opportunity to refinance your home under the lower (percent/percentage) rates.

12. The new investment program is open to all (personal/personnel) and will (sure/surely) build security for (their/there) future.

13. The reason for the increase in deli foods in grocery stores is (that/because) more people are buying food prepared outside the home.

14. I use my personal (stationery/stationary) and please (try to/try and) use yours.

15. Tell Henry to be (sure and/sure to) lock up before he leaves and (sit/set) the late afternoon mail on my desk.

16. We have the document and will forward (it/same) to the actuary so that (you're/your) department is included in the transaction.

17. (Who's/Whose) turn is it to clean the refrigerator because it (sure/surely) needs it?

18. I'll follow the guidelines you (advise/advice), (except/accept) the one involving the (eminent/imminent) staff change in sales.

19. There was wide disparity (between/among) the five candidates, but they supported (each other/one another).

20. Dr. Zhoa was excited about the new job but (eager/anxious) about the research required.

21. Be sure the (cites/sights/sites) are done correctly because we want to do a (good/well) job.

22. What did you (imply/infer) from her (compliment/complement)?

23. The (principle/principal) reason for (their/there/they're) success is the lawyer, (whose/who is) a specialist in international law.

24. A (stationery/stationary) pump for the well was (complemented/complimented) by a mobile emergency backup.

25. They wanted us to work (less/fewer) hours so the (number/amount) of savings could be increased.

■ Formatting Correspondence and Memos

The most common features of business letters, memos, and email are discussed in the following sections and illustrated in Figures 1 and 2.

LETTER AND PUNCTUATION STYLES

The *block style* is the simplest letter style to type because all lines begin at the left margin. In the *modified block style,* the date and closing lines begin at the centre point. Offsetting these parts from the left margin enables the reader to locate them quickly.

The *standard punctuation style*—the most common format—uses a colon (never a comma) after the salutation and a comma after the complimentary closing. The *open punctuation style,* on the other hand, uses no punctuation after these two lines.

STATIONERY AND MARGINS

Most letters are typed on standard-sized stationery. The first page of a business letter is typed on letterhead stationery, which shows company information printed at the top. Subsequent pages of a business letter and all pages of a personal business letter (a letter written to transact one's personal business) are typed on good-quality plain paper.

Side, top, and bottom margins should be 2.5 to 3 cm. Vertically centre one-page letters and memos. Set a tab at the centre point if you're formatting a modified block style letter.

REQUIRED LETTER PARTS

The required letter parts are as follows:

Date Line   Type the current month (spelled out), day, and year on the first line. Begin either at the centre point for modified block style or at the left margin for all other styles.

figure1   CORRESPONDENCE FORMATS

Block style letter

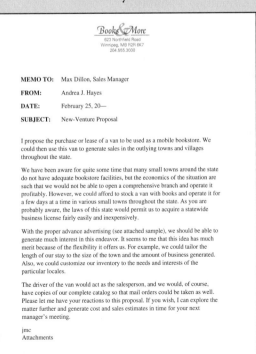

Interoffice memorandum

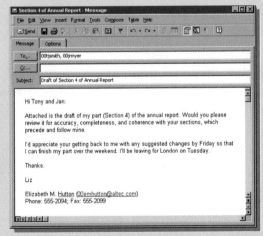

Modified block style letter

Email message

Inside Address   The inside address gives the name and location of the person to whom you're writing. Include a personal title (such as *Mr.*, *Mrs.*, *Miss*, or *Ms.*). If you use the addressee's job title, type it either on the same line as the name (separated from the name by a comma) or on the following line by itself. In the address, use the two-letter Canada post abbreviation, typed in all capitals with no period, and leave one space between the province and the postal code. Type the inside address at the left margin, four lines below the date; that is, press Enter four times. For international letters, type the name of the country in all-capital letters on the last line by itself.

Salutation   Use the same name in both the inside address and the salutation. If the letter is addressed to a job position rather than to a person, use a generic but nonsexist greeting, such as "Dear Human Resources Manager." If you typically address the reader in person by first name, use the first name in the salutation (for example, "Dear Lois:"); otherwise, use a personal title and the surname only (for example, "Dear Ms. Lane:"). Leave one blank line before and after the salutation.

Body   Single-space the lines of each paragraph and leave one blank line between paragraphs.

Page 2 Heading   Use your word processor's page-numbering command to insert the page number in the top right margin. Suppress the page number on page 1. You should carry forward to a second page at least two lines of the body of the message.

Complimentary Closing   Begin the complimentary closing at the same horizontal point as the date line, capitalize the first word only, and leave one blank line before and three blank lines after, to allow room for the signature. If a colon follows the salutation, use a comma after the complimentary closing; otherwise, no punctuation follows.

Signature   Some women insert the personal title they prefer (*Ms.*, *Miss*, or *Mrs.*) in parentheses before their signature. Men never include a personal title.

Writer's Identification   The writer's identification (name or job title or both) begins on the fourth line immediately below the complimentary closing. Do not use a personal title. The job title may go either on the same line as the typed name, separated from the name by a comma, or on the following line by itself.

Reference Initials   When used, reference initials (the initials of the typist) are typed at the left margin in lowercase letters without periods, with one blank line before. Do not include reference initials if you type your own letter.

Envelopes   Business envelopes have a printed return address. You may type your name above this address, if you wish. Use plain envelopes for personal business letters; you should type the return address (your home address) at the upper left corner. Envelopes may be typed either in standard upper- and lowercase style or in all-capital letters without any punctuation. On large (No. 10) envelopes, begin typing the mailing address 5 cm from the top edge and 10 cm from the left edge. On small (No. 6¾) envelopes, begin typing the mailing address 5 cm from the top edge and 6 cm from the left edge. Fold letters as shown in Figure 2.

figure2

ENVELOPES AND FOLDING LETTERS

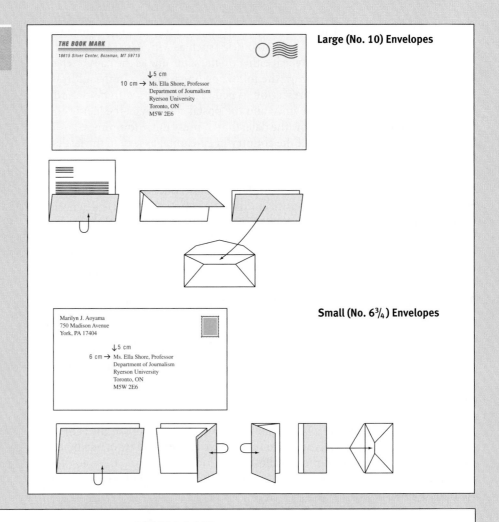

Large (No. 10) Envelopes

THE BOOK MARK
18615 Silver Center, Bozeman, MT 59715

↓5 cm
10 cm → Ms. Ella Shore, Professor
Department of Journalism
Ryerson University
Toronto, ON
M5W 2E6

Small (No. 6³/₄) Envelopes

Marilyn J. Aoyama
750 Madison Avenue
York, PA 17404

↓5 cm
6 cm → Ms. Ella Shore, Professor
Department of Journalism
Ryerson University
Toronto, ON
M5W 2E6

CANADA POST
CANADIAN AND US POSTAL ABBREVIATIONS

Canadian Provinces	*States and Territories*		
Alberta . . . . AB	Alabama . . . . AL	Kentucky . . . . KY	Oklahoma . . . . OK
British Columbia . . . . . BC	Alaska . . . . AK	Louisiana. . . . . LA	Oregon . . . . OR
Labrador. . . . . LB	Arizona . . . . AZ	Maine. . . . . ME	Pennsylvania. . . . . PA
Manitoba . . . . MB	Arkansas . . . . AR	Maryland . . . . MD	Puerto Rico . . . . PR
New Brunswick . . . . . . NB	California. . . . . CA	Massachusetts . . . . MA	Rhode Island . . . . RI
Newfoundland . . . . NF	Colorado . . . . CO	Michigan . . . . MI	South Carolina. . . . . . . SC
Northwest Territories. . NT	Connecticut. . . . . CT	Minnesota . . . . MN	South Dakota. . . . . SD
Nova Scotia . . . . NS	Delaware . . . . DE	Mississippi . . . . MS	Tennessee . . . . TN
Nunavut . . . . NU	District of Columbia . . . . DC	Missouri. . . . . MO	Texas . . . . TX
Ontario . . . . ON	Florida . . . . FL	Montana . . . . MT	Utah . . . . UT
Prince Edward Island . . PE	Georgia . . . . GA	Nebraska. . . . . NE	Vermont . . . . VT
Quebec. . . . . PQ	Guam. . . . . GU	Nevada . . . . NV	Virgin Islands. VI
Saskatchewan . . . . SK	Hawaii . . . . HI	New Hampshire. . . . . . . NH	Virginia. . . . . VA
Yukon Territory. . . . . . . YT	Idaho. . . . . ID	New Jersey. . . . . NJ	Washington . . . . WA
	Illinois IL	New Mexico . . . . NM	West Virginia . . . . WV
	Indiana . . . . IN	New York . . . . NY	Wisconsin . . . . WI
	Iowa. . . . . IA	North Carolina. . . . . NC	Wyoming . . . . WY
	Kansas. . . . . KS	North Dakota. . . . . ND	
		Ohio. . . . . OH	

OPTIONAL LETTER PARTS

Optional letter parts are as follows:

Subject Line   You should include a subject line in most letters (identified by the words *Subject, Re,* or *In Re* followed by a colon) to identify the topic of the letter. Type it below the salutation, with one blank line before and one after.

Numbered or Bulleted Lists in the Body   Use your word processor's number/ bullet feature to insert a numbered list (if the sequence of the items is important) or a bulleted list (when the sequence is not important). If every item takes up only a single line, single-space the items; otherwise, single-space the lines within each item and double-space between items. Either way, leave one blank line before and after the list.

Enclosure Notation   Use an enclosure notation if any additional items are to be included in the envelope. Type "Enclosure" on the line immediately below the reference initials, and as an option, add the description of what is enclosed. (*Note:* For memos, the appropriate term is "Attachment" instead of "Enclosure" if the items are to be physically attached to the memo instead of being enclosed in an envelope.)

Delivery Notation   Type a delivery notation (such as *By Registered Mail, By Fax, By Priority Post*) a single space below the enclosure notation.

Copy Notation   If someone other than the addressee is to receive a copy of the letter, type a copy notation ("c:") immediately below the enclosure notation or reference initials, whichever comes last. Then follow the copy notation with the names of the people who will receive copies.

Postscript   If you add a postscript to a letter, type it as the last item, preceded by one blank line. The heading "PS:" is optional. Postscripts are used most often in sales letters.

■ Formatting Reports

If the reader or organization has a preferred format style, use it. Otherwise, follow these generally accepted guidelines for formatting business reports. Make use of your computer's automatic or formatting features to enhance the appearance and readability of your report and to increase the efficiency of the process.

MARGINS

Memo and letter reports use regular correspondence margins as discussed earlier in this manual. For reports typed in manuscript (formal report) format, use a 5 cm margin for the first page of each special part (for example, the table of contents, the executive summary, the first page of the body of the report, and the first page of the reference list). Leave a 2.5 cm bottom margin for all other pages and at least a 2.5 cm bottom margin on all pages. Use 2.5 to 3 cm side margins on all pages.

SPACING

Memo and letter reports are typed single-spaced. Manuscript reports are also typically single-spaced, unless the reader prefers double spacing to allow for written comments on the pages. Note that double spacing leaves one blank line between each line of type; do not confuse double spacing with 1½ spacing, which leaves only *half* a blank line between lines of type.

Regardless of the spacing used for the body of the report, single spacing is typically used for the table of contents, the executive summary, long quotations, tables, and the reference list. Use a 1.25 cm paragraph indention for double-spaced paragraphs. Do not indent single-spaced paragraphs; instead, double-space between them. Unless directed otherwise, use a 12-point serif font (such as Times New Roman 12).

REPORT HEADINGS

The number of levels of headings used will vary from report to report. Memo reports may have only first-level subheadings, with no part titles or other headings. Long reports may have as many as four levels of headings. One standard format for the various levels is given here. Recognize, however, that the format presented here is only one of several that might be used. Again, consistency and readability should be your major goals. Regardless of the format used, make sure that the reader can instantly tell which are major headings and which are subordinate headings.

Part Title   Using a slightly larger font size than used for the body of the report, centre a part title (for example, "Contents" or "References") in all capitals and in bold on a new page, leaving a 5 cm top margin. Double-space titles of two or more lines, using an inverted pyramid style (the first line longer). Triple-space after the part title.

First-Level Subheading   Begin the first-level subheading at the left margin. Using the same font size as that used in the body of the report, bold the first-level subheading in all capitals. Double-space before and after the heading.

Second-Level Subheading   Begin the second-level subheading at the left margin. Use bold type and capitalize the first letter of the first and last words and all other words except articles, prepositions with four or fewer letters, and conjunctions. Double-space before and after the heading.

Third-Level Subheading   Double-space before the third-level subheading, indent, and bold. Capitalize the first letter of major words as described above. Leave a period and one space after the subheading; begin typing the text on the same line.

PAGINATION

Number the preliminary pages, such as the table of contents, with lowercase roman numerals centred on the bottom margin. The title page is counted as page i, but no page number is shown. Page numbers appear on all other preliminary pages, centred at the bottom margin. For example, the executive summary might be page ii and the table of contents might be page iii.

Number all pages beginning with the first page of the body of the report with arabic numerals. The first page of the body is counted as page 1, but no page number is typed (in word processing terminology, the page number is *suppressed*). Beginning with page 2 of the body and continuing through the reference pages, number all pages consecutively at the top right of the page.

■ Formatting Tables and Charts

FORMATTING TABLES

A **table** is an orderly arrangement of data into columns and rows (see Figure 3 on page 576). Use tables to present numerical information in vertical columns and horizontal rows.

General guidelines for formatting and incorporating tables into a report are as follows:

- Use tables to present a large amount of numerical data in a small space.

- Number tables consecutively and use concise, descriptive headings.

- Ensure that the table is understandable by itself—without reference to the surrounding text.

- Arrange the rows in the table in logical order.

- Use only as much detail as necessary.

- Use common abbreviations and symbols as needed.

- Ensure that the units (e.g., dollars or percentages) are clear.

- Use the same font for the tables that you use for the rest of the report. If needed, tables may be formatted in a slightly smaller size of the same font.

- Format column headings in bold (but not italic) using upper- and lowercase. Centre them if all columns consist of text. Otherwise, block column headings with left alignment for text columns and with right alignment for quantity columns.

- Add a border above a total line and use the word "Total" or "Totals" as appropriate. Do not bold or italicize.

- Introduce each table by number before it appears in the report.

- Whenever possible, avoid splitting a table between two pages.

figure₃

TABLE

the market leader for the past three years. As shown in Table 4, the Central Region led the company's sales force again in 2006.

Table 4. RECYCLED PAPER PRODUCTS Sales Through September 20				
Region	**Year-to-Date Sales***		**% Change**	**Goal Met?**
	2006	**2005**		
Northeast	$ 20	17	15	No
Southeast	183	285	−56	No
Central	2076	1986	4	Yes
West	984	759	23	Yes
Totals	$3263	3047	7	No

Source: *Insurance Leaders DataQuest*, National Insurance Institute, New York, 2006, p. 663.

* Sales in thousands.

All regions but the Southeast experienced an increase in sales through September. According to Wanda Sánchez, regional manager, the main reason for the region's low performance during the past year was primarily the poor local economies in

FORMATTING CHARTS

A chart is used to aid in reader comprehension, emphasize certain data, create interest, and save time and space because the reader can perceive immediately the essential meaning of large masses of statistical data.

Save charts for presenting information that is important and that can best be grasped visually—for example, when the overall picture is more important than the individual numbers. Also, recognize that the more charts your report contains, the less impact each individual chart will have.

The cardinal rule for designing charts is to keep them simple. Trying to cram too much information into one chart will merely confuse the reader and lessen the impact of the graphic. Well-designed charts have only one interpretation, and that interpretation should be clear immediately; the reader shouldn't have to study the chart at length or refer to the surrounding text.

Regardless of their type, label all your charts as *figures*, and assign them consecutive numbers, separate from table numbers. Although tables are captioned at the top, charts may be captioned at the top or bottom. Charts used alone (for example, as an overhead transparency or slide) are typically captioned at the top. Charts preceded or followed by text or containing an explanatory paragraph are typically captioned at the bottom. As with tables, you may use commonly understood abbreviations.

The main types of charts used in business reports and presentations are line charts, bar charts, and pie charts.

A **line chart** is a graph based on a grid of uniformly spaced horizontal and vertical lines. (Figure 4 on page 578 shows three kinds of line charts.) The vertical dimension represents values; the horizontal dimension represents time. Line charts are useful for showing changes in data over long periods of time and for emphasizing the movement of the data—the trends.

A **bar chart** is a graph with horizontal or vertical bars representing values. Bar charts are one of the most useful, simple, and popular graphic techniques. They are particularly appropriate for comparing the magnitude or size of items, either at a specified time or over a period of time (see Figure 5 on page 579).

A **pie chart** is a circle graph whose area is divided into component wedges (see Figure 6 on page 580). Pie charts are useful for showing how component parts add up to make a total when the whole contains three to five component parts. It is customary to include the percentages or other values represented by each wedge and to distinguish each wedge by shading, cross-hatched lines, different colors, or some similar device.

figure4

LINE CHARTS

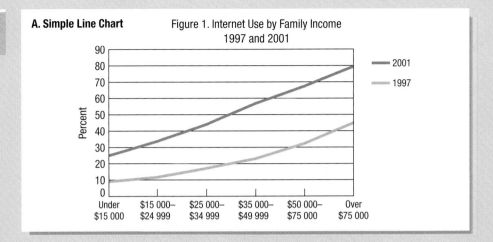

A. Simple Line Chart

Figure 1. Internet Use by Family Income
1997 and 2001

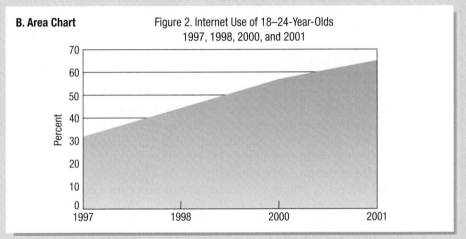

B. Area Chart

Figure 2. Internet Use of 18–24-Year-Olds
1997, 1998, 2000, and 2001

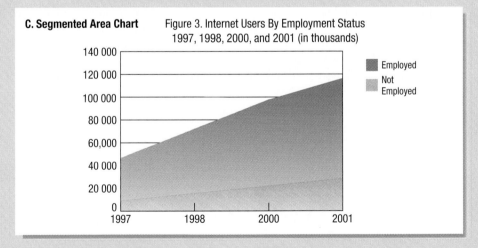

C. Segmented Area Chart

Figure 3. Internet Users By Employment Status
1997, 1998, 2000, and 2001 (in thousands)

A. Vertical Bar Chart

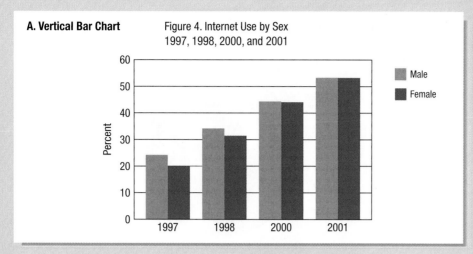

Figure 4. Internet Use by Sex
1997, 1998, 2000, and 2001

figure5

BAR CHARTS

B. Horizontal Bar Chart

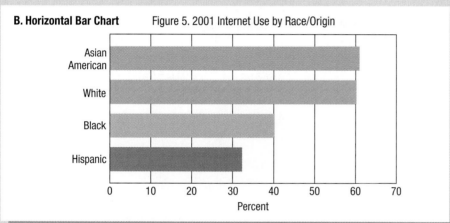

Figure 5. 2001 Internet Use by Race/Origin

C. Stacked Bar Chart

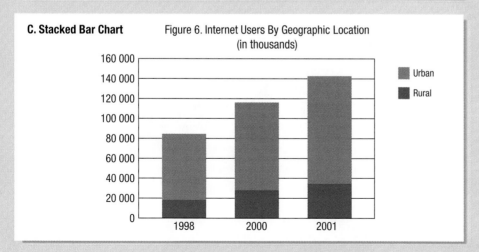

Figure 6. Internet Users By Geographic Location
(in thousands)

figure6

PIE CHARTS

A. Simple Pie Chart

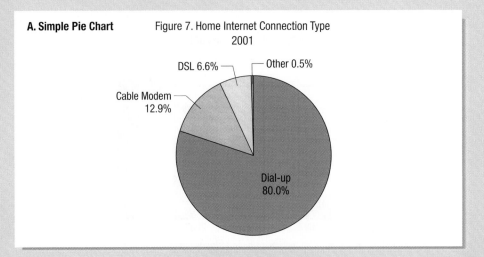

Figure 7. Home Internet Connection Type 2001

B. Three-Dimensional Pie Chart

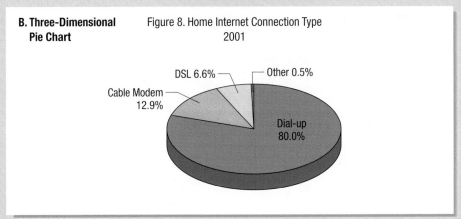

Figure 8. Home Internet Connection Type 2001

C. Three-Dimensional Exploded Pie Chart

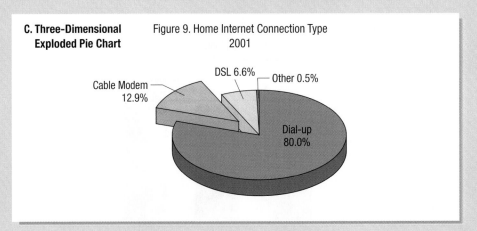

Figure 9. Home Internet Connection Type 2001

General guidelines for formatting and incorporating charts into a report are as follows:

- Use charts only when they will help the reader interpret the data better.

- Label all charts as "figures," and number them consecutively.

- Keep charts simple.

- Prefer two-dimensional charts.

- Use the most appropriate type of chart to achieve your objective.

- Use line charts to show changes in data over a period of time and to emphasize trends.

- Use the horizontal axis for amounts and the vertical axis for time.

- Mark off both axes at equal intervals and clearly label them.

- Begin the vertical axis at zero (use slash marks if needed).

- If you plot more than one variable on a chart, clearly distinguish between them.

❑ Use bar charts to compare the magnitude or relative size of items, either at a specified time or over a period of time.

- Make all bars the same width; vary the length to reflect the value of each item.

- Arrange the bars in a logical order and clearly label each.

❑ Use pie charts to compare the relative parts that make up a whole.

- Begin slicing at the 12 o'clock position, moving clockwise in a logical order.

- Label each wedge, indicate its value, and clearly differentiate between wedges.

■ Citation Styles

Shown below is a representative list of different types of citations formatted in the three most common citation styles—business style (also appropriate for most academic reports), APA style, and MLA style. Although the list is quite extensive, you may occasionally encounter a type of citation not illustrated here. In that case, simply find a similar type of citation and adapt it to your specific source.

Within Document	
	Business Style[1]
One author—not named in text	In fact, fringe benefits are growing in importance as a part of an overall salary package.[1]
One author—named in text	Adams argues that health insurance is the most important benefit of all.[2]
Multiple authors—not named in text	The personalized benefit statement shown in Figure 3 contains all necessary legal information.[3]
Multiple authors—named in text	According to Berelson, Lazarsfield, and Connell,[4] the personalized benefit statement shown in Figure 3 contains all necessary legal information.
Multiple sources	Numerous research studies[5] have shown that white-collar employees prefer an increase in benefits to an increase in salary.
Author not identified	Another variation that is growing in popularity is the cafeteria-style program.[6]
Direct quotation	According to Ivarson, "There is no such creature as a 'fringe benefit' anymore."[7]
	[1]William A. Sabin, *The Gregg Reference Manual,* 9th ed., Westerville, Ohio, Glencoe/McGraw-Hill, 2001.

End of Report	
	Bibliography
Annual report	Abbey Petroleum Industries, *2005 Annual Report,* API, Inc., San Francisco, 2006.
Book—one author	Adams, Josiah B., *Compensation Systems,* Brunswick Press, Boston, 2005.
Book—two authors	Adhams, Ramon, and Seymour Stevens, *Personnel Management,* All-State, Cambridge, MA, 2004.
Book—three or more authors	Berelson, Sarah, et al., *Managing Your Benefit Program,* 13th ed., Novak-Siebold, Chicago, 2006.
Book—organization as author	*Directory of Business and Financial Services,* Corporate Libraries Assoc., New York, 2005.

References

Business Style: William A. Sabin, *The Gregg Reference Manual,* 10th ed.,
McGraw-Hill/Irwin, New York, 2005.

APA Style: *Publication Manual of the American Psychological Association,* 5th ed.,
Washington, D.C., American Psychological Association, 2001.

MLA Style: Joseph Gibaldi, *MLA Handbook for Writers of Research Papers,* 6th ed.
New York, Modern Language Association of America, 2003; "MLA
Style," *MLA Home Page,* September 9, 2003, http://www.mla.org
(June 14, 2004).

APA Style	MLA Style
In fact, fringe benefits are growing in importance as a part of an overall salary package (Ignatio, 2006).	In fact, fringe benefits are growing in importance as a part of an overall salary package (Ignatio 813).
Adams (2005) argues that health insurance is the most important benefit of all.	Adams argues that health insurance is the most important benefit of all (386–87).
The personalized benefit statement shown in Figure 3 contains all necessary legal information (Berelson, Lazarsfield, & Connell, 2006).	The personalized benefit statement shown in Figure 3 contains all necessary legal information (Berelson, Lazarsfield, and Connell 563).
According to Berelson, Lazarsfield, and Connell (2006, p. 563), the personalized benefit statement shown in Figure 3 contains all necessary legal information.	According to Berelson, Lazarsfield, and Connell, the personalized benefit statement shown in Figure 3 contains all necessary legal information (563).
Numerous research studies have shown that white-collar employees prefer an increase in benefits to an increase in salary (Adhams & Stevens, 2004; Ivarson, 2005; White, 2005).	Numerous research studies have shown that white-collar employees prefer an increase in benefits to an increase in salary (Adhams and Stevens 76; Ivarson 29; White).
Another variation that is growing in popularity is the cafeteria-style program ("Let Employees," 2006).	Another variation that is growing in popularity is the cafeteria-style program ("Let Employees").
According to Ivarson (2005), "There is no such creature as a 'fringe benefit' anymore" (p. 27).	According to Ivarson, "There is no such creature as a 'fringe benefit' anymore" (27).

APA Style—References	MLA Style—Works Cited
Abbey Petroleum Industries. (2006). *2005 annual report.* San Francisco: Author.	Abbey Petroleum Industries. *2005 Annual Report, Abbey Petroleum Industries, 2006.* San Francisco: API, Inc., 2006.
Adams, J. B. (2005). *Compensation systems.* Boston: Brunswick Press.	Adams, Josiah B. *Compensation Systems.* Boston: Brunswick; Press, 2005.
Adhams, R., & Stevens, S. (2004). *Personnel management.* Cambridge, MA: All-State.	Adhams, Ramon, and Seymour Stevens. *Personnel Management.* Cambridge: All-State, 2004.
Berelson, S., Lazarsfield, P. F., & Connell, W., Jr. (2006). *Managing your benefit program* (13th ed.). Chicago: Novak-Siebold.	Berelson, Sarah, Paul Lazarsfield, and Will Connell, Jr. *Managing Your Benefit Program.* 13th ed. Chicago: Novak-Siebold, 2006.
Directory of business and financial services. (2005). New York: Corporate Libraries Association.	Corporate Libraries Association. *Directory of Business and Financial Services.* New York: Corporate Libraries Association, 2005.

End of Report (*continued*)

Business Style—Bibliography

Journal article—paged continuously throughout the year	Ignatio, Enar, "Can Flexible Benefits Promote Your Company?" *Personnel Quarterly,* Vol. 20, September 2006, pp. 804–816.
Magazine article—paged starting anew with each issue	Ivarson, Andrew, Jr., "Creating Your Benefit Plan: A Primer," *Business Month,* September 29, 2005, pp. 19–31.
Newspaper article—unsigned	"Let Employees Determine Their Own Benefits," *Manhattan Times,* January 12, 2006, p. C17, col. 2.
Reference work article	"Market Research," *Encyclopedia of Business,* 2d ed., 2006.
Government document	National Institute of Mental Health, *Who Pays the Piper? Ten Years of Passing the Buck,* DHHS Publication No. ADM 82-1195, U.S. Government Printing Office, Washington, 2005.
Interview	O'Brian, Douglas, Interview by author, May 13, 2006.
Paper presented at a meeting	Patts, Regina. *Tuition Reimbursement,* paper presented at the meeting of the National Mayors' Conference, Trenton, NJ, August 5, 2006.
Television/radio broadcast	Preminger, Larry (Executive Producer), *The WKVX-TV Evening News,* Valhalla Broadcasting Co., Los Angeles, August 5, 2006.
CD-ROM article	Petelin, Rosana, "Wage Administration," *Martindale Interactive Business Encyclopedia* (CD-ROM), Martindale, Inc., Pompton Lakes, NJ, 2005.
World Wide Web page	Quincy, Dinah J., "Maxwell Announces New Health Benefit," *Maxwell Corp.,* November 13, 2004, <http://www.maxcorp.com/NEWS/2004/f93500.html> accessed on January 14, 2005.
Online database article	"Salary Survey of Service Industries," *BizInfo,* n.d., <http://www.bizinfo.com/census.gov/ind.lib/tab-0315.html> accessed on July 8, 2004.
Email	Waerov, Denis V., "Reaction to Management's Offer," e-mail message, August 19, 2005.
Electronic discussion message (including Listservs and newsgroups)	Young, Laurel <lyoung2@express.com>, "Training Doesn't Always Last," June 3, 2004, <http:l//groups.yahoo.com/group/personnel/message/51> accessed on April 20, 2005.

APA Style—References	MLA Style—Works Cited
Ignatio, E. (2006). Can flexible benefits promote your company?" *Personnel Quarterly, 20,* 804–816.	Ignatio, Enar. "Can Flexible Benefits Promote Your Company?" *Personnel Quarterly* 20 (2006): 804–16.
Ivarson, A., Jr. (2005, September 29). Creating your benefit plan: A primer. *Business Month, 75,* 19–31.	Ivarson, Andrew, Jr. "Creating Your Benefit Plan: A Primer." *Business Month* 29 Sept. 2005: 19–31.
Let employees determine their own benefits. (2006, January 12). *Manhattan Times,* p. C17.	"Let Employees Determine Their Own Benefits." *Manhattan Times* 12 Jan. 2006: C17.
Market research. (2006). In *The encyclopedia of business* (2nd ed., Vol. 2, pp. 436–441). Cleveland, OH: Collins.	"Market Research." *Encyclopedia of Business,* 2nd ed., Cleveland: Collins, 2006.
National Institute of Mental Health. (2005). *Who pays the piper? Ten years of passing the buck* (DHHS Publication No. ADM 82-1195). Washington, DC: U.S. Government Printing Office.	National Institute of Mental Health. *Who Pays the Piper? Ten Years of Passing the Buck.* DHHS Publication No. ADM 82-1195. Washington: GPO, 2005.
[Not cited in reference list. Cited in text as "D. O'Brian (personal interview, May 13, 2006) suggest that...]	O'Brian, Douglas. Personal interview, 13 May 2006.
Patts, R. (2005, August). *Tuition reimbursement.* Paper presented at the meeting of the National Mayors' Conference, Trenton, NJ.	Patts, Regina. *Tuition Reimbursement.* Paper presented at the meeting of the National Mayors' Conference. Trenton, NJ, 5 Aug. 2005.
Preminger, L. (Executive Producer). (2006, August 5). *The WKVX-TV Evening News* [Television broadcast]. Los Angeles: Valhalla Broadcasting Co.	Preminger, Larry (Executive Producer). *The WKVX-TV Evening News.* Los Angeles: Valhalla Broadcasting Co., 5 Aug. 2006.
Petelin, R. (2005). *Wage administration.* Pompton Lakes, NJ: Martindale, Inc. Retrieved from Martindale database (Martindale Interactive Business Encyclopedia, CD-ROM).	Petelin, Rosana. "Wage Administration," *Martindale Interactive Business Encyclopedia.* CD-ROM. Pompton Lakes, NJ: Martindale, Inc., 2005.
Quincy, D. J. (2004, November 13). Maxwell announces new health benefit. New York: Maxwell. Retrieved January 14, 2005 from http://www.maxcorp.com/NEWS/2004/f93500.html	Quincy, Dinah J. "Maxwell Announces New Health Benefit." *Maxwell Corp. Home Page.* 13 Nov. 2004. 14 Jan. 2005 <http://www.maxcorp.com /NEWS/2004/f93500.html>.
Salary survey of service industries. (n.d.). Retrieved July 8, 2004, from BizInfo database, http://www.bizinfo.com/census.gov/ind.lib /tab-0315.html	"Salary Survey of Service Industries." *BizInfo.* n.d. 8 July 2004 <http://www.bizinfo.com/census.gov/ind.lib /tab-0315.html>.
[Not cited in reference list. Cited in text as "D. V. Waerov (personal communication, August 18, 2003) proposes that . . ."]	Waerov, Denis, V. "Reaction to Management's Offer," E-mail to the author. 19 Aug 2005.
Young, L. (2004, June 3). Training doesn't always last. Message posted to http://groups.yahoo.com/group /personnel/message/51	Young, Laurel. <lyoung2@express.com> "Training Doesn't Always Last." Online posting. 3 June 2004. 20 Apr. 2005 <http://groups.yahoo.com/group /personnel/message/51>.

BUSINESS STYLE POINTERS

❑ The major differences between footnote and bibliographic entries are that (1) footnotes use the normal order for author names (e.g., "Raymond Stevens and Seymour Adams"), whereas bibliographies invert the order of the first author (e.g., "Stevens, Raymond, and Seymour Adams"); and (2) page numbers are included in bibliographic entries only when the material being cited is part of a larger work (for example, a journal or newspaper article).

❑ Type the authors' names exactly as they appear in print. For publications by two authors, arrange only the first name in last-name/first-name order. With three or more authors, type only the first name followed by *et al.* (not in italics). Arrange publications by the same author in alphabetical order, according to the publication title.

❑ Include page numbers only when the material being cited is part of a larger work. Do not italicize edition numbers. Be consistent in formatting the ordinal in raised position (13th) or in normal position (13th).

❑ Include the two-letter province name (using the Canada Post abbreviation) only if confusion might result. Use a shortened form of the publisher's name; e.g., *McGraw-Hill* rather than *McGraw-Hill Book Company,* and use common abbreviations (such as *Assoc.* or *Co.*).

❑ For online citations:

■ For email, insert the type of email (e.g., "office communication" or "personal email").

■ If the date of an online posting cannot be determined, insert the abbreviation *n.d.* (no date)—not in italics.

■ Enclose in parentheses as the last section of the citation the date you accessed the site, followed by a period.

■ Follow the capitalization, punctuation, and spacing exactly as given in the original online address.

■ You may break an online citation *before* (but never after) a dot (.), single slash (/), double slash (//), hyphen (-), underscore (_), at symbol (@), or any other mark of punctuation. Do *not* insert a hyphen within an online address to signify an end-of-line break.

Abstract word   A word that identifies an idea or feeling as opposed to a concrete object.

Active voice   The sentence form in which the subject performs the action expressed by the verb.

Adjustment   A letter written to inform a customer of the action taken in response to the customer's claim letter.

Agenda   An ordered list of topics to be considered at a meeting, along with the name of the person responsible for each topic.

Analytical   A report that not only presents the information but also analyzes it and draws conclusions.

Application letter   A letter from a job applicant to a prospective employer explaining the applicant's interest in and qualifications for a position within the organization; also called a *cover letter*.

Audience   The person or persons with whom you're communicating.

Audience analysis   Identification of the needs, interests, and personality of the receiver of a communication.

Blog   A Web site where regular entries are made, much like an online diary.

Brainstorming   Jotting down ideas, facts, possible leads, and anything else that might be helpful in constructing a message.

Buffer   A neutral and supportive opening statement designed to lessen the impact of negative news.

Business etiquette   The practice of polite and appropriate behaviour in a business setting.

Buzzword   An important sounding term used mainly to impress people.

Central selling theme   The major reader benefit that is introduced early and emphasized throughout a sales letter.

Claim   A letter from the buyer to the seller, seeking some type of action to correct a problem with the seller's product or service.

Cliché   An expression that has become monotonous through overuse.

Communication   The process of sending and receiving messages.

Complex sentence   A sentence that has one independent clause and at least one dependent clause.

Compound-complex sentence   A sentence that has two or more independent clauses and one or more dependent clauses.

Compound sentence   A sentence that has two or more independent clauses.

Consent form   A form that must be signed by participants in research involving human subjects.

Conclusions   The answers to the research questions raised in the introduction to a report.

Concrete word   A word that identifies something the senses can perceive.

Connotation   The subjective or emotional feeling associated with a word.

Dangling expression   Any part of a sentence that does not logically connect to the rest of the sentence.

Defamation   Any false and malicious statement that is communicated to others and that injures a person's good name or reputation.

Denotation   The literal, dictionary meaning of a word.

Derived benefit   The benefit a potential customer would receive from using a product or service.

Direct organizational plan   A plan in which the major purpose of the message is communicated first, followed by any needed explanation.

Direct quotation   The exact words of another.

Diversity   A diverse workplace is one that embraces any traditionally under-represented group and one that recognizes the business advantage of doing so.

Documentation   Giving credit to another person for his or her words or ideas that you have used.

Drafting   Composing a preliminary version of a message.

Editing   The stage of revision which ensures that writing conforms to standard English.

Electronic database   A computer-searchable collection of information on a general subject area, such as business, education, or psychology.

Electronic résumé   A résumé that is stored in a computer database designed to help manage and initially screen job applicants.

Email   A message transmitted electronically over a computer network most often connected by cable, telephone lines, or satellites.

Ethics   Rules of conduct.

Euphemism   An inoffensive expression used in place of an expression that may offend or suggest something unpleasant.

Executive summary   A condensed version of the report body; also called an *abstract* or *synopsis.*

Expletive   An expression such as *there is* or *it has been* that begins a clause and for which the pronoun has no antecedent.

Factoring   Breaking a problem down into its component parts so that data-collection needs are known.

Feedback   The receiver's reaction or response to a message.

Filter   The mental process of perceiving stimuli based on one's knowledge, experience, and viewpoints.

Form letter   A letter with standardized wording that is sent to different people.

Formal communication network   The transmission of prescribed information through downward, upward, horizontal, and cross-channel routes.

Fraud   A deliberate misrepresentation of the truth that is made to induce someone to give up something of value.

Free writing   Writing continuously for five to ten minutes without stopping as a means of generating a large quantity of material that will be revised later.

Generic heading   A report heading that identifies only the topic of a section without giving the conclusion.

Goodwill message   A message that is sent strictly out of a sense of kindness and friendliness.

Groupthink   A barrier to communication that results from an overemphasis on group cohesiveness, which stifles opposing ideas and the free flow of information.

Groupware   A form of software that automates information sharing between two or more remote users and enables them to communicate electronically and coordinate their efforts.

Indirect organizational plan   A plan in which the reasons or rationale are presented first, followed by the major idea.

Informal communication network   The transmission of information through non-official channels within the organization; also called the *grapevine.*

Informational report   A report that objectively details the facts and events surrounding a particular situation, with no attempt to analyze and interpret the data, draw conclusions, or recommend a course of action.

Internet   A worldwide collection of interconnected computers housed in university labs, business offices, government centres, and the like—all filled with massive amounts of information that is accessible to anyone with an Internet account.

Interview guide   A list of questions to ask, with suggested wording and possible follow-up questions.

Invasion of privacy   Any unreasonable intrusion into the private life of another person or denial of a person's right to be left alone.

Jargon   The technical terminology used within specialized groups.

Letter   A written message mailed to someone outside the organization.

Libel   Defamation in a permanent form, such as in writing or on videotape.

Mailing list   An Internet discussion group in which messages are sent directly to members via email; also called a *listserv.*

Mechanics   Those elements in communication that show up only in written form, including spelling, punctuation, abbreviations, capitalization, number expression, and word division.

Medium   The form of a message—for example, a memo or telephone call.

Memorandum   A written message sent to someone within the organization.

Message   The information (either verbal or non-verbal) that is communicated.

Mind mapping   Generating ideas for message content by first writing the purpose of the message in the centre of a page and circling it and then writing possible points to include, linking each one either to the purpose or to another point; also called *clustering.*

Minutes   An official record of the proceedings of a meeting that summarizes what was discussed and what decisions were made.

Misrepresentation   A false statement made innocently with no intent to deceive the other party.

Newsgroup   An Internet discussion group in which messages (called *articles*) are posted at the newsgroup site, rather than being sent directly to the members as email.

Non-discriminatory language   Language that treats everyone equally, making no unwarranted assumptions about any group of people.

Non-verbal message   An unwritten and unspoken signal consisting of facial expressions, gestures, voice qualities, and the like.

Organization   The sequence in which topics are presented in a message.

Parallelism   Using similar grammatical structure to express similar ideas.
Paraphrase   A summary or restatement of a passage in one's own words.
Parliamentary procedure   Written rules of order that permit the efficient transaction of business in meetings.
Passive voice   The sentence form in which the subject receives the action expressed by the verb.
Persuasion   The process of motivating someone to take a specific action or to support a particular idea.
Plagiarism   Using another person's words or ideas without giving proper credit.
Platitude   A trite, obvious statement.
Podcast   An audio program made available for downloading as an MP3. (The name owes its origin to Apple's iPod.)
Policy   A broad operating guideline that governs the general direction or activities of an organization.
Primary audience   The receiver of a message whose cooperation is most crucial if the message is to achieve its objective.
Primary data   Data collected by the researcher to solve the specific problem at hand.
Procedure   The recommended methods or sequential steps to be followed when performing a specific activity.
Proposal   A written report that seeks to persuade a reader outside the organization to do as the writer wants.

Questionnaire   A written instrument containing questions designed to obtain information from the individual being surveyed.

Readability   The ease with which a passage can be understood, based on its style of writing.
Receiver benefits   The advantages a reader would derive from granting the writer's request or from accepting the writer's decision.
Recommendation report   A report that presents the relevant information, interprets it, and then endorses a specific course of action.
Redundancy   The unnecessary repetition of an idea that has already been expressed or intimated.
Reference   A person who has agreed to provide information to a prospective employer regarding a job applicant's fitness for a job.
Report   An orderly and objective presentation of information that assists in decision making and problem solving.
Resale   Information that re-establishes a customer's confidence in the product purchased or in the company that sold the product.
Résumé   A brief record of one's personal history and qualifications that is typically prepared by a job applicant.
Revising   The process of modifying the content and style of a draft to increase its effectiveness.
Rhetorical question   A question asked strictly to get the reader thinking about the topic; a literal answer is not expected.

Secondary audience   Any receiver of a message, other than the primary audience, who will be affected by the message.

Secondary data   Data collected by someone else for some other purpose; it may be published or unpublished.

Simple sentence   A sentence that has one independent clause.

Slander   Defamation in a temporary form, such as in oral communication.

Slang   An expression, often short-lived, that is identified with a specific group of people.

Solicited sales letter   A reply to a request for product information from a potential customer.

Solicited application letter   An application letter written in response to an advertised job vacancy.

Stimulus   An event that creates within an individual the need to communicate.

Style   The manner in which an idea is expressed (rather than the *substance* of the idea).

Survey   A data-collection method that gathers information through questionnaires, telephone inquiries, or interviews.

Table   An orderly arrangement of data into columns and rows.

Talking heading   A report heading that identifies not only the topic of the report section but also the major conclusion.

Team   A group of individuals who depend on one another to accomplish a common objective.

Teleconference   A meeting of three or more people, at least some of whom are in different locations, who communicate via telephone.

Tone   The writer's attitude toward the reader and the subject of the message.

Transmittal document   A letter or memorandum that conveys the finished report to the reader.

Unsolicited application letter   An application letter written to an organization that has not advertised a vacancy; also called a *prospecting letter*.

Unsolicited sales letter   A letter promoting a firm's products mailed to a potential customer who has not expressed any prior interest in the product; also called a *prospecting letter*.

Verbal message   A message comprising spoken or written words.

Videoconference   An interactive meeting between two or more people using video linkups at two or more sites.

Visual aids   Tables, charts, photographs, and other graphic materials used in communication to aid comprehension and add interest.

Weblog   A Web site, created by an individual, interest group, or an organization, in which regular entries are made to provide a forum for discussion and dissemination of information.

Web site   The location of one or more pages of related information that is posted on the World Wide Web and is accessed via the Internet (the main page of a Web site is called its "home page").

Wiki   A web page that is set up to be edited by groups of people.

World Wide Web   The newest and fastest growing segment of the Internet; comprises documents (called *pages*) containing text, graphics, sounds, and video, as well as electronic links (called *hypertext*) that let the user move quickly from one document to another.

Writer's block   The inability to focus one's attention on the writing process and to draft a message.

"You" attitude   A viewpoint that emphasizes what the reader wants to know and how the reader will be affected by the message.

references

Chapter 1

1. *Business Wire*. Ottawa: 12 October 2005. Survey conducted by BackDRAFT.
2. Kristin Goff , "Employers want grads with better skills: Study shows new recruits need more work" in *Examiner*. Barrie, Ontario: April 20, 2000, p. 21.
3. Mark H. McCormack, "Words You Use Tell a Lot About You" in *Arizona Republic*. April 13, 2000, p. D4.
4. David Shenk, *Data Smog: Surviving the Information Glut*. HarperCollins: San Francisco, 1997; David Stipp, "Intellectual Hedonism: Richard Saul Wurman, the King of Access" in *Fortune*. June 23, 1997, p. 106; Richard Saul Wurman, *Information Architects*. New York: Graphics Press Corp., 1996; Richard Saul Wurman, *Information Anxiety*. Garden City, NY: Doubleday, 1989; Peter Lyman and Hal R. Varian, "How Much Information?" on *University of California-Berkeley Home Page*. October 18, 2000. Retrieved from *www.sims.berkeley.edu/research/projects/how-much-info*.
5. John Gerstner, "Executives Evaluate the Importance of Grapevine Communication" in *Communication World*. March 1994, p. 17; James P. Miller, "Work Week" in *Wall Street Journal*, February 1, 2000, p. A1.
6. Donald B. Simmons, "The Nature of the Organizational Grapevine" in *Supervisory Management*. Vol. 30, November 1985, p. 40; Alan Zaremba, "Working with the Organizational Grapevine" in *Personnel Journal*. Vol. 67, July 1988, p. 40; Carol Hymowitz, "Spread the Word: Gossip Is Good" in *Wall Street Journal*. October 4, 1988, p. B1.
7. Lorenzo Sierra, "Tell it to the Grapevine" in *Communication World*. June–July 2002, p. 28.
8. Watson Wyatt Worldwide, *Linking Communications with Strategy to Achieve Business Goals*. Bethesda, MD, 1999, p. 6.
9. Kathleen Driscoll, "Your Voice Can Make or Break You" in *Democrat and Chronicle*. August 26, 1993, p. 10B.
10. Robert L. Montgomery, *Listening Made Easy: How to Improve Listening on the Job, at Home, and in the Community*. New York: American Management Association, 1981, p. 6.
11. David Shenk, *Data Smog: Surviving the Information Glut*. San Francisco: HarperCollins, 1997.
12. Stephen Karel, "Learning Culture the Hard Way" in *Consumer Markets Abroad*. Vol. 7, May 1988, pp. 1, 15.
13. This case was adapted from Brenda R. Sims, "Linking Ethics and Language in the Technical Communication Classroom" in *Technical Communication Quarterly*. Vol. 2, No. 3, summer 1993, p. 285.

Chapter 2

1. Andrea Kay, "Craft Communication to Tasks" in *Indianapolis Star*. June 18, 2003, p. C3.
2. John R. Pierce, "Communication" in *Scientific American*. Vol. 227, September 1972, p. 36.
3. "Conflict Resolution: Don't Get Mad, Get Promoted" in *Training*. June 2002, p. 20.
4. Irving R. Janis, *Victims of Groupthink*. Boston: Houghton Mifflin, 1972.
5. These guidelines are based on principles contained in Peter R. Scholtes, *The Team Handbook: How to Use Teams to Improve Quality*. Madison, WI: Joiner Associates, 1988, pp. 6.23–6.28.
6. Kamil Dib, "Diversity Works" in *Canadian Business*. Vol. 77, Issue 7, March 29, 2004.
7. Valerie Marchant, "The new face of work" in *Canadian Business*. Vol. 77, Issue 7, March 29, 2004.
8. *Ibid.*
9. *Ibid.*
10. Jennifer Coates, *Women, Men, and Language*. New York: Longman, 1986; Deborah Tannen, *You Just Don't Understand*. New York: Ballantine, 1990; John Gray, *Men Are from Mars, Women Are from Venus*. New York: HarperCollins, 1992; Patti Hathaway, *Giving and Receiving Feedback,* rev. ed. Menlo Park, CA: Crisp Publications, 1998; Susan Herring, "Making the Net 'Work'". Retrieved from *www.cs.nott.ac.uk/,azq97c/gender.htm*, May 12, 1999; Deborah Tannen, *Talking from 9 to 5*. New York: William Morrow, 1994.
11. Alice Sargeant, *The Androgynous Manager*. New York: American Management Association, 1983, p. 37.
12. John T. Molloy, "Dress for Success" in *Detroit Free Press*. December 19, 1989, p. 3C.
13. "Telephone On-Hold Statistics" in *National Telephone Message Corporation*. Retrieved from *www.ihearditonhold.com/statistics.html*, September 13, 2003.
14. "Phone Calls Waste a Month Each Year" in *Office Systems*. September 1989, p. 14.
15. Peter F. Drucker, quoted by Bill Boyers in *A World of Ideas*. Garden City, NY: Doubleday, 1990.
16. Albert Mehrabian, "Communicating Without Words" in *Psychology Today*. September 1968, pp. 53–55.
17. "I TYPE THEREFORE IM" in *BC Business*. Vol. 32, No. 12, December 2004. Database: *Canadian Reference Centre*, 0849481X.
18. Teresa Tummillo-Goy, "Being more accessible has made us more inaccessible" in *Guelph Mercury*. June 3, 2006, p. A9.
19. Jason Krause, "Like e-mail only faster" in *ABA Journal*. Vol 91, Issue 5, May 2005, p. 24.
20. *Ibid.*
21. Roberty D. Hof, "Web 2.0 The New Guy at Work" in *Business Week*. Issue 3989, June 19, 2006, pp. 58–59.
22. Natasha Spring and William Briggs. "The Impact of Blogging: Real or Imagined" in *Communication World*. May–June 2006, pp. 29–32.
23. *Wikipedia.com*. Accessed June 23, 2006.
24. Anne Massie, "Blogging Phobia Hits Employers" in *Canadian HR Reporter*. Vol. 18, No. 16, September 26, 2005, pp. 15–16.
25. Andrew Wahl, "Podcast News" in *Canadian Business*. Vol. 78, No. 19, September 26–October 9, 2005, p. 94.
26. Roberty D. Hof, *supra*, note 21, pp. 58–59.
27. David Shenk, *Data Smog: Surviving the Information Glut*. San Francisco: HarperCollins, 1997, p. 97.

28. Quoted in David Stipp, "Intellectual Hedonism" in *Fortune.* June 23, 1997, p. 106.

29. Stephanie Armour, "Meetings Inspire High-Tech Survival Skills" in *USA Today.* January 22, 1999, p. B1; Michael Doyle and David Straus, *How to Make Meetings Work.* New York: Wyden Books, 1976, p. 4; Marcy E. Mullins, "Are Meetings Worthwhile?" in *USA Today.* August 28, 1989, p. B1; "Profile of the Typical Meeting" in *Presentation Products Magazine.* February 1990, p. 8; E. F. Wells, "Rules for a Better Meeting" in *Mainliner.* May 1978, p. 56; E. J. McGarry, "Presentations Can Be Economical and Effective" in *Office Dealer 92.* March/April 1992, p. 18.

30. "Managing Meetings: A Critical Role" in *The Office.* November 1989, p. 20.

31. *Ibid.,* p. 20.

Chapter 3

1. Rick Mercer as quoted in Guy Dixon, "Need the former G-G for a cameo? Just call her up" in *Globe and Mail.* October 21, 2006, p. R9.

2. Marshall Cook, "Seven Steps to Better Manuscripts" in *Writer's Digest.* September 1987, p. 30.

3. Tom Murray, "Canadian Oxford Dictionary affirms national identity" in *University of Alberta Express News.* October 8, 2004 (*www.expressnews.ualberta.ca/article.cfm?id=6125*).

4. Katherine Barber, *www.oup.com/ca/genref/dictionaries/canadian/.* Accessed December 15, 2005.

5. Tom Murray, *supra,* note 3.

6. *Maclean's.* Vol. 118, No. 31/32, August 1–8, 2005, p. 86.

7. Julie Schmit, "Continental's $4 Million Typo" in *USA Today.* May 25, 1993, p. B1.

Chapter 4

1. Marilyn vos Savant, "Ask Marilyn" in *Parade Magazine.* November 3, 1996, p. 8.

2. Scot Ober, "The Difficulty Level of Typewritten Copy in Industry" in *Delta Pi Epsilon Journal.* Vol. 25, January 1983, p. 5.

3. Ge-Lin Zhu, Chief Editor, *Practical Commercial English Handbook.* Beijing, China: Commercial Publishing Company, 1982.

4. Richard A. Lanham, *Revising Business Prose.* New York: Scribner's, 1981, p. 2.

5. Dave Ellis, *Becoming a Master Student.* Boston: Houghton Mifflin, 2000, p. 128; Carol C. Kanar, *The Confident Student.* Boston: Houghton Mifflin, 2001, p. 12.

Chapter 5

1. Alison Bruce, *Chatelaine* (English edition). Vol. 78, No. 2, *February 2005,* p. 21.

2. Robert Thompson, *National Post* (Index only). January 7, 2005, p. FP1.

3. Amy Voida, Wendy C. Newstetter, and Elizabeth D. Mynatt, "When conventions collide: the tensions of instant messaging attributed" in *Chi 2002: Changing the World, Changing Ourselves.* Vol. 4, No. 1, April 20–25, 2002.

4. Tamara Gignac, "Sloppy e-mail taking toll in workplace" in *Calgary Herald.* September 26, 2005, p. A1.

Chapter 6

1. Philippa Campsie, "Email: Productivity tool or productivity drain" in *Municipal World.* November 2005, p. 41.

2. "Unhappy News Travels Fast" in *USA Today.* May 21, 1996, p. 10B.

Chapter 7

1. Herschell Gordon Lewis, *Direct Mail Copy That Sells!* Englewood Cliffs, NJ: Prentice-Hall, 1984, p. iii.

2. Ed Cerny, "Listening for Effect," *American Salesman,* May 1986, p. 28.

3. Linda Lynton, "The Fine Art of Writing a Sales Letter," *Sales & Marketing Management,* August 1988, p. 55.

Chapter 8

1. Wayne Harrison and Peter D. Timmerman, "The Discretionary use of Electronic Media: Four Considerations for Bad News Bearers" in *Journal of Business Communication,* Vol. 42, No. 4, October 2005, pp. 379–389.

2. Gretchen Hoover, "Maintaining Employee Engagement when Communicating Difficult Issues" in *Communication World,* November–December 2005, p. 27.

3. Herschell Gordon Lewis, *Direct Mail Copy That Sells!* Englewood Cliffs, NJ: Prentice-Hall, 1984, p. iii.

4. Ed Cerny, "Listening for Effect" in *American Salesman,* May 1986, p. 28.

5. *www.wired.com/wired/archive/1.02/flux.html,* February 16, 2006.

6. Gretchen Hoover, "Maintaining Employee Engagement when Communicating Difficult Issues" in *Communication World,* November–December 2005, p. 27.

7. Wayne Harrison and Peter D. Timmerman, "The Discretionary use of Electronic Media: Four Considerations for Bad News Bearers" in *Journal of Business Communication,* Vol. 42, No. 4, October 2005, pp. 379–389.

8. *Ibid.,* p. 387.

9. Gretchen Hoover, "Maintaining Employee Engagement when Communicating Difficult Issues" in *Communication World,* November–December 2005, pp. 25–27.

10. *Ibid.*

11. *Ibid.*

Chapter 9

1. Scot Ober, "The Physical Format of Memorandums and Business Reports," *Business Education World,* November–December 1981, pp. 9–10, 24.

2. John Naisbitt, *Megatrends: Ten New Directions Shaping Our Lives.* New York: Warner Books, 1984, p. 17.

3. Martin J. Gannon, *Understanding Global Cultures.* Beverly Hills, CA: Sage, 1994, pp. 3–16; Martin Rosch and Kay Segler, "Communicating with the Japansese," *Management International Review.* Winter 1987, pp. 56–57; Stella Ting-Tommey, "Toward a Theory of Conflict and Culture," *Communication, Culture, and Organizational Processes.* Beverley Hills, CA: Sage,

1985, pp. 71–86; David A. Victor, *International Business Communication.* New York: HarperCollins, 1992, pp. 137–168.

Chapter 10

1. "Stats Can using beer to get Albertans to take part in census" in *Cape Breton Post* (CP), May 3, 2006.
2. "Suck back a Census Brewski" in *The Lethbridge Herald* (AB) (Newswire), May 2, 2006. Database: Canadian Reference Centre, 08394938.
3. *Ibid.*
4. *Ibid.*
5. *www.cbc.ca/story/canada/national/2005/12/16/smarties-claim20051216.html.* Accessed May 1, 2006.
6. "What Makes a Successful Online Student?" in *Illinois Online Network,* April 27, 2001, retrieved from *www.ion.illinois.edu/IONresources/onlineLearning/StudentProfile.asp*; Susan Imel, "Distance Learning: Myths and Realities" in *ERIC,* 1998, retrieved from *www.ericacve.org*; Barry Willis, "Guide #8: Strategies for Learning at a Distance" in *Distance Education at a Glance.* University of Idaho: College of Engineering, December 11, 2000, retrieved from *www.uidaho.edu/evo/dist8.html*; "Is Distance Ed Right for You?," *Channel 3000,* retrieved from *www.channel3000.com,* July 13, 2001.
7. Donald T. Hawkins, "What Is Credible Information?" in *Online,* September 1999, retrieved from *www.onelineinc.com/OL1999/technomonitor9.html,* April 14, 2001.
8. Robert Rosenthal and Ralph L. Rosnow, *The Volunteer Subject.* New York: John Wiley, 1975, at pp. 195–196.
9. "Caslon Analytics Profile: E-mail, SMS, IM & Chat" in *Caslon Analytics Home Page,* retrieved from *www.caslon.com.auemailprofile5.htm,* September 20, 2003.
10. Anne Foy, "Conducting Primary Research Online" in *The Marketing Reivew,* 2004, Vol. 4, pp. 341–360.
11. List compiled from the following sources: Stanley E. Griffis, Thomas J. Goldsby, and Martha Cooper, "Web-based and Mail Surveys: A Comparison of Response, Data, and Cost" in *Journal of Business Logistics,* Vol. 24., No. 2, 2003; Cha Yeow Siah, "All that Gliters is Not Gold: Examining the Perils and Obstacles in Collecting Data on the Internet" in *International Negotiation,* Vol. 10, pp. 115–130, 2005; and Anne Foy, "Conducting Primary Research Online" in *The Marketing Review,* 2004, Vol. 4, pp. 341–360.
12. Palmer Morrel-Samuels, "Web Survey's Hidden Hazards" in *Harvard Business Review,* July 2003, Vol. 81, No. 7, pp. 16–17.
13. As cited by R. Kitchin, *Cyberspace: The World in the Wires.* Chichester: Wiley, at p. 83.

Chapter 11

1. *The Chronicle Herald* (Halifax, NS), May 11, 2006, p. F5 (AN 1C161C161767978510).
2. Kenneth H. Bacon, "U.S. Issues Rules Aimed at Policing Fraud in Research" in *Wall Street Journal,* August 8, 1989, p. B3; Paul M. Barrett, "To Read This Story in Full, Don't Forget to See the Footnotes" in *Wall Street Journal,* May 10, 1988, p. 1; Paul Boller and John George, *They Never Said It.* Oxford: Oxford University Press, 1989; Christopher Cook, "Judge Reportedly Plagiarized in Article" in *Detroit Free Press,* March 19, 1989, p. 3A; John Entine, "Uh-oh: The Feckless Defense of

Fabulists" in *Chicago Tribune,* July 27, 2001, p. 19; John Harris, "Chop-Stuck" in *Forbes,* August 21, 1989, p. 14; Ralph Keyes, "The Greatest Quotes Never Said" in *Reader's Digest,* June 1993, pp. 97–100; Rob Stein, "Plagiarism Charges End in Departure at Harvard" in *Detroit Free Press,* November 29, 1988, p. 8A; Nanci Hellmich, "Stolen Passion: Author Plagiarized Her Rival" in *USA Today,* July 30, 1997, p. 1D; Jay Leno (with Bill Zehme), *Leading with My Chin.* New York: Mass Market Paperbacks, 1997.
3. *From Poverty to Prosperity,* National Council of Welfare, retrieved from *www.ncwcnbes.net/htmdocument/principales/2005NCWPresentationStandingCommitteeFinance.pdf.*

Chapter 12

1. Martin Perelmuter, as quoted in Wallace Immen, "Speakers' Circuit Not Just Talk" in *Globe and Mail—Report on Business,* September 29, 2004.
2. *Ibid.*
3. *Ibid.*
4. *Ibid.*
5. *Ibid.*
6. *Ibid.*
7. Kerry L. Johnson, "You Were Saying" in *Managers Magazine,* February 1989, p. 19.
8. Wharton Applied Center, "A Study of the Effects of the Use of Overhead Transparencies on Business Meetings, Final Report." Philadelphia: University of Pennsylvania, September 14, 1981; Tad Simons, "Study Shows Just How Much Visuals Increase Persuasiveness" in *Presentations Magazine,* March 1998, p. 20.
9. Betty A. Marton, "How to Construct a Winning Presentation" in *Harvard Management Communication Letter,* April 2000, p. 5.
10. As cited in Jeremy Caplan, *Time* (Canadian edition). Toronto: November 14, 2005, Vol. 166, No. 20, p. 70.
11. As quoted in Linda Mahin, "PowerPoint Pedagogy" in *Business Communication Quarterly,* June 2004, Vol. 67, No. 2, p. 219.
12. Cornelius B. Pratt, *Public Relations Quarterly,* Fall 2003, Vol. 48, No. 3, p. 20.
13. Gretchen N. Vik, *Business Communication Quarterly,* June 2004, Vol. 67, No. 2, p. 225.
14. Cornelius B. Pratt, *Public Relations Quarterly,* Fall 2003, Vol. 48, No. 3, p. 22.
15. *Ibid.,* p. 23.
16. *Ibid.,* p. 22.
17. Jim Spellos, "Jim's Hottest Tips for PowerPoint" in *Administrative Assistant's Update,* November 2005, p. 7.
18. *Ibid.,* p. 23.
19. Albert Mehrabian, "Communicating Without Words" in *Psychology Today,* September 1968, pp. 53–55.
20. Teri Kwal Gamble and Michael W. Gamble, *Contacts: Interpersonal Communication in Theory, Practice, and Context.* Houghton Mifflin, 2005, p. 173.
21. Richard M.Harris, "Practically Perfect Presentations" in *Training and Development,* July 1994, p. 56.
22. Dawn E. Waldrop, "What You Wear Is Almost as Important as What You Say" in *Presentations,* July 2000, p. 74.
23. Jolie Solomon, "Executives Who Dread Public Speaking Learn to Keep Their Cool in the Spotlight" in *Wall Street Journal,* May 4, 1990, p. B1.

Chapter 13

1. "The New Reality: Workopolis Reveals the Challenges and Opportunities of a Thriving Job Market", Canada NewsWire, Ottawa, January 31, 2006.
2. Workopolis.com news release, "Jobs in the new millennium: Canadians strike a balance between work and home life; New survey from Workopolis shows Canadians place increasing priority on family", March 15, 2006.
3. Eric Beauchesne, "Most job applicants don't have the right skills for the job" in *CanWest News.* Don Mills, Ontario, March 10, 2004, p. 1.
4. Workopolis.com news release, "School's Out: Let the Job Search Begin", April 13, 2005.
5. Workopolis.com news release, "Jobs in the new millennium: Canadians strike a balance between work and home life; New survey from Workopolis shows Canadians place increasing priority on family", March 15, 2006.
6. Workopolis.com news release, "The New Reality: Workopolis Reveals the Challenges and Opportunities of a Thriving Job Market", January 31, 2006.
7. Sandra L. Latimer, "First Impressions" in *Mt. Pleasant (MI) Morning Sun,* May 8, 1989, p. 6.
8. Elizabeth Blackburn-Brockman and Kelly Belanger, "One Page or Two: A National Study of CPA Recruiters' Preferences for Résumé Length" in *The Journal of Business Communication,* Vol. 38, No. 1, January 2001, p. 42.
9. Elaine Balych, Coordinator, Career Development, Mount Royal College, Calgary. Personal Interview. May 31, 2006.
10. *Ibid.*
11. Career Services. Mount Royal College. Resume Sample Brochure. May 2005.
12. As quoted in Bar Simmons, "Adding Hobbies to Resumes" in *Toronto Star,* February 5, 2004. Accessed from *Workopolis.com* on May 31, 2005.
13. Albert P. Karr, "Labor Letter" in *Wall Street Journal,* September 1, 1992, p. A1.
14. Mark Swartz, "Online Resume Secrets Revealed" in *Toronto Star,* 2004/04/22. Accessed from *Workopolis.com* on May 31, 2006.
15. Mary Bakeman et al., *Job-Seeking Skills Reference Manual,* 3d ed. Minneapolis, MN: Minnesota Rehabilitation Center, 1971, p. 57.
16. With thanks to Keith Black, Mount Royal College, Department of Human Resources.
17. HRDC Web page, *www.hrsdc.gc.ca.* Accessed June 21, 2006.
18. Career Services. Focus on Types of Interviews (brochure), Mount Royal College, June 2006.
19. Barbara Simmons, "Keep you cool during the 'stress interview'" in *The Toronto Star,* December 6, 2006.

Grateful acknowledgment is made to the following companies and individuals for allowing their interviews and photographs to be included in this book:

Chapter 1: Nissan North America, Inc./Debra Sanchez Fair. *Chapter 2:* Farm Credit Canada/John Ryan. *Chapter 3:* Daydream Communications/Bill Bunn. *Chapter 4:* World Wrestling Entertainment/Gary Davis. *Chapter 5:* Heppell Funeral Solutions/Robin Heppell. *Chapter 6:* Annie's Homegrown/Ann Whithey. *Chapter 7:* Communications and Client Strategy for BMO Capital Markets/Martha Durdin. *Chapter 8:* Nortel Calgary/Sandra Falconi. *Chapter 9:* AstraZeneca/Anne K. Cobuzzi. *Chapter 10:* Statistics Canada/Jerry Page. *Chapter 11:* Kent Schroeder. *Chapter 12:* Speakers' Spotlight/Martin and Farah Perelmuter. *Chapter 13:* Workopolis/Patrick Sullivan.

Grateful acknowledgment is made to the following companies for allowing their letterheads to be included in this book. These letters are for text example only; they were not written by employees of the companies.

Chapter 6: Courtesy of Di-Mark.

TEXT CREDITS

Screen shots reprinted with permission from Microsoft Corporation.

Clip art reprinted from "Screen Beans" collections, published by A Bit Better Corporation (phone: 650-948-4766, Web: www.bitbetter.com).

Chapter 2:   *Page 42, Figure 2.2:* From Peter S. Scholtes, *The Team Handbook,* 1998, pp. 6–27. Copyright © 1988 by Joiner Associates, Inc., Madison, WI; 1-800-669-8326. Reprinted with permission. *Page 64, Figure 2.5:* Listserv E-mail Posting screen shot reprinted with permission of AT&T.

Chapter 12:   *Page 424, Figure 11.6:* Copyright 1998 by Dow Jones & Co., Inc. Reproduced with permission of Dow Jones & Co., Inc. in the format Textbook via Copyright Clearance Center.

PHOTO CREDITS

Chapter 1:   *Page 4:* © Chris Chapman. *Page 8:* © Robert Houser (roberthouser.com). *Page 20:* Non Sequitur © 1999 Wiley Miller. Dist. by Universal Press Syndicate. Reprinted with permission. All rights reserved. *Page 33:* © Bill Varie.

Chapter 2:   *Page 37:* © Greg Huszar Photography. *Page 42:* © Jonathan Chick. *Page 62:* © Brian Davis Photography.

Chapter 3:   *Page 87:* John Marshall, The Rick Mercer Report. *Page 91:* CP/Aaron Harris. *Page 97:* CP/Glenn Ogilvie. *Page 98:* Toronto Star/Michael Stuparyk. *Page 113:* © LWA-Dann Tardif/Corbis. *Page 120:* Edmonton Sun/Darryl Dyck.

Chapter 4:   *Page 122:* Dilbert © Scott Adams/Dist. by United Feature Syndicate, Inc. *Page 126:* © Royalty-Free/Corbis.

Chapter 5:   *Page 159:* © Dick Loek/First Light. *Page 162:* By permission of John L. Hart FLP and Creators Syndicate, Inc. *Page 164:* © Toronto Star/Rene Johnson.

Chapter 6:   *Page 190:* Cathy © 1982 Cathy Guisewite. Reprinted with permission of Universal Press Syndicate. All rights reserved. *Page 193:* © Keith Beaty/First Light. *Page 196:* © Dick Loek/First Light. *Page 218:* © Neil Farren/Getty Images.

Chapter 7:   *Page 223:* By permission of Leigh Rubin and Creators Syndicate, Inc. *Page 226:* © 2006 www.davidlevenson.com. *Page 228:* © Bernard Weil/First Light. *Page 263:* © Dan Bosler/Getty Images.

Chapter 8:   *Page 271:* AP Images. *Page 273:* Dilbert © Scott Adams/Dist. by United Feature Syndicate, Inc. *Page 276:* AP Images.

Chapter 9:   *Page 312:* Copyright Grantland Enterprises; www.grantland.net. *Page 320:* Reproduced with permission from Motorola, Inc. © 2007, Motorola, Inc. *Page 322: This Hour has 22 Minutes.* Courtesy of Canadian Broadcasting Corporation.

Chapter 10:   *Page 342:* CP/Mike Sturk. *Page 344:* © Peter Ginter/Getty Images. *Page 364:* © North America Syndicate.

Chapter 11:   *Page 384:* © Kim Kulish/Corbis. *Page 408:* © North America Syndicate. *Page 412:* © John Shanks. *Page 431:* © Elie Bernager/Getty Images.

Chapter 12:   *Page 434:* © Nick Wiebe 2006. *Page 437:* Globe & Mail/Tibor Kolley. *Page 443:* © Debra DeBoise. *Page 445:* Dilbert © Scott Adams/Dist. by United Feature Syndicate, Inc. *Page 447:* CP/Tom Hanson. *Page 456:* © Reuters/Corbis. *Page 478:* © Phil Boorman/Getty Images.

Chapter 13:   *Page 510:* Dilbert © Scott Adams/Dist. by United Feature Syndicate, Inc.

index